To my wife, Linda
  O.C. Ferrell

To Huck and ReRe
  Michael D. Hartline

Brief Contents

PART 1   Setting the Stage for Marketing Strategy

CHAPTER 1   Marketing in Today's Economy   1

CHAPTER 2   Strategic Marketing Planning   27

PART 2   Discovering Market Opportunities

CHAPTER 3   Collecting and Analyzing Marketing Information   53

CHAPTER 4   Developing Competitive Advantage and Strategic Focus   85

PART 3   Developing Marketing Strategy

CHAPTER 5   Customers, Segmentation, and Target Marketing   115

CHAPTER 6   The Marketing Program   149

CHAPTER 7   Branding and Positioning   199

PART 4   Putting Strategy into Action

CHAPTER 8   Ethics and Social Responsibility in Marketing Strategy   227

CHAPTER 9   Marketing Implementation and Control   255

CHAPTER 10   Developing and Maintaining Long-Term Customer Relationships   283

PART 5   Cases

CASE 1   *USA Today*: Innovation in an Evolving Industry   313

CASE 2   Apple's Winning Marketing Strategy   327

CASE 3   Monsanto Balances the Interests of Multiple Stakeholders   339

CASE 4   New Belgium Brewing (A): Gaining Competitive Advantage Through Socially Responsible Marketing   351

CASE 5   New Belgium Brewing (B): Developing a Brand Personality   361

CASE 6   Mattel Confronts Its Marketing Challenges   371

CASE 7   Mistine: Direct Selling in the Thai Cosmetics Market   381

CASE 8   BP Struggles to Repair Its Tarnished Reputation   393

CASE 9   Chevrolet: 100 Years of Product Innovation   405

CASE 10   Wyndham Worldwide Adopts a Stakeholder Orientation Marketing Strategy   419

CASE 11   NASCAR: Can't Keep a Good Brand Down   429

CASE 12   IndyCar: Seeking a Return to Motorsports' Fast Lane   441

CASE 13   Zappos: Delivering Happiness   451

CASE 14   Sigma Marketing: Strategic Marketing Adaptation   461

CASE 15   Netflix Fights to Stay Ahead of a Rapidly Changing Market   471

CASE 16   Gillette: Why Innovation May Not Be Enough   481

CASE 17   IKEA Slowly Expands Its U.S. Market Presence   493

CASE 18   Sushilicious: Standing Out In A Crowded Field   501

CASE 19   Trouble Brews at Starbucks   517

CASE 20   Groupon   533

Appendix   Marketing Plan Worksheets   547

Brands and Companies Index   557
Name Index   571
Subject Index   575

Contents

PART 1 Setting the Stage for Marketing Strategy

CHAPTER 1
Marketing in Today's Economy   1

Introduction   1

Beyond the Pages 1.1 Thriving in Commodity Hell   2

The Challenges and Opportunities of Marketing in Today's Economy   3

Basic Marketing Concepts   7
What Is a Market?   8
What Is Exchange?   9
What Is a Product?   11

Major Marketing Activities and Decisions   14
Strategic Planning   14

Beyond the Pages 1.2 Innovative Marketing Strategies for a Tough Economy   15
Research and Analysis   16
Developing Competitive Advantage   16
Marketing Strategy Decisions   17

Beyond the Pages 1.3 Targeting Consumers via Online Social Networking   18

Social Responsibility and Ethics   20
Implementation and Control   20
Developing and Maintaining Customer Relationships   21

Taking On the Challenges of Marketing Strategy   22

Lessons from Chapter 1   24

Questions for Discussion   25

Exercises   25

CHAPTER 2
Strategic Marketing Planning   27

Introduction   27

Beyond the Pages 2.1 Redbox's Success Story   28

The Strategic Planning Process   29
Organizational Mission versus Organizational Vision   30
Corporate or Business-Unit Strategy   34
Functional Goals and Objectives   35
Functional Strategy   35
Implementation   36
Evaluation and Control   36

The Marketing Plan   36
Marketing Plan Structure   37

Beyond the Pages 2.2 Sell Below Cost, They Will Come   41

Using the Marketing Plan Structure   42

Purposes and Significance of the Marketing Plan   44
Organizational Aspects of the Marketing Plan   44

Maintaining Customer Focus and Balance in Strategic Planning   45
Customer-Focused Planning   46

Beyond the Pages 2.3   Amazon Is on Fire   47

Balanced Strategic Planning   48

Lessons from Chapter 2   50

Questions for Discussion   51

Exercises   51

PART 2   Discovering Market Opportunities

CHAPTER 3
Collecting and Analyzing Marketing Information   53
Introduction   53

Beyond the Pages 3.1   Baby Boomers Deserve Careful Analysis   54

Conducting a Situation Analysis   55
Analysis Alone Is Not a Solution   55
Data Is Not the Same as Information   56
The Benefits of Analysis Must Outweigh the Costs   56
Conducting a Situation Analysis Is a Challenging Exercise   56

The Internal Environment   58
Review of Current Objectives, Strategy, and Performance   59
Availability of Resources   59
Organizational Culture and Structure   60

The Customer Environment   60
Who Are Our Current and Potential Customers?   62
What Do Customers Do with Our Products?   62
Where Do Customers Purchase Our Products?   63
When Do Customers Purchase Our Products?   63

Beyond the Pages 3.2   The Ongoing Challenge of E-Waste   64

Why (and How) Do Customers Select Our Products?   65
Why Do Potential Customers Not Purchase Our Products?   65

The External Environment   66
Competition   66
Economic Growth and Stability   70
Political Trends   71
Legal and Regulatory Issues   71
Technological Advancements   72
Sociocultural Trends   73

Collecting Marketing Data and Information   76
Secondary Information Sources   76

Beyond the Pages 3.3   A Corporate Affairs Primer   77

Primary Data Collection   80
Overcoming Problems in Data Collection   81

Lessons from Chapter 3   82

Questions for Discussion   82

Exercises   83

CHAPTER 4

Developing Competitive Advantage and Strategic Focus   85

Introduction   85

    Beyond the Pages 4.1 Innovation: A Major Key to Success   86

Making SWOT Analysis Productive   87

    Stay Focused   88
    Search Extensively for Competitors   89
    Collaborate with Other Functional Areas   89
    Examine Issues from the Customers' Perspective   90
    Look for Causes, Not Characteristics   92
    Separate Internal Issues from External Issues   92

SWOT-Driven Strategic Planning   93

    Strengths and Weaknesses   93
    Opportunities and Threats   95
    The SWOT Matrix   96

Developing and Leveraging Competitive Advantages   98

Establishing a Strategic Focus   100

    Beyond the Pages 4.2 Successful Product Leadership at 3M   101

Developing Marketing Goals and Objectives   105

    Beyond the Pages 4.3 A Closer Look at Blue Ocean Strategy   106

    Developing Marketing Goals   107
    Developing Marketing Objectives   108
    Moving Beyond Goals and Objectives   111

Lessons from Chapter 4   111

Questions for Discussion   112

Exercises   112

PART 3   Developing Marketing Strategy

CHAPTER 5

Customers, Segmentation, and Target Marketing   115

Introduction   115

    Beyond the Pages 5.1 Data Mining Allows Companies to Know Our Secrets   116

Buyer Behavior in Consumer Markets   117

    The Consumer Buying Process   117
    Factors That Affect the Consumer Buying Process   123

Buyer Behavior in Business Markets   125

    Unique Characteristics of Business Markets   126
    The Business Buying Process   128

Market Segmentation   129

    Traditional Market Segmentation Approaches   129

    Beyond the Pages 5.2 The Challenges and Opportunities of Population Diversity   130
    Individualized Segmentation Approaches   132
    Criteria for Successful Segmentation   134

    Beyond the Pages 5.3 Shifting Strategies in the Cereal Market   135

Identifying Market Segments   135

    Segmenting Consumer Markets   136
    Segmenting Business Markets   141

Target Marketing Strategies   142

Lessons from Chapter 5   143

Questions for Discussion   146

Exercises   146

CHAPTER 6
The Marketing Program   149

Introduction   149

   Beyond the Pages 6.1 Can Good Marketing Save Barnes & Noble?   150

Product Strategy   151
   Strategic Issues in the Product Portfolio   151
   The Challenges of Service Products   154
   Developing New Products   156

Pricing Strategy   158
   Key Issues in Pricing Strategy   159

   Beyond the Pages 6.2 Pricing Around the World   160

   Pricing Service Products   165
   Base Pricing Strategies   166
   Adjusting the Base Price   167

Supply Chain Strategy   169
   Strategic Supply Chain Issues   170
   Trends in Supply Chain Strategy   175

   Beyond the Pages 6.3 Walmart's Supply Chain Advantages   176

Integrated Marketing Communications   179

   Beyond the Pages 6.4 Fragmentation Forever Changes Media Advertising   180

   Strategic Issues in Integrated Marketing Communications   181
   Advertising   182
   Public Relations   184
   Personal Selling and Sales Management   186
   Sales Promotion   188

Lessons from Chapter 6   192

Questions for Discussion   195

Exercises   195

CHAPTER 7
Branding and Positioning   199

Introduction   199

   Beyond the Pages 7.1 Steinway: More Than a Piano   200

Strategic Issues in Branding   202
   Basic Branding Decisions   204
   Strategic Brand Alliances   206
   Brand Value   206
   Packaging and Labeling   209

   Beyond the Pages 7.2 Tropicana's Packaging Debacle   210

Differentiation and Positioning   210
   Bases for Differentiation   212
   Positioning Strategies   214

Mananging Brands over Time   215
Development Stage   217
Introduction Stage   218
Growth Stage   219
Maturity Stage   220

Beyond the Pages 7.3   Nintendo's Rebranding Strategy   222

Decline Stage   223

Lessons from Chapter 7   224

Questions for Discussion   225

Exercises   225

PART 4   Putting Strategy into Action

CHAPTER 8
Ethics and Social Responsibility in Marketing Strategy   227

Introduction   227

Beyond the Pages 8.1   Salesforce.com Adopts a Stakeholder Orientation   228

Ethics and Social Responsibility in Marketing Strategy   229
Dimensions of Social Responsibility   229
Sustainability   232
Marketing Ethics and Strategy   233

Beyond the Pages 8.2   Finding the Real Green Products   234

The Challenges of Being Ethical and Socially Responsible   236

Ethical Issues in the Marketing Program   237
Product-Related Ethical Issues   238
Pricing-Related Ethical Issues   239
Supply Chain-Related Ethical Issues   240
Promotion-Related Ethical Issues   241

Managing and Controlling Ethical Issues   242
Regulating Marketing Ethics   242
Codes of Conduct   243

**Beyond the Pages 8.3   The Consumer Financial Protection Bureau Aims to Build Trust in the
Banking System   244**

Ethical Leadership   245

Relationship to Marketing and Financial Performance   246
Stakeholder Orientation   247
Marketing Financial Performance   247

Incorporating Ethics and Social Responsibility into Strategic Planning   249

Lessons from Chapter 8   250

Questions for Discussion   251

Exercises   251

CHAPTER 9
Marketing Implementation and Control   255

Introduction   255

Beyond the Pages 9.1   Green Mountain Coffee Gets It Done   256

Strategic Issues in Marketing Implementation   257
The Link Between Planning and Implementation   257
The Elements of Marketing Implementation   259

Approaches to Marketing Implementation   263
Implementation by Command   263
Implementation Through Change   263

Beyond the Pages 9.2   The New Rules of CEO Leadership   264

Implementation Through Consensus   265
Implementation as Organizational Culture   266

Internal Marketing and Marketing Implementation   268
The Internal Marketing Approach   268
The Internal Marketing Process   269

Evaluating and Controlling Marketing Activities   270
Formal Marketing Controls   271
Informal Marketing Controls   275
Scheduling Marketing Activities   276

Beyond the Pages 9.3   Managing Risk Through Culture   277

Lessons from Chapter 9   279

Questions for Discussion   280

Exercises   280

CHAPTER 10
Developing and Maintaining Long-Term Customer Relationships   283
Introduction   283

Beyond the Pages 10.1   1-800-Flowers.com Focuses on Customers   284

Managing Customer Relationships   284
Developing Relationships in Consumer Markets   286
Developing Relationships in Business Markets   288

Quality and Value: The Keys to Developing Customer Relationships   290
Understanding the Role of Quality   290
Delivering Superior Quality   293

Beyond the Pages 10.2   Customer Service versus Efficiency   294

Understanding the Role of Value   295
Competing on Value   298

Customer Satisfaction: The Key to Customer Retention   299
Understanding Customer Expectations   299

Beyond the Pages 10.3   Satisfied, But Not Loyal   302

Satisfaction versus Quality versus Value   303
Customer Satisfaction and Customer Retention   304
Customer Satisfaction Measurement   306

Lessons from Chapter 10   308

Questions for Discussion   310

Exercises   310

PART 5   Cases

CASE   1   *USA Today*: Innovation in an Evolving Industry   313

CASE   2   Apple's Winning Marketing Strategy   327

CASE   3   Monsanto Balances the Interests of Multiple Stakeholders   339

CASE **4** New Belgium Brewing (A): Gaining Competitive Advantage Through Socially Responsible Marketing 351

CASE **5** New Belgium Brewing (B): Developing a Brand Personality 361

CASE **6** Mattel Confronts Its Marketing Challenges 371

CASE **7** Mistine: Direct Selling in the Thai Cosmetics Market 381

CASE **8** BP Struggles to Repair Its Tarnished Reputation 393

CASE **9** Chevrolet: 100 Years of Product Innovation 405

CASE **10** Wyndham Worldwide Adopts a Stakeholder Orientation Marketing Strategy 419

CASE **11** NASCAR: Can't Keep a Good Brand Down 429

CASE **12** IndyCar: Seeking a Return to Motorsports' Fast Lane 441

CASE **13** Zappos: Delivering Happiness 451

CASE **14** Sigma Marketing: Strategic Marketing Adaptation 461

CASE **15** Netflix Fights to Stay Ahead of a Rapidly Changing Market 471

CASE **16** Gillette: Why Innovation May Not Be Enough 481

CASE **17** IKEA Slowly Expands Its U.S. Market Presence 493

CASE **18** Sushilicious: Standing Out In A Crowded Field 501

CASE **19** Trouble Brews at Starbucks 517

CASE **20** Groupon 533

Appendix Marketing Plan Worksheets 547

Brands and Companies Index 557
Name Index 571
Subject Index 575

Preface

Welcome to one of the most interesting, challenging, and important topics in your business education. What makes marketing strategy so interesting, challenging, and important you ask? To begin, marketing strategy is interesting because (1) it is inherently people-driven and (2) it is never stagnant. A distinct blend of both art and science, marketing strategy is about people (inside an organization) finding ways to deliver exceptional value by fulfilling the needs and wants of other people (customers, shareholders, business partners, society at large), as well as the needs of the organization itself. Marketing strategy draws from psychology, sociology, and economics to better understand the basic needs and motivations of these people—whether they are the organization's customers (typically considered the most critical), its employees, or its stakeholders. In short, marketing strategy is about people serving people.

For this reason, marketing strategy is interesting because it is never stagnant. The simple fact is that people change. A strategy that works today might not work tomorrow. Products that are popular today are forgotten next week. These truisms are important because truly understanding marketing strategy means accepting the fact that there are few concrete rules for developing and implementing marketing activities. Given the constant state of change in the marketing environment, it is virtually impossible to say that given "this customer need" and "these competitors" and "this level of government regulation" that Product A, Price B, Promotion C, and Distribution D will produce the best results. Marketing simply doesn't work that way. The lack of concrete rules and the ever changing economic, sociocultural, competitive, technological, and political/legal landscapes make marketing strategy a terribly fascinating subject.

Now that you know why marketing strategy is so interesting, it should be easy to see why it is also challenging. A perfect marketing strategy that is executed flawlessly can still fail. Sometimes, organizations are lucky and have success despite having a terrible strategy and/or execution. The nature of marketing can make marketing planning quite frustrating.

Finally, the importance of marketing strategy is undeniable. No other business function focuses on developing relationships with customers—the lifeblood of all organizations (even non-profits). This statement does not diminish the importance of other business functions, as they all are necessary for an organization to be successful. In fact, coordination with other functions is critical to marketing success. However, without customers, and marketing programs in place to cultivate customer relationships, no organization can survive.

Our Focus

Given this marketing landscape, *Marketing Strategy: Text and Cases, 6th Edition* provides a practical, straightforward approach to analyzing, planning, and implementing marketing strategies. Our focus is based on the creative process involved in applying the knowledge and concepts of marketing to the development and implementation of marketing strategy. Our goal is to encourage students of marketing to think and act like a marketer. By discussing the key concepts and tools of marketing strategy, our emphasis on critical thinking, both analytical and creative, allows students to understand the essence of how marketing decisions fit together to create a coherent strategy.

Our approach in *Marketing Strategy: Text and Cases, 6th Edition* is also grounded in the development and execution of the marketing plan. Throughout the text, we provide a comprehensive planning framework based on conducting sound background research, developing market capabilities and competitive advantages, designing integrated marketing programs, and managing customer relationships for the long term. We also emphasize the need for integrity in the strategic planning process, as well as the design of marketing programs that are both ethical and socially responsible. We also stress the integration and coordination of marketing decisions with other functional business decisions as the key to achieving an organization's overall mission and vision. Throughout the text, we offer examples of successful planning and implementation to illustrate how firms face the challenges of marketing strategy in today's economy.

Purpose

We view strategic marketing planning not only as a process for achieving organizational goals, but also as a means of building long-term relationships with customers. Creating a customer orientation takes imagination, vision, and courage, especially in today's rapidly changing economic and technological environments. To help meet these challenges, our text approaches marketing strategy from both "traditional" and "cutting-edge" practices. We cover topics such as segmentation, creating a competitive advantage, marketing program development, and the implementation process with a solid grounding in traditional marketing, but also with an eye toward emerging practices. Lessons learned from the rise, fall, and reemergence of the dotcom sector, recent corporate scandals, and the most recent economic recession illustrate the importance of balancing the traditional and emerging practices of marketing strategy. Our text never loses sight of this balance.

Although our approach allows for the use of sophisticated research and decision-making processes, we have employed a practical perspective that permits marketing managers in any size organization to develop and implement a marketing plan. We have avoided esoteric, abstract, and highly academic material that does not relate to typical marketing strategy decisions in most organizations. The marketing plan framework that we utilize throughout the text has been used by a number of organizations to successfully plan their marketing strategies. Many companies report great success in using our approach partially due to the ease of communicating the plan to all functional areas of the business.

Target Audience

Our text is relevant for a number of educational environments, including undergraduate, graduate, and corporate training courses. At the undergraduate level, our text is appropriate for the capstone course or any upper-level integrating course such as "Marketing Management," "Marketing Strategy," or "Marketing Policy." At this level, the text provides an excellent framework to use with our included text-based cases, live-client cases, or a computer simulation. At the graduate level, our text is appropriate for courses addressing strategic marketing planning, competitive marketing strategies, or as a supplement for any simulation-based course. A growing segment of the market, corporate training, can utilize our text when educating business professionals interested in developing marketing plans of their own, or interpreting and implementing the plans of others.

Each of the twenty cases included in our text describes the strategic situations of real-world, identifiable organizations. Because these cases feature real situations, instructors have the option of using the case material as published, or they may give students the opportunity to update the cases by conducting research to find the latest information. Many additional resources for students and instructors can be found at our text's companion website, www.cengagebrain.com.

Key Features of the 6th Edition

The key features of *Marketing Strategy: Text and Cases, 6th Edition* include:

- *Revised and expanded coverage throughout the text of recent events in marketing practice by well-known global companies.*
- *A focus on the integration of the traditional marketing mix elements (product, price, distribution, and promotion) into a consistent marketing program. Consequently, the four separate marketing mix chapters have been condensed into a single chapter.*
- *A new chapter on Branding and Positioning (Chapter 7) that adds increased emphasis on using every element of the marketing program to achieve branding and positioning success.*
- *Five new cases written specifically for our text:*

  - Case 2, "Apple's Winning Marketing Strategy," focuses on Apple's phenomenal rise to prominence through the use of masterful marketing, an entrepreneurial spirit, and "cool" branding.
  - Case 9, "Chevrolet: 100 Years of Product Innovation," looks at Chevrolet's use of product innovation and branding to create practical, sporty, and affordable automotive products that compete with strong domestic and foreign manufacturers.
  - Case 10, "Wyndham Worldwide Adopts a Stakeholder Orientation Marketing Strategy," examines how Wyndham's focus on stakeholder orientation has positioned the company as a global brand that is synonymous with quality, ethical leadership, customer satisfaction, and sustainability.
  - Case 13, "Zappos: Delivering Happiness," explores the company's unique business model and corporate culture, and how they influence its relationships with customers, employees, the environment, and its communities.
  - Case 15, "Netflix Fights to Stay Ahead of a Rapidly Changing Market," looks at how the dominant rent-by-mail and video streaming company bested its chief rival, Blockbuster, and how the company must prepare for an uncertain future as the DVD rental sector approaches the end of its life cycle.

- *A complete revision of the twelve cases that have been carried over from the 5th edition of our text:*

  - Case 1, "*USA Today*: Innovation in an Evolving Industry," explores how the nation's largest daily newspaper has used continuous innovation to stay ahead of the technological and sociocultural shifts that threaten the very existence of the newspaper industry.
  - Case 3, "Monsanto Balances the Interests of Multiple Stakeholders," focuses on Monsanto's shift from a chemical company to one focused on biotechnology, and the resulting stakeholder concerns about safety and the environment that come with such a change.
  - Case 4, "New Belgium Brewing (A): Gaining Competitive Advantage Through Socially Responsible Marketing," shows how a firm can use social responsibility and customer intimacy as key competitive advantages in the highly competitive craft beer market.
  - Case 5, "New Belgium Brewing (B): Developing a Brand Personality," explains how New Belgium expanded its branding and communication strategy after the development of its "Brand Manifesto."
  - Case 6, "Mattel Confronts Its Marketing Challenges," looks at the threats that Mattel faces in its ongoing global operations, including changing customer preferences, competition, product liability, and declining sales.

- Case 7, "Mistine: Direct Selling in the Thai Cosmetics Market," explores how Mistine's value-based positioning moved the company to the top of the direct selling cosmetics market in Thailand.
  - Case 8, "BP Struggles to Repair Its Tarnished Reputation" considers how BP's growing reputation for sustainability was tarnished by the Gulf oil spill disaster.
  - Case 11, "NASCAR: Can't Keep a Good Brand Down," looks at NASCAR's marketing and branding successes and its newfound struggles to remain on top of the motorsports market and the #1 spectator sport in the U.S.
  - Case 12, "IndyCar: Seeking a Return to Motorsports' Fast Lane," is an excellent companion to the NASCAR case. The case examines the reunification of U.S. open wheel racing and how the new IRL must reconnect with fans to improve its standing in the U.S. motorsports market.
  - Case 14, "Sigma Marketing: Strategic Marketing Adaptation," explores the innovation and market adaptation of this small, family-owned business as it grew from a regional printing company to a global specialty advertising firm.
  - Case 16, "Gillette: Why Innovation May Not Be Enough," examines Gillette's history of product and marketing innovation, and how past success may not be enough to maintain supremacy in the global razor market.
  - Case 17, "IKEA Slowly Expands Its U.S. Market Presence," discusses how IKEA's strategy of operational excellence may stand in the way of further expansion into the U.S. furniture and home furnishings market.

- *The inclusion of three new outside cases from the Ivey School of Business at the University of Western Ontario:*

  - Case 18, "Sushilicious: Standing Out in a Crowded Field," examines the use of social media in the marketing campaign for a California sushi restaurant.
  - Case 19, "Trouble Brews at Starbucks," looks at how the company's rapid expansion actually worked against its long-term brand positioning and equity.
  - Case 20, "Groupon," explores the rapid growth of the online coupon company, its business model, and whether its future growth could depend on finding a business partner to bring needed resources and capabilities to the table.

- *Our complete case package provides up-to-date coverage of topics that are important and relevant to marketing practice in the 21st century. These topics include innovation, social responsibility, sustainability, global sourcing, technology, corporate affairs, and entrepreneurship.*
- *An updated set of Marketing Plan Worksheets, provided in the Appendix. The worksheets reflect a concise approach to marketing plan development. However, the worksheets are comprehensive in scope to help ensure that students and/or managers do not omit important issues in developing strategic marketing plans.*
- *A continued user-friendly writing style that covers essential points without heavy use of jargon. The text has also been reduced from 12 chapters to 10 chapters without a loss in coverage.*

Instructor Resources

The Instructor Resource materials for the 6th edition have been updated to match the new organization of the text. These materials are available via an Instructor's Resource CD-ROM or online at the password-protected instructor's resource website.

These materials include:

- *A revised PowerPoint® package, which incorporates lecture outlines and summary of key points, as well as select figures and tables from the text.*
- *An updated Instructor's Manual, which includes the following:*

    - Chapter lecture outlines—These outlines for each chapter may be used to quickly review chapter content before class or to gain an overview of the entire text. The outlines can also be used by instructors to add their own personal notes and examples before class.
    - Case teaching notes—Our teaching notes use a consistent format to help instructors evaluate cases before use, or to assist instructors in leading case analysis and class discussion. Although there are many different approaches to using cases, our notes will help instructors identify key issues and alternatives as they relate to the content of the case and corresponding text chapters.

- *An updated Test Bank. These examination materials include a variety of multiple choice, true/false, and discussion questions. The Test Bank questions vary in levels of difficulty, and meet a full range of tagging requirements, so that instructors can tailor their testing to meet their specific needs.*

The updated instructor's resource website supports the text and cases. In addition to the instructor resources already mentioned, instructors will find lecture outlines, case teaching notes, and sample syllabi for use in their classes.

Student Resources

Our primary student resource is contained within the text. The Appendix includes a detailed set of marketing plan worksheets that assist students in developing marketing plans. The remaining student resources can be found online at our website:

- *A downloadable Microsoft Word version of the Marketing Plan Worksheets found in the Appendix. The worksheets are designed so students can fill-in material and edit the worksheets outside of class.*
- *Example marketing plans to help illustrate the format and writing style used in creating an actual marketing plan document.*
- *A downloadable Microsoft Word version of the Lessons from each chapter. This document provides a complete outline of each chapter so that students may add to and edit the lessons outside of class. Alternatively, the file can be used during class as a way to organize note taking.*
- *Online exercises for each chapter. These exercises allow students to practice the concepts learned in class.*
- *Online quizzes for each chapter. These quizzes help students prepare for course exams.*
- *A tutorial on how to perform a case analysis. The tutorial provides a suggested way to conduct cases analyses. Instructors may use this tutorial or provide one of their own.*

Acknowledgements

Throughout the development of this text, several extraordinary individuals provided their talent and expertise to make important contributions. A number of individuals have made many useful comments and recommendations as reviewers of this text. We appreciate the generous help of these reviewers:

Lynn Allendorf, *University of Iowa*

Dr. Fazal Ahmed, *University of Pennsylvania*

Julia Cronin-Gilmore, *Bellevue University*

A. Cemal Ekin, *Providence College*

Steven McClung, *Mercer University*

Joseph Ouellette, *Bryant University*

Jeffry Overby, *Belmont University*

Norman Alan Ross, *Northern Arizona University*

Kim Saxton, *Indiana University*

Herbert Sherman, *Long Island University—Brooklyn Campus*

George David Shows, *Louisiana Tech University*

Ziad Swaidan, *University of Houston—Victoria*

Uday Tate, *Marshall University*

Linda Wright, *Longwood University*

We also deeply appreciate the assistance of several individuals who played a major role in developing cases or other materials. Specifically, we thank the following individuals:

Timothy W. Aurand, *Northern Illinois University*

Harper Baird, *University of New Mexico*

Chandani Bhasin, *University of New Mexico*

Christin Copeland, *Florida State University*

Linda Ferrell, *University of New Mexico*

John Fraedrich, *Southern Illinois University - Carbondale*

Bernadette Gallegos, *University of New Mexico*

Jennifer Jackson, *University of New Mexico*

Kimberly Judson, *Illinois State University*

Cassondra Lopez, *University of New Mexico*

Kevin Mihaly, *Florida State University*

Kelsey Reddick, *Florida State University*

Don Roy, *Middle Tennessee State University*

Mike Sapit, *Sigma Marketing*

Jennifer Sawayda, *University of New Mexico*

Beau Shelton, *University of New Mexico*

Bryan Simpson, *New Belgium Brewing Company*

Debbie Thorne, *Texas State University*

Jacqueline Trent, *University of New Mexico*

Robyn Watson, *Florida State University*

Celeste Wood, *Florida State University*

We greatly appreciate the efforts of Jennifer Sawayda, University of New Mexico, for coordinating much of the new case development in this edition. The editorial, production, and marketing staff at Cengage cannot be thanked enough. With a deep since of appreciation, we thank Mike Roche and Sarah Blasco.

Finally, we express appreciation for the support and encouragement of our families, friends, and our colleagues at The University of New Mexico and The Florida State University.

About the Authors

O.C. Ferrell, Ph.D.

The University of New Mexico

O.C. Ferrell (Ph.D., Louisiana State University) is University Distinguished Professor of Marketing and Bill Daniels Professor of Business Ethics at the Anderson School of Management at the University of New Mexico. He served as the Bill Daniels Distinguished Professor of Business Ethics at the University of Wyoming and was Chair of the Marketing Department at Colorado State University. Prior to his arrival at CSU, Dr. Ferrell was the Distinguished Professor of Marketing and Business Ethics at the University of Memphis. He has also served as a professor at the University of Tampa, Texas A&M University, Illinois State University, and Southern Illinois University. His MBA and BA degrees are from Florida State University.

Dr. Ferrell is past president of the Academic Council of the American Marketing Association and former chair of the American Marketing Association Ethics Committee. Under his leadership, the committee developed the AMA Code of Ethics and the AMA Code of Ethics for Marketing on the Internet. He is a Society for Marketing Advances Fellow and the Vice President of Publications for the Academy of Marketing Science. He is a former member of the Board of Governors as a Distinguished Fellow for the Academy of Marketing Science. In addition, he received the first Innovative Educator award from the Marketing Management Association.

Dr. Ferrell has taught a wide variety of courses, including marketing strategy, principles of marketing, marketing ethics, international marketing, as well as most undergraduate courses in marketing. Annually, Dr. Ferrell teaches a graduate course in competitive marketing strategies at Thammasat University in Bangkok, Thailand.

Dr. Ferrell is the co-author of 20 books and more than 100 articles. His research is published in the *Journal of Marketing Research*, the *Journal of Marketing*, the *Journal of Business Ethics*, the *Journal of Business Research*, the *Journal of the Academy of Marketing Science*, as well as other journals. His *Marketing: Concepts and Strategies* text, co-authored with Bill Pride, is one of the most widely adopted principles of marketing texts in the world. Furthermore, his *Business Ethics: Decision Making and Cases* text is the leading business ethics text.

Dr. Ferrell has served as an expert witness in many high-profile civil litigation cases related to marketing ethics. More recently he has assisted international corporations and worked with state regulatory agencies in modifying marketing programs to maintain compliance with both ethical and legal requirements. Currently, he is working with the National Association of State Boards of Accountancy to develop an ethical leadership certification for students. He has appeared on the NBC *Today* show and he has been quoted in national papers such as *USA Today*.

Dr. Ferrell and his wife Linda (also a faculty member at the University of New Mexico) live in Albuquerque. He enjoys golf, skiing, reading, and travel.

Michael D. Hartline, Ph.D.

The Florida State University

Michael D. Hartline (Ph.D., The University of Memphis) is Associate Dean for Strategic Initiatives and Charles A. Bruning Professor of Business Administration in the College of Business at Florida State University, where he is responsible for external relations, executive education, and strategic programs. Prior to joining the FSU faculty in 2001, Dr. Hartline was on faculty at the University of Arkansas at Little Rock, Louisiana State University, and Samford University. His MBA and B.S. degrees are from Jacksonville State University in Alabama.

Dr. Hartline primarily teaches graduate courses in Marketing Strategy and Corporate Affairs Management, as well as undergraduate courses in Services Marketing. He has won many teaching and research awards and made many presentations to industry and academic audiences. Dr. Hartline has also served as a consultant to several for-profit and non-profit organizations in the areas of marketing plan development, market feasibility analysis, customer satisfaction measurement, customer service training, and pricing policy. He has also served on the executive committee of the Academy of Marketing Science, co-chaired two international conferences for the American Marketing Association, and has served on the editorial review boards of a number of leading marketing journals.

Dr. Hartline's research addresses marketing implementation issues in service firms. Specifically, his work examines the role of customer-contact employees and workgroups in the effective delivery of quality service to customers. Dr. Hartline's research appears in the *Journal of Marketing*, the *Journal of Service Research*, the *Journal of Business Research*, the *Journal of Relationship Marketing*, the *Journal of Services Marketing*, the *Cornell Quarterly*, the *Journal of Strategic Marketing*, the *Journal of Business Ethics*, and the *Marketing Science Institute Working Paper Series*.

Dr. Hartline and his wife Marsha live in Tallahassee with their daughters, Meghan, Madison, and Mallory. They have two dogs, Bella and Chief (both Japanese Chins), and a cat, Snickers. Dr. Hartline is a self-professed electronics and gadget enthusiast who enjoys music, reading, computers, travel, college football (Go Seminoles!), and being a dad.

Marketing Strategy

CHAPTER 1

Marketing in Today's Economy

Introduction

As noted in the opening *Beyond the Pages 1.1* story, competing in today's economy means finding ways to break out of commodity status to meet customers' needs better than competing firms. All organizations—both for-profit and nonprofit—require effective planning and a sound marketing strategy to do this effectively. Without these efforts, organizations would not be able to satisfy customers or meet the needs of other stakeholders. For example, having an effective marketing strategy allows Apple to develop popular products, such as the iPhone, iPad, and its MacBook line of notebook computers. Further, effective planning and strategy allows Cola-Cola to continue its leadership in soft drinks, make a key acquisition in its purchase of the Vitamin Water brand, all the while continuing its expansion into the lucrative Chinese market. These and other organizations use sound marketing strategy to leverage their strengths and capitalize on opportunities that exist in the market. Every organization—from your favorite local restaurant to giant multinational corporations; from city, state, and federal governments, to charities such as Habitat for Humanity and the American Red Cross—develops and implements marketing strategies.

How organizations plan, develop, and implement marketing strategies is the focus of this book. To achieve this focus, we provide a systematic process for developing customer-oriented marketing strategies and marketing plans that match an organization to its internal and external environments. Our approach focuses on real-world applications and practical methods of marketing planning, including the process of developing a marketing plan. The chapters of this book focus on the steps of this process. Our goal is to give the reader a deeper understanding of marketing planning, the ability to organize the vast amount of information needed to complete the planning process, and an actual feel for the development of marketing plans.

In this first chapter, we review some of the major challenges and opportunities that exist in planning marketing strategy in today's economy. We also review the nature and scope of major marketing activities and decisions that occur throughout the planning process. Finally, we look at some of the major challenges involved in developing marketing strategy.

B e y o n d   t h e   P a g e s   1 . 1

Thriving in Commodity Hell[1]

Have you noticed that regardless of the industry, most goods and services offered by competing companies are eerily the same? Most household appliances, such as refrigerators, washing machines, and stoves, offer the same basic features and come in white, beige, black, or stainless steel. Virtually all Android-based smartphones offer the same features at similar prices. Even airline flights from New York to Los Angeles are essentially the same. Everywhere you look, most companies offer the same basic products to the same customer groups at roughly the same prices. This situation is referred to as "commodity hell" and it's a tough situation for most companies. Commoditization is everywhere and is the result of mature markets where goods and services lack any real means of differentiation. Unfortunately for companies, when customers begin to see all competing products as offering roughly the same benefits, price is the only thing that matters.

Commoditization is a consequence of mature industries where slowing innovation, extensive product assortment, excess supply, and frugal consumers force margins to the floor. Since firms have few competitive differences, they are unable to increase margins. They must also spend a great deal on promotion to attract new customers. This situation makes firms more vulnerable to the entry of new competitors. Consider the airline industry. Notwithstanding a few minor differences, most air travelers see all airlines as being roughly the same. They all get passengers from Point A to Point B while offering the same basic customer services. This makes price the driving force in consumer decision-making and allows discount airlines such as Southwest and Jet Blue to steal customers away from traditional full-service carriers. This same precarious situation exists in a broad range of industries including telephone service, hotels, packaged goods, automobiles, household appliances, and retailing.

As you might expect, low price leaders can do quite well in commoditized markets. Southwest, for example, was profitable for over 33 years until the economic recession hit the industry hard in 2008. Today, Southwest is expanding routes by acquiring rival companies (such as AirTran). The company also stands apart from others with its innovative "No Bag Fees" promotional campaign. Other firms, however, avoid commodity status through the most basic of marketing tactics: brand building. Here, firms break free from commodity status by developing a distinctive brand position that separates them and their products from the competition. Firms that come to mind are Apple, Coca-Cola, and Chick-fil-A. By offering compelling reasons for consumers to buy products, brand building allows firms to increase margins. Apple, in particular, enjoys the highest profit margins of any firm in the technology sector.

Starbucks is another case in point. Starbucks clearly sells one of the most commoditized, ubiquitous products of all time: coffee. Starbucks Chairman Howard Schultz, however, does not accept that his firm is in the coffee business. Instead, Schultz sees Starbucks as a "third place" to hang out (with home and work being number 1 and number 2, respectively). Through this mentality, Starbucks offers its customers much more than coffee, including wireless Internet access, music, food, and relaxation. Starbucks has continued its brand-building activities by introducing breakfast combos, an instant coffee (Via), and the continued push of its Seattle's Best brand into restaurants, offices, hospitals, and vending machines.

Getting out of commodity hell is not an easy feat. To do so, firms must give consumers a compelling reason to buy their products over competing products. Ultimately, winning the commodity game is all about innovation. Consider the firms that top *BusinessWeek*'s list of the World's Most Innovative Companies for 2011 (in order): Apple, Twitter, Facebook, Nissan, Groupon, and Google. Each of these companies offers innovative products, processes, or experiences that stand apart from the competition; yet each competes in mature industries known for commoditization. These companies prove that innovation and good marketing strategy are the antidotes for commodity hell.

The Challenges and Opportunities of Marketing in Today's Economy

Traditional ideas about marketing strategy began to change forever during the mid 1990s. Advances in computer, communication, and information technology forever changed the world and the ways that marketers reach potential customers. The collapse of the dot-com bubble in the late 1990s was followed by a historic collapse of the world-wide economy in 2008. The powerhouse companies of the past have weakened and lost relevance in an economy marked by constant change and consumer skepticism. Consider these fundamental changes to marketing and business practice, as well as our own personal buying behavior:

- **Power Shift to Customers**. Perhaps the single most important change during the last two decades is the shift in power from marketers to consumers. Rather than businesses having the ability to manipulate customers via technology, customers often manipulate businesses because of their access to information, the ability to comparison shop, and the control they have over spending. Individual consumers and business customers can compare prices and product specifications in a matter of minutes. Using a smartphone and the Amazon app, customers can walk Target's aisles, scan bar codes to check prices on Amazon, and order items for two-day delivery while in the store. In other cases, customers are able to set their own prices, such as purchasing airline tickets at Priceline.com. Customers can now interact with one another, as merchants such as Amazon and eBay allow customers to share opinions on product quality and supplier reliability. As power continues to shift to customers, marketers have little choice but to ensure that their products are unique and of high quality, thereby giving customers a reason to purchase their products and remain loyal to them.
- **Massive Increase in Product Selection**. The variety and assortment of goods and services offered for sale on the Internet and in traditional stores is staggering. In grocery stores alone, customers are faced with countless options in the cereal and soft drink aisles. The growth in online retailing now allows customers to purchase a car from CarsDirect, handmade, exotic gifts from Mojo Tree (www.mojotree.co.uk), or a

© OmniTerra Images

Consumers can instantly find competitors' prices while in the store.

case of their favorite wine from Wine.com. Increased transaction efficiency (e.g., 24/7 access, delivery to home or office) allows customers to fulfill their needs more easily and conveniently than ever before. Furthermore, the vast amounts of information available online has changed the way we communicate, read the news, and entertain ourselves. Customers can now have the news delivered to them automatically via smartphone apps, such as Flipboard, that pull from hundreds of sources. This radical increase in product selection and availability has exposed marketers to inroads by competitors from every corner of the globe.

- **Audience and Media Fragmentation**. Changes in media usage and the availability of new media outlets have forced marketers to rethink the way they communicate with potential customers. Since the advent of cable television in the 1970s, mass media audiences have become increasingly fragmented. Television audiences, for example, shifted from the big three networks (ABC, CBS, NBC) and began watching programming on ESPN, HGTV, Nickelodeon, and the Discovery Channel. When the growth of the Internet, satellite radio, and mobile communication is added to this mix, it becomes increasingly difficult for marketers to reach a true mass audience. Media audiences have become fragmented due to (1) the sheer number of media choices we have available today, and (2) the limited time we have to devote to any one medium. Today, customers increasingly get information and news from Facebook and Twitter rather than the *New York Times* or CBS. They spend a growing amount of time online or interacting with handheld devices than they do reading magazines or watching television. As shown in Exhibit 1.1, consumer usage of traditional media is declining, while the usage of Internet and mobile media is on the rise. However, despite the challenge of reaching mass audiences today, media fragmentation does have a big advantage: It is easier to reach small, highly targeted audiences who are more receptive to specific marketing messages.
- **Changing Value Propositions**. Even before "The Great Recession" began in 2008, consumers and business buyers were already facing increasing costs associated with energy, gasoline, food, and other essentials. Then, as the economy weakened, buyers were forced to tighten their belts and look for other ways to lower expenses. This trend actually began after the dot-com collapse as consumers saw for the first time that they could bypass some types of firms and do things for themselves. For example, travel agents and real estate agents have been hit hard by e-commerce. Many customers now turn to Travelocity and Expedia, rather than travel agents, for

EXHIBIT 1.1   Change in Daily Media Usage by U.S. Adults, 2008–2011

	Percent Change (%)
Television and Video	7.9
Internet	21.9
Radio	-7.8
Mobile	103.1
Newspapers	-31.8
Magazines	-28.0
Other	0.0

Source: Media Literacy Clearinghouse, "Media Use Statistics," http://www.frankwbaker.com/mediause.htm, accessed July 18, 2012.

assistance in booking airline tickets, cruises, or hotel stays. A similar change has taken place in the real estate industry as buyers are moving their house hunting online, while sellers are increasingly taking the "for sale by owner" route. Consequently, many marketers learned a tough lesson: In situations where customers see goods and services as commodities, they will turn to the most convenient, least-expensive alternative.

Today, many of these same consumers face pay cuts or losing their jobs in addition to increased expenses. These and other economic hardships have forced consumer and business buyers to rethink value propositions and focus on the importance of frugality. The effects on business have been dramatic. For example, Kodak filed for Chapter 11 bankruptcy in early 2012 in the face of a highly commoditized market and stiff competition from other camera makers and smartphones with much improved camera technology. As consumers realized that the best camera was the one they had with them (i.e., their smartphones), they began to shy away from traditional camera makers like Kodak.[2] A similar shakeout is happening in the book retailing segment. Borders, for instance, closed its doors after fierce competition from Barnes & Noble, Amazon, Walmart, and Target lured its shoppers away. Likewise, we are just beginning to see the effects of e-book readers, like Amazon's Kindle, and personal publishing solutions, such as Apple's iBooks, on the book publishing industry. Because books have become highly commoditized, consumers typically search for the lowest prices rather than the fringe benefits offered by traditional bookstores. E-book readers add to that by being more ecologically advantageous. This is the essence of being frugal, as customers look for ways to cut spending on unnecessary parts of their lives.

- **Shifting Demand Patterns**. In some cases, changes in technology have shifted customer demand for certain product categories. News is one well-known example, where traditional newspapers are slowing disappearing while online and mobile news continues to grow. Now, many newspaper companies have folded, some are on the brink of folding, while others have cut publication to only a few days per week. Another example is the explosive growth in the digital distribution of music and video. The success of Apple's iPod and iTunes, YouTube, and Netflix, along with the continuing integration of television and computers, has dramatically shifted demand for the recording and movie industries. Hollywood film studios are grappling with soft demand in theatres and the declining popularity of DVDs as customers increasingly look for online movie options, or for other forms of entertainment such as video games. This trend ultimately led to the demise of Blockbuster video in 2011.

- **Privacy, Security, and Ethical Concerns**. Changes in technology have made our society much more open than in the past. As a result, these changes have forced marketers to address real concerns about security and privacy, both online and offline. Businesses have always collected routine information about their customers. Now, customers are much more attuned to these efforts and the purposes for which the information will be used. Though customers appreciate the convenience of e-commerce and mobile access to information, they want assurances that their information is safe and confidential. Concerns over privacy and security are especially acute with respect to online businesses such as Facebook, Google, and mobile devices that can potentially track every move we make, literally. These same concerns are also keen with respect to children. For example, many well-known and respected companies, including Mrs. Fields Cookies, Sony BMG, and Hershey Foods, have been fined for violating the standards of the Children's Online Privacy Protection Act (COPPA). For example, Playdom, Inc., an online gaming company owned by Disney,

---

EXHIBIT 1.2 The Children's Online Privacy Protection Act (COPPA)

The Children's Online Privacy Protection Act applies to operators of commercial websites and online services that attempt to collect personal information from children under the age of 13. The law explains what must be included in the firm's privacy policy, when and how to seek verifiable consent from a parent or guardian, and the firm's responsibilities to protect children's privacy and safety. Firms cannot evade the law's provisions by claiming that children under 13 cannot visit their sites; nor can they make information optional or ask the visitor's age.

In implementing the provisions of COPPA, the FTC issued the Children's Online Privacy Protection Rule, which is designed to give parents control over the information that is collected from their children. The rule requires website operators to:

- Post a description of its privacy policy on the site's homepage and any other area where personal information is collected.
- Provide notice to parents about the site's information collection practices. This full disclosure must describe (1) the type of information collected, (2) why the information is being collected, (3) how the information will be used and stored, (4) whether the information will be disclosed to third parties, and (5) parental rights with regard to information content and usage.
- Obtain verifiable parental consent to the collection and use of a child's personal information for internal use. The operator must also give parents the opportunity to choose not to have this information disclosed to third parties.
- Give parents access to their child's information, give them the right and means to review and/or delete this information, and give parents the choice to opt out of the future collection or use of the information.
- Not require that children provide more information than is reasonably necessary to participate in an activity. Children cannot be required to provide information as a condition of participation.
- Maintain the security, confidentiality, and integrity of all personal information collected from children.

Source: United States Federal Trade Commission, Bureau of Consumer Protection, http://business.ftc.gov/privacy-and-security/children's-privacy.

---

paid a $3 million fine to the Federal Trade Commission for collecting, using, and disclosing personal information from children under the age of 13 without their parents' permission. This was the largest civil penalty ever levied for a violation of COPPA, which is overviewed in Exhibit 1.2.[3]

- **Unclear Legal Jurisdiction**. When a company does business in more than one country (as many Internet-based firms do), that company often faces a dilemma with respect to differing legal systems. Today, this difference is especially keen for firms that do business in both the U.S. and China. Google, for example, faces a difficult situation in dealing with the Chinese government's censorship demands. Though Google is a U.S. firm, it must comply with the Chinese request by operating a completely separate search service that censors information considered sensitive by the Chinese government.[4] Doing business in China is also an issue with respect to protection of intellectual property rights, where Chinese laws do not offer the same protections found in the U.S. For example, the U.S. International Trade Commission estimates that Chinese piracy costs the U.S. economy in excess of $48 billion each year. Most of this is in the information sector, with high-tech and manufacturing also showing sizable losses due to infringements of intellectual property rights by Chinese firms.[5]

Another important legal issue involves the collection of sales tax for online transactions. In the early days of e-commerce, most online merchants did not collect sales taxes for online transactions—giving them a big advantage against store-based merchants. In fact, a 1992 U.S. Supreme Court decision exempted out-of-state retailers from collecting sales taxes in states where they had no physical presence. States countered that they were losing millions in yearly tax revenue, but were poorly organized to mount a collection effort. In 2003, major retailers—including Walmart, Target, and Toys "R" Us—in an agreement with a consortium of 38 states and the District of Columbia, agreed to collect online sales taxes. Amazon plans to collect sales tax from consumers in an additional eight states over the next four years. However, many online merchants still did not charge sales taxes. Today, states—much more organized than before—estimate that they lose a collective $23 billion per year in lost tax revenue. More than a dozen states have passed laws to force the collection of online sales taxes, and similar legislation is pending in ten other states.[6]

Although the full effect of these challenges will not be recognized for some time, circumstances have forced businesses to move ahead by adjusting their marketing activities at both the strategic and tactical levels. As we review the major marketing concepts and activities in this chapter, we will look at how today's challenges have affected strategic planning in these areas.

Basic Marketing Concepts

Marketing is many different things. Many people, especially those not employed in marketing, see marketing as a function of business. From this perspective, marketing parallels other business functions such as production/operations, research, management, human resources, and accounting. As a business function, the goal of marketing is to connect the organization to its customers. Other individuals, particularly those working in marketing jobs, tend to see marketing as a process of managing the flow of products from the point of conception to the point of consumption. The field's major trade organization, the American Marketing Association, has changed the definition of marketing over time to reflect changes in the economic and business environments. From 1985 until 2005, the AMA defined marketing this way:

> *"Marketing is the process of planning and executing the conception, pricing, promotion, and distribution of ideas, goods, and services to create exchanges that satisfy individual and organizational objectives."* [7]

Note how this definition focuses on the four Ps, or the marketing mix. In 2005, the AMA changed the definition to better reflect the realities of competing in the marketplace:

> *"Marketing is an organizational function and a set of processes for creating, communicating, and delivering value to customers and for managing customer relationships in ways that benefit the organization and its stakeholders."* [8]

This definition shifts the focus away from the marketing mix and toward value creation for customers. In 2007, the AMA changed the definition of marketing again:

> *"Marketing is the activity, set of institutions, and processes for creating, communicating, delivering, and exchanging offerings that have value for customers, clients, partners, and society at large."* [9]

Notice that the changes in the definition are not merely cosmetic in nature. The older definitions focused on the process of marketing to deliver value and manage customer relationships. The most recent definition shifts from "value" to "offerings that have value." Also, the notion of stakeholders is made more explicit. Why would the AMA make these changes? One reason has to do with commoditization as discussed in *Beyond the Pages 1.1*. Breaking free from commodity status means finding ways to differentiate the offering. The new definition recognizes that differentiation can come from any part of the offering, whereas older conceptualizations of marketing placed the onus of differentiation on the product itself. The second reason has to do with marketing's broader role in today's corporation. Firms don't just sell products; they sell the firm as a whole. Corporate relationships with partners, media, government, investors, employees, and society are every bit as important as relationships with customers. These types of relationships—which grow and thrive on exceptional value—are an absolute necessity in the commodity-driven status of many product markets. While the older definitions of marketing had a decidedly transactional focus, the new definition emphasizes long-term relationships that provide value for both the firm and its stakeholders.

A final way to think about marketing relates to meeting human and social needs. This broad view links marketing with our standard of living, not only in terms of enhanced consumption and prosperity, but also in terms of society's well being. Through marketing activities, consumers can buy cars from South Korea and wines from South Africa; and organizations can earn a viable profit, making both employees and shareholders happy. However, marketing must also bear responsibility for any negative effects it may generate. This view demands that marketers consider the social and ethical implications of their actions, and whether they practice good citizenship by giving back to their communities. As exemplified in the New Belgium Brewing case at the end of the text, firms can successfully meet human and social needs through socially responsible marketing and business practices.

Let's take a closer look at several basic marketing concepts. As we will see, ongoing changes in today's economy have forever altered our way of thinking about these foundational aspects of marketing.

What Is a Market?

At its most basic level, a *market* is a collection of buyers and sellers. We tend to think of a market as a group of individuals or institutions that have similar needs that can be met by a particular product. For example, the housing market is a collection of buyers and sellers of residential real estate, while the automobile market includes buyers and sellers of automotive transportation. Marketers or sellers tend to use the word "market" to describe only the buyers. This basic understanding of a market has not changed in a very long time. What has changed, however, is not so much the "what" but the "where" of a market; that is, the location of the buyers and sellers. In both consumer markets (like housing and automobiles) and business markets (like replacement parts and raw materials), the answer to the "where" question is quickly becoming "anywhere" as markets become less defined by geography.

Until recently, marketers have considered a market to be a physical location where buyers and sellers meet to conduct transactions. Although those venues (e.g., grocery stores, malls, flea markets) still exist, technology mediates some of the fastest growing markets. The term *marketspace* has been coined to describe these electronic marketplaces unbound by time or space.[10] In a marketspace, physical goods, services, and information are exchanged through computer networks. Some of the largest marketspaces, such as Amazon, eBay, and Monster, are now household names. In fact, Amazon has become the marketspace equivalent of a shopping mall as the company now sells shoes, apparel, jewelry, beauty aids, and sporting goods in addition to its traditional offerings of books and electronics. Marketspaces also exist in the business-to-business realm. The shift from marketplaces to marketspaces has significant ramifications for marketers. The fact that customers can shop, place orders, and exchange information 24/7 means that these businesses must be capable of operating in that same time frame. In effect, marketspace operators never take a break at closing time—they never close. It also means that firms lose some control over the information that is disseminated about their company or products. Through blogs, discussion forums, or even Twitter, customers can exchange information about a marketspace outside the marketspace itself. Furthermore, the substitution of technology for human interaction can be both a blessing and a curse. Some marketspaces, like CarsDirect, are successful because they eliminate the hassle of dealing with another human in the buying process. Many customers, however, have been slow to embrace marketspaces because they lack the human element. In these cases, the design and implementation of the online experience is a serious challenge for marketspace operators. Finally, the wealth of information available through today's marketspaces not only makes customers more educated than ever before, it also gives customers increased power through comparison shopping and price negotiation.

Another interesting shift related to markets is the advent of metamarkets and metamediaries. A *metamarket* is a cluster of closely related goods and services that center around a specific consumption activity. A *metamediary* provides a single access point where buyers can locate and contact many different sellers in the metamarket.[11] Assume for example that you are engaged to be married. How many different buying decisions will you and your fiancé have to make in the coming months? How many newspaper ads, websites, and magazines will you explore? Although the businesses and decisions are diverse, they all converge on the single theme of wedding planning. This is the driving principle behind a metamarket. Exhibit 1.3 shows examples of common metamarkets and metamediaries. Although customers don't use these terms, they fully understand the concept of finding information and solutions in one place. For example, iVillage (www.ivillage.com) has become the Internet's preeminent metamediary with respect to women's issues. One of its most popular sections deals with pregnancy and parenting, which has become the first stop for many anxious parents in need of advice. Metamediaries like iVillage fulfill a vital need by offering quick access and one-stop shopping to a wide variety of information, goods, and services.

What Is Exchange?

Closely related to the concept of a market, our ideas about exchange have changed in recent years. *Exchange* is traditionally defined as the process of obtaining something of value from someone by offering something in return; this usually entails obtaining products for money. For exchange to occur, five conditions must be met:

1. **There must be at least two parties to the exchange**. Although this has always been the case, the exchange process today can potentially include an unlimited number of participants. Online auctions provide a good example. Customers who bid on an item at eBay may be one of many participants to the exchange process. Each participant changes the process for the others, as well as the ultimate outcome for the winning bidder. Some auctions include multiple quantities of an item, so the potential exists for multiple transactions within a single auction process.

2. **Each party has something of value to the other party**. Exchange would be possible, but not very likely, without this basic requirement. The Internet has exposed us to a vast array of goods and services that we did not know existed previously. Today, not

EXHIBIT 1.3   Common Metamarkets and Participants

	Metamarkets		
	Automotive	**Home Ownership**	**Parenting**
Metamediaries	www.edmunds.com http://autos.msn.com www.carsdirect.com www.kbb.com	www.realtor.com http://realestate.msn.com www.bhg.com	www.ivillage.com/pregnancy-parenting www.parenting.com
Metamarket Participants	Buyers Manufacturers Car dealerships Banks Credit unions Credit reporting services Insurance firms Rating services Magazines Television programs Aftermarket parts/accessories Repair services Car rental firms Auction houses	Homeowners Builders Real estate agents Mortgage companies Insurance companies Home inspectors and appraisers Pest control services Magazines Television programs Retailers	Parents Doctors Retailers Baby supply manufacturers Insurance firms Financial planners Educational providers Toy manufacturers Television programs Movies

© Cengage Learning 2013

only can we buy a television or stereo receiver from a local merchant; we also have access to hundreds of online merchants. Furthermore, the ability to comparison shop products and their prices allows customers to seek out the best value.

3. **Each party must be capable of communication and delivery**. The advantages of today's communication and distribution infrastructure are amazing. We can find and communicate with potential exchange partners anywhere and anytime via telephone, computers, interactive television, and smartphones. We can also conduct arm's-length transactions in real time, with delivery of exchanged items occurring in a matter of hours if necessary. For example, you can text message an order to Pizza Hut on your way home from work.

4. **Each party must be free to accept or reject the exchange**. In the online world, this condition of exchange becomes a bit more complicated. Customers have grown accustomed to the ease with which they can return items to local merchants. Easy return policies are among the major strengths of traditional offline merchants. Returning items is more difficult with online transactions. In some cases, the ability to reject an exchange is not allowed in online transactions. Ordering airline tickets on Priceline.com and winning a bid on an item at eBay are contractually binding acts for the customer. Apple has a no refunds policy in its App Store. In other words, once the actual purchasing process has started, the customer is not free to reject the exchange.

5. **Each party believes it is desirable to exchange with the other party**. Customers typically have a great deal of information about, or even a history with, offline merchants. In online exchange, customers often know nothing about the other party. To help resolve this issue, a number of third-party firms have stepped in to provide ratings and opinions about online merchants. Sites like BizRate.com and Epinions.com not only provide these ratings, they also provide product ratings and serve as shopping

portals. eBay and Amazon go one step further by allowing buyers and sellers to rate each other. This gives both parties to the exchange process some assurance that reputable individuals or organizations exist on the other side of the transaction.

The bottom line is that exchange has become all too easy in today's economy. Opportunities for exchange bombard us virtually everywhere we go. Customers don't even have to trouble themselves with giving credit cards or completing forms for shipping information. Most online merchants will remember this information for us if we let them. For example, Amazon's 1-Click* ordering feature allows customers to purchase products with a single mouse click.[12] The ease with which exchange can occur today presents a problem in that individuals who do not have the authority to exchange can still complete transactions. This is especially true for underage customers.

What Is a Product?

It should come as no surprise that the primary focus of marketing is the customer and how the organization can design and deliver products that meet customers' needs. Organizations create essentially all marketing activities as a means toward this end; this includes product design, pricing, promotion, and distribution. In short, an organization would have no reason to exist without customers and a product to offer them.

But what exactly is a product? A very simple definition is that a *product* is something that can be acquired via exchange to satisfy a need or a want. This definition permits us to classify a broad number of "things" as products:[13]

- **Goods**. Goods are tangible items ranging from canned food to fighter jets, from sports memorabilia to used clothing. The marketing of tangible goods is arguably one of the most widely recognizable business activities in the world.
- **Services**. Services are intangible products consisting of acts or deeds directed towards people or their possessions. Banks, hospitals, lawyers, package delivery companies, airlines, hotels, repair technicians, nannies, housekeepers, consultants, and taxi drivers all offer services. Services, rather than tangible goods, dominate modern economies like the U.S. economy.
- **Ideas**. Ideas include issues aimed at promoting a benefit for the customer. Examples include cause-related or charitable organizations such as the Red Cross, the American Cancer Society, Mothers Against Drunk Drivers, or the American Legacy Foundation's campaign against smoking.[14]
- **Information**. Marketers of information include websites, magazine and book publishers, schools and universities, research firms, churches, and charitable organizations. Examples include iTunesU, Khan Academy, and the popular TED Talks website.[15] In the digital age, the production and distribution of information has become a vital part of our economy.
- **Digital Products**. Digital products, such as software, music, and movies are among the most profitable in our economy. Advancements in technology have also wreaked havoc in these industries because pirates can easily copy and redistribute digital products in violation of copyright law. Digital products are interesting because content producers grant customers a license to use them, rather than outright ownership.
- **People**. The individual promotion of people, such as athletes or celebrities, is a huge business around the world. The exchange and trading of professional athletes takes place in a complex system of drafts, contracts, and free agency. Other professions, such as politicians, actors, professional speakers, and news reporters, also engage in people marketing.

- **Places**. When we think of the marketing of a place, we usually think of vacation destinations like Rome or Orlando. However, the marketing of places is quite diverse. Cities, states, and nations all market themselves to tourists, businesses, and potential residents. The state of Alabama, for example, has done quite well in attracting direct investment by foreign firms. Over the last twenty years, Alabama has landed assembly plants from Mercedes, Honda, and Hyundai, as well as many different parts plants and related firms. It's no wonder that some people think of Alabama as the new Detroit.[16]
- **Experiences and Events**. Marketers can bring together a combination of goods, services, ideas, information, or people to create one-of-a-kind experiences or single events. Examples include theme parks such as Disney World and Universal Studios, sporting events like the Daytona 500 or the Super Bowl, or stage and musical performances like *The Phantom of the Opera* or a concert by Rihanna.
- **Real or Financial Property**. The exchange of stocks, bonds, and real estate, once marketed completely offline via real estate agents and investment companies, now occurs increasingly online. For example, Realtor.com is the nation's largest real estate listing service, with almost 4 million searchable listings. Likewise, Schwab.com is the world's largest and top-rated online brokerage.
- **Organizations**. Virtually all organizations strive to create favorable images with the public—not only to increase sales or inquiries, but also to generate customer goodwill. In this sense, General Electric is no different than the United Way: Both seek to enhance their images in order to attract more people (customers, volunteers, and clients) and money (sales, profit, and donations).

We should note that the products in this list are not mutually exclusive. For example, firms that sell tangible goods almost always sell services to supplement their offerings, and vice versa. Charitable organizations simultaneously market themselves, their ideas, and the information that they provide. Finally, special events like the Daytona 500 combine people (drivers), a place (Daytona), an event (the race), organizations (sponsors), and goods (souvenirs) to create a memorable and unique experience for race fans.

To effectively meet the needs of their customers and fulfill organizational objectives, marketers must be astute in creating products and combining them in ways that make them unique from other offerings. A customer's decision to purchase one product or group of products over another is primarily a function of how well that choice will fulfill their needs and satisfy their wants. Economists use the term *utility* to describe the ability of a product to satisfy a customer's desires. Customers usually seek out exchanges with marketers who offer products that are high in one or more of these five types of utility:

- **Form Utility**. Products high in form utility have attributes or features that set them apart from the competition. Often these differences result from the use of high quality raw materials, ingredients, or components; or from the use of highly efficient production processes. For example, Ruth's Chris Steakhouse, considered by many to be one of the nation's top chain restaurants, provides higher form utility than other national chains because of the quality of beef they use. Papa John's Pizza even stresses form utility in its slogan "Better Ingredients. Better Pizza." In many product categories, higher priced product lines offer more form utility because they have more features or bells-and-whistles. Luxury cars are a good example.
- **Time Utility**. Products high in time utility are available when customers want them. Typically, this means that products are available now rather than later. Grocery stores, restaurants, and other retailers that are open around the clock provide exceptional time utility. Often the most successful restaurants around college campuses are those that are open 24/7. Many customers are also willing to pay more for products

available in a shorter time frame (such as overnight delivery via FedEx) or for products available at the most convenient times (such as midmorning airline flights).

- **Place Utility**. Products high in place utility are available where customers want them, which is typically wherever the customer happens to be at that moment (such as grocery delivery to a home) or where the product needs to be at that moment (such as florist delivery to a work place). Home delivery of anything (especially pizza), convenience stores, vending machines, and e-commerce are examples of good place utility. Products that are high in both time and place utility are exceptionally valuable to customers because they provide the utmost in convenience.

- **Possession Utility**. Possession utility deals with the transfer of ownership or title from marketer to customer. Products higher in possession utility are more satisfying because marketers make them easier to acquire. Marketers often combine supplemental services with tangible goods to increase possession utility. For example, furniture stores that offer easy credit terms and home delivery enhance the possession utility of their goods. In fact, any merchant that accepts credit cards enhances possession utility for customers that do not carry cash or checks. Expensive products, like a home or a new factory, require acceptable financing arrangements to complete the exchange process.

- **Psychological Utility**. Products high in psychological utility deliver positive experiential or psychological attributes that customers find satisfying. Sporting events often fall into this category, especially when the competition is based on an intense rivalry. The atmosphere, energy, and excitement associated with being at the game can all create psychological benefits for customers. Conversely, a product might offer exceptional psychological utility because it lacks negative experiential or psychological attributes. For example, a vacation to the beach or the mountains might offer more psychological utility to some customers because it is seen as less stressful than a vacation to Disney World.

The strategic and tactical planning of marketing activities involves the important basic concepts we have explored in this section. Marketers often struggle with finding and

Sporting events deliver psychological utility that goes beyond the actual competition.

© mick20/Shutterstock

reaching the appropriate markets for their products. In other cases, the market is easily accessible, but the product is wrong or does not offer customers a compelling reason to purchase it. The ability to match markets and products in a way that satisfies both customer and organizational objectives is truly an art and a science. Doing so in an environment of never-ending change creates both opportunities and challenges for even the strongest and most respected organizations. As described in *Beyond the Pages 1.2*, Walmart, P&G, and Hulu have found ways to maintain innovative marketing during tough economic times.

The process of planning marketing activities to achieve these ends is the focus of this book. As we turn our attention to an overview of major marketing activities and decisions, we also want to lay out the structure of the text. The chapters roughly coincide with the major activities involved in developing marketing strategy and writing a marketing plan. Although our approach is orderly and straightforward, it provides a holistic representation of the marketing planning process from one period to the next. As we will see, marketing planning is an evolving process that has no definite beginning or ending point.

Major Marketing Activities and Decisions

Organizations must deal with a number of activities and decisions in marketing their products to customers. These activities vary in both complexity and scope. Whether the issue is a local restaurant's change in copy for a newspaper ad, or a large multinational firm launching a new product in a foreign market, all marketing activities have one thing in common: They aim to give customers a reason to buy the organization's product. In this section, we briefly introduce the activities and decisions that will be the focus of the remaining chapters of this book.

Strategic Planning

If an organization is to have any chance of reaching its goals and objectives, it must have a game plan or road map for getting there. A *strategy*, in effect, outlines the organization's game plan for success. Effective marketing requires sound strategic planning at a number of levels in an organization. At the top levels of the organization, planners concern themselves with macro issues such as the corporate mission, management of the mix of strategic business units, resource acquisition and assignments, and corporate policy decisions. Planners at the middle levels, typically a division or strategic business unit, concern themselves with similar issues, but focus on those that pertain to their particular product/market. Strategic planning at the lower levels of an organization is much more tactical in nature. Here, planners concern themselves with the development of marketing plans—more specific game plans for connecting products and markets in ways that satisfy both organizational and customer objectives.

Although this book is essentially about strategic planning, it focuses on tactical planning and the development of the marketing plan. *Tactical planning* addresses specific markets or market segments and the development of marketing programs that will fulfill the needs of customers in those markets. The *marketing plan* provides the outline for how the organization will combine product, pricing, distribution, and promotion decisions to create an offering that customers will find attractive. The marketing plan also addresses the implementation, control, and refinement of these decisions.

To stand a reasonable chance for success, marketing plans should be developed with a keen appreciation of how they fit into the strategic plans of the middle- and upper-levels of the firm. In Chapter 2, we discuss the connection among corporate,

Innovative Marketing Strategies for a Tough Economy[17]

Innovation has long been considered the lifeblood of business, especially in terms of growth and new market opportunities. Unfortunately, our economy's most recent struggles have made it difficult for companies to maintain the pace of innovation they have enjoyed over the past decade. The reason is purely financial: It is hard to be innovative when you are forced to cut costs, layoff employees, close plants, and maintain market standing. The same is true for consumers as they have reigned in spending due to the economy.

Still, some companies have managed to maintain their creativity and innovation even in a weakened economy. They do so by looking for the new opportunities that come along with changing customer spending patterns. Here are three cases in point:

Walmart

When customers have fewer dollars to spend, they try to make those dollars go further. In the grocery business, this translates into stronger sales for store brands (private labels). Many of Walmart's store brands are well known: Great Value, Sam's Choice, Faded Glory, HomeTrends, Ol' Roy, and Equate. To further take advantage of changing shopping patterns, Walmart decided to reinvigorate Great Value—its top-selling private label brand. To do this, Walmart improved the quality of roughly 750 food and grocery products, updated the Great Value logo, and freshened the packaging. In one bold move, Walmart pulled Hefty brand storage bags from its shelves in favor of their lower-priced Great Value brand. The company later returned Hefty to the shelves, but only after Hefty agreed to make the Great Value brand for Walmart. Other chains, such as CVS, Walgreens, Kroger, and Target, are now copying Walmart's strategy. Industry analysts expect other retailers to adopt the same strategy as customers look to private labels as a way to save money.

Procter & Gamble

One result of a weakened economy is that customers forgo buying new cars and instead begin taking better care of the cars they currently own. P&G decided to capitalize on this trend by launching a national chain of franchised car washes under its Mr. Clean brand. Since the car wash industry did not have a dominant national brand, P&G hoped that its Mr. Clean units would capture a good share of the $35 billion industry. To begin, P&G acquired Carnett's—a small car wash chain. Next, P&G took advantage of lower real estate prices to find suitable locations, and rising unemployment to find talented employees. The result, a 14-unit chain of Mr. Clean Car Wash franchisees (most are in the Atlanta area), has been a success. Buoyed by this success, P&G now plans to launch 150 Tide-branded dry cleaners over the next four years. One major benefit of the Tide concept is the lower franchise fee. It costs $950,000 to open a Tide Dry Cleaner, but up to $5 million to open a Mr. Clean Car Wash.

Hulu

When customers have less money to spend on entertainment, they tend to entertain themselves more at home. Hulu.com is perfectly poised to take advantage of this trend. A joint venture between Disney-ABC, NBCUniversal, and Fox Entertainment, Hulu is an advertising-supported, online video streaming service that offers prime-time television programming via the Internet and mobile apps. Hulu's growth comes from a growing trend of watching full-length programming via the Internet instead of network or cable television. The trend is especially prevalent among the prized 18- to 44-year-old demographic—a statistic that has advertisers buzzing. Hulu users spend an average of 206 minutes per month watching videos—each one embedded with advertising from mainstream companies like Best Buy, Bank of America, and Nissan. Customers can also subscribe to Hulu Plus for roughly $10 per month. In only four years, Hulu has become one of the top Internet video websites and generates over $420 million in revenue each year. Hulu's next push is with original programming, including programs such as Battleground and Misfits. The company spends over $500 million each year on programming.

What do these three stories teach us? First, companies can still be innovative in a weakened economy. The key is to conduct research to closely follow changing customer preferences and spending. Second, it's not enough to do the research. Good innovation must be accurately timed to the market. Third, to be creative, companies will often have to step outside their comfort zones. P&G is a great example. Who would have thought that a packaged goods company could become a service provider?

business-unit, and marketing planning, as well as how marketing plans must be integrated with the plans of other functions in the organization (financial plans, production plans, etc.). We also discuss the structure of the marketing plan and some of the challenges involved in creating one.

Research and Analysis

Strategic planning depends heavily on the availability and interpretation of information. Without this lifeblood, strategic planning would be a mindless exercise and a waste of time. Thankfully, today's planners are blessed with an abundance of information due to improving technology and the Internet. However, the challenge of finding and analyzing the right information remains. As many marketing planners have found, having the right information is just as important as having the right product.

Marketers are accustomed to conducting and analyzing research, particularly with respect to the needs, opinions, and attitudes of their customers. Although customer analysis is vital to the success of the marketing plan, the organization must also have access to three other types of information and analysis: internal analysis, competitive analysis, and environmental analysis. *Internal analysis* involves the objective review of internal information pertaining to the firm's current strategy and performance, as well as the current and future availability of resources. Analysis of the competitive environment, increasingly known as *competitive intelligence*, involves analyzing the capabilities, vulnerabilities, and intentions of competing businesses.[18] Analysis of the external environment, also known as *environmental scanning*, involves the analysis of economic, political, legal, technological, and cultural events and trends that may affect the future of the organization and its marketing efforts. Some marketing planners use the term *situation analysis* to refer to the overall process of collecting and interpreting internal, competitive, and environmental information.

The development of a sound marketing plan requires the analysis of information on all fronts. In Chapter 3, we address the collection and analysis of internal, customer, competitive, and environmental information. We also discuss the challenges involved in finding the right information from an overwhelming supply of available information. The uncertainty and continual change in the external environment also create challenges for marketers (as the Internet boom and bust have shown us). As we will see, this type of research and analysis is perhaps the most difficult aspect of developing a marketing plan.

Developing Competitive Advantage

To be successful, a firm must possess one or more competitive advantages that it can leverage in the market in order to meet its objectives. A *competitive advantage* is something that the firm does better than its competitors that gives it an edge in serving customers' needs and/or maintaining mutually satisfying relationships with important stakeholders. Competitive advantages are critical because they set the tone, or strategic focus, of the entire marketing program. When these advantages are tied to market opportunities, the firm can offer customers a compelling reason to buy their products. Without a competitive advantage, the firm and its products are likely to be just one more offering among a sea of commoditized products. Apple, for example, has been quite successful in leveraging innovation and the customer experience to maintain a sizable competitive advantage in computers, portable music players, and music and movie distribution. A typical Mac computer costs substantially more than a comparable PC running Windows. However, Apple bundles multimedia software and a top-rated user experience into the mix. As a result, Apple computers continue to command a price premium, where most PC manufacturers engage in price wars.[19]

In Chapter 4, we discuss the process of developing competitive advantages and establishing a strategic focus for the marketing program. We also address the role of SWOT analysis as a means of tying the firm's strengths or internal capabilities to market opportunities. Further, we discuss the importance of developing goals and objectives. Having good goals and objectives is vital because these become the basis for measuring the success of the entire marketing program. For example, Hampton Inn has a goal of 100% customer satisfaction. Customers do not have to pay for their stay if they are not completely satisfied.[20] Goals like these are not only useful in setting milestones for evaluating marketing performance; they also motivate managers and employees. This can be especially true when marketing goals or objectives help to drive employee evaluation and compensation programs.

Marketing Strategy Decisions

An organization's marketing strategy describes how the firm will fulfill the needs and wants of its customers. It can also include activities associated with maintaining relationships with other stakeholders, such as employees, shareholders, or supply chain partners. Stated another way, marketing strategy is a plan for how the organization will use its strengths and capabilities to match the needs and requirements of the market. A marketing strategy can be composed of one or more marketing programs; each program consists of two elements—a target market or markets and a marketing mix (sometimes known as the four Ps of product, price, place, and promotion). To develop a marketing strategy, an organization must select the right combination of target market(s) and marketing mix(es) in order to create distinct competitive advantages over its rivals.

Market Segmentation and Target Marketing   The identification and selection of one or more target markets is the result of the market segmentation process. Marketers engage in *market segmentation* when they divide the total market into smaller, relatively homogeneous groups or segments that share similar needs, wants, or characteristics. When a marketer selects one or more *target markets*, they identify one or more segments of individuals, businesses, or institutions toward which the firm's marketing efforts will be directed. As described in *Beyond the Pages 1.3*, marketers increasingly use online social networking as a way to target specific markets.

Advances in technology have created some interesting changes in the ways that organizations segment and target markets. Marketers can now analyze customer-buying patterns in real time at the point of purchase via barcode scanning in retail stores, and analyzing clickstream data in online transactions. This allows organizations to target specific segments with product offers or promotional messages.[22] Furthermore, technology now gives marketers the ability to target individual customers through direct mail and e-mail campaigns. This saves considerable time and expense by not wasting efforts on potential customers who may not be interested in the organization's product offering. However, these new opportunities for marketers come at a price: Many potential buyers resent the ability of marketers to reach them individually. Consequently, customers and governmental authorities have raised major concerns over privacy and confidentiality. This is especially true with respect to RFID, or radio frequency identification, which uses tiny radio-enabled chips to track merchandise or process credit card transactions. Since RFID chips can be scanned from distances up to 25 feet, many fear that the technology will allow companies to track consumers even after they leave a store.[23]

Chapter 5 discusses the issues and strategies associated with market segmentation and target marketing. In that discussion, we will examine different approaches to market segmentation and look at target marketing in both consumer and business markets. Effective segmentation and target marketing sets the stage for the development of the

Beyond the Pages 1.3

Targeting Consumers via Online Social Networking[21]

Social networking has proven to be very popular with both users and advertisers. Sites like Facebook, Google+, LinkedIn, Pinterest, and Twitter allow users to share information, find old friends, or network with like-minded individuals. Most users are teens and young adults who use the sites to trade messages, photos, music, and blogs. The largest of these sites currently is Facebook, which boasts over 850 million active users worldwide. Twitter has over 360 million registered users. Other sites are also growing rapidly.

While social networks are very popular, they have attracted a fair amount of criticism. Many argue that these sites make it easier for predators to reach teens and children through the use of their online profiles. Business experts have been skeptical of the long-term success of social networking as a business model. They argue that younger audiences are fickle and will leave these sites for the next hot thing on the Internet. Others argue that the questionable nature of the content on these sites is a risky proposition when tied to advertising strategies.

Despite these criticisms, online social networking appears to have legs for the long-term—forcing media companies and advertisers to take notice. The reason is simple: the demographic profile of the social networking audience is extremely lucrative. MySpace's audience is primarily teens in the 12 to 17 age range. Facebook's fastest growing age segment is the 25 and over crowd. LinkedIn has a different profile of over 150 million members with an older, more professional demographic. However, LinkedIn's profile has been shifting as more students and recent college graduates join the network. Powerful segmentation like this has forced an increasing number of advertisers to consider social networking as a viable media strategy.

In addition to the demographic fortune, social networking also allows firms to carefully target promotions to the right audience and collect a striking amount of information about users. For example, Nike used Facebook Places to target consumers in Portland, Oregon with free athletic jackets for individuals who checked in to a specified location in the city. Vitamin Water used a Facebook campaign asking users to help them choose the next flavor of the popular drink. Domino's also used Facebook to distribute promotional codes to fans of its page. American Airlines and IBM have had similar success using Twitter to reach potential customers.

Social networking sites have become so successful that they are replacing Google, Yahoo!, MSN, and AOL as the web portals of choice. In essence, social networking sites have become one-stop shops for communication, information, and commerce. Consumers can buy products without having to leave these sites, and marketers are paying attention. Recently, Facebook added the ability to rent movies and buy music directly from its site. This has caused competitors, such as Amazon, Netflix, and Apple, to take notice.

---

product offering and the design of a marketing program that can effectively deliver the offering to targeted customers.

Marketing Program Decisions   As we will address in Chapter 6, successful marketing programs depend on a carefully crafted blend of the four major marketing mix elements (i.e., product, price, distribution, and promotion). Earlier in the chapter, we discussed the many different types of products that can be offered to customers. Since the product and its attributes fulfill the basic needs and wants of the customer, it is no surprise that the product and the decisions that surround it are among the most important parts of the marketing program. This importance hinges on the connection between the product and the customers' needs. Even large corporations fail to make this connection at times. McDonald's, for example, spent over $100 million in the mid-1990s to launch the Arch Deluxe—a hamburger designed for adult tastes. The product failed miserably because it was designed for older customers (who are not McDonald's core market), was expensive, and had a very high calorie content. McDonald's customers avoided the Arch Deluxe and the sandwich was eventually discontinued.[24] As this example illustrates, marketing is unlikely to be effective unless there is a solid linkage between a product's benefits and customers' needs.

Pricing decisions are important for several reasons. First, price is the only element of the marketing mix that leads to revenue and profit. All other elements of the marketing mix, such as product development and promotion, represent expenses. Second, price typically has a direct connection with customer demand. This connection makes pricing the most over manipulated element of the marketing mix. Marketers routinely adjust the price of their products in an effort to stimulate or curb demand. Third, pricing is the easiest element of the marketing program to change. There are very few other aspects of marketing that can be altered in real time. This is a huge plus for marketers who need to adjust prices to reflect local market conditions, or for online merchants who want to charge different prices for different customers based on total sales or customer loyalty. Finally, pricing is a major quality cue for customers. In the absence of other information, customers tend to equate higher prices with higher quality.

Distribution and supply chain issues are among the least apparent decisions made in marketing, particularly with customers. The goal of *distribution and supply chain management* is essentially to get the product to the right place, at the right time, in the right quantities, at the lowest possible cost. *Supply chain* decisions involve a long line of activities—from the sourcing of raw materials, through the production of finished products, to ultimate delivery to final customers. Most of these activities, which customers take for granted, take place behind the scenes. Few customers, for example, contemplate how their favorite cereal ends up on their grocer's shelf or how Dell can have a made-to-order computer at your door in days. Customers just expect these things to happen. In fact, most customers never consider these issues until something goes wrong. Suddenly, when the grocer is out of an item or an assembly line runs low on component parts, distribution and supply chain factors become quite noticeable.

Modern marketing has replaced the term *promotion* with the concept of *integrated marketing communication (IMC)*, or the coordination of all promotional activities (media advertising, direct mail, personal selling, sales promotion, public relations, packaging, store displays, website design, personnel) to produce a unified, customer-focused message. Here, the term "customers" not only refers to customers in the traditional sense, but also includes employees, business partners, shareholders, the government, the media, and society in general. IMC rose to prominence in the 1990s as businesses realized that traditional audiences for promotional efforts had become more diverse and fragmented. IMC can also reduce promotional expenses by eliminating the duplication of effort among separate departments (marketing, sales, advertising, public affairs, and information technology) and by increasing efficiencies and economies of scale.

Branding and Positioning   When you think about a company like Southwest Airlines, what comes to mind? Most people will likely say low fares and no bag fees. Others may think of limited routes and destinations. As we will see in Chapter 7, what customers think about a company and its offerings is the focus of branding and positioning strategy. In order to understand branding, the marketer must have a clear understanding of how the elements of the marketing program work together to create the brand. While product decisions (such as design, style, and features) play a prominent role in branding, so do other program elements such as price/value, availability/exclusivity, and image/reputation of both the firm and its offerings. Marketers must also make decisions regarding package design, trademarks, and warranties or guarantees. *Product positioning* involves establishing a mental image, or position, of the product offering relative to competing offerings in the minds of target buyers. The goal of positioning is to distinguish or differentiate the firm's product offering from those of competitors by making the offering stand out among the crowd. As Southwest has shown us, even something as simple as "no bag fees" can be very successful in setting the firm apart from the competition. Another example is the battle between Walmart and Target. The mental image that most customers have of Walmart is associated with everyday low prices. Target has a slightly different position, one that emphasizes value with a stronger sense of style and quality.

Social Responsibility and Ethics

The role of social responsibility and ethics in marketing strategy has come to the forefront of important business issues in today's economy. Our society still reverberates from the effects of corporate scandals at Enron, WorldCom, and ImClone, among others. Although these scandals make for interesting reading, many innocent individuals have suffered the consequences from these companies' unethical behavior. *Social responsibility* refers to an organization's obligation to maximize its positive impact on society, while minimizing its negative impact. In terms of marketing strategy, social responsibility addresses the total effect of an organization's marketing activities on society. A major part of this responsibility is *marketing ethics*, or the principles and standards that define acceptable conduct in marketing activities. Ethical marketing can build trust and commitment and is a crucial ingredient in building long-term relationships with all stakeholders. Another major component of any firm's impact on society is the degree to which it engages in philanthropic activities. Many firms now make philanthropy a key strategic activity.

In Chapter 8, we discuss the economic, legal, ethical, and philanthropic dimensions of social responsibility, along with the strategic management of corporate integrity in the marketing planning process. Although there are occasional lapses, most firms understand their economic and legal responsibilities. However, social and ethical responsibilities, by their nature, are not so clearly understood. Many firms see social responsibility not only as a way to be a good corporate citizen, but also as a good way to build their brands. For example, the Red brand—created by Bono in 2006—has been marketed successfully by firms such as Gap, Apple, Motorola, Armani, Converse, and American Express. These and other companies market Red brand versions of their products with the aim to donate 50 percent of their profits to the Global Fund to fight AIDS in Africa.[25]

Implementation and Control

Once a marketing strategy has been selected and the elements of the marketing mix are in place, the marketer must put the plan into action. *Marketing implementation*, the process of executing the marketing strategy, is the "how" of marketing planning. Rather than being an add-on at the end of the marketing strategy and marketing plan, implementation is actually a part of planning itself. That is, when planning a marketing strategy, the organization must always consider how the strategy will be executed. Sometimes, the organization must revisit the strategy or plan to make revisions during the strategy's execution. This is where marketing control comes into play. Adequate control of marketing activities is essential to ensure that the strategy stays on course and focused on achieving its goals and objectives.

The implementation phase of marketing strategy calls into play the fifth "P" of the marketing program: people. As we will learn in Chapter 9, many of the problems that occur in implementing marketing activities are "people problems" associated with the managers and employees on the frontline of the organization who have responsibility for executing the marketing strategy. Many organizations understand the vital link between people and implementation by treating their employees as indispensable assets. AFLAC, for example, has been named 14 consecutive years by *Fortune* magazine to its list of the "100 Best Companies to Work for in America." The Georgia-based company has developed a corporate culture that focuses on caring for employees and providing for their needs.[26] Other companies cited as having good relationships with their employees include Google, Wegman's Food Markets, Mercedes-Benz USA, and The Container Store.

Developing and Maintaining Customer Relationships

Over the last two decades, marketers have come to the realization that they can learn more about their customers, and earn higher profits, if they develop long-term relationships with them. This requires that markers shift away from transactional marketing and embrace a relationship marketing approach. The goal of *transactional marketing* is to complete a large number of discrete exchanges with individual customers. The focus is on acquiring customers and making the sale, not necessarily on attending to customers' needs and wants. In *relationship marketing*, the goal is to develop and maintain long-term, mutually satisfying arrangements where both buyer and seller focus on the value obtained from the relationship. As long as this value stays the same or increases, the relationship is likely to deepen and grow stronger over time. Exhibit 1.4 illustrates the basic characteristics of transactional versus relationship marketing. Relationship marketing promotes customer trust and confidence in the marketer, who can then develop a deeper understanding of customers' needs and wants. This puts the marketer in a position to respond more effectively to customer's needs, thereby increasing the value of the relationship for both parties.

The principles and advantages of relationship marketing are the same in both business-to-business and consumer markets. Relationship marketing activities also extend beyond customers to include relationships with employees and supply chain partners. In Chapter 10, we discuss these and other aspects of relationship marketing in greater depth. Long-term relationships with important stakeholders will not materialize unless these relationships create value for each participant. This is especially true for customers faced with many different alternatives among firms competing for their business. Since the quality and value of a marketer's product offering typically determine customer value and satisfaction, Chapter 10 will also discuss the role of quality, value, and satisfaction in developing and maintaining customer relationships. Issues associated with quality, value, and satisfaction

---

EXHIBIT 1.4 **Major Characteristics of Transactional and Relationship Marketing**

	Transactional Marketing	Relationship Marketing
Marketing Focus	Customer Acquisition	Customer Retention
Time Orientation	Short-Term	Long-Term
Marketing Goal	Make the Sale	Mutual Satisfaction
Relationship Focus	Create Exchanges	Create Value
Customer Service Priority	Low	High
Customer Contact	Low to Moderate	Frequent
Commitment to Customers	Low	High
Characteristics of the Interaction	Adversarial, Manipulation, Conflict Resolution	Cooperation, Trust, Mutual Respect, Confidence
Source of Competitive Advantage	Production, Marketing	Relationship Commitment

cut across all elements of the marketing program. Hence, we discuss these issues in our final chapter as a means of tying all of the marketing program elements together.

Taking On the Challenges of Marketing Strategy

One of the greatest frustrations and opportunities in marketing is change—customers change, competitors change, and even the marketing organization changes. Strategies that are highly successful today will not work tomorrow. Customers will buy products today that they will have no interest in tomorrow. These are truisms in marketing. Although frustrating, challenges like these also make marketing extremely interesting and rewarding. Life as a marketer is never dull.

Another fact about marketing strategy is that it is inherently people-driven. Marketing strategy is about people (inside an organization) trying to find ways to deliver exceptional value by fulfilling the needs and wants of other people (customers, shareholders, business partners, society at large), as well as the needs of the organization itself. Marketing strategy draws from psychology, sociology, and economics to better understand the basic needs and motivations of these people—whether they are the organization's customers (typically considered the most critical), its employees, or its stakeholders. In short, marketing strategy is about people serving people.

The combination of continual change and the people-driven nature of marketing makes developing and implementing marketing strategy a challenging task. A perfect strategy that is executed perfectly can still fail. This happens because there are very few rules for how to do marketing in specific situations. In other words, it is impossible to say that given "this customer need" and these "competitors" and this "level of government regulation" that Product A, Price B, Promotion C, and Distribution D should be used. Marketing simply doesn't work that way. Sometimes, an organization can get lucky and be successful despite having a terrible strategy and/or execution. The lack of rules and the ever changing economic, sociocultural, competitive, technological, and political/legal landscapes make marketing strategy a terribly fascinating subject.

Most of the changes that marketers have faced over the past twenty years deal with the basic evolution of marketing and business practice in our society. One of the most basic shifts involves the increasing demands of customers. Today, customers have very high expectations about basic issues such as quality, performance, price, and availability. American customers in particular have a passion for instant gratification that marketers struggle to fulfill. Some evidence suggests that marketers have not met this challenge. The American Customer Satisfaction Index, computed by the National Quality Research Center at the University of Michigan, indicates that customer satisfaction has only recently recovered since the Center first computed the index in 1994. As shown in Exhibit 1.5, some industries such as newspapers and airlines have suffered large declines in customer satisfaction. Satisfaction in other industries, such as the automotive industry and soft drinks, has remained fairly high and stable.

The decline in satisfaction can be attributed to several reasons. For one, customers have become much less brand loyal than in previous generations. Today's customers are very price sensitive, especially in commoditized markets where products lack any real means of differentiation. Consequently, customers constantly seek the best value and thrive on their ability to compare prices among competing alternatives. Customers are also quite cynical about business in general and are not that trusting of marketers. In short, today's customers not only have more power; they also have more attitude. This combination makes them a formidable force in the development of contemporary marketing strategy.

Marketers have also been forced to adapt to shifts in markets and competition. In terms of their life cycles, most products compete today in very mature markets. Many

EXHIBIT 1.5   American Customer Satisfaction Index

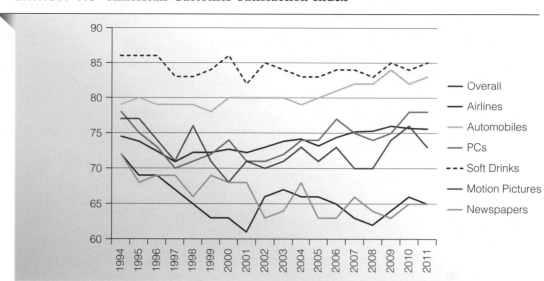

Source: American Customer Satisfaction Index and the University of Michigan Business School, http://www.theacsi.org, 2012.

firms also compete in markets where product offerings have become commoditized by a lack of differentiation (e.g., customers perceive competing offerings as essentially the same). Some examples include airlines, wireless phone service, department stores, laundry supplies, and household appliances. Product commoditization pushes margins lower and reduces brand loyalty even further. To meet this challenge, U.S. firms have moved aggressively into foreign markets in an effort to increase sales and find new growth opportunities. At the same time, however, foreign firms have moved into U.S. markets to meet the challenges of maturing markets in their own countries. It is interesting that while Apple has pushed iTunes aggressively into other nations, Spotify, a Swedish-based music streaming service, has launched its wildly popular service in the United States. The company's integration with Facebook allowed it to add more than 7 million new subscribers in only two months.[27]

In the face of increasing competition and maturing markets, businesses have been forced to cut expenses in order to remain competitive. Some businesses do this by eliminating products or product lines. GM, for example, dropped its Saturn division—a move similar to its dropping of Oldsmobile and the Hummer H1. Others have maintained their product mix, but have aggressively sought ways to lower their distribution costs. The growth in direct distribution (manufacturer to end user) is a result of these efforts. Still other firms have been forced to take drastic measures, such as downsizing and laying off employees to trim expenses.

Needless to say, developing a viable and effective marketing strategy has become extremely challenging. Even the most admired marketers in the world like McDonald's, Procter & Gamble, Anheuser-Busch, and Toyota occasionally have problems meeting the demands of the strategic planning process and developing the "right" marketing strategy. Our goal in this book is not to teach you to develop the "right" strategy. Rather, our approach will give you a framework for organizing the planning process, and the ability to see how all of the pieces fit together. Think of it as a mindset or way to think about marketing strategy. The remainder of this text dedicates itself to these goals.

Lessons from Chapter 1

Marketing challenges and opportunities in the new economy include:

- a shift in power to customers caused by increased access to information.
- a massive increase in product selection due to line extensions and global sourcing.
- greater audience and media fragmentation as customers spend more time with interactive media and less time with traditional media.
- changing customer perceptions of value and frugality.
- shifting demand patterns for certain product categories, especially those delivered digitally.
- increasing concerns over privacy, security, and ethics.
- unclear legal jurisdictions, especially in global markets.

Marketing:

- is parallel to other business functions such as production, research, management, human resources, and accounting. The goal of marketing is to connect the organization to its customers.
- is defined as the activity, set of institutions, and processes for creating, communicating, delivering, and exchanging offerings that have value for customers, clients, partners, and society at large.
- has changed in focus over the past 20 years. Today, marketing stresses value and customer relationships, including relationships with all potential stakeholders.
- is linked with our standard of living, not only in terms of enhanced consumption and prosperity, but also in terms of society's well being.

Basic marketing concepts include:

- market—a collection of buyers and sellers.
- marketplace—a physical location where buyers and sellers meet to conduct transactions.
- marketspace—an electronic marketplace not bound by time or space.
- metamarket—a cluster of closely related goods and services that centers on a specific consumption activity.
- metamediary—a single access point where buyers can locate and contact many different sellers in the metamarket.
- exchange—the process of obtaining something of value from someone by offering something in return; this usually involves obtaining products for money. There are five conditions of exchange:
  1. There must be at least two parties to the exchange.
  2. Each party has something of value to the other party.
  3. Each party must be capable of communication and delivery.
  4. Each party must be free to accept or reject the exchange.
  5. Each party believes it is desirable to exchange with the other party.
- product—something that can be acquired via exchange to satisfy a need or a want.
- utility—the ability of a product to satisfy a customer's needs and wants. The five types of utility provided through marketing exchanges are form utility, time utility, place utility, possession utility, and psychological utility.

Major marketing activities and decisions include:

- strategic and tactical planning.
- research and analysis.
- developing competitive advantages and a strategic focus for the marketing program.
- marketing strategy decisions, including decisions related to market segmentation and target marketing, as well as the marketing program (i.e., product, pricing, distribution, and promotion) and branding/positioning.
- social responsibility and ethics.
- implementing and controlling marketing activities.
- developing and maintaining long-term customer relationships, including a shift from transactional marketing to relationship marketing.

Some of the challenges involved in developing marketing strategy include:

- unending change—customers change, competitors change, and even the marketing organization changes.
- the fact that marketing is inherently people-driven.
- the lack of rules for choosing appropriate marketing activities.
- the basic evolution of marketing and business practice in our society.
- the increasing demands of customers.
- an overall decline in brand loyalty and an increase in price sensitivity among customers.
- increasing customer cynicism about business and marketing activities.
- competing in mature markets with increasing commoditization and little real differentiation among product offerings.
- increasing expansion into foreign markets by U.S. and foreign firms.
- aggressive cost-cutting measures in order to increase competitiveness.

Questions for Discussion

1. Increasing customer power is a continuing challenge to marketers in today's economy. In what ways have you personally experienced this shift in power; either as a customer or as a business person? Is this power shift uniform across industries and markets? How so?

2. How concerned are you about privacy and security in today's economy? Why do so many people, particularly younger people, seem to be unconcerned about privacy? Will these issues still be important in 10 years? Explain.

3. The text argues that marketing possesses very few rules for choosing the appropriate marketing activities. Can you describe any universal rules of marketing that might be applied to most products, markets, customers, and situations?

Exercises

1. The pace of change in our economy was frenetic from 1999 to 2001 (the so called dot-com boom) because of rapidly expanding technology and the growth of the Internet. Shortly thereafter, the bubble burst and many dot-com pioneers disappeared. Conduct some research to determine the reasons for the collapse. Most experts contend that a similar type of shakeout is unlikely today. What is different about today's technology and the Internet that points to this conclusion? How can firms prevent another collapse?

2. Logon to a metamediary in the automobile metamarket (e.g., www.edmunds.com, www.autos.msn.com, www.kbb.com, or www.carsdirect.com). What aspects of the car buying experience does the metamediary offer? Which aspects of the experience are missing? How does the metamediary overcome these missing aspects?

3. Think about all of the exchanges that you participate in on a weekly or monthly basis. How many of these exchanges have their basis in long-term relationships? How many are simple transaction-based exchanges? Which do you find most satisfying? Why?

End Notes

1. These facts are from Justin Bachman, Mary Schlangenstein, and John Hughes, "Southwest Charts a New Flight Plan," *Business-Week Online*, September 29, 2010 (http://www.businessweek.com/magazine/content/10_41/b4198022740823.htm); "Best Buy: How to Break Out of Commodity Hell," *BusinessWeek Online*, March 27, 2006 (http://www.businessweek.com/magazine/content/06_13/b3977007.htm); Leslie Patton, "Starbucks Targets Folks Who Shun Starbucks," *BusinessWeek Online*, April 21, 2011 (http://www.businessweek.com/magazine/content/11_18/b4226026215941.htm); and "The World's Most Innovative Companies 2011," Fast Company (http://www.fastcompany.com/most-innovative-companies/2011), accessed February 13, 2012.

2. "Kodak to Phase Out Its Camera, Digital Picture Frame Business as Part of Cost Cuts," *Washington Post*, February 11, 2012 (http://www.washingtonpost.com/business/kodak-to-phase-out-it-camera-digital-picture-frame-business-as-part-of-cost-cuts/2012/02/09/gIQABjSJ1Q_story.html).

3. William B. Baker, "Sony Pays Record Civil Penalty to Settle COPPA Violations," *Privacy in Focus*, January 2009 (http://www.wileyrein.com/publication.cfm?publication_id=14098); and Kevin Khurana, "COPPA Violations? Cop a Settlement for $3 Million," Proskauer.com, May 18, 2011 (http://privacylaw.proskauer.com/2011/05/articles/childrens-online-privacy-prote/coppa-violations-cop-a-settlement-for-3-million).

4. "Google, Internet Portals Targeted by Chinese Crackdown Apologize," *ABS-CBN News*, January 8, 2009 (http://www.abs-cbnnews.com/technology/01/08/09/google-internet-portals-targeted-chinese-crackdown-apologize); and Laura Sydell, "Google Unveils Censored Search Engine in China," *All Things Considered*, January 25, 2006 (http://www.npr.org/templates/story/story.php?storyId=5172204).

5. "U.S. ITC Report on China Piracy Shows Billions in Losses: Senators Demand Action," *Intellectual Property Watch*, May 18, 2011 (http://www.ip-watch.org/2011/05/18/us-itc-report-on-china-piracy-shows-billions-in-losses-senators-demand-action).

6. Sandra Block, "Momentum Growing for Sales Taxes on Online Purchases," *USA Today Online*, February 8, 2012 (http://www.usatoday.com/money/perfi/taxes/story/2012-02-08/online-sales-taxes/53015142/1).

7. American Marketing Association (http://www.marketingpower.com).

8. Ibid.

9. Ibid.

10. Jeffrey F. Rayport and Bernard J. Jaworski, *e-Commerce* (Boston: McGraw-Hill/Irwin, 2001), 3.

11. Mohanbir Sawhney, "Making New Markets," *Business 2.0,* May 1999, 116–121.

12. Amazon.com (http://www.amazon.com).

13. William M. Pride and O. C. Ferrell, *Marketing* (Mason, OH: Cengage Learning, 2012), pp. 320–22.

14. Legacy Foundation (http://www.legacyforhealth.org).

15. TED (http://www.ted.com/talks).

16. Alabama Development Office, "Teamwork Drives Hyundai to Alabama!" *Developing Alabama,* Spring 2002.

17. These facts are from Ellen Byron, "Mr. Clean Takes Car-Wash Gig," *Wall Street Journal Online,* February 5, 2009 (http://online.wsj.com/article/SB123379252641549893.html); Andria Cheng, "Retailers Try New Tricks Amid Global Downturn," *MarketWatch,* March 23, 2009 (http://www.marketwatch.com/story/wal-marts-great-value-signals-coming); Lauren Coleman-Lochner and Mark Clothier, "P&G Looks to Franchise Tide Dry Cleaning," *Business-Week Online,* September 2, 2010 (http://www.businessweek.com/magazine/content/10_37/b4194020958182.htm); Andy Fixmer, "Hulu Plans to Raise Money to Fund Expansion into Original Shows," *BusinessWeek Online,* January 18, 2012 (http://www.businessweek.com/news/2012-01-18/hulu-plans-to-raise-money-to-fund-expansion-into-original-shows.html); Mr. Clean Car Wash website (http://mrcleancarwash.com), accessed February 14, 2012; Reena Jana, "P&G's Trickle-Up Success: Sweet as Honey," *BusinessWeek Online,* March 31, 2009 (http://www.businessweek.com/innovate/content/mar2009/id20090331_127029.htm?chan=innovation_innovation+%2B+design_innovation+strategy); Parija Kavilanz, "Dumped! Brand Names Fight to Stay in Stores," *Fortune,* February 16, 2010 (http://money.cnn.com/2010/02/15/news/companies/walmart_dropping_ brands/index.htm); Tom Lowry, "NBC and New Corp.'s Hulu is Off to a Strong Start," *BusinessWeek Online,* September 25, 2008 (http://www.businessweek.com/magazine/content/08_40/b4102052685561.htm); and Jeneanne Rae, "Innovative Ways to Grow During the Downturn," *BusinessWeek Online,* April 15, 2009 (http://www.businessweek.com/innovate/content/apr2009/id20090415_238678.htm).

18. The Society of Competitive Intelligence Professionals (http://www.scip.org).

19. These facts are from Arik Hesseldahl, "Mac vs. PC: What You Don't Get for $699," *BusinessWeek Online,* April 15, 2009 (http://www.businessweek.com/technology/content/apr2009/tc20090415_602968.htm?chan=rss_topStories_ssi_5).

20. Hampton Inn's Satisfaction Guarantee (http://hamptoninn.hilton.com/en/hp/promotions/satisfaction_guarantee/index.jhtml), accessed February 14, 2012.

21. These facts are from Joe Brown, "You Can Rent Movies on Facebook Now," *Gizmodo,* August 19, 2011 (http://gizmodo.com/5832713/you-can-rent-movies-on-facebook); "8 Cool Marketing Campaigns Using Facebook Places," *AllFacebook.com* (http://www.allfacebook.com/8-cool-marketing-campaigns-using-facebook-places-2011-08), accessed February 15, 2012; LinkedIn website (http://press.linkedin.com/about), accessed February 15, 2012; Graeme McMillan, "How Many People Actually Use Twitter? Good Question," *Time Online,* August 29, 2011 (http://techland.time.com/2011/08/29/how-many-people-actually-use-twitter-good-question); "Need Facebook Marketing Inspiration? 20 of the Most Innovative Campaigns," *SimplyZesty.com,* February 7, 2011 (http://www.allfacebook.com/8-cool-marketing-campaigns-using-facebook-places-2011-08); and Jeffrey F. Rayport, "Social Networks are the New Web Portals," *BusinessWeek Online,* January 21, 2009 (http://www.businessweek.com/technology/content/jan2009/tc20090121_557202.htm).

22. Michael Grigsby, "Getting Personal," *Marketing Research* 14 (Fall 2002), 18–22.

23. Grant Gross, "RFID and Privacy: Debate Heating up in Washington," *InfoWorld* (IDG News Service), May 28, 2004 (http://www.infoworld.com/article/04/05/28/HNrfidprivacy_1.html).

24. These facts are from Mark Kassof & Company, "McDonald's Arch McFlop," *Research Insights: Lessons from Marketing Flops,* Summer 1997.

25. These facts are from (RED) (http://www.joinred.com), accessed February 15, 2012.

26. These facts are from the Aflac corporate website (http://www.aflac.com); and "The 100 Best Companies to Work For 2012," *Fortune* (http://money.cnn.com/magazines/fortune/best-companies/2012), accessed February 15, 2012.

27. "Spotify: A Perfect Platform for Apps," *MarketWatch,* November 30, 2011 (http://www.marketwatch.com/story/spotify-a-perfect-platform-for-apps-2011-11-30).

CHAPTER **2**

Strategic Marketing Planning

Introduction

The process of strategic marketing planning can either be quite complex or relatively straightforward. As evidenced in *Beyond the Pages 2.1*, strategic planning in today's market often requires partnering with other firms and carefully planning for the actions of others, such as supply sources or competitors. Whether a multinational corporation, like Ford Motor Company, or a sole-proprietorship, like a local bakery, the planning process is the same in many ways. Ultimately, the goals and objectives can be quite similar. Large or small, all marketers strive to meet the needs of their customers while meeting their own business and marketing objectives.

The marketing planning process typically requires the coordination of broad-based decisions at the top of the corporate hierarchy with more narrowly defined actions at the bottom. At the top are important corporate decisions dealing with the firm's mission, vision, goals, and the allocation of resources among business units. Planning at this level also involves decisions regarding the purchase or divestment of the business units themselves. Delta's merger with Northwest and GM's closing of its Pontiac division are good examples of the decision-making complexity that is often typical of major corporate decisions. These decisions trickle down the corporate structure to the business-unit level, where planning focuses on meeting goals and objectives within defined product markets. Planning at this level must take into account and be consistent with decisions made at the corporate level. However, in organizations having only one business unit, corporate and business unit strategy are the same. The most specific planning and decision making occurs at the bottom of the structure. It is at this level where organizations make and implement tactical decisions regarding marketing strategy (target markets and the marketing program) as well as marketing plans.

In this chapter, we examine the planning process at different points in this process. We begin by discussing the overall process by considering the hierarchy of decisions that must be made in strategic marketing planning. Next, we introduce the marketing plan and look at the marketing plan framework used throughout the text. We also discuss the role and importance of the marketing plan in marketing strategy. Finally, we explore other advances in strategic planning such as strategy mapping and the balanced performance scorecard.

Redbox's Success Story[1]

One buck for one night. That was the initial strategy of Redbox, now a hugely successful DVD rental company that distributes movies and video games from roughly 36,000 kiosks in supermarkets, drugstores, restaurants, convenience stores, and other retailers around the country. The idea is simple: With the push of a button and the swipe of a credit card, customers can rent a movie or video game from a bright red machine about the size of a refrigerator. Each kiosk holds up to 630 discs and 200 different movie and game titles, virtually all of which are six months old or less. Customers can reserve movies and games online or with a mobile app before visiting a kiosk, and simply return the rented discs to a Redbox kiosk anywhere in the country. Although the price of a movie rental has risen to $1.20 (video games start at $2.00 per day), Redbox has been undeniably successful: The company has rented over 1.5 billion discs since it launched, or roughly 5 discs per second over a ten-year period. Today, the company's rental rate is roughly 40 rentals per second and growing.

Surprisingly, the idea for Redbox began as a new business venture for McDonald's in 2002. At that time, McDonald's was experimenting with vending machines to sell a variety of different items. The concept was based on research that indicated customers prefer dealing with machines, rather than people, for some transactions (think banking, choosing airline seats, movie tickets at theaters, etc.). After the concept proved to be a success, Redbox was sold to Coinstar— a Bellevue, WA company that also operates coin-counting machines and gift card dispensers. Soon after, Coinstar inked deals with Walmart, Kroger, Winn-Dixie, Walgreens, Kangaroo (gas stations), and other national outlets to place Redbox kiosks in high-traffic locations. As it turned out, the timing couldn't have been better. As the recession of 2008 lingered over the next few years, customers began to see Redbox as a bargain compared to their $15 per month Netflix plans or $5 on-demand movie rentals.

Redbox has achieved phenomenal sales growth in a very short time: from 200 million cumulative rentals in 2008, to 500 million in 2009, to 1.5 billion total rentals in 2012. These numbers are startling when compared to the 43.9 percent decline in DVD sales from 2009 to 2012. Further evidence of success can be found in the penetration of Redbox into mainstream America. The Redbox mobile apps have been downloaded 4.7 million times on Android and 6.5 million times on iPhone. The company claims that 68 percent of the U.S. population lives within a five-minute drive of a Redbox kiosk.

Despite this success, Redbox's growth has been greeted with trepidation by Hollywood movie studios. Universal Studios and 20th Century Fox, for example, asked distributors to stop supplying Redbox with DVDs until six weeks after their release dates. Redbox, in return, filed suit claiming abuse of copyright and a violation of antitrust law. The company's distribution agreement with Time Warner collapsed after Time Warner demanded that Redbox wait 56 days (up from 28 days) before renting new releases. Coinstar stated that it would get new movies through traditional retail channels instead. Although movie studios are powerless to stop Redbox in this action, paying the higher retail cost for DVDs significantly cuts into Redbox's revenue.

For movie studios, the issue boils down to money and reducing or eliminating the number of previously viewed DVDs in the market. When a customer buys a DVD from Walmart, the studio collects $17 per disc. That number drops to $0.60 for a Redbox rental. Studios receive nothing when a company sells used DVDs. In deciding the fate of Redbox, the movie studios have a fundamental question to answer: Should they supply Redbox with DVDs and promote the company's incredible growth, or should they try to kill it? Redbox contends that customers are more likely to buy DVDs after renting them—not unlike what happens in the music industry. Needless to say, movie executives are afraid that Redbox will continue to erode demand for higher-priced DVD purchases.

Rather than worry about the studios, Redbox continues to move ahead. The company agreed to acquire all Blockbuster Express kiosks from NCR for $100 million. This acquisition expanded the Redbox footprint to over 46,000 kiosks nationwide. The company also inked a deal with Verizon to launch a video-streaming service to compete with Netflix and Amazon Prime.

The Strategic Planning Process

Whether at the corporate, business unit, or functional level, the planning process begins with an in-depth analysis of the organization's internal and external environments—sometimes referred to as a *situation analysis*. As we will discuss in Chapter 3, this analysis focuses on the firm's resources, strengths, and capabilities vis-à-vis competitive, customer, and environmental issues. Based on an exhaustive review of these relevant environmental issues, the firm establishes its mission, goals, and/or objectives, its strategy, and several functional plans. As indicated in Exhibit 2.1, planning efforts within each functional area will result in the creation of a strategic plan for that area. Although we emphasize the issues and processes concerned with developing a customer-oriented marketing strategy and marketing plan, we should stress that organizations develop effective marketing strategies and plans in concert with the organization's mission and goals, as well as the plans from other functional areas. Senior management must coordinate these functional plans in a manner that will achieve the organization's mission, goals, and objectives.

In this text, we are interested in a particular type of functional plan—the marketing plan. A *marketing plan* is a written document that provides the blueprint or outline of the organization's marketing activities, including the implementation, evaluation, and control of those activities. The marketing plan serves a number of purposes. For one, the marketing plan clearly explains how the organization will achieve its goals and

EXHIBIT 2.1   The Strategic Planning Process

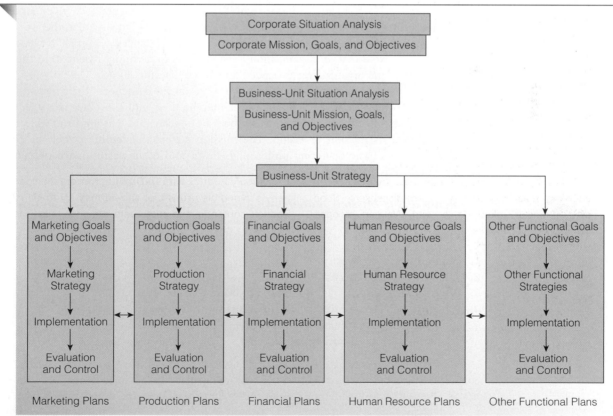

© Cengage Learning 2013

objectives. This aspect of marketing planning is vital—not having goals and objectives is like driving a car without knowing your destination. In this sense, the marketing plan serves as the "road map" for implementing the marketing strategy. It instructs employees as to their roles and functions in fulfilling the plan. It also provides specifics regarding the allocation of resources and includes the specific marketing tasks, responsibilities of individuals, and the timing of all marketing activities.

Although our focus is on marketing planning and strategy, we cannot emphasize enough that marketing decisions must be made within the boundaries of the organization's overall mission, goals, and objectives. The sequencing of decision stages outlined in the following sections begins with broad decisions regarding the organizational mission, followed by a discussion of the corporate or business-unit strategy. It is within these contexts that marketing goals/objectives and marketing strategies must be developed and implemented.

Organizational Mission versus Organizational Vision

To adequately address the role of the organizational mission in strategic planning, we must first understand the differences between the organization's mission and its vision. A *mission*, or *mission statement*, seeks to answer the question "What business are we in?" It is a clear and concise statement (a paragraph or two at most) that explains the organization's reason for existence. By contrast, a *vision* or *vision statement* seeks to answer the question "What do we want to become?" For example, Texas Instruments—one of the world's largest technology companies—defines its mission this way: "Texas Instruments Incorporated provides innovative semiconductor technologies to help our customers create the world's most advanced electronics." Compare this to the company's vision: "… to use the company's unique technical skills to fundamentally change markets and create entirely new ones."[2] Similarly, Google's mission is "to organize the world's information and make it universally accessible and useful." Google's vision is "Never settle for the best." Note that an organization's vision tends to be future oriented, in that it represents where the organization is headed and where it wants to go.

If you ask many businesspeople "What is your reason for existence?" their response is likely to be "To make money." Although that may be their ultimate objective, it is not their raison d'être. Profit has a role in this process, of course, but it is a goal or objective of the firm, not its mission or vision. The mission statement identifies what the firm stands for and its basic operating philosophy. Profit and other performance outcomes are ends, and thus are out of place and confuse the mission of the firm.

Elements of the Mission Statement   A well-devised mission statement for any organization, unit within an organization, or single-owner business should answer the same five basic questions. These questions should clarify for the firm's stakeholders (especially employees):

1. Who are we?
2. Who are our customers?
3. What is our operating philosophy (basic beliefs, values, ethics, etc.)?
4. What are our core competencies or competitive advantages?
5. What are our responsibilities with respect to being a good steward of our human, financial, and environmental resources?

A mission statement that delivers a clear answer to each of these questions installs the cornerstone for the development of the marketing plan. If the cornerstone is weak, or not in line with the foundation laid in the preliminary steps, the entire plan will have no real chance of long-term success. Exhibit 2.2 outlines several mission statements considered to be among the best. As you read these statements, consider how well they answer these five questions.

EXHIBIT 2.2 **The Best Mission Statements**

In their book, *Say It and Live It: The 50 Corporate Mission Statements That Hit the Mark*, Patricia Jones and Larry Kahaner identified 50 companies that possess outstanding mission statements. This exhibit lists several of these companies, along with their 1995, 2000, and 2012 mission statements. Remember that these organizations customized their mission statements to fit their own needs and goals, not to match the criteria established in this chapter.

Boeing

1995 To be the number one aerospace company in the world and among the premier industrial concerns in terms of quality, profitability, and growth.

2000 Our mission is bigger and broader than ever. It is to push not just the envelope of flight, but the entire envelope of value relating to our customers and shareholders.

2012 People working together as a global enterprise for aerospace leadership.

Leo Burnett

1995 The mission of the Leo Burnett Company is to create superior advertising. In Leo's words: "Our primary function in life is to produce the best advertising in the world, bar none. This is to be advertising so interrupting, so daring, so fresh, so engaging, so human, so believable and so well-focused as to themes and ideas that, at one and the same time, it builds a quality reputation for the long haul as it produces sales for the immediate present."

2000 Our Vision: To be an indispensable source of our clients' competitive advantage. Our Mission: We will work with our clients as a community of star-reachers whose ideas build leadership brands through imagination and a sensitive and deeper understanding of human behavior.

2012 At Leo Burnett our purpose is to be the world's best creator of ideas that truly move people… bar none. Together with our partners, we strive to put a meaningful human purpose at the center of our clients' brands, to transform the way people thing, feel and ultimately behave.

Celestial Seasonings

1995 Our mission is to grow and dominate the U.S. specialty tea market by exceeding consumer expectations with the best tasting, 100 percent natural hot and iced teas, packaged with Celestial art and philosophy, creating the most valued tea experience. Through leadership, innovation, focus, and teamwork we are dedicated to continuously improving value to our consumers, customers, employees, and stakeholders with a quality-first organization.

2000 We believe in creating and selling healthful, naturally oriented products that nurture people's bodies and uplift their souls. Our products must be

- superior in quality,
- of good value,
- beautifully artistic, and
- philosophically inspiring.

Our role is to play an active part in making this world a better place by unselfishly serving the public. We believe we can have a significant impact on making people's lives happier and healthier through their use of our products.

2012 In 1969, a group of passionate young entrepreneurs founded Celestial Seasonings upon the belief that their flavorful, all-natural herbal teas could help people live healthier lives. They harvested fresh herbs from the Rocky Mountains by hand, and then dried, blended and packaged them in hand-sewn muslin bags to be sold at local health food stores. By staying committed to their vision, the founders of Celestial Seasonings turned their cottage industry into an almost overnight success. Today, Celestial Seasonings is one of the largest specialty tea manufacturers in North America. We serve more than 1.6 billion cups of tea every year, and we source more than 100 different ingredients from over 35 countries to create our delicious, all-natural herbal, green, red, white, chai and wellness teas. But most importantly, we're still about people and passion.

Intel Corporation

1995 Do a great job for our customers, employees and stockholders by being the preeminent building block supplier to the computing industry.

2000 Intel's mission is to be the preeminent building block supplier to the worldwide Internet economy.

2012 This decade we will create and extend computing technology to connect and enrich the lives of every person on earth.

Sources: Patricia Jones and Larry Kahaner, *Say It and Live It: The 50 Corporate Mission Statements That Hit the Mark* (New York: Doubleday, 1995); and the websites of these companies.

The mission statement is the one portion of the strategic plan that should not be kept confidential. It should tell everyone—customers, employees, investors, competitors, regulators, and society in general—what the firm stands for and why it exists. Mission statements facilitate public relations activities and communicate to customers and others important information that can be used to build trust and long-term relationships. The mission statement should be included in annual reports and major press releases, framed on the wall in every office, and personally owned by every employee of the organization. Goals, objectives, strategies, tactics, and budgets are not for public viewing. A mission statement kept secret, however, is of little value to the organization.

Mission Width and Stability   In crafting a mission statement, management should be concerned about the statement's width. If the mission is too broad, it will be meaningless to those who read and build upon it. A mission to "make all people happy around the world by providing them with entertaining products" sounds splendid but provides no useful information. Overly broad missions can lead companies to establish plans and strategies in areas where their strengths are limited. Such endeavors almost always result in failure. Exxon's past venture into office products and Sears' expansion into real estate and financial services serve as reminders of the problems associated with poorly designed mission statements. Although a well-designed mission statement should not stifle an organization's creativity, it must help keep the firm from moving too far from its core competencies.

Overly narrow mission statements that constrain the vision of the organization can prove just as costly. Early in this century, the railroads defined their business as owning and operating trains. Consequently, the railroad industry had no concerns about the invention of the airplane. After all, they thought, the ability to fly had nothing to do with trains or the railroad business. Today, we know that firms such as American Airlines, Southwest Airlines, and Federal Express, rather than Burlington, Union Pacific, or Santa Fe, dominate the passenger and time-sensitive freight business. The railroads missed this major opportunity because their missions were too narrowly tied to railroads, as opposed to a more appropriate definition encompassing the transportation business.

© tr3gin/Shutterstock

What business does the railroad industry find itself in today?

Mission stability refers to the frequency of modifications in an organization's mission statement. Of all the components of the strategic plan, the mission should change the least frequently. It is the one element that will likely remain constant through multiple rounds of strategic planning. Goals, objectives, and marketing plan elements will change over time, usually as an annual or quarterly event. When the mission changes, however, the cornerstone has been moved and everything else must change as well. The mission should change only when it is no longer in sync with the firm's capabilities, when competitors drive the firm from certain markets, when new technology changes the delivery of customer benefits, or when the firm identifies a new opportunity that matches its strengths and expertise. As we discussed in Chapter 1, the growth of the Internet and electronic commerce has affected many industries. The importance and role of travel agents, stockbrokers, and car dealers has changed dramatically as customers changed the way they shop for travel, financial products, and automobiles. Organizations in these and other industries have been forced to refocus their efforts by redefining their mission statements.

Customer-Focused Mission Statements In recent years, firms have realized the role that mission statements can play in their marketing efforts. Consequently, mission statements have become much more customer oriented. People's lives and businesses should be enriched because they have dealt with the organization. A focus on profit in the mission statement means that something positive happens for the owners and managers of the organization, not necessarily for the customers or other stakeholders. For example, a focus on customers is one of the leading reasons for the long running success of Southwest Airlines. The company's mission has not changed since 1988:

> *The mission of Southwest Airlines is dedication to the highest quality of Customer Service delivered with a sense of warmth, friendliness, individual pride, and Company Spirit.*[3]

The mission statement of cultural icon Ben & Jerry's Ice Cream consists of three interrelated parts, and is a good example of how an organization can work to have a positive impact on customers and society:[4]

> *Social Mission: To operate the company in a way that actively recognizes the central role that business plays in society by initiating innovative ways to improve the quality of life locally, nationally and internationally.*

> *Product Mission: To make, distribute and sell the finest quality all natural ice cream and euphoric concoctions with a continued commitment to incorporating wholesome, natural ingredients and promoting business practices that respect the Earth and the Environment.*

> *Economic Mission: To operate the Company on a sustainable financial basis of profitable growth, increasing value for our stakeholders and expanding opportunities for development and career growth for our employees.*

The infamous 1982 Tylenol cyanide tragedy illustrated the importance of a customer-oriented mission statement. After several deaths occurred as a result of outside tampering with Tylenol capsules, McNeilab and Johnson & Johnson immediately pulled all Tylenol capsules from the market at a direct cost of $100 million. When asked about the difficulty of this decision, executives said that the choice was obvious given Johnson & Johnson's mission statement. That statement, developed decades earlier by the firm's founders, established that Johnson & Johnson's primary responsibility is to the doctors, nurses, patients, parents, and children who prescribe or use the company's products. Because the mission dictated the firm's response to the crisis, Tylenol became an even more dominant player in the pain-reliever market after the tragedy.[5] Since that time, Johnson & Johnson has faced similar recalls. In 2010, the company recalled several pain relief products, including Tylenol and Motrin, due to an unusual moldy smell. Similarly in 2012, all infant Tylenol was pulled from U.S. shelves when parents complained about the company's redesigned bottles. In each case, the company's mission statement was a guiding forcing in making the recall decisions.[6]

Customer-focused mission statements are the norm for charities and humanitarian organizations. These nonprofit organizations—just like their for-profit counterparts—strive to fulfill their missions through effective marketing programs. For instance, the mission of the American Red Cross reads:

> *The American Red Cross, a humanitarian organization led by volunteers and guided by its Congressional Charter and the Fundamental Principles of the International Red Cross and Red Crescent Movement, will provide relief to victims of disaster and help people prevent, prepare for, and respond to emergencies.*

Unlike other charitable organizations, the American Red Cross holds a key competitive advantage: its Congressional charter. This gives the American Red Cross the authority needed to respond no matter the nature or complexity of the crisis. During the aftermath of Hurricanes Katrina, Rita, and Wilma in 2005, the American Red Cross initiated its single largest disaster response in the organization's history. Through a massive promotional campaign and significant corporate sponsorships, the American Red Cross was able to raise the $2.1 billion needed for relief efforts.[7]

Corporate or Business-Unit Strategy

All organizations need a *corporate strategy*, the central scheme or means for utilizing and integrating resources in the areas of production, finance, research and development, human resources, and marketing, to carry out the organization's mission and achieve the desired goals and objectives. In the strategic planning process, issues such as competition, differentiation, diversification, coordination of business units, and environmental issues all tend to emerge as corporate strategy concerns. In small businesses, corporate strategy and business-unit strategy are essentially the same. Although we use both terms, corporate and business-unit strategy apply to all organizations, from large corporations to small businesses and nonprofit organizations.

Larger firms often find it beneficial to devise separate strategies for each strategic business unit (SBU), subsidiary, division, product line, or other profit center within the parent firm. Business-unit strategy determines the nature and future direction of each business unit, including its competitive advantages, the allocation of its resources, and the coordination of the functional business areas (marketing, production, finance, human resources, etc.). Many organizations manage their differing SBUs in ways that create synergies by providing customers a single-branded solution across multiple markets. Sony, for example, has a number of SBUs including the Consumer Products and Services Group (computers and home entertainment), the Professional, Device and Solutions Group (semiconductors), Sony Music Entertainment (record labels such as Arista, Epic, Columbia, and LaFace), Sony Pictures Entertainment (Columbia TriStar studios, movie distribution), Sony Mobile Communications (mobile multimedia and phones), and Sony Financial Holdings.[8]

An important consideration for a firm determining its corporate or business-unit strategy is the firm's capabilities. When a firm possesses capabilities that allow it to serve customers' needs better than the competition, it is said to have a *competitive*, or *differential*, *advantage*. Although a number of advantages come from functions other than marketing—such as human resources, research and development, or production—these functions often create important competitive advantages that can be exploited through marketing activities. For example, Walmart's long-running strategic investments in logistics allow the retailer to operate with lower inventory costs than its competitors—an advantage that translates into lower prices at retail. The 3M Company is highly regarded for its expertise in research and development. In fact, 3M defines itself as a science company. Their advantage in research and innovation allows its 89-plus product categories to excel in eight different business units: home and leisure; office; manufacturing and industry; transportation; safety and security; health care; electronics, electrical, and communication; and display and graphics.[9]

Competitive advantages cannot be fully realized unless targeted customers see them as valuable. The key issue is the organization's ability to convince customers that its advantages are superior to those of the competition. Walmart has been able to convey effectively its low price advantage to customers by adhering to an everyday low-price policy. The company's advertising plays on this fact by using "roll back" prices. Interestingly, Walmart's prices are not always the lowest for a given product in a given geographic area. However, Walmart's perception of offering low prices translates into a key competitive advantage for the firm.

Functional Goals and Objectives

Marketing and all other business functions must support the organization's mission and goals, translating these into objectives with specific quantitative measurements. For example, a corporate or business unit goal to increase return on investment might translate into a marketing objective to increase sales, a production objective to reduce the cost of raw materials, a financial objective to rebalance the firm's portfolio of investments, or a human resources objective to increase employee training and productivity. All functional objectives should be expressed in clear, simple terms so that all personnel understand what type and level of performance the organization desires. In other words, objectives should be written so that their accomplishment can be measured accurately. In the case of marketing objectives, units of measure might include sales volume (in dollars or units), profitability per unit, percentage gain in market share, sales per square foot, average customer purchase, percentage of customers in the firm's target market who prefer its products, or some other measurable achievement.

It is also important for all functional objectives to be reconsidered for each planning period. Perhaps no strategy arose in the previous planning period to meet the stated objectives. Or perhaps the implementation of new technology allowed the firm to greatly exceed its objectives. In either case, realism demands the revision of functional objectives to remain consistent with the next edition of the functional area plan.

Functional Strategy

Organizations design functional strategies to provide a total integration of efforts that focus on achieving the area's stated objectives. In production, this might involve strategies for procurement, just-in-time inventory control, or warehousing. In human resources, strategies dealing with employee recruitment, selection, retention, training, evaluation, and compensation are often at the forefront of the decision-making process. In marketing strategy, the process focuses on selecting one or more target markets and developing a marketing program that satisfies the needs and wants of members of that target market. AutoZone, for example, targets do-it-yourself "shade tree mechanics" by offering an extensive selection of automotive replacement parts, maintenance items, and accessories at low prices.

Functional strategy decisions do not develop in a vacuum. The strategy must: (1) fit the needs and purposes of the functional area with respect to meeting its goals and objectives, (2) be realistic given the organization's available resources and environment, and (3) be consistent with the organization's mission, goals, and objectives. Within the context of the overall strategic planning process, each functional strategy must be evaluated to determine its effect on the organization's sales, costs, image, and profitability.

Implementation

Implementation involves activities that actually execute the functional area strategy. One of the more interesting aspects of implementation is that all functional plans have at least two target markets: an external market (i.e., customers, suppliers, investors, potential employees, the society at large) and an internal market (i.e., employees, managers, executives). This occurs because functional plans, when executed, have repercussions both inside and outside the firm. Even seemingly disconnected events in finance or human resources can have an effect on the firm's ultimate customers—the individuals and businesses that buy the firm's products.

In order for a functional strategy to be implemented successfully, the organization must rely on the commitment and knowledge of its employees—its internal target market. After all, employees have a responsibility to perform the activities that will implement the strategy. For this reason, organizations often execute internal marketing activities designed to gain employee commitment and motivation to implement functional plans.

Evaluation and Control

Organizations design the evaluation and control phase of strategic planning to keep planned activities on target with goals and objectives. In the big picture, the critical issue in this phase is coordination among functional areas. For example, timely distribution and product availability almost always depend on accurate and timely production. By maintaining contact with the production manager, the marketing manager helps to ensure effective marketing strategy implementation (by ensuring timely production) and, in the long run, increased customer satisfaction. The need for coordination is especially keen in marketing where the fulfillment of marketing strategy always depends on coordinated execution with other functional strategies.

The key to coordination is to ensure that functional areas maintain open lines of communication at all times. Although this can be quite a challenge, it is helpful if the organizational culture is both internally and externally customer oriented. Maintaining a customer focus is extremely important throughout the strategic planning process, but especially so during the implementation, evaluation, and control phases of the process. Functional managers should have the ability to see the interconnectedness of all business decisions and act in the best interests of the organization and its customers.

In some ways, the evaluation and control phase of the planning process is an ending and a beginning. On one hand, evaluation and control occur after a strategy has been implemented. In fact, the implementation of any strategy would be incomplete without an assessment of its success and the creation of control mechanisms to provide and revise the strategy or its implementation—or both if necessary. On the other hand, evaluation and control serve as the beginning point for the planning process in the next planning cycle. Because strategic planning is a never-ending process, managers should have a system for monitoring and evaluating implementation outcomes on an ongoing basis.

The Marketing Plan

The result of the strategic planning process described in the first portion of this chapter is a series of plans for each functional area of the organization. For the marketing department, the marketing plan provides a detailed formulation of the actions necessary to carry out the marketing program. Think of the marketing plan as an action document—it is the handbook for marketing implementation, evaluation, and control. With that in mind, it is important to note that a marketing plan is not the same as a business plan. Business plans, although they typically contain a marketing plan, encompass other issues such as business organization and ownership, operations, financial strategy, human resources, and risk management. Although business plans and marketing plans are not synonymous, many small businesses will consolidate their corporate, business-unit, and marketing plans into a single document.

A good marketing plan requires a great deal of information from many different sources. An important consideration in pulling all of this information together is to maintain a big picture view while simultaneously keeping an eye on the details. This requires looking at the marketing plan holistically rather than as a collection of related elements. Unfortunately, adopting a holistic perspective is rather difficult in practice. It is easy to get deeply involved in developing marketing strategy only to discover later that the strategy is inappropriate for the organization's resources or marketing environment. The hallmark of a well-developed marketing plan is its ability to achieve its stated goals and objectives.

In the following sections, we explore the marketing plan in more detail, including the structure of a typical marketing plan. This structure matches the marketing plan worksheets in the Appendix and the sample marketing plan available on our website. As we work through the marketing plan structure, keep in mind that a marketing plan can be written in many different ways. Marketing plans can be developed for specific products, brands, target markets, or industries. Likewise, a marketing plan can focus on a specific element of the marketing program, such as a product development plan, a promotional plan, a distribution plan, or a pricing plan.

Marketing Plan Structure

All marketing plans should be well organized to ensure that all relevant information is considered and included. Exhibit 2.3 illustrates the structure or outline of a typical marketing plan. We say this outline is "typical," but there are many other ways to organize a marketing plan. Although the actual outline used is not that important, most plans will share common elements described here. Regardless of the specific outline you use to develop a marketing plan, you should keep in mind that a good marketing plan outline is:

- **Comprehensive.** Having a comprehensive outline is essential to ensure that there are no omissions of important information. Of course, every element of the outline may not be pertinent to the situation at hand, but at least each element receives consideration.
- **Flexible.** Although having a comprehensive outline is essential, flexibility should not be sacrificed. Any outline you choose must be flexible enough to be modified to fit the unique needs of your situation. Because all situations and organizations are different, using an overly rigid outline is detrimental to the planning process.
- **Consistent.** Consistency between the marketing plan outline and the outline of other functional area plans is an important consideration. Consistency may also include the connection of the marketing plan outline to the planning process used at the corporate- or business-unit levels. Maintaining consistency ensures that executives and employees outside of marketing will understand the marketing plan and the planning process.
- **Logical.** Because the marketing plan must ultimately sell itself to top managers, the plan's outline must flow in a logical manner. An illogical outline could force top managers to reject or underfund the marketing plan.

The marketing plan structure that we discuss here has the ability to meet all four of these points. Although the structure is comprehensive, you should freely adapt the outline to match the unique requirements of your situation.

Executive Summary The *executive summary* is a synopsis of the overall marketing plan, with an outline that conveys the main thrust of the marketing strategy and its execution. The purpose of the executive summary is to provide an overview of the plan

---

EXHIBIT 2.3   Marketing Plan Structure

 I. **Executive Summary**

   a. Synopsis

   b. Major aspects of the marketing plan

 II. **Situation Analysis**

   a. Analysis of the internal environment

   b. Analysis of the customer environment

   c. Analysis of the external environment

 III. **SWOT Analysis (Strengths, Weaknesses, Opportunities, and Threats)**

   a. Strengths

   b. Weaknesses

   c. Opportunities

   d. Threats

   e. Analysis of the SWOT matrix

   f. Developing competitive advantages

   g. Developing a strategic focus

 IV. **Marketing Goals and Objectives**

   a. Marketing goals

   b. Marketing objectives

 V. **Marketing Strategy**

   a. Primary (and secondary) target market

   b. Overall branding strategy

   c. Product strategy

   d. Pricing strategy

   e. Distribution/supply chain strategy

   f. Integrated marketing communication (promotion) strategy

 VI. **Marketing Implementation**

   a. Structural issues

   b. Tactical marketing activities

 VII. **Evaluation and Control**

   a. Formal controls

   b. Informal controls

   c. Implementation schedule and timeline

   d. Marketing audits

© Cengage Learning 2013

so the reader can quickly identify key issues or concerns related to his or her role in implementing the marketing strategy. Therefore, the executive summary does not provide detailed information found in the following sections, or any other detailed information that supports the final plan. Instead, this synopsis introduces the major aspects of the marketing plan, including objectives, sales projections, costs, and performance evaluation measures. Along with the overall thrust of the marketing strategy, the executive summary should also identify the scope and time frame for the plan. The idea is to give the reader a quick under-standing of the breadth of the plan and its time frame for execution.

Individuals both within and outside of the organization may read the executive summary for reasons other than marketing planning or implementation. Ultimately, many users of a marketing plan ignore some of the details because of the role they play. The CEO, for exam-ple, may be more concerned with the overall cost and expected return of the plan, and less interested in the plan's implementation. Financial institutions or investment bankers may want to read the marketing plan before approving any necessary financing. Likewise, suppli-ers, investors, or others who have a stake in the success of the organization sometimes receive access to the marketing plan. In these cases, the executive summary is critical, as it must convey a concise overview of the plan and its objectives, costs, and returns.

Although the executive summary is the first element of a marketing plan, it should always be the last element to be written because it is easier and more meaningful to write after the entire marketing plan has been developed. There is another good reason to write the executive summary last: It may be the only element of the marketing plan read by a large number of people. As a result, the executive summary must accurately represent the entire marketing plan.

Situation Analysis The next section of the marketing plan is the situation analysis, which summarizes all pertinent information obtained about three key environments: the internal environment, the customer environment, and the firm's external environ-ment. The analysis of the firm's internal environment considers issues such as the avail-ability and deployment of human resources, the age and capacity of equipment or technology, the availability of financial resources, and the power and political struggles within the firm's structure. In addition, this section summarizes the firm's current mar-keting objectives and performance. The analysis of the customer environment examines the current situation with respect to the needs of the target market (consumer or busi-ness), anticipated changes in these needs, and how well the firm's products presently meet these needs. Finally, the analysis of the external environment includes relevant external factors—competitive, economic, social, political/legal, and technological—that can exert considerable direct and indirect pressures on the firm's marketing activities.

A clear and comprehensive situation analysis is one of the most difficult parts of developing a marketing plan. This difficulty arises because the analysis must be both comprehensive and focused on key issues in order to prevent information overload—a task actually made more complicated by advances in information technology. The infor-mation for a situation analysis may be obtained internally through the firm's marketing information system, or it may have to be obtained externally through primary or second-ary marketing research. Either way, the challenge is often having too much data and information to analyze rather than having too little.

SWOT (Strengths, Weaknesses, Opportunities, and Threats) Analysis SWOT *analysis* focuses on the internal factors (strengths and weaknesses) and external factors (opportunities and threats)—derived from the situation analysis in the preceding section—that give the firm certain advantages and disadvantages in satisfying the needs of its target market(s). These strengths, weaknesses, opportunities, and threats should be analyzed relative to market needs and competition. This analysis helps the company determine what it does well and where it needs to make improvements.

SWOT analysis has gained widespread acceptance because it is a simple framework for organizing and evaluating a company's strategic position when developing a market-ing plan. However, like any useful tool, SWOT analysis can be misused unless one conducts the appropriate research to identify key variables that will affect the performance of the firm. A common mistake in SWOT analysis is the failure to separate internal issues from external issues. Strengths and weaknesses are internal issues unique to the firm conducting the analysis. Opportunities and threats are external issues that exist independently of the firm conducting the analysis. Another common mistake is to list the firm's strategic alternatives as opportunities. However, alternatives belong in the discussion of marketing strategy, not in the SWOT analysis.

At the conclusion of the SWOT analysis, the focus of the marketing plan shifts to address the strategic focus and competitive advantages to be leveraged in the strategy. The key to developing strategic focus is to match the firm's strengths with its opportunities to create capabilities in delivering value to customers. The challenge for any firm at this stage is to create a compelling reason for customers to purchase its products over those offered by competitors. It is this compelling reason that then becomes the framework or strategic focus around which the strategy can be developed. As explained in *Beyond the Pages 2.2*, a common way to deliver good value to customers is to sell below cost, or even give the product away.

Marketing Goals and Objectives   Marketing goals and objectives are formal statements of the desired and expected outcomes resulting from the marketing plan. *Goals* are broad, simple statements of what will be accomplished through the marketing strategy. The major function of goals is to guide the development of objectives and to provide direction for resource allocation decisions. Marketing *objectives* are more specific and are essential to planning. Marketing objectives should be stated in quantitative terms to permit reasonably precise measurement. The quantitative nature of marketing objectives makes them easier to implement after development of the strategy.

This section of the marketing plan has two important purposes. First, it sets the performance targets that the firm seeks to achieve by giving life to its strategic focus through its marketing strategy (i.e., what the firm hopes to achieve). Second, it defines the parameters by which the firm will measure actual performance in the evaluation and control phase of the marketing plan (i.e., how performance will actually be measured). At this point, it is important to remember that neither goals nor objectives can be developed without a clearly defined mission statement. Marketing goals must be consistent with the firm's mission, while marketing objectives must flow naturally from the marketing goals.

Marketing Strategy   This section of the marketing plan outlines how the firm will achieve its marketing objectives. In Chapter 1, we said that marketing strategies involve selecting and analyzing target markets and creating and maintaining an appropriate marketing program (product, distribution, promotion, and price) to satisfy the needs of those target markets. It is at this level where the firm will detail how it will gain a competitive advantage by doing something better than the competition: Its products must be of higher quality than competitive offerings, its prices must be consistent with the level of quality (value), its distribution methods must be as efficient as possible, and its promotions must be more effective in communicating with target customers. It is also important that the firm attempt to make these advantages sustainable. Thus, in its broadest sense, marketing strategy refers to how the firm will manage its relationships with customers in a manner that gives it an advantage over the competition.

Marketing Implementation   The implementation section of the marketing plan describes how the marketing program will be executed. This section of the marketing plan answers several questions with respect to the marketing strategies outlined in the preceding section:

Beyond the Pages 2.2

Sell Below Cost, They Will Come[10]

Sometimes the best marketing strategy involves giving the product away for free, especially if the firm is looking for rapid adoption among customers. This has long been the case in computer software where manufacturers give away restricted "trial" versions of their software to encourage use and, hopefully, purchase. Adobe, for example, gives away its popular Reader to help maintain branding of its other software products. McAfee and Norton freely package their antivirus programs with new computer purchases in hopes that buyers will subscribe to their continuous update services (priced between $40 and $200 per year based on features). The strategy is also used in consumer products. Procter & Gamble gives away (or sells below cost) its razors in the anticipation that it will sell more blades in the future.

The free or below cost strategy is common among products that are sold as platforms. A platform product is one that consists of a base product with numerous add-ons or supplemental products. Video gaming systems are a good example. When Microsoft launched the Xbox 360, it did so using a "neutral gross margin" strategy that sold each console at a loss. When the cost of parts, cables, and controllers are factored in, Microsoft loses roughly $150 per console. Sony follows a similar strategy with its PlayStation gaming system. Both Microsoft and Sony make up for the losses with higher profit margins on games and accessories, as well as brand licensing. In the future, Microsoft may shift that strategy to make the next edition of the Xbox (due in 2014 or 2015) profitable from the outset. The risk, however, is that Sony will continue to sell its consoles at a loss in an effort to undercut Microsoft's dominance in the gaming market.

A similar model is used in music. For example, many experts believe that Apple employs a neutral profit strategy in its operation of the iTunes store. It is estimated that for each $1.29 song sold on iTunes, Apple earns only 10 to 20 cents after paying royalties, micropayment fees, and infrastructure fees. Apple must then use that revenue to cover its operating and marketing costs. However, Apple more than makes up for these losses via the high profit margins of its iPod, iPhone, iPad, Apple TV, and MacBook computers.

There are many other examples of products sold at a loss to stimulate sales of other products. Mobile app developers have adopted a "freemium" strategy where the base app is provided free of charge, but a premium is charged for added features or functionality. These "lite" versions, such as Angry Birds Lite, are among the most popular apps available today. Further, inkjet printers are typically sold at or below cost because they stimulate future sales of ink and toner. Wireless phones are sold at a loss, or are subsidized at lower prices, in exchange for a one- or two-year service agreement. In grocery retailing, this practice is referred to as a loss-leader strategy. Common grocery loss leaders include milk, eggs, cereal, and soft drinks.

1. What specific marketing activities will be undertaken?
2. How will these activities be performed?
3. When will these activities be performed?
4. Who is responsible for the completion of these activities?
5. How will the completion of planned activities be monitored?
6. How much will these activities cost?

Without a good plan for implementation, the success of the marketing strategy is seriously jeopardized. For this reason, the implementation phase of the marketing plan is just as important as the marketing strategy phase. You should remember, too, that implementation hinges on gaining the support of employees: Employees implement marketing strategies, not organizations. As a result, issues such as leadership, employee motivation, communication, and employee training are critical to implementation success.

Frontline employees are important assets in developing and implementing marketing strategy.

Evaluation and Control   The final section of the marketing plan details how the results of the marketing program will be evaluated and controlled. *Marketing control* involves establishing performance standards, assessing actual performance by comparing it with these standards, and taking corrective action if necessary to reduce discrepancies between desired and actual performance. Performance standards should be tied back to the objectives stated earlier in the plan. These standards can be based on increases in sales volume, market share, or profitability, or even advertising standards such as brand name recognition or recall. Regardless of the standard selected, all performance standards must be agreed upon before the results of the plan can be assessed.

The financial assessment of the marketing plan is also an important component of evaluation and control. Estimates of costs, sales, and revenues determine financial projections. In reality, budgetary considerations play a key role in the identification of alternative strategies. The financial realities of the firm must be monitored at all times. For example, proposing to expand into new geographic areas or alter products without financial resources is a waste of time, energy, and opportunity. Even if funds are available, the strategy must be a "good value" and provide an acceptable return on investment to be a part of the final plan.

Finally, should it be determined that the marketing plan has not lived up to expectations; the firm can use a number of tools to pinpoint potential causes for the discrepancies. One such tool is the marketing audit—a systematic examination of the firm's marketing objectives, strategy, and performance. The marketing audit can help isolate weaknesses in the marketing plan and recommend actions to help improve performance. The control phase of the planning process also outlines the actions that can be taken to reduce the differences between planned and actual performance.

Using the Marketing Plan Structure

In the Appendix, you will find marketing plan worksheets that expand the marketing plan structure into a comprehensive framework for developing a marketing plan. These worksheets are designed to be *comprehensive*, *flexible*, and *logical*. The consistency of this framework with other planning documents will depend on the planning structure used in other functional areas of an organization. However, this framework is certainly capable of being consistent with the plans from other functional areas.

Although you may not use every single portion of the worksheets, you should at least go through them in their entirety to ensure that all important information is present. You should note that the sample marketing plan provided on our website uses this same framework. However, this plan does not match the framework *exactly* because the framework was adapted to match the characteristics of a unique planning situation.

Before we move ahead, we offer the following tips for using the marketing plan framework to develop a marketing plan:

- **Plan ahead**. Writing a comprehensive marketing plan is very time consuming, especially if the plan is under development for the first time. Initially, most of your time will be spent on the situation analysis. Although this analysis is very demanding, the marketing plan has little chance for success without it.

- **Revise, then revise again**. After the situation analysis, you will spend most of your time revising the remaining elements of the marketing plan to ensure that they mesh with each other. Once you have written a first draft of the plan, put it away for a day or so. Then, review the plan with a fresh perspective and fine tune sections that need changing. Because the revision process always takes more time than expected, it is wise to begin the planning process far in advance of the due date for the plan.

- **Be creative**. A marketing plan is only as good as the information it contains and the effort and creativity that go into its creation. A plan developed half-heartedly will collect dust on the shelf.

- **Use common sense and judgment**. Writing a marketing plan is an art. Common sense and judgment are necessary to sort through all of the information, weed out poor strategies, and develop a sound marketing plan. Managers must always weigh any information against its accuracy, as well as their own intuition, when making marketing decisions.

- **Think ahead to implementation**. As you develop the plan, you should always be mindful of how the plan will be implemented. Great marketing strategies that never see the light of day do little to help the organization meet its goals. Good marketing plans are those that are realistic and doable given the organization's resources.

- **Update regularly**. Once the marketing plan has been developed and implemented, it should be updated regularly with the collection of new data and information. Many organizations update their marketing plans on a quarterly basis to ensure that the marketing strategy remains consistent with changes in the internal, customer, and external environments. Under this approach, you will always have a working plan that covers 12 months into the future.

- **Communicate to others**. One critical aspect of the marketing plan is its ability to communicate to colleagues, particularly top managers who look to the marketing plan for an explanation of the marketing strategy, as well as for a justification of needed resources, like the marketing budget.[11] The marketing plan also communicates to line managers and other employees by giving them points of reference to chart the progress of marketing implementation. A survey of marketing executives on the importance of the marketing plan revealed that:

".... the process of preparing the plan is more important than the document itself.... A marketing plan does compel attention, though. It makes the marketing team concentrate on the market, on the company's objectives, and on the strategies and tactics appropriate to those objectives. It's a mechanism for synchronizing action."[12]

Research indicates that organizations that develop formal, written strategic marketing plans tend to be more tightly integrated across functional areas, more specialized, and more decentralized in decision making. The end result of these marketing planning efforts is improved financial and marketing performance.[13] Given these benefits, it is surprising that many firms do not develop formal plans to guide their marketing efforts. For example, a survey of CEOs done by the American Banking Association found that only 44 percent of community banks have a formal marketing plan.[14]

Purposes and Significance of the Marketing Plan

The purposes of a marketing plan must be understood to appreciate its significance. A good marketing plan will fulfill these five purposes in detail:

1. It explains both the present and future situations of the organization. This includes the situation and SWOT analyses and the firm's past performance.
2. It specifies the expected outcomes (goals and objectives) so that the organization can anticipate its situation at the end of the planning period.
3. It describes the specific actions that are to take place so that the responsibility for each action can be assigned and implemented.
4. It identifies the resources that will be needed to carry out the planned actions.
5. It permits the monitoring of each action and its results so that controls may be implemented. Feedback from monitoring and control provides information to start the planning cycle again in the next time frame.

These five purposes are very important to various persons in the firm. Line managers have a particular interest in the third purpose (description of specific actions) because they are responsible for ensuring the implementation of marketing actions. Middle-level managers have a special interest in the fifth purpose (monitoring and control), as they want to ensure that tactical changes can be made if needed. These managers must also be able to evaluate why the marketing strategy does or does not succeed.

The most pressing concern for success, however, may lie in the fourth purpose: identifying needed resources. The marketing plan is the means of communicating the strategy to top executives who make the critical decisions regarding the productive and efficient allocation of resources. Very sound marketing plans can prove unsuccessful if implementation of the plan is not adequately funded. It is important to remember that marketing is not the only business function competing for scarce resources. Other functions such as finance, research and development, and human resources have strategic plans of their own. It is in this vein that the marketing plan must sell itself to top management.

Organizational Aspects of the Marketing Plan

Who writes the marketing plan? In many organizations, the marketing manager, brand manager, or product manager writes the marketing plan. Some organizations develop marketing plans through committees. Others will hire professional marketing consultants to write the marketing plan. However, in most firms, the responsibility for planning lies at the level of a marketing vice president or marketing director.[15] The fact that top managers develop most marketing plans does not necessarily refute the logic of having the brand or product manager prepare the plan. However, except in small organizations where one person both develops and approves the plan, the authority to approve the marketing plan is typically vested in upper-level executives. At this stage, top managers usually ask two important questions:

1. Will the proposed marketing plan achieve the desired marketing, business unit, and corporate goals and objectives?
2. Are there alternative uses of resources that would better meet corporate or business unit objectives than the submitted marketing plan?

In most cases, *final* approval actually lies with the president, chairperson, or CEO of the organization.[16] Many organizations also have executive committees that evaluate and screen

EXHIBIT 2.4   Major Obstacles to Developing and Implementing Marketing Plans

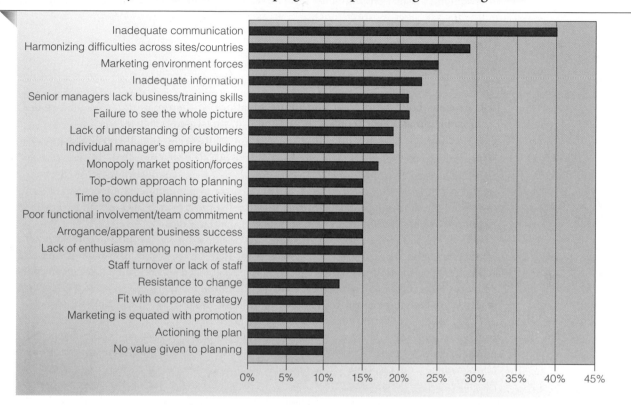

Source: Lyndon Simkin, "Barriers Impeding Effective Implementation of Marketing Plans—A Training Agenda," *Journal of Business and Industrial Marketing*, 17 (Winter 2002): 13. Permission granted by Emerald Group Publishing Corp., http://www.emeraldinsight.com.

marketing plans before submission to the approving executive. In the end, regardless of who writes the marketing plan, the plan must be clear and persuasive to win the approval of the decision makers who make the evaluation. It is also critical that these individuals make efficient and timely decisions with respect to the marketing plan. To give the plan every chance for success, very little time should elapse between the completion of the plan and its implementation.

Once a marketing plan has been approved, it still faces many obstacles before its marketing programs can come to fruition. Exhibit 2.4 outlines some of these obstacles. One major hurdle involves the relative time horizon of the organization's key stakeholders, particularly its managers and investors. It is quite common for U.S. firms to ignore long-range strategy and focus on the near term. Typically, this is caused by a compensation structure that rewards executives for short-term financial results such as profit, market capitalization, or stock price. Unfortunately, this mindset can play havoc on many marketing activities—such as advertising to build brand awareness—because their results are only apparent over longer time horizons. Consequently, many firms will shift strategies "midstream" rather than wait for results to emerge.

Maintaining Customer Focus and Balance in Strategic Planning

In the past two decades, many firms have changed the focus and content of their strategic planning efforts and marketing plans. Of these changes, two stand out: (1) renewed emphasis on the customer and (2) the advent of balanced strategic planning. These changes require shifting focus from the company's products to the unique requirements of specific target market segments. Firms have also had to become more astute at linking marketing activities to other functional areas.

Customer-Focused Planning

Focusing on the customer has not been the hallmark of strategic planning throughout history. Early in the twentieth century, planning focused on production ideals such as efficiency and quality. Automobile pioneer Henry Ford has long been credited with the statement that customers could have any color car that they wanted, as long as it was black. This mentality, though it worked well in its day, meant that strategic planning proceeded with little regard for customer needs and wants. Today, cars, trucks, and SUVs come in an array of colors that Henry Ford would have never contemplated. By the middle of the twentieth century, strategic planning focused on *selling* products to customers rather than making products for customers. Marketing strategies during this time concentrated on overcoming customer resistance and convincing them to buy products whether they needed them or not. Today, we no longer see door-to-door sales of vacuum cleaners, brushes, or encyclopedias.

The cornerstone of marketing thought and practice during the mid-to-late twentieth century was the marketing concept, which focused on customer satisfaction and the achievement of the firm's objectives. Having a market or customer orientation meant putting customers' needs and wants first. This shift in thinking led to the growth of marketing research to determine unmet customer needs and systems for satisfying those needs. Today's twenty-first century marketing organizations move one step beyond the marketing concept to focus on long-term, value-added relationships with customers, employees, suppliers, and other partners. The focus has shifted from customer transactions to customer relationships, from customers to all stakeholders, and from competition to collaboration. As explained in *Beyond the Pages 2.3*, Amazon has created a series of relationships with authors, book publishers, movie studios, music companies, customers, and potential competitors in the creation of the ecosystem for its Kindle tablets and e-book readers.

Market-oriented firms are those that successfully generate, disseminate, and respond to market information. These firms focus on customer analysis, competitor analysis, and integrating the firm's resources to provide customer value and satisfaction, as well as long-term profits.[18] To be successful, the firm must be able to focus its efforts and resources toward understanding their customers in ways that enhance the firm's ability to generate sustainable competitive advantages.[19] By creating organizational cultures that put customers first, market-oriented firms tend to perform at higher levels and reap the benefits of more highly satisfied customers. Exhibit 2.5 depicts the difference between a traditional and market-oriented organizational structure. Where traditional structures are very authoritative, with decision-making authority emanating from the top of the hierarchy; market-oriented structures decentralize decision making.

In a market-oriented organization, every level of the organization has its focus on serving customer needs. Each level serves the levels above it by taking any actions necessary to ensure that each level performs its job well. In this case, the role of the CEO is to ensure that his or her employees have everything they need to perform their jobs well. This same service mentality carries through all levels of the organization, including customers. Thus, the job of a frontline manager is to ensure that frontline employees are capable and efficient. The end result of the market-oriented design is a complete focus on customer needs.

In today's business environment, an orientation towards customers also requires that the organization's suppliers and even competitors be customer oriented as well. Though competing firms can continue to serve customers separately, customers can also be served through cooperative efforts that place market needs ahead of competitive interests. For example, Toyota has a number of partnerships with rival carmakers, particularly

Beyond the Pages 2.3

Amazon Is on Fire[17]

Amazon CEO Jeff Bezos has a history of pushing the envelope by expanding into areas that don't seem to fit the mold of an online retailer. Once billed as "Earth's biggest bookstore," Amazon now sells everything from electronics to fishing gear and cosmetics. Always searching for the next revolutionary product or business process, Bezos is no stranger to failure. The company's moves into search (with A9) and online auctions are good examples. However, with the launch of the Kindle in 2007, Amazon forever changed book retailing and personal media consumption.

On the surface, the first Kindle was a simple e-book reader. Both it and its successors use an e-ink screen that is very easy to read without causing eyestrain. They offer long battery life and the ability to store thousands of e-books. Although all Kindle models include WiFi capabilities, some models also incorporate 3G radios that allow customers to download e-books in almost any location. Most newly released e-books sell for $9.99 to $12.99, far less than typical hardcover new releases. Newspaper subscriptions are also available for less than $20 per month. The ability to buy an e-book directly from the Kindle without using a computer completely revolutionized book retailing and spawned a number of competing products, most notably the Apple iPad and Barnes & Noble's Nook. Today, Amazon offers over 1 million e-books through its Kindle Store, with over 800,000 titles selling for $9.99 or less. That selection, combined with the ease of buying e-books wirelessly, has converted many book purchases into impulse buys. Today, Amazon sells more e-book versions than it does hardback or paperback versions of the same title.

After Apple introduced the iPad in 2010, many began to see traditional e-book readers as passé. After all, the Kindle and its competitors lacked a color display, smooth web browsing, and the ability to watch video. At the same time, competitors such as Sony, Motorola, and Blackberry had failed to gain any traction against the iPad. One of the main reasons for the iPad's popularity was and is the tightly integrated ecosystem of apps, music, and movies that Apple had built around it. The significance of this was not lost on Bezos and Amazon. Very quietly, the company began to develop relationships with companies in the music and movie industries. Once those were in place, Amazon began to offer music downloads (often at prices that beat the iTunes Music Store), online movie rentals, and a movie streaming service through its Amazon Prime membership program.

With the ecosystem in place, Amazon was poised to move to the next level. Just in time for the 2011 holiday season, Amazon released the Kindle Fire—a 7" tablet based on the Android operating system. The Kindle Fire is similar to the iPad in that it can access an expansive library of books, magazines, music, movies, and apps. However, it is priced at only $199, much lower than the $499 for the lowest priced iPad. Given its features and lower price, no one was surprised when Amazon sold over 5 million Kindle Fire units during the first six months.

Despite its early success, however, industry analysts suggest that the Kindle Fire is vulnerable to competition, especially from the updated iPad and Google's Nexus 7 tablet. The main difference between the Kindle Fire and the Nexus 7, however, is the ecosystem. To date, only Apple and Amazon have been able to create the multimedia ecosystem required to support a tablet device. Many believe that the future battle among these and other companies will take place in textbooks for K-12 and colleges/universities. Currently, Amazon and Barnes & Noble do very well in selling physical textbooks. However, Apple and its newly released iBooks Author (for creating e-textbooks) will certainly make waves in the industry. The college textbook market alone is a roughly $12 billion per-year business. Time will tell whether Amazon can successfully transition from physical textbooks to e-textbooks along with the rest of the industry.

focused on hybrid technology. Nissan uses Toyota's hybrid fuel system in its vehicles, while GM has collaborated with Toyota in developing new fuel-cell technologies. Recently, Toyota inked agreements with BMW to develop next generation lithium-ion batteries, and with Ford to develop hybrid technology for light trucks and SUVs. Toyota's partnership with BMW also includes the use of BMW's diesel engines in cars destined for the European market.[20]

EXHIBIT 2.5 Traditional versus Market-Oriented Organizational Structures

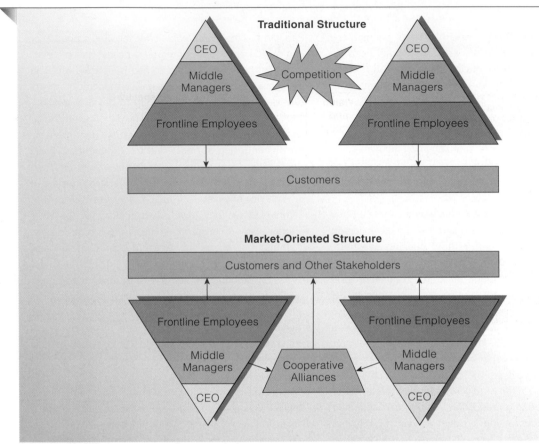

© Cengage Learning 2013

Balanced Strategic Planning

The shift to balanced strategic planning was borne out of necessity. As firms approached the twenty-first century, they realized that traditional planning and measurement approaches were not able to capture value created by the organization's intangible assets. These assets—including such vital issues as customer relationships, processes, human resources, innovation, and information—were becoming increasingly important to business success, but they were not being reported through traditional financial measures. One solution to this problem was the development of the balanced performance scorecard by Robert Kaplan and David Norton of Harvard University.[21] Their approach to strategic planning is illustrated in Exhibit 2.6.

The basic tenet of the balanced performance scorecard is that firms can achieve better performance if they align their strategic efforts by approaching strategy from four complementary perspectives: financial, customer, internal process, and learning and growth. The financial perspective is the traditional view of strategy and performance. This perspective is vital, but should be balanced by the other components of the scorecard. The customer perspective looks at customer satisfaction metrics as a key indicator of firm performance, particularly as the firm moves ahead. Financial measures are not suited to this task because they report past performance rather than current performance. The internal process perspective focuses on the way the business is running by looking at

EXHIBIT 2.6   The Balanced Performance Scorecard

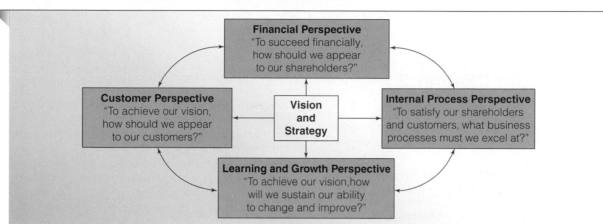

Source: From Robert S. Karlan and David P. Norton, "The Strategy-Focused Organization: How Balanced Scorecard Companies Thrive in the New Business Environment" (Boston, MA: Harvard Business School Press, 2001). Used by permission of Harvard Business School Publishing.

both mission-critical and routine processes that drive day-to-day activity. Finally, the learning and growth perspective focuses on people and includes such vital issues as corporate culture, employee training, communication, and knowledge management.[22]

The balanced scorecard has been used successfully by many public and private sector organizations. Kaplan and Norton found that these successful firms typically adhered to five common principles when implementing the balanced scorecard:[23]

1. **Translate the Strategy into Operational Terms**. Successful firms are able to illustrate the cause-and-effect relationships that show how intangible assets are transformed into value for customers and other stakeholders. This provides a common frame of reference for all employees.
2. **Align the Organization to Strategy**. Successful firms link different functional areas through common themes, priorities, and objectives. This creates synergy within the organization that ensures that all efforts are coordinated.
3. **Make Strategy Everyone's Everyday Job**. Successful firms move the strategy from the executive boardroom to the front lines of the organization. They do this through communication, education, allowing employees to set personal objectives, and tying incentives to the balanced scorecard.
4. **Make Strategy a Continual Process**. Successful firms hold regular meetings to review strategy performance. They also establish a process whereby the firm can learn and adapt as the strategy evolves.
5. **Mobilize Change through Executive Leadership**. Successful firms have committed energetic leaders who champion the strategy and the balanced scorecard. This ensures that the strategy maintains momentum. Good leaders also prevent the strategy from becoming an obstacle to future progress.

The balanced scorecard doesn't refute the traditional approach to strategic planning. It does, however, caution business leaders to look at strategy and performance as a multidimensional issue. Financial measures, though important, simply cannot tell the whole story. One of the major benefits of the balanced scorecard is that it forces organizations to explicitly consider *during strategy formulation* those factors that are critical to strategy execution. We cannot stress this point enough. Good strategy is always developed with an eye toward how it will be implemented. Issues within the balanced scorecard such as employee training, corporate culture, organizational learning, and executive leadership are critical to the implementation of any strategy.

Lessons from Chapter 2

Strategic marketing planning:

- begins with broad decisions, then flows into more specific decisions as the process proceeds through subsequent planning stages.
- involves establishing an organizational mission, corporate or business-unit strategy, marketing goals and objectives, marketing strategy, and ultimately a marketing plan.
- must be consistent with the organization's mission and the corporate or business-unit strategy.
- must be coordinated with all functional business areas to ensure that the organization's goals and objectives will be considered in the development of each functional plan, one of which is the marketing plan.
- establishes marketing-level goals and objectives that support the organization's mission, goals, and objectives.
- develops a marketing strategy, which includes selecting and analyzing target markets and creating and maintaining an appropriate marketing program to satisfy the needs of customers in those target markets.
- ultimately results in a strategic market plan that outlines the activities and resources required to fulfill the organization's mission and achieve its goals and objectives.

The organizational mission:

- answers the broad question "What business are we in?"
- identifies what the firm stands for and its basic operating philosophy by answering five basic questions:

    1. Who are we?
    2. Who are our customers?
    3. What is our operating philosophy (basic beliefs, values, ethics, etc.)?
    4. What are our core competencies or competitive advantages?
    5. What are our responsibilities with respect to being a good steward of our human, financial, and environmental resources?

- is not the same as the organization's vision, which seeks to answer the question "What do we want to become?"
- should not be too broad or too narrow, thereby rendering it useless for planning purposes.
- should be customer oriented. People's lives and businesses should be enriched because they have dealt with the organization.
- should never focus on profit. A focus on profit in the mission means that something positive happens for the owners and managers of the organization, not necessarily for the customers or other stakeholders.
- must be owned and supported by employees if the organization has any chance of success.
- should not be kept secret but instead communicated to everyone—customers, employees, investors, competitors, regulators, and society in general.
- should be the least changed part of the strategic plan.

Business-unit strategy:

- is the central scheme or means for utilizing and integrating resources in the areas of production, finance, research and development, human resources, and marketing to carry out the organization's mission and achieve the desired goals and objectives.
- is associated with developing a competitive advantage where the firm leverages its capabilities in order to serve customers' needs better than the competition.
- determines the nature and future direction of each business unit, including its competitive advantages, the allocation of its resources, and the coordination of functional business areas (marketing, production, finance, human resources, etc.).
- is essentially the same as corporate strategy in small businesses.

The marketing plan:

- provides a detailed explanation of the actions necessary to execute the marketing program and thus requires a great deal of effort and organizational commitment to create and implement.
- should be well organized to ensure that it considers and includes all relevant information. The typical structure or outline of a marketing plan includes these elements:

    - executive summary
    - situation analysis
    - SWOT analysis
    - marketing goals and objectives
    - marketing strategies
    - marketing implementation
    - evaluation and control

- should be based on an outline that is comprehensive, flexible, consistent, and logical.
- fulfills five purposes:

    - explains both the present and future situations of the organization

- specifies expected outcomes (goals and objectives)
- describes the specific actions that are to take place and assigns responsibility for each action
- identifies the resources needed to carry out the planned actions
- permits the monitoring of each action and its results so that controls may be implemented
- serves as an important communication vehicle to top management and to line managers and employees.
- is an important document, but not nearly as important as the knowledge gained from going through the planning process itself.
- is most often prepared by the director or vice president of marketing, but is ultimately approved by the organization's president, chairman, or CEO.

Customer-focused strategic planning:

- requires that organizations shift focus from products to the requirements of specific target market segments, from customer transactions to customer relationships, and from competition to collaboration.
- puts customers' needs and wants first and focuses on long-term, value-added relationships with customers, employees, suppliers, and other partners.
- must be able to focus its efforts and resources toward understanding customers in ways that enhance the firm's ability to generate sustainable competitive advantages.
- instills a corporate culture that places customers at the top of the organizational hierarchy.

- finds ways to cooperate with suppliers and competitors to serve customers more effectively and efficiently.

Balanced strategic planning:

- was borne out of necessity since traditional planning and measurement approaches were not able to capture value created by an organization's intangible assets (customer relationships, processes, human resources, innovation, and information).
- was advocated strongly by Kaplan and Norton with their creation of the balanced performance scorecard.
- considers traditional financial indicators of performance, but also looks at planning from three additional perspectives: customers, internal processes, and learning and growth.
- is used successfully by many public and private sector organizations. Successful firms are those that adhere to five principles when implementing the balanced scorecard:
  - translate the strategy into operational terms
  - align the organization to strategy
  - make strategy everyone's everyday job
  - make strategy a continual process
  - mobilize change through executive leadership
- does not refute the traditional approach to strategic planning, but it does caution business leaders to look at strategy and performance as a multidimensional issue.
- forces organizations to explicitly consider *during strategy formulation* those factors that are critical to strategy execution. Good strategy is always developed with an eye toward how it will be implemented.

Questions for Discussion

1. In many organizations, marketing does not have a place of importance in the organizational hierarchy. Why do you think this happens? What are the consequences for a firm that gives little importance to marketing relative to other business functions?

2. Defend or contradict this statement: Developing marketing strategy is more important than imple-menting marketing strategy because if the strategy is flawed, its implementation doesn't matter.

3. What are some of the potential difficulties in approaching strategic planning from a balanced perspective? Isn't financial performance still the most important perspective to take in planning? Explain.

Exercises

1. Review each of the mission statements listed in Exhibit 2.2. Do they follow the guidelines discussed in this chapter? How well does each answer the five basic questions? What do you make of the changes or lack thereof in these mission statements over time?

2. Talk with a small business owner about the strategic planning process he or she uses. Do they have a mission statement? Marketing goals and objectives? A marketing plan? What are the major issues he or she faces in implementing their marketing program?

3. Palo Alto Software maintains a website devoted to business and marketing plans. Log on to www.mplans.com/sample_marketing_plans.php and take a look at a few of the sample marketing plans available. Do these plans use the same framework discussed in this chapter?

End Notes

1. These facts are from Chris Davies, "Verizon and Redbox Partner on Netflix Streaming Rival for 2H 2012," *Slashgear*, February 6, 2012 (http://www.slashgear.com/verizon-and-redbox-partner-on-netflix-streaming-rival-for-2h-2012-06212204); Ryan Nakashima, "Whither Redbox? Hollywood Studios are Conflicted," *BusinessWeek Online*, August 7, 2009 (http://www.businessweek.com/ap/tech/D99U8BT00.htm); Terrence O'Brien, "Redbox Snatches Up NCR's Entertainment Division, Swallows Blockbuster Express Business," *Engadget*, February 6, 2012 (http://www.engadget.com/2012/02/06/redbox-snatches-up-ncrs-entertainment-division-future-of-block); Dorothy Pomerantz, "Red Menace," *Forbes*, March 6, 2009 (http://www.forbes.com/2009/03/06/redbox-blockbuster-rentals-business-media-rebox.html); Redbox website (http://www.redbox.com), accessed February 21, 2012; Eli Rosenberg, "DVD Sales Dive, While Netflix Soars," *The Atlantic Wire*, May 12, 2011 (http://www.theatlanticwire.com/national/2011/05/add-dvds-list-dying-industries/37664); Paul Suarez, "Hollywood Hates Redbox's $1 DVD Rentals," *Macworld*, August 10, 2009 (http://www.macworld.com/article/142192/2009/08/redbox.html); and Michael White, "Coinstar Soars on Profit, Buyout of NCR Unit: Los Angeles Mover," *BusinessWeek Online*, February 8, 2012 (http://www.businessweek.com/news/2012-02-08/coinstar-soars-on-profit-buyout-of-ncr-unit-los-angeles-mover.html).

2. The Texas Instruments mission and vision statements are from their company website (http://www.ti.com/corp/docs/company/factsheet.shtml), accessed February 21, 2012.

3. The Southwest Airlines mission statement is from their company website (http://www.southwest.com/html/about-southwest/index.html), accessed February 21, 2012.

4. The Ben & Jerry's mission statement is from their company website (http://www.benjerry.com/activism/mission-statement), accessed February 21, 2012.

5. "Johnson & Johnson Reincarnates a Brand," *Sales and Marketing Management*, January 16, 1984, 63; and Elyse Tanouye, "Johnson & Johnson Stays Fit by Shuffling Its Mix of Businesses," *Wall Street Journal*, December 22, 1992, A1, A4.

6. These facts are from "All Infant Tylenol Recalled by J&J," *CBS News*, February 17, 2012 (http://www.cbsnews.com/8301-504763_162-57380543-10391704/all-infant-tylenol-recalled-by-j-j); and Parija Kavilanz, "Tylenol Recall: FDA Slams Company," *CNN Money*, October 19, 2010 (http://money.cnn.com/2010/01/15/news/companies/over_the_counter_medicine_recall/index.htm).

7. These facts are taken from "Turning Compassion into Action—Donor Dollars at Work: Hurricanes Katrina, Rita and Wilma," Red Cross (http://www.redcross.org/news/ds/hurricanes/support05/report.html).

8. These facts are from the Sony Corporate website (http://www.sony.net/SonyInfo/CorporateInfo/Data/organization.html), accessed February 21, 2012.

9. These facts are from the 3M corporate website (http://solutions.3m.com/en_US/Products), accessed February 21, 2012.

10. These facts are from James Brightman, "Sony Expects Big Losses on PS3 Launch," *GameDaily*, May 1, 2006 (http://www.businessweek.com/innovate/content/may2006/id20060501_525587.htm); Eric Caoili, "iSuppli: Sony Still Losing $50 With Each PS3 Sold," *Gamasutra*, December 23, 2008 (http://www.gamasutra.com/php-bin/news_index.php?story=21657); Arik Hesseldahl, "Microsoft's Red-Ink Game," *BusinessWeek Online*, November 22, 2005 (http://www.businessweek.com/technology/content/nov2005/tc20051122_410710.htm); Armando Rodriguez, "Biggest News of the Week: Microsoft Xbox Division Loses

$31 Million," *411Mania*, April 27, 2009 (http://www.411mania.com/wrestling/tv_reports/103060); Matt Rosoff, "Microsoft's Board is Now Worried About How Much Money Xbox Will Lose," *Business Insider*, April 21, 2011 (http://articles.businessinsider.com/2011-04-21/tech/29975028_1_windows-phone-microsoft-nintendo); and Christian Zibreg, "Opinion: Apple Should Open Up the iTunes Store," *Geek.com*, August 6, 2009 (http://www.geek.com/articles/mobile/opinion-apple-should-open-up-the-itunes-store-2009086).

11. Howard Sutton, *The Marketing Plan in the 1990s* (New York: The Conference Board, Inc., 1990).

12. Sutton, *The Marketing Plan in the 1990s*, 9.

13. Cindy Claycomb, Richard Germain, and Cornelia Droge, "The Effects of Formal Strategic Marketing Planning on the Industrial Firm's Configuration, Structure, Exchange Patterns, and Performance," *Industrial Marketing Management* 29 (May 2000), 219–234.

14. "Marketing Plan Help," *ABA Banking Journal* 95 (October 2003), 18.

15. Sutton, *The Marketing Plan in the 1990s*, 16.

16. Sutton, *The Marketing Plan in the 1990s*, 17.

17. These facts are from the Amazon website (http://www.amazon.com), accessed February 24, 2012; "Amazon Unwraps the New Kindle," *BusinessWeek Online*, February 9, 2009 (http://www.businessweek.com/bwdaily/dnflash/content/feb2009/db2009029_964407.htm); Philip Elmer-DeWitt, "Amazon re-Kindles the iPhone," *Fortune Online*, May 11, 2009 (http://apple20.blogs.fortune.cnn.com/2009/05/11/amazon-re-kindles-the-iphone); Douglass MacMillan, "Amazon's Kindle is Off to College," *BusinessWeek Online*, May 4, 2009 (http://www.businessweek.com/technology/content/may2009/tc2009054_280910.htm); Jeffrey M. O'Brien, "Amazon's Next Revolution," *Fortune Online*, May 26, 2009 (http://money.cnn.com/2009/05/26/technology/obrien_kindle.fortune/index.htm?postversion=2009052605); and Trefis Team, "Amazon, Apple and the Case of Converging Tablets," February 24, 2012 (http://www.forbes.com/sites/greatspeculations/2012/02/24/amazon-apple-and-the-case-of-converging-tablets).

18. Bernard J. Jaworski and Ajay K. Kohli, "Market Orientation: Antecedents and Consequences," *Journal of Marketing* 57 (July 1993), 53–70.

19. Ibid; and Stanley F. Slater and John C. Narver, "Market Orientation and the Learning Organization," *Journal of Marketing* 59 (July 1995), 63–74.

20. These facts are from "Ford, Toyota to Collaborate on Developing New Hybrid System for Light Trucks, SUVs; Future Telematic Standards," Toyota Newsroom (http://pressroom.toyota.com/releases/ford+toyota+hybrid+trucks+suvs+telematics.htm), accessed February 26, 2010; "Nissan Altima Hybrid: A Better Toyota," The Car Family Blog, July 15, 2008 (http://carfamily.wordpress.com/2008/07/15/nissan-altima-hybrid-a-better-toyota); and Jason Siu, "Toyota and BMW Form Official Partnership for Eco-Friendly Projects," *AutoGuide*, January 12, 2011 (http://www.autoguide.com/auto-news/2011/12/toyota-and-bmw-form-official-partnership-for-eco-friendly-projects.html).

21. The material in this section is adapted from Robert S. Kaplan and David P. Norton, *The Strategy-Focused Organization* (Boston, MA: Harvard Business School Press, 2001).

22. Descriptions of each perspective are adapted from "What is the Balanced Scorecard?" The Balanced Scorecard Institute (http://www.balancedscorecard.org/BSCResources/AbouttheBalancedScorecard/tabid/55/Default.aspx), accessed February 26, 2012.

23. Kaplan and Norton, *The Strategy-Focused Organization*, 8–17.

CHAPTER **3**

Collecting and Analyzing Marketing Information

Introduction

In this chapter, we begin the process of developing a marketing plan by examining key issues in collecting and structuring marketing information to assist in the formulation of marketing strategies. Managers in all organizations, large and small, devote a major portion of their time and energy to developing plans and making decisions. As shown in *Beyond the Pages 3.1*, continuous tracking of the buying preferences of target consumers over time is critical. However, the ability to do so requires access to and analysis of data to generate usable information in a timely manner. Staying abreast of trends in the marketing environment is but one of several tasks performed by marketing managers. However, it is perhaps the most important task as practically all planning and decision making depends on how well this analysis is conducted.

One of the most widely used approaches to the collection and analysis of marketing information is the situation analysis. The purpose of the situation analysis is to describe current and future issues and key trends as they affect three key environments: the internal environment, the customer environment, and the external environment. As shown in Exhibit 3.1, there are many issues to be considered in a situation analysis. When viewed together, the data collected during the situation analysis gives the organization a big picture of the issues and trends that affect its ability to deliver value to stakeholders. These efforts drive the development of the organization's competitive advantages and strategic focus as discussed in the next chapter.

In this chapter, we examine several issues related to conducting a situation analysis, the components of a situation analysis, and the collection of marketing data and information to facilitate strategic marketing planning. Although situation analysis has traditionally been one of the most difficult aspects of market planning, recent advances in technology have made the collection of market data and information much easier and more efficient. A wealth of valuable data and information are free for the asking. This chapter examines the different types of marketing data and information needed for planning, as well as many sources where such data may be obtained.

Baby Boomers Deserve Careful Analysis[1]

Baby boomers—the 77 million people born between 1946 and 1964—have long been the holy grail of marketers aimed at growing their business. The simple numbers have always made boomers a powerful force and a favored target of marketers for decades. However, today's boomers have reached a critical milestone: The youngest boomers are now approaching the age of 50. Currently, more than half of all baby boomers are over 50, with the oldest boomers now over the age of 65. These numbers are significant because 50 is the typical age at which marketers give up on consumers. Tradition says that by the age of 50, a consumer has developed deeply entrenched buying preferences and brand loyalty that no amount of marketing can undo. Today's marketers, however, are finding that tradition is wrong.

Marketers have rediscovered baby boomers for a number of reasons. One reason is the incredible buying potential. Thanks to better health and longer life expectancies, most boomers plan to continue working well into their 60s in order to shore up their retirement savings. Recent declines in the stock market and the retirement accounts of most boomers have forced them to look for ways to stay in the workforce longer. That extra earning potential makes boomers even more attractive. Boomers now control over 80 percent of our nation's financial assets and are responsible for more than half of all consumer spending—a whopping $1 trillion every year. A second reason is that today's 50+ consumers are much more active than their parents. Unlike previous generations, boomers are much more likely to change careers, have more children, go back to school, remarry, pursue new hobbies, and inherit more money from their parents. Consequently, marketers are finding that boomers' brand preferences and shopping habits are not as entrenched as once thought. Finally, marketers cannot give up on boomers due to the relatively smaller number of Generation X consumers—only 50 million strong—that are following behind them. In the years ahead, marketers must continue to reach out to boomers until the 74 million Generation Y consumers (those born roughly between 1982 and 1999) reach their peak earning potential.

Reaching out to boomers has become a challenge for many marketers because they have to throw out their stereotypical ideas about 50+ consumers. Gap, for example, tried to reach out to boomers using advertising featuring well-known boomer celebrities. That strategy backfired, however, because Gap's clothes do not suit boomers' tastes. Other marketers have found success simply by catering to boomers' ideals and needs. For example, Dove saw its sales increase after it dropped attractive models from its advertising in favor of ordinary, 40-something women. Cover Girl adopted a similar strategy by launching its first line of makeup targeted at older women. Further, Home Depot added renovation services to its mix in addition to its assortment of products for do-it-yourselfers. And even Honda was surprised when it learned that 40 percent of its minivan buyers were older customers who needed to haul grandchildren rather than their own children. As a result, Honda introduced a version of its popular Odyssey minivan to cater to the needs of older consumers.

The picture is not uniformly rosy; however, as real estate developers and makers of luxury products have seen a rapid falloff in both interest and sales among their traditional boomer clients. As their retirement savings have dwindled, boomers today are less interested in buying second homes, cars, vacations, and other luxury items. This fact has forced most retirement planning professionals to change tactics. For example, most financial ads targeted at boomers today discuss practical and measured investment strategies rather than spending on "the good life." In fact, some investment analysts question whether boomers will ever be able to retire.

Experts agree that the key to tapping the boomer market is to not assume that they are of one mind. Researchers at Duke University have discovered that boomers are the most diverse of all current generations. Consequently, marketers must continually gather research on boomers to ensure that their marketing resonates with the correct boomer segment.

EXHIBIT 3.1   Issues to Be Considered in a Situation Analysis

---

The Internal Environment

Review of current objectives, strategy, and performance

Availability of resources

Organizational culture and structure

The Customer Environment

Who are our current and potential customers?

What do customers do with our products?

Where do customers purchase our products?

When do customers purchase our products?

Why (and how) do customers select our products?

Why do potential customers not purchase our products?

The External Environment

Competition

Economic growth and stability

Political trends

Legal and regulatory issues

Technological advancements

Sociocultural trends

© Cengage Learning 2013

Conducting a Situation Analysis

Before we move forward in our discussion, it is important to keep in mind four important issues regarding situation analysis. We hope our advice helps you overcome potential problems throughout the situation analysis.

Analysis Alone Is Not a Solution

Although it is true that a comprehensive situation analysis can lead to better planning and decision making, analysis itself is not enough. Put another way, situation analysis is a necessary, but insufficient, prerequisite for effective strategic planning. The analysis must be combined with intuition and judgment to make the results of the analysis useful for planning purposes. Situation analysis should not replace the manager in the decision-making process. Its purpose is to empower the manager with information for more effective decision making.

A thorough situation analysis empowers the marketing manager because it encourages both analysis and synthesis of information. From this perspective, situation analysis involves taking things apart: whether it's a customer segment (in order to study the heavy users), a product (in order to understand the relationship between its features and customers' needs), or competitors (in order to weigh their strengths and weaknesses against your own). The purpose of taking things apart is to understand why people, products, or organizations perform the way they do. After this dissection is complete, the manager can then synthesize the information to gain a big picture view of the complex decisions to be made.

Data Is Not the Same as Information

Throughout the planning process, managers regularly face the question: "How much data and information do I need?" The answer sounds simple, but in practice it is not. Today, there is no shortage of data. In fact, it is virtually impossible to know everything about a specific topic. Thankfully, the cost of collecting and storing vast amounts of data has dropped dramatically over the past decade. Computer-based marketing information systems are commonplace. Online data sources allow managers to retrieve data in a matter of seconds. The growth of wireless technology now gives managers access to vital data while in the field. The bottom line is that managers are more likely to be overwhelmed with data rather than face a shortage.

While the vast amount of available data is an issue to be resolved, the real challenge is that good, useful information is not the same as data. Data are easy to collect and store, but good information is not. In simple terms, data are a collection of numbers or facts that have the potential to provide information. Data, however, do not become informative until a person or process transforms or combines them with other data in a manner that makes them useful to decision makers. For example, the fact that your firm's sales are up 20 percent is not informative until you compare it with the industry's growth rate of 40 percent. It is also important to remember that information is only as good as the data from which it comes. As the saying goes, "Garbage in, garbage out." It is a good idea to be curious about, perhaps even suspicious of, the quality of data used for planning and decision making.

The Benefits of Analysis Must Outweigh the Costs

Situation analysis is valuable only to the extent that it improves the quality of the resulting marketing plan. For example, data that cost $4,000 to acquire, but improve the quality of the decision by only $3,999, should not be part of the analysis process. Although the costs of acquiring data are easy to determine, the benefits of improved decisions are quite difficult to estimate. Managers must constantly ask questions such as: "Where do I have knowledge gaps?", "How can these gaps be filled?", "What are the costs of filling these gaps?", and "How much improvement in decision making will be gained by acquiring this information?". By asking these questions, managers can find a balance between jumping to conclusions and "paralysis by analysis," or constantly postponing a decision due to a perceived lack of information. Perpetually analyzing data without making any decisions is usually not worth the additional costs in terms of time or financial resources.

Conducting a Situation Analysis Is a Challenging Exercise

Situation analysis is one of the most difficult tasks in developing a marketing plan. Managers have the responsibility of assessing the quality, adequacy, and timeliness of the data and information used for analysis and synthesis. The dynamic nature of internal and external environments often creates breakdowns in the effort to develop effective information flows. This dynamism can be especially troubling when the firm attempts to collect and analyze data in international markets.

It is important that any effort at situation analysis be well organized, systematic, and supported by sufficient resources (e.g., people, equipment, information, budget). However, the most important aspect of the analysis is that it should be an ongoing effort. The analysis should not only take place in the days and weeks immediately preceding the formation of strategies and plans; the collection, creation, analysis, and dissemination of pertinent marketing data and information must be ingrained in the culture of the organization. While this is not an easy task, if the organization is going to be successful

EXHIBIT 3.2   **The Relationship Among the Internal, Customer, and External Environments**

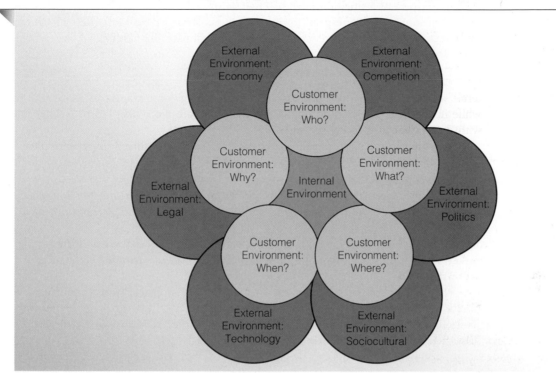

© Cengage Learning 2013

it must have the ability to assess its current situation in real time. This type of live data is especially important when tracking customers and competitors.

A final challenge is the task of tracking all three environments (internal, customer, external) simultaneously. Although the rapid pace of change in today's economy is one cause of this difficulty, the relationship among all three environments creates challenges as well. As shown in Exhibit 3.2, the internal, customer, and external environments do not exist independently. Changes in one portion of the external environment can cause subsequent shifts in the customer environment or the internal environment. For example, after Mattel sued MGA Entertainment, Inc. for copyright infringement for its Bratz doll design, Mattel won a $100 million verdict against MGA. The company was ordered to transfer its Bratz line and all intellectual property associated with the product to Mattel. That verdict was eventually overturned on appeal. Later, MGA won a separate suit against Mattel for theft of intellectual property. Although the final outcome of the battle is still unknown, this single dispute from the legal environment represents a major threat to both Mattel and MGA Entertainment.[2]

As we turn our attention to the three major components of the situation analysis, keep in mind that data and information about these environments will come from both internal and external sources. Even information about the firm's internal environment can be collected via external sources such as third-party analysis and ratings, financial commentaries, or customer opinion ratings. Finally, it is important to remember that the type of data and information source is not as important as having ready access to a wide variety of sources.

The Internal Environment

The first aspect of a situation analysis involves the critical evaluation of the firm's internal environment with respect to its objectives, strategy, performance, allocation of resources, structural characteristics, and political climate. In Exhibit 3.3, we provide a framework for analyzing the internal environment.

EXHIBIT 3.3   A Framework for Analyzing the Internal Environment

---

Review of Current Marketing Objectives, Strategy, and Performance

1. What are the current marketing goals and objectives?
2. Are the marketing goals and objectives consistent with the corporate or business-unit mission, goals, and objectives? Are they consistent with recent changes in the customer or external environments? Why or why not?
3. How are current marketing strategies performing with respect to anticipated outcomes (for example, sales volume, market share, profitability, communication, brand awareness, customer preference, customer satisfaction)?
4. How does current performance compare to other organizations in the industry? Is the performance of the industry as a whole improving or declining? Why?
5. If performance is declining, what are the most likely causes? Are marketing objectives inconsistent? Is the strategy flawed? Was the strategy poorly implemented?
6. If performance is improving, what actions can be taken to ensure that performance continues to improve? Is the improvement in performance due to a better-than-anticipated environment or superior planning and implementation?

Review of Current and Anticipated Organizational Resources

1. What is the state of current organizational resources (for example, financial, human, experience, relationships with key suppliers or customers)?
2. Are these resources likely to change for the better or worse in the near future? How?
3. If the changes are for the better, how can these added resources be used to better meet customers' needs?
4. If the changes are for the worse, what can be done to compensate for these new resource constraints?

Review of Current and Anticipated Cultural and Structural Issues

1. What are the positive and negative aspects of the current and anticipated organizational culture?
2. What issues related to internal politics or management struggles might affect the organization's marketing activities?
3. What is the overall position and importance of the marketing function as seen by other functional areas? Are key executive positions expected to change in the future?
4. How will the overall market- or customer-orientation of the organization (or lack thereof) affect marketing activities?
5. Does the organization emphasize a long- or short-term planning horizon? How will this emphasis affect marketing activities?
6. Currently, are there positive or negative issues with respect to motivating employees, especially those in frontline positions (for example, sales and customer service)?

Review of Current Objectives, Strategy, and Performance

First, the marketing manager must assess the firm's current marketing objectives, strategy, and performance. A periodic assessment of marketing objectives is necessary to ensure that they remain consistent with the firm's mission and the changing customer and external environments. It may also be necessary to reassess the firm's marketing goals if the objectives prove to be out-of-date or ineffective. This analysis serves as an important input to later stages of the marketing planning process.

The marketing manager should also evaluate the performance of the current marketing strategy with respect to sales volume, market share, profitability, and other relevant measures. This analysis can take place at many levels: by brand, product line, market, business unit, division, and so on. It is also important to analyze the marketing strategy relative to overall industry performance. Poor or declining performance may be the result of: (1) holding on to marketing goals or objectives inconsistent with the current realities of the customer or external environments, (2) a flawed marketing strategy, (3) poor implementation, or (4) changes in the customer or external environments beyond the control of the firm. The causes for poor or declining performance must be pinpointed before marketing strategies can be developed to correct the situation.

For example, in the mid-1990s Pepsi was locked in a seemingly endless market share battle with Coca-Cola. By all accounts, the battle was not going well for Pepsi: its profits trailed Coke's by 47 percent, while its market value was less than half of its chief rival.[3] But losing out to Coke in the cola wars was just the kick that Pepsi needed to regroup. Forced to look outside of the soft drink industry for new growth opportunities, PepsiCo, Inc. moved aggressively into noncarbonated drinks, sports beverages, food, and snacks. Today, PepsiCo's Aquafina bottled water and Gatorade are dominant over Coke's Dasani bottled water and Powerade in their respective markets. Pepsi's Frito-Lay division commands over 60 percent of the U.S. snack food market. PepsiCo's other leading brands, such as Tropicana and Quaker, are also doing well. However, all of the focus on these other brands caused the company to lose focus on its flagship Pepsi brand. After profit increases of over 100 percent during the early and mid 2000s, Pepsi's profits actually fell somewhat in 2012. A new $600 million marketing boost is planned to reinvigorate Pepsi's core brands.[4]

Availability of Resources

Second, the marketing manager must review the current and anticipated levels of organizational resources that can be used for marketing purposes. This review includes an analysis of financial, human, and experience resources, as well as any resources the firm might hold in key relationships with supply chain partners, strategic alliance partners, or customer groups. An important element of this analysis is to gauge whether the availability or level of these resources is likely to change in the near future. Additional resources might be used to create competitive advantages in meeting customer needs. If the marketing manager expects resource levels to decline, he or she must find ways to compensate when establishing marketing goals, objectives, and strategies for the next planning period.

In bad economic times, financial shortfalls get most of the attention. However, many experts predict that a shortage of skilled labor will be a major problem in the U.S. over the next few years. The problem is not the raw number of workers, but the skill set that each one brings to the job. After years of increasing technological innovation, workers must now possess the right set of skills to work with technology. Likewise, workers of today must possess knowledge-related skills such as abstract reasoning, problem solving, and communication. Firms are also trying to increase labor productivity by doing the same or more work with fewer employees. Companies in many industries—most notably services—have turned to off shoring jobs to other countries where highly-educated,

English speaking employees will work for less pay than their U.S. counterparts. Of all white-collar jobs that have been offshored, a full 90 percent are now located in India. An interesting irony is that the same technology that demands increased skills from employees allows these jobs to be offshored to other countries. Experts suggest that 30 to 80 percent of work for any company can be potentially offshored to other countries.[5]

Organizational Culture and Structure

Finally, the marketing manager should review current and anticipated cultural and structural issues that could affect marketing activities. One of the most important issues in this review involves the internal culture of the firm. In some organizations, marketing does not hold a prominent position in the political hierarchy. This situation can create challenges for the marketing manager in acquiring resources and gaining approval of the marketing plan. The internal culture also includes any anticipated changes in key executive positions within the firm. The marketing manager, for example, could have difficulty in dealing with a new production manager who fails to see the benefits of marketing. Other structural issues to be considered include the overall customer orientation of the firm (or lack thereof), issues related to employee motivation and commitment to the organization (particularly among unionized employees), and the relative emphasis on long-term versus short-term planning. Top managers who concern themselves only with short-term profits are unlikely to see the importance of a marketing plan that attempts to create long-term customer relationships.

For most firms, culture and structure are relatively stable issues that do not change dramatically from one year to the next. In fact, changing or reorienting an organization's culture is a difficult and time-consuming process. In some cases, however, the culture and structure can change swiftly, causing political and power struggles within the organization. Consider the effects when two organizations combine their separate cultures and structures during a merger. For example, the largest merger in U.S. history took place in 2001 when AOL acquired Time Warner. At the time, the $162 billion merger was hailed as visionary in its combination of old and new media to lead the convergence of communication, entertainment, and media. However, the massive size of the merger, the differences in corporate cultures, and intense competition in the Internet advertising business conspired to lessen the potential payoff from the merger. In fact, Time Warner's stock fell almost 80 percent after the merger. Eventually, the two companies split apart. The move, which came on the heels of Time Warner's spinoff of Time Warner Cable, was designed to refocus Time Warner's efforts on its core cable networks and magazines. Today, the AOL/Time Warner merger is considered the worst in U.S. history.[6]

The Customer Environment

In the second part of the situation analysis, the marketing manager must examine the current and future situation with respect to customers in the firm's target markets. During this analysis, information should be collected that identifies: (1) the firm's current and potential customers, (2) the prevailing needs of current and potential customers, (3) the basic features of the firm's and competitors' products perceived by customers as meeting their needs, and (4) anticipated changes in customers' needs.

In assessing the firm's target markets, the marketing manager must attempt to understand all relevant buyer behavior and product usage characteristics. One method that the manager can use to collect this information is the 5W Model: Who, What, Where, When, and Why. We have adapted and applied this model to customer analysis, as shown in Exhibit 3.4. Organizations that are truly market- or customer-oriented should

---

EXHIBIT 3.4 **The Expanded 5W Model for Customer Analysis**

Who Are Our Current and Potential Customers?

1. What are the demographic, geographic, and psychographic characteristics of our customers?
2. Who actually purchases our products?
3. How do these purchasers differ from the users of our products?
4. Who are the major influencers of the purchase decision?
5. Who is financially responsible for making the purchase?

What Do Customers Do with Our Products?

1. In what quantities and in what combinations are our products purchased?
2. How do heavy users of our products differ from light users?
3. Do purchasers use complementary products during the consumption of our products? If so, what is the nature of the demand for these products, and how does it affect the demand for our products?
4. What do our customers do with our products after consumption?
5. Are our customers recycling our products or packaging?

Where Do Customers Purchase Our Products?

1. From what types of vendors are our products purchased?
2. Does e-commerce have an effect on the purchase of our products?
3. Are our customers increasing their purchasing from nonstore outlets?

When Do Customers Purchase Our Products?

1. Are the purchase and consumption of our products seasonal?
2. To what extent do promotional events affect the purchase and consumption of our products?
3. Do the purchase and consumption of our products vary based on changes in physical/social surroundings, time perceptions, or the purchase task?

Why (and How) Do Customers Select Our Products?

1. What are the basic features provided by our products and our competitors' products? How do our products compare to those of competitors?
2. What are the customer needs fulfilled by our products and our competitors' products? How well do our products meet these needs? How well do our competitors' products meet these needs?
3. Are the needs of our customers expected to change in the future? If so, how?
4. What methods of payment do our customers use when making a purchase? Is the availability of credit or financing an issue with our customers?
5. Are our customers prone to developing close long-term relationships with us and our competitors, or do they buy in a transactional fashion (primarily based on price)?
6. How can we develop, maintain, or enhance the relationships we have with our customers?

Why Do Potential Customers Not Purchase Our Products?

1. What are the basic needs of noncustomers that our products do not meet?
2. What are the features, benefits, or advantages of competing products that cause noncustomers to choose them over our products?
3. Are there issues related to distribution, promotion, or pricing that prevent noncustomers from purchasing our products?
4. What is the potential for converting noncustomers into customers of our products?

Source: Adapted from Donald R. Lehmann and Russell S. Winer, *Analysis for Marketing Planning*, 6th edition (Boston: McGraw-Hill/Irwin, 2005). Copyright 2005 The McGraw-Hill Companies, Inc.

know their customers well enough that they have easy access to the types of information that answer these questions. If not, the organization may need to conduct primary marketing research to fully understand its target markets.

Who Are Our Current and Potential Customers?

Answering the "who" question requires an examination of the relevant characteristics that define target markets. This includes demographic characteristics (gender, age, income, etc.), geographic characteristics (where customers live, density of the target market, etc.), and psychographic characteristics (attitudes, opinions, interests, etc.). Depending on the types of products sold by the firm, purchase influencers or users, rather than actual purchasers, may be important as well. For example, in consumer markets it is well known that the influence of children is critical for purchases such as cars, homes, meals, toys, and vacations. In business markets, the analysis typically focuses on the buying center. Is the buying decision made by an individual or by a committee? Who has the greatest influence on the purchase decision?

The analysis must also assess the viability of potential customers or markets that may be acquired in the future. This involves looking ahead to situations that may increase the firm's ability to gain new customers. For example, firms around the world are particularly excited about the further opening of the Chinese market and its 1.3 billion potential consumers. Many firms, including Procter & Gamble, Walmart, Starbucks, and Pepsi have established a presence in China that they hope to leverage for future growth opportunities. The excitement about the Chinese market stems from its strong middle-class of over 250 million consumers.[7]

What Do Customers Do with Our Products?

The "what" question entails an assessment of how customers consume and dispose of the firm's products. Here the marketing manager might be interested in identifying the rate of product consumption (also called the usage rate), differences between heavy and light users of products, whether customers use complementary products during consumption, and

Many firms see China as the world's most lucrative market with over 1.3 billion potential consumers.

what customers do with the firm's products after consumption. In business markets, customers typically use the firm's products in the creation of their own products. As a result, business customers tend to pay very close attention to product specifications and quality.

In some cases, marketers cannot fully understand how customers use their products without looking at the complementary products that go with them. In these cases of *derived demand*—where the demand for one product depends on (is derived from) the demand of another product—the marketer must also examine the consumption and usage of the complementary product. For example, tire manufacturers concern themselves with the demand for automobiles, and makers of computer accessories closely watch the demand for desktop and laptop computers. By following the demand for and consumption of complementary products, marketers are in a much better position to understand how customers use their own products.

Before customers and marketers became more concerned about the natural environment, many firms looked only at how their customers used products. Today, marketers have become increasingly interested in how customers dispose of products, such as whether customers recycle the product or its packaging. Another postconsumption issue deals with the need for reverse channels of distribution to handle product repairs. Car manufacturers, for example, must maintain an elaborate network of certified repair facilities (typically through dealers) to handle maintenance and repairs under warranty.

Sometimes recycling and repair issues come into conflict. The relatively low cost of today's home electronics leads many customers to buy new televisions, computers, or cell phones rather than have old ones repaired. As discussed in *Beyond the Pages 3.2*, this causes a problem: What do consumers do with e-waste, or broken and obsolete electronic devices? Though e-waste makes up only 1 percent of our country's garbage volume, state governments and local communities have struggled for years with the e-waste that enters our nation's landfills.

Where Do Customers Purchase Our Products?

The "where" question is associated mainly with distribution and customer convenience. Until recently, most firms looked solely at traditional channels of distribution, such as brokers, wholesalers, and retailers. Thus, the marketing manager would have concerns about the intensity of the distribution effort and the types of retailers that the firm's customers patronized. Today, however, many other forms of distribution are available. The fastest growing form of distribution today is nonstore retailing—which includes vending machines; direct marketing through catalogs, home sales, or infomercials; and electronic retailing through the Internet, interactive television, and video kiosks. Business markets have also begun to capitalize on the lower costs of procurement via the Internet. Likewise, many manufacturers have bypassed traditional distribution channels in favor of selling through their own outlet stores or websites. For example, there are so now many different avenues for downloading or streaming movies, either online or via cable, that the traditional movie rental business is in jeopardy.

When Do Customers Purchase Our Products?

The "when" question refers to any situational influences that may cause customer purchasing activity to vary over time. This includes broad issues, such as the seasonality of the firm's products and the variability in purchasing activity caused by promotional events or budgetary constraints. Everyone knows that consumer purchasing activity increases just after payday. In business markets, budgetary constraints and the timing of a firm's fiscal year often dictate the "when" question. For example, many schools and universities buy large quantities of supplies just before the end of their fiscal years.

The Ongoing Challenge of E-Waste[8]

What do you do with an old computer, television, DVD player, cell phone, or any other consumer electronic device when it no longer works? Having the device repaired is typically not justifiable given the high repair cost relative to buying a new item. If you are like most people, you throw these devices into the trash, a drawer, or give them away. Therein lies the problem with electronic waste, or e-waste; which is now a major problem for electronics manufacturers, state and local governments, and the U.S. Environmental Protection Agency. Recent data shows that over 86 percent of discarded electronics (2 million tons) ends up in our nation's landfills. Many of these discarded items contain toxins such as mercury, cadmium, and lead which can contaminate the soil and water if they are not disposed of properly.

Because of the growing problem of e-waste, many state and local governments have taken steps to solve the problem. In 2007, for example, Minnesota required manufacturers to collect and recycle 60 percent of discarded electronics they sold in the state. Oregon followed suit in 2009. Today, only 20 states ban electronics from landfills. California, for example, mandates 100 percent recycling of used electronics, but adds $8 to $25 to the price of new items to help offset the recycling costs. To date, there is no federal law that governs e-waste, though Congress has been looking into the issue. One such proposal adds recycling requirements for electronics retailers as well as manufacturers. Such actions put enormous pressure on these companies, many of which do not have reverse supply chain procedures in place to handle incoming e-waste. Television manufacturers face the biggest obstacles in recycling. Old televisions are big, heavy, and often very difficult for consumers to haul to recycling facilities. Further, the number of recycled televisions is growing rapidly as consumers switch from analog CRT televisions to flat-panel digital models. Consumers are also confused about what they are supposed to do with obsolete and broken electronics.

To handle the growing demands for recycling, the industry established the Electronic Manufacturers Recycling Management Company, which is funded by its members—including Toshiba, Sharp, and Panasonic. Other companies use third-party recyclers, such as Waste Management, to handle recycling. Electronic Recyclers International, the country's largest recycler of electronic waste, processes 15 million pounds of e-waste every month at seven locations in six states. The company has over 2,000 clients, including Best Buy. Dell and Goodwill Industries developed an innovative strategy—the Reconnect Partnership—where Dell provides training and financial support to refurbish old computers. The effort saves over 2.7 million pounds of computer waste from going into landfills each year. The strategy is a huge win for Goodwill, which like other charities has been inundated with donations of unwanted electronics.

E-waste is now a lucrative business for recyclers as the industry generates over $3 billion in annual revenue. It also generated a fair amount of controversy when it was discovered that some recyclers were exporting e-waste to other countries (mostly Asia, Mexico, and Africa) for disposal. These countries have lax environmental laws that make the e-waste problem much more difficult in communities where the e-waste is stored. Such actions are a violation of the Basel Convention—an international agreement that restricts trade in hazardous waste. The U.S. has yet to ratify the agreement. However, the EPA does require approval before U.S. companies can export CRT displays (computer monitors and televisions with picture tubes), which are among the most dangerous types of e-waste. Due to the growing importance of the e-waste problem, many companies—like Dell—have published formal polices regarding e-waste and e-recycling. In addition to electronics manufacturers, retailers and service companies are now on board. Amazon, for example, recently launched an electronics trade-in program. The company will accept trade-ins for over 2,500 devices in exchange for credit good for future Amazon purchases.

The "when" question also includes more subtle influences that can affect purchasing behavior, such as physical and social surroundings, time perceptions, and the purchase task. For example, a consumer may purchase a domestic brand of beer for regular home consumption, but purchase an import or microbrew when visiting a bar (physical surroundings), going out with friends (social surroundings), or hosting a party. Customers can also vary their purchasing behavior based on the time of day or how much time they have to search for alternatives. Variation by purchase task depends on what the customer intends to accomplish with the purchase. For example, a customer may purchase brand A for her own use, brand B for her children, and brand C for her coworker as a gift.

Why (and How) Do Customers Select Our Products?

The "why" question involves identifying the basic need-satisfying benefits provided by the firm's products. The potential benefits provided by the features of competing products should also be analyzed. This question is important because customers may purchase the firm's products to fulfill needs that the firm never considered. For example, most people think of vinegar as an ingredient in salad dressings. However, vinegar boasts many other uses, including cleaning floors, loosening rusted screws or nuts, tenderizing meat, and softening hard paint brushes.[9] The answer to the "why" question can also aid in identifying unsatisfied or undersatisfied customer needs. During the analysis, it is also important to identify potential changes in customers' current and future needs. Customers may purchase the firm's products for a reason that may be trumped by newly launched competitive products in the future.

The "how" part of this question refers to the means of payment that customers use when making a purchase. Although most people use cash (which also includes checks and debit cards) for most transactions, the availability of credit makes it possible for customers to take possession of high-priced products like cars and homes. The same is true in business markets where credit is essential to the exchange of goods and services in both domestic and international transactions. Recently, a very old form of payment has reemerged in business markets—barter. Barter involves the exchange of goods and services for other goods or services; no money changes hands. Barter arrangements are very good for small businesses short on cash. According to the International Reciprocal Trade Association, over $12 billion of international trade in goods and services is conducted annually on a non-cash basis—a number that represents over 15 percent of the global economy. Barter has grown at the rate of roughly 8 percent each year, thanks in part to the advent of barter networks on the Internet.[10]

Why Do Potential Customers Not Purchase Our Products?

An important part of customer analysis is the realization that many potential customers choose not to purchase the firm's products. Although there are many potential reasons why customers might not purchase a firm's products, some reasons include:

- Noncustomers have a basic need that the firm's product does not fulfill.
- Noncustomers perceive that they have better or lower-priced alternatives, such as competing substitute products.
- Competing products actually have better features or benefits than the firm's product.
- The firm's product does not match noncustomers' budgets or lifestyles.
- Noncustomers have high switching costs.
- Noncustomers do not know that the firm's product exists.
- Noncustomers have misconceptions about the firm's product (weak or poor image).
- Poor distribution makes the firm's product difficult to find.

Once the manager identifies the reasons for non-purchase, he or she should make a realistic assessment of the potential for converting noncustomers into customers.

Although conversion is not always possible, in many cases converting noncustomers is as simple as taking a different approach. For example, Australian-based Casella Wines was able to convert noncustomers into wine drinkers by fundamentally changing their approach to the wine industry. Through its [yellow tail] brand, Casella converted non-wine drinkers by positioning itself as being easy to drink, easy to understand, easy to buy, and fun. [yellow tail] ignored long-held wine attributes such as prestige and complexity to make wine more approachable to the masses. The end result is that [yellow tail] is now the best selling imported wine brand in the U.S.[11]

Once the marketing manager has analyzed the firm's current and potential customers, the information can be used to identify and select specific target markets for the revised marketing strategy. The firm should target those customer segments where it can create and maintain a sustainable advantage over its competition.

The External Environment

The final and broadest issue in a situation analysis is an assessment of the external environment, which includes all the external factors—competitive, economic, political, legal/regulatory, technological, and sociocultural—that can exert considerable direct and indirect pressures on both domestic and international marketing activities. Exhibit 3.5 provides a framework for analyzing factors in the external environment. As this framework suggests, the issues involved in examining the external environment can be divided into separate categories (i.e., competitive, economic, legal, etc.). However, some environmental issues can fall into multiple categories.

One such example is the explosive growth in direct-to-consumer (DTC) advertising in the pharmaceutical industry. In 2010, the industry spent roughly \$4.4 billion on DTC advertising through "ask your doctor" style ads aimed at encouraging consumers to request drugs by name from their physicians. This promotional strategy has been praised and criticized on a number of fronts. Some argue that DTC advertising plays an important role in educating the population about both disease and available treatments. Critics—including the U.S. Congress—argue that DTC advertising encourages consumers to self-diagnose and is often misleading about a drug's benefits and side effects. In response to these criticisms, the pharmaceutical industry developed a set of guiding principles for DTC advertising. However, most expect Congress to eventually pass legislation curtailing or barring the practice.[12]

Issues in the external environment can often be quite complex. For example, a 1997 strike by UPS employees not only put UPS employees out of work, it also led to economic slowdowns in UPS hub cities. The strike also became a political issue for President Bill Clinton as he was continually pressured to invoke the Taft-Hartley Act to force striking UPS employees back to work. Although the effects of the UPS strike were short-lived, some changes have a lasting impact. The tragic events of September 11, 2001 led to many changes in the competitive, economic, political, legal, technological, and sociocultural environments that will be felt for decades to come. Thankfully, complex situations like these occur infrequently. As we examine each element of the external marketing environment, keep in mind that issues that arise in one aspect of the environment are usually reflected in other elements as well.

Competition

In most industries, customers have preferences and choices in terms of the goods and services they can purchase. Thus, when a firm defines the target markets it will serve, it simultaneously selects a set of competing firms. The current and future actions of these

---

EXHIBIT 3.5 A Framework for Analyzing the External Environment

Competition

1. Who are our major brand, product, generic, and total budget competitors? What a~~ ~~ teristics in terms of size, growth, profitability, strategies, and target markets?
2. What are our competitors' key strengths and weaknesses?
3. What are our competitors' key capabilities and vulnerabilities with respect to their marketi~~ ~~ gram (for example, products, distribution, promotion, and pricing)?
4. What response can we expect from our competitors if environmental conditions change or if we change our marketing strategy?
5. How is our set of competitors likely to change in the future? Who are our new competitors likely to be?

Economic Growth and Stability

1. What are the general economic conditions of the country, region, state, and local area in which our firm operates?
2. What are the economic conditions of our industry? Is our industry growing? Why or why not?
3. Overall, are customers optimistic or pessimistic about the economy? Why?
4. What are the buying power and spending patterns of customers in our industry? Are our industry's customers buying less or more of our products? Why?

Political Trends

1. Have recent elections changed the political landscape within our domestic or international markets? If so, how?
2. What type of industry regulations do elected officials favor?
3. What are we doing currently to maintain good relations with elected officials? Have these activities been effective? Why or why not?

Legal and Regulatory Issues

1. What proposed changes in international, federal, state, or local laws and regulations have the potential to affect our marketing activities?
2. Do recent court decisions suggest that we should modify our marketing activities?
3. Do the recent rulings of federal, state, local and self-regulatory agencies suggest that we should modify our marketing activities?
4. What effect will changes in global trade agreements or laws have on our international marketing opportunities?

Technological Advancements

1. What impact has changing technology had on our customers?
2. What technological changes will affect the way that we operate or manufacture our products?
3. What technological changes will affect the way that we conduct marketing activities such as distribution or promotion?
4. Are there any current technologies that we do not use to their fullest potential in making our marketing activities more effective and efficient?
5. Do any technological advances threaten to make our products obsolete? Does new technology have the potential to satisfy previously unmet or unknown customer needs?

Sociocultural Trends

1. How are society's demographics and values changing? What effect will these changes have on our customers, products, pricing, distribution, promotion, and our employees?

continued

...anges in the diversity of our customers and employees

...bout our industry, company, and products? Could we take

...e be addressing?

...ust be constantly monitored, and hopefully even anticipated. One of the ...ns in analyzing competition is the question of identification. That is, how ...nager answer the question "Who are our current and future competitors?" ...an answer, the manager must look beyond the obvious examples of competition. Most firms face four basic types of competition:

1. **Brand competitors**, which market products with similar features and benefits to the same customers at similar prices.
2. **Product competitors**, which compete in the same product class, but with products that are different in features, benefits, and price.
3. **Generic competitors**, which market very different products that solve the same problem or satisfy the same basic customer need.
4. **Total budget competitors**, which compete for the limited financial resources of the same customers.

Exhibit 3.6 presents examples of each type of competition for selected product markets. In the compact SUV segment of the automotive industry, for example, the Chevrolet Equinox, Ford Escape, Honda CR-V, and Jeep Compass are brand competitors.

EXHIBIT 3.6 **Examples of Major Types of Competition**

Product Category (Need Fulfilled)	Brand Competitors	Product Competitors	Generic Competitors	Total Budget Competitors
Compact SUVs (Transportation)	Chevrolet Equinox Ford Escape Honda CR-V Jeep Compass	Mid-size SUVs Trucks Passenger cars Minivans	Rental cars Motorcycles Bicycles Public transportation	Vacation Debt reduction Home remodeling
Soft Drinks (Refreshment)	Coca-Cola Zero Diet Coke Pepsi Cola Diet Pepsi	Tea Orange juice Bottled water Energy drinks	Tap water	Candy Gum Potato chips
Movies (Entertainment)	*Harry Potter* *Twilight* *Star Trek*	Cable TV Pay-Per-View Video rentals	Athletic events Arcades Concerts	Shopping Reading Fishing
Colleges (Education)	New Mexico Florida State LSU	Trade School Community college Online programs	Books CDs Apprenticeship	New Cars Vacations Investments

However, each faces competition from other types of automotive products, such as mid-size SUVs, trucks, minivans, and passenger cars. Some of this product competition comes from within each company's own product portfolio (e.g., Honda's Pilot SUV, Accord sedan, Odyssey minivan, and Ridgeline truck compete with the CR-V). Compact SUVs also face generic competition from motorcycles, bicycles, rental cars, and public transportation—all of which offer products that satisfy the same basic customer need for transportation. Finally, customers have many alternative uses for their money rather than purchasing a compact SUV: They can take a vacation, install a pool in the backyard, buy a boat, start an investment fund, or pay off debt.

All four types of competition are important, but brand competitors rightfully receive the greatest attention as customers see different brands as direct substitutes for each other. For this reason, strategies aimed at getting customers to switch brands are a major focus in any effort to beat brand competitors. For example, Gatorade, far and away the dominant sports drink, has lost market share in recent years to competitors such as Vitamin Water, Propel, and Powerade. To refresh the Gatorade brand, Pepsi plans to expand its reach from sports drinks (a $7 billion industry) to sports nutrition (a $20 billion industry). Using research from its Florida-based Sports Science Institute, Pepsi plans to expand its Gatorade line to include energy bars, gels, protein shakes, and any other nutrition-related products that athletes use to boost energy, performance, endurance, and recovery. The first outward sign of the shift came in the repackaging of its core G-series lines into 01 Prime (pre-workout products), 02 Perform (during-workout products), and 03 Recover (post-workout products). The second launch was a line of energy chews designed to boost athletic performance. The new strategy is challenging in that Gatorade must shift its distribution system from one that is solely focused on beverages, to one that can handle the assortments and sizes of new product lines.[13]

Competitive analysis has received greater attention recently for several reasons: more intense competition from sophisticated competitors, increased competition from foreign firms, shorter product life cycles, and dynamic environments, particularly in the area of technological innovation. A growing number of companies have adopted formalized methods of identifying competitors, tracking their activities, and assessing their strengths and weaknesses—a process referred to as competitive intelligence. Competitive intelligence involves the legal and ethical observation, tracking, and analysis of the total range of competitive activity; including competitors' capabilities and vulnerabilities with respect to sources of supply, technology, marketing, financial strength, manufacturing capacities and qualities, and target markets. It also attempts to predict and anticipate competitive actions and reactions in the marketplace.[14] Competitive analysis should progress through the following stages:

1. **Identification**. Identify all current and potential brand, product, generic, and total budget competitors.
2. **Characteristics.** Focus on key competitors by assessing the size, growth, profitability, objectives, strategies, and target markets of each one.
3. **Assessment**. Assess each key competitor's strengths and weaknesses, including the major capabilities and vulnerabilities that each possesses within its functional areas (marketing, research and development, production, human resources, etc.).
4. **Capabilities.** Focus the analysis on each key competitor's marketing capabilities in terms of its products, distribution, promotion, and pricing.
5. **Response**. Estimate each key competitor's most likely strategies and responses under different environmental situations, as well as its reactions to the firm's own marketing efforts.

Many sources are available for gathering information on current or potential competitors. Company annual reports are useful for determining a firm's current performance and future direction. An examination of a competitor's mission statement can also provide information, particularly with respect to how the company defines itself. A thorough scan of a competitor's website can also uncover information—such as product specifications and prices—that can greatly improve the competitive analysis. Other, clever ways to collect competitive information include data mining techniques, patent tracking to reveal technological breakthroughs, creating psychological profiles of competitor's key executives, searching consumer review and blog websites, and attending trade shows and conferences.[15] Other valuable information sources include business periodicals and trade publications that provide newsworthy tidbits about companies. There are also numerous commercial databases, such as ABI/INFORM, InfoTrac, EBSCO, Hoover's, and Moody's, which provide a wealth of information on companies and their marketing activities. The information contained in these databases can be purchased in print form, on CD-ROM, or through an online connection with a data provider such as a school or public library.

Economic Growth and Stability

If there is one truism about any economy, it is that it will inevitably change. Therefore, current and expected conditions in the economy can have a profound impact on marketing strategy. A thorough examination of economic factors requires marketing managers to gauge and anticipate the general economic conditions of the nation, region, state, and local area in which they operate. These general economic conditions include inflation, employment and income levels, interest rates, taxes, trade restrictions, tariffs, and the current and future stages of the business cycle (prosperity, stagnation, recession, depression, and recovery). For example, the annual U.S. inflation rate trended downward for 16 years until it began to rise again in 2003. The upward trend ended in 2009 when inflation actually became negative (i.e., deflation). This means that general price levels began to fall during the economic downturn, brought on by contractions in spending by the government and individuals. Today, inflation is roughly 1.7 percent per year in the U.S.[16]

Equally important economic factors include consumers' overall impressions of the economy and their ability and willingness to spend. Consumer confidence (or lack thereof) can greatly affect what the firm can or cannot do in the marketplace. In times of low confidence, consumers may not be willing to pay higher prices for premium products, even if they have the ability to do so. In other cases, consumers may not have the ability to spend, regardless of the state of the economy. Another important factor is the current and anticipated spending patterns of consumers in the firm's target market. If consumers buy less (or more) of the firm's products, there could be important economic reasons for the change.

One of the most important economic realities in the United States over the last 50 years has been a steady shift away from a tangibles-dominant economy (goods, equipment, manufacturing) to one dominated by intangibles such as services and information. In fact, virtually everyone is aware that the U.S. economy is a knowledge-based economy. However, our methods of measuring and reporting on the economy have not kept pace with this change. Our methods are very good at capturing manufacturing output, capital expenditures, and investments in other tangible assets; but they cannot capture investments in intangibles such as innovation, employee training, brand equity, or product design. Consequently, the true nature of our economy is underreported by virtually all current statistics, such as the revered GDP. Innovation, creativity, and human assets—the main drivers behind the success of most U.S. businesses—are not counted as a part of yearly GDP statistics. Furthermore, intangible assets are woefully underreported on corporate balance sheets. The value of intangible assets in public U.S. companies is estimated at $14.5 trillion, over 60 percent of which is not reported on balance sheets. One of the major challenges as we move forward is finding ways of capturing these intangibles in our regular reporting and economic analyses.[17]

Political Trends

Although the importance will vary from firm to firm, most organizations should track political trends and attempt to maintain good relations with elected officials. Organizations that do business with government entities, such as defense contractors, must be especially attuned to political trends. Elected officials who have negative attitudes toward a firm or its industry are more likely to create or enforce regulations unfavorable for the firm. For example, the anti-tobacco trend in the United States has been in full swing since the late 1990s. Today, many states and local communities have passed laws to prevent smoking in public places. One of the most hotly contested business-related political issues of late has been the status of illegal immigrants crossing the U.S. border, especially from Mexico. This single issue has potential ramifications for our economy (employment, healthcare, trade), our society (language, culture), and our political relations with other nations. As these examples show, political discussions can have serious, lasting consequences for an industry or firm.

Many organizations view political factors as beyond their control and do little more than adjust the firm's strategies to accommodate changes in those factors. Other firms, however, take a more proactive stance by seeking to influence elected officials. For example, some organizations publicly protest legislative actions, while others seek influence more discreetly by routing funds to political parties or lobbying groups. Whatever the approach, managers should always stay in touch with the political landscape.

Legal and Regulatory Issues

As you might suspect, legal and regulatory issues have close ties to events in the political environment. Numerous laws and regulations have the potential to influence marketing decisions and activities. The simple existence of these laws and regulations causes many firms to accept this influence as a predetermined aspect of market planning. For example, most firms comply with procompetitive legislation rather than face the penalties of noncompliance. In reality, most laws and regulations are fairly vague (for instance, the Americans with Disabilities Act), which often forces firms to test the limits of certain laws by operating in a legally questionable manner. The vagueness of laws is particularly troubling for e-commerce firms who face a number of ambiguous legal issues involving copyright, liability, taxation, and legal jurisdiction. For reasons such as these, the marketing manager should carefully examine recent court decisions to better understand the law or regulation in question. New court interpretations can point to future changes in existing laws and regulations. The marketing manager should also examine the recent rulings of federal, state, local and self-regulatory trade agencies to determine their effects on marketing activities.

One of the most profound legislative shifts in corporate governance occurred with President Bush's signing of the Sarbanes-Oxley Act on July 30, 2002. Sarbanes-Oxley was essentially the federal government's response to a string of corporate scandals—most notably Enron, Tyco, and WorldCom. The law introduced very stringent rules for financial practice and corporate governance designed to protect investors by increasing the accuracy and reliability of corporate disclosures of financial information. An interesting result of Sarbanes-Oxley is the intense media and public attention that it garnered. The accuracy of corporate disclosures is now such a closely watched issue that organizations are forced into compliance both legally and practically. It is estimated that compliance with the law—in the form of new information and reporting systems—has cost the average company $2.3 million per year in compliance costs. Recently, the Sarbanes-Oxley act survived a constitutionality test in the U.S. Supreme Court, although some minor provisions of the law were to be changed.[18]

Organizations that engage in international business should also be mindful of legal issues surrounding the trade agreements among nations. The implementation of the North American Free Trade Agreement (NAFTA), for example, created an open market of roughly 374 million consumers. Since NAFTA went into effect, many U.S. firms have begun, or expanded, operations in Canada and Mexico. Conversely, national governments sometimes use trade agreements to limit the distribution of certain products into member countries. Recurring disagreements between the U.S., Canada, and Argentina and the European Union over genetically modified foods, for example, prompted the U.S. to file a complaint with the World Trade Organization in 2003. The EU has banned all genetically modified food and crops since 1998. The complaint argued that the ban lacked scientific support and amounted to an unfair trade barrier. The WTO ruled against the EU in 2006, opening the way for genetically modified foods to enter the EU. However, individual EU nations, such as Germany, have continued to ban the use of genetically modified seeds and food. Today, only 0.06 percent of farmland in the EU is used to grow genetically modified food, most of that in Spain. Even if the market eventually opens to U.S. producers, the going will be tough. The vast majority of European consumers believe that genetically modified foods are unsafe for consumption.[19]

Technological Advancements

When most people think about technology, they tend to think about new high-tech products such as wireless telephones, broadband Internet access, medical breakthroughs, GPS systems, or interactive television. However, technology actually refers to the way we accomplish specific tasks or the processes we use to create the "things" we consider as new. Of all the new technologies created in the past 30 years, none has had a greater impact on marketing than advances in computer and information technology. These technologies have changed the way consumers and employees live and the way that marketers operate in fulfilling their needs. In some cases, changes in technology can be so profound that they make a firm's products obsolete, such as with vinyl long-playing (LP) records, typewriters, cassette tapes, and pagers. We see this process occurring today as consumers slowly shift from CDs, DVDs, and newspapers to digital music, movies, and news.

Many changes in technology assume a frontstage presence in creating new marketing opportunities. By frontstage technology, we mean those advances that are most noticeable to customers. For example, products such as wireless phones, microwave ovens, and genetic engineering have spawned entirely new industries aimed at fulfilling previously unrecognized customer needs. Many frontstage technologies, such as smartphones and GPS satellite navigation systems, aim to increase customer convenience. Likewise, companies continue to push toward even more substantial changes in the ways that marketers reach customers through the use of interactive marketing via computers and digital television.

These and other technological changes can also assume a backstage presence when their advantages are not necessarily apparent to customers. Advances in backstage technology can affect marketing activities by making them more efficient and effective. For example, advances in computer technology have made warehouse storage and inventory control more efficient and less expensive. Similar changes in communication technology have made field sales representatives more efficient and effective in their dealings with managers and customers.

© Albert Lozano/Shutterstock

Radio frequency identification (RFID) tags are used in a variety of frontstage and backstage applications.

In some cases, technology can have both a frontstage and a backstage presence. One of the most promising breakthroughs is radio frequency identification (RFID), which involves the use of tiny radio-enabled chips that can be attached to a product or its packaging, or embedded in electronic devices such as GPS receivers and smartphones. The radio signals emitted or reflected from the chip (or tag) can be used to track inventory levels, prevent theft, or make wireless payments. One of the newest forms of RFID, near field communication (NFC), can be used for short-range wireless data transmission between smartphones and payment terminals such as vending machines, point-of-sale terminals, and ticket kiosks in subways, movie theaters, or airports. By 2014, 20 percent of smartphones will be NFC-enabled and compatible with payment systems from MasterCard, Visa, and American Express. RFID technology is also used in other applications such as patient tracking in hospitals, real-time data analysis in Indy racecars, and EZ-Pass systems on the nation's toll roads.[20]

Sociocultural Trends

Sociocultural factors are those social and cultural influences that cause changes in attitudes, beliefs, norms, customs, and lifestyles. These forces profoundly affect the way people live and help determine what, where, how, and when customers buy a firm's products. The list of potentially important sociocultural trends is far too long to examine each one here. Exhibit 3.7 illustrates examples of some of these trends. Two of the more important trends, however, are changes in demographics and customer values.

There are many changes taking place in the demographic makeup of the U.S. population. For example, most of us know that the population as a whole has grown older as a result of advances in medicine and healthier lifestyles. As shown in Exhibit 3.8, research suggests that the number of Americans age 65 and older will increase 106 percent by 2030—from 13 to 20 percent of the population.[21] Experts project that by 2050, the worldwide population of older people will be larger than the population of children ages 0–14 for the first time in human history. As a result, marketers of healthcare, recreation, tourism, and retirement housing can expect large increases in demand over the next several decades. Other important changes include a decline in the teenage

---

EXHIBIT 3.7　Trends in the U.S. Sociocultural Environment

Demographic Trends

Aging of the American population

Increasing population diversity, especially in the number of Hispanic Americans

Increasing number of single-member/individual households

Increasing number of single-parent families

Decline in the teen population (as a percentage of the total population)

Population growth in Sun Belt states

Increasing immigration (legal and illegal)

Increasing number of wealthy Americans

Lifestyle Trends

Many Americans are postponing retirement

Clothing has become more casual, especially at work

Growing participation in body modification (e.g., tattoos, piercings)

Americans have less time for leisure activities

Vacationing at home (a "staycation") is more common

Less shopping in malls, more shopping from home

Continuing focus on health, nutrition, and exercise

Increasing importance of leisure time versus work time

Time spent watching television and reading newspapers has declined

Growing popularity of fuel efficient hybrid vehicles

Value Trends

Growing disconnect with government

Greater focus on ethics and social responsibility

Increased interest in giving back to the community

Shorter attention spans and less tolerance for waiting

More value-oriented consumption (good quality, good price)

Importance of maintaining close, personal relationships with others

Increasing concerns about the natural environment

Less tolerance of smoking in public places

More tolerance of individual lifestyle choices

Growing skepticism about business

population, an increasing number of singles and single-parent households, and still greater participation of women in the workforce. The increase in the number of two-income and single-parent families has, for example, led to a massive increase in demand and retail shelf space for convenient frozen entrees and meals. Our growing focus on health and nutrition has led many of the marketers of these meals to offer lower calorie and carbohydrate content in their products.

EXHIBIT 3.8   **Growth in the Number of Older Americans**

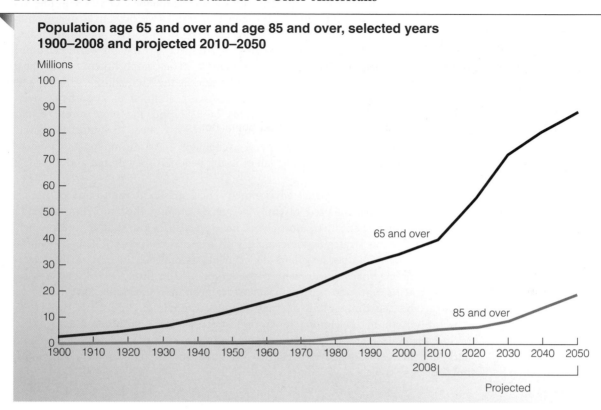

Population age 65 and over and age 85 and over, selected years 1900–2008 and projected 2010–2050

Millions

65 and over

85 and over

2008

Projected

Note: Data for 2010–2050 are projections of the population.
Reference population: These data refer to the resident population.
Source: U.S. Census Bureau, Decennial Census, Population Estimates and Projections.

One of the other most important demographic changes taking place is the increasing diversity of the U.S. population. The number of legal immigrants coming to the United States has risen steadily during the past 30 years. Between now and 2050, minority population growth will account for a full 90 percent of the growth of the total U.S. population. This trend is especially true among the Hispanic population, which has increased 43 percent since 2000 (the national population has grown by 9.7 percent since 2000). By 2050, almost one quarter of the U.S. population will be of Hispanic decent—up from 16.4 percent today.[22] These changes in diversity will create both threats and opportunities for most organizations. A diverse population means a diverse customer base. Firms must alter their marketing practices, including the way they recruit and select employees, to match these changing customer segments. For example, women of color, ignored by cosmetics companies for a long time, used to have a very difficult time finding makeup in shades appropriate for their skin tones. Now, virtually all cosmetics companies offer product lines designed specifically for these previously unserved markets. Furthermore, most well known companies now specifically target Hispanic consumers. Not only is the Hispanic market growing, it also has a number of positive characteristics such as low household debt, two-income households, and an affinity for branded merchandise. Kraft Foods, for example, recently tripled its ad spending directed at the Hispanic market. On the whole, however, less than 5 percent of total media spending is targeted at Hispanics, suggesting that marketers have a ways to go in reaching out to this lucrative market segment.[23]

Changes in our cultural values—the guiding principles of everyday life—can also create opportunities and challenges for marketers. Values influence our views of how to live, the decisions we make, the jobs we do, and the brands we buy. In a major study of American values, researchers found that the four most important values regardless of age, gender, race, income, or region are: (1) self-respect, (2) having warm relationships with others, (3) security, and (4) having a sense of accomplishment. Over the past 30 years, self-respect has been the dominant value in the U.S. culture. Having a sense of belonging and the need for security have actually declined in importance over the same time period, despite the tragic events of 9/11 and the most recent economic recession. Interestingly, the fastest growing value with respect to importance over the same time period is fun, enjoyment, and excitement.[24] Astute marketers can use this information to reflect our prevailing values in the products they design and the advertising they create.

As you can see, the external environment encompasses a wide array of important factors that must be analyzed carefully before developing the marketing plan. These issues are so important that most firms have specialists on staff to track emerging trends and develop strategies for dealing with external concerns. These specialists are typically housed in corporate affairs departments as outlined in *Beyond the Pages 3.3*. Although the external environment is the largest of the three environments we have discussed, it is not necessarily the most important. Depending on the firm, its industry, and the timing, the internal and/or customer environments can be much more important in developing marketing strategy. The important issue is that all three environments must be analyzed prior to developing a marketing strategy and marketing plan. Good analysis requires the collection of relevant data and information, our next topic.

Collecting Marketing Data and Information

To perform a complete situation analysis, the marketing manager must invest time and money to collect data and information pertinent to the development of the marketing plan. This effort will always involve the collection of secondary data, which must be compiled inside or outside the organization for some purpose other than the current analysis. However, if the required data or information is unavailable, primary data may have to be collected through marketing research. Accessing secondary data sources is usually preferable as a first option because these sources can be obtained more quickly and at less cost than collecting primary data. In this section, we will examine the different sources of environmental data and challenges in collecting this data.

Secondary Information Sources

There are four basic sources of secondary data and information: internal, government, periodicals/books, and commercial data sources. Most of these sources are available in both print and electronic formats. Let's look at the major strengths and weaknesses of these sources.

Internal Data Sources   The firm's own records are the best source of data on current objectives, strategy, performance, and available resources. Internal sources may also be a good source of data on customer needs, attitudes, and buying behavior. Internal data also has the advantage of being relevant and believable because the organization itself has responsibility for its collection and organization.

Beyond the Pages 3.3

A Corporate Affairs Primer[25]

What is corporate affairs? In its broadest sense, corporate affairs is a collection of strategic activities aimed at marketing an organization, its issues, and its ideals to potential stakeholders (consumers, general public, shareholders, media, government, etc.). One way to think about corporate affairs is that it includes all of the organization's marketing activities not directed at the end users of its products. The activities that define corporate affairs vary; however, most organizations maintain departments that engage in the following strategic activities:

- **Corporate Communication**—activities aimed at telling the organization's story and promoting goodwill among a variety of stakeholders. It includes activities such as public relations, employee relations, corporate image advertising, public affairs, and media relations.
- **Government Relations**—activities aimed at educating and influencing elected officials, government officials, and regulatory agencies with respect to key issues that are pertinent to the firm. The most visible form of government relations is lobbying.
- **Investor Relations**—activities designed to promote investment in the organization through the sale of financial instruments such as stocks and bonds. It includes activities such as developing the annual report, planning shareholders' meetings, and other customer service activities directed at corporate shareholders.
- **Corporate Philanthropy**—activities aimed at serving the needs of the community at large (either domestically or globally) through product or cash donations, volunteerism, or support of humanitarian initiatives.
- **Corporate Sustainability**—activities aimed at reducing the organization's impact on the environment. It includes activities such as reducing the organization's carbon footprint, recycling of its products, and promoting environmental stewardship.
- **Policy Analysis**—activities designed to influence the national or international dialogue with respect to public or economic policy in an industry-related area. It includes research and analysis designed to provide needed information for making policy decisions.

Perhaps the best way to understand corporate affairs is to see what several major organizations have to say about it. Here are a few examples:

Microsoft—Legal and Corporate Affairs Group

The Microsoft Legal and Corporate Affairs Group (LCA) works on the cutting edge of business and regulatory issues around the world. A diverse and multidisciplinary team of legal, business, and corporate affairs professionals operates from 57 locations in 40 countries/regions worldwide.

LCA supports Microsoft by pioneering solutions. People are encouraged to play a proactive and engaged role not only in identifying problems, but also in forging new legal and corporate affairs solutions that will advance business goals and also benefit consumers, industry partners, and the communities where we live and work.

LCA strives to be a valued partner demonstrating world-class leadership in corporate and legal relations. We build constructive relationships, champion business integrity, and pioneer innovative solutions that earn the public's trust and build Microsoft's enduring value.

Tesco—Corporate and Legal Affairs

Our Corporate Affairs team promotes and protects the Tesco brand, influencing what people think of us and affecting the way we do things.

Operating 24 hours a day across the Group, we're here to inform the public about the company's activities. Essentially, it's about delivering clear messages that put our customers first. However, we also advise on policy and communications, organise key conferences and influence events. We keep staff, customers and other stakeholders up-to-date on the company's latest special offers and business developments—not to mention our support for good causes and communities. In fact, we're one of the most people-facing functions in the business.

SABMiller—Corporate Affairs

Our Corporate Affairs teams exemplify SABMiller's dedication to make a difference through beer.

How can we brew more beer using less water? How can we reduce irresponsible drinking? How can we continue to reduce our carbon footprint? How do we track, monitor and communicate our outstanding

continued

successes in corporate social responsibility and sustainable development? These are some of the questions that our Corporate Affairs teams answer and the challenges they help to resolve.

We're in the business of brewing beer, but we're committed to doing this in the most ethical, environmentally sustainable and transparent way possible. SABMiller is determined to give back to society and has a commitment to doing what is right.

SABMiller offers Corporate Affairs careers across a wide range of opportunities at every level, including: Media Relations, Investor Relations, Government Relations, Alcohol Industry Affairs, Corporate Social Responsibility, Sustainable Development, Internal Communications and Reputation Management.

BlueScope Steel (Australia)—Corporate Affairs (External Relations)

BlueScope Steel Corporate Affairs manages Blue-Scope Steel's corporate relationships with a number of key external stakeholders including media, governments, industry bodies, and other steelmakers. Corporate Affairs produces regular media releases and announcements, and is responsible for managing the production of corporate reports, including the Annual Report and the Community, Safety & Environment Report. Corporate Affairs is also responsible for the management of communications with the company's 21,000 plus employees around the globe,

including production of the company-wide employee newspaper, Steel Connections.

IBM—Corporate Citizenship

It is only logical that responsibility for good corporate citizenship extends to all divisions of the company, because corporate citizenship at IBM consists of far more than community service. IBM is a company of more than 425,000 employees, doing business in nearly 170 countries. We manage a supply chain of more than 27,000 suppliers. We support a vast network of stakeholders—from clients, employees and business partners to community leaders and investors. And the work we do impacts not only other companies' business success, but also the efficiency and innovation of countries, cities, governments, communities and our planet's critical infrastructure.

For these reasons, IBM's business is inherently required to pursue the highest standards of social responsibility, from how we support and empower our employees, to how we work with our clients, to how we govern the corporation.

Given the complexity of the external environment in today's economy, strategic planning regarding corporate affairs is every bit as important as developing sound strategy for reaching the organization's customers. No organization exists in isolation. Consequently, all organizations must actively manage their relationships with potential stakeholders to ensure continued success.

One of the biggest problems with internal data is that it is often not in a readily accessible form for planning purposes. Box after box of printed company records that sit in a warehouse are hardly useful for marketing planning. To overcome this problem, many organizations maintain complex information systems that make data easily accessible and interactive. These systems enable employees to access internal data such as customer profiles and product inventory, and to share details of their activities and projects with other company employees across the hall or the world. These systems also provide an opportunity for company-wide marketing intelligence that permits coordination and integration of efforts to achieve a true market orientation.

Government Sources   If it exists, the U.S. government has collected data about it. The sheer volume of available information on the economy, our population, and business activities is the major strength of most government data sources. Government sources also have the added advantages of easy accessibility and low cost—most are even free. The major drawback to government data is timeliness. Although many government sources have annual updates, some are done much less frequently (e.g., the census every decade). As a result, some government sources may be out-of-date and not particularly useful for market planning purposes.

Still, the objectivity and low cost of government sources make them an attractive answer to the data need of many organizations. Some of the best government sources available on the Internet include:

- **Federal Trade Commission** (www.ftc.gov) provides reports, speeches, and other facts about competitive, antitrust, and consumer protection issues.
- **FedWorld** (www.fedworld.gov) offers links to various federal government sources of industry and market statistics.
- **Edgar Database** (www.sec.gov/edgar.shtml) provides comprehensive financial data (10K reports) on public corporations in the United States.
- **U.S. Small Business Administration** (www.sba.gov) offers numerous resources for small businesses, including industry reports, maps, market analyses (national, regional, or local), library resources, and checklists.

Book and Periodical Sources The articles and research reports available in books and periodicals provide a gamut of information about many organizations, industries, and nations. Forget any notion about books and periodicals appearing only in print. Today, many good sources exist only in electronic format. Timeliness is a major strength of these sources, as most are about current environmental trends and business practices. Some sources, such as academic journals, provide detailed results of research studies that may be pertinent to the manager's planning efforts. Others, such as trade publications, focus on specific industries and the issues that characterize them.

Many of these sources are freely available on the Internet. Most, however, require paid subscriptions. Some of the better examples include:

- **Subscription services** such as *Moody's* (www.moodys.com), *Hoover's* (www.hoovers.com), *Standard and Poor's* (www.standardandpoors.com), and *Dismal Scientist* (www.economy.com/dismal) offer in-depth analyses and current statistics about major industries and corporations.
- **Major trade associations** such as the *American Marketing Association* (www.marketingpower.com) and *Sales and Marketing Executives* (www.smei.org) and trade publications such as *Adweek* (www.adweek.com) and *Chain Store Age* (www.chainstoreage.com) offer a wide range of news and information to their membership and readers.
- **Academic journals**, such as the *Harvard Business Review* (http://hbr.org) and the *Sloan Management Review* (http://sloanreview.mit.edu), are good sources of cutting-edge thinking on business and marketing.
- **General business publications**, such as the *Wall Street Journal* (www.wsj.com), *Fortune* (www.fortune.com), and *Business Week* (www.businessweek.com), offer a wealth of information on a wide variety of industries and companies.

The two biggest drawbacks to book and periodical sources are information overload and relevance to the specific problem at hand. That is, despite the sheer volume of information that is available, finding data or information that pertains to the manager's specific and unique situation can feel like looking for that proverbial needle in a haystack.

Commercial Sources Commercial sources are almost always relevant to a specific issue because they deal with the actual behaviors of customers in the marketplace. Firms such as Nielsen monitor a variety of behaviors from food purchases in grocery stores to media usage characteristics. Commercial sources generally charge a fee for their services. However, their data and information are invaluable to many companies. Some commercial sources provide limited information on their websites:

- **The Nielsen Company** (www.nielsen.com) and *SymphonyIRI Group* (www.symphonyiri.com) supply data and reports on point-of-purchase sales.
- **GfK Mediamark Research and Intelligence** (www.gfkmri.com) and *Arbitron* (www.arbitron.com) specialize in multimedia audience research by providing a wealth of customer demographic, lifestyle, and product usage data to major media and advertising companies.
- **The Audit Bureau of Circulations** (www.accessabc.com) provides independent, third party audits of print circulation, readership and website activity.
- **Surveys.com** (www.surveys.com) uses an online consumer panel to provide information to businesses about the products and services they provide.

The most obvious drawback to these and other commercial sources is cost. Although this is not a problem for large organizations, small companies often cannot afford the expense. However, many commercial sources provide limited, free access to some data and information. Additionally, companies often find "off-the-shelf" studies less costly than conducting primary research.

Primary Data Collection

The situation analysis should always begin with an examination of secondary data sources due to their availability and low cost. Since each secondary data source has its advantages and disadvantages, the best approach is one that blends data and information from a variety of sources. However, if the needed secondary data is not available, out of date, inaccurate or unreliable, or irrelevant to the specific problem at hand, an organization may have little choice but to collect primary data through marketing research. Primary marketing research has the major advantages of being relevant to the specific problem, as well as trustworthy due to the control the manager has over data collection. However, primary research is extremely expensive and time consuming. There are four major types of primary data collection:

- **Direct observation**, where the researcher records the overt behaviors of customers, competitors, or suppliers in natural settings. Historically, researchers have used direct observation to study the shopping and buying behaviors of customers. However, behavior can be observed today through the use of technology such as bar code scanners, RFID tags, and the analysis of clickstream data in online settings. The main advantage of observation research is that it accurately describes behavior without influencing the target under observation. However, the results of observation research are often overly descriptive and subject to a great deal of bias and researcher interpretation.
- **Focus groups**, where the researcher moderates a panel discussion among a gathering of 6 to 10 people who openly discuss a specific subject. Focus group research is an excellent means of obtaining in-depth information about a particular issue. Its flexibility also allows it to be used in a variety of settings and with different types of panel members (i.e., customers, suppliers, and employees). Focus groups are also very useful in designing a large-scale survey to ensure that questions have the appropriate wording. The main disadvantage is that focus groups require a highly skilled moderator to help limit the potential for moderator bias.
- **Surveys**, where the researcher asks respondents to answer a series of questions on a particular topic. Surveys can be administered using the paper-and-pencil method, either in person or through the mail; or they can be administered interactively via telephone, email, or the Internet. Although surveys are a very useful and time-efficient way to collect primary data, it has become increasingly difficult to convince people to

participate. Potential respondents have become skeptical of survey methods due to overly long questionnaires and the unethical practices of many researchers. These concerns are one of the reasons behind the creation of the national Do Not Call Registry for telemarketers (www.donotcall.gov).

- **Experiments**, where the researcher selects matched subjects and exposes them to different treatments while controlling for extraneous variables. Because experiments are well suited to testing for cause-and-effect relationships, researchers use them quite often in test marketing programs. Marketers can experiment with different combinations of marketing mix variables to determine which combination has the strongest effect on sales or profitability. The major obstacles to effective experimentation in marketing are the expense and the difficulty of controlling for all extraneous variables in the test.

As with secondary data, often the best approach to primary data collection is to use a combination of data sources. Focus groups and direct observation can be used to gain a more complete understanding of a particular issue or marketing phenomenon. Surveys can then be used to further test for certain tendencies or effects before launching into a full-scale test-marketing program. At this point, the process comes full circle as observation and focus groups can be used to explore the outcomes of the test-marketing program.

Overcoming Problems in Data Collection

Despite the best intentions, problems usually arise in collecting data and information. One of the most common problems is an incomplete or inaccurate assessment of the situation that the gathering of data should address. After expending a great degree of effort in collecting data, the manager may be unsure of the usefulness or relevance of what has been collected. In some cases, the manager might even suffer from severe information overload. To prevent these problems from occurring, the marketing problem must be accurately and specifically defined before the collection of any data. Top managers who do not adequately explain their needs and expectations to marketing researchers often cause the problem.

Another common difficulty is the expense of collecting environmental data. Although there are always costs associated with data collection (even if the data are free), the process need not be prohibitively expensive. The key is to find alternative data collection methods or sources. For example, an excellent way for some businesses to collect data is to engage the cooperation of a local college or university. Many professors seek out marketing projects for their students as a part of course requirements. Likewise, to help overcome data collection costs, many researchers have turned to the Internet as a means of collecting both quantitative and qualitative data on customer opinions and behaviors.

A third issue is the time it takes to collect data and information. Although this is certainly true with respect to primary data collection, the collection of secondary data can be quite easy and fast. Online data sources are quite accessible. Even if the manager has no idea where to begin the search, the powerful search engines and indexes available on the Internet make it easy to find data. Online data sources have become so good at data retrieval that the real problem involves the time needed to sort through all of the available information to find something that is truly relevant.

Finally, it can be challenging to find a way to organize the vast amount of data and information collected during the situation analysis. Clearly defining the marketing problem and blending different data sources are among the first steps toward finding all of the pieces to the puzzle. A critical next step is to convert the data and information into a form that will facilitate strategy development. Although there are a variety of tools that can be used to analyze and organize environmental data and information, one of the most effective of these tools is SWOT analysis. As we will see in the next chapter, SWOT analysis—which involves classifying data and information into strengths, weaknesses, opportunities and threats—can be used to organize data and information and used as a catalyst for strategy formulation.

Lessons from Chapter 3

Collecting and analyzing marketing information through a situation analysis:

- is perhaps the most important task of the marketing manager because practically all decision making and planning depends on how well he or she conducts the analysis.
- should be an ongoing effort that is well organized, systematic, and supported by sufficient resources.
- involves analysis and synthesis to understand why people, products, and organizations perform the way they do.
- is not intended to replace the marketing manager in the decision-making process, but to empower him or her with information for decision making.
- recognizes that data and information are not the same. Data is not useful until converted into information.
- forces managers to ask continually, "How much data and information do I need?"
- is valuable only to the extent that it improves the quality of the resulting decisions. Marketing managers must avoid "paralysis by analysis."
- should provide as complete a picture as possible about the organization's current and future situation with respect to the internal, customer, and external environments.

Analysis of the internal environment:

- includes an assessment of the firm's current goals, objectives, performance, and how well the current marketing strategy is working.
- includes a review of the current and anticipated levels of organizational resources.
- must include a review of current and anticipated cultural and structural issues that could affect marketing activities.

Analysis of the customer environment:

- examines the firm's current customers in its target markets, as well as potential customers that currently do not purchase the firm's product offering.
- can be conducted by using the expanded 5W model:

- Who are our current and potential customers?
- What do customers do with our products?
- Where do customers purchase our products?
- When do customers purchase our products?
- Why (and how) do customers select our products?
- Why do potential customers not purchase our products?

Analysis of the external environment:

- examines the competitive, economic, political, legal and regulatory, technological, and sociocultural factors in the firm's external environment.
- includes an examination of the four basic types of competitors faced by all businesses: brand competitors, product competitors, generic competitors, and total budget competitors.
- is often handled by a team of specialists within an organization's corporate affairs department.

Marketing data and information:

- can be collected from a wide array of internal, government, periodical, book, and commercial sources, as well as through primary marketing research.
- are often collected through four different types of primary research: direct observation, focus groups, surveys, and experiments.
- must be blended from many different sources to be the most useful for planning purposes.

Problems that can occur during data collection include:

- an incomplete or inaccurate definition of the marketing problem.
- ambiguity about the usefulness or relevance of the collected data.
- severe information overload.
- the expense and time associated with data collection.
- finding ways to organize the vast amount of collected data and information.

Questions for Discussion

1. Of the three major environments in a situation analysis (internal, customer, external), which do you think is the most important in a general sense? Why? What are some situations that would make one environment more important than the others?

2. Understanding the motivations of a firm's noncustomers is often just as important as understanding its customers. Look again at the reasons why an individual would not purchase a firm's products. How can a firm reach out to noncustomers and successfully convert them into customers?

Exercises

1. Choose a specific product that you use on a daily basis (such as food items, toiletries, or your car) and apply the 5W model in Exhibit 3.4 to yourself:
   a. Who are you (demographics, psychographics, etc.)?
   b. What do you do with the product (consumption, storage, disposal, etc.)?
   c. Where do you purchase the product? Why?
   d. When do you purchase the product? Why?
   e. Why and how do you select the product?
   f. Why do you not purchase competing products?

   Assume your responses are similar to millions of other consumers. Given this profile, how would you approach the marketing strategy for this particular product?

3. Do you think the Internet has made it easier or more difficult to collect marketing data and information? Why? How might the major data collection issues of today compare to the issues that occurred in the pre-Internet era?

2. Consider the last purchase you made (maybe it was lunch or a soft drink). List all of the brand, product, generic, and total budget competitors for that product. In a general sense, what would it take for you to switch to another type of competitor? Are there situations that would encourage you to switch to a generic competitor? When would total budget competitors become more relevant to your decision making process?

3. Review the sociocultural trends in Exhibit 3.7. What other trends could be added to the list? What trends are specific to your generation that cannot be universally applied to all Americans?

End Notes

1. These facts are from Parija Bhatnagar, "Home Depot Looking to Age Well," *CNNMoney*, January 17, 2006 (http://money.cnn.com/2006/01/17/news/companies/home_depot/index.htm); Alicia Clegg, "Mining the Golden Years," *BusinessWeek Online*, May 4, 2006 (http://www.businessweek.com/print/innovate/content/may2006/id20060504_612679.htm); Karen E. Klein, "Reaching Out to an Older Crowd," *BusinessWeek Online*, April 3, 2006 (http://www.businessweek.com/print/smallbiz/content/apr2006/sb20060403_549646.htm); Louise Lee, "Love Those Boomers," *BusinessWeek*, October 25, 2005; Devin Leonard and Caroline Winter, "In Financial Ads, the Dream Comes Down to Earth," *BusinessWeek Online*, October 27, 2011 (http://www.businessweek.com/magazine/in-financial-ads-the-dream-comes-down-to-earth-10272011.html); Janet Novak, "The Biggest Market Losers: The Boomers," *Forbes Online*, May 14, 2009 (http://www.forbes.com/2009/05/14/stock-market-losses-survey-personal-finance-retirement-worried-baby-boomers.html); David Serchuk, "Boomers Leave the Table," *Forbes Online*, November 21, 2008 (http://www.forbes.com/2008/11/20/intelligent-investing-baby-boomer-retirement-Nov20-panel.html); and Ed Wallace, "The Boomers Stop Buying," *BusinessWeek Online*, February 26, 2009 (http://www.businessweek.com/lifestyle/content/feb2009/bw20090226_384582.htm).

2. These facts are from "Mattel Tells Federal Jury MGA Stole Bratz Doll Idea, Should Pay," *BusinessWeek Online*, April 8, 2001 (http://www.businessweek.com/news/2011-04-08/mattel-tells-federal-jury-mga-stole-bratz-doll-idea-should-pay.html); and "MGA Asks Appeals Court to Halt Transfer of Bratz," *BusinessWeek Online*, May 27, 2009 (http://www.businessweek.com/ap/financialnews/D98ET0AG3.htm).

3. These facts are from Katrina Brooker, "The Pepsi Machine," *Fortune*, February 6, 2006, 68–72.

4. These facts are from Burt Helm, "Blowing Up Pepsi," *BusinessWeek Online*, April 23, 2009 (http://www.businessweek.com/magazine/content/09_17/b4128032006687.htm); Duane D. Stanford, "PepsiCo May Boost Marketing Budget to Take on Coca-Cola: Retail," *BusinessWeek Online*, January 30, 2012 (http://www.businessweek.com/news/2012-01-30/pepsico-may-boost-marketing-budget-to-take-on-coca-cola-retail.html); and Duane D. Stanford, "PepsiCo to Cut 8,700 Jobs, Spend More on Marketing Brands," *BusinessWeek Online*, February 10, 2012 (http://www.businessweek.com/news/2012-02-10/pepsico-to-cut-8-700-jobs-spend-more-on-marketing-brands.html).

5. These facts are from Nanette Byrnes, "The Jobs that Employers Can't Fill," *BusinessWeek Online*, May 29, 2009 (http://www.businessweek.com/careers/managementiq/archives/2009/05/the_jobs_that_e.html); Bruce Einhorn and Ketaki Gokhale, "India Outsources Feel Unloved in the U.S.," *BusinessWeek Online*, November 4, 2010 (http://www.businessweek.com/magazine/content/10_46/b4203016835355.htm); and Robert J. Grossman, "The Truth About the Coming Labor Shortage," *HR Magazine* 50 (3), March 2005.

6. These facts are from Emma Barnett and Amanda Andrews, "AOL Merger Was 'The Biggest Mistake in Corporate History', Believes Time Warner Chief Jeff Bewkes," *The Telegraph*, September 28, 2010 (http://www.telegraph.co.uk/finance/newsbysector/mediatechnologyandtelecoms/media/8031227/AOL-merger-was-the-biggest-mistake-in-corporate-history-believes-Time-Warner-chief-Jeff-Bewkes.html); and Aaron Smith, "Time Warner to Split Off AOL," *CNN Money*, May 28, 2009 (http://money.cnn.com/2009/05/28/technology/timewarner_aol/index.htm).

7. These facts are from Shaun Rein, "China's Consumers are Still Spending," *BusinessWeek Online*, March 25, 2009 (http://www.businessweek.com/globalbiz/content/mar2009/gb20090325_370224.htm).

8. These facts are from Susan Carpenter, "Paring Down Our E-Waste Heap: TVs, Cellphones and Other Electronics Don't Belong in the Trash," *Chicago Tribune*, July 26, 2011 (http://articles.chicagotribune.com/2011-07-26/classified/sc-home-0718-ewaste-20110723_1_e-waste-electronic-waste-electronic-trash); Gina-Marie Cheeseman, "Amazon Joins the eWaste Trade-In Movement," *TriplePundit*, May 23, 2011 (http://www.triplepundit.com/2011/05/amazon-ewaste-trade-in); Ben Elgin and Brian Grow, "E-Waste: The Dirty Secret of Recycling Electronics," *BusinessWeek Online*, October 15, 2008 (http://www.businessweek.com/magazine/content/08_43/b4105000160974.htm); Olga Kharif, "E-Waste: Whose Problem is It?" *BusinessWeek Online*, March 17, 2008 (http://www.businessweek.com/technology/content/mar2008/tc20080317_718350.htm); Jessica Mintz, "Dell Bans E-Waste Export to Developing Countries," *BusinessWeek Online*, May 12, 2009 (http://www.businessweek.com/ap/tech/D9850TS80.htm); and Gerry Smith, "Will E-Waste Recycling Law Compute?" *Chicago Tribune*, April 3, 2011 (http://articles.chicagotribune.com/2011-04-03/news/ct-met-e-waste-20110403_1_e-waste-recycling-goals-benchmarks).

9. Mary Ellen Pinkham, "20 Surprising Uses for Vinegar," iVillage (http://i.ivillage.com/PP/MomTourage/pdf/momtourage_vinegar.pdf).

10. International Reciprocal Trade Association (http://www.irta.com), accessed February 28, 2012.

11. These facts are from W. Chan Kim and Renee Mauborgne, *Blue Ocean Strategy* (Boston, MA: Harvard Business School Press, 2005), 24–35; and Mike Steinberger, "Not Such a G'Day," *Slate*, April 8, 2009 (http://www.slate.com/id/2215153).

12. These facts are from John Mack, "Double Dip in DTC Spending Plus 33% Drop in Internet Display Ad Spending!" *Pharma Marketing Blog*, October 22, 2011 (http://pharmamkting.blogspot.com/2011/10/double-dip-in-dtc-spending-plus-33-drop.html); and Arlene Weintraub, "Ask Your Doctor if This Ad is Right for You," *BusinessWeek Online*, November 4, 2009 (http://www.businessweek.com/magazine/content/09_46/b4155078964719.htm).

13. These facts are from Duane Stanford, "Gatorade Goes Back to the Lab," *BusinessWeek Online*, November 23, 2011 (http://www.businessweek.com/magazine/gatorade-goes-back-to-the-lab-11232011.html).

14. This definition of competitive intelligence is adapted from The Society of Competitive Intelligence Professionals (http://www.scip.org/ci).

15. Ibid.

16. This information is from InflationData.com (http://www.inflationdata.com), accessed March 1, 2012.

17. These facts are from Jane Denny, "The US's $14.5 Trillion Intangible Economy and a Failure of Accountancy," *Intellectual Asset Management Blog*, November 4, 2011 (http://www.iam-magazine.com/blog/Detail.aspx?g=8426421b-14fc-4227-846f-78e8f3f4bddc); Ken Jarboe, "Measuring Innovation and Intangibles," *The Intangible Economy*, Athena Alliance weblog, January 16, 2009 (http://www.athenaalliance.org/weblog/archives/2009/01/measuring_innovation_and_intangibles.html); and Michael Mandel, "GDP: What's Counted, What's Not," *BusinessWeek Online*, February 13, 2006 (http://www.businessweek.com/magazine/content/06_07/b3971010.htm).

18. These facts are from "Court to Review Anti-Fraud Law," *BusinessWeek Online*, May 18, 2009 (http://www.businessweek.com/ap/financialnews/D988NL482.htm); Nick Gillespie, "The Worst Ideas of the Decade: Sarbanes-Oxley," *The Washington Post* (http://www.washingtonpost.com/wp-srv/special/opinions/outlook/worst-ideas/sarbanes-oxley.html), accessed March 1, 2012; "Sarbanes-Oxley is Here to Stay," *The ERM Current*, June 28, 2010 (http://wheelhouseadvisors.com/category/sarbanes-oxley); and The Sarbanes-Oxley Act Community Forum (http://www.sarbanes-oxley-forum.com), accessed March 1, 2012.

19. Kerry Capell, "Now, Will Europe Swallow Frankenfoods?" *BusinessWeek Online*, February 8, 2006 (http://www.businessweek.com/bwdaily/dnflash/feb2006/nf2006028_3575_db039.htm); Germany Bans Monsanto's GMO Corn," *BusinessWeek Online*, April 16, 2009 (http://www.businessweek.com/globalbiz/content/apr2009/gb20090416_667169.htm); "Greece Extends Ban on U.S. Biotech Corn Seeds," *BusinessWeek Online*, May 27, 2009 (http://www.businessweek.com/ap/financialnews/D98EL0TG2.htm); and "Industry Figures Confirm GM Food is a Commercial Flop in Europe," Greenpeace Press Release, February 7, 2012 (http://www.greenpeace.org/eu-unit/en/News/2012/GM-figures).

20. These facts are from Marie Mawad, "Gemalto Plans to Introduce Smart Chip for Mobile Payment," *BusinessWeek Online*, February 28, 2012 (http://www.businessweek.com/news/2012-02-28/gemalto-plans-to-introduce-smart-chip-for-mobile-payment.html); and RFID Journal (http://www.rfidjournal.com), accessed March 2, 2012.

21. Administration on Aging website (http://www.aoa.gov).

22. These facts are from Michael Martinez and David Ariosto, "Hispanic Population Exceeds 50 Million, Firmly Nation's No. 2 Group," *CNN*, March 24, 2011 (http://articles.cnn.com/2011-03-24/us/census.hispanics_1_hispanic-population-illegal-immigration-foreign-born?_s=PM:US).

23. These facts are from Ronald Grover, "U.S. Marketers Say Hola! To Hispanic Consumers," *BusinessWeek Online*, April 9, 2009 (http://www.businessweek.com/magazine/content/09_16/b4127076302996.htm); and Todd Spangler, "Hispanic TV Summit: Level of Ad Spending is 'Disgusting': Vidal's Ruiz," *VegaPages*, September 21, 2011 (http://www.vegapages.com/article/hispanic-tv-summit-level-of-ad-spending-is-disgusting-vidals-ruiz.html).

24. Eda Gurel-Atay, Guang-Xin Xie, Johnny Chen, and Lynn Richard Kahle, "Changes in Social Values in the United States, 1976-2007: 'Self-Respect' is on the Upswing as a 'Sense of Belonging' Becomes Less Important," *Journal of Advertising Research*, 50 (March), 57–67.

25. The organizational descriptions of corporate affairs are taken from websites of these companies: BlueScope Steel (http://www.bluescopesteel.com/utilities-menu/contact-us/corporate-affairs); IBM (http://www.ibm.com/ibm/responsibility); Microsoft (http://www.microsoft.com/About/Legal/EN/US/Default.aspx); Tesco (http://www.tesco-careers.com/home/about-us/our-company/corporate-and-legal-affairs); and SABMiller (http://www.sabmiller.com/index.asp?pageid=1281).

CHAPTER **4**

Developing Competitive Advantage and Strategic Focus

Introduction

Situation analysis, as discussed in Chapter 3, can generate a great deal of data and information for marketing planning. But information, in and of itself, provides little direction to managers in preparing a marketing plan. If the analysis does not structure the information in a meaningful way that clarifies both present and anticipated situations, the manager will be unable to see how the pieces fit together. This synthesis of information is critical in developing competitive advantages and the strategic focus of the marketing plan. As illustrated in *Beyond the Pages 4.1*, this synthesis often comes from enhanced innovation, a stronger focus on customer needs, and tighter integration within the firm. Understanding the connectedness of the external environment is vital to enhanced innovation across a number of industries.

How should the marketing manager organize and use the information collected during the situation analysis? One widely used tool is SWOT analysis (strengths and weaknesses, opportunities and threats). A SWOT analysis encompasses both the internal and external environments of the firm. Internally, the framework addresses a firm's strengths and weaknesses on key dimensions such as financial performance and resources, human resources, production facilities and capacity, market share, customer perceptions, product quality, product availability, and organizational communication. The assessment of the external environment organizes information on the market (customers and competition), economic conditions, social trends, technology, and government regulations.

Many consider SWOT analysis to be one of the most effective tools in the analysis of marketing data and information. SWOT analysis is a simple, straightforward framework that provides direction and serves as a catalyst for the development of viable marketing plans. It fulfills this role by structuring the assessment of the fit between what a firm can and cannot do (strengths and weaknesses), and the environmental conditions working for and against the firm (opportunities and threats). When performed correctly, a SWOT analysis not only organizes data and information, it can be especially useful in uncovering competitive advantages that can be leveraged in the firm's marketing strategy.

Beyond the Pages 4.1

Innovation: A Major Key to Success[1]

Innovation is the buzzword of business in the twenty-first century. Of course, innovation has always been important, especially with respect to developing new products. What has changed, however, is the focus of innovation in most companies. The twentieth-century model of innovation was about quality control, cost cutting and operational efficiency. Today, innovation is more about reinventing business processes, collaborating and integrating within the firm, and creating entirely new markets to meet untapped customers needs. Increasing globalization, the growth of the Internet, and more demanding customers are forcing marketers to find innovative ways of conducting business.

An important lesson that many companies have learned is that innovation is not always about technology or offering the latest gee-whiz product. Differences in innovation style are apparent in *BusinessWeek*'s most recent list of the World's Most Innovative Companies. The top 20 companies on the list include both cultural icons and manufacturing giants (U.S. companies except where noted):

Rank	Company	Stock Returns % 2006-09	Revenue Growth % 2006-09	Margin Growth % 2006-09
1.	Apple	35	30	29
2.	Google	10	31	2
3.	Microsoft	3	10	-4
4.	IBM	12	2	11
5.	Toyota (Japan)	-20	-11	NA
6.	Amazon	51	29	6
7.	LG Electronics (South Korea)	31	16	707
8.	BYD (China)	99	42	-1
9.	General Electric	-22	-1	-25
10.	Sony (Japan)	-19	-5	NA
11.	Samsung (South Korea)	10	17	-9
12.	Intel	3	0	12
13.	Ford	10	-12	NA
14.	Research in Motion (Canada)	17	75	-6
15.	Volkswagen (Germany)	8	0	14
16.	Hewlett-Packard	9	8	9
17.	Tata Group (India)	Private	Private	Private
18.	BMW (Germany)	-8	0	NA
19.	Coca-Cola	9	9	1
20.	Nintendo (Japan)	-8	22	3

Several types of innovation are evident in this list. For example, in launching the iPod, iPhone, iPad, and the App Store, Apple combined innovations in product design, branding, strategic alliances, and business model to create a cultural phenomenon. Innovation at Google is based on applications such as Google Voice and Google Docs that are not related to its ubiquitous search engine. Toyota makes the list (despite negative financial performance due to a major recall) due to relentless manufacturing expertise, tight integration within the firm, and advancements in hybrid technology with its Prius. Other Asian companies, such as LG, Samsung, BYD (lithium batteries), and Hyundai (number 22) made a strong showing in the list as well.

One thing that all innovative companies have in common is a laser-like focus on customer needs. Innovative companies find new ways of learning from customers in addition to traditional methods. For example, many companies closely watch blogs and online communities to learn what customers are thinking. Focusing on customers may not sound innovative, but increasing competition and shorter product cycles are forcing marketers to shift away from the price- and efficiency-driven approaches of the past. To escape from commodity hell, marketers must find innovation in unfamiliar places. For example, Procter & Gamble (number 25 on the list) recently launched Tide Pods after 8 years of research and 6,000 consumer tests. Tide Pods are ball-shaped, premeasured packages of detergent and fabric softener that consumers simply toss into the wash. A lot of the research for Tide Pods was conducted at P&G's Beckett Ridge Innovation Center just outside of the company's Cincinnati headquarters. There, P&G's researchers watched consumers to learn how to make a laundry detergent that was easier to use, less confusing, and more convenient to carry.

As reflected in the table, innovation is obviously good for the bottom line. Through increased growth, better collaboration, and a broader product mix, the most innovative companies are able to pull their products out of commodity status and increase their operating revenue. It is clear that innovation has become a key driver of competitive advantage and success in today's market.

EXHIBIT 4.1 **Major Benefits of SWOT Analysis**

Simplicity

SWOT analysis requires no extensive training or technical skills to be used successfully. The analyst needs only a comprehensive understanding of the nature of the company and the industry in which it competes.

Lower Costs

Because specialized training and skills are not necessary, the use of SWOT analysis can actually reduce the costs associated with strategic planning. As firms begin to recognize this benefit of SWOT analysis, many opt to downsize or eliminate their strategic planning departments.

Flexibility

SWOT analysis can enhance the quality of an organization's strategic planning even without extensive marketing information systems. However, when comprehensive systems are present, they can be structured to feed information directly into the SWOT framework. The presence of a comprehensive information system can make repeated SWOT analyses run more smoothly and efficiently.

Integration and Synthesis

SWOT analysis gives the analyst the ability to integrate and synthesize diverse information, both of a quantitative and a qualitative nature. It organizes information that is widely known, as well as information that has only recently been acquired or discovered. SWOT analysis can also deal with a wide diversity of information sources. In fact, SWOT analysis helps transform information diversity from a weakness of the planning process into one of its major strengths.

Collaboration

SWOT analysis fosters collaboration and open information exchange between different functional areas. By learning what their counterparts do, what they know, what they think, and how they feel, the marketing analyst can solve problems, fill voids in the analysis, and eliminate potential disagreements before the finalization of the marketing plan.

© Cengage Learning 2013

These competitive advantages help establish the strategic focus and direction of the firm's marketing plan.

As a planning tool, SWOT analysis has many benefits, as outlined in Exhibit 4.1. In fact, SWOT analysis is so useful and logical that many underestimate its value in planning. However, this simplicity often leads to unfocused and poorly conducted analyses. The most common criticisms leveled against SWOT analysis are that (1) it allows firms to create lists without serious consideration of the issues and (2) it often becomes a sterile academic exercise of classifying data and information. It is important to remember that SWOT analysis, by itself, is not inherently productive or unproductive. Rather, the way that one uses SWOT analysis will determine whether it yields benefits for the firm.

Making SWOT Analysis Productive

Whether a firm receives the full benefits of SWOT analysis depends on the way the manager uses the framework. If done correctly and smartly, SWOT analysis can be a viable mechanism for the development of the marketing plan. If done haphazardly or

---

EXHIBIT 4.2   Directives for a Productive SWOT Analysis

Stay Focused

A single, broad analysis leads to meaningless generalizations. Separate analyses for each product–market combination are recommended.

Search Extensively for Competitors

Although major brand competitors are the most important, the analyst must not overlook product, generic, and total budget competitors. Potential future competitors must also be considered.

Collaborate with Other Functional Areas

SWOT analysis promotes the sharing of information and perspective across departments. This cross-pollination of ideas allows for more creative and innovative solutions to marketing problems.

Examine Issues from the Customers' Perspective

Customers' beliefs about the firm, its products, and marketing activities are important considerations in SWOT analysis. The views of employees and other key stakeholders must also be considered.

Look for Causes, Not Characteristics

Rather than simply list characteristics of the firm's internal and external environments, the analyst must also explore the resources possessed by the firm and/or its competitors that are the true causes for the firm's strengths, weaknesses, opportunities, and threats.

Separate Internal Issues from External Issues

If an issue would exist even if the firm did not exist, the issue should be classified as external. In the SWOT framework, opportunities (and threats) exist independently of the firm and are associated with characteristics or situations present in the economic, customer, competitive, cultural, technological, political, or legal environments in which the firm resides. Marketing options, strategies, or tactics are not a part of the SWOT analysis.

© Cengage Learning 2013

---

incorrectly, it can be a great waste of time and other valuable resources. To help ensure that the former, and not the latter, takes place, we offer the following directives to make SWOT analysis more productive and useful. Exhibit 4.2 outlines these directives.

Stay Focused

Marketing planners often make the mistake of conducting one generic SWOT analysis for the entire organization or business unit. Such an approach produces stale, meaningless generalizations that come from the tops of managers' heads or from press release files. Although this type of effort may make managers feel good and provide a quick sense of accomplishment, it does little to add to the creativity and vision of the planning process.

When we say SWOT analysis, we really mean SWOT *analyses*. In most firms, there should be a series of analyses, each focusing on a specific product/market combination. For example, a single SWOT analysis for the Chevrolet division of General Motors would not be focused enough to be meaningful. Instead, separate analyses for each product category (passenger cars, trucks, SUVs) or brand (Corvette, Impala, Avalanche, Tahoe) in the division would be more appropriate. Such a focus enables the marketing manager to look at the specific mix of competitors, customers, and external factors that are present in a given market. Chevrolet's Tahoe, for example, competes in the crowded

SUV market where competitors release new models and competing crossover vehicles at a staggering pace. Consequently, market planning for the Tahoe should differ substantially from market planning for Chevrolet's Corvette. If needed, separate product/market analyses can be combined to examine the issues relevant for the entire strategic business unit, and business unit analyses can be combined to create a complete SWOT analysis for the entire organization. The only time a single SWOT analysis would be appropriate is when an organization has only one product/market combination.

Search Extensively for Competitors

Information on competitors and their activities is an important aspect of a well-focused SWOT analysis. The key is not to overlook any competitor, whether a current rival or one on the horizon. As we discussed in Chapter 3, the firm will focus most of its efforts on brand competition. During the SWOT analysis, however, the firm must watch for any current or potential direct substitutes for its products. Product, generic, and total budget competitors are important as well. Looking for all four types of competition is crucial because many firms and managers never look past brand competitors. Although it is important for the SWOT analysis to be focused, it must not be myopic.

Even industry giants can lose sight of their potential competitors by focusing exclusively on brand competition. Kodak, for example, had always taken steps to maintain its market dominance over rivals Fuji, Konica, and Polaroid in the film industry. However, the advent of digital photography added Sony, Nikon, Canon and others to Kodak's set of competing firms. And, as digital cameras became integrated into wireless phones, Kodak was forced to add Apple, Motorola, LG, Samsung, and Nokia to its competitive set. Given the significant increase in competitive pressures facing the firm, it is of little surprise that Kodak was forced to declare bankruptcy. A similar trend has occurred in financial services as deregulation has allowed brokers, banks, and insurance firms to compete in each other's traditional markets. State Farm, for example, offers mortgage loans, credit cards, mutual funds, and traditional banking services alongside its well-known insurance products. This shift has forced firms such as Charles Schwab and Wells Fargo to look at insurance companies in a different light.

Collaborate with Other Functional Areas

One of the major benefits of SWOT analysis is that it generates information and perspective that can be shared across a variety of functional areas in the firm. The SWOT process should be a powerful stimulus for communication outside normal channels. The final outcome of a properly conducted SWOT analysis should be a fusion of information from many areas. Managers in sales, advertising, production, research and development, finance, customer service, inventory control, quality control, and other areas should learn what other managers see as the firm's strengths, weaknesses, opportunities, and threats. This allows the marketing manager to come to terms with multiple perspectives before actually creating the marketing plan.

When combining the SWOT analyses from individual areas, the marketing manager can identify opportunities for joint projects and cross selling of the firm's products. In a large firm, the first time a SWOT analysis takes place may be the initial point at which managers from some areas have ever formally communicated with each other. Such cross-pollination can generate a very conducive environment for creativity and innovation. Moreover, research has shown that the success of introducing a new product, especially a radically new product, is extremely dependent on the ability of different functional areas to collaborate and integrate their differing perspectives. For example,

Collaboration with other functional areas is a necessary ingredient in a well-crafted SWOT analysis.

every time BMW develops a new car, they relocate 200 to 300 engineering, design, production, marketing, and finance employees from their worldwide locations to the company's research and innovation center in Munich, Germany. For up to three years, these employees work alongside BMW's research and development team in a manner that speeds communication and car development.[2]

Examine Issues from the Customers' Perspective

In the initial stages of SWOT analysis, it is important to identify issues exhaustively. However, all issues are not equally important with respect to developing competitive advantages and strategic focus for the marketing plan. As the analysis progresses, the marketing manager should identify the most critical issues by looking at each one through the eyes of the firm's customers. To do this, the manager must constantly ask questions such as:

- What do customers (and noncustomers) believe about us as a company?
- What do customers (and noncustomers) think of our product quality, customer service, price and overall value, convenience, and promotional messages in comparison to our competitors?
- Which of our weaknesses translate into a decreased ability to serve customers (and decreased ability to convert noncustomers)?
- How do trends in the external environment affect customers (and noncustomers)?
- What is the relative importance of these issues, not as we see them, but as customers see them?

Marketing planners must also gauge the perceptions of each customer segment that the firm attempts to target. For example, older banking customers, due to their reluctance to use ATMs and online banking services, may have vastly different perceptions of a bank's convenience than younger customers. Each customer segment's perceptions of external issues, such as the economy or the environment, are also important. It matters little,

EXHIBIT 4.3 **Breaking Down Managerial Clichés into Customer-Oriented Strengths and Weaknesses**

Clichè	Potential Strengths	Potential Weaknesses
"We are an established firm."	Stable after-sales service	Old-fashioned
	Experienced	Inflexible
	Trustworthy	Weak innovation
"We are a large supplier."	Comprehensive product line	Bureaucratic
	Technical expertise	Focused only on large accounts
	Longevity	Impersonal
	Strong reputation	Weak customer service
"We have a comprehensive product line."	Wide variety and availability	Shallow assortment
	One-stop supplier	Cannot offer hard-to-find products
	Convenient	Limited in-depth product expertise
	Customized solutions	
"We are the industry standard."	Wide product adoption	Vulnerable to technological changes
	High status and image	Limited view of competition
	Good marketing leverage	Higher prices (weaker value)
	Extensive third-party support	

Source: Adapted from Nigel Piercy, *Market-Led Strategic Change* (Oxford, UK: Butterworth-Heineman, 2002).

for example, that managers think the economic outlook is positive if customers have curbed their spending because they think the economy is weak.

Examining issues from the customers' perspective also includes the firm's internal customers: its employees. The fact that management perceives the firm as offering competitive compensation and benefits is unimportant. The real issue is what the employees think. Employees are also a valuable source of information on strengths, weaknesses, opportunities, and threats that management may have never considered. Some employees, especially frontline employees, are closer to the customer and can offer a different perspective on what customers think and believe. Other key stakeholders, such as investors, the general public, and government officials, should also be considered. The key is to examine every issue from the most relevant perspective. Exhibit 4.3 illustrates how taking the customers' perspective can help managers interpret the clichés they might develop, and then break them down into meaningful customer-oriented strengths and weaknesses.

Taking the customers' perspective is a cornerstone of a well-done SWOT analysis. Managers have a natural tendency to see issues the way they think they are (e.g., "We offer a high quality product"). SWOT analysis forces managers to change their perceptions to the way customers and other important groups see things (e.g., "The product offers weak value given its price and features as compared against the strongest brand competitor."). The contrast between these two perspectives often leads to the identification of a gap between management's version of reality and customers' perceptions. As the planning process moves ahead, managers must reduce or eliminate this gap and determine whether their views of the firm are realistic.

Look for Causes, Not Characteristics

Although taking the customers' perspective is important, it often provides just enough information to get into serious trouble. That is, it provides a level of detail that is often very descriptive, but not very constructive. The problem lies in listing strengths, weaknesses, opportunities, and threats as simple descriptions or characteristics of the firm's internal and external environments without going deeper to consider the causes for these characteristics. Although the customers' perspective is quite valuable, customers do not see behind the scenes to understand the reasons for a firm's characteristics. More often than not, the causes for each issue in a SWOT analysis can be found in the resources possessed by the firm and/or its competitors.

From a resource-based viewpoint, every organization can be considered as a unique bundle of tangible and intangible resources. Major types of these resources include:[3]

- **Financial resources**—cash, access to financial markets, physical facilities, equipment, raw materials, systems and configurations
- **Intellectual resources**—expertise, discoveries, creativity, innovation
- **Legal resources**—patents, trademarks, contracts
- **Human resources**—employee expertise and skills, leadership
- **Organizational resources**—culture, customs, shared values, vision, routines, working relationships, processes and systems
- **Informational resources**—customer intelligence, competitive intelligence, marketing information systems
- **Relational resources**—strategic alliances, relations with customers, vendors, and other stakeholders, bargaining power, switching costs
- **Reputational resources**—brand names, symbols, image, reputation

The availability or lack of these resources are the causes for the firm's strengths and weaknesses in meeting customers' needs, and determine which external conditions represent opportunities and threats. For example, Walmart's strength in low-cost distribution and logistics comes from its combined resources in terms of distribution, information, and communication infrastructure; and strong relationships with vendors. Likewise, 3M's strength in product innovation is the result of combined financial, intellectual, legal, organizational, and informational resources. These resources not only give Walmart and 3M strengths or advantages in serving customers; they also create imposing threats for their competitors.

Separate Internal Issues from External Issues

For the results of a SWOT analysis to be truly beneficial, we have seen that the analyst must go beyond simple descriptions of internal and external characteristics to explore the resources that are the foundation for these characteristics. It is equally important, however, for the analyst to maintain a separation between internal issues and external issues. Internal issues are the firm's strengths and weaknesses, while external issues refer to opportunities and threats in the firm's external environments. The key test to differentiate a strength or weakness from an opportunity or threat is to ask, "Would this issue exist if the firm did not exist?" If the answer is yes, the issue should be classified as external to the firm.

At first glance, the distinction between internal and external issues seems simplistic and immaterial. However, the failure to understand the difference between internal and external issues is one of the major reasons for a poorly conducted SWOT analysis. This happens because managers tend to get ahead of themselves and list their marketing options or strategies as opportunities. For example, a manager might state that the firm has "an opportunity to move into global markets." However, such a move is a strategy or action that the firm might take to expand market share. In the SWOT framework, opportunities (and threats) exist independently of the firm and are associated with characteristics or situations present in the economic, customer, competitive, cultural, technological, political, or legal environments in which the firm resides. For example, an opportunity in this case could be "increasing customer demand for U.S. products," or that a "competitor recently pulled out of the foreign market." Once the opportunities (and threats) are known, the manager's options, strategies, or tactics should be based on what the firm intends to do about its opportunities and threats relative to its own strengths and weaknesses. The development of these strategic options occurs at a later point within the marketing plan framework.

In summary, a SWOT analysis should be directed by Socrates' advice: "Know thyself." This knowledge should be realistic, based on how customers (external and internal) and other key stakeholders see the company, and viewed in terms of the firm's resources. If managers find it difficult to make an honest and realistic assessment of these issues, they should recognize the need to bring in outside experts or consultants to oversee the process.

SWOT-Driven Strategic Planning

As we discussed in Chapter 3, the collection of marketing information via a situation analysis identifies the key factors that should be tracked by the firm and organizes them within a system that will monitor and distribute information on these factors on an ongoing basis. This process feeds into and helps define the boundaries of a SWOT analysis that will be used as a catalyst for the development of the firm's marketing plan. The role of SWOT analysis then is to help the marketing manager make the transition from a broad understanding of the marketing environment to the development of a strategic focus for the firm's marketing efforts. The potential issues that can be considered in a SWOT analysis are numerous and will vary depending on the particular firm or industry being examined. To aid your search for relevant issues, we have provided a list of potential strengths, weaknesses, opportunities, and threats in Exhibit 4.4. This list is not exhaustive, as these items illustrate only some of the potential issues that may arise in a SWOT analysis.

Strengths and Weaknesses

Relative to market needs and competitors' characteristics, the marketing manager must begin to think in terms of what the firm can do well and where it may have deficiencies. Strengths and weaknesses exist either because of resources possessed (or not possessed) by the firm, or in the nature of the relationships between the firm and its customers, its employees, or outside organizations (e.g., supply chain partners, suppliers, lending institutions, government agencies, etc.). Given that SWOT analysis must be customer focused to gain maximum benefit, strengths are meaningful only when they serve to satisfy a customer need. When this is the case, that strength becomes a capability.[4] The marketing manager can then develop marketing strategies that leverage these capabilities in the form of strategic competitive advantages. At the same time, the manager can develop strategies to overcome the firm's weaknesses, or find ways to minimize the negative effects of these weaknesses.

A great example of strengths and weaknesses in action occurs in the U.S. airline industry. As a whole, the industry was in trouble even before September 11, 2001. Big carriers—such as American, Delta, and US Airways—have strengths in terms of sheer

---

EXHIBIT 4.4   Potential Issues to Consider in a SWOT Analysis

---

Potential Internal Strengths	**Potential External Opportunities**
Abundant financial resources	Rapid market growth
Well-known brand name	Complacent rival firms
Number 1 ranking in the industry	Changing customer needs/tastes
Economies of scale	Opening of foreign markets
Proprietary technology	Mishap of a rival firm
Patented products or processes	New product or process discoveries
Lower costs (raw materials or processes)	Economic boom/downturn
Respected company/brand image	Government deregulation
Superior management talent	New technology
Better marketing skills	Demographic shifts
Superior product quality	Other firms seeking alliances
Alliances with other firms	High brand switching
Good distribution skills	Sales decline for a substitute product
Committed employees	Evolving business models in the industry

Potential Internal Weaknesses	**Potential External Threats**
Lack of strategic direction	Entry of foreign competitors
Limited financial resources	Introduction of new substitute products
Weak spending on R&D	Product life cycle in decline
Very narrow product line	Evolving business models in the industry
Limited distribution	Changing customer needs/tastes
Higher costs (raw materials or processes)	Declining consumer confidence
Out-of-date products or technology	Rival firms adopting new strategies
Internal operating problems	Increased government regulation
Internal political problems	Economic boom/downturn
Weak market image	Change in Federal Reserve policy
Poor marketing skills	New technology
Alliances with weak firms	Demographic shifts
Limited management skills	Foreign trade barriers
Undertrained employees	Poor performance of ally firm
	International political turmoil
	Weakening currency exchange rates

© Cengage Learning 2013

---

size, passenger volume, and marketing muscle. However, they suffer from a number of weaknesses related to internal efficiency, labor relations, and business models that cannot compensate for changes in customer preferences. These weaknesses are especially dramatic when compared to low-cost airlines such as Southwest, Virgin America, Allegiant Air, and JetBlue. Initially, these carriers offered low-cost service in routes ignored by the big carriers. Their strengths in terms of internal efficiency, flexible operations, and lower cost equipment gave low-cost carriers a major advantage with respect to cost economies. The differences in operating expenses per available seat mile (an industry benchmark) are eye opening: ExpressJet (7.9¢), Atlantic Southeast (9.7¢), Spirit (9.9¢), Virgin America (11.1¢), JetBlue (11.3¢), Allegiant (11.6¢), and Southwest (12.6¢) versus American (15.9¢), Delta (16.4¢), United (16.7¢), and US Airways (17.8¢). The ability of low-cost carriers to operate more efficiently and at reduced costs has changed the way customers look at air travel. Today, most customers see air travel as a commodity product, with price being the only real distinguishing feature among competing brands.[5]

Opportunities and Threats

In leveraging strengths to create capabilities and competitive advantages, the marketing manager must be mindful of trends and situations in the external environment. Stressing internal strengths while ignoring external issues can lead to an organization that, although efficient, cannot adapt when external changes either enhance or impede the firm's ability to serve the needs of its customers. Opportunities and threats exist outside the firm, independently of internal strengths, weaknesses, or marketing options. Opportunities and threats typically occur within the competitive, customer, economic, political/ legal, technological, and/or sociocultural environments. After identifying opportunities and threats, the manager can develop strategies to take advantage of opportunities and minimize or overcome the firm's threats.

Market opportunities can come from many sources. For example, when CEO Howard Schultz first envisioned the idea of Starbucks coffeehouses in 1983, he never dreamed that his idea would create an entire industry. Schultz was on a trip to Milan, Italy when he first conceived of a chain of American coffee bars. At that time, there was essentially no competition in coffee, as most consumers considered it a commodity. He knew that the demand for coffee was high, as it is only second to water in terms of consumption around the world. However, the U.S. coffee market was largely found on grocery store shelves and in restaurants. In fact, only 200 coffeehouses existed in the U.S. when Starbucks began its expansion. This clear lack of competition gave Schultz the impetus to take Starbucks from its humble Seattle, Washington beginnings to the rest of the world. Today there are over 17,000 Starbucks coffeehouses around the world—63 percent of them are in the U.S. Coffee is now a cultural phenomenon as there are thousands of coffeehouses in the U.S. today, most being mom-and-pop businesses that piggyback on Starbucks's success. Starbucks customers eagerly spend $3 for a cup of coffee, but they get more than a mere drink. Starbucks is a place to meet friends, talk business, listen to music, or just relax. Starbucks' popularity has spread to grocery store shelves were the brand is now a major threat to traditional in-store competitors. The combination of an obvious market opportunity and Schultz's idea has forever changed the worldwide coffee market.[6]

Starbucks' founder Howard Schultz seized an open market opportunity and forever changed the coffee industry.

The SWOT Matrix

As we consider how a firm can use its strengths, weaknesses, opportunities, and threats to drive the development of its marketing plan, remember that SWOT analysis is designed to synthesize a wide array of information and aid the transition to the firm's strategic focus. To address these issues properly, the marketing manager should appraise every strength, weakness, opportunity, and threat to determine their total impact on the firm's marketing efforts. To utilize SWOT analysis successfully, the marketing manager must be cognizant of four issues:[7]

1. The assessment of strengths and weaknesses must look beyond the firm's resources and product offering(s) to examine processes that are key to meeting customers' needs. This often entails offering "solutions" to customers' problems, rather than specific products.
2. The achievement of the firm's goals and objectives depends on its ability to create capabilities by matching its strengths with market opportunities. Capabilities become competitive advantages if they provide better value to customers than competing offerings.
3. Firms can often convert weaknesses into strengths or even capabilities by investing strategically in key areas (e.g., customer support, research and development, supply chain efficiency, employee training). Likewise, threats can often be converted into opportunities if the right resources are available.
4. Weaknesses that cannot be converted into strengths become the firm's limitations. Limitations that are obvious and meaningful to customers or other stakeholders must be minimized through effective strategic choices.

One useful method of conducting this assessment is to visualize the analysis via a SWOT matrix. Exhibit 4.5 provides an example of this four-cell array that can be used to visually evaluate each element of a SWOT analysis. At this point, the manager must evaluate the

---

EXHIBIT 4.5 **The SWOT Matrix**

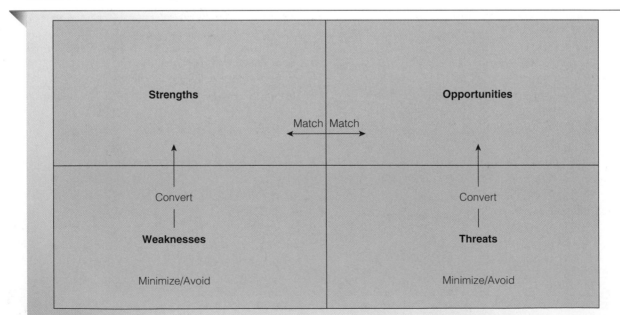

Source: Adapted from Nigel Piercy, *Market-Led Strategic Change* (Oxford, UK: Butterworth-Heineman, 2002).

issues within each cell of the matrix in terms of their magnitude and importance. As we have stated before, this evaluation should ideally be based on customers' perceptions. If customers' perceptions cannot be gathered, the manager should base the ratings on the input of employees, business partners, or their own intuition and expertise.

It is not mandatory that the SWOT matrix be assessed quantitatively, but it can be informative to do so. Exhibit 4.6 illustrates how this assessment might be conducted

---

EXHIBIT 4.6   Quantitative Assessment of the SWOT Matrix

This analysis was conducted for the VirPharm marketing plan example found on our website. The ratings in each cell have their basis in a thorough analysis of the company and the industry.

Strengths	M	I	R	Opportunities	M	I	R
BOPREX approved to treat arthritis, migraine headache, and general pain	3	3	9	FDA has approved the transition of prescription NSAIDs into OTC market	3	3	9
Patent exclusivity for three years	3	3	9	Consumers will try new products as they become available	3	3	9
New product entry	3	2	6	NSAIDs can be used as general pain reliever and fever reducer	3	3	9
Prescription-strength pain relief available OTC	3	2	6	Potential market channels not currently exploited	3	3	9
Effective migraine treatment	3	2	6	Competing prescription pain relievers have been pulled from the market	3	2	6
Talented and motivated workforce	2	2	4	Weak product differentiation among OTC competitors	3	2	6
Lower cost of raw materials	3	1	3	U.S. population is increasingly seeking convenience of online shopping	2	3	6
Wide range of products	1	2	2	Increase in aging population	2	2	4
Weaknesses	**M**	**I**	**R**	**Threats**	**M**	**I**	**R**
Limited marketing budget	-3	3	-9	Competition from both prescription pain relievers and OTC pain relievers	-3	3	-9
Market position (number 6 in market)	-3	3	-9	Extremely crowded OTC market	-3	3	-9
Weak product differentiation	-3	3	-9	Consumer loyalty with existing competitors	-3	2	-6
Current brand name (new to market)	-3	2	-6	Negative publicity regarding NSAIDs	-2	3	-6
Mid-sized company	-2	2	-4	Declining physician recommendation of NSAIDs	-1	3	-3
BOPREX associated with gastrointestinal side effects	-1	3	-3	OTC NSAIDs not indicated for long-term use	-1	2	-2
Variability in offshore suppliers	-1	2	-2	Regulations on drug advertisements could intensify	-1	2	-2

M = magnitude of the element, I = importance of the element, R = total rating of the element.
Magnitude scale ranges from 1 (low magnitude) to 3 (high magnitude).
Importance scale ranges from 1 (low importance) to 3 (high importance).

using information from the VirPharm marketing plan example found on our website. The first step is to quantify the magnitude of each element within the matrix. Magnitude refers to how strongly each element affects the firm. A simple method is to use a scale of 1 (low magnitude), 2 (medium magnitude), or 3 (high magnitude) for each strength and opportunity, and -1 (low magnitude), -2 (medium magnitude), or -3 (high magnitude) for each weakness and threat. The second step is to rate the importance of each element using a scale of 1 (weak importance), 2 (average importance), or 3 (major importance) for all elements in the matrix. The final step is to multiply the magnitude ratings by the importance ratings to create a total rating for each element. Remember that the magnitude and importance ratings should be heavily influenced by customer perceptions, not just the perceptions of the manager.

Those elements with the highest total ratings (positive or negative) should have the greatest influence in developing the marketing strategy. A sizable strength in an important area must certainly be emphasized in order to convert it into a capability or competitive advantage. On the other hand, a fairly small and insignificant opportunity should not play a central role in the planning process. The magnitude and importance of opportunities and threats will vary depending on the particular product or market. For example, a dramatic increase in new housing starts would be very important for the lumber, mortgage, or real estate industries, but inconsequential for industries involving semiconductors or telecommunications. In this example, the magnitude of the opportunity would be the same for all industries; however, the importance ratings would differ across industries.

Developing and Leveraging Competitive Advantages

After the magnitude and importance of each element in the SWOT matrix have been assessed, the manager should focus on identifying competitive advantages by matching strengths to opportunities. The key strengths most likely to be converted into capabilities will be those that have a compatibility with important and sizable opportunities. Remember that capabilities that allow a firm to serve customers' needs better than the competition give it a competitive advantage. As outlined in Exhibit 4.7, competitive advantages can arise from many internal or external sources.

When we refer to competitive advantages, we usually speak in terms of real differences between competing firms. After all, competitive advantages stem from real strengths possessed by the firm or in real weaknesses possessed by rival firms. However, competitive advantages can also be based more on perception than reality. For example, Apple's iPad dominates the market for tablet computers despite the fact that competing products from Google, Motorola, RIM (Blackberry), Samsung, Acer, and Amazon typically match, or even beat, the iPad in terms of features and performance. Customers who are unaware of better tablets (or those that simply don't care) buy the iPad because of its slick image, integration with iTunes and the App Store, and the availability of third-party accessories. Because consumers maintain the perception that the iPad is better than competing products, competing products have a difficult time breaking through.

Effectively managing customers' perceptions has been a challenge for marketers for generations. The problem lies in developing and maintaining capabilities and competitive advantages that customers can easily understand, and that solve their

---

EXHIBIT 4.7   Common Sources of Competitive Advantage

Relational Advantages

Brand-loyal customers

High customer-switching costs

Long-term relationships with supply chain partners

Strategic alliance agreements

Comarketing or cobranding agreements

Tight coordination and integration with supply chain partners

Strong bargaining power

Legal Advantages

Patents and trademarks

Strong and beneficial contracts

Tax advantages

Zoning laws

Global trade restrictions

Government subsidies

Organizational Advantages

Abundant financial resources

Modern plant and equipment

Effective competitor and customer intelligence systems

Culture, vision, and shared goals

Strong organizational goodwill

Human Resource Advantages

Superior management talent

Strong organizational culture

Access to skilled labor

Committed employees

World-class employee training

Product Advantages

Brand equity and brand name

Exclusive products

Superior quality or features

Production expertise

Guarantees and warranties

Outstanding customer service

Research and development

Superior product image

Pricing Advantages

Lower production costs

Economies of scale

Large-volume buying

Low-cost distribution

Bargaining power with vendors

Promotion Advantages

Company image

Large promotion budget

Superior sales force

Creativity

Extensive marketing expertise

Distribution Advantages

Efficient distribution system

Real-time inventory control

Extensive supply chain integration

Superior information systems

Exclusive distribution outlets

Convenient locations

Strong e-commerce capabilities

© Cengage Learning 2013

---

specific needs. Capabilities or competitive advantages that do not translate into specific benefits for customers are of little use to a firm. In recent years, many successful firms have developed capabilities and competitive advantages based on one of three basic strategies: operational excellence, product leadership, and customer intimacy:

- **Operational Excellence.** Firms employing a strategy of operational excellence focus on efficiency of operations and processes. These firms operate at lower costs than their competitors, allowing them to deliver goods and services to their customers at lower prices or a better value. Low-cost airlines, like JetBlue and Southwest Airlines, are a prime example of operational excellence in action. Southwest's no-frills service and use of nearly identical aircraft keep operating costs quite low compared to other air carriers. Other firms that employ operational excellence include Dell and Walmart.[8]

- **Product Leadership**. Firms that focus on product leadership excel at technology and product development. As a result, these firms offer customers the most advanced, highest quality goods and services in the industry. For example, Microsoft, which dominates the market for personal computer operating systems and office productivity suites, continues to upgrade and stretch the technology underlying its software, while creating complementary products that solve customers' needs. Pfizer, Intel, and 3M are other examples of companies that pursue a product leadership strategy. *Beyond the Pages 4.2* explains some of the secrets to 3M's product leadership success.

- **Customer Intimacy**. Working to know your customers and understand their needs better than the competition is the hallmark of customer intimacy. These firms attempt to develop long-term relationships with customers by seeking their input on how to make the firm's goods and services better or how to solve specific customer problems. Nordstrom, for example, organizes its store layout by fashion and lifestyle rather than by merchandise categories. The company offers high quality products with impeccable customer service. In fact, Nordstrom is consistently ranked tops in customer service among all retail chains.[9] Other firms that pursue customer intimacy include Amazon, DHL, and Ritz-Carlton.

To be successful, firms should be able to execute all three strategies. However, the most successful firms choose one area at which to excel, and then actively manage customer perceptions so that customers believe that the firm does indeed excel in that area. To implement any one of these strategies effectively, a firm must possess certain core competencies, as outlined in Exhibit 4.8. Firms that boast such competencies are more likely to create a competitive advantage than those that do not. However, before a competitive advantage can be translated into specific customer benefits, the firm's target markets must recognize that its competencies give it an advantage over the competition. Exhibit 4.8 includes a list of attributes that customers might use to describe a company that possesses each particular competitive advantage. The core competencies are internal (strength) issues, while specific attributes refer to activities that customers will notice as they interact with the firm.

Establishing a Strategic Focus

At the conclusion of the SWOT analysis, the marketing manager must turn his or her attention toward establishing the strategic focus of the firm's marketing program. By strategic focus, we mean the overall concept or model that guides the firm as it weaves various marketing elements together into a coherent strategy. A firm's strategic focus is typically tied to its competitive advantages. However, depending on the situation, the strategic focus can shift to compensate for the firm's weaknesses or to defend against its vulnerabilities. A firm's strategic focus can change over time to reflect the dynamic nature of the internal and external environments. The direction taken depends on how the firm's strengths and weaknesses match up with its external opportunities and threats.

Beyond the Pages 4.2

Successful Product Leadership at 3M[10]

Most people know that 3M is the maker of everyday items such as Post-It Notes and Scotch Tape. Some might know that 3M makes other products such as O-Cel-O sponges, Clarity braces (for teeth), and Littmann stethoscopes. What most people don't know about 3M, however, is that the company has been developing innovative products like these for over 107 years. After all that time, what is most amazing about 3M is that the company's appetite for product innovation has never waned.

3M (Minnesota Mining and Manufacturing) began as an abrasives maker in 1902. However, the company didn't become well known until the invention of masking tape in 1925. Even then, the company didn't become a household name until the invention of Post-It Notes in 1980. Today, the company sells an expansive line of Scotch tape products and has innovated Post-It into picture paper and index cards.

What is 3M's secret to successful product leadership? When Larry Wendling, former vice-president of 3M's corporate research labs was asked that question, he summed up the company's success based on a list of seven key factors:

1. **Commitment to Innovation.** Every employee, from the CEO down, is firmly committed to innovation. 3M backs up this commitment with massive spending on R&D: over $1 billion per year, or 6 percent of its total revenue.

2. **Active Maintenance of the Corporate Culture.** Probably the main factor in 3M's success, the company's culture is based on hiring good people, giving them the freedom to do their work, and tolerating mistakes. A common characteristic of highly innovative companies is that they tolerate failure and try to learn from it.

3. **Broad Base of Underlying Technology.** Having a diverse expertise across many different technologies allows 3M to apply ideas from one area of the company to another. This is one of the secrets to why 3M never seems to run out of ideas.

4. **Active Networking.** 3M actively promotes networking and internal conversations among its scientists and engineers. They host an annual Technical Forum where the roughly 10,000 members of the R&D staff talk and share ideas.

5. **Reward Employees for Outstanding Work.** 3M maintains a dual-career track so experienced scientists and engineers can move up the career ladder without moving into corporate management. The company also honors its employees with scientific achievement awards each year.

6. **Measure Results.** A key benchmark for 3M is the percentage of revenue that comes from products introduced during the past four years. This prevents the company from resting on its laurels and allows management to determine if R&D dollars are well spent.

7. **Listen to the Customer.** 3M employees spend a great deal of time learning about customer needs and expectations. They take these ideas back to the lab where innovative products are developed. For example, the idea for Post-It Photo Paper came directly from customers.

Wendling argues that innovation at 3M is not an accident. Throughout the company's history, these seven pillars of innovation have been developed, managed, and nurtured. It is no wonder that 3M regularly appears in the *BusinessWeek* rankings of the world's most innovative and most admired companies.

In addition to innovation, 3M also maintains product leadership through strategic acquisitions. The company's most recent acquisition is Avery Dennison's office and consumer products division, the undisputed market leader in the labeling business. The acquisition gave 3M control over the Avery label brand and other market leading products such as Marks-A-Lot pens and Hi-Liter markers. The addition of the Avery label line helps to round out 3M's own line of office products, including the ubiquitous Post-It Notes and Scotch Tape.

EXHIBIT 4.8 Core Competencies Necessary for Competitive Advantage Strategies

Operational Excellence—Example Firms: Walmart, Southwest Airlines, Dell

Core Competencies

- Low cost operations
- Totally dependable product supply
- Expedient customer service
- Effective demand management

Common Attributes of Operationally Excellent Firms

- Deliver compelling value through the use of low prices, standardized product offerings, and convenient buying processes
- Target a broad, heterogeneous market of price-sensitive buyers
- Invest to achieve scale economies and efficiency-driven systems that translate into lower prices for buyers
- Develop information systems geared toward capturing and distributing information on inventories, shipments, customer transactions, and costs in real time
- Maintain a system to avoid waste and highly reward efficiency improvement

Product Leadership—Example Firms: Pfizer, Intel, 3M

Core Competencies

- Basic research/rapid research interpretation
- Applied research geared toward product development
- Rapid exploitation of market opportunities
- Excellent marketing skills

Common Attributes of Product-Leading Firms

- Focus their marketing plans on the rapid introduction of high quality, technologically sophisticated products in order to create customer loyalty
- Constantly scan the environment in search of new opportunities; often making their own products obsolete through continuous innovation
- Target narrow, homogeneous market segments
- Maintain organizational cultures characterized by decentralization, adaptability, entrepreneurship, creativity, and the expectation of learning from failure
- Have an attitude of "How can we make this work?" rather than "Why can't we make this work?"

Customer Intimacy—Example Firms: Nordstrom, Amazon, Ritz-Carlton

Core Competencies

- Exceptional skills in discovering customer needs
- Problem solving proficiency
- Flexible product/solution customization
- A customer relationship management mind-set
- A wide presence of collaborative (win-win) negotiation skills

Common Attributes of Customer-Intimate Firms

- See customer loyalty as their greatest asset as they focus their efforts on developing and maintaining an intimate knowledge of customer requirements
- Consistently exceed customer expectations by offering high quality products and solutions without an apology for charging higher prices
- Decentralize most decision-making authority to the customer-contact level
- Regularly form strategic alliances with other companies to address customers' needs in a comprehensive fashion
- Assess all relationships with customers or alliance partners on a long-term, even lifetime basis

Source: From 'Discipline of Market Leaders: Choose Your Customers' in "CSC Index" by Michael Treacy and Fred Wiersema (Addison-Wesley, 1995). Reprinted with permission from Helen Rees Literary Agency, Michael Treacy, and Fred Wiersema.

Using the results of the SWOT analysis as a guide, a firm might consider four general directions for its strategic efforts:[11]

- **Aggressive (many internal strengths/many external opportunities).** Firms in this enviable position can develop marketing strategies to aggressively take on multiple opportunities. Expansion and growth, with new products and new markets, are the keys to an aggressive approach. These firms are often so dominant that they can actually reshape the industry or the competitive landscape to fit their agenda. Google offers a good example of this approach in its development of web-based applications that serve multiple needs and markets. Google Voice, Google Plus, Google Docs, Gmail, and YouTube are a few examples of Google's offerings.

- **Diversification (many internal strengths/many external threats).** Firms in this position have a great deal to offer, but external factors weaken their ability to pursue aggressive strategies. To help offset these threats, firms can use marketing strategy to diversify their portfolio of products, markets, or even business units. A good example of this strategy in action is the Altria Group, whose divisions include Philip Morris USA, U.S. Smokeless Tobacco Company, John Middleton (cigars), Chateau Ste. Michelle Wine Estates, Philip Morris Capital Corporation (leasing), and partial ownership of SABMiller (the world's second largest brewer). Although Altria owns many of the world's most recognizable brands (Marlboro, Virginia Slims, Skoal, Copenhagen, Prince Albert), the firm faces innumerable threats from low-cost competitors, taxes, and litigation.[12]

- **Turnaround (many internal weaknesses/many external opportunities).** Firms often pursue turnaround strategies because they find themselves in the situation—often temporary—of having too many internal problems to consider strategies that will take advantage of external opportunities. In these cases, firms typically have to put their own house back in order before looking beyond their current products or markets. For example, GM was once the dominant carmaker in the world. However, a weak product portfolio, high pension costs, stiff competition, and the downturn in the world economy created a perfect storm that forced GM into bankruptcy in 2009. To keep the company solvent, the U.S. government provided a $50 billion bailout and acquired a major ownership stake in GM. As a part of its turnaround strategy, GM sold off or closed four non-core brands—Saturn, Hummer, Pontiac, and Saab—and took steps to drastically reduce costs. Today, GM is once again the world's leading automaker. The U.S. government still holds 32 percent of GM, but plans to sell it in the open market.[13]

- **Defensive (many internal weaknesses/many external threats).** Firms take a defensive posture when they become overwhelmed by internal and external problems simultaneously. For example, pharmaceutical giant Merck was dealt a serious blow in 2004 when it was announced that patients taking the company's pain reliever Vioxx were at an increased risk of heart attacks. Merck withdrew Vioxx from the market, which marked the beginning of a string of potentially damaging litigation against the firm. However, Merck won 10 out of 15 major lawsuits against them, and then eventually settled all remaining suits for $4.85 billion in 2007. Next, Merck began looking for ways to defend its market position given that many of its most popular drugs—including Zocor, Fosamax, and Singulair—would lose patent protection over the next several years. Merck announced a solution in 2009 with a $41 billion merger with Schering-Plough, which gave the company a strong development pipeline of 18 new drugs in Phase III trials. One of the company's most promising new drugs is Incivek, a treatment for Hepatitis C. Roughly 170 million people worldwide have the disease and represent a roughly $3 billion market for medicines to combat it.[14]

Although these four stances are quite common, other combinations of strengths, weaknesses, opportunities, and threats are possible. For example, a firm may have few internal strengths but many external opportunities. In this situation, the firm cannot take advantage of opportunities because it does not possess the needed resources to create capabilities or competitive advantages. To resolve this problem, the firm might focus all of its efforts toward small niche markets, or it might consider establishing alliances with firms that possess the necessary resources. It is also possible that a firm will possess many internal strengths but few external opportunities. In this situation, the firm might pursue a strategy of diversification by entering new markets or acquiring other companies. This strategy is dangerous, however, unless these new pursuits are consistent with the mission of the firm. Business history is replete with stories of firms that explored new opportunities that were outside of their core mission and values. Sears's expansion into real estate, financial services, and credit cards in the 1980s should remind us all that stepping beyond core strengths is often a bad idea.

Establishing a solid strategic focus is important at this stage of the planning process because it lays the groundwork for the development of marketing goals and objectives that follow. Unfortunately, many firms struggle with finding a focus that translates into a strategy that offers customers a compelling reason for purchasing the firm's products. Firms can use any number of tools and techniques for identifying a compelling strategic focus. We believe that one of the most useful tools is the strategy canvas, which was developed by professors W. Chan Kim and Renee Mauborgne in their book *Blue Ocean Strategy*.[15]

In essence, a strategy canvas is a tool for visualizing a firm's strategy relative to other firms in a given industry. As an example, consider the strategy canvas for Southwest Airlines depicted in Exhibit 4.9.[16] The horizontal axis of a strategy canvas identifies the key factors that the industry competes on with the products that are offered to customers. In the case of the airline industry, these factors include price, meals, seating choices, and service among others. The vertical axis indicates the offering level that firms offer to buyers across these factors. The central portion of the strategy canvas is the value curve, or the graphic

EXHIBIT 4.9   **Strategy Canvas for Southwest Airlines**

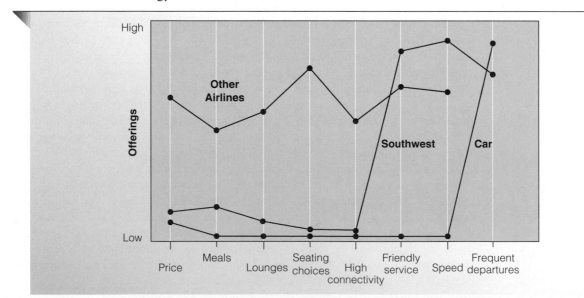

Source: From W. Chan Kim and Renee Mauborgne, "Blue Ocean Strategy" (Boston, MA: Harvard Business School Press, 2005), p. 38. Used by permission of Harvard Business School Publishing.

representation of the firm's relative performance across its industry's factors. The key to using the strategy canvas (and the key to developing a compelling strategic focus) lies in identifying a value curve that stands apart from the competition.

As illustrated in the exhibit, Southwest's strategic focus is based on downplaying the traditional competitive factors used in the airline industry (price, meals, etc.), stressing other factors (service, speed), and creating a new factor upon which to base its competitive advantage (frequent departures). In doing this, Southwest offers a compelling alternative to customers who dislike making the tradeoffs between air travel and car travel. Southwest's strategic focus, then, is offering fast, friendly, and frequent air travel at prices that appeal to customers who would have customarily opted to travel by car. As we have seen earlier in this chapter, Southwest is able to support this focus through its competitive advantages based on operational excellence. It should be no surprise that Southwest has been one of the most successful and profitable carriers in the industry for quite some time.

To use the strategy canvas successfully, the marketing manager must identify a value curve with two major characteristics.[17] First, the value curve should clearly depict the firm's strategic focus. As shown in Exhibit 4.9, Southwest Airlines' focus on service, speed, and frequent departures is clear. All other competitive factors are downplayed in Southwest's strategy. Second, the value curve should be distinctively different from competitors. Again, this is the case for Southwest as its combination of competitive factors clearly separates the firm from the competition. More information on the blue ocean approach to developing a strategic focus can be found in *Beyond the Pages 4.3*.

The combination of the SWOT matrix and the strategy canvas offers a useful and powerful means of visualizing the firm's competitive advantage and strategic focus. Clearly articulating the firm's focus is crucial as the marketing manager moves ahead in developing the marketing plan. In the next phase of the planning process, the manager must identify the firm's marketing goals and objectives in order to connect the strategic focus to the outcomes that are desired and expected. These goals and objectives will also be crucial at the latter stages of planning as the manager identifies standards that will be used to assess the performance of the marketing strategy. In the next section, we look at the development of marketing goals and objectives in more detail.

Developing Marketing Goals and Objectives

After identifying a strategic focus, the marketing manager may have some ideas about potential marketing activities that can be used to leverage the firm's competitive advantages relative to the opportunities available in the market. At this stage, however, there are likely to be many different goals and objectives that coincide with the anticipated strategic direction. Because most firms have limited resources, it is typically difficult to accomplish everything in a single planning cycle. At this point, the manager must prioritize the firm's strategic intentions and develop specific goals and objectives for the marketing plan.

We reiterate that marketing goals and objectives must be consistent with the overall mission and vision of the firm. Once the firm has a mission statement that clearly delineates what it is, what it stands for, and what it does for others, the marketing manager can then begin to express what he or she hopes to achieve in the firm's marketing program. These statements of desired accomplishments are goals and objectives. Some use the terms "goals" and "objectives" interchangeably. However, failure to understand the key differences between them can severely limit the effectiveness of the marketing plan. Goals are general desired accomplishments, while objectives provide specific, quantitative benchmarks that can be used to gauge progress toward the achievement of the marketing goals.

A Closer Look at Blue Ocean Strategy[18]

In addition to the strategy canvas discussed in the chapter, Professors Chan and Mauborgne developed a companion tool called the four actions framework. Where the strategy canvas graphically depicts the firm's strategic focus relative to competitors and the factors that define competition within an industry, the four actions framework is a tool for discovering how to shift the strategy canvas and reorient the firm's strategic focus. As shown in the diagram, the four actions framework is designed to challenge traditional assumptions about strategy by asking four questions about the firm's way of doing business.

As an example of how the four actions framework can be used, Chan and Mauborgne drew on the experiences of Casella Wine's successful launch of [yellow tail]. First, Casella *eliminated* traditional competitive factors such as impenetrable wine terminology, aging qualities, and heavy marketing expenditures. Casella reasoned that these factors made wine inaccessible to the mass of buyers who were unfamiliar with wine culture. Second, Casella *reduced* the importance of other factors such as wine complexity, range of wine selections, and prestige. At launch, for example, Casella introduced only two wines: Chardonnay and Shiraz. They also used a nontraditional label featuring an orange and yellow kangaroo on a black background to reduce the prestige or "snob appeal" common in most wines. Third, Casella *raised* the importance of

competitive factors such as store involvement. Casella involved store employees by giving them Australian clothing to wear at work. This created a laid back approach to wine that made the employees eager to recommend [yellow tail] to their customers. Finally, Casella *created* easy to drink, easy to buy, and fun as new competitive factors. [yellow tail] has a soft fruity taste that makes it more approachable. Casella also put red and white wines in the same-shaped bottle—an industry first. This simple change greatly reduces manufacturing costs and makes point-of-sale displays simpler and more eye catching.

The blue ocean approach is also used successfully by Southwest Airlines, Cirque du Soleil, and Curves (a chain of women-only fitness centers), among others. Chan and Mauborgne argue that successfully reorienting a firm's strategic focus requires the firm to give up long-held assumptions about how business should be conducted. They caution firms to avoid benchmarking and extensive customer research because these approaches tend to create a typical "more for less" mentality that guides the strategic focus of most firms. Instead, the blue ocean approach requires firms to fundamentally alter their strategic logic. Therein lies the challenge of blue ocean thinking: it is very, very difficult for most businesses to change. Consequently, true blue ocean approaches tend to be a rare occurrence.

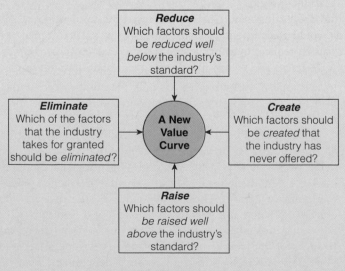

The Four Actions Framework

Developing Marketing Goals

As statements of broad, desired accomplishments, goals are expressed in general terms and do not contain specific information about where the organization presently stands or where it hopes to be in the future. Home Depot, for example, has a goal of having lower prices than the competition. This goal is not specific, however, because it does not specify a benchmark that defines what a lower price is. To achieve this goal, Home Depot offers a price guarantee that matches then beats competitors' prices by 10 percent.[19] Goals like these are important because they indicate the direction in which the firm attempts to move, as well as the set of priorities it will use in evaluating alternatives and making decisions.

It is also important that all functional areas of the organization be considered in the goal-setting process. In developing goals for the marketing plan, it is important to keep in mind that marketing goals should be attainable, consistent, comprehensive, and involve some degree of intangibility. Failure to consider these issues will result in goals that are less effective, and perhaps even dysfunctional. Let's look more closely at these characteristics.

Attainability Setting realistic goals is important because the key parties involved in reaching them must see each goal as reasonable. Determining whether a goal is realistic requires an assessment of both the internal and external environments. For example, it would not be unrealistic for a firm in second place in market share, trailing the leading brand by just 2 percent, to set a goal of becoming the industry leader. Other things being equal, such a goal could help motivate employees toward becoming "number one." In contrast, a firm in sixth place, trailing the fifth place firm by 5 percent and the leader by 30 percent, could set the same goal—but it would not be realistic. Unrealistic goals can be demotivational because they show employees that management is out of touch. Since one of the primary benefits of having goals is to motivate employees toward better performance, setting unrealistic goals can cause major problems.

Consistency In addition to being realistic, management must work to set goals that are consistent with one another. Enhancing market share and working to have the highest profit margins in the industry are both reasonable goals by themselves, but together they are inconsistent. Goals to increase both sales and market share would be consistent, as would goals to enhance customer service and customer satisfaction. However, setting goals to reduce inventory levels and increase customer service are usually incompatible. Goals across and within functional areas should also mesh together. This is a major concern in large organizations, and it highlights the need for a great deal of information sharing during the goal-formulation process.

Comprehensiveness The goal-setting process should also be comprehensive. This means that each functional area should be able to develop its own goals that relate to the organization's goals. For example, if goals are set only in terms of advancing the technology associated with a firm's products, members of the marketing department may wonder what role they will play in this accomplishment. The goal should be stated so that both marketing and research and development can work together to help advance the organizational goal of offering the most technologically advanced products. Marketing will need to work on the demand side of this effort (measuring customer needs and staying attuned to trends in the external environment), while research and development will focus on the supply side (conducting basic and applied research, as well as staying abreast of all major technological innovations). Goals should help clarify the roles of all parties in the organization. Functional areas that do not match any of the organization's goals should question their need for future resources and their ability to acquire them.

Intangibility   Finally, goals should involve some degree of intangibility. Some planners have been known to confuse strategies, and even tactics, with goals. A goal is not some action the firm can take; rather, it is an outcome the organization hopes to accomplish. Actions such as hiring 100 new salespeople or doubling the advertising budget are not goals, as any firm with adequate resources can accomplish both tasks. However, having "the best-trained sales force in the industry" or "the most creative and effective advertising campaign in the industry" are suitable goals. Note the intangibility associated with the use of terms such as *best trained*, *most creative*, and *most effective*. These terms are motivational because they promote comparisons with rival firms. They also continually push for excellence, as their open-ended nature always leaves room for improvement.

Developing Marketing Objectives

Objectives provide specific and quantitative benchmarks that can be used to gauge progress toward the achievement of the marketing goals. In some cases, a particular goal may require several objectives for its progress to be adequately monitored, usually across multiple business functions. For example, a goal of "creating a high-quality image for the firm" cannot be accomplished by better inventory control if accounts receivable makes mistakes and customer complaints about the firm's salespeople are on the rise. Similarly, the marketing department alone could not have accomplished Home Depot's phenomenal growth from two Atlanta-based stores in 1979 to over 2,200 worldwide stores today.[20] Such an endeavor requires a carefully coordinated effort across many departments.

Goals without objectives are essentially meaningless because progress is impossible to measure. A typical marketing objective might be: "The sales division will decrease unfilled customer orders from 3 percent to 2 percent between January and June of this fiscal year." Note that this objective contains a high degree of specificity. It is this specificity that sets goals and objectives apart. Objectives involve measurable, quantitative outcomes, with specifically assigned responsibility for their accomplishment, and a definite time period for their attainment. Let's look at the specific characteristics of marketing objectives.

Attainability   As with goals, marketing objectives should be realistic given the internal and external environments identified during the situation and SWOT analyses. A good objective is one that is attainable with a reasonable amount of effort. Easily attainable objectives will not motivate employees to achieve higher levels of performance. Likewise, good objectives do not come from false assumptions that everything will go as planned or that every employee will give 110 percent effort. In some cases, competitors will establish objectives that include taking customers and sales away from the firm. Setting objectives that assume inanimate or inept competitors, when history has proven otherwise, creates objectives that quickly lose their value as employees recognize them as being unreasonable.

Continuity   The need for realism brings up a second consideration, that of continuity. Marketing objectives can be either continuous or discontinuous. A firm uses continuous objectives when its current objectives are similar to objectives set in the previous planning period. For example, an objective "to increase market share from 20 to 22 percent in the next fiscal year" could be carried forward in a similar fashion to the next period: "to increase market share from 22 to 24 percent in the next fiscal year." This would be a continuous objective because the factor in question and the magnitude of change are similar, or even identical, from period to period.

An important caveat about continuous objectives: Objectives that are identical, or only slightly modified, from period to period often do not need new strategies, increased effort, or better implementation to be achieved. Marketing objectives should lead employees to perform at higher levels than would otherwise have been the case. Employees naturally tend to be objective oriented. Once they meet the objective, the level of creativity and effort tends to fall off. There are certainly circumstances where continuous objectives are appropriate, but they should not be set simply as a matter of habit.

Discontinuous objectives significantly elevate the level of performance on a given outcome factor, or bring new factors into the set of objectives. If sales growth has been averaging 10 percent, and the SWOT analysis suggests that this is an easily obtainable level, an example of a discontinuous objective might be "to increase sales 18 percent during the next fiscal year." This would require new strategies to sell additional products to existing customers, to expand the customer base, or at the very least to develop new tactics and/or enhance the implementation of existing strategies. Discontinuous objectives require more analysis and linkage to strategic planning than continuous objectives.

Developing discontinuous objectives is one of the major benefits a company can gain from applying for the Malcolm Baldrige National Quality Award. Exhibit 4.10 identifies the performance criteria for the Baldrige Award. To demonstrate proficiency in these areas, a firm must first establish benchmarks, which typically are the quantitative performance levels of the leaders in an industry. The firm then develops objectives that center on improving performance in each area. Many companies feel that simply applying for the Baldrige Award has positive effects on performance, if for no other reason than the process forces the company to set challenging discontinuous objectives. This is also true for organizations that use the Baldrige guidelines as a planning aid.

Time Frame   Another key consideration in setting objectives is the time frame for their achievement. Although companies often establish marketing plans on an annual basis, marketing objectives may differ from this period in their time frame. Sales volume, market share, customer service, and gross margin objectives may be set for terms less than, equal to, or greater than one year. The time frame should be appropriate and allow for accomplishment with reasonable levels of effort. To set a target of doubling sales for a well-established company within six months would likely be unreasonable. On the other hand, objectives having an excessively long time frame may be attained without any increased effort or creativity. The combination of managerial expertise and experience, along with the information acquired during the situation and SWOT analyses, should lead to the establishment of an appropriate time frame.

For objectives with longer time frames, it is important to remind employees of the objective on a regular basis and to provide feedback on progress toward its achievement. For example, employees at FedEx's terminal in Memphis, Tennessee can see a real-time accuracy gauge that displays the company's current performance in terms of getting packages to their rightful destinations. FedEx also uses a nightly countdown clock to remind employees of the speed needed to turnaround packages and load them on outbound cargo planes. Whether a weekly announcement, a monthly newsletter, or a

EXHIBIT 4.10   Malcolm Baldrige Award: Criteria for Performance Excellence

Categories and Items		Point Values
1	**Leadership**	120
	1.1 Senior Leadership	70
	1.2 Governance and Societal Responsibilities	50
2	**Strategic Planning**	85
	2.1 Strategy Development	40
	2.2 Strategy Implementation	45
3	**Customer Focus**	85
	3.1 Voice of the Customer	40
	3.2 Customer Engagement	45
4	**Measurement, Analysis, and Knowledge Management**	90
	4.1 Measurement, Analysis, and Improvement of Organizational Performance	45
	4.2 Management of Information, Knowledge, and Information Technology	45
5	**Workforce Focus**	85
	5.1 Workforce Environment	40
	5.2 Workforce Engagement	45
6	**Operations Focus**	85
	6.1 Work Systems	45
	6.2 Work Processes	40
7	**Results**	450
	7.1 Product and Process Outcomes	120
	7.2 Customer-Focused Outcomes	90
	7.3 Workforce-Focused Outcomes	80
	7.4 Leadership and Governance Outcomes	80
	7.5 Financial and Market Outcomes	80
	Total Points	**1,000**

Source: "2011-2012 Criteria for Performance Excellence," *Baldrige Performance Excellence Program* (Gaithersburg, MD: National Institute of Standards and Technology, U.S. Department of Commerce, 2011), 3.

real-time gauge on the wall that charts progress toward the objective, feedback is a critical part of the objective-setting process, particularly for longer-term objectives.

Assignment of Responsibility   One final aspect of objectives that sets them apart from goals is that the marketing manager must identify the person, team, or unit responsible for achieving each objective. By explicitly assigning responsibility, the firm can limit the problems of stealing credit and avoiding responsibility. A bank might give the marketing department the responsibility of achieving an objective of "having 40 percent of its customers list the bank as their primary financial institution within one year." If by the end of the year, 42 percent of all customers list the bank as their primary financial institution, the marketing department gets credit for this outcome. If the figure is only 38 percent, the marketing department must provide an explanation.

Moving Beyond Goals and Objectives

Marketing goals and objectives identify the desired ends, both general and specific, that the organization hopes to achieve during the planning period. However, companies do not fulfill properly set goals and objectives automatically or through wishing and hoping. They set into motion a chain of decisions and serve as a catalyst for the subsequent stages in the planning process. Organizational goals and objectives must lead to the establishment of consistent goals and objectives for each functional area of the firm. Having recognized the desired ends, each area, including marketing, must next determine the means that will lead to these targeted results.

As we move forward, we focus our attention on the means issue as we address marketing strategy development. Although a firm might consider the steps of the market planning process sequentially, in reality the firm must move back and forth between steps. If marketing strategies that have the potential to achieve the marketing goals and objectives cannot be developed, the goals and objectives may not be reasonable and need to be reevaluated before the development of the marketing strategy. Given that the marketing plan must be a working document, the cycling among planning steps never truly ends.

Lessons from Chapter 4

SWOT analysis:

- is considered to be one of the most useful tools in analyzing marketing data and information.
- links a company's ongoing situation analysis to the development of the marketing plan.
- structures the information from the situation analysis into four categories: strengths, weaknesses, opportunities, and threats.
- uses the structured information to uncover competitive advantages and guide the selection of the strategic focus for the firm's marketing strategy.

To make SWOT analysis as productive as possible, the marketing manager should:

- stay focused by using a series of SWOT analyses, each focusing on a specific product/market combination.
- search extensively for competitors, whether they are a present competitor or one in the future.
- collaborate with other functional areas by sharing information and perspectives.
- examine issues from the customers' perspective by asking questions such as "What do customers (and noncustomers) believe about us as a company?" and "Which of our weaknesses translate into a decreased ability to serve customers (and a decreased ability to convert noncustomers)?" This includes examining the issues from the perspective of the firm's internal customers, its employees.
- look for causes, not characteristics by considering the firm's resources that are the true causes for the firm's strengths, weaknesses, opportunities, and threats.
- separate internal issues from external issues using this key test to differentiate: "Would this issue exist if the firm did

not exist?" If the answer is yes, the issue should be classified as external to the firm.

Strengths and weaknesses:

- exist because of resources possessed (or not possessed) by the firm, or they exist due to the nature of key relationships between the firm and its customers, its employees, or outside organizations.
- must be leveraged into capabilities (in the case of strengths) or overcome (in the case of weaknesses).
- are meaningful only when they assist or hinder the firm in satisfying customer needs.

Opportunities and threats:

- are not potential marketing actions. Rather, they involve issues or situations that occur in the firm's external environments.
- should not be ignored as the firm gets caught up in developing strengths and capabilities for fear of creating an efficient, but ineffective, organization.
- may stem from changes in the competitive, customer, economic, political/legal, technological, and/or socio-cultural environments.

The SWOT matrix:

- allows the marketing manager to visualize the analysis.
- should serve as a catalyst to facilitate and guide the creation of marketing strategies that will produce desired results.
- allows the manager to see how strengths and opportunities might be connected to create capabilities that are key to meeting customer needs.
- involves assessing the magnitude and importance of each strength, weakness, opportunity, and threat.

Competitive advantage:

- stems from the firm's capabilities in relation to those held by the competition.
- can be based on both internal and external factors.
- is based on both reality and customer perceptions.
- is often based on the basic strategies of operational excellence, product leadership, and/or customer intimacy.

Establishing a strategic focus:

- is based on developing an overall concept or model that guides the firm as it weaves various marketing elements together into a coherent strategy.
- is typically tied to the firm's competitive advantages.
- involves using the results of the SWOT analysis as the firm considers four major directions for its strategic efforts: aggressiveness, diversification, turnaround, or defensiveness.
- can help ensure that the firm does not step beyond its core strengths to consider opportunities that are outside its capabilities.
- can be visualized through the use of a strategy canvas where the goal is to develop a value curve that is distinct from the competition.
- is often done by downplaying traditional industry competitive factors in favor of new approaches.

- is an important stage of the planning process because it lays the groundwork for the development of marketing goals and objectives and connects the outcomes of the SWOT analysis to the remainder of the marketing plan.

Marketing goals:

- are broad, desired accomplishments that are stated in general terms.
- indicate the direction the firm attempts to move in, as well as the set of priorities it will use in evaluating alternatives and making decisions.
- should be attainable, realistic, internally consistent, and comprehensive and help to clarify the roles of all parties in the organization.
- should involve some degree of intangibility.

Marketing objectives:

- provide specific and quantitative benchmarks that can be used to gauge progress toward the achievement of the marketing goals.
- should be attainable with a reasonable degree of effort.
- may be either continuous or discontinuous, depending on the degree to which they depart from present objectives.
- should specify the time frame for their completion.
- should be assigned to specific areas, departments, or individuals who have the responsibility to accomplish them.

Questions for Discussion

1. Strengths, weaknesses, opportunities, and threats: Which is the most important? Why? How might your response change if you were the CEO of a corporation? What if you were a customer of the firm? An employee? A supplier?
2. Support or contradict this statement: "Given the realities of today's economy and the rapid changes occurring in business technology, all competitive advantages are short-lived. There is no such thing as a *sustainable* competitive advantage that lasts over the long term." Defend your position.
3. Is it possible for an organization to be successful despite having a value curve that is not distinct from the competition? In other words, can an organization be successful by selling a me-too product (a product that offers no compelling differences when compared to the competition)? Explain.

Exercises

1. Perform a SWOT analysis using yourself as the product. Be candid about your resources and the strengths and weaknesses you possess. Based on the opportunities and threats you see in the environment, where do you stand in terms of your ability to attend graduate school, get a job, begin a career, or change careers?
2. Choose two companies from the same industry: one that is quite successful and one that is struggling. For each company, list every strength and weakness you believe it possesses (both the company and its products). Compare your answers with those of your colleagues. What could these companies learn from your analysis?
3. Using the same companies from question #2, draw a strategy canvas that depicts the value curve of both firms, as well as the "average" firm in the industry (i.e., draw three value curves). What does the successful firm offer that the struggling firm does not offer? What might a firm do to break away from the industry's traditional competitive factors?

End Notes

1. These facts are from Mae Anderson, "From Idea to Store Shelf: A New Product is Born," *Associated Press*, March 4, 2012; and "The 50 Most Innovative Companies 2010," *BusinessWeek Online* (http://www.businessweek.com/interactive_reports/innovative_companies_2010.html?chan=magazine+channel_special+report), accessed March 4, 2012.

2. These facts are from Gail Edmondson, "BMW's Dream Factory," *BusinessWeek Online*, October 16, 2006 (http://www.businessweek.com/magazine/content/06_42/b4005072.htm).

3. This list and most of this section are based on E. K. Valentin, "SWOT Analysis from a Resource-Based View," *Journal of Marketing Theory and Practice* 9 (Spring 2001), 54–69.

4. Shelby D. Hunt, *A General Theory of Competition* (Thousand Oaks, CA: Sage Publications, 2000), 67–68.

5. These facts are from the Bureau of Transportation Statistics, Airline Domestic Unit Costs (Cents per Mile), Tables 10, 11, and 12, 2nd Quarter 2011 (http://www.bts.gov/press_releases/2011/bts055_11/html/bts055_11.html).

6. These facts are from Starbucks Company 2011 Annual Report (phx.corporate-ir.net/External.File?item=UGFyZW50SUQ9MTI0MzYyfENoaWxkSUQ9LTF8VHlwZT0z&t=1); and Starbuck Company Timeline (http://assets.starbucks.com/assets/aboutustimelinefinal72811.pdf), accessed March 6, 2012.

7. George Stalk, Philip Evans, and Lawrence E. Shulman, "Competing on Capabilities: The New Rules of Corporate Strategy," *Harvard Business Review*, 70 (March–April 1992), 57–69.

8. Michael Treacy and Fred Wiersema, *The Discipline of Market Leaders* (Reading, MA: Addison-Wesley, 1995).

9. These facts are from Department Store Rankings, American Customer Satisfaction Index (http://theacsi.org/index.php?option=com_content&view=article&id=147&catid=&Itemid=212&i=Department+%26+Discount+Stores), accessed March 6, 2012.

10. These facts are from Michael Arndt, "3M's Seven Pillars of Innovation," *BusinessWeek Online*, May 10, 2006 (http://www.businessweek.com/innovate/content/may2006/id20060510_682823.htm); Thomas Black, "3M Rises Highest Since August on $550 Million Acquisition," *BusinessWeek Online*, January 3, 2012 (http://www.businessweek.com/news/2012-01-03/3m-rises-highest-since-august-on-550-million-acquisition.html); Charlotte Li, "3M: Years of Commitment to Green Business," *BusinessWeek Online*, May 14, 2009 (http://www.businessweek.com/magazine/content/09_21/b4132043810940.htm); and "Who We Are," 3M Company website (http://solutions.3m.com/wps/portal/3M/en_US/3M-Company/Information/AboutUs/WhoWeAre), accessed March 6, 2012.

11. This material is based on Cornelis A. De Kluyver, *Strategic Thinking: An Executive Perspective* (Upper Saddle River, NJ: Prentice Hall, 2000), 53–56; and Philip Kotler, *A Framework for Marketing Management*, 2nd ed. (Upper Saddle River, NJ: Prentice Hall, 2003), 67.

12. These facts are from Altria Group's website (http://www.altria.com/en/cms/About_Altria/At_A_Glance/default.aspx?src=top_nav); and Bob Van Voris, "Altria, Reynolds American Begin Trial of 600 Smoking Claims," *BusinessWeek Online*, October 26, 2011 (http://www.businessweek.com/news/2011-10-26/altria-reynolds-american-begin-trial-of-600-smoking-claims.html).

13. These facts are from David Goldman, "GM to Sell Saturn to Penske," *BusinessWeek Online*, June 5, 2009 (http://money.cnn.com/2009/06/05/news/companies/saturn_penske/index.htm); and Tim Higgins, "GM Earns Record $9.19 Billion Net Income; Opel Posts Loss," *BusinessWeek Online*, February 17, 2012 (http://www.businessweek.com/news/2012-02-17/gm-earns-record-9-19-billion-net-income-opel-posts-loss.html).

14. These facts are from Alyssa Abkowitz, "Big Pharma's New Landscape," *CNNMoney*, March 12, 2009 (http://money.cnn.com/2009/03/11/news/companies/pharma.fortune/index.htm); Robert Langreth, "Merck Hepatitis C Drug May 'Anchor' Future Worldwide Regimen," *BusinessWeek Online*, January 18, 2012 (http://www.businessweek.com/news/2012-01-18/merck-hepatitis-c-drug-may-anchor-future-worldwide-regimen.html); and Arlene Weintraub, "What Merck Gains by Settling," *BusinessWeek Online*, November 9, 2007 (http://www.businessweek.com/technology/content/nov2007/tc2007119_133486.htm).

15. The material in this section is adapted from W. Chan Kim and Renee Mauborgne, *Blue Ocean Strategy* (Boston, MA: Harvard Business School Press, 2005).

16. The strategy canvas for Southwest Airlines is from Kim and Mauborgne, *Blue Ocean Strategy*, page 38.

17. Ibid, page 39.

18. This information is from W. Chan Kim and Renee Mauborgne, *Blue Ocean Strategy* (Boston, MA: Harvard Business School Press, 2005), 29–37.

19. Home Depot website (http://www.homedepot.com/webapp/catalog/servlet/ContentView?pn=SF_MS_In-Store_Low_Price_Guarantee).

20. Home Depot Corporate Financial Overview (http://corporate.homedepot.com/OurCompany/Documents/Corp_Financial_Overview.pdf).

CHAPTER **5**

Customers, Segmentation, and Target Marketing

Introduction

In this chapter, we begin our discussion of marketing strategy by examining customers, segments, and target markets. In Chapter 1, we referred to a market as a collection of buyers and sellers. Now, we focus our attention on the buyers who collectively make up the major portion of most markets. From this perspective, we concern ourselves with markets as individuals, institutions, or groups of individuals or institutions that have similar needs that can be met by a particular product offering. As we shall see, firms can attempt to reach all buyers in a market, smaller groups or segments of the market, or even specific buyers on an individual level. Whether the firm aims for the entire market or smaller market segments, the goal of marketing strategy is to identify specific customer needs, then design a marketing program that can satisfy those needs. To do this effectively, the firm must have a comprehensive understanding of its current and potential customers, including their motivations, behaviors, needs, and wants.

The ability to determine in-depth information about customers is a fairly recent phenomenon in marketing. Fifty years ago, for example, technology and marketing know-how were less sophisticated. Marketers of the day were unable to fully understand customers' needs and wants, much less make fine distinctions among smaller segments of the total market. Marketers tended to offer products that came in only one variety, flavor, or style. Today, market segmentation is critical to the success of most firms. Segmentation allows marketers to more precisely define and understand customer needs, and gives them the ability to tailor products to better suit those needs. As discussed in *Beyond the Pages 5.1*, the level of detailed information available about customers today has changed the way firms do business. However, the use of such information raises concerns about consumer privacy. Still, without segmentation we would not enjoy the incredible variety of products available today. Consider the number of choices we have in categories such as soft drinks, cereals, packaged goods, automobiles, and clothing. In many respects, segmentation has improved our standard of living. Customers now expect firms to delve into their needs and wants, and to tailor products accordingly. This fact makes market segmentation a vital part of marketing

Beyond the Pages 5.1

Data Mining Allows Companies to Know Our Secrets[1]

Consider a world where what you eat, read, wear, listen to, watch, buy, and do can be reduced to a mathematical formula. Every move you make is tracked with such a level of specificity that your entire life can be captured in a computer model. Sound far-fetched? It's not. Today, the combination of computer science, mathematics, and business is changing our view of consumers and their behavior. The ability to track consumer behavior has never been more advanced than it is today. The new insights gained from the mathematical modeling of consumer behavior is creating new avenues for business, allowing marketers to develop one-to-one relationships with consumers, and causing a fair amount of anxiety. It is also causing a sharp increase in the hiring of math graduates from our nation's universities.

None of this is really new. Through advanced math, computer modeling, and data mining, businesses have been able to track consumer attitudes and behaviors for some time. The difference today is the unprecedented access to data made available via the Internet and other technologies. Over the past ten years, a sizable portion of the consuming public has moved its work, play, conversation, and shopping online. These integrated networks collect vast amounts of data and store our lives in databases that can be connected in ways that allow us to capture a more complete picture of consumer behavior. For example, researchers at companies like Facebook, Yahoo!, Google, and Amazon are developing mathematical models of customers. These firms are also working with other companies and government agencies to develop models that can predict voting behavior, how patients respond to disease intervention, or which employee is best suited for a job assignment. For example, Target's data mining expertise raised a few eyebrows when the *New York Times* uncovered that the retailer was able to tell when a customer was pregnant or about to deliver. Target's statisticians are able to tie millions of purchases together to

reveal patterns in their data. One of their insights: When women become pregnant, they buy a lot of supplements such as calcium, magnesium, and zinc. When their delivery date is close, pregnant women tend to buy a lot of scent-free products, large bags of cotton balls, hand sanitizer, and washcloths. Target uses this information to target ads and coupons to the right consumers. Data mining results like these are one of the reasons for Target's incredible growth from $44 billion in revenue in 2002 to roughly $70 billion in 2011.

Retailers are not the only companies that use data mining. The advertising and media industries are perhaps the most affected by this shift. As mass audience advertising has declined, marketers have been looking for ways to target customers more directly. Google is a pioneer in this effort because the company has amassed an unfathomable about of data on what customers do online. Other companies now provide data mining solutions. In research conducted with SPSS, for example, Italian carmaker Fiat was able to improve customer relations and increase customer retention by 6 to 7 percent. Microsoft uses its own analytical techniques to study the productivity of its workforce. Furthermore, Harrah's Entertainment (a major player in the casino industry) has increased their annual growth rate by using computer models to predict which customers will respond to the company's targeted advertising and promotional offers.

Of course, all of this sophistication comes at a price. The ability of companies to track customers and model their behavior raises a number of privacy concerns. Most companies take great pains to protect individual consumer identities and their private information. However, the continuing erosion of consumer privacy is likely to continue. A key question for marketers is at what point will consumers say enough is enough? How far can firms push the boundaries of data collection and analysis before consumers mount a backlash?

strategy. Until a firm has chosen and analyzed a target market, it cannot make effective decisions regarding other elements of the marketing strategy.

In this chapter, we examine issues associated with buyer behavior in both consumer and business markets. We also discuss traditional and individualized approaches to market segmentation, the criteria for successful market segmentation, and specific target marketing strategies. The potential combinations of target markets and marketing programs are essentially limitless. Choosing the right target market from among many possible alternatives is one of the key tests in developing a good marketing strategy.

Buyer Behavior in Consumer Markets

Trying to understand the buyer behavior of consumers is a very trying and challenging task. The behavior of consumers is often irrational and unpredictable. Consumers often say one thing but do another. Still, the effort spent trying to understand consumers is valuable because it can provide needed insight on how to design products and marketing programs that better meet consumer needs and wants. One of the most recent trends in learning about customers is the rising use of ethnography, a qualitative research technique designed to understand cultural phenomena such as communication, shared meanings, and personal interests. Computer maker Lenovo, for example, has used ethnographic research to learn more about how families in India use consumer electronics. One interesting finding is that the family social center in Indian homes is the parents' bedroom. The kitchen serves the same social function in American homes. Lenovo uses this type of information to develop consumer electronics that better fit differing family lifestyles in India and the U.S. With the continuing growth of the Internet, marketers have been scouring social sites such as Facebook, Twitter, and MySpace to gain cultural insights about consumers. One of the most useful of these sites is Pinterest, where people can "pin" anything that interests them. Pinterest's phenomenal growth (daily site visits grew 145 percent during the first half of 2012) and its open nature make it a treasure trove of information about American culture.[2]

In this section, we look key issues with respect to buyer behavior in consumer markets. Here, we examine the consumer buying process and the factors that alter the ways consumers buy goods and services. As we will see, successful marketing strategy depends on a clear understanding of customers with respect to who they are, what they need, what they prefer, and why they buy. Although this understanding clearly has relevance for designing the product offering, it also impacts the pricing, distribution, and promotion decisions in the marketing program.

The Consumer Buying Process

The consumer buying process shown in Exhibit 5.1 depicts five stages of activities that consumers may go through in buying goods and services. The process begins with the recognition of a need, and then passes through the stages of information search, evaluation of alternatives, purchase decision, and postpurchase evaluation. A marketer's interest in the buying process can go well beyond these stages to include actual consumption behaviors, product uses, and product disposal after consumption. As we consider each stage of the buying process, it is important to keep a few key issues in mind.

First, the buying process depicts the possible range of activities that may occur in making purchase decisions. Consumers, however, do not always follow these stages in sequence and may even skip stages en route to making a purchase. For example, impulse purchases, such as buying a pack of chewing gum or a newspaper, do not involve lengthy search or evaluation activities. On the other hand, complex purchases like buying a home are often quite lengthy as they incorporate every stage of the buying process. Likewise, consumers who are loyal to a product or brand will skip some stages and are most likely to simply purchase the same product they bought last time. Consequently, marketers

---

EXHIBIT 5.1 **The Consumer Buying Process**

Stages	Key Issues
Need Recognition	• Consumer needs and wants are not the same.
	• An understanding of consumer wants is essential for market segmentation and the development of the marketing program.
	• Marketers must create the appropriate stimuli to foster need recognition.
Information Search	• Consumers trust internal and personal sources of information more than external sources.
	• The amount of time, effort, and expense dedicated to the search for information depends on (1) the degree of risk involved in the purchase, (2) the amount of experience the consumer has with the product category, and (3) the actual cost of the search in terms of time and money.
	• Consumers narrow their potential choices to an evoked set of suitable alternatives that may meet their needs.
Evaluation of Alternatives	• Consumers translate their needs into wants for specific products or brands.
	• Consumers evaluate products as bundles of attributes that have varying abilities to satisfy their needs.
	• Marketers must ensure that their product is in the evoked set of potential alternatives.
	• Marketers must take steps to understand consumers' choice criteria and the importance they place on specific product attributes.
Purchase Decision	• A consumer's purchase intention and the actual act of buying are distinct concepts. Several factors may prevent the actual purchase from taking place.
	• Marketers must ensure that their product is available and offer solutions that increase possession utility.
Postpurchase Evaluation	• Postpurchase evaluation is the connection between the buying process and the development of long-term customer relationships.
	• Marketers must closely follow consumers' responses (delight, satisfaction, dissatisfaction, cognitive dissonance) to monitor the product's performance and its ability to meet customers' expectations.

© Cengage Learning 2013

have a difficult time promoting brand switching because they must convince these customers to break tradition and take a look at what different products have to offer.

Second, the buying process often involves a parallel sequence of activities associated with finding the most suitable merchant of the product in question. That is, while consumers consider which product to buy, they also consider where they might buy it. In the case of name brand products, this selection process may focus on the product's price and availability at different stores or online merchants. A specific model of Sony television, for example, is often available from many different retailers and may even be available at Sony's website (www.sonystyle.com). Conversely, in the case of private-label merchandise, the choices of product and merchant are made simultaneously. If a customer is interested only in Gap brand clothing, then that customer must purchase the clothing from a Gap store or the Gap website.

Third, the choice of a suitable merchant may actually take precedence over the choice of a specific product. In some cases, customers are so loyal to a particular merchant that they will not consider looking elsewhere. For example, many older consumers are fiercely loyal to American car manufacturers. These customers will limit their product selection to a single brand or dealership, greatly limiting their range of potential product choices. In other cases, customers might be loyal to a particular merchant because they hold that merchant's credit card or are a member of its frequent customer program. Finally, some

When consumers purchase products like candy or gum on impulse, they rarely go through each stage of the buying process.

merchants become so well known for certain products that customers just naturally execute their buying process with that merchant. Sears, for example, is well known for its selection of name-brand appliances and tools. For many customers, Sears is the natural place to go when they are in the market for a new refrigerator, washer, or wrenches.

Need Recognition   The buying process begins when consumers recognize that they have an unmet need. This occurs when consumers realize that there is a discrepancy between their existing level of satisfaction and their desired level of satisfaction. Consumers can recognize needs in a variety of settings and situations. Some needs have their basis in internal stimuli, such as hunger, thirst, and fatigue. Other needs have their basis in external stimuli, such as advertising, window shopping, interacting with salespeople, or talking with friends and family. External stimuli can also arouse internal responses, such as the hunger you might feel when watching an advertisement for Pizza Hut.

Typically, we think of needs as necessities, particularly with respect to the necessities of life (food, water, clothing, safety, shelter, health, or love). However, this definition is limited because everyone has a different perspective on what constitutes a need. For example, many people would argue that they need a car when their real need is for transportation. Their need for a car is really a "want" for a car. This is where we draw the distinction between needs and wants. A need occurs when an individual's current level of satisfaction does not equal their desired level of satisfaction. A want is a consumer's desire for a specific product that will satisfy the need. Hence, people need transportation, but they choose to fulfill that need with a car, rather than with alternative products like motorcycles, bicycles, public transportation, a taxi, or a horse.

The distinction between needs and wants is not simply academic. In any marketing effort, the firm must always understand the basic needs fulfilled by their products. For example, people do not need drills; they need to make holes or drive screws. Similarly, they do not need lawnmowers; they need shorter, well-manicured grass. Understanding these basic needs allows the firm to segment markets and create marketing programs that can translate consumer needs into wants for their specific products. An important part of this effort involves creating the appropriate stimuli that will foster need recognition among consumers. The idea is to build on the basic need and convince potential consumers to want your product because it will fulfill their needs better than any competing product.

It is also important to understand that wants are not the same thing as demand. Demand occurs only when the consumer's ability and willingness to purchase a specific product backs up their want for the product. Many customers want a luxury yacht, for example, but only a few are able and willing to buy one. In some cases, consumers may actually need a product, but not want it. So-called "unsought products" like life insurance, cemetery plots, long-term health insurance, and continuing education are good examples. In these cases, the marketer must first educate consumers on the need for the product, and then convince consumers to want their products over competing products. For example, Allstate's "Are You in Good Hands?" campaign specifically questions whether potential customers are sure about their insurance coverage. Creating the seed of doubt in the consumer's mind is a good first step toward educating potential customers about the need for adequate insurance.

Understanding consumers' needs and wants is an important consideration in market segmentation. Some markets can be segmented on the basis of needs alone. College students, for example, have needs that are very different from senior citizens; and single consumers have very different needs than families with small children. However, the marketing of most products does not occur on the basis of need-fulfillment alone. In the automobile market, for example, essentially no manufacturer promotes their products as being the best to get you from Point A to Point B (the basic need of transportation). Rather, they market their products on the basis of consumer wants such as luxury (Lexus), image (Mercedes), sportiness (Jaguar), durability (Ford trucks), fuel economy (Honda Civic), and value (Kia). These wants are the hot buttons for consumers, and the keys to promoting further activity in the buying process.

Information Search   When done correctly, marketing stimuli can prompt consumers to become interested in a product, leading to a desire to seek out additional information. This desire can be passive or active. In a passive information search, the consumer becomes more attentive and receptive to information, such as noticing and paying attention to automobile advertisements if the customer has a want for a specific car brand. A consumer engages in an active information search when he or she purposely seeks additional information, such as browsing the Internet, asking friends, or visiting dealer showrooms. Information can come from a variety of sources. Internal sources, including the personal experiences and memories, are typically the first type of information that consumers search. Information can also come from personal sources, including word-of-mouth advice from friends, family, or coworkers. External sources of information include advertising, magazines, websites, packaging, displays, and salespeople. Although external sources are the most numerous, consumers typically trust these sources less than internal and personal sources of information.

The amount of time, effort, and expense dedicated to the search for information depends on a number of issues. First, and perhaps most important, is the degree of risk involved in the purchase. Consumers by nature are naturally risk averse; they use their search for information to reduce risk and increase the odds of making the right choice. Risk comes in many forms, including financial risk (buying a home), social risk (buying the right clothing), emotional risk (selecting a wedding photographer), and personal risk (choosing the right surgeon). In buying a car, for example, consumers regularly turn to *Consumer Reports* magazine, friends, and government safety ratings to help reduce these types of risk. A second issue is the amount of expertise or experience the consumer has with the product category. If a first-time buyer is in the market for a notebook computer, they face a bewildering array of choices and brands. This buyer is likely to engage in an extensive information search to reduce risk and narrow the potential set of product choices. The same buyer, several purchases later, will not go through the same process. Finally, the actual cost of the search in terms of time and money will limit the degree to which consumers search for information. In some situations, such as time deadlines or emergencies, consumers have little time to consult all sources of information at their disposal.

Throughout the information search, consumers learn about different products or brands and begin to remove some from further consideration. They evaluate and reevaluate their initial set of products or brands until their list of potential product choices has been narrowed to only a few products or brands that can meet their needs. This list of suitable alternatives is called the evoked set, and it represents the outcome of the information search and the beginning of the next stage of the buying process.

Evaluation of Alternatives In evaluating the alternative product or brand choices among the members of the evoked set, the consumer essentially translates his or her need into a want for a specific product or brand. The evaluation of alternatives is the black box of consumer behavior because it is typically the hardest for marketers to understand, measure, or influence. What we do know about this stage of the buying process is that consumers base their evaluation on a number of different criteria, which usually equate with a number of product attributes.

Consumers evaluate products as bundles of attributes that have varying abilities to satisfy their needs. In buying a car, for example, each potential choice represents a bundle of attributes, including brand attributes (e.g., image, reputation, reliability, safety), product features (e.g., power windows, automatic transmission, fuel economy), aesthetic attributes (e.g., styling, sportiness, roominess, color), and price. Each consumer has a different opinion as to the relative importance of these attributes—some put safety first, while others consider price the dominant factor. Another interesting feature of the evaluation stage is that the priority of each consumer's choice criteria can change during the process. Consumers may visit a dealership with price as their dominant criterion, only to leave the dealership with price dropping to third on their list of important attributes.

There are several important considerations for marketers during the evaluation stage. First and foremost, the firm's products must be in the evoked set of potential alternatives. For this reason, marketers must constantly remind consumers of their company and its product offerings. Second, it is vital that marketers take steps to understand consumers' choice criteria and the importance they place on specific product attributes. As we will see later in this chapter, understanding the connection between customers' needs and product attributes is an important consideration in market segmentation and target marketing decisions. Finally, marketers must often design marketing programs that change the priority of choice criteria or change consumers' opinions about a product's image. Microsoft, for example, has moved to combat the rapid growth of the iPhone and Android smartphones by aggressively promoting its own Windows Phone. Their phone and its innovative interface have received glowing reviews from experts who tout its ease of use and speed. Unfortunately, the chic of the iPhone and the ubiquity of Android have dampened consumers' enthusiasm for the Windows Phone. Microsoft will continue to fight back with a flurry of advertisements touting the reliability and ease of use of its phone and operating system.[3]

Purchase Decision After the consumer has evaluated each alternative in the evoked set, he or she forms an intention to purchase a particular product or brand. However, a purchase intention and the actual act of buying are distinct concepts. A consumer may have every intention of purchasing a new car, for example, but several factors may

© Stephen Coburn/Shutterstock

Free delivery is one of the most common ways to increase possession utility during the purchase stage of the consumer buying process.

prevent the actual purchase from taking place. The customer may postpone the purchase due to unforeseen circumstances, such as an illness or job loss. The salesperson or the sales manager may anger the consumer, leading them to walk away from the deal. The buyer may not be able to obtain financing for their purchase due to a mistake in their credit file. Or the buyer may simply change his or her mind. Marketers can often reduce or eliminate these problems by reducing the risk of purchase through warranties or guarantees, making the purchase stage as easy as possible, or finding creative solutions to unexpected problems.

Assuming these potential intervening factors are not a concern, the key issues for marketers during the purchase stage are product availability and possession utility. Product availability is critical. Without it, buyers will not purchase from you, but from someone else who can deliver the product. The key to availability—which is closely related to the distribution component of the marketing program—is convenience. The goal is to put the product within the consumer's reach wherever that consumer happens to be. This task is closely related to possession utility (i.e., ease of taking possession). To increase possession utility, the marketer may have to offer financing or layaway for large dollar purchases, delivery and installation of products like appliances or furniture, home delivery of convenience items like pizza or newspapers, or the proper packaging and prompt shipment of items through the mail.

Postpurchase Evaluation   In the context of attracting and retaining buyers, post-purchase evaluation is the connection between the buying process and the development of long-term customer relationships. Marketers must closely follow consumers' responses during this stage to monitor the product's performance and its ability to meet consumers' expectations. In the postpurchase stage, consumers will experience one of these four outcomes:

- **Delight**—the product's performance greatly exceeds the consumer's expectations
- **Satisfaction**—the product's performance matches the consumer's expectations
- **Dissatisfaction**—the product's performance falls short of the consumer's expectations
- **Cognitive Dissonance (Postpurchase Doubt)**—the consumer is unsure of the product's performance relative to their expectations

Consumers are more likely to experience dissatisfaction or cognitive dissonance when the dollar value of the purchase increases, the opportunity costs of rejected alternatives are high, or the purchase decision is emotionally involving. Firms can manage these responses by offering liberal return policies, providing extensive post-sale support, or reinforcing the wisdom of the consumer's purchase decision. The firm's ability to manage dissatisfaction and dissonance is not only a key to creating customer satisfaction; it also has a major influence on the consumer's intentions to spread word-of-mouth information about the company and its products.

Factors That Affect the Consumer Buying Process

As we mentioned previously, the stages in the buying process depict a range of possible activities that may occur as consumers make purchase decisions. Consumers may spend relatively more or less time in certain stages, they may follow the stages in or out of sequence, or they may even skip stages entirely. This variation in the buying process occurs because consumers are different, the products that they buy are different, and the situations in which consumers make purchase decisions are different. There are a number of factors that affect the consumer buying process, including the complexity of the purchase and decision, individual influences, social influences, and situational influences. Let's briefly examine each factor.

Decision-Making Complexity   The complexity of the purchase and decision-making process is the primary reason why the buying process will vary across consumers and with the same consumer in different situations. For example, highly complex decisions, like buying a first home, a first car, selecting the right college, or choosing elective surgery, are very involving for most consumers. These purchases are often characterized by high personal, social, or financial risk; strong emotional involvement; and the lack of experience with the product or purchase situation. In these instances, consumers will spend a great deal of time, effort, and even money to help ensure that they make the right decision. In contrast, purchase tasks that are low in complexity are relatively non-involving for most consumers. In some cases, these purchase tasks can become routine in nature. For example, many consumers buy groceries by selecting familiar items from the shelf and placing them in their carts without considering alternative products.

For marketers, managing decision-making complexity is an important consideration. Marketers of highly complex products must recognize that consumers are quite risk averse, and need a great deal of information to help them make the right decision. In these situations, access to high quality and useful information should be an important consideration in the firm's marketing program. Firms that sell less complex products do not have to provide as much information, but they do face the challenges of creating a brand image and ensuring that their products are easily recognizable. For these marketers, issues like branding, packaging, advertising, and point-of-purchase displays are key considerations in the marketing program.

Individual Influences   The range of individual influences that can affect the buying process is quite extensive. Some individual factors, such as age, life cycle, occupation, and socioeconomic status, are fairly easy to understand and incorporate into the marketing strategy. For the most part, these individual factors dictate preferences for certain types of products or brands. Married consumers with three children will clearly have different needs and preferences than young, single consumers. Likewise, more affluent consumers will have the same basic needs as less affluent consumers; however, their "wants" will be quite different. These individual factors are quite useful for marketers in target market selection, product development, and promotional strategy.

Other individual factors, such as perceptions, motives, interests, attitudes, opinions, or lifestyles, are much harder to understand because they do not clearly coincide with demographic characteristics like age, gender, or income levels. These individual factors are also very difficult to change. For that reason, many marketers adapt their products and promotional messages to fit existing attitudes, interests, or lifestyles. For example, Kia has turned to human-size rapping hamsters to market its Soul wagon. The hip-hop inspired ads are targeted at a younger, non-conformist demographic that loves music and social activities.[4]

Social Influences   Like individual influences, there is a wide range of social influences that can affect the buying process. Social influences such as culture, subculture, social class, reference groups, and family have a profound impact on what, why, and how consumers buy. Among these social influences, none is more important than the family. From birth, individuals become socialized with respect to the knowledge and skills needed to be an effective consumer. As adults, consumers typically exhibit the brand and product preferences of their parents. The influence of children on the buying process has grown tremendously over the last 50 years.

Reference groups and opinion leaders also have an important impact on consumers' buying processes. Reference groups act as a point of comparison and source of product information. A consumer's purchase decisions tend to fall in line with the advice, beliefs, and actions of one or more reference groups. Opinion leaders can be part of a reference group or may be specific individuals that exist outside of a reference group. When consumers feel like they lack personal expertise, they seek the advice of opinion leaders, who they view as being well informed in a particular field of knowledge. In some cases, marketers will seek out opinion leaders before trying to reach more mainstream consumers. Software manufacturers, for example, release beta (test) versions of their products to opinion leaders before a full-scale launch. Not only does this practice work the bugs out of the product, it also starts a word-of-mouth buzz about the upcoming software release.

Situational Influences   There are a number of situational influences that can affect the consumer buying process. Exhibit 5.2 illustrates some of the most common situational influences; many of which affect the amount of time and effort that consumers devote to the purchase task. For example, hungry consumers who are in a hurry often grab the quickest lunch they can find—even if it comes from a vending machine. This fact accounts for the quick success of Pret a Manger ("ready to eat" in French), a chain of fast-food restaurants that offers prepackaged fare focusing on fresh, all-natural, and organic foods. The company strives to serve customers in 60 seconds or less.[5] Furthermore, consumers facing emergency situations have little time to reflect on their product choices and whether they will make the right decision. Consumers may also devote less time and effort to the buying process if they are uncomfortable. For this reason, sit-down restaurants should be inviting and relaxing to encourage longer visits and add-ons such as dessert or coffee after the meal.

EXHIBIT 5.2 Common Situational Influences in the Consumer Buying Process

Situational Influences	Examples	Potential Influences on Buying Behavior
Physical and spatial influences	Retail atmospherics Retail crowding Store layout and design	A comfortable atmosphere or ambience promotes lingering, browsing, and buying. Crowded stores may cause customers to leave or buy less than planned.
Social and interpersonal influences	Shopping in groups Sales people Other customers	Consumers are more susceptible to the influences of other consumers when shopping in groups. Rude sales people can end the buying process. Obnoxious "other" customers may cause the consumer to leave or be dissatisfied.
Temporal (time) influences	Lack of time Emergencies Convenience	Consumers will pay more for products when they are in a hurry or face an emergency. Lack of time greatly reduces the search for information and the evaluation of alternatives. Consumers with ample time can seek information on many different product alternatives.
Purchase task or product usage influences	Special occasions Buying for others Buying a gift	Consumers may buy higher quality products for gifts or special occasions. The evoked set will differ when consumers are buying for others as opposed to themselves.
Consumer dispositional influences	Stress Anxiety Fear Fatigue Emotional involvement Good/bad mood	Consumers suffering from stress or fatigue may not buy at all or they may indulge in certain products to make themselves feel better. Consumers who are in a bad mood are exceptionally difficult to please. An increase in fear or anxiety over a purchase may cause consumers to seek additional information and take great pains to make the right decision.

Other situational influences can affect specific product choices. For example, if you have your boss over for dinner, your product choices would likely differ from those you make in everyday purchases of food and drink. Likewise, customers may purchase more expensive items for gifts, or when they shop with friends. Product choices also change when customers make the purchase for someone else, such as buying clothing for children. In fact, many parents will purposely buy less expensive clothing for their children if they are growing rapidly or are exceptionally active. These parents want to save money on clothing that will quickly wear out or become too small.

Buyer Behavior in Business Markets

As we shift our attention to buyer behavior in business markets, keep in mind that business markets and consumer markets have many things in common. Both contain buyers and sellers who seek to make good purchases and satisfy their personal or organizational objectives. Both markets use similar buying processes that include stages associated with need identification, information search, and product evaluation. Finally, both processes focus on customer satisfaction as the desired outcome. However, business markets differ from consumer markets in important ways. One of the most important differences involves the consumption of the purchased products. Consumers buy products for their personal use or consumption. In contrast, organizational buyers purchase products for use in their operations. These uses can be direct, as in acquiring raw materials to produce finished goods; or indirect, as in buying office supplies or leasing cars for sales-people. There are four types of business markets:

- **Commercial Markets**. These markets buy raw materials for use in producing finished goods, and they buy facilitating goods and services used in the production of finished goods. Commercial markets include a variety of industries, such as aerospace, agriculture, mining, construction, transportation, communication, and utilities.
- **Reseller Markets**. These markets consist of channel intermediaries such as wholesalers, retailers, or brokers that buy finished goods from the producer market and resell them at a profit. As we will see in Chapter 6, channel intermediaries have the responsibility for creating the variety and assortment of products offered to consumers. Therefore, they wield a great deal of power in the supply chain.
- **Government Markets**. These markets include federal, state, county, city, and local governments. Governments buy a wide range of finished goods ranging from aircraft carriers to fire trucks to office equipment. However, most government purchases are for the services provided to citizens, such as education, fire and police protection, maintenance and repair of roads, and water and sewage treatment.
- **Institutional Markets**. These markets consist of a diverse group of non-commercial organizations such as churches, charities, schools, hospitals, or professional organizations. These organizations primarily buy finished goods that facilitate their ongoing operations.

Unique Characteristics of Business Markets

Business markets differ from consumer markets in at least four ways. These differences concern the nature of the decision-making unit, the role of hard and soft costs in making and evaluating purchase decisions, reciprocal buying relationships, and the dependence of the two parties on each other. As a general rule, these differences are more acute for firms attempting to build long-term client relationships. In business markets, buying needed products at the lowest possible price is not necessarily the most important objective. Since many business transactions are based on long-term relationships, trust, reliability, and overall goal attainment are often much more important than the price of the product.

The Buying Center   The first key difference relates to the role of the *buying center*— the group of people responsible for making purchase decisions. In consumer markets, the buying center is fairly straightforward: The adult head-of-household tends to make most major purchase decisions for the family, with input and assistance from children and other family members as applicable. In an organization, however, the buying center tends to be much more complex and difficult to identify, in part because it may include three distinct groups of people—economic buyers, technical buyers, and users—each of which may have its own agenda and unique needs that affect the buying decision.

Any effort to build a relationship between the selling and buying organization must include economic buyers—those senior managers with the overall responsibility of achieving the buying firm's objectives. In recent years, economic buyers have become increasingly influential as price has become less important in determining a product's true value to the buying firm. This has made economic buyers a greater target for promotional activities. Technical buyers—employees with the responsibility of buying products to meet needs on an ongoing basis—include purchasing agents and materials managers. These buyers have the responsibility of narrowing the number of product options and delivering buying recommendations to the economic buyer(s) that are within budget. Technical buyers are critical in the execution of purchase transactions and are also important to the day-to-day maintenance of long-term relationships. Users—managers and employees who have the responsibility of using a product purchased by the firm—comprise the last group of people in the buying center. The user is often not the ultimate decision maker, but frequently has a place in the decision process, particularly in the case of technologically advanced products. For example, the head of information technology often has a major role in computer and IT purchase decisions.

Hard and Soft Costs   The second difference between business and consumer markets involves the significance of hard and soft costs. Consumers and organizations both consider *hard costs*, which include monetary price and associated purchase costs such as shipping and installation. Organizations, however, must also consider *soft costs*, such as downtime, opportunity costs, and human resource costs associated with the compatibility of systems, in the buying decision. The purchase and implementation of a new payroll system, for example, will decrease productivity and increase training costs in the payroll department until the new system has been fully integrated.

Reciprocity   The third key difference involves the existence of reciprocal buying relationships. With consumer purchases, the opportunity for buying and selling is usually a one-way street: The marketer sells and the consumer buys. Business marketing, however, is more often a two-way street, with each firm marketing products that the other firm buys. For example, a company may buy office supplies from another company that in turn buys copiers from the first firm. In fact, such arrangements can be an upfront condition of purchase in purely transaction-based marketing. Reciprocal buying is less likely to occur within long-term relationships unless it helps both parties achieve their respective goals.

Mutual Dependence   Finally, in business markets, the buyer and seller are more likely to be dependent on one another. For consumer–marketer relationships, this level of dependence tends to be low. If a store is out of a product, or a firm goes out of business, customers simply switch to another source to meet their needs. Likewise, the loss of a particular customer through brand switching, relocation, or death is unfortunate for a company, but not in itself particularly damaging. The only real exception to this norm is when consumers are loyal to a brand or merchant. In these cases, consumers become dependent on a single brand or merchant, and the firm can become dependent on the sales volume generated by these brand loyal consumers.

This is not the case in business markets where sole-source or limited-source buying may leave an organization's operations severely distressed when a supplier shuts down or cannot deliver. The same is true for the loss of a customer. The selling firm has invested significantly in the client relationship, often modifying products and altering information or other systems central to the organization. Each client relationship represents a significant portion of the firm's profit, and the loss of a single customer can take months or even years to replace. For example, after Rubbermaid's relationships with Walmart, Lowe's, and Home Depot soured in the mid-1990s, these retailers pulled Rubbermaid products from their shelves and turned to Sterilite, a small Massachusetts-based manufacturer, to supply plastic products (storage bins, containers, etc.) for their stores. Along with damaging Rubbermaid's reputation and profits, the considerable buying power of Walmart, Lowe's, and Home Depot turned Sterilite into a major competitor for Rubbermaid. Today, Sterilite is the world's largest independent manufacturer of plastic housewares.[6]

The Business Buying Process

Like consumers, businesses follow a buying process. However, given the complexity, risk, and expense of many business purchases, business buyers tend to follow these stages in sequence. Some buying situations can be quite routine, such as the daily or weekly purchase and delivery of raw materials or the purchase of office consumables like paper and toner cartridges. Nonetheless, business buyers often make even routine purchases from prequalified or single source suppliers. Consequently, virtually all business purchases have gone through the following stages of the buying process at one time or another:

1. **Problem Recognition**. The recognition of needs can stem from a variety of internal and external sources, such as employees, members of the buying center, or outside salespeople. Business buyers often recognize needs due to special circumstances, such as when equipment or machinery breaks or malfunctions.
2. **Develop Product Specifications**. Detailed product specifications often define business purchases. This occurs because new purchases must be integrated with current technologies and processes. Developing product specifications is typically done by the buying center.
3. **Vendor Identification and Qualification**. Business buyers must ensure that potential vendors can deliver on needed product specifications, within a specified time frame, and in the needed quantities. Therefore, business buyers will conduct a thorough analysis of potential vendors to ensure they can meet their firm's needs. The buyers then qualify and approve the vendors that meet their criteria to supply goods and services to the firm.
4. **Solicitation of Proposals or Bids**. Depending on the purchase in question, the buying firm may request that qualified vendors submit proposals or bids. These proposals or bids will detail how the vendor will meet the buying firm's needs and fulfill the purchase criteria established during the second stage of the process.
5. **Vendor Selection**. The buying firm will select the vendor or vendors that can best meet its needs. The best vendor is not necessarily the one offering the lowest price. Other issues such as reputation, timeliness of delivery, guarantees, or personal relationships with the members of the buying center are often more important.
6. **Order Processing**. Often a behind-the-scenes process, order processing involves the details of processing the order, negotiating credit terms, setting firm delivery dates, and any final technical assistance needed to complete the purchase.
7. **Vendor Performance Review**. The final stage of the buying process involves a review of the vendor's performance. In some cases, the product may flawlessly fulfill the needed specifications, but the vendor's performance is poor. In this stage, both product and vendor specifications can be reevaluated and changed if necessary. In the end, the result of these evaluations will affect future purchase decisions.

Like consumer markets, there are a number of factors that can influence the business buying process. Environmental conditions can have a major influence on buyer behavior by increasing the uncertainty, complexity, and risk associated with a purchase. In situations of rapid environmental change, business buyers may alter their buying plans, postpone purchases, or even cancel purchases until things settle down. Environmental conditions not only affect the purchase of products; they also affect decisions regarding the recruitment and hiring of employees.

Organizational factors can also influence corporate buying decisions. These factors include conditions within the firm's internal environment (resources, strategies, policies, objectives), as well as the condition of relationships with business or supply chain partners. A shift in the firm's resources can change buying decisions, such as a temporary delay in purchasing until favorable credit terms can be arranged. Likewise, if a supplier suddenly cannot provide needed quantities of products or cannot meet a needed delivery schedule, the buying firm will be forced to identify and qualify new suppliers. Internal changes in information technology can also affect the buying process, such as when technicians integrate electronic procurement systems with the legacy systems of the firm and its vendors. Finally, interpersonal relationships and individual factors can affect the buying process. A common example occurs when members of the buying center are at odds over purchase decisions. Power struggles are not uncommon in business buying, and they can bring the entire process to a halt if not handled properly. Individual factors, such as a manager's personal preferences or prejudices, can also affect business buying decisions. The importance of interpersonal and individual factors depends on the specific buying situation and its importance to the firm's goals and objectives. Major purchases typically create the most conflict among members of the buying center.

Market Segmentation

Understanding the processes that consumers and businesses use to make purchase decisions is critical to the development of long-term, mutually beneficial relationships with customers. It is also a necessary first step in uncovering similarities among groups of potential buyers that can be used in market segmentation and target marketing decisions. From a strategic perspective, we define *market segmentation* as the process of dividing the total market for a particular product or product category into relatively homogeneous segments or groups. To be effective, segmentation should create groups where the members within the group have similar likes, tastes, needs, wants, or preferences; but where the groups themselves are dissimilar from each other. As noted in *Beyond the Pages 5.2*, the increasing diversity of the U.S. population creates a number of opportunities and challenges when it comes to segmenting markets.

In reality, the most fundamental segmentation decision is really whether to segment at all. When a firm makes the decision to pursue the entire market, it must do so on the basis of universal needs that all customers possess. However, most firms opt to target one or more segments of the total market because they find that they can be more successful when they tailor products to fit unique needs or requirements. In today's economy, segmentation is often mandated by customers due to their search for unique products and their changing uses of communication media. The end result is that customer segments have become even more fragmented and more difficult to reach. Many firms today take segmentation to the extreme by targeting small niches of a market, or even the smallest of market segments: individuals.

Traditional Market Segmentation Approaches

Many segmentation approaches are traditional in the sense that firms have used them successfully for decades. It is not our intention to depict these approaches as old or out-of-date, especially when compared to individualized segmentation strategies that we discuss later. In fact, many of today's most successful firms use these tried-and-true approaches. Some organizations actually use more than one type of segmentation, depending on the brand, product, or market in question.

Beyond the Pages 5.2

The Challenges and Opportunities of Population Diversity[7]

Although there are obvious differences among the members of our population, many people are surprised to learn that the U.S. is more diverse than they would have realized. However, we should not be surprised. After all, the U.S. was founded as a melting pot of cultures. That pot of cultural differences creates many challenges and opportunities in finding and serving target markets. Consider the following statistics:

- Today, roughly one-third of the U.S. population is a minority. If these consumers were a separate country, they would be the twelfth largest in the world. By 2045, approximately half of the U.S. population will be part of a minority group.
- Texas, California, Hawaii, New Mexico, and the District of Columbia now have "majority–minority" populations where more than 50 percent of the population is part of a minority group.
- Minority populations have a large middle-class with strong buying power. For instance, the combined buying power of minorities, which stands at $1.6 trillion today, will rise to $2.1 trillion by 2015. Hispanics alone account for $1 trillion in buying power today. That number makes the U.S. Hispanic population the 15th largest economy in the world.
- The defining characteristics of minority markets are not based on skin color or language. Instead, core values such as family, faith, nationalism, respect for the elderly and community leaders, and cultural institutions are the dominant features that define minority populations.
- Minority populations have stopped trying to "fit in" with traditional U.S. customs. Instead, these groups work hard to preserve their ethnic values and customs.

- Distinct minority populations have little in common with each other, other than their emotional connections to their own ethnic traditions.

Given these stark facts, it becomes clear that firms will have a hard time reaching a mass audience of U.S. consumers using a one-size-fits-all marketing approach. So, how can a firm reach across segments of society for maximum marketing effectiveness and efficiency? The truth is that most firms don't bother. Still, targeting specific minority groups has become more difficult. The tactics of yesterday—simple language translation, hiring diverse employees, or using photos of ethnic minorities in promotional images—won't work anymore.

McDonald's is pursuing one interesting approach to this challenge. Although the company still does targeted advertising specifically to minority groups, McDonald's newest strategy is to take lessons from minority groups in its approach to targeting Caucasians. Ethnic trends and tastes are now being used to reshape McDonald's menu and advertising decisions. For example, the fruit combinations in the company's smoothies are based on the taste preferences of minorities. Likewise, the "Fiesta Menu" offered in many Western states is now equally popular with both Hispanics and Caucasians. McDonald's advertising has shifted as well. The company uses a higher percentage of minorities in its advertising than other restaurant chains. The results have been impressive. Sales have increased 1.5 percent since the strategy went into effect. Even more impressive is that McDonald's sales are growing at a time when the rest of the restaurant industry has been struggling to grow.

Mass Marketing   It seems odd to call mass marketing a segmentation approach, as it involves no segmentation whatsoever. Companies aim mass marketing campaigns at the total (whole) market for a particular product. Companies that adopt mass marketing take an undifferentiated approach that assumes that all customers in the market have similar needs and wants that can be reasonably satisfied with a single marketing program. This marketing program typically consists of a single product or brand (or, in the case of retailers, a homogeneous set of products), one price, one promotional program, and one distribution system. Duracell, for example, offers a collection of different battery sizes (D, C, A, AA, AAA, 9-volt), but they are all disposable batteries marketed to consumers for use in toys and small electronic devices. They also offer a line of rechargeable and ultra power batteries for high power devices. Likewise, the WD-40 Company offers an assortment of brands—including WD-40, 3-IN-ONE Oil, Lava Soap, 2000 Flushes, Carpet Fresh, and X14 Cleaner—used in a variety of household tasks.

Mass marketing works best when the needs of an entire market are relatively homogeneous. Good examples include commodities like oil and agricultural products. In reality, very few products or markets are ideal for mass marketing, if for no other reason than companies, wanting to reach new customers, often modify their product lines. For most of its existence, Vaseline manufactured and offered a single product. To reach new customers, Vaseline modified this strategy by launching its Intensive Care line of products and extending customers' perception of Vaseline's uses to various needs in the home, including in the garage/workshop. Furthermore, think of the many products that contain Arm & Hammer Baking Soda, a product that at one time was sold only as a baking ingredient.

Although mass marketing is advantageous in terms of production efficiency and lower marketing costs, it is inherently risky. By offering a standard product to all customers, the organization becomes vulnerable to competitors that offer specialized products that better match customers' needs. In industries where barriers to entry are low, mass marketing runs the risk of being seen as too generic. This situation is very inviting for competitors who use more targeted approaches. Mass marketing is also very risky in global markets, where even global brands like Coca-Cola must be adapted to match local tastes and customs.

Differentiated Marketing   Most firms use some form of market segmentation by: (1) dividing the total market into groups of customers having relatively common or homogeneous needs, and (2) attempting to develop a marketing program that appeals to one or more of these groups. This approach may be necessary when customer needs are similar within a single group, but their needs differ across groups. Through well-designed and carefully conducted research, firms can identify the particular needs of each market segment to create marketing programs that best match those needs and expectations. Within the differentiated approach there are two options: the multisegment approach and the market concentration approach.

Firms using the *multisegment approach* seek to attract buyers in more than one market segment by offering a variety of products that appeal to different needs. Firms using this option can increase their share of the market by responding to the heterogeneous needs of different segments. If the segments have enough buying potential, and the product is successful, the resulting sales increases can more than offset the increased costs of offering multiple products and marketing programs. The multisegment approach is the most widely used segmentation strategy in medium- to large-sized firms. It is extremely common in packaged goods and grocery products. Maxwell House, for example, began by marketing one type of coffee and one brand. Today, this division of Kraft Foods offers 22 different brand varieties under the Maxwell House, Sanka, and Yuban labels, in addition to providing private label brands for retailers. A walk down the cereal aisle of your local supermarket offers additional examples. Firms such as Kellogg's and Nabisco offer seemingly hundreds of brands of breakfast cereals targeted at specific segments, including children (e.g., Fruity Pebbles, Apple Jacks), health-conscious adults (e.g., Shredded Wheat, Total), parents looking for healthier foods for their children (e.g., Life, Kix), and so on.

Firms using the *market concentration* approach focus on a single market segment. These firms often find it most efficient to seek a maximum share in one segment of the market. For example, Armor All markets a well-known line of automotive cleaners, protectants, and polishes targeted primarily to young, driving-age males. The main advantage of market concentration is specialization, as it allows the firm to focus all of its resources toward understanding and serving a single segment. Specialization is also the major disadvantage of this approach. By "putting all of its eggs in one basket," the firm can be vulnerable to changes in its market segment, such as economic downturns and demographic shifts. Still, the market concentration approach can be highly success-ful. In the arts, where market concentration is almost universal, musical groups hone their talents and plan their performances to satisfy the tastes of one market segment, divided by genres of music such as country, rock, or jazz.

Niche Marketing   Some companies narrow the market concentration approach even more and focus their marketing efforts on one small, well-defined market segment or niche that has a unique, specific set of needs. Customers in niche markets will typically pay higher prices for products that match their specialized needs. One example of suc-cessful niche marketing is found in the gym industry. For example, Curves—a health club for women—now has 10,000 locations in 85 countries around the world. Other niche gyms for children and the over-55 age group are popping up around the U.S. The Little Gym—designed for kids ages four months through 12 years—has over 300 locations worldwide. The goal of these gyms is to create highly customized workout experiences for niche markets that don't fit the profile of a typical health club member.[8] As the gym industry has learned, the key to successful niche marketing is to understand and meet the needs of target customers so completely that, despite the small size of the niche, the firm's substantial share makes the segment highly profitable. An attractive market niche is one that has growth and profit potential, but is not so appealing that it attracts competitors. The firm should also possess a specialization or provide a unique offering that customers find highly desirable.

Individualized Segmentation Approaches

Due to advances in communication and Internet technology, individualized segmenta-tion approaches have emerged. These approaches are possible because organizations now have the ability to track customers with a high degree of specificity. By combining demographic data with past and current purchasing behavior, organizations can tweak their marketing programs in ways that allow them to precisely match customers' needs, wants, and preferences. Three types of individualized segmentation approaches are one-to-one marketing, mass customization, and permission marketing.

One-to-One Marketing   When a company creates an entirely unique product or marketing program for each customer in the target segment, it employs one-to-one marketing. This approach is common in business markets where companies design unique programs and/or systems for each customer. For example, providers of enterprise software—such as Oracle, SAP, and Business Objects—create customized solutions that allow firms to track customers, business processes, and results in real time. Insurance companies or brokers, such Britain's Sedgwick Group, design insurance and pension programs to meet a corporation's specific needs. The key to one-to-one marketing is personalization, where every element of the marketing program is customized to meet the specifics of a particular client's situation.

Historically, one-to-one marketing has been used less often in consumer markets, although Burger King was an early pioneer in this approach, with its "Have It Your Way" effort that continues today. One-to-one marketing is quite common in luxury and custom-made products, such as when a consumer buys a large sailboat, airplane, or a custom-built home. In such instances, the product has significant modifications made to it to meet unique customer needs and preferences. Many service firms—such as hairstylists, lawyers, doctors, and educational institutions—also customize their marketing programs to match individual consumer needs. One-to-one marketing has grown rapidly in electronic commerce where customers can be targeted very precisely. Amazon, for example, maintains complete profiles on customers who browse and buy from its site. These profiles assist Amazon with the customization of web pages in real time, product suggestions, and reminder e-mails sent to customers.

Mass Customization   An extension of one-to-one marketing, mass customization refers to providing unique products and solutions to individual customers on a mass scale. Along with the Internet, advances in supply chain management—including real-time inventory control—have allowed companies to customize products in ways that are both cost effective and practical. For example, Dell builds thousands of custom-ordered computers every day. Each customer gets to choose from a variety of options (hard drives, screen sizes, colors, etc.) to configure the computer as they want it. Dell gets to take advantage of scale economies because it builds thousands of the same basic computer for its other customers. Other firms that use mass customization include 1-800-Flowers.com (custom flower arrangements, plants, or other gifts) and Build-A-Bear Workshop (custom teddy bears or other animals).

Mass customization also occurs in business markets. Through a buying firm's electronic procurement system, employees can order products ranging from office supplies to travel services. The system allows employees to requisition goods and services via a customized catalog—unique to the firm—where the buying firm has negotiated the products and prices. E-procurement systems like these have become quite popular for good reason: They allow firms to save a great deal of money—not only on prices but also on the costs of placing orders. Selling firms benefit as well by customizing their catalogs to specific buying firms, allowing them to sell more goods and services at a reduced cost.

Permission Marketing   Permission marketing, although similar to one-to-one marketing, is different in that customers choose to become part of a firm's market segment. In permission marketing, customers give companies permission to specifically target them in their marketing efforts. The most common tool used in permission marketing is the opt-in e-mail list, where customers permit a firm—or a third-party partner of the firm—to send periodic e-mail about goods and services that they have interest in purchasing. This scenario is ubiquitous in business-to-consumer e-commerce, so much so that many consumers fail to notice it. When customers order products online, they receive the option of receiving or not receiving future e-mail notifications about new products. In many cases, the customer must deselect a box at the end of the order form or they will be added to the e-mail list.

Permission marketing has a major advantage over other individualized segmentation approaches: Customers who opt-in have already shown interest in the goods and services offered by the firm. This allows the firm to precisely target only those individuals with an interest in their products, thereby eliminating wasted marketing effort and expense. For example, many airlines have the permission of their customers to send weekly e-mail notices of airfare and other travel-related specials. This system is in stark contrast to traditional mass media advertising where only a portion of the viewing or reading audience has a real interest in the company's product.

One-to-one marketing, mass customization, and permission marketing will become even more important in the future because their focus on individual customers makes them critical to the development and maintenance of long-term relationships.

The simple truth is that customers will maintain relationships with firms that best fulfill their needs or solve their problems. Unfortunately, individualized segmentation approaches can be prohibitively expensive. To make these approaches viable, firms must be mindful of two important issues. First, the delivery of the marketing program must be automated to a degree that makes it cost efficient. The Internet makes this possible by allowing for individual customization in real time. Second, the marketing program must not become so automated that the offering lacks personalization. Today, personalization means much more than simply calling customers by name. We use the term to describe the idea of giving customers choices—not only in terms of product configuration, but also in terms of the entire marketing program. Firms like Dell and Amazon offer a great deal of personalization by effectively mining their customer databases. Customers can choose payment terms, shipping terms, delivery locations, gift-wrapping, and whether to opt-in to future e-mail promotions. Also, by monitoring click stream data in real time, the best e-commerce firms can offer product suggestions on the fly—while customers visit their sites. This sort of customized point-of-sale information not only increases sales; it also better fulfills customers' needs and increases the likelihood of establishing long-term customer relationships.

Criteria for Successful Segmentation

It is important to remember that not all segmentation approaches or their resulting market segments are viable in a marketing sense. For example, it makes little sense to segment the soft drink market based on eye color or shoe size, as these characteristics have nothing to do with the purchase of soft drinks. Although markets can be segmented in limitless ways, the segmentation approach must make sense in terms of at least five related criteria:

- **Identifiable and Measurable**. The characteristics of the segment's members must be easily identifiable. This allows the firm to measure identifying characteristics, including the segment's size and purchasing power.
- **Substantial**. The segment must be large and profitable enough to make it worthwhile for the firm. The profit potential must be greater than the costs involved in creating a marketing program specifically for the segment.
- **Accessible**. The segment must be accessible in terms of communication (advertising, mail, telephone, etc.) and distribution (channels, merchants, retail outlets, etc.).
- **Responsive.** The segment must respond to the firm's marketing efforts, including changes to the marketing program over time. The segment must also respond differently than other segments.
- **Viable and Sustainable**. The segment must meet the basic criteria for exchange, including being ready, willing, and able to conduct business with the firm. The segment must also be sustainable over time to allow the firm to effectively develop a marketing strategy for serving the needs of the segment.

It is possible for a market segment to meet these criteria, yet still not be viable in a business sense. Markets for many illegal products, such as illicit drugs or pornography, can easily meet these criteria. However, ethical and socially responsible firms would not pursue these markets. Other markets, like gaming or gambling, may be legal in some geographical areas, but are often not in the best interests of the firm. More commonly, firms will identify perfectly viable market segments; however, these segments will rest outside of the firm's expertise or mission. Just because a market segment is viable or highly profitable does not mean the firm should pursue it.

Shifting Strategies in the Cereal Market[9]

Cereal has long been thought of as a healthy breakfast. Yet in terms of sugar, parents might as well feed their children a cookie to start their day. Some sugary cereals are as much as 50 percent sugar. Kellogg's Honey Smacks, for example contains 15 grams of sugar per serving, which is 3 grams more than in a glazed donut. In spite of their poor nutritional profiles, it is often the sweetest cereals that are targeted toward children. In response, many upset parents have filed lawsuits against cereal companies. In order to deal with the backlash and to gain a competitive advantage, companies like Kellogg's have worked to reformulate and reposition their cereals as healthy breakfast choices.

Cereal companies began specifically marketing to children in the 1950s, the same decade in which sugar became a common additive in cereal. As one might imagine, kids gravitated toward these sugary sweets. Cereal companies also introduced cartoon characters to get kids interested in their brands. Tony the Tiger and Trix the Rabbit became beloved child icons. Companies also began placing free toys into cereal boxes. These marketing ploys worked; children craved these fun cereals, making sugary cereals a popular item on the breakfast table for decades.

In a string of lawsuits filed over the past twenty years, consumers have argued that cereal companies, such as Kellogg's and General Mills, engage in deceptive advertising regarding nutritional information and in making exaggerated claims about physical strength, happiness, or even magical powers. Today,

cereal companies have reworked their advertising and most have stopped co-branding their products with well-known cartoon characters. Other lawsuits have focused on nutritional content or labeling, such as a suit filed against Kellogg's Froot Loops by a woman who was upset that the cereal did not actually contain fruit.

In response to these concerns, Kellogg's has taken a proactive stance to shift its marketing strategy. The company stopped advertising cereals that do not meet the Institute of Medicine and World Health Organization's health guidelines for cereal. No longer will you find a Kellogg's cereal advertised if it contains over 12 grams of sugar or 200 calories per serving. The company also created guidelines advising consumers to eat sugary cereals in moderation. Additionally, cereals like Special K and the Kashi brand have become popular, although these cereals will never hold the same cache with children as Lucky Charms or Fruity Pebbles. Many major cereal companies are going further to respond to criticism by listing health benefits prominently on cereal labels. Even sugary cereals are trying to appeal to the health-conscious customer with claims that they contain essential vitamins and minerals. A few brands, such as Frosted Flakes, have even introduced reduced sugar versions. As long as consumers remain concerned, however, cereal companies must continue to shift their marketing to keep up with the public's changing health preferences.

Identifying Market Segments

A firm's segmentation strategy and its choice of one or more target markets depend on its ability to identify the characteristics of buyers within those markets. This involves selecting the most relevant variables to identify and define the target market or markets. Many of these variables, including demographics, lifestyles, product-usage, or firm size, derive from the situation analysis section of the marketing plan. However, a new or revised marketing strategy often requires changes in target market definition to correct problems in the previous marketing strategy. Target markets also shift in response to required changes in specific elements of the marketing program; such as reducing price to enhance value, increasing price to connote higher quality, adding a new product feature to make the benefits more meaningful, or selling through retail stores instead of direct distribution to add the convenience of immediate availability. In short, the target market and the marketing program are interdependent, and changes in one typically require changes in the other. *Beyond the Pages 5.3* outlines how major cereal companies have addressed changing customers' demands in the cereal market.

Segmenting Consumer Markets

The goal in segmenting consumer markets is to isolate individual characteristics that distinguish one or more segments from the total market. The key is to segment the total market into groups with relatively homogeneous needs. As you may recall from our earlier discussion, consumers buy products because the benefits they provide can fulfill specific needs or wants. The difficulty in segmenting consumer markets lies in isolating one or more characteristics that closely align with these needs and wants. For example, marketers of soft drinks do not necessarily concern themselves with the age or gender of their customers, but rather in how age and gender relate to customers' needs, attitudes, preferences, and lifestyles.

In the discussion that follows, we look more closely at segmentation in consumer markets by examining the different factors that can be used to divide these markets into homogeneous groupings. As Exhibit 5.3 illustrates, these factors fall into one of four general categories: behavioral segmentation, demographic segmentation, psychographic segmentation, and geographic segmentation.

Behavioral Segmentation   Behavioral segmentation is the most powerful approach because it uses actual consumer behavior or product usage to make distinctions among market segments. Typically, these distinctions are tied to the reasons that customers buy and use products. Consequently, behavioral segmentation, unlike other types of consumer segmentation, is most closely associated with consumers' needs. A common use of behavioral segmentation is to group consumers based on their extent of product usage—heavy, medium, and light users. Heavy users are a firm's bread-and-butter customers and they should always be served well. Marketers often use strategies to increase product usage among light users, as well as non-users of the product or brand. One of the best uses of behavioral segmentation is to create market segments based on specific consumer benefits. Exhibit 5.4 illustrates how benefit segmentation might be applied in the snack food market. Once different benefit segments have been identified, marketers can conduct research to develop profiles of the consumers in each segment.

Behavioral segmentation is a powerful tool; however, it is also quite difficult to execute in practice. Conducting research to identify behavioral segments is quite expensive and time consuming. Also, the personal characteristics associated with behavioral segments are not always clear. For example, although some consumers buy a new car solely for transportation, most buy specific makes and models for other reasons. Some consumers want cars that are sporty, fun to drive, and that enhance their image. The problem lies in identifying the characteristics of these consumers. Are they older or younger, men or women, single or married, and do they live in urban or suburban areas? In some cases, consumer characteristics are easy to identify. Families purchase minivans because they want more room for their children and cargo. Older consumers tend to opt for comfortable and luxurious models. The key to successful behavioral segmentation is to clearly understand the basic needs and benefits sought by different consumer groups. Then this information can be combined with demographic, psychographic, and geographic segmentation to create complete consumer profiles.

Demographic Segmentation   Demographic segmentation divides markets into segments using demographic factors such as gender (e.g., Secret deodorant for women), age (e.g., Abercrombie & Fitch clothing for teens and young adults), income (e.g., Lexus automobiles for wealthy consumers), and education (e.g., online executive MBA

EXHIBIT 5.3   **Common Segmentation Variables Used in Consumer Markets**

Category	Variables	Examples
Behavioral Segmentation	Benefits sought	Quality, value, taste, image enhancement, beauty, sportiness, speed, excitement, entertainment, nutrition, convenience
	Product usage	Heavy, medium, and light users; nonusers; former users; first-time users
	Occasions or situations	Emergencies, celebrations, birthdays, anniversaries, weddings, births, funerals, graduation
	Price sensitivity	Price sensitive, value conscious, status conscious (not price sensitive)
Demographic Segmentation	Age	Newborns, 0–5, 6–12, 13–17, 18–25, 26–34, 35–49, 50–64, 65+
	Gender	Male, female
	Income	Under $15,000, $15,000–$30,000, $30,000–$50,000, $50,000–$75,000, $75,000–$100,000, over $100,000
	Occupation	Blue collar, white collar, technical, professional, managers, laborers, retired, homemakers, unemployed
	Education	High school graduate, some college, college graduate, graduate degree
	Family life cycle	Single, married no children, married with young children, married with teenage children, married with grown children, divorced, widowed
	Generation	Generation Y, Generation X, baby boomers, seniors
	Ethnicity	Caucasian, African American, Hispanic, Asian
	Religion	Protestant, Catholic, Muslim, Hindu
	Nationality	American, European, Japanese, Australian, Korean
	Social class	Upper class, middle class, lower class, working class, poverty level
Psychographic Segmentation	Personality	Outgoing, shy, compulsive, individualistic, materialistic, civic minded, anxious, controlled, venturesome
	Lifestyle	Outdoor enthusiast, sports-minded, homebody, couch potato, family-centered, workaholic
	Motives	Safety, status, relaxation, convenience
Geographic Segmentation	Regional	Northeast, Southeast, Midwest, New England, Southern France, South Africa
	City/county size	Under 50,000; 50,000–100,000; 100,000–250,000; 250,000–500,000; 500,000–1,000,000, over 1,000,000
	Population density	Urban, suburban, rural

programs for busy professionals). Demographic segmentation tends to be the most widely used basis for segmenting consumer markets because demographic information is widely available and relatively easy to measure. In fact, much of this information is easily obtainable during the situation analysis through secondary sources.

Some demographic characteristics are often associated with true differences in needs that can be used to segment markets. In these cases, the connection between demographics, needs, and desired product benefits can make demographic segmentation quite easy. For example, men and women have clearly different needs with respect to

EXHIBIT 5.4   Benefit Segmentation of the Snack Food Market

	Nutritional Snackers	Weight Watchers	Guilty Snackers	Party Snackers	Indiscriminant Snackers	Economical Snackers
Benefits Sought	Nutritious, all-natural ingredients	Low calorie, quick energy	Low calorie, good tasting	Can be served to guests, goes well with beverages	Good tasting, satisfies hunger cravings	Low price, best value
Types of Snacks Eaten	Fruits, vegetables, cheeses	Yogurt, vegetables	Yogurt, cookies, crackers, candy	Potato chips, nuts, crackers, pretzels	Candy, ice cream, cookies, potato chips, pretzels, popcorn	No specific products
Snack Consumption Level	Light	Light	Heavy	Average	Heavy	Average
Percentage of Snackers	23%	15%	10%	16%	16%	19%
Demographic Characteristics	Better educated, have young children	Younger, single	Less educated, lower incomes	Middle aged, suburban	Teens	Better educated, larger families
Psychographic Characteristics	Self-assured, controlled	Outdoorsy, influential, venturesome	Anxious, isolated	Sociable, outgoing	Hedonistic, time deprived	Self-assured, price sensitive

Source: Adapted from Charles W. Lamb, Jr., Joseph F. Hair, Jr., and Carl McDaniel, *Marketing* 7th ed. (Mason, OH: South-Western, 2004), p. 224.

clothing and healthcare. Large families with children have a greater need for life insurance, laundry detergent, and food. Children prefer sweeter-tasting food and beverages than do adults. Unfortunately, demographic segmentation becomes less useful when the firm has a strong interest in understanding the motives or values that drive buying behavior. Often, the motives and values that drive actual purchases do not necessarily have anything to do with demographics. For example, how would you describe the demographic characteristics of a price sensitive, value-conscious consumer? Before you answer, remember that Walmart customers come from all walks of life. Likewise, how would you describe the demographics of an adventuresome, outdoor-oriented consumer? When Honda first introduced its Element utility vehicle, the company targeted adventuresome, high school and college-aged consumers. To its surprise, Honda quickly discovered that the Element was just as popular with 30- and 40-somethings who used it to haul kids and groceries. The problem in understanding consumer motives and values is that these variables depend more on what consumers *think and feel* rather than whom they are. Delving into consumer thoughts and feelings is the subject of psychographic segmentation.

Psychographic Segmentation   Psychographic segmentation deals with state-of-mind issues such as motives, attitudes, opinions, values, lifestyles, interests, and personality. These issues are more difficult to measure, and often require primary marketing research to properly determine the makeup and size of various market segments. Once the firm identifies one or more psychographic segments, they can be combined with demographic, geographic, or behavioral segmentation to create fully developed consumer profiles.

One of the most successful and well-known tools of psychographic segmentation is VALS, developed by Strategic Business Insights.[10] VALS, which stands for "values and lifestyles," divides adult U.S. consumers into one of eight profiles based on their level of resources and one of three primary consumption motives: ideals (knowledge and principles), achievement (demonstrating success to others), or self-expression (social or physical activity, variety, and risk taking). Exhibit 5.5 describes the eight VALS profiles. Many companies use VALS in a variety of marketing activities including new product development, product positioning, brand development, promotional strategy, and media placement. There is also a geographic version of VALS, called GeoVALS, which links each consumer profile with geographic information such as ZIP codes. This tool is quite useful in direct marketing campaigns and retail site selection.

EXHIBIT 5.5 VALS Consumer Profiles

Innovators

These consumers have abundant resources and high self-esteem. Innovators are successful, sophisticated consumers who have a taste for upscale, innovative, and specialized goods and services. Innovators are concerned about image as an expression of self, but not as an expression of status or power.

Example products: fine wines, upscale home furnishings, lawn maintenance services, recent technology, luxury automobiles

Thinkers

Thinkers are well-educated consumers who value order, knowledge, and responsibility. These consumers like to be as well informed about the products they buy as they are about world and national events. Although Thinkers have resources that give them many choices or options, they tend to be conservative consumers who look for practicality, durability, functionality, and value.

Example products: news and information services, low-emission vehicles, conservative homes and home furnishings

Achievers

The lifestyle of an Achiever is focused and structured around family, a place of worship, and career. Achievers are conventional, conservative, and respect authority and the status quo. These individuals are very active consumers who desire established, prestigious products and services that demonstrate their success. Achievers lead busy lives; hence, they value products that can save them time and effort.

Example products: SUVs, family vacations, products that promote career enhancement, online shopping, swimming pools

Experiencers

Experiencers are young, enthusiastic, and impulsive consumers who are motivated by self-expression. These consumers emphasize variety, excitement, the offbeat, and the risky. Experiencers enjoy looking good and buying "cool" products.

Example products: fashion, entertainment, sports/exercise, outdoor recreation and social activities

Believers

Believers are conservative, conventional consumers who hold steadfast beliefs based on traditional values related to family, religion, community, and patriotism. These consumers are predictable in that they follow established routines centered on family, community, or organizational membership. Believers prefer familiar and well-known American brands and tend to be very loyal customers.

Example products: membership in social, religious, or fraternal organizations; American made products; charitable organizations

continued

Strivers

Strivers are motivated by achievement, yet they lack the resources to meet all their desires. As a group, Strivers are trendy, fun loving, and concerned with the opinions and approval of others. These consumers see shopping as a social activity and an opportunity to demonstrate their purchasing power up to the limits imposed by their financial situations. Most Strivers think of themselves as having jobs rather than careers. *Example products:* stylish products, impulse items, credit cards, designer "knock-offs," shopping as entertainment

Makers

Makers, like Experiencers, are motivated by self-expression. However, these consumers experience the world by engaging in many do-it-yourself activities such as repairing their own cars, building houses, or growing and canning their own vegetables. Makers are practical consumers who value self-sufficiency and have the skills to back it up. Makers are also unimpressed by material possessions, new ideas, or big business. They live traditional lives and prefer to buy basic items. *Example products:* Auto parts, home-improvement supplies, gardening supplies, sewing supplies, discount retailers

Survivors

Survivors live narrowly focused lives and have few resources with which to cope. They are primarily concerned with safety, security, and meeting needs rather than fulfilling wants. As a group, Survivors are cautious consumers who represent a fairly small market for most products. They are loyal to favorite brands, especially if they can buy them on sale. *Example products:* Basic necessities and staples; old, established brands

Source: Strategic Business Insights, http://www.strategicbusinessinsights.com/vals/ustypes.shtml.

Psychographic segmentation is useful because it transcends purely descriptive characteristics to help explain personal motives, attitudes, emotions, and lifestyles directly connected to buying behavior. For example, companies such as Michelin and State Farm appeal to consumers motivated by issues such as safety, security, and protection when buying tires or insurance. Other firms, such as Subaru, Kia, and Hyundai, appeal to consumers whose values and opinions about transportation focus more on economy than status. Online degree programs appeal to consumers whose active lifestyles do not allow them to attend classes in the traditional sense.

Geographic Segmentation   Geographic characteristics often play a large part in developing market segments. For example, firms often find that their customers are geographically concentrated. Even ubiquitous products like Coca-Cola sell better in the southern United States than in other parts of the country. Consumer preferences for certain purchases based on geography are a primary consideration in developing trade areas for retailers such as grocery stores, gas stations, and dry cleaners. For example, geodemographic segmentation, or geoclustering, is an approach that looks at neighborhood profiles based on demographic, geographic, and lifestyle segmentation variables. One of the best-known geoclustering tools is Nielsen's PRIZM segmentation system, which classifies every neighborhood in the United States into one of 14 different demographic and behavioral clusters. The "Big Fish, Small Pond" cluster contains older, upper-class, highly educated professionals who enjoy success. The adults in this cluster are typically 45 to 64 years old, empty-nesting couples with a median household income of just over

$87,000. They are prime targets for financial services, upscale cars, and charitable causes. PRIZM is useful to marketers because it allows them to focus their marketing programs only in areas where their products are more likely to be accepted. Not only does this make their marketing activities more successful, it also greatly reduces marketing expenditures.[11]

Segmenting Business Markets

One of the most basic methods of segmenting business markets involves the four types of markets we discussed earlier in the chapter: commercial markets, reseller markets, government markets, and institutional markets. Marketers may focus on one or more of these markets, as each has different requirements. However, even within one type of market, marketers will discover that buying firms have unique and varying characteristics. In these cases, further segmentation using additional variables might be needed to further refine the needs and characteristics of business customers. For example, Canon sells a line of wide format printers aimed at CAD and architectural design users, as well as other segments such as fine art, photography, office, and signage. Each segment has different uses for wide format printing, as well as different requirements with respect to the types of inks used in the printers. In addition to the types of business markets, firms can also segment business buyers with respect to:

- **Type of Organization**. Different types of organizations may require different and specific marketing programs, such as product modifications, different distribution and delivery structures, or different selling strategies. A glass manufacturer, for example, might segment customers into several groups, such as car manufacturers, furniture makers, window manufacturers, or repair and maintenance contractors.
- **Organizational Characteristics**. The needs of business buyers often vary based on their size, geographic location, or product usage. Large buyers often command price discounts and structural relationships that are appropriate for their volume of purchases. Likewise, buyers in different parts of the country, as well as in different nations, may have varying product requirements, specifications, or distribution arrangements. Product usage is also important. Computer manufacturers often segment markets based on how their products will be used. For example, K–12 educational institutions have different requirements for computers and software than do major research universities.
- **Benefits Sought or Buying Processes**. Organizations differ with respect to the benefits they seek and the buying processes they use to acquire products. Some business buyers seek only the lowest cost provider, while others require extensive product support and service. Additionally, some businesses buy using highly structured processes, most likely through their buying center. Others may use online auctions or even highly informal processes.
- **Personal and Psychological Characteristics**. The personal characteristics of the buyers themselves often play a role in segmentation decisions. Buyers will vary according to risk tolerance, buying influence, job responsibilities, and decision styles.
- **Relationship Intensity**. Business markets can also be segmented based on the strength and longevity of the relationship with the firm. Many organizations structure their selling organization using this approach with one person or team dedicated to the most critical relationships. Other members of the selling organization may be involved in business development strategies to seek out new customers.

As we have seen, segmentation in business markets addresses many of the same issues found in consumer markets. Despite some differences and additional considerations that must be addressed, the foundation remains the same. Marketers must understand the needs of their potential customers and how these needs differ across segments within the total market.

Target Marketing Strategies

Once the firm has completed segmenting a market, it must then evaluate each segment to determine its attractiveness and whether it offers opportunities that match the firm's capabilities and resources. Remember that just because a market segment meets all criteria for viability does not mean the firm should pursue it. Attractive segments might be dropped for several reasons, including a lack of resources, no synergy with the firm's mission, overwhelming competition in the segment, an impending technology shift, or ethical and legal concerns over targeting a particular segment. Based on its analysis of each segment, the firm's current and anticipated situation, and a comprehensive SWOT analysis, a firm might consider five basic strategies for target market selection. Exhibit 5.6 depicts the following strategies.[12]

- **Single Segment Targeting**. Firms use single segment targeting when their capabilities are intrinsically tied to the needs of a specific market segment. Many consider the firms using this targeting strategy to be true specialists in a particular product category. Good examples include New Belgium Brewing (craft beer), Porsche, and Ray-Ban. These and other firms using single segment targeting are successful because they fully understand their customers' needs, preferences, and lifestyles. These firms also constantly strive to improve quality and customer satisfaction by continuously refining their products to meet changing customer preferences.
- **Selective Targeting.** Firms that have multiple capabilities in many different product categories use selective targeting successfully. This strategy has several advantages, including diversification of the firm's risk and the ability to cherry pick only the most attractive market segment opportunities. Procter & Gamble uses selective targeting to offer customers many different products in the family care, household care, and personal care markets. Besides the familiar deodorants, laundry detergents, and hair care products, P&G also sells products in the cosmetics, snack food and beverages, cologne, and prescription drug markets. One of the keys to P&G's success is that the company does not try to be all things for all customers. The company carefully selects product/market combinations where its capabilities match customers' needs.
- **Mass Market Targeting.** Only the largest firms have the capability to execute mass market targeting, which involves the development of multiple marketing programs to

---

EXHIBIT 5.6   **Basic Strategies for Target Market Selection**

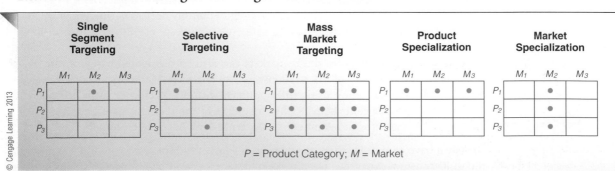

P = Product Category; M = Market

© Cengage Learning 2013

serve all customer segments simultaneously. For example, Coca-Cola offers roughly 400 branded beverages across many segments that fulfill different consumer needs in over 200 countries around the world. Likewise, Frito-Lay sells hundreds of different varieties of snack foods around the world.

- **Product Specialization**. Firms engage in product specialization when their expertise in a product category can be leveraged across many different market segments. These firms can adapt product specifications to match the different needs of individual customer groups. For example, many consider Littmann Stethoscopes, a division of 3M, as the worldwide leader in auscultation technology. Littmann offers high performance electronic stethoscopes for cardiologists, specially designed stethoscopes for pediatric/infant use, lightweight stethoscopes for simple physical assessment, and a line of stethoscopes for nursing and medical students. The company also offers a line of veterinary stethoscopes.[13]

- **Market Specialization**. Firms engage in market specialization when their intimate knowledge and expertise in one market allows them to offer customized marketing programs that not only deliver needed products, but also provide needed solutions to customers' problems. The Follett Corporation is a prime example. Follett specializes in the education market and serves over 800 schools, colleges, and universities in the U.S. and Canada. The company's slogan "Simplifying the delivery of education everywhere" is based on the firm's goal to be the leading provider of educational solutions, services and products to schools, libraries, colleges, students and life-long learners.[14]

In addition to targeting a subset of current customers within the product/market, firms can also take steps to target noncustomers. As we discussed in Chapter 3, there are many reasons why noncustomers do not purchase a firm's products. These reasons can include unique customer needs, better competing alternatives, high switching costs, lack of product awareness, or the existence of long-held assumptions about a product. For example, products associated with tooth whitening were at one time associated only with dentists. Consequently, consumers were hesitant to use these products due to the expense, effort, and anxiety involved. Oral care companies were able to break this tradition and reach out to noncustomers by developing high-quality, low-price over-the-counter alternatives that were much easier to purchase. Today, these at-home tooth-whitening products—such as Procter & Gamble's Crest Whitestrips—are a $300 million market in the U.S.[15]

As this example illustrates, the key to targeting noncustomers lies in understanding the reasons why they do not buy, and then finding ways to remove these obstacles. Removing obstacles to purchase, whether they exist in product design, affordability, distribution convenience, or product awareness, is a major strategic issue in developing an effective marketing program. Over the next two chapters, we turn our attention to the important strategic issues involved in creating the marketing program, including branding and positioning the product offering.

Lessons from Chapter 5

Buyer behavior in consumer markets:
- is often irrational and unpredictable as consumers often say one thing but do another.
- can progress through five stages: need recognition, information search, evaluation of alternatives, the purchase decision, and postpurchase evaluation.

- does not always follow these stages in sequence and may even skip stages en route to the purchase.
- may be characterized by loyalty where consumers simply purchase the same product that they bought last time.
- often involves a parallel sequence of activities associated with finding the most suitable merchant. That is, while

consumers consider which product to buy, they also consider where they might buy it.

- may occur with only one merchant for a particular product category if the consumer is fiercely loyal to that merchant.

Keys to understanding consumer needs and wants:

- Defining needs as "necessities" has limitations because everyone has a different perspective on what constitutes a need.
- Needs occur when a consumer's current level of satisfaction does not equal the desired level of satisfaction.
- Wants are a consumer's desire for a specific product that will satisfy a need.
- The firm must always understand the basic needs fulfilled by its products. This understanding allows the firm to segment markets and create marketing programs that can translate consumer needs into wants for their specific products.
- Although some products and markets can be segmented on the basis of needs alone, most product categories are marketed on the basis of wants, not need fulfillment.
- Wants are not the same thing as demand, as demand occurs only when the consumer's ability and willingness to pay backs up a want for a specific product.

The information search stage of the consumer buying process:

- can be passive—where the consumer becomes more attentive and receptive to information—or active—where the consumer engages in a more aggressive information search by seeking additional information.
- depends on a number of issues, including the degree of risk involved in the purchase, the amount of expertise or experience the consumer has with the product category, and the actual cost of the search in terms of time and money.
- culminates in an evoked set of suitable buying alternatives.

During the evaluation of alternatives:

- consumers essentially translate their needs into wants for specific products or brands.
- consumers evaluate products as bundles of attributes that have varying abilities to satisfy their needs.
- the priority of each consumer's choice criteria can change.
- marketers must ensure that their product is in the evoked set of potential alternatives by constantly reminding consumers of their company and its product offerings.

During the purchase stage of the buying process:

- it is important to remember that the intention to purchase and the actual act of buying are distinct concepts.
- the key issues for marketers are product availability and possession utility.

During postpurchase evaluation:

- the outcome of the buying process is linked to the development of long-term customer relationships. Marketers must closely follow customers' responses to monitor the product's performance and its ability to meet customers' expectations.
- consumers will experience one of four potential outcomes: delight, satisfaction, dissatisfaction, or cognitive dissonance.

Overall, the consumer buying process can be affected by:

- the complexity of the purchase and decision-making process.
- individual factors, such as age, life cycle, occupation, socioeconomic status, perceptions, motives, interests, attitudes, opinions, and lifestyles.
- social influences such as culture, subculture, social class, family, reference groups, and opinion leaders.
- situational influences, such as physical and spatial influences, social and interpersonal influences, time, purchase task or usage, and the consumer's disposition.

Business markets:

- purchase products for use in their operations, such as acquiring raw materials to produce finished goods or buying office supplies or leasing cars.
- consist of four types of buyers: commercial markets, reseller markets, government markets, and institutional markets.
- possess four unique characteristics not typically found in consumer markets:
  - the buying center: economic buyers, technical buyers, and users.
  - hard and soft costs: soft costs (downtime, opportunity costs, human resource costs) are just as important as hard costs (monetary price or purchase costs).
  - reciprocity: business buyers and sellers often buy products from each other.
  - mutual dependence: sole-source or limited-source buying makes both buying and selling firms mutually dependent.

The business buying process:

- follows a well-defined sequence of stages, including: (1) problem recognition, (2) development of product specifications, (3) vendor identification and qualification, (4) solicitation of proposals or bids, (5) vendor selection, (6) order processing, and (7) vendor performance review.
- can be affected by a number of factors, including environmental conditions, organizational factors, and interpersonal and individual factors.

Market segmentation:

- is the process of dividing the total market for a particular product or product category into relatively homogeneous segments or groups.

- should create groups where the members are similar to each other, but where the groups are dissimilar from each other.
- involves a fundamental decision of whether to segment at all.
- typically allows firms to be more successful due to the fact that they can tailor products to meet the needs or requirements of a particular market segment.

Traditional market segmentation approaches:

- have been used successfully for decades, are not out-of-date, and are used by many of today's most successful firms.
- are sometimes used in combination with newer approaches by the same firm, depending on the brand/product or market in question.

Mass marketing:

- involves no segmentation whatsoever as it is aimed at the total (whole) market for a particular product.
- is an undifferentiated approach that assumes that all customers in the market have similar needs and wants that can be reasonably satisfied with a single marketing program.
- works best when the needs of an entire market are relatively homogeneous.
- is advantageous in terms of production efficiency and lower marketing costs.
- is inherently risky because a standardized product is vulnerable to competitors that offer specialized products that better match customers' needs.

Differentiated marketing:

- involves dividing the total market into groups of customers having relatively common or homogeneous needs, and attempting to develop a marketing program that appeals to one or more of these groups.
- may be necessary when customer needs are similar within a single group but their needs differ across groups.
- involves two options: the multisegment approach and the market concentration approach.

Niche marketing:

- involves focusing marketing efforts on one small, well-defined market segment or niche that has a unique, specific set of needs.
- requires that firms understand and meet the needs of target customers so completely that, despite the small size of the niche, the firm's substantial share makes the segment highly profitable.

Individualized segmentation approaches:

- have become viable due to advances in technology, particularly communication technology and the Internet.

- are possible because organizations now have the ability to track customers with a high degree of specificity.
- allow firms to combine demographic data with past and current purchasing behavior so they can tweak their marketing programs in ways that allow them to precisely match customers needs, wants, and preferences.
- will become even more important in the future because their focus on individual customers makes them critical to the development and maintenance of long-term relationships.
- can be prohibitively expensive to deliver.
- depend on two important considerations: automated delivery of the marketing program and personalization.

One-to-one marketing:

- involves the creation of an entirely unique product or marketing program for each customer in the target segment.
- is common in business markets where unique programs and/or systems are designed for each customer.
- is growing rapidly in consumer markets, particularly in luxury and custom-made products, as well as in services and electronic commerce.

Mass customization:

- refers to providing unique products and solutions to individual customers on a mass scale.
- is now cost effective and practical due to advances in supply chain management, including real-time inventory control.
- is used quite often in business markets, especially in electronic procurement systems.

Permission marketing:

- is different from one-to-one marketing because customers choose to become a member of the firm's target market.
- is commonly executed via the opt-in e-mail list, where customers permit a firm to send periodic e-mail about goods and services that they have an interest in purchasing.
- has a major advantage in that customers who opt-in are already interested in the goods and services offered by the firm.
- allows a firm to precisely target individuals, thereby eliminating the problem of wasted marketing effort and expense.

Successful segmentation:

- requires that market segments fulfill five related criteria: segments must be identifiable and measurable, substantial, accessible, responsive, and viable and sustainable.
- involves avoiding ethically and legally sensitive segments that are profitable but not viable in a business sense.

- involves avoiding potentially viable segments that do not match the firm's expertise or mission.

Identifying market segments:

- involves selecting the most relevant variables to identify and define the target market, many of which come from the situation analysis section of the marketing plan.
- involves the isolation of individual characteristics that distinguish one or more segments from the total market. These segments must have relatively homogeneous needs.
- in consumer markets involves the examination of factors that fall into one of four general categories:
  - behavioral segmentation; the most powerful approach because it uses actual consumer behavior or product usage helps to make distinctions among market segments.
  - demographic segmentation; which divides markets using factors such as gender, age, income, and education.
  - psychographic segmentation; which deals with state-of-mind issues such as motives, attitudes, opinions, values, lifestyles, interests, and personality.

- geographic segmentation; which is often most useful when combined with other segmentation variables. One of the best examples is geodemographic segmentation, or geoclustering.
- in business markets is often based on type of market (commercial, reseller, government, or institutional) or on other characteristics such as type of organization, organizational characteristics, benefits sought or buying processes, personal or psychological characteristics, or relationship intensity.

Target marketing strategies:

- are based on an evaluation of the attractiveness of each segment and whether each offers opportunities that match the firm's capabilities and resources.
- include single segment targeting, selective targeting, mass market targeting, product specialization, and market specialization.
- should also consider issues related to noncustomers such as reasons why they do not buy and finding ways to remove obstacles to purchase.

Questions for Discussion

1. Many people criticize marketing as being manipulative based on the argument that marketing activities create needs where none previously existed. Marketers of SUVs, tobacco products, diet programs, exercise equipment, and luxury products are typically the most criticized. Given what you now know about the differences between needs and wants, do you agree with these critics? Explain.
2. Many consumers and consumer advocates are critical of individualized segmentation approaches due to personal privacy concerns. They argue that technology has made it far too easy to track buyer behavior and personal information. Marketers

counter that individualized segmentation can lead to privacy abuses, but that the benefits to both consumers and marketers far outweigh the risks. Where do you stand on this issue? What are the benefits and risks associated with individualized segmentation?
3. As we have seen thus far, the size of the consuming population over the age of 50 continues to grow. What are some of the current ethical issues involved in targeting this age group? As this group gets older, will these issues become more or less important? Explain.

Exercises

1. Consider the last purchase you made in these categories: personal electronics, clothing, and vacation destination. To what extent was your purchase decision influenced by decision-making complexity, individual influences, social influences, and situational influences? What specific issues were the most influential in making the decision? How could a marketer have swayed your decision in each case?
2. One of the most exciting advances in market segmentation is the increasing use of geographic information systems (GIS) to map target markets. Go to www.gis.com and get a feel for the use of GIS in business and other fields. Then, go to http://mapapps.esri.com/create-map/index.html and enter your ZIP code to make a demographic map about where you live. What are the advantages of using GIS in market segmentation?

3. As discussed in the chapter, VALS is one of the most popular proprietary segmentation tools used in marketing segmentation. Go to the VALS website (www.strategicbusinessinsights.com/vals/ presurvey.shtml) and take the free VALS survey. Do you agree with the survey results? Why or why not?

End Notes

1. These facts are from Stephen Baker, "Data Mining Moves to Human Resources," *BusinessWeek Online*, March 12, 2009 (http://www.businessweek.com/magazine/content/09_12/b4124046224092.htm); Charles Duhigg, "How Companies Learn Your Secrets," *New York Times*, February 16, 2012 (http://www.nytimes.com/2012/02/19/magazine/shopping-habits.html?_r=2&pagewanted=1&hp); Tim Ferguson, "How Europeans are Using Data Mining," *BusinessWeek Online*, May 17, 2009 (http://www.businessweek.com/global biz/content/may2009/gb20090517_529807.htm); Kashmir Hill, "How Target Figured Out a Teen Girl Was Pregnant Before Her Father Did," *Forbes*, February 16, 2012 (http://www.forbes.com/sites/kashmirhill/2012/02/16/how-target-figured-out-a-teen-girl-was-pregnant-before-her-father-did); "Math Will Rock Your World," *BusinessWeek*, January 23, 2006; and Chris Taylor, "Imagining the Google Future," *Business 2.0*, February 1, 2006 (http://money.cnn.com/magazines/business2/business2_archive/2006/01/01/8368125/index.htm).

2. These facts are from Robert Berner, "The Ethnography of Marketing," *BusinessWeek Online*, June 12, 2006 (http://businessweek.com/innovate/content/jun2006/id20060612_919537.htm); Jordan Crook, "This is Everything You Need to Know About Pinterest," *TechCrunch*, March 14, 2012 (http://techcrunch.com/2012/03/14/this-is-everything-you-need-to-know-about-pinterest-infographic); and Grant McCracken, "Pinterest as Free Market Research," *Harvard Business Review Blog*, February 17, 2012 (http://blogs.hbr.org/cs/2012/02/pinterest_is_free_market_resea.html).

3. Peter Burrows, "How Microsoft is Fighting Back," *BusinessWeek Online*, April 9, 2009 (http://www.businessweek.com/magazine/content/09_16/b4127063278613.htm); and Cornelius Rahn and Diana ben-Aaron, "Microsoft Plans More Ads for Windows Phone to 'Smoke' Rivals," *BusinessWeek Online*, February 29, 2012 (http://www.businessweek.com/news/2012-02-29/microsoft-plans-more-ads-for-windows-phone-to-smoke-rivals.html).

4. Alan Ohnsman and Sookyung Seo, "Korea's Kia is Drawing Drivers," *BusinessWeek Online*, November 24, 2010 (http://www.businessweek.com/magazine/content/10_49/b4206023212567.htm).

5. Stephanie Clifford, "Would You Like a Smile with That?" *New York Times*, August 6, 2011 (http://www.nytimes.com/2011/08/07/business/pret-a-manger-with-new-fast-food-ideas-gains-a-foothold-in-united-states.html?pagewanted=all).

6. These facts are from Matthew Boyle, "Joe Galli's Army," *Fortune*, December 30, 2002, 135; and the Sterilite Corporate website (http://www.sterilite.com/about_sterilite.html), accessed March 9, 2012.

7. These facts are from "2010 Census Shows America's Diversity," U.S. Census Bureau Press Release, March 24, 2011 (http://2010.census.gov/news/releases/operations/cb11-cn125.html); Sam Fahmy, "Despite Recession, Hispanic and Asian Buying Power Expected to Surge in U.S.," Selig Center for Economic Growth, Terry College of Business, University of Georgia, November 4, 2010 (http://www.terry.uga.edu/news/releases/2010/minority-buying-power-report.html); Burt Helm, "Ethnic Marketing: McDonald's is Lovin' It," *BusinessWeek Online*, July 8, 2010 (http://www.businessweek.com/magazine/content/10_29/b4187022876832.htm); and Esther Novak, "We the People: A Memo on Multiculturalism," *BusinessWeek Online*, December 9, 2008 (http://www.businessweek.com/bwdaily/dnflash/content/dec2008/db2008128_536371.htm).

8. Curves website (http://www.curvesinformation.com), accessed March 9, 2012; The Little Gym website (http://www.thelittlegym.com/Pages/our-story.aspx), accessed March 9, 2012; and Allison Van Dusen, "Is a Custom Gym Membership for You?" *Forbes Online*, September 9, 2008 (http://www.forbes.com/2008/09/29/custom-gym-popularity-forbeslife-cx_avd_0929health.html).

9. These facts are from Salynn Boyles, "Kids' Cereals: Some Are 50% Sugar," WebMD, October 1, 2008 (http://www.webmd.com/food-recipes/news/20081001/kids-cereals-some-are-50-percent-sugar); "Froot Loops Not Made of Real Fruit: The Cereal Lawsuits," *Law Vibe Blog*, May 1, 2010 (http://lawvibe.com/froot-loops-not-made-of-real-fruit-the-cereal-lawsuits); and Jennifer Mariani and Matt Schottmiller, "2009 Marketing and the Cereal Industry Case," The University of New Mexico.

10. This discussion is based on information obtained from the VALS website (http://www.strategicbusinessinsights.com/vals).

11. These facts are from the PRIZM website (http://www.claritas.com/MyBestSegments/Default.jsp).

12. This material is adapted from Charles W. Lamb, Jr., Joseph F. Hair, Jr., and Carl McDaniel, *Marketing*, 7th ed. (Mason, OH: South-Western, 2004), 228–231; and Philip Kotler, *A Framework for Marketing Management*, 2nd ed. (Upper Saddle River, NJ: Prentice-Hall, 2003), 181–185.

13. These facts are from 3M Littmann Stethoscopes (http://solutions.3m.com/wps/portal/3M/en_US/3M-Littmann/stethoscope), accessed July 27, 2012.

14. These facts are from Follett (http://www.follett.com), accessed March 9, 2012.

15. These facts are from Allison Van Dusen, "The Price of a Perfect Smile," *Forbes.com*, January 17, 2008 (http://www.forbes.com/2008/01/16/health-smile-perfect-forbeslife-cx_avd_0117health.html).

CHAPTER **6**

The Marketing Program

Introduction

With a clearly defined target market in hand, the organization turns its attention toward developing a marketing program that will fulfill the target's needs and wants better than the competition. When we say *marketing program*, we are referring to the strategic combination of the four basic marketing mix elements: product, price, distribution, and promotion. Although each element is vitally important to the success of the marketing strategy, the product usually receives the most attention because it is most responsible for fulfilling the customers' needs and wants. However, since customers' needs and wants are multifaceted, we prefer to think of the outcome of the marketing program as a complete "offering" that consists of an array of physical (tangible), service (intangible), and symbolic (perceptual) attributes designed to satisfy customers' needs and wants. In other words, the best marketing strategy is likely to be one that combines the product, price, distribution, and promotion elements in a way that maximizes the tangible, intangible, and perceptual attributes of the complete offering.

Good marketing strategy considers all four elements of the marketing program and the offering rather than emphasizing a single element. We have noted throughout this text how most firms today compete in rather mature markets characterized by commoditization. In these cases, the core product (the element that satisfies the basic customer need) typically becomes incapable of differentiating the offering from those of the competition. Consequently, most organizations work to enhance the service and symbolic elements of their offerings by changing price, distribution, or promotion in order to stand out from the crowd. As described in *Beyond the Pages 6.1*, this makes marketing strategy even more challenging for the firm. It also requires that the marketing program be considered holistically rather than sequentially. This means that products must be designed with an eye toward how they will be priced, distributed, and promoted. It does a company no good to develop a standout product that is not price competitive, difficult to ship or store, and hard to convey in promotional messages. All four elements of the marketing program must be developed simultaneously.

Beyond the Pages 6.1

Can Good Marketing Save Barnes & Noble?[1]

Like many companies in the Internet economy, Barnes & Noble is at a crossroads. The largest U.S. bookstore chain made retailing history when it opened the first category-killer bookstore in the late 1980s. At that time, the store was five times the size of a typical bookstore. Customers flocked to the spacious and comfortable stores that offered a comprehensive inventory of books, music, and DVDs. Most of the stores also included a café where customers could have coffee, a snack, and enjoy a good book. Barnes & Noble had successfully converted the small, mall-based bookstore to a true destination for book-loving customers.

But that was in the 1980s and 1990s. As the Internet economy took off in the late 1990s and into the 2000s, Barnes & Noble was forced to move online. At the launch of Barnesandnoble.com in 1997, the company offered a staggering 1 million titles for immediate delivery, plus access to a nationwide network offering over 30 million listings from out-of-print, rare, and used book dealers. This move came at roughly the same time as the launch of an unusual online bookstore called Amazon.com. Amazon offered a limited selection and was a pure Internet-based company, so few people gave the company any chance of succeeding. Plus, Amazon was losing money. At the time, Barnes & Noble wasn't worried about Amazon because their book superstore concept was a huge success. And, everyone knew that book lovers preferred to browse in the store, sit in comfortable chairs, and enjoy a coffee. Didn't they?

Fast-forward to today and we all know that Amazon has been remarkably successful. So much so that other book retailers, namely Borders and Waldenbooks, have since closed. We also know that both Amazon and Barnes & Noble sell more e-books than physical books. E-readers such as Amazon's Kindle and Barnes & Noble's Nook (plus a variety of tablets like the iPad) are wildly popular among a variety of target customers, old and young. In addition, other competitors have entered the market. Apple, for example, offers e-books through its iBooks app on the iPad and iPhone. Google now offers free access to millions of public domain books. The rapid changes in the book retailing market have forced Barnes & Noble to adapt, and these changes now threaten the future of the once-dominant book retailer.

What can Barnes & Noble do to remain relevant and viable in this market? To answer that question, we need to look at the company's current marketing program:

- **Products**. Barnes & Noble competes in a highly commoditized product market. Books, whether offered in print or as e-books, are the same no matter where they are purchased. Barnes & Noble does have an advantage in the textbook market, but the differences between its selection and the selection at Amazon are disappearing fast. Amazon, on the other hand, offers a very broad selection of products ranging from electronics to beauty supplies. Barnes & Noble offers a much narrower variety of books, music, movies, and some toys. Both companies' e-readers are competitively matched in terms of features and benefits.

- **Pricing**. Given the commoditized nature of the market, price would be one logical place to compete against Amazon and other competitors. However, there is very little price differentiation in the book market. This is especially true with respect to e-books, where prices are roughly the same across multiple competitors.

- **Distribution**. Barnes & Noble has invested a lot of resources into its distribution system. However, Amazon is also no slouch at supply chain management. One area where Barnes & Noble has a distinct advantage is on college campuses. The company operates over 640 college bookstores serving 4 million students and 250,000 faculty in all 50 states. The company's physical footprint also includes roughly 700 traditional Barnes & Noble stores that draw millions of customers annually. These stores are still destinations for true book lovers, something that Amazon cannot copy.

- **Promotion**. It is very hard to build a competitive advantage based on promotion alone, and neither Barnes & Noble nor Amazon stand out per se. Both have strong brands and positioning. Both also offer membership programs. However, Amazon's program—Amazon Prime—beats Barnes & Noble by a wide margin. For a $79 per year fee, Prime members get free two-day shipping on millions of products, free instant streaming of thousands

continued

of movies and television programs, and the ability to borrow one Kindle e-book each month. By contrast, Barnes & Noble's members get free shipping and small discounts on books and Nook e-readers.

It is clear that carving out a strong competitive advantage is difficult for any book retailer. Barnes & Noble has an edge in college campus distribution and a loyal customer following. Amazon, however, has an edge in terms of the total digital ecosystem and a loyal following of price conscious customers. In some ways the two companies compete using different paradigms.

Despite the challenges, one other thing Barnes & Noble has in its favor is the deep distrust of Amazon by companies such as Microsoft, Apple, and Google, who see Amazon as a major threat. This fact prompted Microsoft to invest $300 million in Barnes & Noble in exchange for roughly 18 percent of the company's digital and college businesses. In return, Barnes & Noble will spin off its digital and college businesses into a new subsidiary, which will be co-owned by Barnes & Noble and Microsoft. The infusion of new capital is critical for Barnes & Noble in order to expand its growing e-book business. For Microsoft, access to a large digital library is critical to its launch of Windows 8 and the Surface tablet. Moving forward, it will be interesting to watch how a Barnes & Noble/Microsoft partnership will use its combined marketing muscle to compete against Amazon.

In this chapter, we examine the four elements of the marketing program in more detail. Issues such as product design, affordability, distribution convenience, and product awareness are major considerations in developing an effective marketing program. Problems in any one area can create obstacles that customers may be unwilling to overlook as they search for the best offering that will fulfill their needs.

Product Strategy

Of all the strategic decisions to be made in the marketing plan, the design, development, branding, and positioning of the product are perhaps the most critical. At the heart of every organization lie one or more products that define what the organization does and why it exists. As we stated in Chapter 1, the term "product" refers to something that buyers can acquire via exchange to satisfy a need or a want. This is a very broad definition that allows us to classify many different things as products: food, entertainment, information, people, places, ideas, etc. An organization's product offering is typically composed of many different elements—usually some combination of tangible goods, services, ideas, image, or even people. As we consider product decisions here, it is important to remember that product offerings in and of themselves have little value to customers. Rather, an offering's real value comes from its ability to deliver benefits that enhance a customer's situation or solve a customer's problems. For example, customers don't buy pest control; they buy a bug-free environment. Lexus customers don't buy a car; they buy luxury, status, comfort, and social appeal. Students who frequent a local nightclub are not thirsty; they want to fulfill their need for social interaction. Likewise, companies do not need computers; they need to store, retrieve, distribute, network, and analyze data and information. Marketers who keep their sights set on developing product offerings that truly meet the needs of the target market are more likely to be successful.

Strategic Issues in the Product Portfolio

Products fall into two general categories. Products used for personal use and enjoyment are called consumer products; while those purchased for resale, to make other products, or for use in a firm's operations are called business products. Exhibit 6.1 illustrates

EXHIBIT 6.1   Types of Consumer and Business Products

	Type of Product	Examples
Consumer Products	**Convenience Products** Inexpensive, routinely purchased products that consumers spend little time and effort in acquiring.	Soft drinks Candy and gum Gasoline Dry cleaning
	Shopping Products Products that consumers will spend time and effort to obtain. Consumers shop different options to compare prices, features, and service.	Appliances Furniture Clothing Vacations
	Specialty Products Unique, one-of-a-kind products that consumers will spend considerable time, effort, and money to acquire.	Sports memorabilia Antiques Plastic surgery Luxury items
	Unsought Products Products that consumers are unaware of or a product that consumers do not consider purchasing until a need arises.	True innovations Repair services Emergency medicine Insurance
Business Products	**Raw Materials** Basic natural materials that become part of a finished product. They are purchased in very large quantities based on specifications or grades.	Iron ore Chemicals Agricultural products Wood pulp
	Component Parts Finished items that become part of a larger finished product. They are purchased based on specifications or industry standards.	Spark plugs Computer chips Pane glass Hard drives
	Process Materials Finished products that become unidentifiable upon their inclusion in the finished product.	Food additives Wood sealants Paint colorings
	Maintenance, Repair, and Operating Products Products that are used in business processes or operations but do not become part of the finished product.	Office supplies Janitorial services Building security Bathroom supplies
	Accessory Equipment Products that help facilitate production or operations but do not become part of the finished product.	Tools Office equipment Computers Furniture
	Installations Major purchases, typically of a physical nature, that are based on customized solutions including installation/construction, training, financing, maintenance, and repair.	Enterprise software Buildings Heat and air systems
	Business Services Intangible products that support business operations. These purchases often occur as a part of outsourcing decisions.	Legal services Accounting services Consulting Research services

Source: This material is adapted from William M. Pride and O.C. Ferrell, *Marketing* (Mason, OH: Cengage Learning, 2010), pp. 285–289.

examples of each type of product category. Although the distinction may seem simplistic, it is important in a strategic sense because the type of product in question can influence its pricing, distribution, or promotion. For example, marketing strategy for consumer convenience products must maximize availability and ease of purchase—both important distribution considerations. The strategy associated with consumer shopping products often focuses more on differentiation through image and symbolic attributes—both important branding and promotion issues. Marketing strategies for raw materials are especially challenging because these products are commodities by definition. Here, conformance to exacting product specifications and low acquisition costs are the keys to effective strategy. Many business products are also characterized by derived demand; where the demand for the product is derived from, or dependent upon, the demand for other business or consumer products. For example, the demand for business products such as glass, steel, rubber, chrome, leather, and carpeting is dependent upon the demand for automobiles.

It is very rare for a company to sell only one product. Most firms sell a variety of products to fulfill a variety of different needs. In general terms, the products sold by a firm can be described with respect to product lines and product mixes. A *product line* consists of a group of closely related product items. As shown in Exhibit 6.2, Procter & Gamble sells a number of famous brands in its line of household care products, including Tide, Bounty, Pringles, and Duracell. Most companies sell a variety of different product lines. The different product lines at General Motors carry well-known brand names like Corvette, Chevrolet, Cadillac, and Buick. Likewise, FedEx offers a number of logistics and supply chain services in its family of brands, such as FedEx Express, FedEx Ground, and FedEx Freight. A firm's *product mix* or *portfolio* is the total group of products offered by the company. For example, Procter & Gamble's entire product portfolio consists of beauty and grooming products, health and wellness products, baby and family products, and pet nutrition and care products in addition to the products in its household care line.

Decisions regarding product lines and product mixes are important strategic considerations for most firms. One of these important decisions is the number of product lines to offer, referred to as the width or variety of the product mix. By offering a wide variety of product lines, the firm can diversify its risk across a portfolio of product offerings.

EXHIBIT 6.2   Procter & Gamble's Portfolio of Household Care Products

	Product Mix Width (Variety)					
	Dish Washing	Household Cleaners	Batteries	Laundry and Fabric Care	Paper Products	Snacks
Product Mix Depth (Assortment)	Ariel Dawn Cascade	Mr. Clean Bounty Swiffer	Duracell	Tide Cheer Bounce Gain Downy Dreft Era Febreze Bold Ace	Charmin Bounty Puffs	Pringles

Source: From the Procter & Gamble website (http://www.pg.com/en_US/brands/household_care/index.shtml), accessed May 17, 2012.

Also, a wide product mix can be used to capitalize on the strength and reputation of the firm. Sony, for example, enjoys this advantage as it uses its name to stake out a strong position in electronics, music, and movies. The second important decision involves the depth of each product line. Sometimes called *assortment*, product line depth is an important marketing tool. Firms can attract a wide range of customers and market segments by offering a deep assortment of products in a specific line. Each brand or product in the assortment can be used to fulfill different customer needs. For example, Hilton, Inc. offers ten different lodging brands—including Hilton, Hilton Garden Inn, Hampton Inn, Conrad, and Embassy Suites—that cater to different segments of the hospitality market.

Although offering a large portfolio of products can make the coordination of marketing activities more challenging and expensive, it also creates a number of important benefits:

- **Economies of Scale**. Offering many different product lines can create economies of scale in production, bulk buying, and promotion. Many firms advertise using an umbrella theme for all products in the line. Nike's "Just Do It" and Maxwell House's "Good to the Last Drop" are examples of this. The single theme covering the entire product line saves considerably on promotional expenses.
- **Package Uniformity**. When all packages in a product line have the same look and feel, customers can locate the firm's products more quickly. It also becomes easier for the firm to coordinate and integrate promotion and distribution. For example, Duracell batteries all have the same copper look with black and copper packaging.
- **Standardization**. Product lines often use the same component parts. For example, Toyota's Camry and Highlander use many of the same chassis and engine components. This greatly reduces Toyota's manufacturing and inventory handling costs.
- **Sales and Distribution Efficiency**. When a firm offers many different product lines, sales personnel can offer a full range of choices and options to customers. For the same reason, channel intermediaries are more accepting of a product line than they are of individual products.
- **Equivalent Quality Beliefs**. Customers typically expect and believe that all products in a product line are about equal in terms of quality and performance. This is a major advantage for a firm that offers a well-known and respected line of products. For example, Crest's portfolio of oral care products all enjoys the same reputation for high quality.

A firm's product portfolio must be carefully managed to reflect changes in customers' preferences and the introduction of competitive products. Product offerings may be modified to change one or more characteristics that enhance quality, style, or lower the product's price. Firms may introduce product line extensions that allow it to compete more broadly in an industry. The recent trend of flavored soft drinks, such as Vanilla Coke, Diet Pepsi Vanilla, Sprite Zero, and Dr. Pepper Cherry Vanilla, is a good example of this. Sometimes, a firm may decide that a product or product line has become obsolete or is just not competitive against other products. When this happens, the firm can decide to contract the product line, as GM did when it dropped its Pontiac, Saturn, and Hummer divisions.

The Challenges of Service Products

It is important to remember that products can be intangible services and ideas as well as tangible goods. Service firms such as airlines, hospitals, movie theaters, and hair stylists, as well as nonprofit organizations, charitable causes, and government agencies, all develop and implement marketing strategies designed to match their portfolio of intangible products to the needs of target markets. Products lie on a continuum ranging from tangible-dominant goods (salt, soap) to intangible-dominant services (education, consulting). Firms lying closer to the intangible end of this spectrum face unique challenges in developing marketing strategy. These challenges are the direct result of the unique characteristics of services as shown in Exhibit 6.3. Obviously, the primary difference between a good and a service is that a service is intangible. Some services, such as business consulting and education, are almost completely intangible, while others have more tangible elements. The services provided by UPS and FedEx, for example, include tangible airplanes, trucks, boxes, and invoices. Another challenging characteristic of services is that they cannot be stored for future use. This lack of inventory means that service firms experience major problems in balancing service supply (capacity) and service demand. Likewise, the demand for services is extremely time-and-place dependent because customers must typically be present for service to be delivered. Consider the issues faced by popular restaurants every Friday and Saturday night. The increased demand forces restaurant managers to pre-schedule the right amount of food ingredients and employees to accommodate the increase in guests. And, given that the restaurant's capacity is fixed, the manager and employees must serve guests efficiently and effectively in a crowded,

EXHIBIT 6.3   Unique Characteristics of Services and Resulting Marketing Challenges

Service Characteristics	Marketing Challenges
Intangibility	It is difficult for customers to evaluate quality, especially before purchase and consumption.
	It is difficult to convey service characteristics and benefits in promotion. As a result, the firm is forced to sell a promise.
	Many services have few standardized units of measurement. Therefore, service prices are difficult to set and justify.
	Customers cannot take possession of a service.
Simultaneous Production and Consumption	Customers or their possessions must be present during service delivery.
	Other customers can affect service outcomes including service quality and customer satisfaction.
	Service employees are critical because they must interact with customers to deliver service.
	Converting high-contact services to low-contact services will lower costs but may reduce service quality.
	Services are often difficult to distribute.
Perishability	Services cannot be inventoried for later use. Therefore, unused service capacity is lost forever.
	Service demand is very time-and-place sensitive. As a result, it is difficult to balance supply and demand, especially during periods of peak demand.
	Service facilities and equipment sit idle during periods of off-peak demand.
Heterogeneity	Service quality varies across people, time, and place, making it very difficult to deliver good service consistently.
	There are limited opportunities to standardize service delivery.
	Many services are customizable by nature. However, customization can dramatically increase the costs of providing the service.
Client-Based Relationships	Most services live or die by maintaining a satisfied clientele over the long term.
	Generating repeat business is crucial for the service firm's success.

noisy atmosphere. This precarious balance is quite common across most industries in the services sector of our economy.

Because of the intangibility of service, it is quite difficult for customers to evaluate a service before they actually purchase and consume it. Third-party evaluations and recommendations for services are not as prevalent as they are with respect to tangible goods. Of course, customers can ask friends and family for recommendations, but in many cases a good assessment of quality is hard to obtain. This forces customers to place some degree of trust in the service provider to perform the service correctly and in the time frame promised or anticipated. This problem is the reason for the launch of Angie's List, a membership-based referral and recommendation service that provides member ratings for local service providers. One way that companies can address this issue is by providing satisfaction guarantees to customers. For example, Hampton Inn, a national chain of mid-priced hotels, offers guests a free night if they are not 100 percent satisfied with their stay.[2] Midas, H&R Block, and FedEx offer similar guarantees.

Moreover, because most services are dependent upon people (employees, customers) for their delivery, they are susceptible to variations in quality and inconsistency. Such variations can occur from one organization to another, from one outlet to another within the same organization, from one service to another within the same outlet, and even from one employee to another within the same outlet. Service quality can further vary from week to week, day to day, or even hour to hour. Also, because service quality is a subjective phenomenon, it can also vary from customer to customer, and for the same customer from one visit to the next. As a result, standardization and service quality are very difficult to control. The lack of standardization, however, actually gives service firms one advantage: Services can be customized to match the specific needs of any customer. Such customized services are frequently very expensive for both the firm and its customers. This creates a dilemma: How does a service firm provide efficient, standardized service at an acceptable level of quality while simultaneously treating every customer as a unique person? This dilemma is especially prevalent in the health care industry today, where care is managed to carefully control both access and cost.

Another major challenge for service marketers is to tie services directly to customers' needs. Although customers typically have few problems in expressing needs for tangible goods, they often have difficulty in expressing or explaining needs for services. In some cases, the need is vague. For example, you may decide that you need a relaxing vacation, but how do you know which services will best meet your need? Which is best for relaxation: a trip to the beach, a cruise, or a stay at a bed-and-breakfast? The answer depends on how you personally define "relaxing." Since different customers have different definitions, the vacation provider has a more difficult job in connecting their service offerings to customers' needs. In other cases, customers may not understand the need for a specific service. For example, business consultants, insurance agents, financial planners, and wedding consultants often have to educate customers on why their services are needed. This is a necessary first hurdle to overcome before these service providers can offer their products as the solution that will best fulfill the need.

Developing New Products

One of the key issues in product strategy deals with the introduction of new products. The development and commercialization of new products is a vital part of a firm's efforts to sustain growth and profits over time. The success of new products depends on the product's fit with the firm's strengths and a defined market opportunity. Market characteristics and the competitive situation will also affect the sales potential of new products. For example, manufacturers such as Garmin, TomTom, and Magellan are consistently developing new GPS devices. However, the future of standalone GPS devices is unclear given that GPS functionality is now an option on most new cars, and is fully integrated into many wireless phones. As these GPS-enabled devices add more features, consumers are going to be much less likely to purchase standalone GPS units. This is why many GPS units can now sync with telephones or serve as music players. Some manufacturers, such as Garmin, are looking to enter the wireless phone business as a way to remain competitive.[3]

Many firms base their new product introductions on key themes such as product or technological superiority. New product introductions in the electronics, computer, and automotive industries often take this approach. In other firms and industries, new product introductions may stem from only minor tweaking of current products. This approach is common in packaged goods and household items. Truthfully, what is considered to be a new product depends on the point of view of both the firm and its customers. Although some product introductions are actually new, others may only be *perceived* as being new. There are six strategic options related to the newness of products. These options follow, in decreasing degrees of product change:

- **New-to-the-World Products (Discontinuous Innovations)**. These products involve a pioneering effort by a firm that eventually leads to the creation of an entirely new market. New-to-the-world products are typically the result of radical thinking by individual inventors or entrepreneurs. For example, Fred Smith's idea for an overnight package delivery service gave us FedEx.
- **New Product Lines**. These products represent new offerings by the firm, but the firm introduces them into established markets. For example, P&G's launch of a national chain of car washes is a new product line for the company. New product lines are not as risky as true innovation, and they allow the firm to diversify into closely related product categories.
- **Product Line Extensions**. These products supplement an existing product line with new styles, models, features, or flavors. Anheuser-Busch's introduction of Budweiser Select and Honda's launch of the Civic Hybrid are good examples. Product line extensions allow the firm to keep its products fresh and exciting with minimal development costs and risk of market failure.
- **Improvements or Revisions of Existing Products**. These products offer customers improved performance or greater perceived value. The common "new and improved" strategy used in packaged goods and the yearly design changes in the automobile industry are good examples. Clorox, for example, now offers "splashless" and "anti-allergen" bleach in addition to its perennial "regular" bleach product. The common "shampoo plus conditioner" formulas of many shampoos are another example.
- **Repositioning**. This strategy involves targeting existing products at new markets or segments. Repositioning can involve real or perceived changes to a product. An example is Carnival Cruise Line's effort to attract senior citizens to supplement its younger crowd. Likewise, many design schools have repositioned themselves toward a growing business need for employees who are well versed in the art of innovation. As such, these design schools are now competing with top MBA programs around the country.
- **Cost Reductions**. This strategy involves modifying products to offer performance similar to competing products at a lower price. Book publishers use this strategy when they convert hardback books to paperbacks or e-books. Similarly, a firm may be able to lower a product's price due to improved manufacturing efficiency or a drop in the price of raw materials. For example, many computer manufacturers offer lower-priced products that use standard or slightly dated technology.

The first two options are the most effective and profitable when the firm wants to significantly differentiate its product offering from competitors. However, there are often good reasons to pursue one of the remaining four options, particularly if resource constraints are an issue or if the firm's management does not want to expose the firm to increased market risk. The key to new product success is to create a differential advantage for the new product. What unique benefit does the new product offer to customers? Although this benefit can be based on real differences or based entirely on image, it is the customers' *perception* of differentiation that is critical. For example, despite *Consumer Reports* tests that 5-blade or battery-powered razors do not provide a closer shave than traditional 3-blade razors, many consumers believe that they do. This belief is based primarily on the back-and-forth marketing battle between Gillette (Fusion razor) and Schick (Quattro and Hydro razors). A number of low-price competitors also exist to serve consumers who do not buy into the new product hype. Whether five blades are truly better than three blades is immaterial. In the battle for supremacy in the razor market, customer perceptions are all that matter.

Customer perceptions are also critical in the process of developing new products. Although the new product development process varies across firms, most firms will go through the following stages:

- **Idea Generation**. New product ideas can be obtained from a number of sources, including customers, employees, basic research, competitors, and supply chain partners.
- **Screening and Evaluation**. New product ideas are screened for their match with the firm's capabilities and the degree to which they meet customers' needs and wants. In some cases, prototype products are developed to further test the commercial viability of a product concept. New product concepts are also evaluated with respect to projected costs, revenues, and profit potential.
- **Development**. At this stage, product specifications are set, the product design is finalized, and initial production begins. In addition, the full marketing plan is developed in order to acquire the resources and collaboration needed for a full-scale launch.
- **Test Marketing**. As a final test before launch, the new product is test marketed in either real or simulated situations to determine its performance relative to customer needs and competing products.
- **Commercialization**. In this final stage, the product is launched with a complete marketing program designed to stimulate customer awareness and acceptance of the new product.

Many firms try to think outside the box in designing new products. Kia, for example, turned to Peter Schreyer, a German automotive designer, to reinvigorate the South Korean company's brand image. When he was hired away from Volkswagen, Schreyer's first task was to design two new vehicles—the Kia Forte and the Kia Soul—to compete against new designs from Nissan and Scion. He then redesigned Kia's popular Sorento SUV and the midsize Optima sedan. The results have been impressive: Kia's sales increased 22 percent overall in 2012, with the Optima up 69 percent and the Rio up 56 percent.[4] Kia's success highlights the importance of maintaining proactive product innovation even in a down economy.

Pricing Strategy

There is no other component of the marketing program that firms become more infatuated with than pricing. There are at least four reasons for the attention given to pricing. First, the revenue equation is simple: Revenue equals the price times quantity sold. There are only two ways for a firm to grow revenue: increase prices or increase the volume of product sold. Rarely can a firm do both simultaneously. Second, pricing is the easiest of all marketing variables to change. Although changing the product and its distribution or promotion can take months or even years, changes in pricing can be executed immediately in real time. Real-time price changes are the norm in many industries, including air travel, hotels, and electronic commerce. As illustrated in *Beyond the Pages 6.2*, prices for the same product vary around the world to account for differences in currencies, taxes/tariffs, and consumer demand.

Third, firms take considerable pains to discover and anticipate the pricing strategies and tactics of other firms. Salespeople learn to read a competitor's price sheet upside down at a buyer's desk. Retailers send "secret shoppers" into competitors' stores to learn what they charge for the same merchandise. Even buyers spend considerable time comparison shopping to find the best deal. Finally, pricing receives a great deal of attention because it is considered to be one of the few ways to differentiate a product in commoditized and mature markets. When customers see all competing products as offering the same features and benefits, their buying decisions are primarily driven by price.

Key Issues in Pricing Strategy

Given the importance of pricing in marketing strategy, pricing decisions are among the most complex decisions to be made in developing a marketing plan. Decisions regarding price require a tightly integrated balance among a number of important issues. Many of these issues possess some degree of uncertainty regarding the reactions to pricing among customers, competitors, and supply chain partners. These issues are critically important in establishing initial prices, and to modifying the pricing strategy over time. As we review these issues, keep in mind that they are interrelated and must be considered in the context of the firm's entire marketing program. For example, increases in product quality or the addition of new product features often come with an increase in price. Pricing is also influenced by distribution, especially the image and reputation of the outlets where the good or service is sold. Finally, companies often use price as a tool of promotion. Coupons, for example, represent a combination of price and promotion that can stimulate increased sales in many different product categories. In services, price changes are often used to fill unused capacity (e.g., empty airline or theater seats) during non-peak demand.

The Firm's Cost Structure   The firm's costs in producing and marketing a product are an important factor in setting prices. Obviously, a firm that fails to cover both its direct costs (e.g., finished goods/components, materials, supplies, sales commission, transportation) and its indirect costs (e.g., administrative expenses, utilities, rent) will not make a profit. Perhaps the most popular way to associate costs and prices is through breakeven pricing, where the firm's fixed and variable costs are considered:

$$\text{Breakeven in Units} = \frac{\text{Total Fixed Costs}}{\text{Unit Price} - \text{Unit Variable Costs}}$$

To use breakeven analysis in setting prices, the firm must look at the feasibility of selling more than the breakeven level in order to make a profit. The breakeven number is only a point of reference in setting prices, as market conditions and customer demand must also be considered.

Another way to use the firm's cost structure in setting prices is to use cost-plus pricing—a strategy that is quite common in retailing. Here, the firm sets prices based on average unit costs and its planned markup percentage:

$$\text{Selling Price} = \frac{\text{Average Unit Cost}}{1 - \text{Markup Percent (decimal)}}$$

Beyond the Pages 6.2

Pricing Around the World[5]

If you do much traveling around the world, you'll quickly learn that products are not priced the same in different countries. In fact, despite widespread American sentiment to the contrary, the prices we pay in the U.S. are among the lowest in the world. In the latest survey done by the Economist Intelligence Unit, New York, the most expensive U.S. city, ranked 15th on the list of the world's most expensive cities. The top ten cities, shown below, are dominated by Asian and European cities due to their strong currencies, high consumer confidence, and low interest rates. Cities at the bottom of the list are mostly from the Middle East. For example, Karachi, Pakistan is the least expensive city in the survey with an index of 46.

Differences in pricing across national boundaries are also true with respect to typical purchases. In most cases, the products sold around the world under the same brand name are virtually identical. They are even sold using similar promotional campaigns to the same types of target markets who consume these products in roughly the same manner. Yet, the prices set in different markets can vary dramatically. Consider the examples noted below.

In some cases, there are logical differences in pricing, such as higher costs of transportation or other extra costs associated with bringing a product to market. Other differences are associated with currency valuation. The U.S. dollar is relatively weak compared to other currencies, so it buys less in some cases. Other differences are based on the tax and tariff structures in each country. The U.S. and Britain, for example, impose very high taxes on tobacco sales. Firms have a great deal of latitude in setting prices, and will often raise prices in some countries simply because consumers are willing to pay the cost to acquire a popular product with few substitutes.

Generally speaking, average prices will be lower in developing countries than in mature, developed countries. This is especially true in services, which are less expensive to deliver due to lower wage rates. The lower cost of labor in developing countries has spawned a groundswell of activity in outsourcing of services to other countries.

Rank	City	Index
1	Zurich, Switzerland	170
2	Tokyo, Japan	166
3	Geneva, Switzerland	157
4	Osaka Kobe, Japan	157
5	Olso, Norway	156
6	Paris, France	150
7	Sydney, Australia	147
8	Melbourne, Australia	145
9	Singapore	142
10	Frankfurt, Germany	137

Note: Index is based on New York at 100.

	Zurich	Sydney	London	New York	Beijing	New Delhi
Loaf of bread	$6.15	$3.48	$2.26	$6.06	$1.85	$0.76
White rice (1 kg)	$5.38	$2.97	$4.81	$3.78	$2.23	$2.18
Gas (1 gallon)	$8.56	$5.68	$8.14	$4.20	$4.96	$5.26

Note: All prices shown in U.S. dollars.

Cost-plus pricing is not only intuitive; it is also very easy to use. Its weakness, however, lies in determining the correct markup percentage. Industry norms often come into play at this point. For example, average markups in grocery retailing are typically in the 20 percent range, while markups can be several hundred percent or more in furniture or jewelry stores. Customer expectations are also an important consideration in determining the correct markup percentage.

Although breakeven analysis and cost-plus pricing are important tools, they should not be the driving force behind pricing strategy. The reason is often ignored: Different firms have different cost structures. By setting prices solely on the basis of costs, firms run a major risk in setting their prices too high or too low. If one firm's costs are relatively higher than other firms, it will have to accept lower margins in order to compete effectively. Conversely, just because a product costs very little to produce and market does not mean that the firm should sell it at a low price (movie theater popcorn is a good example). Even if the firm covers its costs, the fact is that customers may not be willing to pay their prices. Hence, market demand is also a critical factor in pricing strategy. In the final analysis, cost is best understood as an absolute floor below which prices cannot be set for an extended period of time.

Perceived Value Both the firm and its customers are concerned with value. Value is a difficult term to define because it means different things to different people.[6] Some customers equate good value with high product quality, while others see value as nothing more than a low price. We define *value* as a customer's subjective evaluation of benefits relative to costs to determine the worth of a firm's product offering relative to other product offerings. A simple formula for value might look like this:

$$\text{Perceived Value} = \frac{\text{Customer Benefits}}{\text{Customer Costs}}$$

Customer benefits include everything the customer obtains from the product offering such as quality, satisfaction, prestige/image, and the solution to a problem. Customer costs include everything the customer must give up such as money, time, effort, and all non-selected alternatives (opportunity costs). Although value is a key component in setting a viable pricing strategy, good value depends on much more than pricing. In fact, value is intricately tied to every element in the marketing program and is a key factor in customer satisfaction and retention. We will discuss the strategic implications of value more fully in Chapter 10.

The Price/Revenue Relationship All firms understand the relationship between price and revenue. However, firms cannot always charge high prices due to competition from their rivals. In the face of this competition, it is natural for firms to see price-cutting as a viable means of increasing sales. Price cutting can also move excess inventory and generate short-term cash flow. However, all price cuts affect the firm's bottom line. When setting prices, many firms hold fast to these two general pricing myths:[7]

Myth #1: When business is good, a price cut will capture greater market share.

Myth #2: When business is bad, a price cut will stimulate sales.

Unfortunately, the relationship between price and revenue challenges these assumptions and makes them a risky proposition for most firms. The reality is that any price cut must be offset by an increase in sales volume just to maintain the same level of revenue. Let's look at an example. Assume that a consumer electronics manufacturer sells 1,000 high-end stereo receivers per month at $1,000 per system. The firm's total cost is $500 per system, which leaves a gross margin of $500. When the sales of this high-end system decline, the firm decides to cut the price to increase sales. The firm's strategy is to offer a $100 rebate to anyone who buys a system over the next three months. The rebate is consistent with a 10 percent price cut, but it is in reality a 20 percent reduction in gross margin (from $500 to $400). To compensate for the loss in gross margin, the firm must increase the volume of receivers sold. The question is by how much? We can find the answer using this formula:

$$\text{Percent Change in Unit Volume} = \frac{\text{Gross Margin \%}}{\text{Gross Margin \%} \pm \text{Price Change \%}} - 1$$

$$0.25 = \frac{0.50}{0.50 - 0.10} - 1$$

As the calculation indicates, the firm would have to increase sales volume by 25 percent to 1,250 units sold in order to maintain the same level of total gross margin. How likely is it that a $100 rebate will increase sales volume by 25 percent? This question is critical to the success of the firm's rebate strategy. In many instances, the needed increase in sales volume is too high. Consequently, the firm's gross margin may actually be lower after the price cut.

Rather than blindly use price cutting to stimulate sales and revenue, it is often better for a firm to find ways to build value into the product and justify the current price, or even a higher price, rather than cutting the product's price in search of higher sales volume. In the case of the stereo manufacturer, giving customers $100 worth of music or movies with each purchase is a much better option than a $100 rebate. Video game manufacturers, such as Microsoft (Xbox) and Sony (PlayStation 3), often bundle games and accessories with their system consoles to increase value. The cost of giving customers these free add-ons is low because the marketer buys them in bulk quantities. This added expense is almost always less costly than a price cut. And the increase in value may allow the marketer to charge higher prices for the product bundle.

Pricing Objectives   Setting specific pricing objectives that are realistic, measurable, and attainable is an important part of pricing strategy. As shown in Exhibit 6.4, there are a number of pricing objectives that firms may pursue. Remember that firms make money on profit margin, volume, or some combination of the two. A firm's pricing objectives will always reflect this market reality.

Price Elasticity   Price elasticity is perhaps the most important overall consideration in setting effective prices. Simply defined, *price elasticity* refers to customers' responsiveness or sensitivity to changes in price. A more precise definition defines elasticity as the relative impact on the demand for a product, given specific increases or decreases in the price charged for that product. Firms cannot base prices solely on price elasticity calculations because they will rarely know the elasticity for any product with great precision over time. Further, the same product can have different elasticities in different times, places, and situations. Since the actual price elasticity calculation is difficult to pinpoint precisely, firms often consider price elasticity in regard to differing customer behavior patterns or purchase situations. Understanding when, where, and how customers are more or less sensitive to price is crucial in setting fair and profitable prices.

Generally speaking, customers become much more sensitive to price when they have many different choices or options for fulfilling their needs and wants. Price elasticity is higher (more elastic) in the following situations:

- **Availability of Substitute Products.** When customers can choose among a number of different substitutes, they will be much more sensitive to price differences. This situation occurs very frequently among name-brand products and in markets where product offerings have become commoditized (airlines, for example).

EXHIBIT 6.4   Description of Common Pricing Objectives

Pricing Objectives	Description
Profit-Oriented	Designed to maximize price relative to competitors' prices, the product's perceived value, the firm's cost structure, and production efficiency. Profit objectives are typically based on a target return, rather than simple profit maximization.
Volume-Oriented	Sets prices in order to maximize dollar or unit sales volume. This objective sacrifices profit margin in favor of high product turnover.
Market Demand	Sets prices in accordance with customer expectations and specific buying situations. This objective is often known as "charging what the market will bear."
Market Share	Designed to increase or maintain market share regardless of fluctuations in industry sales. Market share objectives are often used in the maturity stage of the product life cycle.
Cash Flow	Designed to maximize the recovery of cash as quickly as possible. This objective is useful when a firm has a cash emergency or when the product life cycle is expected to be quite short.
Competitive Matching	Designed to match or beat competitors' prices. The goal is to maintain the perception of good value relative to the competition.
Prestige	Sets high prices that are consistent with a prestige or high status product. Prices are set with little regard for the firm's cost structure or the competition.
Status Quo	Maintains current prices in an effort to sustain a position relative to the competition.

- **Higher Total Expenditure.** As a general rule, the higher the total expense, the more elastic the demand for that product will be. This effect is actually easier to see if we look at a low priced product. A 20 percent increase in the price of a newspaper, from $1.00 to $1.20 for example, would not have a large impact on demand. However, if the price of a $20,000 car increases by 20 percent, then the impact is a much more noticeable $4,000. At that rate of change, some customers will look for a different car or pull out of buying all together.
- **Noticeable Price Differences.** Products having heavily promoted prices tend to experience more elastic demand. Gasoline is a classic example. An increase of three cents per gallon is only 45 cents more on a 15-gallon fill-up. However, many customers will drive several miles out of their way to find a lower price (often spending more in gas consumption than they save). Noticeable price differences sometimes occur at specific pricing thresholds. Using the gasoline example, many customers will not notice price increases until gas reaches $4.00 per gallon. At this price, these customers suddenly move from an inelastic mindset to an elastic mindset. The move from $3.80 to $3.90 may not have an impact on these customers, but the jump from $3.90 to $4.00 totally changes their mental framework.
- **Easy Price Comparisons.** Regardless of the product or product category, customers will become more price sensitive if they can easily compare prices among competing products. In industries such as retailing, supermarkets, travel, toys, and books, price has become a dominant purchase consideration because

customers can easily compare prices. It should come as no surprise that these industries have also experienced a shift from physical stores to online sales.

In general, customers become much less sensitive to price when they have few choices or options for fulfilling their needs and wants. Price elasticity is lower (more inelastic) in these situations:

- **Lack of Substitutes.** When customers have few choices in terms of substitutes, they will be much less sensitive to price. This situation is common in some categories, including baking/cooking ingredients, add-on or replacement parts, one-of-a-kind antiques, collectables or memorabilia, unique sporting events, and specialized vacation destinations. The more unique or specialized the product, the more customers will pay for it.

- **Real or Perceived Necessities.** Many products, such as food, water, medical care, cigarettes, and prescription drugs, have extremely inelastic demand because customers have real or perceived needs for them. Some product categories are price inelastic because customers perceive those products as true necessities. It matters little whether a customer truly has a need for a specific product. If that customer perceives the product as a necessity, then that customer becomes much less sensitive to price increases for that product.

- **Complementary Products.** Complementary products have an effect on the price sensitivity of related products. If the price of one product falls, customers will become less sensitive to the price of complementary products. For example, when the price of a cruise goes down, the price of shore excursions becomes more inelastic. With more travelers on board, and each having more money to spend, excursion operators realize that travelers are less sensitive to the prices they charge.

- **Perceived Product Benefits.** For some customers, certain products are just worth the price. For these purchases, the phrase "expensive but worth it" comes to mind. All of us have certain products that we indulge in from time to time, such as fine wines, gourmet chocolates, imported coffee, or trips to a day spa. Since these products do not comprise the bulk of our purchasing activities, customers rarely notice, or simply ignore, price increases.

- **Situational Influences.** The circumstances surrounding a purchase situation can vastly alter the price elasticity for a product. Many of these situational influences occur because time pressures or purchase risk increase to the point that an immediate purchase must be made (emergencies, for example). Other common situational influences revolve around purchase risk, typically the social risk involved in making a bad decision. In a general sense, customers tend to be much less price sensitive when they purchase items for others or for gift giving.

- **Product Differentiation.** Differentiation reduces the number of perceived substitutes for a product. For example, Coke's differentiation strategy has worked so well that Coke drinkers will buy the soft drink at $2.49 or $3.49 per six-pack. Product differentiation does not have to be based on real differences in order to make customers less price sensitive. Many times the differences are perceptual. Blindfolded, a person may not know the difference between Coke and Pepsi, but consumers do not buy or consume soft drinks blindfolded. The look of the can, the advertising, and prior experiences all come together to differentiate the product.

In a strategic sense, product differentiation is the best way to ensure that customers are not sensitive to price changes. The ultimate goal of this effort is to differentiate the product so well that customers perceive that no competing product can take its place. When this happens, customers will become brand loyal and the demand for the product will become very inelastic. Nike, for example, commands extreme brand loyalty because the firm has successfully differentiated its products through technological innovation, effective advertising, and the ubiquitous swoosh. Likewise, Intel has done a great job using real and perceived differentiation to become the dominant supplier of processor chips in the computer industry.

Pricing Service Products

When it comes to buying services, customers have a difficult time determining quality prior to purchase. Consequently, service pricing is critical because it may be the only quality cue that is available in advance of the purchase experience. If the service provider sets prices too low, customers will have inaccurate perceptions and expectations about quality. If prices are too high, customers may not give the firm a chance. In general, services pricing becomes more important—and more difficult—when:

- service quality is hard to detect prior to purchase
- the costs associated with providing the service are difficult to determine
- customers are unfamiliar with the service process
- brand names are not well established
- the customer can perform the service themselves
- advertising within a service category is limited
- the total price of the service experience is difficult to state beforehand

Setting prices for professional services (lawyers, accountants, consultants, doctors, and mechanics) is especially difficult as they suffer from a number of the conditions in the list above. Customers often balk at the high prices of these service providers because they have a limited ability to evaluate the quality or total cost until the service process has been completed. The heterogeneous nature of these services limits standardization; therefore, customer knowledge about pricing is limited. Heterogeneity also limits price comparison among competing providers. The key for these firms it to be up-front about the expected quality and costs of the service. This is often done through the use of binding estimates and contractual guarantees of quality.

Due to the limited capacity associated with most services, service pricing is also a key issue with respect to balancing supply and demand during peak and off-peak demand times. In these situations, many service firms use yield management systems to balance pricing and revenue considerations with their need to fill unfilled capacity. Exhibit 6.5 depicts an example of yield management for a hotel.

Yield management allows the service firm to simultaneously control capacity and demand in order to maximize revenue and capacity utilization. This is accomplished in two ways. First, the service firm controls capacity by limiting the available capacity at certain price points. Airlines do this by selling a limited number of seats at discount prices three or more weeks prior to a flight's departure. Southwest Airlines, for example, sells limited seats in three categories: Wanna Get Away (the lowest priced seats), Anytime, and Business Select (the highest priced seats).[8] Second, the service firm controls demand through price changes over time and by overbooking capacity. These activities ensure that service demand will be consistent and that any unused capacity will be minimized. These practices are common in services characterized by high fixed costs and low variable costs, such as airlines, hotels, rental cars, cruises, transportation firms, and hospitals. Since variable costs in these services are quite low, the profit for these firms directly relates to sales and capacity utilization. Consequently, these firms will sell some capacity at reduced prices in order to maximize utilization.

EXHIBIT 6.5   Yield Management for a Hypothetical Hotel

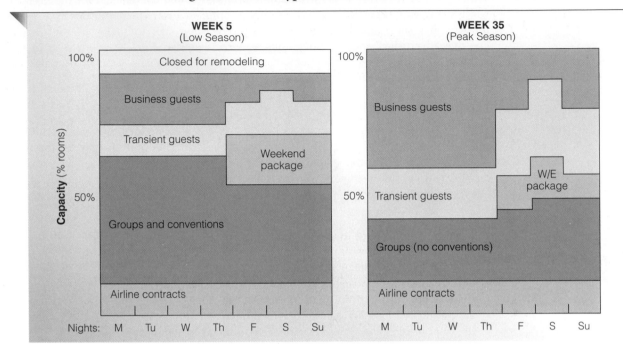

Source: Lovelock, Christopher, *Services Marketing: People, Technology, Strategy,* 4th Edition, © 2001. Reprinted by permission of Pearson Education Inc., Upper Saddle River, New Jersey.

Yield management systems are also useful in their ability to segment markets based on price elasticity. That is, yield management allows a firm to offer the same basic service to different market segments at different price points. Customers who are very price sensitive with respect to travel services—vacation travelers and families with children—can get a good deal on a hotel if they book it early. Conversely, consultants are less price-sensitive because their clients reimburse them for expenses. Likewise, business travelers book flights on the spur of the moment, so they are more forgiving of the higher prices just prior to departure. Other firms can reach different market segments with attractive off-peak pricing. Many customers take advantage of the lower prices at theme parks and beach resorts by traveling during the off-season. Similar situations occur in lower-priced movie matinees and lower prices for lunch items at most restaurants.

Base Pricing Strategies

Although prices for individual products are made on a case-by-case basis, most firms have developed a general and consistent approach—or base pricing strategy—to be used in establishing prices. The relationship between price and other elements of the marketing program dictates that pricing decisions cannot be made in isolation. In fact, price changes may result in minor modifications to the product, distribution, or promotion strategies. As we have discussed, it is not so much the actual price being charged that influences buying decisions as the way that members of the target market perceive the price. This reality reminds us that many of the strategic issues involved in pricing have close ties with customer psychology and information processing: What customers think about prices is what those prices are to them.

A firm's base pricing strategy establishes the initial price and sets the range of possible price movements throughout the product's life cycle. The initial price is critical, not only for initial success, but also for maintaining the potential for profit over the long term. There are several different approaches to base pricing. Some of the most common approaches include:

- **Price Skimming**. This strategy intentionally sets a high price relative to the competition, thereby "skimming" off the profits early after the product's launch. Price skimming is designed to recover the high R&D and marketing expenses associated with developing a new product. For example, new prescription drugs are priced high initially and only drop in price once their patent protection expires.

- **Price Penetration**. This strategy is designed to maximize sales, gain widespread market acceptance, and capture a large market share quickly by setting a relatively low initial price. This approach works best when customers are price sensitive for the product or product category, research and development and marketing expenses are relatively low, or when new competitors will quickly enter the market. To use penetration pricing successfully, the firm must have a cost structure and scale economies that can withstand narrow profit margins.

- **Prestige Pricing**. This strategy sets prices at the top end of all competing products in a category. This is done to promote an image of exclusivity and superior quality. Prestige pricing is a viable approach in situations where it is hard to objectively judge the true value of a product. Ritz-Carlton Hotels, for example, never compete with other hotels on price. Instead, the company competes only on service and the value of the unique, high quality experience that they deliver to hotel guests.

- **Value-Based Pricing (EDLP).** Firms that use a value-based pricing approach set reasonably low prices, but still offer high quality products and adequate customer services. Many different types of firms use value-based pricing; however, retailing has widely embraced this approach, where it is known as everyday low pricing or EDLP. Prices are not the highest in the market, nor are they the lowest. Instead, value-based pricing sets prices so they are consistent with the benefits and costs associated with acquiring the product. Many well-known firms use value-based pricing, including Walmart, Lowe's, Home Depot, IKEA, and Southwest Airlines.

- **Competitive Matching.** In many industries, pricing strategy focuses on matching competitors' prices and price changes. Although some firms may charge slightly more or slightly less, these firms set prices at what most consider to be the "going rate" for the industry. This is especially true in commoditized markets such as airlines, oil, and steel.

- **Non-Price Strategies.** This strategy builds the marketing program around factors other than price. By downplaying price in the marketing program, the firm must be able to emphasize the product's quality, benefits, and unique features; as well as customer service, promotion, or packaging in order to make the product stand out against competitors, many of whom will offer similar products at lower prices. For example, theme parks like Disney World, Sea World, and Universal Studios generally compete on excellent service, unique benefits, and one-of-a-kind experiences rather than price. Customers willingly pay for these experiences because they cannot be found in any other setting.

Adjusting the Base Price

In addition to a base pricing strategy, firms also use other techniques to adjust or fine-tune prices. These techniques can involve permanent adjustments to a product's price, or temporary adjustments used to stimulate sales during a particular time or situation.

Although the list of potentially viable pricing techniques is quite long, five of the most common techniques in consumer markets are:

- **Discounting.** This strategy involves temporary price reductions to stimulate sales or store traffic. Customers love a sale and that is precisely the main benefit of discounting. Virtually all firms, even those using value-based pricing, will occasionally run special promotions or sales to attract customers and create excitement. Dillard's, for example, will hold a quick sale early in a selling season, and then return prices to their normal levels. Near the end of the season, Dillard's will begin to make these sale prices (or markdowns) permanent as time draws closer to the end-of-season clearance sale.

- **Reference Pricing.** Firms use reference pricing when they compare the actual selling price to an internal or external reference price. All customers use internal reference prices, or the internal expectation for what a product should cost. As consumers, our experiences have given us a reasonable expectation of how much to pay for a combo meal at McDonald's or a gallon of gas. In other cases, the firm will state a reference price, such as "Originally $99, Now $49." These comparisons make it easier for customers to judge prices prior to purchase.

- **Price Lining**. This strategy, where the price of a competing product is the reference price, takes advantage of the simple truth that some customers will always choose the lowest-priced or highest-priced product. Firms use this to their advantage by creating lines of products that are similar in appearance and functionality, but are offered with different features and at different price points. For example, Sony can cut a few features off its top-of-the-line Model A1 digital camcorder and Model B2 can be on the shelf at $799 rather than the original $999. Cut a few more features and the price can drop to $599 for Model C3. Here, each model in the Sony line establishes reference prices for the other models in the line. The same is true for all competing camcorders from other manufacturers.

- **Odd Pricing.** Everyone knows that prices are rarely set at whole, round numbers. The concert tickets are $49.95, the breakfast special is $3.95, and the gallon of gas is $3.799. The prevalence of odd pricing is based mostly on psychology: Customers perceive that the seller did everything possible to get the price as fine (and thus as low) as he or she possibly could. To say you will cut my grass for $47 sounds like you put a lot more thought into it than if you just said, "I will do it for $40," even though the first figure is $7 higher.

- **Price Bundling.** Sometimes called solution-based pricing or all-inclusive pricing, price bundling brings together two or more complementary products for a single price. At its best, the bundled price is less than if a company sold the products separately. Slow moving items can be bundled with hot sellers to expand the scope of the product offering, build value, and manage inventory. All-inclusive resorts, including Sandals and Club Med, use price bundling because many customers want to simplify their vacations and add budget predictability.

Many of these techniques are also used in business markets to adjust or fine-tune base prices. However, there are a number of pricing techniques unique to business markets, including:

- **Trade Discounts**. Manufacturers will reduce prices for certain intermediaries in the supply chain based on the functions that the intermediary performs. In general, discounts are greater for wholesalers than for retailers because the manufacturer wants to compensate wholesalers for the extra functions they perform, such as selling, storage, transportation, and risk taking. Trade discounts vary widely and have become more complicated due to the growth of large retailers who now perform their own wholesaling functions.

- **Discounts and Allowances**. Business buyers can take advantage of sales just like consumers. However, business buyers also receive other price breaks, including discounts for cash, quantity or bulk discounts, seasonal discounts, or trade allowances for participation in advertising or sales support programs.
- **Geographic Pricing**. Selling firms often quote prices in terms of reductions or increases based on transportation costs or the actual physical distance between the seller and the buyer. The most common examples of geographic pricing are uniform delivered pricing (same price for all buyers regardless of transportation expenses) and zone pricing (different prices based on transportation to predefined geographic zones).
- **Transfer Pricing**. Transfer pricing occurs when one unit in an organization sells products to another unit.
- **Barter and Countertrade**. In business exchanges across national boundaries, companies sometimes use products, rather than cash, for payments. Barter involves the direct exchange of goods or services between two firms or nations. Countertrade refers to agreements based on partial payments in both cash and products, or to agreements between firms or nations to buy goods and services from each other.

Another important pricing technique used in business markets is price discrimination, which occurs when firms charge different prices to different customers. When this situation occurs, firms set different prices based on actual cost differences in selling products to one customer relative to the costs involved in selling to other customers. Price discrimination is a viable technique because the costs of selling to one firm are often much higher than selling to others.

Supply Chain Strategy

Distribution and supply chain relationships are among the most important strategic decisions for any firm. Walmart, Best Buy, Amazon, and even Starbucks depend on effective and highly efficient supply chains to provide competitive advantage. Unfortunately, customers rarely appreciate how companies connect to their supply lines because the processes occur behind the scenes. Customers take supply chain issues for granted and only notice when supply lines are interrupted. The picture is drastically different from the firm's perspective. Today, most companies rank supply chain concerns at the top of the list for achieving a sustainable advantage and true differentiation in the marketplace. Prices can be copied easily, even if only for the short term. Products can become obsolete almost overnight. Good promotion and advertising in September can easily be passé when the prime selling season in November and December comes around. The lesson is clear: Supply chain strategy is vital to the success and survival of every firm.

When we think of supply chain management, we tend to think of two interrelated components:

- **Marketing channels**—an organized system of marketing institutions, through which products, resources, information, funds, and/or product ownership flow from the point of production to the final user. Some channel members or intermediaries physically take possession or title of products (e.g., wholesalers, distributors, retailers), while others simply facilitate the process (e.g., agents, brokers, financial institutions).
- **Physical distribution**—coordinating the flow of information and products among members of the channel to ensure the availability of products in the right places, in the right quantities, at the right times, and in a cost-efficient manner. Physical

distribution (or logistics) includes activities such as customer service/order entry, administration, transportation, storage, and materials handling, (warehousing) inventory carrying and the systems and equipment necessary for these activities.

The term *supply chain* expresses the connection and integration of all members of the marketing channel. Velocity or the need to speed inventory to and from channel members requires collaborating with technology, transportation, and other outside logistics experts. This supply chain process is designed to increase inventory turns, and get the right products to the right place at the right time maintaining the appropriate service and quality standards.[9] The linchpin of effective supply chain management in today's economy is integration. Through informational, technological, social, and structural linkages, the goal of supply chain integration is to create a seamless network of collaborating suppliers, vendors, buyers, and customers. When done correctly, this level of integration results in an extended enterprise that manages value by coordinating the flow of information, goods, and services toward end users, as well as reverse flows away from end users. Creating an extended enterprise requires investments in and commitment to three key factors:[10]

- **Connectivity**—the informational and technological linkages among firms in the supply chain network. Connectivity ensures that firms can access real-time information about the flow in the supply chain network.
- **Community**—the sense of compatible goals and objectives among firms in the supply chain network. All firms must be willing to work together to achieve a common mission and vision.
- **Collaboration**—the recognition of mutual interdependence among members of the supply chain network. Collaboration goes beyond contractual obligations to establish principles, processes, and structures that promote a level of shared understanding. Firms learn to put the needs of the supply chain ahead of their own because they understand that the success of each firm separately has a strong connection to the success of other firms, as well as the entire supply chain.

Supply chain integration and creating an extended enterprise are extremely challenging goals. In the most seamlessly integrated supply chains, the boundaries among channel members blur to the point where it is difficult to tell where one firm ends and another firm begins. As shown in Exhibit 6.6, this level of integration requires a tenuous balance of trust, cooperation, interdependence, and stability in order to create mutual benefits.[11]

Strategic Supply Chain Issues

The importance of the supply chain ultimately comes down to providing time, place, and possession utility for consumer and business buyers. Without good distribution, buyers would not be able to acquire goods and services when and where they need them. However, the expense of distribution requires that firms balance customers' needs with their own need to minimize total costs. Exhibit 6.7 provides a breakdown of total distribution costs across key activities. Note that 42 percent of these expenses are associated with storing and carrying inventory—key factors in ensuring product availability for customers. To manage these costs efficiently, distribution strategy must balance the needs of customers with the needs of the firm.

Marketing Channel Functions   Marketing channels make our lives easier because of the variety of functions performed by channel members. Likewise, channel members, particularly manufacturers, can cut costs by working through channel intermediaries.

EXHIBIT 6.6   **Factors in Successful Supply Chain Integration**

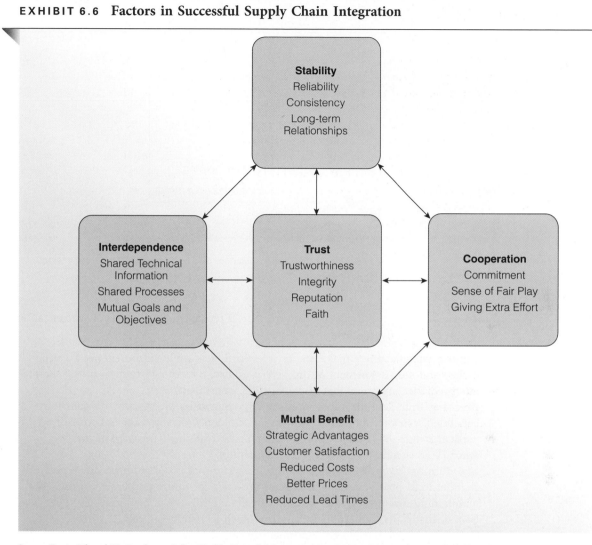

Source: Davis, Edward W.; Speckman, Robert E., *The Extended Enterprise: Gaining Competitive Advantage through Collaborative Supply Chains,* 1st ed., © 2004.

The most basic benefit of marketing channels is contact efficiency, where channels reduce the number of contacts necessary to exchange products. Without contact efficiency, we would have to visit a bakery, poultry farm, slaughterhouse, and dairy just to assemble the products necessary for breakfast. Likewise, contact efficiency allows companies such as Del Monte Foods to maximize product distribution by selling to select intermediaries. For Del Monte, Walmart stores account for over 31 percent of the company's sales volume. Del Monte's next nine largest customers account for another 30 percent of the company's sales. These percentages will increase if additional consolidation among food retailers and growth of mass merchandisers continues.[12]

Throughout a marketing channel, some firms are good at manufacturing, some are good at transportation or storage, and others are better at selling to consumers. Given the costs involved, it is virtually impossible for a single firm to perform all channel

EXHIBIT 6.7   Breakdown of Total Distribution Costs

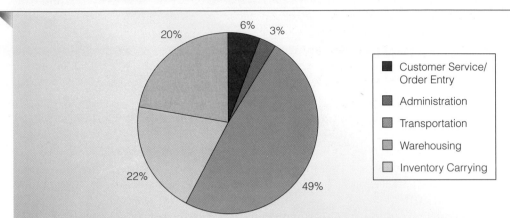

Source: From 'Proportion Cost of Each Distribution Function as a Percentage of Total Distribution Costs' in "Logistics Cost and Service 2009," © 2009 Establish, Inc. (Forth Lee, NJ), www.establishinc.com. Reprinted by permission of Establish, Inc.

functions well. As a result, channel intermediaries typically attain a level of specialization in one or more of the following functions:

- **Sorting**. Manufacturers make one or a few products while customers need a wide variety and deep assortment of different products. By sorting products in the channel, intermediaries overcome this discrepancy of assortment.
- **Breaking Bulk**. Manufacturers produce large quantities of a product to gain the benefits of economies of scale. However, customers typically want only one of a particular item. By breaking bulk in the channel, intermediaries—particularly retailers—overcome this discrepancy of quantity.
- **Maintaining Inventories**. Since manufacturers cannot make products on demand, the channel must provide for the storage of products for future purchase and use. By maintaining inventories, intermediaries overcome this temporal (time) discrepancy. Note that this does not apply to services—such as haircuts or airline flights—where the product is produced and consumed simultaneously.
- **Maintaining Convenient Locations**. Since manufacturers and customers are separated geographically, the channel must overcome this spatial discrepancy by making products available in convenient locations.
- **Provide Services**. Channels add value to products by offering facilitating services (e.g., insurance, storage, financing) and standardizing the exchange process (e.g., payment processing, delivery, pricing).

With the exception of highly intangible services like consulting, education, or counseling, the fulfillment of these functions occurs in every marketing channel. Also, these functions must be fulfilled in order for the channel to operate effectively. It does not matter which intermediary performs these functions; the fact remains that they must be performed. For example, Sam's Club does not break bulk in the traditional sense. Sam's customers buy in large quantities and actually break bulk after purchase. Further, many emerging trends in distribution and supply chain management have blurred the responsibilities of different intermediaries. Today, large retailers are essentially a one-stop channel of distribution. Due to their immense size and bulk buying ability, these firms now fulfill virtually all traditional channel functions.

Marketing Channel Structure   There are many strategic options for the structure of a marketing channel; these strategies are often complex and very costly to implement. However, a good distribution strategy is essential for success because once a firm selects a channel and makes commitments to it, distribution often becomes highly inflexible due to long-term contracts, sizable investments, and commitments among channel members. There are three basic structural options for distribution in terms of the amount of market coverage and level of exclusivity between vendor and retailer:

- **Exclusive Distribution.** Exclusive distribution is the most restrictive type of market coverage. Firms using this strategy give one merchant or outlet the sole right to sell a product within a defined geographic region.
- **Selective Distribution**. Firms using selective distribution give several merchants or outlets the right to sell a product in a defined geographic region. Selective distribution is desirable when customers need the opportunity to comparison shop, and after-sale services are important.
- **Intensive Distribution.** Intensive distribution makes a product available in the maximum number of merchants or outlets in each area to gain as much exposure and as many sales opportunities as possible.

Channel structure is clearly linked to other elements in the marketing program and can be an integral part of both branding strategy and product positioning. For example, exclusive distribution is commonly associated with prestige products, major industrial equipment, or with firms that attempt to give their products an exclusive or prestige image (for example, BMW, Jaguar, and Mercedes). Firms that pursue exclusive distribution usually target a single, well-defined market segment. Selective distribution is used across many product categories, including clothing (Tommy Hilfiger), cosmetics (Clinique), electronics (Bose), franchising (McDonald's), and premium pet food (Science Diet). These and other companies carefully screen the image and selling practices of merchants to ensure that they match those of the manufacturer and its products. Intensive distribution is the best option for most consumer convenience goods, such as candy, soft drinks, over-the-counter drugs, or cigarettes; and for business office supplies like paper and toner cartridges. To gain this visibility and sales volume, the manufacturer must give up a good degree of control over pricing and product display. If a customer cannot find one firm's products in a given location, they will simply substitute another brand to fill the need.

Clinique's line of upscale cosmetics is an example of a product made available through selective distribution.

Power in the Supply Chain   True supply chain integration requires a fundamental change in how channel members work together. Among these changes is a move from a "win–lose" competitive attitude to a "win–win" collaborative approach in which there is a common realization that all firms in the supply chain must prosper. Consider the Toro Company that sells turf maintenance equipment, irrigation systems, landscaping equipment, and yard products to both professional and residential markets. This requires many different distributors and dealers (many of which are quite small), as well as supplying products to large national retailers such as Home Depot. If one of Toro's products is made available in Home Depot, it is likely to have a lower retail price (due to bulk buying) than the same or similar product at a local tractor supply company. This situation is clearly not in the best interests of the local firm, so it will strive to put its interests ahead of others in the supply chain. However, the local tractor supply company also understands that it must service Toro equipment—no matter where it was purchased—if it is to remain a certified service facility. For the local firm, putting the needs of the supply chain ahead of its own needs is likely to create tension and conflict with the Toro Company. In situations like this, each firm will exhibit a different degree of authority or power in managing or controlling the activities within the supply chain. There are five basic sources of power in a supply chain:[13]

- **Legitimate Power**. This power source is based on the firm's position in the supply chain. Historically, manufacturers held most of the legitimate power, but this power balance shifted to retailers in the 1990s. In today's economy, retailers still wield a great deal of power; but consumers are clearly in charge.
- **Reward Power**. The ability to help other parties reach their goals and objectives is the crux of reward power. Rewards may come in terms of higher volume sales, sales with more favorable margins, or both. Individual salespeople at the buyer end of the channel may be rewarded with cash payments, merchandise, or vacations to gain more favorable presentation of a manufacturer's or wholesaler's products.
- **Coercive Power**. The ability to take positive outcomes away from other channel members, or the ability to inflict punishment on other channel members. For example, a manufacturer may slow down deliveries or postpone the availability of some portions of a product line to a wholesaler or retailer. Likewise, a retailer can decide to not carry a product, not promote a product, or to give a product unfavorable placement on its shelves.
- **Information Power**. Having and sharing knowledge is the root of information power. Such knowledge makes channel members more effective and efficient. Information power may stem from knowledge concerning sales forecasts, market trends, competitive intelligence, product uses and usage rates, or other critical pieces of information. In many supply chains, retailers hold the most information power because their close proximity to customers gives them access to data and information that is difficult to obtain from other sources.
- **Referent Power**. Referent power has its basis in personal relationships and the fact that one party likes another party. It has long been said that buyers like to do business with salespeople they enjoy being around. This is still true, but increasingly referent power has its roots in firms wanting to associate with other firms, as opposed to individual one-on-one relationships. Similar cultures, values, and even information systems can lead to the development of referent power.

Powerful channel members have the ability to get other firms to do things they otherwise would not do. Depending on how the channel member uses its influence, power can create considerable conflict, or it can make the entire supply chain operate more smoothly and effectively. Today, discount mass merchandise retailers—like Walmart,

Costco, and Target—and category focused retailers (also known as category killers)—such as Best Buy, Barnes & Noble, Office Depot, and AutoZone—hold the power in most consumer channels. The sheer size and buying power of these firms allows them to demand price concessions from manufacturers. They also perform their own whole-saling functions; therefore, they receive trade discounts traditionally reserved for true wholesalers. Likewise, their control over retail shelf space allows them to dictate when and where new products will be introduced. Manufacturers typically must pay hefty fees, called *slotting allowances*, just to get a single product placed on store shelves. Finally, their closeness to millions of customers allows these large retailers to gather valu-able information at the point of sale. As mentioned previously, control over information is a valuable commodity and a source of power in virtually all supply chains.

Trends in Supply Chain Strategy

In addition to the strategic supply chain issues discussed to this point, a number of trends have shaped the structure of marketing channels and the ways that supply chains function. In this section, we examine a number of these trends.

Technological Improvements   Significant advancements in information processing and digital communication have created new methods for placing and filling orders for both business buyers and consumers. The growth of the Internet and electronic com-merce is the most obvious sign of these changes. As business buyers and consumers more fully embrace these technologies, the growth of e-commerce is expected to flourish. For example, e-commerce accounted for fewer than 20 percent of transactions in the manufacturing sector in 2002. Today, that number is over 46 percent. In the wholesaling sector, e-commerce accounts for roughly 25 percent of all transactions. Conversely, e-commerce accounts for only 4.4 percent of all retail transactions, and only 2.3 percent of transactions in service-based industries. Still, e-commerce in these consumer markets is growing at roughly 16 percent per year. These statistics show that electronic commerce still has a great deal of room to grow, especially in consumer markets.[14]

Another promising technology is radio frequency identification (RFID), which involves the use of tiny computer chips with radio transmission capability that can be attached to a product or its packaging. The radio signals reflected from the chip can be used to track inventory levels and product spoilage, or prevent theft. They can also be used for instantaneous checkout of an entire shopping cart of items. As addressed in *Beyond the Pages 6.3*, large retailers and packaged goods manufacturers have adopted RFID, which will eventually replace bar codes as a means to manage inventory.[15] Innovations in web-based communication technologies such as global positioning, are also taking rail and truck equipment to a new level of service in sup-ply chain integration.

Outsourcing Channel Functions   Outsourcing—shifting work activities to businesses outside the firm—is a rapidly growing trend across many different industries and supply chains.[17] In the past, outsourcing was used primarily as a way of cutting expenses asso-ciated with labor, transportation, or other overhead costs. Today, though cutting expenses is still a main factor, the desire of many firms to focus on core competencies drives outsourcing. By outsourcing non-core activities, firms can improve their focus on what they do best, free resources for other purposes, and enhance product differentiation—all of which lead to greater opportunities to develop and maintain competitive advantages. The hourly labor costs in countries such as China, India, and Mexico are far less than in the United States or Europe. These developing countries have improved their manufacturing

Beyond the Pages 6.3

Walmart's Supply Chain Advantages[16]

Walmart Stores Inc.—the world's largest retailer—is possibly the most controversial business in America. With over 10,000 stores globally, sales over $444 billion in 2012, and approximately 2.2 million employees worldwide (of these, 1.4 million are U.S. employees), managing stakeholder relationships is a major challenge. The Walmart that saves the average family an estimated $2,300 per year has its critics. Walmart claims that it is committed to improving the standard of living for its customers throughout the world. Their key strategy is a broad assortment of quality merchandise and services at everyday low prices (EDLP) while fostering a culture that claims to reward and embrace mutual respect, integrity, and diversity. Walmart uses the data it collects about customers, as well as data collected throughout its distribution system to maintain its competitive advantage and low costs.

Walmart is not only the world's largest retailer, it also operates the world's largest data warehouse, an organization-wide data collection and storage system that gathers data from all of the firm's critical operating systems as well as from selected external data sources. Walmart's data warehouse contains more than 2,000 terabytes (or 2 petabytes) of data with sales information on every item it sells (roughly 200 million transactions per week).

Walmart collects reams of data about products and customers primarily from checkout scanners at its Walmart discount and Sam's Club membership stores. Clerks and managers may also use wireless handheld units to gather additional inventory data. The company stores the detailed data and classifies it into categories such as product, individual store, or region. The system also serves as a basis for the Retail Link decision-support system between Walmart and its suppliers. Retail Link permits some vendors, like Kraft, to access data about how well their products are selling at Walmart stores.

The mountain of data Walmart collects helps boost efficiency dramatically by matching product supplies to demand. This information, for example, helped the firm determine to stock not only flashlights but also extra strawberry Pop-Tarts prior to a hurricane strike on the coast. (It seems that Pop-Tart sales increase as much as seven times their normal rate ahead of a hurricane.) The data may also help the company track supplier performance, set ideal prices, and even determine how many cashiers to schedule at a certain store on a certain day. Most importantly, it helps the retailer avoid carrying too much inventory or not having enough to satisfy demand.

Technology is a driving force in operational efficiency that lowers costs for Walmart. The merchandise-tracking system uses RFID to ensure that a product can be tracked from the time it leaves the supplier's warehouse to the time it enters and leaves a Walmart store. Walmart began the move to RFID in 2004 by insisting that its top 100 suppliers adopt RFID technology. Supplier adoption has been slowed because the cost to suppliers is much larger than the cost to Walmart (suppliers must continually buy RFID tags while Walmart only needs a system to read the tags). The cost to adopt and implement RFID technology has been estimated to be roughly $9 million per supplier.

RFID helps Walmart keep its shelves stocked and curbs the loss of retail products as they travel through the supply chain. RFID at Walmart has directly resulted in a 16 percent reduction in stockouts and a 67 percent drop in replenishment times. As customers go through checkout, the RFID system swiftly combines point-of-sale data on their purchases with RFID-generated data on what is available in the stockroom to produce pick lists that are automatically created in real time. It also ensures that suppliers are notified when products are sold and can ensure that enough of a product is always at a particular store. This strategy also results in time and labor savings because Walmart associates no longer need to scan shelves to determine what is out of stock; nor do they have to scan cartons and cases arriving at the stockroom. The scanners tag incoming pallets and translate the data into supply chain management database forecasting models to address out-of-stock items and reduce stocking/restocking mix-ups.

capabilities, infrastructure, and technical and business skills, making them more attractive regions for global sourcing.

On the other hand, the costs and risks of outsourcing halfway around the world must be taken into consideration. Firms that outsource give up a measure of control over key factors such as data security and the quality of service delivered to customers. To combat these issues, many firms have shifted from outsourcing to offshoring of their own activities. These companies set up their own offshore operations (called captives) to handle business processes where wage rates are lower. ANZ Bank (Australia and New Zealand Banking Group), for example, uses a captive operation in India to handle back-office processing for credit cards, mortgages, wealth management, human resources, and IT development.[18]

As illustrated in Exhibit 6.8, information technology is the primary activity outsourced today. Currently, however, firms are shifting supporting processes to outside businesses. These supporting processes include administrative activities, distribution, human resources, financial analysis, call centers, and even sales and marketing. When a firm has significant needs and insufficient in-house expertise, the importance of outsourcing will increase. For example, an entire industry known as 3PLs (third party logistics providers) has emerged in the United States and Europe as retailers look toward outside expertise as a way to reduce costs and make their products more readily available. In fact, roughly 77 percent of *Fortune* 500 firms use 3PLs to manage inventories and handle the physical movement of products in the supply chain to ensure that items are in the right amounts and in the right places when needed.[19]

EXHIBIT 6.8   The Trend in Outsourcing

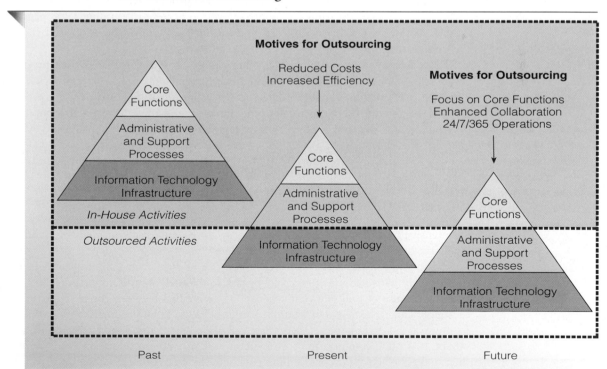

Source: Adapted from Edward W. Davis and Robert E. Speckman, *The Extended Enterprise* (Upper Saddle River, NJ: Prentice Hall Financial Times, 2004), p. 111, based on information from Forrester Research, Inc.

The Growth of Nontraditional Channels While the traditional marketing channel of manufacturer to wholesaler to retailer is alive and well today, customers' demands for lower prices and greater convenience have put pressure on all channel intermediaries to justify their existence. Every time a different intermediary handles a product, the cost to the final customer increases. This places a great deal of downward pressure on profit margins as firms struggle to balance their need for profit with the need to offer customers good value and fair prices. Under such circumstances, the channel typically evolves into a more direct form. Keep in mind, however, that channel evolution does not replace or alter the basic functions that all channels must perform (e.g., sorting, breaking bulk, holding inventory, etc.). Even after the elimination of certain channel intermediaries, other firms—or even the customer—will have to step in and fulfill these basic functions.

A number of nontraditional channels have emerged to expand opportunities for more direct distribution. The fastest growing example of this trend is e-commerce. However, there are other forms of direct distribution that occur outside the traditional "bricks-and-mortar" of physical stores:

- **Catalog and Direct Marketing**. Some of the most popular and successful direct merchants, including Lands' End, J. Crew, IKEA, Cabela's, and GEICO Insurance, are catalog and direct marketers.
- **Direct Selling**. These merchants sell through face-to-face contact with sales associates. Examples include Avon, Tupperware, Discovery Toys, and Pampered Chef. Avon is far and away the largest with over $11 billion in sales each year.
- **Home Shopping Networks**. Networks like QVC and the Home Shopping Network serve millions of satisfied customers every week.
- **Vending**. The advantage of vending is 24/7/365 product availability in virtually any location. Though soft drinks account for over 50 percent of vending sales, products such as flowers, toothpaste, movies, and fishing bait can now be purchased via vending machines.
- **Direct Response Advertising**. Many companies sell music, toy, and book products via television commercials and 1-800 phone numbers. One of the largest is Time Life, which sells millions of books, CDs, and DVDs each year. Infomercials, a cross between an advertisement, a news program, and a documentary, are also popular programs for products such as exercise equipment and kitchen appliances.

One of the benefits of nontraditional channels for manufacturers is the ability to offer two or more lines of the same merchandise through two or more channels (often called dual distribution), thus increasing sales coverage. For example, Hallmark sells its highly respected Hallmark line of greeting cards primarily through selective distribution at Hallmark stores. They make their Ambassador and Shoebox Greetings card lines available on an intensive basis through supermarkets, drug stores, and discount retailers. In addition, Hallmark offers both cards and e-cards online. One of the consequences of using multiple channels, however, is that it increases the risk of disintermediation, where customers deal directly with manufacturers and bypass traditional channel intermediaries. Consequently, the use of multiple channels can create conflict between the manufacturer and its supply chain partners. For example, Apple sells the same products in its online store, its physical stores, at large retailers (Best Buy, Walmart, Target), and at Amazon, among others. It is quite common for customers to look at Apple products in retail stores, but then make the actual purchase online at either Apple or Amazon (sometimes even while standing in the store). Amazon's low prices, free shipping, and lack of sales tax in many states also puts physical stores at a disadvantage. For these reasons, manufacturers must carefully weigh the benefits of dual distribution against its potential drawbacks.

Integrated Marketing Communications

Without a doubt, promotion and marketing communications are the most ubiquitous elements of any firm's marketing program. This is not surprising because promotional activities are necessary to communicate the features and benefits of a product to the firm's intended target markets. Marketing communications includes conveying and sharing meaning between buyers and sellers, either as individuals, firms, or between individuals and firms. Integrated marketing communications (IMC) refers to the strategic, coordinated use of promotion to create one consistent message across multiple channels to ensure maximum persuasive impact on the firm's current and potential customers. IMC takes a 360-degree view of the customer that considers each and every contact that a customer or potential customer may have in his or her relationship with the firm. The key to IMC is consistency and uniformity of message across all elements of promotion as shown in Exhibit 6.9.

Due to the many advantages associated with IMC, most marketers have adopted integrated marketing as the basis for their communication and promotion strategies. By coordinating all communication "touch points," firms using IMC convey an image of truly knowing and caring about their customers that can translate into long-term customer relationships. Likewise, IMC reduces costs and increases efficiency because it can reduce or eliminate redundancies and waste in the overall promotional program. Many firms have embraced IMC because mass-media advertising has become more expensive and less predictable than in the past. As discussed in *Beyond the Pages 6.4*, marketers are being forced to adopt new marketing strategies as advancing technology and customer preferences are threatening to make traditional forms of promotion obsolete. Many firms are also embracing technology in order to target customers directly through product placement and online promotion. This increased focus on individual customers requires that the overall promotional program be integrated and focused as well.

EXHIBIT 6.9   **Components of IMC Strategy**

Fragmentation Forever Changes Media Advertising[20]

The increasing fragmentation of consumer audiences has forever changed the way both media and advertisers do business. The problem is that consumers' attention is being spread across an increasing array of media and entertainment choices, including the Internet, targeted cable programming, video-on-demand, DVR, iPods/iPads, video games, movies, and mobile devices such as smartphones. Today, mass audiences are dwindling fast as consumers spend less time with traditional media such as television, magazines, and newspapers. Consumers now expect to use media whenever and wherever they want, and on any device. They are no longer wed to full-length television programming or to leisurely reading the newspaper. For advertisers, the trend is alarming because their traditional bread-and-butter demographic is fragmenting the most. For example, the number of 18- to 34-year-old men who watch primetime television has declined steadily since 2000. Those who do watch television increasingly use DVR devices to skip advertising. Today, DVR usage accounts for 8 percent of all U.S. TV viewing time, which is higher than both video games and DVDs.

These changes are forcing marketers to adapt by finding newer, more effective ways to reach their target audiences. One way marketers are countering the trend is by linking sales promotion to target markets through strategic integration into related media programming. Company sponsorship of programming or events can allow a close connection between brand and target market. For example, Bravo's *Top Chef* has successfully partnered with Toyota, Clorox, *Food & Wine Magazine*, Campbell Soup, Diet Dr. Pepper, and Quaker. Sponsorship opportunities like these work better than traditional advertising, especially with respect to brand recall. Bank of America, for example, achieves an astounding 39 percent average recall when it sponsors a sporting event. Nike (21 percent), Buick (14 percent), American Express (13 percent), and FedEx (11 percent) have reported similar successes with sports sponsorships.

In addition to outright sponsorship of popular programs, marketers also make deals with television and cable networks, as well as movie studios, to place their products into actual programs and films. In-program product placements have been successful in reaching consumers as they are being entertained, rather than during the competitive commercial breaks. Reality programming in particular has been a natural fit for product placement because of the close interchange between the participants and the products (e.g. Coca Cola and *American Idol*; Sears and *Extreme Makeover: Home Edition*). Furthermore, sixteen brands were prominently featured in the recent hit movie, *The Avengers*. Acura, in particular, signed a multi-picture deal with Marvel to showcase its cars in upcoming films.

Media companies themselves have also been forced to adapt, most notably by fragmenting their content and business models to match their fragmented audiences. One way that companies have addressed the problem is by making their content available on multiple platforms. CBS, for example, first experimented with its broadcast of the 2008 NCAA Basketball Tournament by broadcasting live action on the Internet. The service, called March Madness on Demand, attracted roughly 5 million different online viewers and over $30 million in advertising revenue during the tournament. More recently, CBS switched to a paid model with March Madness Live. For $3.99, fans could watch high quality streams on their Apple and Android devices. The games were still available for free on CBSSports.com. As these and other examples illustrate, the key to meeting the demands of fragmented audiences is to disaggregate content and make it available *a la carte* style. Consumers prefer to access content (songs, movies, TV shows, news) when, where, and how they want it without having to purchase entire albums, programs, or networks.

Despite the challenges of reaching fragmented audiences, the trend actually has a big side benefit. The science behind traditional broadcast television ratings and audience measurement has always been uncertain. With on-demand services, advertisers are able to precisely measure audience characteristics whether the content is delivered via the Internet, cable, or wireless devices. This one-two punch of profits and precise measurement may mark the death of the traditional 30-second primetime television spot.

Strategic Issues in Integrated Marketing Communications

When selecting elements to include in the IMC program, it is important to take a holistic perspective that coordinates not only all promotional elements but also the IMC program with the rest of the marketing program (product, price, and supply chain strategy). Taking this approach allows a firm to communicate a consistent message to target customers from every possible angle, thereby maximizing the total impact on those customers. For example, if the advertising campaign stresses quality, the sales force talks about low price, the supply chain pushes wide availability, and the website stresses product innovation, then what is the customer to believe? Not readily seeing that a product can deliver all these benefits, the customer is likely to become confused and go to a competitor with a more consistent message.

All too frequently, firms rush to launch an intensive IMC campaign that has no clear promotional objectives. The vast majority of promotion activities do not create results in the short term, so firms must focus on long-term promotional objectives and have the patience to continue the program long enough to gauge true success. It takes a great deal of time, effort, and resources to build a solid market position. Promotion based on creativity alone, unlinked to the rest of the marketing strategy, can waste limited and valuable marketing resources.

Ultimately, the goals and objectives of any promotional campaign culminate in the purchase of goods or services by the target market. The classic model for outlining promotional goals and achieving this ultimate outcome is the AIDA model—attention, interest, desire, and action:

- **Attention**. Firms cannot sell products if the members of the target market do not know they exist. As a result, the first major goal of any promotional campaign is to attract the attention of potential customers.
- **Interest**. Attracting attention seldom sells products. Therefore, the firm must spark interest in the product by demonstrating its features, uses, and benefits.
- **Desire.** To be successful, firms must move potential customers beyond mere interest in the product. Good promotion will stimulate desire by convincing potential customers of the product's superiority and its ability to satisfy specific needs.
- **Action**. After convincing potential customers to buy the product, promotion must then push them toward the actual purchase.

The role and importance of specific promotional elements vary across the steps in the AIDA model. Mass-communication elements, such as advertising and public relations, tend to be used more heavily to stimulate awareness and interest due to their efficiency in reaching large numbers of potential customers. Along with advertising, sales promotion activities, such as product samples or demonstrations, are vital to stimulating interest in the product. The enhanced communication effectiveness of personal selling makes it ideally suited to moving potential customers through internal desire and into action. Other sales promotion activities, such as product displays, coupons, and trial-size packaging, are well suited to pushing customers toward the final act of making a purchase.

Alongside the issue of promotional goals and objectives, the firm must also consider its promotional goals with respect to the supply chain. In essence, the firm must decide whether it will use a pull strategy, a push strategy, or some combination of the two. When firms use a pull strategy, they focus their promotional efforts toward stimulating demand among final customers, who then exert pressure on the supply chain to carry the product. The coordinated use of heavy advertising, public relations, and consumer sales promotion has the effect of pulling products through the supply chain, hence its name. In a push strategy, promotional efforts focus on members of the supply chain, such as wholesalers and retailers, to motivate them to spend extra time and effort on selling the product. This strategy relies heavily on personal selling and trade sales promotion to push products through the supply chain toward final customers.

Coordinating promotional elements within the context of the entire marketing program requires a complete understanding of the role, function, and benefits of each element. The advantages and disadvantages of each element must be carefully balanced against the promotional budget and the firm's IMC goals and objectives. To ensure a constant and synergistic message to targeted customers, the firm must ultimately decide how to weigh each promotional element in the overall IMC strategy. The next sections take a closer look at the four key elements that comprise most IMC programs.

Advertising

Advertising is a key component of promotion and is usually one of the most visible elements of an integrated marketing communications program. Advertising is paid, non-personal communication transmitted through media such as television, radio, magazines, newspapers, direct mail, outdoor displays, the Internet, and mobile devices. Exhibit 6.10 outlines the changing trends in U.S. media advertising. Note that after tremendous growth over the last decade, spending on Internet advertising has slowed dramatically.

EXHIBIT 6.10 **Change in U.S. Measured Ad Spending, 2010-2011**

Media Sector	Percent Change
Television	2.4
• Network	−2.0
• Cable	7.7
• Spot TV	−4.5
• Syndication	15.4
• Spanish Language	8.3
Magazines	−0.4
• Consumer	0.0
• B-to-B	0.8
• Sunday	−7.2
• Local	−2.9
• Spanish Language	24.9
Newspaper	−3.7
• Local	−3.8
• National	−3.6
• Spanish Language	1.9
Internet	0.4
• Paid Search	−2.8
• Display	5.5
Radio	−0.6
Outdoor Media	6.5

Source: Kantar Media (http://kantarmediana.com/intelligence/press/us-advertising-expenditures-increased-08-percent-2011), March 12, 2012.

Newspapers, magazines, and radio continue to struggle with meaningful declines in ad revenues. This spending pattern follows trends in media usage as consumers are spending more time online and less time with traditional media. The major bright spot in recent ad spending figures is the growth in Spanish language advertising. This is not surprising considering the rapid growth of the Hispanic population in the United States. In addition, Hispanics wield nearly $1 trillion in buying power—a number expected to increase to $1.5 trillion by 2015. By then, Hispanics will account for 11 percent of the total buying power in the United States.[21]

As the use of traditional media declines, advertisers are accelerating their use of Internet-based advertising methods. As shown in Exhibit 6.11, the bulk of Internet-based ad spending—which now totals almost $32 billion in the U.S.—comes from search advertising (despite the recent decline noted in Exhibit 6.10), followed by display/banner ads and classifieds. The fastest growing segment is in mobile advertising, which is up over 128 percent since 2010. Most of the top Internet advertisers come from the retail (22 percent of spending), financial services (13 percent), and telecom (12 percent) sectors. Although firms in these and other industries enjoy the large number of impressions that can be generated via Internet-based advertising, their efforts suffer from the fleeting nature of most online ads. Getting a potential customer to click on a banner ad or look at a message for more than a few seconds can be quite challenging.

Despite the many advantages of advertising, its use does create a number of challenges for companies. First, the initial expense for advertising is typically quite high, especially for television. Although media buys like airtime on the Super Bowl gets a lot of attention, the actual production cost for a 30-second commercial can also be expensive (the U.S. average is just under $400,000).[22] Second, many companies struggle to determine the correct amount of money to allocate to advertising because the effects of advertising are difficult to measure. There are many factors that can determine a firm's decision about the appropriate level to fund advertising activities, including the geographic size of the market, the distribution or density of customers, the types of products advertised, sales volume relative to the competition, and the firm's budget. While setting the budget too high will obviously result in waste and lower profits, setting

EXHIBIT 6.11   Internet Ad Revenues by Advertising Format, 2011

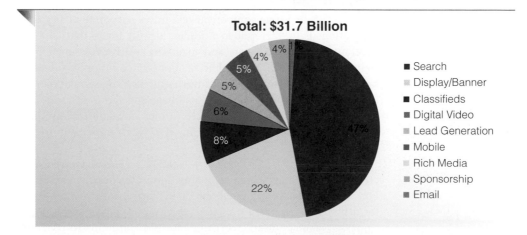

Source: "IAB Internet Advertising Revenue Report 2011," Interactive Advertising Bureau, April 2012 (http://www.iab. net/media/file/IAB_Internet_Advertising_Revenue_Report_FY_2011.pdf).

the budget too low may be worse. Firms that do not spend enough on advertising find it very difficult to stand out in an extremely crowded market for customer attention.

Third, it is usually very difficult to evaluate the effectiveness of advertising. Many of the effects and outcomes of advertising take a long time to develop, especially regarding important outcomes such as enhanced brand image, corporate reputation, and positive product attitudes. The effect of advertising on sales lags in some cases, with the effect occurring long after the campaign has ended. The seemingly unending methods that can be used to evaluate advertising effectiveness further complicate the task of measuring advertising results. Some methods include evaluating the achievement of advertising objectives; assessing the effectiveness of advertising copy, illustrations, and layouts; and evaluating the effectiveness of various media. Effectiveness measures can also look at different market segments and their responses to advertising—including brand image; attitudes toward the advertising, the brand, or the firm; and actual customer purchasing behavior.

Finally, most marketers struggle with the fine line between what is permissible and not permissible in advertising. In addition to cultural and stylistic considerations, marketers must also carefully consider how they portray their products to potential customers. For example, the Federal Trade Commission fined both Skechers ($40 million) and Reebok ($25 million) for false claims about their fitness shoes. The FTC found that both companies misled consumers with ads claiming that using their shoes would lead to a more perfect body.[23] Product claims are also important in comparative advertising, which occurs when one firm compares its product with one or more competing products on specific features or benefits. Comparative advertising is common in product categories such as soft drinks, automobiles, computers, and over-the-counter medications. In some cases, this comparison is direct, as in Burger King's "Whopper Virgin" taste test, where the company had people who had never tasted a hamburger before compare a McDonald's Big Mac with the Burger King Whopper. In other cases, the comparison used in the advertisement is indirect or implied. Procter & Gamble uses this tactic when promoting its Gillette razors as "The Best a Man Can Get." The implied comparison in this case involves all competing razors on the market. Under the provisions of the Trademark Law Revision Act, marketers using comparative advertising must ensure they do not misrepresent the characteristics of competing products.

Public Relations

Public relations is one component of a firm's corporate affairs activities. The goal of public relations is to track public attitudes, identify issues that may elicit public concern, and develop programs to create and maintain positive relationships between a firm and its stakeholders. A firm uses public relations to communicate with its stakeholders for the same reasons that it develops advertisements. Public relations can be used to promote the firm, its people, its ideas, and its image and can even create an internal shared understanding among employees. Because various stakeholders' attitudes toward the firm affect their decisions relative to the firm, it is very important to maintain positive public opinion.

Public relations can improve the public's general awareness of a company and can create specific images such as quality, innovativeness, value, or concern for social issues. For example, New Belgium Brewery in Fort Collins, Colorado, has a strong reputation for its stance on environmental efficiency and conservation. The brewery takes an aggressive stance toward recycling and uses windmills to generate electricity.[24] Likewise, Starbucks has gained international awareness through its fair treatment of employees. The company was also the first coffee retailer to establish a global code of conduct for fair treatment of agricultural suppliers—the small farmers who supply the coffee beans for its products.

Firms use a number of public relations methods to convey messages and to create the right attitudes, images, and opinions. Public relations is sometimes confused with publicity. Although publicity is one part of public relations, it is more narrowly defined to include the firm's activities designed to gain media attention through articles, editorials, or news stories. By encouraging the media to report on a firm's accomplishments, publicity helps maintain positive public awareness, visibility, and a desired image. Publicity can be used for a single purpose, such as to launch a new product or diminish the public's opinion regarding a negative event, or it can be used for multiple purposes to enhance many aspects of the firm's activities. Having a good publicity strategy is important because publicity can have the same effect as advertising, though typically with greater credibility. There are a number of different methods used in public relations and publicity efforts:

- **News (or Press) Releases**. A news release is a few pages of typewritten copy— typically fewer than 300 words—used to draw attention to a company event, product, or person affiliated with the firm. News releases can be submitted to newspapers, magazines, television contacts, suppliers, key customers, or even the firm's employees.
- **Feature Articles**. A feature article is a full-length story prepared for a specific purpose or target audience. For example, a firm building a new production facility in northeast Georgia might supply a feature article to regional and local media outlets, chambers of commerce, local governments, and major firms in the area. Feature articles typically focus on the implications or economic impact of a firm's actions. They are also very useful when responding to negative events or publicity.
- **White Papers**. White papers are similar to feature articles; however, they are more technical and focus on very specific topics of interest to the firm's stakeholders. White papers promote a firm's stance on important product or market issues and can be used to promote the firm's own products and solutions. White papers have been used extensively in the information technology field where firms continually work to establish standards and keep up with technological innovation.
- **Press Conferences**. A press conference is a meeting with news media called to announce or respond to major events. Media personnel receive invitations to a specific location, with written materials, photographs, exhibits, and even products given to them. Multimedia materials may be distributed to broadcast stations in hopes that they will air some of the activities that occurred at the press conference. Firms typically hold press conferences when announcing new products, patents, mergers or acquisitions, philanthropic efforts, or internal administrative changes.
- **Event Sponsorship**. Corporate sponsorship of major events has become an entire industry in itself. Sponsorships can range from local events, such as high school athletics and local charities, to international events such as the Tour de France or NASCAR. Another popular sponsorship strategy involves the naming of sports stadiums and venues, such as Gillette Stadium, home to the New England Patriots.
- **Employee Relations**. Employee relations are every bit as important as public and investor relations. Employee relations' activities provide organizational support for employees with respect to their jobs and lives. Employee relations can encompass many different activities including internal newsletters, training programs, employee assistance programs, and human resource programs.

When these methods generate publicity in the media, the public perceives the message as having more credibility due to the implied endorsement of the media that carries the story. The public will typically consider news coverage more truthful and credible than advertising because the firm has not paid for the media time. One major drawback of public relations activities is that the firm has much less control over how the message will be delivered. For example, many media personnel have a reputation for inserting their own opinions and biases when communicating a news story. Another drawback involves the risk of spending a great deal of time and effort in developing public relations messages that fail to attract media attention.

Personal Selling and Sales Management

Personal selling is paid personal communication that attempts to inform customers about products and persuade them to purchase those products. Personal selling takes place in many forms. For example, a Best Buy salesperson who describes the benefits of a HP laptop to a customer engages in personal selling. So does the salesperson who attempts to convince a large industrial organization to purchase photocopy machines. Some types of personal selling are highly complex and relational in nature. The complexity of these types of contracts requires a long-term, personal relationship between salespeople and companies.

Compared to other types of promotion, personal selling is the most precise form of communication because it assures companies that they are in direct contact with an excellent prospect. Though one-on-one contact is highly advantageous, it does not come without disadvantages. The most serious drawback of personal selling is the cost per contact. In business markets, a single sales presentation can take many months and thousands of dollars to prepare. For instance, to give government officials a real feel for the design and scope of a bridge construction project, Parsons, Inc. (a large engineering and construction firm) must invest thousands of dollars in detailed scale models of several different bridge designs. Personal selling is also expensive due to the costs associated with recruiting, selecting, training, and motivating salespeople. Despite the high costs, personal selling plays an increasingly important role in IMC and overall marketing strategy.

The goals of personal selling vary tremendously based on its role in a long-run approach to integrated communications. These goals typically involve finding prospects, informing prospects, persuading prospects to buy, and keeping customers satisfied through follow-up service after the sale. To effectively deliver on these goals, salespeople have to be not only competent in selling skills but also thoroughly trained in technical product characteristics. For example, pharmaceutical salespeople (drug reps) who sell to physicians and hospitals must have detailed training in the technical medical applications of the drugs and medical devices that they sell. In fact, it is not unusual for salespeople who sell medical implants such as knee or hip replacements to have as much technical training about the product as the physicians who actually implant these devices during surgery. Obviously, when the products and buyers are less sophisticated, salespeople will require much less training.

Very few businesses can survive on the profits generated from purely transactional marketing (one-time purchases). For long-term survival, most firms depend on repeat sales and the development of ongoing relationships with customers. For this reason, personal selling has evolved to take on elements of customer service and marketing research. More than any other part of the firm, salespeople are closer to the customer and have many more opportunities for communication with them. Every contact with a customer gives the sales force a chance to deliver exceptional service and learn more about the customer's needs. Salespeople also have the opportunity to learn about competing products and the customer's reaction toward them. These relational aspects are important—whether the salesperson makes a sale or not. In today's highly competitive markets, the frontline knowledge held by the sales force is one of the most important assets of the firm. In fact, the knowledge held by the sales force is often an important strength that can be leveraged in developing marketing strategy.

Because the sales force has a direct bearing on sales revenue and customer satisfaction, the effective management of the sales force is vital to a firm's marketing program. In addition to generating performance outcomes, the sales force often creates the firm's reputation, and the conduct of individual salespeople determines the perceived ethicalness of the entire firm. The strategic implementation of effective sales management requires a number of activities:

- **Developing Sales Force Objectives**. The technical aspects of establishing sales force objectives involve desired sales dollars, sales volume, or market share. These sales objectives can be translated into guidelines for recruiting new salespeople as well as setting quotas for individual salespeople. Further, individual sales objectives might be based on order size, the number of sales calls, or the ratio of orders to calls. Ultimately, sales objectives help evaluate and control sales force activities, as well as compensate individual salespeople.
- **Determining Sales Force Size**. The size of the sales force is a function of many variables including the type of salespeople used, specific sales objectives, and the importance of personal selling within the overall IMC program. The size of the sales force is important because the firm must find a balance between sales expenses and revenue generation. Having a sales force that is too large or too small can lead to inflated expenses, lost sales, and lost profit.
- **Recruiting and Training Salespeople**. Recruiting the right types of salespeople should be closely tied to the personal selling and IMC strategies. Firms usually recruit potential salespeople from a number of sources including within the firm, competing firms, employment agencies, educational institutions, and direct-response advertisements placed on the Internet, in magazines, or in newspapers. Salesperson recruitment should be a continuous activity because firms must ensure that new salespeople are consistently available to sustain the sales program.
- **Controlling and Evaluating the Sales Force**. Controlling and evaluating the sales force require a comparison of sales objectives with actual sales performance. To effectively evaluate a salesperson, predetermined performance standards must be in place. These standards also determine the compensation plan for the sales force. Exhibit 6.12 provides a comparison of various sales force compensation systems.

Across many industries, sales forces have shrunk due to advances in communications technology and mobile computing. The development of integrated supply chains and the procurement of standardized products over the Internet have reduced the need for salespeople in many industries. Although these developments reduce selling costs, they create a major management challenge for most firms: How can firms use new technology to reduce costs and increase productivity while maintaining personalized, one-to-one client relationships?

One of the keys to using sales technology effectively is to seamlessly integrate it with customer relationship management systems, competitive intelligence activities, and internal customer databases. By automating many repetitive selling tasks, like filling repeat orders, sales technology can actually increase sales, productivity, and one-to-one client relationships at the same time. Although many firms develop and maintain their own sales automation systems, others who lack the resources to do so can turn to third-party providers like Salesforce.com—an on-demand, web-based provider of integrated CRM and sales automation solutions. Whether in-house or third party, the key to these solutions is integration. By pushing integrated customer, competitive, and product

---

EXHIBIT 6.12   Comparison of Sales Force Compensation Methods

Method	Most Useful When:	Advantages	Disadvantages
Straight Salary	• Salespeople are new • Salespeople move into new territories • Products require intense presale and postsale service	• Easy to administer • Gives salespeople more security • Greater control over salespeople • More predictable selling expenses	• Little or no incentive for salespeople • Salespeople require close supervision
Straight Commission	• Aggressive selling is required • Nonselling tasks can be minimized • The firm outsources some selling functions	• Gives salespeople maximum incentive • Ties selling expenses to sales volume • Can use differential commissions for different products to boost sales	• Less security for salespeople • Managers have less control over salespeople • Small accounts may receive less service
Combination	• Sales territories have similar sales potential • The firm wants to provide incentive and still have some control	• Good balance of incentive and security for salespeople	• Selling expenses are less predictable • May be difficult to administer

Source: Adapted from William M. Pride and O.C. Ferrell, *Marketing* (Mason, OH: South-Western: Cengage Learning, 2010), p. 530.

information toward the salesperson, technology can increase salesperson productivity and sales revenue by allowing the sales force to serve customers' needs more effectively.

Sales Promotion

Despite the attention paid to advertising, sales promotion activities account for the bulk of promotional spending in many firms. This is especially true for firms selling consumer products in grocery stores and mass-merchandise retailers where sales promotion can account for up to 70 percent of the firm's promotional budget.[25] Sales promotion involves activities that create buyer incentives to purchase a product or that add value for the buyer or the trade. Sales promotion can be targeted toward consumers, channel intermediaries, or the sales force. Roughly a third of all sales promotion expenditures are targeted toward the trade (wholesalers and retailers). Direct mail comprises the next largest expense at between 15 and 20 percent. Regardless of the activity and toward whom it is directed, sales promotion has one universal goal: to induce product trial and purchase.

Most firms use sales promotion in support of advertising, public relations, or personal selling activities rather than as a stand-alone promotional element. Advertising is frequently coordinated with sales promotion activities to provide free product samples, premiums, or value-added incentives. For example, a manufacturer might offer free merchandise to channel intermediaries who purchase a stated quantity of product within a specified time frame. A 7-Up bottler, for example, might offer a free case of 7-Up for every ten cases purchased by a retailer. On the consumer side, Coca-Cola's innovative "Don't Dew it" promotion took steps to increase market share of the company's Vault brand over Pepsi's Mountain Dew. In a bold move, Coca-Cola offered free samples of Vault by giving away 16, 20, or 24-ounce Vaults to consumers who purchased a 20-ounce Mountain Dew.[26]

Consumer Sales Promotion   Any member of the supply chain can initiate consumer sales promotions, but manufacturers and retailers typically offer them. For manufacturers, sales promotion activities represent an effective way to introduce new products or promote established brands. Coupons and product sampling are frequently used during new product launches to stimulate interest and trial. Retailers typically offer sales promotions to stimulate customer traffic or increase sales at specific locations. Coupons and free products are common examples, as are in-store product demonstrations. Many retailers are known for their sales promotions such as the free toys that come with kid's meals at McDonald's, Burger King, and other fast food establishments. A potentially limitless variety of sales promotion methods can be used in consumer markets. Truthfully, developing and using these methods is limited only by the creativity of the firm offering the promotion. However, firms will typically offer one or more of the following types of sales promotions to consumers:

- **Coupons**. Coupons reduce the price of a product and encourage customers to try new or established brands. Coupons can be used to increase sales volume quickly, to attract repeat purchasers, or even to introduce new product sizes or models. While coupon cutting (cutting coupons from newspapers or direct mail) was once quite common, the practice declined over the years. This mentality changed with the latest economic recession as many consumers returned to using coupons, especially new mobile coupons. Exhibit 6.13 demonstrates the remarkable growth in mobile coupon users and its connection to smartphone ownership.

- **Rebates**. Rebates are very similar to coupons except that they require more effort on the consumer's part to obtain the price reduction. Although consumers prefer coupons because of the ease of use, most firms prefer rebates for several reasons. First, firms have more control over rebates because they can be launched and ended very quickly. Second, a rebate program allows the firm to collect important consumer information that can be used to build customer databases. The best reason is that

EXHIBIT 6.13   Growth in Mobile Coupon Users

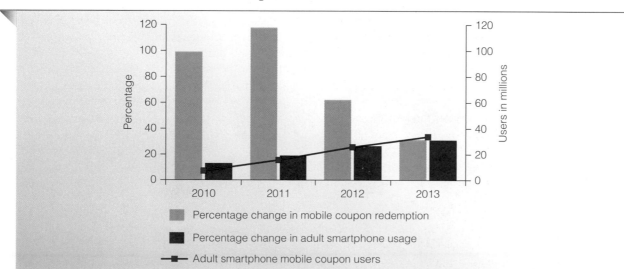

Source: "One in Ten Users Redeem Mobile Coupons," *Mobile Marketing Watch*, September 7, 2011, (http://www.mobilemarketingwatch.com/one-in-ten-users-redeem-mobile-coupons-18438).

most consumers never bother to redeem rebate offers. This allows a firm to entice customers to purchase a product with only a minimal loss of profit.

- **Samples**. Free samples are one of the most widely used consumer sales promotion methods. Samples stimulate trial of a product, increase volume in the early stages of the product's life cycle, and encourage consumers to actively search for a product. Samples can be distributed through the mail, attached to other products, and given out through personal selling efforts or in-store displays. Samples can also be distributed via less direct methods. For example, free samples of soap, shampoo, coffee, or sunscreen might be placed in hotel rooms to create consumer awareness of new products.

- **Loyalty Programs**. Loyalty programs, or frequent-buyer programs, reward loyal customers who engage in repeat purchases. These programs are popular in many industries due to their potential to dramatically increase profits over the long term. We are all familiar with the frequent-flier programs offered by major airlines. Other companies, such as hotels, auto rental agencies, and credit card companies, offer free goods or services for repeat purchases. For instance, the Discover Card provides a one percent cash-back bonus to each cardholder at the end of the year, and Hallmark rewards loyal customers with the Hallmark Gold Crown Card, which allows frequent buyers to accrue points that are redeemable for merchandise and discounts.

- **Point-of-Purchase Promotion**. Point-of-purchase (POP) promotion includes displays, in-store demonstrations, counter pieces, display racks, or self-service cartons that are designed to build traffic, advertise a product, or induce impulse purchases. POP promotions are highly effective because they are used in a store where consumers make roughly 70 to 80 percent of all purchase decisions.

- **Premiums**. Premiums are items offered free or at a minimum cost as a bonus for purchasing a product. Examples of premiums include a free car wash with a gasoline fill-up, a free toothbrush with a purchase of a tube of toothpaste, and the toys offered inside a McDonald's Happy Meal. Premiums are good at increasing consumption and persuading consumers to switch brands.

The toy prizes inside a McDonald's Happy Meal may be the best-known consumer sales promotion of all time.

- **Contests and Sweepstakes**. Consumer contests, games, and sweepstakes encourage potential consumers to compete for prizes or try their luck by submitting their names in a drawing for prizes. In addition to being valuable information collection tools, contests and sweepstakes are good at attracting a large number of participants and generating widespread interest in a product. Because they require no skill to enter, sweepstakes are an effective way to increase sales or market share in the short term.
- **Direct Mail**. Direct mail, which includes catalog marketing and other printed material mailed to individual consumers, is a unique category because it incorporates elements of advertising, sales promotion, and distribution into a coordinated effort to induce customers to buy. The use of direct mail has grown tremendously in recent years due to consumer time constraints, relatively low cost, and the advent of sophisticated database management tools.

Firms can use any one or all of these consumer promotion methods in their overall IMC program. However, the choice of one or more methods must be made in consideration of the firm's IMC objectives. Furthermore, the choice must also consider the use of sales promotions by competitors and whether a particular method involves ethical or legal dimensions. Consumer sweepstakes, in particular, have specific legal requirements to ensure that each entrant has an equally likely chance of winning.

Business (Trade) Sales Promotion   Sales promotion in business markets, or trade promotion, is generally the largest expense in a firm's total sales promotion budget. By targeting channel intermediaries with promotional activities, manufacturers hope to push their products through the channel by increasing sales and encouraging increased effort among their channel partners. Manufacturers use many of the same promotional methods that target consumers; however, a number of sales promotion methods are unique to business markets:

- **Trade Allowances**. Manufacturers offer a number of different trade allowances, or price reductions, to their channel intermediaries. Buying allowances are price reductions for purchasing specified quantities of a product at a single time (the equivalent of a bulk discount). Related to this is a buy-back allowance where the reduction is proportional to the total amount of product purchased during the time frame of the promotional offer. Finally, a merchandise allowance is a manufacturer's agreement to pay intermediaries a specific sum of money in exchange for specific promotional efforts such as special displays or advertising. In each case, the goal of the allowance is to induce intermediaries to perform specific actions.
- **Free Merchandise**. Manufacturers sometimes offer free merchandise to intermediaries instead of quantity discounts. Typically, they provide the free merchandise to reduce invoice costs as a way of compensating the intermediary for other activities that assist the manufacturer.
- **Cooperative Advertising**. Cooperative advertising is an arrangement whereby a manufacturer agrees to pay a certain amount of an intermediary's media cost for advertising the manufacturer's products. This is a very popular sales promotion method among retailers.
- **Training Assistance and Sales Incentives**. In some cases, a manufacturer can offer free training to an intermediary's employees or sales staff. This typically occurs when the products involved are rather complex. Selling incentives come in two general forms: push money and sales contests. The intermediary's sales staff receives push money in the form of additional compensation to encourage a more aggressive selling effort for a particular product. This method is expensive and should be used carefully to avoid any ethical or legal issues. Sales contests encourage outstanding performance

within an intermediary's sales force. Sales personnel can be recognized for outstanding achievements by receiving money, vacations, computers, or even cars for meeting or exceeding certain sales targets.

Trade sales promotion encompasses a wide variety of activities and is vital when a manufacturer needs the cooperation and support of the channel to fulfill its own sales and marketing objectives. This is particularly true when a manufacturer must obtain support for a new product launch or a new consumer sales promotion. Given the importance of integrated supply chains, it should not be surprising that effective trade promotion is also vital to fulfilling a firm's distribution strategy.

Lessons from Chapter 6

The marketing program:

- refers to the strategic combination of the four basic marketing mix elements: product, price, distribution, and promotion.
- has as its outcome a complete offering that consists of an array of physical (tangible), service (intangible), and symbolic (perceptual) attributes designed to satisfy customers' needs and wants.
- strives to overcome commoditization by enhancing the service and symbolic elements of the offering.

Product strategy:

- lies at the heart of every organization in that it defines what the organization does and why it exists.
- is about delivering benefits that enhance a customer's situation or solve a customer's problems.

The product portfolio:

- is used in both consumer (convenience, shopping, specialty, and unsought products) and business (raw materials, component parts, process materials, MRO supplies, accessory equipment, installations, and business services) markets.
- is used in most firms due to the advantages of selling a variety of products rather than a single product.
- consists of a group of closely related product items (product lines) and the total group of products offered by the firm (product mix).
- involves strategic decisions such as the number of product lines to offer (variety), as well as the depth of each product line (assortment).
- can create a number of important benefits for firms, including economies of scale, package uniformity, standardization, sales and distribution efficiency, and equivalent quality beliefs.

The challenges of service products:

- stem mainly from the fact that services are intangible. Other challenging characteristics of services include simultaneous production and consumption, perishability, heterogeneity, and client-based relationships.

- include the following issues:
  - service firms experience problems in balancing supply (capacity) with demand.
  - service demand is time-and-place dependent because customers or their possessions must be present for delivery.
  - customers have a difficult time evaluating the quality of a service before it is purchased and consumed.
  - service quality is often inconsistent and very difficult to standardize across many customers.
  - the need for some services is not always apparent to customers. Consequently, service marketers often have trouble tying their offerings directly to customers' needs.

New product development:

- is a vital part of a firm's efforts to sustain growth and profits.
- considers six strategic options related to the newness of products:
  - New-to-the-world products (discontinuous innovations)— which involve a pioneering effort by a firm that leads to the creation of an entirely new market.
  - New product lines—which represent new offerings by the firm, but they become introduced into established markets.
  - Product line extensions—which supplement an existing product line with new styles, models, features, or flavors.
  - Improvements or revisions of existing products— which offer customers improved performance or greater perceived value.
  - Repositioning—which involves targeting existing products at new markets or segments.
  - Cost reductions—which involves modifying products to offer performance similar to competing products at a lower price.
- depends on the ability of the firm to create a differential advantage for the new product.

- typically proceeds through five stages: idea generation, screening and evaluation, development, test marketing, and commercialization.

Pricing:

- is a key factor in producing revenue for a firm.
- is the easiest of all marketing variables to change.
- is an important consideration in competitive intelligence.
- is considered to be the only real means of differentiation in mature markets plagued by commoditization.
- is among the most complex decisions to be made in developing a marketing plan.

The key issues in pricing strategy include:

- the firm's cost structure.
- perceived value.
- the price/revenue relationship.
- pricing objectives.
- price elasticity.

The firm's cost structure:

- is typically associated with pricing through the use of breakeven analysis or cost-plus pricing.
- should not be the driving force behind pricing strategy because different firms have different cost structures.
- should be used to establish a floor below which prices cannot be set for an extended period of time.

Perceived value:

- is a difficult term to define because it means different things to different people.
- is defined as a customer's subjective evaluation of benefits relative to costs to determine the worth of a firm's product offering relative to other product offerings.

The price/revenue relationship:

- is usually based on two general pricing myths: (1) when business is good, a price cut will capture greater market share, and (2) when business is bad, a price cut will stimulate sales.
- means that firms should not always cut prices, but should instead find ways to build value into the product and justify the current, or a higher, price.

Price elasticity:

- refers to customers' responsiveness or sensitivity to changes in price.
- can increase under these conditions:
  - when substitute products are widely available.
  - when the total expenditure is high.
  - when changes in price are noticeable to customers.
  - when price comparison among competing products is easy.

- can decrease under these conditions:
  - when substitute products are not available.
  - when customers perceive products as being necessities.
  - when the prices of complementary products go down.
  - when customers believe that the product is just worth the price.
  - when customers are in certain situations associated with time pressures or purchase risk.
  - when products are highly differentiated from the competition.

Pricing strategy in services:

- is critical because price may be the only cue to quality that is available in advance of the purchase experience.
- becomes more important—and more difficult—when:
  - service quality is hard to detect prior to purchase.
  - the costs associated with providing the service are difficult to determine.
  - customers are unfamiliar with the service process.
  - brand names are not well established.
  - the customer can perform the service themselves.
  - the service has poorly defined units of consumption.
  - advertising within a service category is limited.
  - the total price of the service experience is difficult to state beforehand.
- is often based on yield management systems that allow a firm to simultaneously control capacity and demand in order to maximize revenue and capacity utilization.

Major base pricing strategies include:

- price skimming.
- price penetration.
- prestige pricing.
- value-based pricing (EDLP).
- competitive matching.
- non-price strategies.

Strategies for adjusting prices in consumer markets include:

- discounting.
- reference pricing.
- price lining.
- odd pricing.
- price bundling.

Strategies for adjusting prices in business markets include:

- trade discounts.
- discounts and allowances.
- geographic pricing.
- transfer pricing.
- barter and countertrade.

Supply chain strategy:

- is one of the most important strategic decisions for many marketers.
- has remained essentially invisible to customers because the processes occur behind the scenes.
- is important to providing time, place, and possession utility for consumer and business buyers.
- consists of two interrelated components: marketing channels and physical distribution.
- is only effective when all channel members are integrated and committed to connectivity, community, and collaboration.

Marketing channels:

- are organized systems of marketing institutions through which products, resources, information, funds, and/or product ownership flow from the point of production to the final user.
- greatly increase contact efficiency by reducing the number of contacts necessary to exchange products.
- perform a variety of functions: sorting, breaking bulk, maintaining inventories, maintaining convenient locations, and providing services.

Marketing channel structures include:

- exclusive distribution, where a firm gives one merchant or outlet the sole right to sell a product within a defined geographic region.
- selective distribution, where a firm gives several merchants or outlets the right to sell a product in a defined geographic region.
- intensive distribution, which makes a product available in the maximum number of merchants or outlets in each area to gain as much exposure and as many sales opportunities as possible.

Power in the supply chain:

- can lead to conflict as each firm attempts to fulfill its mission, goals, objectives, and strategies by putting its own interests ahead of other firms.
- can result from five different sources: legitimate power, reward power, coercive power, information power, and referent power.

Trends in marketing channels include:

- technological improvements, such as the growth of electronic commerce and the increasing use of radio frequency identification (RFID).
- outsourcing and offshoring of work activities, particularly information technology operations and supporting functions.
- the growth of nontraditional channels, such as ecommerce, catalog and direct marketing, direct selling, home shopping networks, vending, and direct response advertising.

- the growth of dual distribution, as firms use multiple channels to reach various markets.

Integrated marketing communications:

- includes conveying and sharing meaning between buyers and sellers, either as individuals, firms, or between individuals and firms.
- includes the traditional elements of the promotion mix: advertising, public relations, personal selling, and sales promotion.
- refers to the strategic, coordinated use of promotion to create one consistent message across multiple channels to ensure maximum persuasive impact on the firm's current and potential customers.
- takes a 360-degree view of the customer that considers every contact that a customer or potential customer may have in his relationship with the firm.
- typically sets goals and objectives for the promotional campaign using the AIDA model—attention, interest, desire, and action.
- can change depending on whether the firm uses a pull or push strategy with respect to its supply chain.

Advertising:

- is identified as paid, nonpersonal communication transmitted through the media such as television, radio, magazines, newspapers, direct mail, outdoor displays, the Internet, and mobile devices.
- is rapidly expanding online as consumers spend less time with traditional media.
- offers many benefits because it is extremely cost efficient when it reaches a large number of people. On the other hand, the initial outlay for advertising can be expensive.
- is hard to measure in terms of its effectiveness in increasing sales.

Public relations:

- is the element of an IMC program that tracks public attitudes, identifies issues that may elicit public concern, and develops programs to create and maintain positive relationships between a firm and its stakeholders.
- can be used to promote the firm, its people, its ideas, and its image and even to create an internal shared understanding among employees.
- can improve the public's general awareness of a company and can create specific images such as quality, innovativeness, value, or concern for social issues.
- is often confused with publicity; however, publicity is more narrowly defined to include the firm's activities designed to gain media attention through articles, editorials, or news stories.
- can involve the use of a wide variety of methods, including news or press releases, feature articles, white papers, press conferences, event sponsorship, product placement, and employee relations.

Personal selling:

- is paid, personal communication that attempts to inform customers about products and persuade them to purchase those products.
- is the most precise form of communication because it assures companies that they are in direct contact with an excellent prospect.
- has a serious drawback of high cost per contact.
- goals are typically associated with finding prospects, informing prospects, persuading prospects to buy, and keeping customers satisfied through follow-up service after the sale.
- has evolved to take on elements of customer service and marketing research in order to generate repeat sales and develop ongoing relationships with customers.
- and sales management activities include the development of sales force objectives, determining the size of the sales force, recruiting and training salespeople, and controlling and evaluating the sales force.
- has been greatly impacted by technological advances, especially online sales training and sales automation systems that push integrated customer, competitive, and product information toward the salesperson.

Sales promotion:

- involves activities that create buyer incentives to purchase a product or that add value for the buyer or the trade.

- can be targeted toward consumers, channel intermediaries, or the sales force.
- has one universal goal: to induce product trial and purchase.
- is typically used in support of advertising, public relations, or personal selling activities rather than as a stand-alone promotional element.
- directed toward consumers:
  - can be initiated by any member of the supply chain, but manufacturers or retailers typically offer them.
  - represents an effective way to introduce new products or promote established brands.
  - can include such activities as coupons, rebates, samples, loyalty programs, point-of-purchase promotion, premiums, contests and sweepstakes, and direct mail.
- directed toward the trade (business markets):
  - is undertaken to push products through the channel by increasing sales and encouraging increased effort among channel partners.
  - uses many of the same promotional methods that are targeted toward consumers; however, it involves a number of unique methods including trade allowances, free merchandise, training assistance, cooperative advertising, and selling incentives offered to an intermediary's sales force.

Questions for Discussion

1. Consider the number of product choices available in the U.S. consumer market. In virtually every product category, consumers have many options to fulfill their needs. Are all of these options really necessary? Is having this many choices a good thing for consumers? Why or why not? Is it a good thing for marketers and retailers that have to support and carry all of these product choices? Why or why not?

2. Pricing strategy associated with services is typically more complex than the pricing of tangible goods. As a consumer, what pricing issues do you consider when purchasing services? How difficult is it to compare prices among competing services, or to determine the complete price of the service before purchase? What could service providers do to solve these issues?

3. Some manufacturers and retailers advertise that customers should buy from them because they "eliminate the middleman." Evaluate this comment in light of the functions that must be performed in a marketing channel. Does a channel with fewer members always deliver products to customers at lower prices? Defend your position.

4. Review the steps in the AIDA model. In what ways has promotion affected you in various stages of this model? Does promotion affect you differently based on the type of product in question? Does the price of the product (low versus high) make a difference in how promotion can affect your choices? Explain.

Exercises

1. You are in the process of planning a hypothetical airline flight from New York to St. Louis. Visit the websites of three different airlines and compare prices for this trip. Try travel dates that include a Saturday night layover and those that do not. Try dates less than seven days away, and compare

those prices with flights that are more than twenty-one days out. How do you explain the similarities and differences you see in these prices?

2. Locate a product offered by a manufacturer using a dual distribution approach. Are there differences between the customers targeted by each channel? How do the purchase experiences differ? In the end, why would a customer buy directly from a manufacturer if the prices are higher?

3. Shadow a salesperson for a day and talk about how his or her activities integrate with other promotional elements used by their firm. How does the

salesperson set objectives? How is he or she made aware of the firm's overall IMC strategy? Does the sales force participate in planning marketing or promotional activities?

4. Visit the Cents Off website (www.centsoff.com) and browse the available coupons and read the FAQs. What are the benefits of the Cents Off service for advertisers and consumers? If you were a manufacturer that issues coupons, what factors would favor using the Cents Off website for distribution rather than the traditional Sunday newspaper insert?

End Notes

1. "Investor Relations," Barnes & Noble Corporate website (http://www.barnesandnobleinc.com/for_investors/for_investors.html), accessed May 17, 2012; Matt Townsend, "Barnes & Noble Investor Pushes Management to Spin Off Nook," *BusinessWeek Online*, February 18, 2012 (http://www.businessweek.com/news/2012-02-18/barnes-noble-investor-pushes-management-to-spin-off-nook.html); and Tim Worstall, "Barnes and Noble and the Efficient Markets Hypothesis," *Forbes*, May 1, 2012 (http://www.forbes.com/sites/timworstall/2012/05/01/barnes-and-noble-and-the-efficient-markets-hypothesis).

2. The Hampton Inn Guarantee (http://hamptoninn3.hilton.com/en/about/satisfaction.html).

3. David Twiddy, "Garmin to Sell Wireless Phone in Asia," *BusinessWeek Online*, June 5, 2009 (http://www.businessweek.com/ap/financialnews/D98KP9QG0.htm).

4. These facts are from "Kia April Sales Rise Slightly in US," *BusinessWeek Online*, May 1, 2012 (http://www.businessweek.com/ap/2012-05/D9UG3Q281.htm).

5. These facts are from Economic Intelligence Unit, "Worldwide Cost of Living 2012" (http://www.eiu.com/public/thankyou_download.aspx?activity=download&campaignid=wcol2012).

6. Valarie A. Zeithaml, "Consumer Perceptions of Price, Quality, and Value: A Means-End Model and Synthesis of Evidence," *Journal of Marketing*, 52 (July 1988), 2–22.

7. This discussion is based on material from Charley Kyd, "Tempted to Cut Prices? It's Probably Time to *Raise* Them," *Today's Business*, Fall 2000, 3.

8. For further information, see the Southwest Airlines website (http://www.southwest.com).

9. Deborah Catalano Ruriani, "Inventory Velocity: All the Right Moves," *Inbound Logistics*, November 2005, 36.

10. See Edward W. Davis and Robert E. Speckman, *The Extended Enterprise* (Upper Saddle River, NJ: Prentice-Hall Financial Times, 2004).

11. Ibid, 15.

12. James Watson, "Del Monte Foods Company," *Wikinvest* (http://www.wikinvest.com/stock/Del_Monte_Foods_Company_%28DLM%29), accessed August 12, 2009.

13. Robert Dawson, *Secrets of Power Negotiation*, 2nd ed. (Franklin Lakes, NJ: Career Press, 1999).

14. U.S. Census Bureau, *E-Commerce 2010 Report*, May 10, 2012 (http://www.census.gov/econ/estats/2010/2010reportfinal.pdf).

15. "What is RFID?" *RFID Journal* (http://www.rfidjournal.com/article/articleview/1339/1/129), accessed May 10, 2012.

16. These facts are from EcoSensa, "The Up and Down of Walmart RFID Implementation," *RFID Blog*, March 24, 2009 (http://ecosensa.com/rfidblog/2009/03/24/Walmart-rfid-implementation); Constance L. Hays, "What Walmart Knows About Customers' Habits," *New York Times*, November 14, 2004; Hollis Tibbetts, "Integration on the Edge: Data Explosion and Next-Gen Integration," EbizQ, September 24, 2010 (http://www.ebizq.net/blogs/integrationedge/2010/09/how-fast-things-change.php); Thomas Wailgum, "Walmart is Dead Serious About RFID," *CIO*, January 18, 2008 (http://www.cio.com/article/173702/Wal_Mart_Is_Dead_Serious_About_RFID); and Walmart corporate website (http://www.walmartstores.com/AboutUs), accessed May 21, 2012.

17. The material in this section is based on Davis and Speckman, *The Extended Enterprise*, 109–129.

18. These facts are from Mark Atterby, "Captive Outsourcing is Alive and Well," *The Sauce*, August 31, 2011 (http://thesauce.net.au/2011/08/captive-outsourcing-is-alive-and-well).

19. Martin Murray, "3PL's Used by Three Quarters of the Fortune 500," *Martin's Logistics Blog*, January 28, 2009 (http://logistics.about.com/b/2009/01/28/3pls-used-by-three-quarters-of-the-fortune-500.htm).

20. These facts are from Nicholas Cameron, "Sponsorship Overview & Case Studies," SponsorMap, March 29, 2010 (http://www.slideshare.net/SponsorMap/some-sponsorship-roi-case-studies); Andrew Hampp, "How 'Top Chef Cooks Up Fresh Integrations," *Advertising Age*, October 30, 2008 (http://adage.com/madisonandvine/article?article_id=132146); Pat McDonough, "As TV Screens Grow, So Does U.S. DVR Usage," *Nielsenwire*, February 29, 2012 (http://blog.nielsen.com/nielsenwire/media_entertainment/as-tv-screens-grow-so-does-u-s-dvr-usage); Abe Sauer, "The Avengers Product Placement Brandcameo Scorecard," *brandchannel*, May 7, 2012 (http://www.brandchannel.com/home/post/Brandcameo-050712-The-Avengers.aspx); Rich Thomaselli, "How CBS Sports Can Use March Madness Success to Grow Online," March 11, 2009 (http://adage.com/digital/article?article_id=135186); and Don Walker, "March Madness on Demand Goes to a Pay Model," *Milwaukee*

Journal Sentinel, February 18, 2012 (http://www.jsonline.com/blogs/sports/139574443.html).

21. Sam Fahmy, "Despite Recession, Hispanic and Asian Buying Power Expected to Surge in U.S.," Terry College of Business Press Release, University of Georgia (http://www.terry.uga.edu/news/releases/2010/minority-buying-power-report.html), accessed May 21, 2012.

22. Vidopp website (http://www.vidopp.com/uncategorized/tv-ad-production-cost-study-released), accessed May 10, 2012.

23. Brian Hartman, "Reebok to Refund $25 Million for False Advertising," *ABC News*, September 28, 2011 (http://abcnews.go.com/blogs/health/2011/09/28/reebok-to-refund-25-million-for-false-advertising); and Jennifer Kerr, "FTC: Skechers Deceived Consumers with Shoe Ads," *Chicago Sun-Times*, May 16, 2012 (http://www.suntimes.com/business/12574235-420/ftc-skechers-deceived-consumers-with-shoe-ads.html).

24. New Belgium Brewery website (http://www.newbelgium.com).

25. Promotion Marketing Association, "State of the Promotion Industry Report," © 2005 Promotion Marketing Association (http://www.pmalink.org/resources/pma2005report.pdf).

26. Nathalie Zmuda, "Coke: Buy 1 Rival, Get our Brand Free," *Advertising Age*, March 9 and 16, 2009, 1 and 19; "Coke Promotion Gives Free Vault to Mountain Dew Customers," *Convenience Store News*, April 10, 2009, 1; and "Coca Cola Brings Vault Drink Head to Head with Mtn Dew," *yumsugar*, March 11, 2009 (http://www.yumsugar.com/2912146).

CHAPTER **7**

Branding and Positioning

Introduction

As the elements of the marketing program come together to create the complete offering, marketers must also consider how the marketing program will be used to create effective branding and positioning. These decisions are critical because they create differentiation among competing offerings in the marketplace. This differentiation is the antidote to commoditization; however, it is becoming increasingly difficult for firms to brand and position their offerings in meaningful ways. For the firms that are successful, having a solid branding and positioning strategy is truly priceless. As *Beyond the Pages 7.1* illustrates, individuals who purchase a Steinway piano buy much more than a musical instrument. They also get exceptional craftsmanship, unparalleled customer service, a highly prestigious brand name, and 160 years of technical innovation.

While the concept of a brand may seem relatively simple to understand, branding strategy can actually be quite complex. From a technical point of view, a *brand* is a combination of name, symbol, term, or design that identifies a specific product. Brands have two parts: the brand name and the brand mark. The brand name is the part of a brand that can be spoken, including words, letters, and numbers (Honda, 7-Eleven, WD-40, GMC, Citi). The brand mark—which includes symbols, figures, or a design—is the part of a brand that cannot be spoken. Good brand marks, like McDonald's golden arches, Nike's swoosh, and Prudential's rock, effectively communicate the brand and its image without using spoken words. Brand marks are also useful in advertising and product placement, such as when college football broadcasts clearly depict the Nike logo on the clothing and uniforms of both coaches and players.

While these technical aspects of branding are important, branding strategy involves much more than developing a clever brand name or unique brand mark. To be truly effective, a brand should succinctly capture the total offering in a way that answers a question in the customer's mind.[2] Good brands are those that immediately come to mind when a customer has a problem to be solved or a need to be fulfilled. Consider these questions that might be asked by a customer:

Steinway: More Than a Piano[1]

One of the most dominant strengths any firm can possess occurs when the firm enjoys a superior brand image that is backed by patent protection. Such is the case for Steinway and Sons, makers of the world's finest pianos. For 160 years, Steinway's art and craftsmanship have made it the world's most renowned brand for high-end, "concert hall quality" pianos. In fact, virtually every top pianist in the world performs on a Steinway.

The company holds 130 technical patents and innovations that distinguish its pianos from all others. Each piano made in the Astoria (New York) and Hamburg (Germany) factories takes 9 to 12 months to complete and is hand assembled from 12,000 parts—most of them also made by hand. Despite its reputation, Steinway is not a large company. It makes roughly 2,500 pianos a year—a number dwarfed by other firms in the industry. Steinway, however, does not define success in terms of numbers, but in its reputation. Steinway is the piano of choice for concert halls, composers, professional musicians, and wealthy customers. Although the company accounts for only 2 percent of piano sales in the United States, it earns over 35 percent of the industry's profit. Customers enjoy the quality, beauty, and reputation of a Steinway piano, and don't mind paying the $40,000 to $250,000 price tag. In fact, many argue that a Steinway is more akin to a work of art than a musical instrument. The advantages earned from this type of reputation and customer loyalty are hard to beat.

However, Steinway's stellar image and reputation presented a problem for the company at one point in its history. While Steinway dominated the upper-end of the piano market, the company did not compete in the rapidly growing and much larger entry-level and mid-level piano markets. These markets were dominated by Asian brands such as Yamaha and Kawai—good names in their own right, but not in the same league as Steinway. Piano dealers were forced to stock these brands alongside Steinways in order to meet the needs of other customer segments. The challenge for Steinway was to find a way to compete in these markets without damaging the brand equity in the Steinway name.

The company's solution involved the launch of two new brands: "Boston" for the mid-level market and "Essex" for the entry-level market. Both the Boston and the Essex are manufactured in Japan and sold through exclusive channels. The decision to launch these new brands was agonizing for Steinway's management. The company's top management once said, "There is no such thing as a cheaper Steinway." With that in mind, the launch of the Boston and Essex represented a real risk for the company.

Steinway argues that the only way to maintain brand equity, especially with a name like Steinway, is to take a long-term view and move very slowly. This is the company's strategy with its move into Asian markets—the home turf of Steinway's less expensive rivals. The company has expanded distribution in Japan and China to the point where it now earns over 30 percent of its business from outside the United States. Steinway's sales in China alone are growing at an average of 20 percent each year. Steinway also raises its prices 3 to 4 percent each year—another long-term strategy aimed at maintaining brand equity. The company argues that you cannot put a discounted price on the passion associated with a worldwide icon like Steinway.

- Where can I find information quickly?
- Where can I get a quick meal and make my kids happy?
- Where can I buy everything I need, all at decent prices?
- Where can I get the best deal on car insurance?
- How do I find a value-priced hotel in midtown Manhattan?

How do you answer these questions? How many customers do you think would give the following answers: Google, McDonald's, Walmart, GEICO, and Expedia? To successfully develop a brand, the firm should position the offering (which

© KarSol/Shutterstock

This symbol, recognizable around the world, embodies a number of important branding attributes.

includes all tangible, intangible, and symbolic elements arising from the marketing program) as the answer to questions like these. Customers tend to buy offerings whose combination of attributes is the best solution to their problems. As shown in Exhibit 7.1, brands may have many different attributes that make up the way customers think about them. For example, the iPhone possesses many different attributes that make up customers' overall knowledge about the brand: alliances (AT&T, Verizon, Sprint, Twitter), company (Apple), extensions (iTunes, access-ories), employees (Tim Cook, Steve Jobs), endorsers (celebrities such as Samuel L. Jackson and Zooey Deschanel), events (Macworld Expo, Apple keynote speeches), and channels (the Apple Store). Other brands are enhanced via strong country-of-origin (Guinness, IKEA), branded ingredients (Dell computers use Microsoft and Intel components), causes (Ben and Jerry's), and endorser (Nike) effects.

EXHIBIT 7.1   **Potential Brand Attributes**

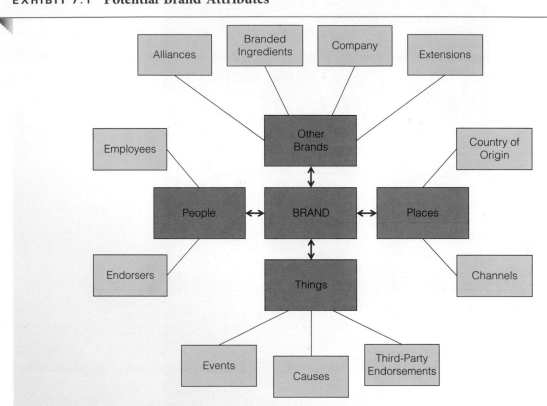

Source: Kotler, Philip; Keller, Kevin; *Simulations, Interpretive, Framework for Marketing Management: Integrated PharmaSim Simulation Experience*, 4th Edition, © 2009. Reprinted by permission of Pearson Education, Inc., Upper Saddle River, NJ.

Strategic Issues in Branding

When a firm considers its branding strategy, the marketing program, especially the product, becomes a central focus. Before we examine some of the key strategic issues in branding strategy, however, we need to discuss the closely related topic of corporate branding. Most firms consider their corporate brands to be equally as important as individual product-related brands. In fact, product-related brands and corporate brands are clearly intertwined. Ben & Jerry's Ice Cream, for example, is an ardent participant in many social causes such as global warming and social injustice. In this case, the company's corporate brand clearly plays a role in branding and positioning its ice cream products. In some companies, the corporate brand dominates. For example, IBM advertises that it provides infrastructure and solutions for e-business. Although the company offers a wide array of products for e-business, many of IBM's advertisements do not name these products or explain how their infrastructure and solutions actually work. Instead, the purpose of the advertisements is to give potential customers the impression that IBM is a company that understands e-business and that has the ability to solve problems.

Corporate branding activities are typically aimed at a variety of stakeholders, including customers, shareholders, advocacy groups, government regulators, and the public at large. These activities are designed to build and enhance the firm's reputation among these groups, and to rebuild the firm's reputation when unexpected and unfavorable events occur. Corporate branding and reputation are critical to effective product-related

---

EXHIBIT 7.2   The Strongest and Weakest U.S. Corporate Reputations

---

Rank	Company	Reputation Quotient*
	The Strongest Reputations	
1.	Apple	85.62
2.	Google	82.82
3.	The Coca-Cola Company	81.99
4.	Amazon.com	81.92
5.	Kraft Foods	81.62
6.	The Walt Disney Company	81.28
7.	Johnson & Johnson	80.45
8.	Whole Foods Market	80.14
9.	Microsoft	79.87
10.	UPS	79.75
11.	Sony	79.22
12.	Honda	78.95
13.	Samsung	78.11
14.	Home Depot	78.11
15.	Procter & Gamble	78.09
	The Weakest Reputations	
46.	Chevron	64.72
47.	Sears	64.26
48.	Time Warner	63.38
49.	T-Mobile	62.82
50.	Chrysler	60.30
51.	ExxonMobil	60.01
52.	Wells Fargo	59.50
53.	Comcast	59.10
54.	News Corp	57.14
55.	Citigroup	55.95
56.	JPMorgan Chase	54.84
57.	BP	53.50
58.	Bank of America	49.85
59.	Goldman Sachs	47.57
60.	AIG	46.18

Source: From Harris Interactive, "The Annual RQ 2008: The Reputations of the Most Visible Companies™." Copyright 2008 Harris Interactive, (http://www.harrisinteractive.com/services/pubs/HI_BSC_REPORT_AnnualRQ2008_Rankings.pdf), accessed July 31, 2009.

branding and positioning as they create trust between the firm and its stakeholders. Exhibit 7.2 lists U.S. firms having some of the strongest and weakest public reputations. Note that firms with lower reputation scores, such as BP and Goldman Sachs, have experienced a number of scandals and legal problems in recent years. Many major financial corporations currently have weak reputations because of the financial scandals that recently plagued the industry. Faith in the financial sector is at an all-time low, and it may take years for these companies to rebuild their reputations.

The range of scores in Exhibit 7.2 is quite telling of the effects that positive and negative reputations can have on a firm. Apple's reputation score, the highest in the history of the poll, is closely tied to its quality products, financial performance, social responsibility, and executive leadership. This reputation is clearly intertwined with the brand caché of the iPad and iPhone. Contrast this to AIG, which has been at the bottom of the ratings for many years. Not only was AIG implicated in financial scandals and required government bailout money, but AIG rewarded top executives with bonuses and hosted conferences in luxurious resorts after receiving the money. AIG's actions clearly worsened its reputation and made it harder to compete in the competitive financial services industry. It is not surprising that AIG's stock price has declined over 98 percent in the last five years. These examples demonstrate the important connections between corporate branding and reputation and the activities that companies use to successfully brand and position their product offerings.

Basic Branding Decisions

To brand or not to brand: There really is no question. Virtually every product is associated with some type of branding. So-called "generic" products generally don't exist today, except in some grocery items and perhaps commodities like sugar, wheat, and corn. The advantages of branding are so compelling that the real question is not "why?" but "how?" Some of the many advantages of branding include:

- **Product Identification**. Brands make identifying and locating products easier for customers.
- **Comparison Shopping**. Brands assist customers in evaluating competing products.
- **Shopping Efficiency**. Brands speed up the buying process and make repeat purchases easier by reducing search time and effort.
- **Risk Reduction**. Brands allow customers to buy known products, thereby reducing the risk of purchase.
- **Product Acceptance**. New products released under a known brand name are accepted and adopted more quickly.
- **Enhanced Self-Image**. Brands can convey status, image, and prestige.
- **Enhanced Product Loyalty**. Branding increases psychosocial identification with a product.

In addition to these general benefits of branding, specific branding decisions can also create other benefits. For example, one key branding decision involves the distinction between manufacturer brands and private-label brands (brands owned by the merchants that sell them). Private-label brands, sometimes called store brands (but never generic brands), range from well-known products like Gap clothing and Craftsman tools, to other products such as Walmart's Ol' Roy dog food, Equate aspirin, or Sam's Choice soft drinks. Strategically, the choice to sell manufacturer brands or private-label brands is not an either-or decision. As Exhibit 7.3 illustrates, both types of brands have important advantages. For that reason, many distributors, wholesalers, and retailers carry both types of brands. For example, department stores carry manufacturer brands—such as Nike, Polo, and Hilfiger—because customers expect to find them. Hence, manufacturer brands are important in driving customer traffic. They also give customers confidence that they are buying a widely known brand from a respected company. Department stores also carry a number of private label brands because of the increased profit margins associated with them. JCPenney, for example, is well-known for its popular private label

---

EXHIBIT 7.3   Manufacturer (Name) Brands versus Private-Label Brands

---

Unique Advantages of Selling Manufacturer (Name) Brands

Reduced Costs	Heavy promotion by the manufacturer reduces the marketing costs of the merchant that carries the brand.
Built-In Loyalty	Manufacturer brands come with their own cadre of loyal customers.
Enhanced Image	The image and prestige of the merchant are enhanced.
Lower Inventory	Manufacturers are capable of time-certain delivery, which allows the merchant to carry less inventory and reduce inventory costs.
Less Risk	Poor quality or product failures become attributed to the manufacturer rather than the merchant.

Unique Advantages of Selling Private-Label (Store) Brands

Increased Profit	The merchant maintains a higher margin on its own brands and faces less pressure to cut prices to match the competition.
Less Competition	Where manufacturer brands are carried by many different merchants, private-label brands are exclusive to the merchant that sells them.
Total Control	The merchant has total control over the development, pricing, distribution, and promotion of the brand.
Merchant Loyalty	Customers who are loyal to a private-label brand are automatically loyal to the merchant.

© Cengage Learning 2013

brands. Over 40 percent of Penney's sales come from private-label brands; seven of which—including Arizona, Worthington, and St. John's Bay—individually sell over $1 billion each year. Penney's has also added a private brand of clothing and home furnishings called American Living, which is manufactured by Polo Ralph Lauren. Further, JCPenney acquired the Liz Claiborne brand (a former manufacturer brand) in late 2011. The move was part of Penney's full brand makeover to emphasize "Fair and Square Pricing" instead of frequent sales.[3]

A second important branding decision involves individual versus family branding. A firm uses individual branding when it gives each of its product offerings a different brand name. A number of well-known firms use individual branding, including Sara Lee (Hanes, L'eggs, Jimmy Dean, Ball Park), Reckitt Benckiser (Air Wick, Clearasil, French's, and Woolite), and Procter & Gamble (Tide, Duracell, Cover Girl, Scope). The key advantage of individual branding is that the potential poor performance of one product does not tarnish the brand image of other products in the firm's portfolio. It is also useful in market segmentation when the firm wants to enter many segments of the same market. Procter & Gamble uses this strategy in the laundry detergent market (Tide, Cheer, Bold, Gain, Ariel).

Conversely, family branding occurs when a firm uses the same name or part of the brand name on every product. For example, every cereal in the Kellogg's portfolio uses the Kellogg's name (Kellogg's Frosted Flakes, Kellogg's Rice Krispies, etc.). Campbell's uses the same strategy in its soup portfolio (Campbell's Tomato Soup, Campbell's Chunky, etc.) and with many of its other brands such as Pepperidge Farm, Pace, Swanson, and V8. The key advantage of family branding is that the promotion (and brand image) of one product reflects on other products under the same family brand. However, in addition to the obvious risk of releasing a poor product under a family brand, family branding also runs the risk of overextension. Too many brand extensions, especially into unrelated areas, can confuse customers and promote brand switching. Examples include Bic perfume (the company is known for pens and lighters), Bayer Aspirin Free Pain Reliever (Bayer is the dominant aspirin maker), and Miller Chill (not exactly the "High Life").

Strategic Brand Alliances

As we have stated in previous chapters, relationships with other firms are among the most important competitive advantages that can be held by an organization. Many of these relationships are based on a variety of brand alliances. For example, *cobranding* is the use of two or more brands on one product. Cobranding leverages the image and reputation of multiple brands to create distinctive products with distinctive differentiation. Cobranding is quite common in processed foods and credit cards. For example, General Mills partners with Hershey's on its Betty Crocker chocolate cake mixes with Hershey's cocoa. This brand alliance gives Betty Crocker a distinct advantage over competitors like Duncan Hines. Likewise, credit card companies like Visa and MasterCard offer cobranded versions of their cards emblazoned with the logos of sports teams, universities, professions, or other firms like Delta Airlines and Disney World. Cobranding is quite successful because the complimentary nature of the brands used on a single product increases perceived quality and customer familiarity.

Brand licensing is another type of branding alliance. *Brand licensing* involves a contractual agreement where a company permits an organization to use its brand on noncompeting products in exchange for a licensing fee. Although this royalty can be quite expensive, the instant brand recognition that comes with the licensed brand is often worth the expense. Fashion brands such as Calvin Klein, Ralph Lauren, Bill Blass, and Tommy Hilfiger appear on numerous products in a variety of product categories. Licensing is also quite common in toys where manufacturers will license the characters and images from popular movies like *Cars* or *Harry Potter* to create a variety of products. Even Jack Daniels and Jim Beam whiskeys have licensed barbeque sauces that bear their famous brands.

Brand Value

What is a brand worth? The answer depends on whether you ask customers or the firm. For customers, brands offer a number of advantages as mentioned above. However, customers also have attitudinal and emotional attachments to brands that create value. One of the most common types of customer brand value is brand loyalty. *Brand loyalty* is a positive attitude toward a brand that causes customers to have a consistent preference for that brand over all other competing brands in a product category. There are three degrees of brand loyalty:

- **Brand recognition**—exists when a customer knows about the brand and is considering it as one of several alternatives in the evoked set. This is the lowest form of brand loyalty and exists mainly due to the awareness of the brand rather than a strong desire to buy the brand.
- **Brand preference**—a stronger degree of brand loyalty where a customer prefers one brand to competitive brands and will usually purchase this brand if it is available. For example, a customer may hold a brand preference for Diet Coke. However, if this brand is not available, the customer will usually accept a substitute such as Diet Pepsi or Coke Zero rather than expending extra effort to find and purchase Diet Coke.

- **Brand insistence**—the strongest degree of brand loyalty, occurs when customers will go out of their way to find the brand and will accept no substitute. Customers who are brand insistent will expend a great deal of time and effort to locate and purchase their favorite brand.

Marketers clearly want to develop brand insistence for their products. However, brand loyalty is declining overall because of increasing commoditization and the overuse of sales promotion activities. A recent study revealed the top ten brands having the highest customer loyalty: Amazon, Apple (iPhone), Facebook, Samsung (phones), Apple (Mac), Zappos, Hyundai, Kindle, Patron, and Mary Kay.[4] Brand loyalty also remains quite high in many product categories, including cigarettes, mayonnaise, toothpaste, coffee, bath soap, medicines, body lotion, makeup, soft drinks, ketchup, and diapers. Note that most of these examples include products that customers put in their mouths or on their bodies— a common trait of products that enjoy strong brand loyalty.

The value of a brand to the firm is often referred to as *brand equity*. Another way of looking at brand equity is the marketing and financial value associated with a brand's position in the marketplace. Brand equity usually has ties to brand name awareness, brand loyalty, brand quality, and other attributes shown in Exhibit 7.1. Brand awareness and brand loyalty increase customer familiarity with a brand. Customers familiar or comfortable with a specific brand are more likely to consider the brand when making a purchase. When this familiarity is combined with a high degree of brand quality, the inherent risk in purchasing the brand decreases dramatically. Brand associations include the brand's image, attributes, or benefits that either directly or indirectly give the brand a certain personality. For example, customers associate 7-Up with "uncola," Charmin tissue with "squeezably soft," Michelin tires with family safety, Allstate insurance with "the good hands," Coca-Cola with "happiness," and Honeycomb cereal with a "big, big bite." Associations like these are every bit as important as quality and loyalty, and they also take many years to develop.

Unfortunately, it is also possible for brand associations (and brand equity) to be negative. Although Kia has enjoyed recent success through new product development (especially with the Optima and Sorento), the South Korean carmaker has struggled with a weak quality image associated with its brands. To counteract this negative brand association, Kia backs its products with a 10-year, 100,000-mile powertrain warranty.[5]

Although brand equity is hard to measure, it represents a key asset for any firm and an important part of marketing strategy. Exhibit 7.4 lists the world's 25 most valuable brands. Brands like these take years to develop and nurture into the valuable assets that they have come to represent. This reality makes it easier and less expensive for firms to buy established brands than to develop new brands from scratch. For example, Johnson & Johnson's acquisition of Pfizer's consumer products unit allowed the company to add several powerful brands to its portfolio—Listerine, Sudafed, Visine, Neosporin, and Nicorette. The equity associated with these brands would have taken Johnson & Johnson decades to develop on its own.[6] The same can be said for Microsoft's purchase of Skype and Facebook's purchase of Instagram.

Given the value of brands like these, it is no surprise that firms go to great lengths to protect their brand assets. Registering a brand with the U.S. Patent and Trademark Office is only the first step in protecting the value of a brand. While the U.S. legal system provides many laws to protect brands, most of the responsibility for enforcing this protection falls on the company to find and police abuses. Firms must diligently monitor competitive behavior for signs of potential brand infringement that could confuse or deceive customers. For example, Auto Shack was forced to change its name to AutoZone after the Tandy Corporation, owner of Radio Shack, sued the company. McDonald's is also aggressive in protecting its brand and has brought lawsuits against many companies

EXHIBIT 7.4   The World's Twenty-Five Most Valuable Brands

Brand Rank	Brand	2012 Brand Value ($M)	% Change in Brand Value 2012 vs. 2011	Country of Ownership
1	Apple	182,951	19	U.S.
2	IBM	115,985	15	U.S.
3	Google	107,857	-3	U.S.
4	McDonald's	95,188	17	U.S.
5	Microsoft	76,651	-2	U.S.
6	Coca-Cola	74,286	1	U.S.
7	Marlboro	73,612	9	U.S.
8	AT&T	68,870	-1	U.S.
9	Verizon	49,151	15	U.S.
10	China Mobile	47,041	-18	China
11	GE	45,810	-9	U.S.
12	Vodafone	43,033	-1	UK
13	ICBC	41,518	-7	China
14	Wells Fargo	39,754	8	U.S.
15	Visa	38,284	34	U.S.
16	UPS	37,129	4	U.S.
17	Walmart	34,436	-8	U.S.
18	Amazon.com	34,077	-9	U.S.
19	Facebook	33,233	74	U.S.
20	Deutsche Telecom	26,837	-10	Germany
21	Louis Vuitton	25,920	7	France
22	SAP	25,715	-1	Germany
23	BMW	24,623	10	Germany
24	China Construction Bank	24,517	-4	China
25	Baidu	24,326	8	China

Source: BrandZ™ Top 100 Most Valuable Global Brands 2012 (http://www.wpp.com/NR/rdonlyres/4B44C834-AEA8-4951-871A-A5B937EBFD3E/0/brandz_2012_top_100.pdf).

who use "Mc" in their names. Due to the differing and often lax legal systems in other nations, brand abuse is quite common in foreign markets. It is not surprising that patent, copyright, and intellectual property law has become a growth industry both in the United States and around the world. Without these protections in place, firms run the real risk of having their brand become synonymous with an entire product category. Scotch tape, Xerox copiers, Band-Aid adhesive bandages, Coca-Cola, FedEx, and Kleenex constantly fight this battle. To protect their brands, firms obtain trademarks to legally designate that the brand owner has exclusive use of the brand and to prohibit others from using the brand in any way. Former brand names that their parent companies did not protect sufficiently include aspirin, escalator, nylon, linoleum, kerosene, and shredded wheat.

Packaging and Labeling

At first glance, the issues of packaging and labeling might not seem like important considerations in branding strategy. Although packaging and labeling strategy does involve different goals than branding, the two often go hand-in-hand in developing a product, its benefits, its differentiation, and its image. Consider, for instance, the number of products that use distinctive packaging as part of their branding strategy. Obvious examples include the brand names and brand marks that appear on all product packaging. The color used on a product's package or label is also a vital part of branding, such as Tide's consistent use of bright orange on its line of laundry detergents. The size and shape of the label is sometimes a key to brand identification. For example, Heinz uses a unique crown-shaped label on its ketchup bottles. The physical characteristics of the package itself sometimes become part of the brand. Coca-Cola's unique 10-ounce glass bottle, Pringles' potato chip canister, and the bottles used by Absolut vodka and Crown Royal whiskey are good examples. Finally, products that use recyclable packaging are gaining favor. For example, NatureWorks LLC has developed a biopolymer known as Ingeo—a fully compostable bio-plastic made from corn. Ingeo is used in many different packaging applications because it biodegrades easily—usually within 75 to 80 days. Biota Water uses Ingeo for all of its packaging. Similarly, Coca-Cola introduced the PlantBottle, a recyclable bottle made from 70 percent petroleum and 30 percent sugar and molasses. The PlantBottle logo is now featured prominently on the company's Dasani bottled water. Unlike Ingeo, the PlantBottle can be recycled.[7]

Packaging serves a number of important functions in marketing strategy. Customers take some functions—like protection, storage, and convenience—for granted until the package fails to keep the product fresh, or they discover that the package will not conveniently fit in the refrigerator, medicine cabinet, or backpack. Packaging can also play a role in product modifications and repositioning. An improved cap or closure, an "easy open" package, a more durable box or container, or the introduction of a more conveniently sized package can create instant market recognition and a competitive advantage. Sometimes, a change in package design can create major problems for a brand, as described in *Beyond the Pages 7.2*. Packaging can also be used as a part of a co-branding strategy. Hillshire Farms, for example, formed an alliance with The Glad Products Company to package its Deli Select line of lunchmeats in GladWare reusable plastic containers. The package is easy to seal and completely reusable once the lunchmeat has been consumed.[8]

Labeling, in and of itself, is an important consideration in marketing strategy. Product labels not only aid in product identification and promotion; they also contain a great deal of information to help customers make proper product selections. Labeling is also an important legal issue as several federal laws and regulations specify the information that must be included on a product's packaging. The Nutritional Labeling and Education Act of 1990 was one of the most sweeping changes in federal labeling law in history. The law mandated that packaged food manufacturers must include detailed nutritional information on their packaging. The law also set standards for health claims such as "low fat," "light," "low calorie," and "reduced cholesterol." The Food Allergy Labeling and Consumer Protection Act, passed in 2004, required labeling of any food containing peanuts, soybeans, milk, eggs, shellfish, tree nuts, and wheat. The U.S. Supreme Court has ruled that manufacturers bear full responsibility for the content of the labeling and warnings on their packaging. This ruling also applies to manufacturers of products that are inspected and certified by the government, such as foods and pharmaceuticals.[10]

Beyond the Pages 7.2

Tropicana's Packaging Debacle[9]

In January 2009 as a part of a major overhaul of brands in the PepsiCo family, Tropicana dropped the long-familiar labeling of its popular Pure Premium brand of orange juice. That labeling, which contained the familiar logo of a straw sticking out of an orange, was replaced with a more modern, streamlined look with a glass of juice and the "Tropicana" brand written vertically on the packaging. The move was a part of a $35 million "Squeeze: It's a Natural" campaign, which promoted fresh taste and family imagery.

Unfortunately for Tropicana, the redesigned packaging met with instant criticism and complaints from loyal consumers. Many consumers argued that the packaging was "ugly" and that it looked like "a generic or store brand." Others complained that the new packaging made it harder for consumers to recognize Tropicana on supermarket shelves. In fact, many consumers complained that they had bought the wrong orange juice. After less than two months in its redesigned packaging, Tropicana Pure Premium sales fell 20 percent, or roughly $33 million. At the same time, competing brands—such as Minute Maid, Florida's Natural, and Tree Ripe—enjoyed double-digit sales growth. Sales of private-label brands also increased.

After the rapid drop in sales and thousands of consumer letters, emails, and telephone calls, PepsiCo announced that it would scrap the new packaging and return to the old packaging. Industry critics lauded the move and compared it with Coke's "New Coke" fiasco from 1985. Pepsi, like Coke at the time, had failed to see the deep bond that loyal consumers had with Tropicana's packaging. Once the old packaging had returned, Tropicana's sales returned to normal.

While the Tropicana story is an important lesson against meddling with an iconic brand, it also points out the clout that consumers have today. It is easier to connect with, and harder to avoid, customers who can easily and effectively interact with companies and each other through social technologies. Just ten years ago, it would have taken Tropicana months to determine that there was a backlash against its packaging. Now, through email, Facebook, and Twitter, companies can discover customer reactions in real time.

Differentiation and Positioning

Though we have focused solely on branding issues to this point in the chapter, it is vital to remember that branding is intricately tied to differentiation and positioning within the marketing program. People sometimes confuse differentiation and positioning with market segmentation and target marketing. *Differentiation* involves creating differences in the firm's product offering that set it apart from competing offerings. Differentiation typically has its basis in distinct product features, additional services, or other characteristics. *Positioning* refers to creating a mental image of the product offering and its differentiating features in the minds of the target market. This mental image can be based on real or perceived differences among competing offerings. Whereas differentiation is about the product and the marketing program, positioning is about customers' perceptions of the real or perceived benefits that the offering possesses.

Although differentiation and positioning can be based on actual product features or characteristics, the principle task for the firm is to develop and maintain a *relative position* for the product in the minds of the target market. The process of creating a favorable relative position involves several steps:

1. Identify the needs, wants, and preferences desired by the target market.
2. Evaluate the differentiation and positioning of current and potential competitors.
3. Compare the firm's current relative position vis-à-vis the competition across the needs, wants, and preferences desired by the target market.

4. Identify unique differentiation and positioning not offered by the competition that matches the firm's capabilities.
5. Develop a marketing program to create the firm's position in the minds of the target market.
6. Continually reassess the target market, the firm's position, and the position of competing offerings to ensure that the marketing program stays on track and to identify emerging positioning opportunities.

The concept of relative position can be addressed using a number of tools. One of the most commonly used tools is perceptual mapping. A *perceptual map* represents customer perceptions and preferences spatially by means of a visual display. A hypothetical perceptual map for automotive brands is shown in Exhibit 7.5. The axes represent underlying dimensions that customers might use to form perceptions and preferences of brands. Any number of dimensions can be represented using computer algorithms such as multidimensional scaling or cluster analysis. However, simple two-dimensional maps are the most common form because a limited number of dimensions are typically the most salient for consumers.

A second commonly used tool is the *strategy canvas*, which we discussed in Chapter 4 and Exhibit 4.9. In addition to its usefulness in the planning process, the strategy canvas is an excellent tool for demonstrating the firm's relative position in terms of the competitive factors that are important to the target market. In *Beyond the Pages 6.1*, we discussed the marketing program of Barnes & Noble relative to Amazon, its strongest competitor. A hypothetical strategy canvas for this market is shown in Exhibit 7.6. Note that while Barnes & Noble maintains an advantage in book selection (primarily on the strength of its textbook

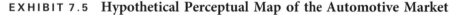

EXHIBIT 7.5 **Hypothetical Perceptual Map of the Automotive Market**

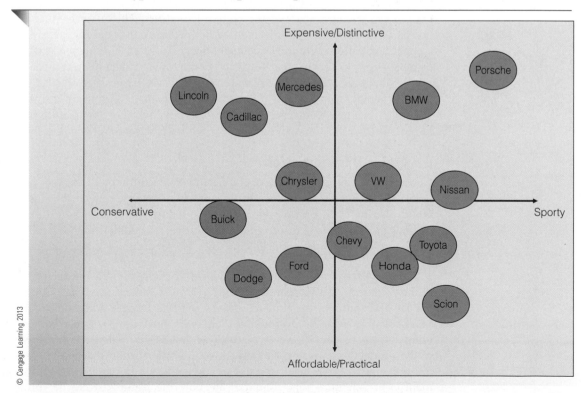

© Cengage Learning 2013

EXHIBIT 7.6 **Hypothetical Strategy Canvas for the Book Retailing Market**

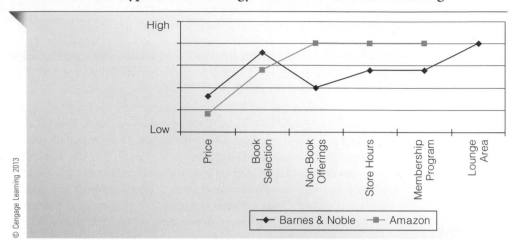

© Cengage Learning 2013

market) and having a comfortable lounge area for customers, Amazon has dominant advantages in non-book offerings, store hours, and its membership program.

The perceptual map and strategy canvas illustrate two basic issues in positioning strategy. First, they indicate products/brands that are similar in terms of relative mental position. In the example perceptual map, customers are likely to see the offerings of Toyota and Honda as being very similar. Positioning a brand to coincide with competing brands becomes more difficult when many brands occupy the same relative space. In the book retailing market, this is the case with pricing and book selection. Second, these tools illustrate voids in the current mindscape for a product category. In the perceptual map, note the empty space in the bottom-left corner. This indicates that consumers do not perceive any current products to be both conservative and inexpensive. This lack of competition within the mindspace might occur because (1) customers have unmet needs or preferences, or (2) customers have no desire for a product offering with this combination of dimensions. In the case of the strategy canvas, Barnes & Noble has a clear advantage in being a comfortable place to browse, lounge, and enjoy a coffee. However, additional research would be needed to determine whether this feature is more or less important to customers than having a strong book selection or membership program.

Bases for Differentiation

Generally, the most important tool of differentiation is the brand. Customer perceptions of a brand are of utmost importance in differentiation because differences among competing brands can be based on real qualities (e.g., product characteristics, features, or style) or psychological qualities (e.g., perception and image). In addition to the brand, other important bases for differentiation include product descriptors and customer support services.

Product Descriptors Firms generally provide information about their products in one of three contexts, as shown in Exhibit 7.7. The first context is *product features*, which are factual descriptors of the product and its characteristics. For example, Apple's 13-inch MacBook Pro includes key features such as an Intel Core i7 processor and aluminum unibody construction. However, features—although they tell something about the nature of the product—are not generally the pieces of information that lead customers to buy. Features must be translated into the second context, advantages. *Advantages* are performance characteristics that communicate how the features make the product behave,

EXHIBIT 7.7   Using Product Descriptors as a Basis for Differentiation

Product	Features	Advantages	Benefits
Apple MacBook Pro 13-inch Laptop	Intel Core i7 processor Mac OS X operating system with iLife Precision aluminum unibody construction Less than 1" thick and only 4.5 lbs High performance Intel HD graphics 7-hour, 63.5 watt lithium-polymer battery Integrated WiFi and Bluetooth	Very lightweight and compact Blazingly fast multimedia performance Out-of-the-box photo, video, and audio editing Long-lasting battery Hassle-free connectivity	Ultimate mobility Rugged entertainment on the road No need to purchase separate photo- or video-editing software Stay connected wherever you are
Chevrolet Camaro	6.2L, 426-horsepower SS V8 Variable-ratio power steering Low, wide, aggressive stance and 52/48 front/rear weight distribution Active fuel management	0 to 60 in 5 seconds Superb handling Better road grip 24 mpg highway	Enhanced self image Fun to drive Easy to drive Fuel-efficient muscle Safety
Bounty Select-a-Size Paper Towels	Sheets can be torn in varying sizes More sheets per roll Increased wet strength	Great for any size cleaning job Less waste Superior absorbency Won't run out as often	More control over cleaning Reduces cost of buying paper towels Can be sized for use as placemats

hopefully in a fashion that is distinctive and appealing to customers. The advantages of the MacBook Pro include a lightweight, compact design, fast performance, and long battery life. However, as we have said before, the real reason customers buy products is to gain *benefits*—the positive outcomes or need satisfaction they acquire from purchased products. Thus, the benefits of the MacBook Pro include ultimate mobility and rugged entertainment on the road. Other benefits, like increased productivity and connectivity, might also be implied in Apple's promotional program.

One aspect of a product's description that customers value highly is quality. Product characteristics that customers associate with quality include reliability, durability, ease of maintenance, ease of use, and a trusted brand name. In business markets, other characteristics, such as technical suitability, ease of repair, and company reputation, become included in this list of quality indicators. In general, higher product quality—real or imagined—means that a company can charge a higher price for their product and simultaneously build customer loyalty. In the case of Apple and the MacBook Pro, this is certainly true. The relationship between quality and price (inherent in the concept of value) forces the firm to consider product quality carefully when making decisions regarding differentiation, positioning, and the overall marketing program.

Customer Support Services   A firm may have difficulty differentiating its products when all products in a market have essentially the same quality, features, or benefits. In such cases, providing good customer support services—both before and after the sale—may be the only way to differentiate the firm's products and move them away from a price-driven commodity status. For example, over the past ten years, small, locally owned bookstores have disappeared at an alarming rate as competition from Barnes & Noble, Books-A-Million, and Amazon has taken its toll. The local stores that have remained in business thrive because of the exceptional, personalized service they provide to their customers. Many local bookstores create customer loyalty by being actively involved in the community, including contributing to local schools, churches, and charities. Many customers value this level of personalization so highly that they will pay slightly higher prices and remain loyal to *their* bookstore.

Support services include anything the firm can provide in addition to the main product that adds value to that product for the customer. Examples include assistance in identifying and defining customer needs, delivery and installation, technical support for high-tech systems and software, financing arrangements, training, extended warranties and guarantees, repair, layaway plans, convenient hours of operation, affinity programs (e.g., frequent flier/buyer programs), and adequate parking. If you buy a Kenmore refrigerator, for example, you can expect Sears to provide financing, delivery and installation, and warranty repair service, if necessary. Through research, the firm can discover the types of support services that customers value most. In some cases, customers may want lower prices rather than an array of support services. Low-cost airlines—such as JetBlue and Allegiant Air— and budget hotels—such as Motel 6 and La Quinta—are good examples. The importance of having the proper mix of support services has increased in recent years, causing many firms to design their customer services as carefully as they design their products.

Regardless of the basis for differentiation, reality is often not as important as perception. Firms that enjoy a solid image or reputation can differentiate their offerings based solely on the company or brand name alone. Examples of firms that have this ability include BMW, Mercedes, Michelin, Budweiser, Campbell's, Ritz-Carlton Hotels, Disney World, and Princess Cruises. But what if the firm doesn't have this ability? What if there are no credible bases for differentiation? In other words, what if your market is commoditized? In this case, creating a perception may be the firm's only choice. Consider the car rental industry. In the industry's early years, Hertz not only stood in first place, the company also maintained a vast lead over second-place Avis. The management of Avis, intent on capturing a larger portion of Hertz's customers, asked its advertising agency to develop an effective positioning strategy relative to Hertz. After searching for any advantage that Avis held over Hertz, the agency concluded that the only difference was that Avis was number two. Avis management decided to claim this fact as an advantage, using the theme "We're number two. We try harder!" Avis rentals soared, putting the company in a much stronger number-two position.

Positioning Strategies

A firm can design its marketing program to position and enhance the image of its offering in the minds of target customers. To create a positive image for a product, a firm can choose to strengthen its current position or find a new position. The key to strengthening a product's current position is to monitor constantly what target customers want and the extent to which customers perceive the product as satisfying those wants. Any complacency in today's dynamic marketplace is likely to result in lost customers and sales. For example, a firm known for excellent customer service must continue to invest time, money, talent, and attention to its product position to protect its market share and sales from competitive activity. This is especially true for firms such as Ritz-Carlton and Nordstrom that pursue competitive advantage based on customer intimacy.

Strengthening a current position is all about continually raising the bar of customer expectations. For example, Honda has always been known for quality and reliability. Recently, however, Honda has shifted its positioning focus to wrap quality and value in the context of long-term value. The company's promotional campaigns explain how its cars have a lower cost of ownership when factors such as insurance, fuel, and maintenance are taken into consideration.[11] Honda's positioning is different than the strategies pursued by Toyota (hybrid technology), Kia (style), and Volkswagen (engineering). By tweaking its positioning strategy, Honda understands that it must constantly raise expectations about value if it is to hold its position and remain competitive.

At times, declining sales or market share may signal that customers have lost faith in a product's ability to satisfy their needs. In such cases, a new position may be the best response, as strengthening the current position may well accelerate the downturn in performance. Repositioning may involve a fundamental change in any of the marketing mix elements, or perhaps even all of them. J.C. Penney, for example, hired Ron Johnson away from Apple to help transform the 110-year old chain. Johnson began by changing to a "Fair and Square" pricing strategy using three price points rather than frequent sales: Every Day, Month Long Value, and Best Prices. Prices were also changed to end in 0 instead of .99 to help remove the discount stigma associated with the company. Johnson also created dozens of "store within a store" boutiques around a "Town Square" theme to freshen Penney's merchandising strategy. Even the company's logo was changed to incorporate a square design (matching the pricing strategy) and patriotic red, white, and blue colors. The initial results were not kind to Johnson: Same store sales dropped a whopping 24 percent after the changes went into effect. However, Johnson's plan to revitalize Penney's is expected to take four years to complete.[12]

Some of the most memorable marketing programs involve attempts to move to new positions. The "Not Just for Breakfast Anymore" campaign for orange juice and the "Pork: The Other White Meat" campaign are good examples. A continuing example is Cadillac's attempt to reposition the brand because of the aging of its traditional target. The erosion of Cadillac's share of the luxury car market has forced the company to focus on and attract younger audiences to the brand. Cadillac's recent marketing programs have been headlined by the "Fusion of Design and Technology," "Heritage Reborn," "Break Through," "It's a Lifestyle," and "Red Blooded Luxury" campaigns. In some cases, repositioning requires a focus on new products. For example, Sony, the third-largest camera manufacturer in the world (behind Canon and Nikon), was not taken seriously as a camera brand until it acquired Konica Minolta and launched the Alpha—a digital SLR camera aimed at the high-end of the market. Before the Alpha, Sony offered only point-and-shoot models.

Mananging Brands over Time

Decisions related to branding and positioning are ongoing strategic issues. So is managing the marketing program over time. To address this issue, we use the traditional product life cycle—shown in Exhibit 7.8—to discuss marketing strategy in terms of the brand or product's conception, through its growth and maturity, and to its ultimate death. Our use of the product life cycle is based on its ability to describe the strategic issues and key objectives that should be considered during each phase of a brand's life. We note, however, that the product life cycle has many limitations. For one, most new brands and products never get past development and most successful brands and products never die. Second, the product life cycle really refers to the life of a product/market, industry, sector, or product category—not to specific brands or firms. Hence, if we trace the life cycle of the bricks-and-mortar book retailing business, we deal with market characteristics for this sector and not single firms like Barnes & Noble or Books-a-Million. Further, the length of each stage and the time involved in the overall cycle depends heavily on the actions of the firms within the industry. Firms and industries constantly reinvent themselves; which can cause the life cycle to speed up, slow down, or even recycle.

EXHIBIT 7.8   Stages of the Product Life Cycle

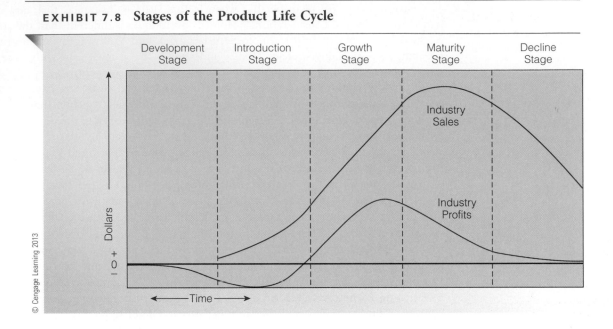

Despite these issues, the product life cycle offers a useful framework for discussing marketing strategy over time. Exhibit 7.9 summarizes the strategic considerations for each stage of the life cycle. It is important for firms to consider the stage of their market's life cycle with respect to planning in the current period, as well as planning for the future. Using the product life cycle as a framework has the distinct advantage of forcing firms to consider the future of their industry and their brand. For example, the traditional DVD rental industry is clearly in the early stages of its decline phase. The advent of DVD distribution via mail and kiosks, and technological innovations such as video on demand, streaming video content, and the growing use of mobile platforms, offer a dramatic increase in convenience for consumers. Given this fact, it is not surprising that traditional rental companies such as Blockbuster and Movie Gallery have either closed their doors or are near death. Conversely, Netflix embraced newer technologies and now boasts over 26 million streaming customers around the world. Redbox, the dominant player in kiosk-based DVD rentals, has also been growing at a rapid pace. In both examples, Netflix and Redbox were able to shift their strategies over time in order to capitalize on changes in the movie rental industry.[13]

The change in Netflix's strategy over time also highlights the strong connections between the marketing program and branding. For many years, the Netflix brand stood for easy, convenient access to DVDs through a customizable, and relatively inexpensive, rental program. Distribution and price were the company's key strengths. Over time, however, movie distributors became threatened by Netflix and became less willing to work with the company over issues such as pricing and distribution rights. This caused Netflix's operating costs to increase. As the technology shifted away from DVDs and more toward digital distribution, Netflix took the opportunity to begin its move in the same direction. This necessitated changes in the marketing program in terms of program structure, pricing, and distribution that were not well received by customers. Many protested the changes and over 800,000 cancelled their subscriptions. Suddenly, the Netflix brand was not held in high regard. Over time, customers began to come back to Netflix because, despite the price increases, the Netflix service still offers exceptional value to customers. Looking forward, however, Netflix will have to be mindful of competitive

EXHIBIT 7.9   **Strategic Considerations During the Product Life Cycle**

	Life Cycle Stages			
	Introduction	**Growth**	**Maturity**	**Decline**
Overall Marketing Goals	Stimulate product awareness and trial	Increase market share by acquiring new customers; discover new needs and market segments	Maximize profit by defending market share or stealing it from competitors	Reduce expenses and marketing efforts to maximize the last opportunity for profit
Product Strategy	Introduce limited models with limited features; frequent product changes	Introduce new models with new features; pursue continuous innovation	Full model line; increase supplemental product offerings to aid in product differentiation	Eliminate unprofitable models and brands
Pricing Strategy	Penetration pricing to establish a market presence or price skimming to recoup development costs	Prices fall due to competition; price to match or beat the competition	Prices continue to fall; price to beat the competition	Prices stabilize at a lower level
Distribution Strategy	Gradually roll out product to expand availability; get channel intermediaries on board	Intensify efforts to expand product reach and availability	Extensive product availability; retain shelf space; phase out unprofitable outlets or channels	Maintain a level necessary to keep brand loyal customers; continue phasing out unprofitable channels
Promotion Strategy	Advertising and personal selling to build awareness; heavy sales promotion to stimulate product trial	Aggressive brand advertising, selling, and sales promotion to encourage brand switching and continued trial	Stress brand differences and benefits; encourage brand switching; keep the brand/product fresh	Reduce to a minimal level or phase out entirely

Source: Adapted from William M. Pride and O.C. Ferrell, *Marketing*: 2010 Edition (Mason, OH: Cengage Learning, 2010), pp. 290-295.

moves by Apple, Amazon, and others if the brand is to remain synonymous with movie streaming and DVD rentals by mail.

Development Stage

As Exhibit 7.8 indicates, a firm has no sales revenue during the development stage. In fact, the firm experiences a net cash outflow due to the expenses involved in product innovation and development. For most innovations, the firm assumes a great deal of financial, market, and opportunity risk due to the uncertainty involved in developing new products and brands. For example, the pharmaceutical industry understands the challenges of new product development like no other industry. Firms such as Merck, Pfizer, and AstraZeneca spend millions each year developing new drugs. Upon identifying a new drug, it takes years of testing before earning FDA approval. Then, once the new drug is on the market, the firm has only a few years to recoup their investment before patent protection expires and the market opens to generic competition. In this highly competitive industry, pharmaceutical firms live or die based on the number and quality of drugs they have in their development pipelines.

The development stage usually begins with a concept, which has several components: (1) an understanding of the specific uses and benefits that target customers seek in a new product, (2) a description of the product, including its potential uses and benefits, (3) the potential for creating a complete product line that can create synergy in sales, distribution, and promotion, and (4) an analysis of the feasibility of the product concept, including such issues as anticipated sales, required return on investment, time of market introduction, and length of time to recoup the investment. Given the odds stacked against most new products, it is not surprising that over 80 percent of all new products fail. This unfortunate fact of life underscores the need to correctly identify target customer needs *before* developing the product strategy. Through effective test marketing, the firm can gauge customer response to a new product before the full-scale launch. New products that closely match customers' needs and have strong advantages over competing products are much easier to market as the new product enters the introduction stage of its life cycle.

Introduction Stage

The introduction stage begins when development is complete and ends when sales indicate that target customers widely accept the product. The marketing strategy devised during the development stage is fully implemented during the introduction stage, and should be tightly integrated with the firm's competitive advantages and strategic focus. Marketing strategy goals common to the introduction stage include:

- Attracting customers by raising awareness of, and interest in, the product offering through advertising, public relations, and publicity efforts that connect key product benefits to customers' needs and wants.
- Inducing customers to try and buy the product through the use of various sales tools and pricing activities. Common examples include free samples of the product and the use of price incentives.
- Engaging in customer education activities that teach members of the target market how to use the new product.
- Strengthening or expanding channel and supply chain relationships to gain sufficient product distribution to make the product easily accessible by target customers.
- Building on the availability and visibility of the product through trade promotion activities that encourage channel intermediaries to stock and support the product.
- Setting pricing objectives that will balance the firm's need to recoup investment with the competitive realities of the market.

Although all elements of the marketing program are important during the introduction stage, good promotion and distribution are essential to make customers aware that the new product is available, teach them how to use it correctly, and tell them where to purchase it. Although this is typically a very expensive undertaking, it doesn't have to be. For example, when Mozilla released its open-source Firefox web browser, it garnered 150 million downloads and 10 million permanent users in only 18 months without any marketing staff. The secret to Mozilla's success was a word-of-mouth buzz campaign that centered on its SpreadFirefox.com website. Today, Firefox users can still post ideas on how to market Firefox or volunteer to put other ideas into action.[14]

The length of the introduction stage can vary. In business markets, new products often have long introduction periods while buyers become convinced to adopt them. In consumer markets, many products experience an immediate upsurge in sales as consumers and retailers take advantage of special introductory offers. After the introduction, the firm must continually track market share, revenues, store placement, channel support, costs, and product usage rates to assess whether the new product pays back the firm's investment. Even when the firm has patent protection or hard-to-copy technology, it must carefully track competitors' reactions. Tracking this information is critical if the product is to make the grade, continue along the gradually rising sales curve, and enter the profitable growth stage.

Unfortunately, most new product introductions start off very slowly and never enjoy rising demand or profits. Or, they start with a bang and decline rapidly. Failures during introduction are even more expensive than in the development stage, as marketing and distribution costs accrue to the total expenses involved in the product's launch.

Growth Stage

The firm should be ready for the growth stage, as sustained sales increases may begin quickly. The product's upward sales curve may be steep, and profits should rapidly increase, and then decline, toward the end of the growth stage. The length of the growth stage varies according to the nature of the product and competitive reactions. For example, disposable diapers had a long growth stage as they experienced over 30 percent yearly growth for a decade. A short growth stage is typical for new technologies, such as the latest iPhone or new video games.

Regardless of the length of the growth stage, the firm has two main priorities: (1) establishing a strong, defensible market position, and (2) achieving financial objectives that repay investment and earn enough profit to justify a long-term commitment to the product. Within these two priorities, there are a number of pertinent marketing strategy goals:

- Leverage the product's *perceived* differential advantages in terms of branding, quality, price, value, and so on, to secure a strong market position.
- Establish a clear brand identity through coordinated promotional campaigns aimed at both customers and the trade.
- Create unique positioning through the use of advertising that stresses the product's benefits for target customers relative to other available solutions or products.
- Maintain control over product quality to assure customer satisfaction.
- Maximize availability of the product through distribution and promotion activities that capitalize on the product's popularity.
- Maintain or enhance the product's ability to deliver profits to key channel and supply chain partners, especially retailers that control shelf space and product placement.
- Find the ideal balance between price and demand as price elasticity becomes more important as the product moves toward the maturity stage.
- Always keep an eye focused on the competition.

During the growth stage, the overall strategy shifts from acquisition to retention, from stimulating product trial to generating repeat purchases and building brand loyalty. This is not only true for customers, but also for wholesalers, retailers, and other supply chain members. The key is to develop long-term relationships with customers and partners in order to prepare for the maturity stage. As the market matures, the firm will need loyal customers and good friends in the supply chain in order to remain competitive. Maintaining key relationships is a challenging and expensive proposition. For this reason, the growth stage is the most expensive stage for marketing.

Pricing also becomes more challenging during the growth stage. As more competitors enter the market, the firm must balance its need for cash flow with its need to be competitive. The relationship between price and perceived quality is a complicating factor, as is the increasing price sensitivity of customers. It is not surprising during the growth stage to see competitors stake out market positions based on premium or value-based pricing strategies. Other firms solve the pricing dilemma by offering different products at different price points. You can see this strategy in action in the wireless phone market, where each service provider offers tiered service offerings (i.e., minutes and features) at different pricing levels. FedEx implements the same strategy with its tiered service offerings (overnight by 8:30 A.M., overnight by 10:30 A.M., etc.).

Another major challenge during the growth stage is the increasing number of competitors entering the market. There is a tendency for many firms to pay less attention to competitors during the growth stage. After all, the market has grown rapidly and there is enough business for everyone to have a piece. Why not worry about competitors later? Because growth will eventually end and the market will become mature. To protect itself, the firm must build a defensible market position as it prepares for market maturity. This position may be based on image, price, quality, or perhaps some technological standard. Eventually, the market will go through a shakeout period and the dominant firms will emerge. In the U.S., this process is already underway in markets such as wireless phones, airlines, and Internet technology.

Maturity Stage

After the shakeout occurs at the end of the growth stage, the strategic window of opportunity will all but close for the market and it will enter the maturity stage. No more firms will enter the market unless they have found some product innovation significant enough to attract large numbers of customers. The window of opportunity often remains open, however, for new product features and variations. A good example is the introduction of light, dry, ice, microbrew, low-alcohol, and low-carb products in the beer industry. These variations can be quite important as firms attempt to gain market share. In the face of limited or no growth within the market, one of the few ways for a firm to gain market share is to steal it from a competitor. Such theft often comes only with significant promotional investments or cuts in gross margin because of the lowering of prices. The stakes in this chess match are often very high. For example, just a fractional change in market share in the soft drink industry means millions in additional revenue and profit for the lucky firm.

In the typical product life cycle, we expect maturity to be the longest stage. For the firm that has survived the growth stage, maturity can be a relatively status quo period of time. As long as one maintains sales volume to keep market share constant, a longer-term perspective can be taken due to decreasing market uncertainty. Typically, a firm has four general goals that can be pursued during the maturity stage:

- **Generate Cash Flow**. By the time a market reaches maturity, the firm's products should be yielding a very positive cash flow. This is essential to recoup the initial investment and to generate the excess cash necessary for the firm to grow and develop new products.
- **Hold Market Share**. Marketing strategy should stress holding market share among the dominant brands in the market. Firms having marginal market share must decide whether they have a reasonable chance of improving their position. If not, they should consider pulling out of the market.
- **Steal Market Share**. Any firm in a mature market can pursue this goal; however, it is more likely to be used by firms holding weaker market positions. The key to this strategy is to create incentives that encourage brand switching, even if only temporarily. Even small gains in market share can lead to large increases in profits.
- **Increase Share of Customer**. Share of customer refers to the percentage of each customer's needs in a particular area met by the firm. This strategy is quite common in financial services. Likewise, many large grocery chains increase share of customer by adding features ranging from ready-to-eat meals to dry cleaning services in an effort to create one-stop shopping for family needs.

To achieve these goals, the firm has at least four general options for strategy selection throughout the maturity stage: (1) develop a new product image, (2) find and attract new users to the product, (3) discover new applications and uses for the product, or (4) apply new technology to the product. Kraft Foods, for example, launched a massive promotional campaign to create a new product image for Jell-O after a long decline in sales. Today, Jell-O has once again achieved gourmet status with America's children. Similarly, Whirlpool used product innovation to shake itself free from the "sea of white," a phrase that is often used to describe the bland range of offerings in household appliances. Whirlpool's Duet washers and dryers—industry leaders in design, ease of use, and energy efficiency—now command 40 percent of the front-loading market.[15] Finally, as described in *Beyond the Pages 7.3*, Nintendo used a rebranding strategy to attract casual gamers to its handheld and home gaming systems.

Stealing customers away from the competition involves creating incentives for non-customers to try the firm's product. This may entail heavy expenditures in sales promotion activities such as product sampling, couponing, or trade promotion to encourage prominent display of the product on the store's shelves. In some cases, once the brand switch has been accomplished, customers can be locked in through the use of contractual agreements. This is common among wireless phone providers, health clubs, and satellite television providers. A more common approach is to simply match competitive prices, as is the case among many competing retail firms. For example, most pizza chains will accept competitor's coupons and match their promotional incentives to gain business.

PRNewsFoto/Whirlpool

Whirlpool was able to breathe new life into a stagnant market through the use of innovative product design.

Beyond the Pages 7.3

Nintendo's Rebranding Strategy[16]

Admit it. You've always thought of Nintendo's line of game systems as being strictly for kids. You're not alone. Most people associate the Nintendo 64, Gamecube, Wii, GameBoy, and DSi with famous characters such as Mario, Luigi, and Princess Peach. However, after several years of sales declines, Nintendo embarked on a rebranding strategy to change everyone's opinions about video games and the gamers that enjoy them. The company discovered that casual gamers, and even non-gamers, were a much larger market than hard-core gamers. Since hard-core gamers already preferred the Xbox and PlayStation, Nintendo took a Blue Ocean Strategy approach to remake the company and specifically target the casual and non-gamer markets.

Nintendo's first step toward rebranding occurred in early 2006 with the redesign of its original DS handheld game system. Dubbed the DS Lite, the handheld was a smaller, lighter, brighter-screened, and distinctly iPod-looking version of the original DS system. It boasted a touch sensitive screen, a stylus, long battery life, and the ability to play all DS and GameBoy Advance games. To coincide with the launch, Nintendo rebranded many of its popular puzzle and skill-building games under the "Touch Generations" label. Titles in the series—including *Brain Age*, *Big Brain Academy*, *Tetris DS*, *Nintendogs*, *Magnetica*, *Electroplankton*, *Sudoku Gridmaster*, and *True Swing Golf*—had been available for a while; however, they had not been collectively branded and targeted toward a particular audience. That audience included 40- and 50-something men and women in the so-called casual gamer market. Unlike younger gamers that enjoy playing for long periods of time, casual gamers prefer to play games in smaller portions: waiting for the kids to finish dance class, riding in mass transit, or as a fun way to fill 10 minutes before a meeting. At the time of launch, Nintendo's Touch Generations website stated this market's needs perfectly:

> Not a hard-core gamer? That's OK. We've made games for you in mind. Nintendo's Touch Generations series, exclusive to the Nintendo DS handheld game system, allows you simple, engaging interaction with games that promote production over destruction, contemplation over domination. No complex instructions. No

steep learning curve. Play a little. Play a lot. It's up to you.

Nintendo's second step toward rebranding occurred in late 2006 with the launch of the Wii home gaming console. The defining characteristic of the Wii was its wireless controller—the Wii Remote. It allowed gamers to play games interactively by moving their arms and body in distinct game-like motions (such as playing tennis, baseball, or driving a car). Nintendo also expanded the Touch Generations brand to include Wii games such as *Wii Fit*, *Wii Music*, and *Big Brain Academy*. After launch, both the DS Lite and the Wii quickly became the best selling gaming platforms in the world.

In 2009, Nintendo further refined its strategy with the launch of the DSi handheld gaming system. Although the system looked very much like the DS Lite, it incorporated larger screens, front- and rear-facing cameras, an online game store, removable storage, and picture-editing software. The handheld was further updated in 2011 to the 3DS featuring 3D graphics. Together, these changes made the DSi and 3DS much more social than the original system. In fact, Nintendo's goal was to create a system that did more than play games. The company wanted to create a system that enriched people's lives. This shift necessitated a change in Nintendo's marketing about Touch Generations:

> The Touch Generations family of software lets people from all walks of life connect with each other through fun and engaging interactive experiences—no matter what their age, gender, or background. Titles like Wii Fit™ Plus and Art Academy™ can bring families together in new and exciting ways. After all, fun is a universal idea. Just look for the distinctive orange logo on the game box at your local retailer.

Nintendo's Touch Generations strategy takes advantage of trends in the gaming market. The average age of frequent game purchasers is 40, with a full 25 percent of all gamers being over the age of 50. Nintendo believes that there is large segment of "dormant" gamers in the market who enjoyed playing *Pac-Man* and *Pong* as children or young adults. Many experts agree and point to the huge success of *The Sims* as an example of a game that appeals to this market.

Decline Stage

A product's sales plateau will not last forever, and eventually a persistent decline in revenue begins. A firm has two basic options during the decline stage: (1) attempt to postpone the decline, or (2) accept its inevitability. Should the firm attempt to postpone the decline, the product's demand must be renewed through repositioning, developing new uses or features for the product, or applying new technology. For example, despite the decline in sales of muscle cars over the past two decades, Ford, Chrysler, and GM have successfully launched redesigned versions of their famous brands. The Ford Mustang Shelby GT 500 was introduced in 2007 to eager buyers willing to pay $20,000 over sticker (which was around $40,000) to get the first Shelbys produced. Chrysler's Dodge Challenger debuted in 2008, with GM's Chevy Camaro launching in 2009.[17] Today, all three brands are still selling quite well. Postponing a product's decline in this manner takes a great deal of time and a substantial investment of resources. Many firms, however, do not have the resources or opportunity to renew a product's demand and must accept the inevitability of decline. In such instances, the firm can either harvest profits from the product while demand declines or divest the product, taking steps to abandon it or sell it to another firm.

The *harvesting* approach calls for a gradual reduction in marketing expenditures, and uses a less resource-intensive marketing mix. A harvesting strategy also allows the firm to funnel its increased cash flow into the development of new products. For example, GM phased out the Oldsmobile brand over several years by offering discounts and other special incentives, such as longer product warranties, to allay customer fears of limited product support. A company using the *divesting* option withdraws all marketing support from the product. It may continue to sell the product until it sustains losses, or arrange for the product to be acquired by another firm. For example, Procter & Gamble dropped its Oxydol brand laundry detergent and sold it to Redox Brands (now known as CR Brands) for $7 million. Though P&G had sold Oxydol for 73 years, the company decided to delete the brand after its sales fell from a high of $64 million in 1950 to only $5.5 million just before the sale. CR Brands now markets the brand as Oxydol Extreme Clean and targets Generation X consumers with liquid versions and vibrant packaging.[18]

There are several factors that the firm should take into consideration before deciding on an appropriate marketing strategy during the decline stage:

- **Market Segment Potential**. The firm might have loyal customer segments that will continue to buy the product. If these segments are viable and profitable, the firm should postpone the decline or slowly harvest the product. For example, despite the decline in the DVD rental market, a substantial number of customers like Redbox for its convenience and low prices.
- **The Market Position of the Product**. A product in a leading market position with a solid image may be profitable and generate excess cash by attracting customers from competitors' abandoned products.
- **The Firm's Price and Cost Structure**. If the firm is a low cost producer in the industry and can maintain its selling price, the product can remain viable even in a declining market. The firm's cost structure could also be enhanced by no longer having to invest in the product's marketing program.
- **The Rate of Market Deterioration**. The faster the rate of market deterioration, the sooner the firm should divest the product.

Although the firm should carefully consider these factors, it should not be sentimental about dropping a failing product or brand. On the other hand, the firm should not quickly dismiss a renewal attempt, particularly if the firm does not have a better alternative use for its resources.

Throughout the product life cycle, it is imperative that the firm stays focused on changes in the market, not on its products or brands. Products and brands have life cycles only because markets and customers change. By focusing on changing markets, the firm can attempt to create new and better quality products to match customers' needs. Only in this way can a firm grow, prosper, remain competitive, and continue to be seen as a source of solutions by the target market.

Lessons from Chapter 7

Branding strategy:

- is critical to the effective differentiation and positioning of the complete offering.
- involves selecting the right combination of name, symbol, term, or design that identifies a specific product or firm.
- has two parts: the brand name (words, letters, and numbers) and the brand mark (symbols, figures, or a design).
- involves more than developing a brand name or brand mark. To be truly successful, a brand should succinctly captures the product offering in a way that answers a question in the customer's mind.
- involves the many different attributes that make up the way customers think about brands: people (employees and endorsers), places (country of origin and channels), things (events, causes, and third-party endorsements), and other brands (alliances, branded ingredients, the company, and extensions).
- also involves corporate branding, which includes activities aimed at a variety of stakeholders to build and enhance the firm's reputation.
- is important because of the many advantages of branding, including making it easier for customers to find and buy products.
- involves decisions such as selling manufacturer versus private-label brands. Although private-label brands are generally more profitable, manufacturer brands have built-in demand, recognition, and product loyalty.
- involves decisions related to individual versus family branding.
- involves managing strategic brand alliances, such as cobranding or brand licensing, that involve developing close relationships with other firms.
- involves developing customers' loyalty to brands. Brand loyalty is a positive attitude toward a brand that causes customers to have a consistent preference for that brand over all other competing brands in a product category. Three levels of loyalty include brand recognition, brand preference, and brand insistence.
- involves building the brand's value to the firm with respect to its equity, or the marketing and financial value associated with a brand's position in the marketplace.

- also involves taking steps to protect brand names and brand marks from trademark infringement by other firms.

Packaging and labeling:

- are important considerations in branding strategy because packaging often goes hand-in-hand in developing a product, its benefits, its differentiation, and its image.
- includes issues such as color, shape, size, and convenience of the package or the product's container.
- are often used in product modifications or cobranding to reposition the product or give it new and improved features.
- are vital in helping customers make proper product selections.
- can have important environmental and legal consequences.

Differentiation and positioning:

- involves creating differences in the firm's product offering that set it apart from competing offerings (differentiation), as well as the development and maintenance of a relative position for a product offering in the minds of the target market (positioning).
- can be monitored through the use of several tools including perceptual mapping (a visual, spatial display of customer perceptions on two or more key dimensions) and the strategy canvas (a visual tool that depicts how the firm stacks up against the competition across several competitive factors that are important to the target market).
- is fundamentally based on the brand, but can include other bases for differentiation including product descriptors (features, advantages, benefits) and customer support services.
- includes the positioning strategies of strengthen the current position and repositioning.

Managing brands over time:

- can be addressed via the traditional product life cycle, which traces the evolution of a product's or brand's development and birth, growth and maturity, and decline and death over five stages:

- development—a time of no sales revenue, negative cash flow, and high risk
- introduction—a time of rising customer awareness, extensive marketing expenditures, and rapidly increasing sales revenue
- growth—a time of rapidly increasing sales revenue, rising profits, market expansion, and increasing numbers of competitors
- maturity—a time of sales and profit plateaus, a shift from customer acquisition to customer retention, and strategies aimed at holding or stealing market share
- decline—a time of persistent sales and profit decreases, attempts to postpone the decline, or strategies aimed at harvesting or divesting the product

- can be influenced by shifts in the market, or by the actions of the firms within the industry as they constantly reinvent themselves.

Questions for Discussion

1. Consider the notion that a truly effective brand is one that succinctly captures the product offering in a way that answers a question in the customer's mind. Now, consider these brands (or choose your own): Coca-Cola, Disney, Marlboro, American Express, and Ford. What questions do these brands answer? Why are these effective brands?
2. Compare the corporate reputation scores in Exhibit 7.2 with the brand valuations in Exhibit 7.4. Why does Apple sit at the top of both lists? How has the company used good branding and positioning strategy to achieve this result? How is it that Wells Fargo can have a very high brand valuation, but a very low corporate reputation score?
3. Look back at the Top 10 brands in Exhibit 7.4. What bases do these brands use for differentiation? What strategies do they use to create a relative position in their respective markets? Why do these brands hold so much value?

Exercises

1. Using the brand attribute framework in Exhibit 7.1, construct an overall branding statement about yourself. How would others, especially potential employers, look at your brand? What areas do you need to improve? Does your brand answer key questions or create questions about your abilities?
2. Do some background research on the following markets: wireless phone service, DVD players, and pizza. Which stage of the product life cycle is each of these markets in currently? What market characteristics lead you to feel this way? Is there evidence that any of these markets are on the verge of moving into the next stage of the life cycle? Explain.
3. Think about the last purchase you made in each of the following product categories. What were the features, advantages, and benefits of the specific product or brand that you selected? After completing the table, consider the positioning of the product or brand in the market. Does its positioning match your responses in the table? Explain.

	Features	Advantages	Benefits
Athletic Shoes Brand _____			
Sit-Down Restaurant Name or Franchise _____			
Airline Brand _____			

End Notes

1. These facts are from Fred Mackerodt, "Defending a Brand Isn't Easy," *CEO Magazine*, April/May 2006, 54–55; Maya Roney, "Steinway: Worth Much More than a Song," *BusinessWeek Online*, March 6, 2007 (http://www.businessweek.com/bwdaily/dnflash/content/mar2007/db20070305_637888.htm); Steinway corporate website (http://www.steinway.com/about), accessed May 23, 2012; and Chen Yingqun and Yang Yang, "Music to Their Ears," *China Daily USA*, March 30, 2012 (http://usa.chinadaily.com.cn/weekly/2012-03/30/content_14947510.htm).

2. These concepts are adapted from Jennifer Rice's Brand Blog, Mantra Brand Consulting (http://brand.blogs.com).

3. Douglas A. McIntyre, "JCPenney Buys Liz Claiborne, a Brand No One Else Wants," *24/7 Wall Street*, October 13, 2011 (http://247wallst.com/2011/10/13/jcpenney-buys-liz-claiborne-a-brand-no-one-else-wants); Mark J. Miller, "JCPenney Re-Refreshes Brand – Third Time's the Charm?" *brandchannel*, January 26, 2012 (http://www.brandchannel.com/home/post/JCPenney-Rebrands-012612.aspx); and Aarthi Sivaraman, "Buy or Sell—Will Penney Emerge Stronger from the Downturn?" *Forbes*, April 17, 2009 (http://www.forbes.com/feeds/afx/2009/04/17/afx6306069.html).

4. Robert Passikoff, "Top-100 Loyalty Leaders for 2011," *Forbes*, September 13, 2011 (http://www.forbes.com/sites/marketshare/2011/09/13/top-100-loyalty-leaders-for-2011).

5. Kia website (http://www.kia.com/#/warranty).

6. "J&J to Buy Pfizer Unit for $16B" *CNN Money* (from Reuters), June 26, 2006 (http://money.cnn.com/2006/06/26/news/companies/pfizer_jnj.reut/index.htm).

7. These facts are from BIOTA Spring Water website (http://www.biotaspringwater.com/?q=bottle), accessed May 24, 2012; Coca-Cola PlantBottle website (http://www.thecoca-colacompany.com/citizenship/plantbottle_benefits.html), accessed May 24, 2012; and the NatureWorks LLC website (http://www.natureworksllc.com/the-ingeo-journey.aspx), accessed May 24, 2012.

8. "Lunchmeats Launch in Reusable PP Containers," *Packaging World*, June 2, 2003 (http://www.packworld.com/package-type/thermoformed-packaging/lunchmeats-launch-reusable-pp-containers).

9. These facts are from Stuart Elliott, "Tropicana Discovers Some Buyers are Passionate about Packaging," *New York Times*, February 22, 2009 (http://www.nytimes.com/2009/02/23/business/media/23adcol.html); David Kiley, "Arnell Strikes Again: Orange You Glad You Hired Him Tropicana?" *BusinessWeek Online*, February 27, 2009 (http://www.businessweek.com/the_thread/brandnewday/archives/2009/02/arnell_strikes.html); David Kiley, "More Piling on Arnell's Tropicana Fiasco," *BusinessWeek Online*, March 18, 2009 (http://www.businessweek.com/the_thread/brandnewday/archives/2009/03/more_piling_on.html); and David Kiley, "Tropicana Fiasco from Arnell is Gift that Keeps Giving," *BusinessWeek*

Online, April 3, 2009 (http://www.businessweek.com/the_thread/brandnewday/archives/2009/04/tropicana_fiasc.html).

10. Eric Greenberg, "Drug Makers Not Preempted from Lawsuits," *Packworld*, April 17, 2009 (http://www.packworld.com/webonly-27416).

11. Brian Morrissey, "Honda Touts Value Message," *Adweek*, April 6, 2009 (http://www.adweek.com/aw/content_display/esearch/e3iff50ba6951560a30c30555cab2e882ef).

12. These facts are from Rebecca Cullers, "JCPenney Gets All Patriotic With Its New Logo," *Adweek*, January 27, 2012 (http://www.adweek.com/adfreak/jcpenney-gets-all-patriotic-its-new-logo-137786); Rafi Mohammed, "J.C. Penney's Risky New Pricing Strategy," *BusinessWeek*, January 31, 2012 (http://www.businessweek.com/management/jc-penneys-risky-new-pricing-strategy-01312012.html); and Jennifer Reingold, "Ron Johnson: Retail's New Radical," *CNN Money*, March 7, 2012 (http://management.fortune.cnn.com/2012/03/07/jc-penney-ron-johnson).

13. These facts are from Chloe Albanesius, "Netflix: Users Who Left After Price Hike are Re-Joining," *PC Magazine*, May 16, 2012 (http://www.pcmag.com/article2/0,2817,2404523,00.asp).

14. "Open-Source Ad Campaigns," *Business 2.0*, April 2006, 92; and the Firefox website (http://affiliates.mozilla.org/en-US), accessed May 25, 2012.

15. Corporate Design Foundation, "Branding that Speaks to the Eyes," *BusinessWeek Online*, March 16, 2006 (http://www.businessweek.com/innovate/content/mar2006/id20060316_504093.htm).

16. Kenji Hall, "Has Nintendo Peaked?" *BusinessWeek Online*, May 7, 2009 (http://www.businessweek.com/globalbiz/content/may2009/gb2009057_844946.htm); Reena Jana, "Nintendo's Brand New Game," *BusinessWeek Online*, June 22, 2006 (http://www.businessweek.com/innovate/content/jun2006/id20060622_124931.htm); Sarah Lacy, "Social Gaming Scores in the Recession," *BusinessWeek Online*, April 30, 2009 (http://www.businessweek.com/technology/content/apr2009/tc20090429_963394.htm); and Nintendo's Touch Generations website (http://www.nintendo.com/games/touchgenerations), accessed May 25, 2012.

17. Alex Taylor III, "Bankruptcy Baby: 2010 Chevrolet Camaro Coupe," *Fortune*, June 2, 2009 (http://thewheeldeal.blogs.fortune.cnn.com/2009/06/02/bankruptcy-baby-2010-chevrolet-camaro-coupe); and Peter Valdes-Dapena, "Shelby Mustangs: $20,000 Over Sticker," *CNNMoney.com* (Autos Section), May 19, 2006 (http://www.cnn.com/2006/AUTOS/05/17/shelby_over_sticker/index.html).

18. These facts are from CR Brands Oxydol website (http://www.oxydol.com/Products.html), accessed May 25, 2012; Matthew Swibel, "Spin Cycle," *Forbes*, April 2, 2001, 118; and Randy Tucker, "Liquid Oxydol Aimed at Gen X," *Cincinnati Inquirer*, May 3, 2001 (http://www.enquirer.com/editions/2001/05/03/fin_liquid_oxydol_aimed.html).

CHAPTER 8
Ethics and Social Responsibility in Marketing Strategy

Introduction

The importance of marketing ethics and social responsibility has grown in recent years, and their role in the strategic planning process has become increasingly important. Many firms have seen their images, reputations, and marketing efforts destroyed by problems in these areas. The failure to see ethical conduct as part of strategic marketing planning can destroy the trust and customer relationships that are necessary for success. Ethics and social responsibility are also necessary in light of stakeholder demands, and many aspects of ethics can become legal issues. For example, price fixing, bribery, conflicts of interest, fraud, and deceptive advertising and sales practices all have legal implications. Marketing ethics does not just happen by hiring ethical people; it requires strategic decisions that become a part of the overall marketing strategy and culture of the firm.

The traditional view of marketing holds that ethics and social responsibility are good supplements to business activities but may not be essential. Some marketers believe that ethics and social responsibility initiatives drain resources that could be better used for other marketing activities. Yet research has shown that ethical behavior can not only enhance a company's reputation, but also contribute significantly to its bottom line.[2] As demonstrated by Salesforce.com's success in *Beyond the Pages 8.1*, social responsibility and sustainability are becoming increasingly popular among businesses as a way to reduce a company's carbon footprint and create a positive image among stakeholders. Ample evidence demonstrates that ignoring stakeholders' demands for responsible marketing can destroy customers' trust and even prompt increased government regulation. Irresponsible actions that anger customers, employees, or competitors may jeopardize a firm's financial standing and also lead to legal repercussions. For instance, GlaxoSmithKline settled with the U.S. Justice Department for $3 billion after the Justice Department accused it of defrauding Medicaid and marketing certain drugs illegally. One of the accusations levied against GlaxoSmithKline was that it marketed its drug Wellbutrin for uses not approved by the Food and Drug Administration. Such off-label marketing is illegal.[3] Today, most CEOs recognize that companies must do better. As Indra Nooyi, chairperson and CEO of PepsiCo, states: "performance without purpose is not a long-term sustainable formula."[4]

Beyond the Pages 8.1

Salesforce.com Adopts a Stakeholder Orientation[1]

Salesforce.com truly believes in sharing the wealth. Salesforce.com is a cloud computing organization that provides software, such as customer relationship management applications, to a variety of clients including Dell, Qualcomm, NBCUniversal, and Symantec. The various applications in the Salesforce.com platform bring people and data together to provide information the sales force needs to be successful. Additionally, Salesforce.com is a known and respected leader in social responsibility.

Salesforce.com secured the number one spot in *Fortune*'s ranking of the 25 top-paying companies. Believing that employees are largely responsible for making Salesforce.com what it is today, Salesforce.com provides large bonuses to its top performers, pays for "incentive trips" to Hawaii, and allows some of its employees to own stock in the company. The average total pay at Salesforce.com exceeds $300,000.

To hold the company accountable to its investors, Salesforce.com has implemented several policies to ensure objectivity and accountability. Most of the company's board members are independent, reducing the chance that board members might experience conflicts of interest in their responsibilities. The company has also adopted an ethics code and has an ethics office to ensure that the company's ethical expectations are met.

Additionally, Salesforce.com views the environment as an important stakeholder. The company continually strives to reduce its environmental impact. Its buildings meet LEED (Leadership in Energy and Environmental Design) standards, and Salesforce.com communicates its environmental expectations throughout the company and its supply chain. Salesforce.com also creates products to help its customers measure their environmental impact. The company claims that its cloud computing model reduces greenhouse gas emissions by 95 percent compared to traditional hardware or software. Salesforce.com also discloses its carbon emissions data for independent assessment. The Carbon Disclosure Institute, which analyzes S&P 500 companies on its carbon emissions data, awarded Salesforce.com 85 percent for its disclosure. Although Salesforce.com still has many ways it can improve its efforts toward sustainability, its willingness to disclose information about the sustainability of its operations demonstrates the company's commitment toward the environment.

In 2011, for the fourth consecutive year, Salesforce.com was named as one of the "World's Most Ethical" companies by the Ethisphere Institute. Much of this has to do with Salesforce.com's 1/1/1 Model, which stands for 1 percent time (in which employees are given 1 percent time to volunteer), 1 percent equity (in which 1 percent of its capital is given to the Salesforce.com Foundation), and 1 percent product. As a result of this program, Salesforce.com has donated more than 240,000 employee-hours to community causes, has donated or discounted licenses for its software to more than 10,000 organizations (many of them nonprofits), and has awarded more than $21 million in grants. By integrating corporate social responsibility into the company culture, Salesforce.com hopes to make a positive difference in communities and nonprofit organizations.

All of these ethical initiatives have not diminished Salesforce.com's profitability. In fact, it's quite the contrary. Salesforce.com has experienced rapid growth and was added into the S&P 500 in 2008. Social responsibility has appeared to pay off for the company's bottom line.

In this chapter, we look at the dimensions of ethics and social responsibility, sustainability issues in marketing, the role of ethics and social responsibility in connection to marketing strategy, and the challenges of ethical behavior. We also address specific ethical issues within the firm's marketing program, as well as organizational and self-regulating methods of preventing misconduct. We examine the organizational context of marketing ethics, including codes of ethics and the impact of ethical leadership. Additionally, we show the role of ethics and social responsibility in improving both marketing and financial performance. Finally, we discuss how ethics and social responsibility can be incorporated into strategic planning.

Ethics and Social Responsibility in Marketing Strategy

In response to customer demands, along with the threat of increased regulation, firms increasingly incorporate ethics and social responsibility into the strategic marketing planning process. Any organization's reputation can be damaged by poor performance or ethical misconduct. Obviously, stakeholders who are most directly affected by negative events will have a corresponding shift in their perceptions of a firm's reputation. However, even those indirectly connected to negative events can shift their attitudes toward the firm. Some scandals may lead to boycotts and aggressive campaigns to dampen sales and earnings. Nestlé experienced a backlash when Greenpeace revealed that the company used non-sustainable palm oil in its Kit-Kat bars. Palm oil plantations have destroyed thousands of acres of rainforests and have threatened the habitat of many native species, including orangutan populations. Consumers were outraged and posted angry messages to Nestlé's Facebook page. The backlash prompted the company to sever ties with its palm oil supplier and allow the Forest Trust to perform audits of its supply chain.[5]

Dimensions of Social Responsibility

Social responsibility is a broad concept that relates to an organization's obligation to maximize its positive impact on society while minimizing its negative impact. As shown in Exhibit 8.1, social responsibility consists of four dimensions: economic, legal, ethical, and philanthropic.[6]

Economic and Legal Responsibilities   From an economic perspective, firms must be responsible to all stakeholders for financial success. The economic responsibility of making a profit serves employees and the community at large due to its impact on employment and income levels in the area that the firm calls home. Firms also have expectations, at a minimum, to obey laws and regulations. This is a challenge because the legal and regulatory environment is hard to navigate and interpretations of the law change frequently. Laws and regulations are designed to keep U.S. companies' actions within the range of acceptable conduct and fair competition. When customers, interest groups, or competitors become concerned over what they perceive as misconduct on the part of a marketing organization, they may urge their legislators to draft new laws to regulate the behavior or engage in litigation to force the organization to "play by the rules." For example, complaints from merchants about high debit card fees prompted new legislation that capped how much banks can charge for processing debit card transactions.[7] Economic and legal responsibilities are the most basic levels of social responsibility for a good reason: failure to consider them may mean that a firm is not around long enough to engage in ethical or philanthropic activities.

Ethical Responsibilities   At the next level of the pyramid, marketing ethics refers to principles and standards that define acceptable marketing conduct as determined by the public, government regulators, private-interest groups, competitors, and the firm itself. The most basic of these principles have been codified as laws and regulations to induce marketers to conform to society's expectations of conduct. However, it is important to

---

EXHIBIT 8.1 **The Pyramid of Corporate Social Responsibility**

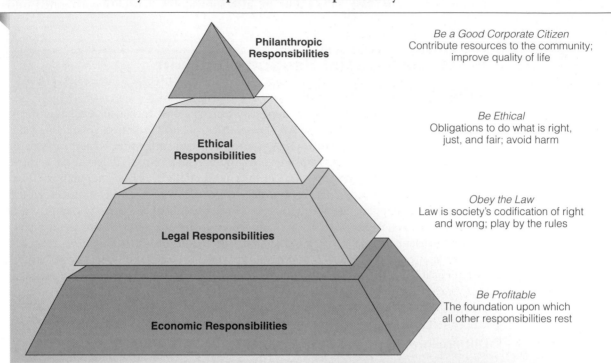

Source: Reprinted from *Business Horizons* 34(4) (July/August 1991), Archie Carroll, "The Pyramid of Corporate Social Responsibility: Toward the Moral Management of Organizational Stakeholders" p. 42, Copyright © 1991, with permission from Elsevier.

understand that marketing ethics go beyond legal issues: Ethical marketing decisions foster trust, which helps build long-term marketing relationships. Marketing ethics includes decisions about what is right or wrong in the organizational context of planning and implementing marketing activities in a global business environment to benefit (1) organizational performance, (2) individual achievement in a work group, (3) social acceptance and advancement in the organization, and (4) stakeholders. This definition of marketing ethics recognizes that ethical decisions occur in a complex social network within a marketing organization. Marketers are often asked by upper-level management to help make the numbers by reaching almost impossible sales targets. In fact, most marketing misconduct is done to help the organization. Being a team player and bending the rules to make targets may result in a promotion. On the other hand, it has destroyed the careers of some of those willing to do anything that they are asked to do.

Evidence shows that ignoring ethical issues can destroy stakeholder trust and prompt government intervention. When firms engage in activities that deviate from accepted principles to further their own interests, continued marketing exchanges become difficult, if not impossible. The best way to deal with such problems is during the strategic planning process, not after major problems materialize. For example, Google was forced to pay $500 million to settle allegations that it had knowingly displayed illegal advertisements from Canadian pharmacies. The Justice Department alluded to emails involving Google employees that suggested they had helped pharmacies avoid controls Google had in place to prevent such misconduct. The Justice Department claimed that the prescription drugs being advertised could be unsafe for consumers, which led to the harsh penalty levied against Google.[8]

Discussing and addressing potential problems during the strategic planning process could save a company millions in the long term. As a result, more and more companies create extensive ethics and compliance programs to identify problems early on. For instance, Lockheed Martin, a technology aerospace manufacturer and global security company, has a comprehensive ethics program. These programs address the key ethical risks facing marketing. Every firm has unique risks based on the industry and the firm's unique marketing strategy. For example, in the direct selling industry, recruiting and compensating sales representatives requires transparent and truthful communication. Therefore, the self-regulatory Direct Selling Association has developed a code of ethics to deal with this as well as other risk areas.

Ethical and socially responsible behavior requires commitment. Some firms simply ignore these issues and focus instead on satisfying their economic and legal responsibilities, with an eye toward the overall bottom line of profits. Although the firm may do nothing wrong, it misses out on the long-term strategic benefits that can be derived from satisfying ethical and philanthropic responsibilities. Firms that choose to take these extra steps concern themselves with increasing their overall positive impact on society, their local communities, and the environment, with the bottom line of increased goodwill toward the firm, as well as increased profits. The focus on ethical and philanthropic dimensions has the potential to build trust and long-term customer loyalty. These should be the goals of every effective marketing program.

Philanthropic Responsibilities   At the top of the pyramid are philanthropic responsibilities. These responsibilities, which go beyond marketing ethics, are not required of a company, but they promote human welfare or goodwill above and beyond the economic, legal, and ethical dimensions of social responsibility. Many companies demonstrate philanthropic responsibility, which is evidenced by the more than $15 billion in annual corporate donations and contributions to environmental and social causes.[9] Even small companies participate in philanthropy through donations and volunteer support of local causes and national charities, such as the Red Cross and the United Way. For example, Charlotte Street Computers in Asheville, North Carolina has developed a refurbishing center that refurbishes computers and then donates them to those in need. The small business also sponsors several community events and fundraising for charities.[10]

More companies than ever are adopting a strategic approach to corporate philanthropy. Many firms link their products to a particular social cause on an ongoing or short-term basis, a practice known as *cause-related marketing*. General Mills, for example, uses its Box Tops for Education program to raise money for schools. Consumers can raise money for their children's schools by cutting Box Top coupons found on participating products. Schools can then redeem these coupons for cash. The program has generated approximately $400 million for schools since it was implemented in 1996.[11] Such cause-related programs tend to appeal to consumers because they provide an additional reason to "feel good" about a particular purchase. Marketers like these programs because they often increase sales and create feelings of respect and admiration for the companies involved. Indeed, research suggests that 85 percent of American consumers have a more positive opinion of an organization when it supports causes that they care about.[12]

On the other hand, some companies are beginning to extend the concept of corporate philanthropy beyond financial contributions by adopting a *strategic philanthropy* approach, the synergistic use of organizational core competencies and resources to address key stakeholders' interests and achieve both organizational and social benefits. Strategic philanthropy involves employees, organizational resources and expertise, and

Philanthropic activities are not only good for society, they can also be useful in promoting the corporation.

the ability to link those assets to the concerns of key stakeholders, including employees, customers, suppliers, and social needs. Strategic philanthropy involves both financial and nonfinancial contributions to stakeholders (employee time, goods and services, company technology and equipment, etc.), while also benefiting the company.[13] For instance, California-based apparel company Patagonia incorporates environmental concerns into its operations. Patagonia uses environmentally friendly materials such as organic cotton or recycled polyester. In addition, the company recycles garments that have reached the end of their life. Patagonia also believes it must be an active participant in preserving the environment. The company donates 1 percent of its sales toward preserving and restoring the environment.[14]

Philanthropic activities make very good marketing tools. Thinking of corporate philanthropy as a marketing tool may seem cynical, but it points out the reality that philanthropy can be very good for a firm. Coca-Cola, for example, has embarked on an initiative to research, test, and develop hygiene intervention and sustainable water solutions at schools in Kenya. As part of the initiative, teachers at the schools will learn how to treat the water supply with chlorine to help prevent illnesses. Coca-Cola's efforts indicate that it is willing to take these stakeholders' concerns seriously to improve the environment and consumer health.[15]

Sustainability

One of the more common ways marketers demonstrate social responsibility is through programs designed to protect and preserve the natural environment. Sustainability includes the assessment and improvement of business strategies, economic sectors, work practices, technologies, and lifestyles—all while maintaining the natural environment. Many companies make contributions to sustainability by adopting more eco-friendly business practices and/or supporting environmental initiatives. For instance, Walmart has taken steps to reduce waste and decrease greenhouse gas emissions in its supply chain. Walmart's example is convincing other large retailers to take similar actions.[16] Another green practice many companies adopt involves building new facilities that adhere to Leadership in Energy and Environmental Design (LEED) standards. These standards provide a framework for incorporating greener building materials and more efficient operations into construction.[17] Recreation Equipment, Inc. (REI) has built six facilities that are LEED certified.[18] Because buildings produce 40 percent of greenhouse gas emissions, green building construction can have a significant impact toward sustainability. Such efforts generate positive publicity and often increase sales for the companies involved.

Many products have been certified as "green" by environmental organizations such as Green Seal and carry a special logo identifying their organization as green marketers. Lumber products at Home Depot, for example, may carry a seal from the Forest Stewardship Council to indicate that they were harvested from sustainable forests using environmentally friendly methods.[19] Likewise, most Chiquita bananas are certified through the Rainforest Alliance's Better Banana Project as having been grown with more environmentally and labor-friendly practices.[20] In Europe, companies can voluntarily apply for the EU Ecolabel to indicate that their products are less harmful to the environment than competing products, based on scientifically determined criteria.

The emphasis on sustainability has led many firms to engage in green marketing, a strategic process involving stakeholder assessment to create meaningful long-term relationships with customers, while maintaining, supporting, and enhancing the natural environment. In contrast, some companies choose to engage in a deceptive marketing practice called greenwashing, which involves misleading a consumer into thinking that a good or service is more environmentally friendly than it actually is. This generally takes the form of misleading product labels, which can range from making environmental claims that are required by law and are therefore irrelevant (for example, saying that a product is CFC-free when CFCs have been banned by the government) to puffery (exaggerating environmental claims) to fraud.[21] Firms need to be careful when using words like green, sustainable, or environmentally friendly so as not to mislead consumers and face potential litigation. The federal government has taken a tougher stand on environmental issues, and as greenwashing becomes more prevalent, it is likely that legal action will increase. Since 2000, the FTC has taken legal action against three companies for greenwashing. Since one-third of consumers rely exclusively on labels to decide if a product is environmentally friendly, it is important that labels tell the truth.[22]

Some organizations have developed a certification system to help consumers make informed decisions when buying supposedly green products. For example, the Carbon Trust offers a certification that validates claims about reducing carbon output. However, certification organizations are not always trustworthy either. Some of them charge a fee and do not hold products to rigorous standards. As explained in *Beyond the Pages 8.2*, the best way for consumers to be informed about eco-friendly products is to do their research before going shopping.

Despite the problem of greenwashing, many firms take proactive steps to become more sustainable. General Motors is investigating more sustainable solutions for its vehicles partially to meet the 2025 mandate that vehicles must get 54.5 miles per gallon.[24] Other firms are choosing to experiment with alternative energy solutions as a form of social responsibility. IKEA is using geothermal energy—energy derived from the natural heat inside the Earth—to power some of its stores, while Walmart is experimenting with solar energy.[25] As support for sustainability continues to increase, companies are quickly recognizing that sustainability initiatives are a smart marketing move.

Marketing Ethics and Strategy

Marketing ethics includes the principles and standards that guide the behavior of individuals and groups in making marketing decisions. Marketing strategy must consider stakeholders—including managers, employees, customers, government regulators, suppliers, shareholders, the community, and special-interest groups—all of whom contribute to

Beyond the Pages 8.2

Finding the Real Green Products[23]

What makes a green product green? This question is actually quite complicated. The growing popularity of eco-friendly products is encouraging businesses to create and sell more green items. However, some businesses cut corners by touting their products as green when they really aren't—a form of misconduct known as greenwashing. Greenwashers make unjustifiable "green" claims about their products to appeal to the eco-friendly consumer. One study determined that as many as 95 percent of products marketed as green were guilty of at least one form of greenwashing. As a result, many consumers claim they don't know how to ensure that a company is really eco-friendly.

One common way that companies engage in greenwashing is by sustainably sourcing one product ingredient while the other ingredients remain unsustainable. This might be akin to a company claiming that its product is green since one of the ingredients is organic cotton, while simultaneously glossing over the fact that the product also consists of nonrecyclable products or chemicals. Unfortunately, the subjective nature of greenwashing makes it harder to detect, as consumers themselves differ on what is green and what is greenwashing. For instance, some consumers feel misled by Cascade Farm's logo of a small idyllic farm when they discover that the brand is actually owned by General Mills. Others are unconcerned as long as the brand's organic claims are true. Being green often requires tradeoffs as well—some of

which consumers might find to be unacceptable. Compact fluorescent light bulbs save energy, but they also contain mercury that could harm consumers if they break. The question of how far to go to create a green product can be controversial.

The issue of greenwashing has become so pervasive that it is prompting government intervention. The Federal Trade Commission (FTC) has released green guidelines to define what is acceptable in green advertising. The FTC has also begun cracking down on companies for making false claims. For example, it sent warning letters to 78 retailers including Walmart, Kohl's, and The Gap after they advertised that their rayon products were made from bamboo. However, guidelines do not have the same effect as laws, particularly as individual consumers may have their own views of what constitutes a "green" product. The best way consumers can avoid greenwashing is to investigate green claims for themselves. Such an investigation could include looking for third-party certification of a product's "greenness," paying attention to ingredient lists, and looking for information on trustworthy websites. At the same time, it is important for consumers to realize that all products have some effect on the environment. Rather than looking for a 100 percent green product, consumers could instead look for ways that companies have increased sustainability throughout its operations to decrease its negative environmental impact.

accepted standards and society's expectations. The most basic of these standards have been codified as laws and regulations to encourage companies to conform to society's expectations of business conduct. These laws were usually passed due to societal concerns about misconduct that was damaging to competition or to consumers.

The standards of conduct that determine the ethics of marketing activities require both organizations and individuals to accept responsibility for their actions and to comply with established value systems. Repeated ethical misconduct in a particular business or industry sometimes requires the government to intervene, a situation that can be expensive and inconvenient for businesses and consumers. Early in the twenty-first century, business ethics appeared to be improving after Enron, WorldCom, and the passage of the Sarbanes-Oxley Act in 2002. However, misconduct in the financial and banking sectors, as well as high-profile failures of companies like GM during the 2008–2009 financial crisis, created a dramatic erosion of consumer confidence and trust. Not surprisingly, this sentiment peaked during the height of the financial crisis. Marketing deceptions, such as lying or misrepresenting information, increased consumer distrust of some businesses and industries, such as the mortgage industry, and contributed to economic instability during the crisis. Misleading consumers, investors, and other stakeholders not only caused the ruin of established companies like Lehman Brothers and Countrywide Financial, but also led to the arrests of major company officials and the loss of billions of investor's dollars. Without a shared view of appropriate and acceptable business conduct, companies often fail to balance their desires for profits against the wishes and needs of society.

When companies deviate from the prevailing standards of industry and society, the result is customer dissatisfaction, lack of trust, and legal action. The reputation of the firm is one of the most important considerations for consumers. Marketers should be aware of stakeholders and the need to build trust. When marketing activities deviate from accepted standards, the exchange process can break down, resulting in customer dissatisfaction, lack of trust, and lawsuits. A recent study shows that only about 50 percent of U.S. consumers trust businesses today, which can significantly affect the relationship between consumers and business.[26] Trust is an important concern for marketers since it is the foundation for long-term relationships. Consumer lack of trust has increased in recent years due to the financial crisis and deep recession. The questionable conduct of high-profile financial institutions and banks has caused many consumers to critically examine the conduct of all companies. Trust must be built or restored to gain the confidence of customers. Exhibit 8.2 describes the trust Americans have for different institutions. Once trust is lost, it can take a lifetime to rebuild. The way to deal with ethical issues is proactively during the strategic planning process, not after major problems materialize.

Given that so much of a company's success depends on the public's perceptions of the firm, a firm's reputation is one of its greatest internal resources that directly affect the success of the marketing strategy. The value of a positive reputation is difficult to quantify, but it is very important and once lost can be difficult to regain. Consider that 70 percent of the market value of McDonald's is based on intangible assets such as brand

EXHIBIT 8.2   American Trust in Different Institutions

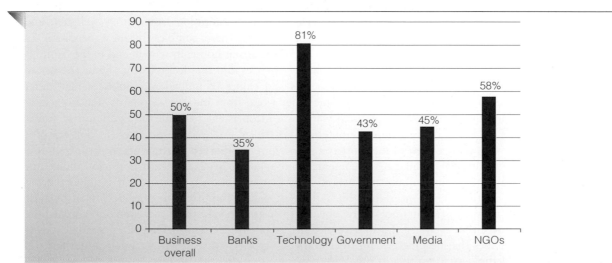

Source: Edelman, *2012 Edelman Trust Barometer Global Results* (http://trust.edelman.com/trust-download/global-results), accessed May 28, 2012.

value and goodwill.[27] A single negative incident can influence perceptions of a firm's image and reputation for years afterward. Corporate reputation, image, and branding are more important than ever and are among the most critical aspects of sustaining relationships with key stakeholders. Although an organization does not control its reputation in a direct sense, its actions, choices, behaviors, and consequences do influence its reputation. For example, BP's reputation based on sustainability and its Beyond Petroleum image was destroyed by the Gulf oil spill disaster.

The Challenges of Being Ethical and Socially Responsible

Although most consider the values of honesty, respect, and trust to be self-evident and universally accepted, business decisions involve complex and detailed discussions in which correctness may not be so apparent. Both employees and managers need experience within their specific industry to understand how to operate in gray areas or to handle close calls in evolving areas, such as Internet privacy. For example, how much personal information should be stored on a firm's website without customers' permission? In Europe, the European Union Directive on Data Protection prohibits selling or renting mailing lists—consumers' data cannot be used without their permission.[28] In the United States, firms have more freedom to decide how to collect and use customers' personal data, but advancing technology raises new questions every day. As businesses continue to push the limits of privacy, the government has begun to crack down on what it sees as privacy infringement. Facebook agreed to undergo independent privacy audits for the next 20 years after the Federal Trade Commission decided that Facebook's 2009 changes to its privacy policies were done without warning users. The FTC felt such changes violated users' rights to know what information was being made public.[29] Issues related to personal privacy, unsolicited e-mail, and misappropriation of copyrighted intellectual property cause ethical problems. Protecting trademarks and brand names becomes more difficult as digital communication and social media expands.

Individuals who have limited business experience often find themselves required to make sudden decisions about product quality, advertising, pricing, bribery, hiring practices, privacy, and pollution control. For example, how do advertisers know when they make misleading statements as opposed to simple puffery or exaggeration? Bayer claims to be "the world's best aspirin"; Hush Puppies are "the earth's most comfortable shoes"; and Firestone (before its famous recall of 6.5 million tires) promised "quality you can trust."[30] The personal values learned through socialization from family, religion, and school may not provide specific guidelines for these complex business decisions. In other words, a person's experiences and decisions at home, in school, and in the community may be quite different from the experiences and the decisions that he or she has to make at work. Moreover, the interests and values of individual employees may differ from those of the company in which they work, from industry standards, and from society in general. When personal values are inconsistent with the configuration of values held by the work group, the potential for ethical misconduct increases. Exhibit 8.3 provides an overview of the most common types of observed misconduct in organizations.

Although Exhibit 8.3 documents many types of issues that exist in organizations, due to the almost infinite number of ways that misconduct can occur, it is impossible to identify every conceivable ethical issue. It is also important to note that most of these potential issues are not clearly obvious to customers. However, any type of manipulation, deceit, or even just the absence of transparency in decision making can potentially create issues that become evident to customers, supply chain partners, or other important stakeholders. With that in mind, we now turn our attention to specific ethical issues in the marketing program.

EXHIBIT 8.3   Types of Misconduct Observed in Organizations

	2009 (%)	2011 (%)
Misuse of company time	N/A	33
Abusive behavior	22	21
Lying to employees	19	20
Company resource abuse	23	20
Violating company Internet use policies	N/A	16
Discrimination	14	15
Conflicts of interest	16	15
Inappropriate social networking	N/A	14
Health or safety violations	11	13
Lying to outside stakeholders	12	12
Stealing	9	12
Falsifying time reports or hours worked	N/A	12
Employee benefits violations	11	12
Sexual harassment	7	11
Employee privacy breach	10	11

Source: From "2007 National Business Ethics Survey: An Inside View of Private Sector Ethics". Copyright © 2007 Ethics Resource Center. Used with permission of the Ethics Resource Center, 2345 Crystal Drive, Suite 201, Arlington, VA 22202, www.ethics.org.

Ethical Issues in the Marketing Program

An *ethical issue* is an identifiable problem, situation, or opportunity that requires an individual or organization to choose from among several actions that must be evaluated as right or wrong, ethical or unethical. Any time an activity causes marketing managers or customers to feel manipulated or cheated, an ethical issue exists, regardless of the legality of that activity. It is therefore imperative that firms become familiar with many of the ethical issues that can potentially occur in the marketing program so that these issues can be identified and resolved when they occur. Some examples of potential ethical issues in the marketing program appear in Exhibit 8.4. These and other issues can develop into legal problems if they are not addressed in the strategic planning process.

While customers and other stakeholders may think a firm is engaged in unethical conduct, the final decision is usually determined by legal action or a self-regulatory body such as the Better Business Bureau (BBB). The National Advertising Division (NAD), a division of the Better Business Bureau, reviews complaints about unfair advertising and recommends whether the advertising in question should be discontinued. For instance, NAD determined that Verizon's claim that consumers rated its FiOS Internet service number one was misleading. NAD agreed with Comcast that the claims implied that Verizon's competitors were ranked lower than Verizon, which was not the case. Verizon agreed to discontinue these claims.[31]

Regardless of the reasons behind specific ethical issues, marketers must be able to identify those issues and decide how to resolve them. Doing so requires familiarity with the many kinds of ethical issues that may arise in marketing. Research suggests that the greater the consequences associated with an issue, the more likely it will be recognized as an ethics issue and the more important it will be in making an ethical decision.[32] Let's look at several potential ethical issues in more detail.

EXHIBIT 8.4   **Potential Ethical Issues in the Marketing Program**

Overall

Misrepresenting the firm's capabilities

Manipulation or misuse of data or information

Exploitation of children or disadvantaged groups

Invasion of privacy

Anticompetitive activities

Abusive behavior

Misuse of firm resources

Product Issues

Misrepresentation of goods or services

Failure to disclose product defects

Counterfeit or gray market products

Misleading warranties

Reducing package contents without reducing package size

Pricing Issues

Price deception

Reference pricing claims

Price discrimination

Predatory pricing

Fraudulent refund policies

Distribution (Supply Chain) Issues

Opportunistic behavior among members of the supply chain

Exclusive distribution arrangements

Slotting fees

Tying contracts

Failure to honor product and promotional support

Promotion Issues

False or misleading advertising or selling

Bait-and-switch advertising

High-pressure sales tactics

Entertainment and gift giving

Stereotypical portrayals of women, minorities, or senior citizens

Failure to honor sales promotion promises

© Cengage Learning 2013

Product-Related Ethical Issues

Product-related ethical issues generally arise when the firm fails to disclose risks associated with a product or information regarding the function, value, or use of a product. These issues are common in many industries, including automobiles, toys, pharmaceuticals, and other industries where safety or design issues come into play. For instance, Johnson & Johnson, a company long known for its high ethical standards, came under fire recently for not adequately disclosing the dangers associated with acetaminophen, the key ingredient in Tylenol. After several consumers overdosed on the drug, Johnson & Johnson was forced to pay damages after a judge determined that the company knew about the product's risks, but did not sufficiently warn consumers about them.[33]

Ethical issues can arise in product design as pressures build to substitute inferior materials or product components to reduce costs. For example, many laptop makers created and sold "Ultrabooks" in an attempt to emulate the astounding success of the MacBook Air. These ultra-light, Windows-based machines use the same type of brushed-metal casing found in the Air. However, in order to drive prices down, Ultrabook makers have turned to less expensive plastic casings, many of which look like brushed metal.[34] If Ultrabook makers do not clearly explain that the change in price is due to a significant change in product design, the switch to less expensive plastic could become an ethical issue. Similarly, ethical issues can arise when the firm fails to inform customers about changes in quality or quantity of product sold. For example, if a cereal maker reduced the amount of cereal in the package without reducing the package size or the price, the company would have a serious ethical issue on its hands.

Another common product-related ethical issue involves counterfeit products. Counterfeit products abound today, particularly in the areas of clothing, audio and video products, and computer software. Any product that can be easily copied is vulnerable to counterfeit activities. Some people argue that only manufacturers become injured when consumers purchase counterfeit products. This is clearly mistaken reasoning. For example, the loss of tax revenues has a huge impact on governments, as they can't collect both direct and indirect taxes on the sale of counterfeit products. Likewise, counterfeits leech profits necessary for ongoing product development away from the firm, as well as thousands of jobs at legitimate companies. Customers also feel the impact of counterfeit products, as their quality almost never lives up to the quality of the original. For example, faced with increasing risks associated with counterfeit drugs, the Food and Drug Administration (FDA) has strongly endorsed the use of RFID to combat the growing problem and to protect American consumers. The FDA is monitoring the use of RFID, but has yet to declare that RFID is acceptable for identifying drugs as they move through the U.S. pharmaceutical supply chain.[35]

Pricing-Related Ethical Issues

Pricing is one of the most heavily watched and regulated of all marketing activities. Given that a difference in price can create such a significant competitive advantage, any effort to artificially give one company an edge over another is subject to legal or regulatory intervention. The emotional and subjective nature of price creates many situations where misunderstandings between the seller and buyer cause ethical problems. Firms have the right to price their products to earn a reasonable profit, but ethical issues may crop up when a company seeks to earn high profits at the expense of its customers. Some pharmaceutical companies, for example, have been accused of price gouging, or pricing products at exorbitant levels, and taking advantage of customers who must purchase the medicine to survive or to maintain their quality of life. Likewise, various forms of bait and switch pricing attempt to gain consumer interest with a low-priced product, and then switch the buyer to a more expensive product or add-on service. While there is an endless potential for ethical violations in pricing strategy, four key issues garner the most attention: price discrimination, price fixing, predatory pricing, and superficial discounting.

Price discrimination occurs when firms charge different prices to different customers. This is fairly common in consumer markets, such as when cable and satellite companies offer lower prices to new customers, or when fast-food restaurants offer lower-priced meals for children. Price discrimination is very common in business markets where it typically occurs among different intermediaries in the supply chain. In general, price discrimination is illegal, unless the price differential has a basis in actual cost differences in selling products to one customer relative to another (such as volume discounts and competitive price matching). The overriding question in cases of price discrimination is whether the price differential injures competition. The Robinson-Patman Act and the Clayton Act both regulate discriminatory pricing. The intent of these regulations is to provide a level playing field for all competitors.

Price fixing occurs when rival firms collaborate to set prices. Although such arrangements are illegal under the Sherman Act, price fixing is exceedingly difficult to prove. Usually, one firm in an industry will be a price leader and others will be the price followers. The Justice Department has determined that, while following a competitor's lead in an upward or downward trend is acceptable, there can be no signaling of prices to competitors in this process. Sizable fines and prison terms for those convicted of price fixing are the norm. Consumer-goods manufacturers Henkel, Procter & Gamble, and Colgate Palmolive were fined $484 million by French authorities for allegedly engaging in price fixing on soap products.[36]

Predatory pricing occurs when a firm charges very low prices for a product with the intent of driving competition out of business or out of a specific market. Prices then return to normal once the competitors have been eliminated. Predatory pricing is illegal; however, like price fixing, it is extremely difficult to prove in court. The challenge in predatory pricing cases is to prove that the predatory firm had the willful intent to ruin the competition. The court must also be convinced that the low price charged by the predator is below their average variable cost. The variable cost definition of predatory pricing is a major reason why very few lawsuits for predatory pricing are successful. The reality is that large firms with lean, efficient cost structures dominate today's competitive landscape. These firms have lower variable costs that allow them to legitimately charge lower prices than the competition in many cases. This is the reason that large retailers such as Walmart, Home Depot, Lowe's, and Barnes and Noble have slowly and methodically put smaller retailers out of business. These large firms are not necessarily guilty of predatory pricing—they are only guilty of being more efficient and competitive than other firms.

Superficial discounting occurs when a firm advertises a sale price as a reduction below the normal price when it is not the case. Typically, the firm does not sell the product at the regular price in any meaningful quantities, or the sale price period is excessively long. This pricing tactic is clearly an ethical issue because most customers are not aware that they are being intentionally misled. Most of the legal activity regarding superficial discounting has taken place at the state attorney general level. To avoid legal action, a firm should offer a product at the original price, discount the price in a specified dollar amount for a specified period, and then revert to the original price at the end of that period. If the product is a discontinued item, that fact should be noted in the advertisement.

Supply Chain-Related Ethical Issues

Managing ethical issues in distribution and supply chain strategy is one of the greatest difficulties in marketing today. The reasons deal with the complexity of most supply chains and the fact that supply chains today are global. For instance, the chocolate industry has been criticized for sourcing from suppliers that use child labor on cocoa plantations. Hershey pledged that it would improve its supply chain practices and invest

$10 million in its West African suppliers after the International Labor Rights Forum threatened to publicize the child labor used at some of the company's cocoa suppliers.[37] Supply chain issues can occur in any industry. Even Apple, the top brand in terms of both value and reputation, has experienced instances of forced overtime, underage workers, explosions, and improperly disposed waste in its supplier's factories. Although Apple has a Supplier Code of Conduct, problems at its supplier factories have continued.[38]

The issues that Hershey and Apple have faced highlight the numerous risks that occur in global supply chains. Although companies often create a Supplier Code of Conduct, they are required to conduct regular audits to ensure that factories are following compliance standards—which in turn can incur significant costs to companies in both time and finances. Countries with lax labor laws, such as China and Russia, require even more diligent monitoring. Often suppliers hire sub-contractors to do some of the work, which increases a company's network of suppliers and the costs of trying to monitor all of them. Finally, company compliance requirements may conflict with the mission of the procurement office. Because it is the procurement division's job to procure resources at the lowest price possible, the division may very well opt to source from less expensive suppliers with questionable ethical practices rather than from more expensive ethical suppliers. Nike faced this problem during the 1990s when it was highly criticized for worker abuses in its supplier factories.[39]

Managing supply chain ethics is important because many stakeholders hold the firm responsible for all ethical conduct related to product availability. This requires the company to exercise oversight over all of the suppliers used in producing a product. Developing good supply chain ethics is important because it ensures the integrity of the product and the firm's operations in serving customers. For instance, leading healthcare supply company Novation has been recognized for its strong corporate governance and reporting mechanisms in its supply chain. To encourage its suppliers to report misconduct, the company has instituted a vendor grievance and feedback system. This system allows vendors to report potential problems before they reach the next level of the supply chain, which reduces the damage such problems will cause if the products continue down the supply chain unchecked.[40]

Fortunately, organizations have developed solutions to promote ethical sourcing practices. First, it is essential for all companies who work with global suppliers to adopt a Global Supplier Code of Conduct and ensure that it is effectively communicated to its suppliers. Additionally, companies should encourage compliance and procurement employees to work together to find ethical suppliers at reasonable costs. Marketers must also work to make certain that their company's supply chains are diverse. This can be difficult because sometimes the best product manufacturers are located in a single country. Although it is expensive to diversify a company's supply chain, disasters can incapacitate a firm.[41] Companies such as Jabil Circuit and Goodyear Tire & Rubber found their supply chains at risk due to the Japanese tsunami and severe flooding in Thailand during 2011.[42] Finally, and perhaps most importantly, companies must perform regular audits on their suppliers and, if necessary, discipline those found to be in violation of company standards.

Promotion-Related Ethical Issues

Marketing practices that are false or misleading can destroy customers' trust in an organization. The Federal Trade Commission monitors businesses for deceptive practices and takes disciplinary action when needed. It fined Reebok $25 million for making unsubstantiated claims that its toning sneakers strengthen muscles and lead to a toned body.[43] The FTC also joined with the FDA in sending warning letters to companies marketing the weight-loss properties of human chorionic gonadotropin (HCG) drugs.

Although the HCG hormone has certain medicinal properties, weight-loss has not been proven as one of them. The FTC sees such claims as deceptive marketing.[44] No matter how vigilant, it is difficult for the FTC to catch all forms of deceptive marketing, particularly in the area of promotion.

Ethical issues also arise when firms use ambiguous statements, in which claims are so weak that the viewer, reader, or listener must infer the advertiser's intended message. Because it is inherently vague, using ambiguous wording allows the firm to deny any intent to deceive. The verb "help" is a good example (as in expressions such as "helps prevent," "helps fight," or "helps make you feel"). Consumers may view such advertisements as unethical because they fail to communicate all the information needed to make a good purchasing decision or because they deceive the consumer outright. In another example, the FTC and other agencies now monitor more closely the promotions for work-at-home business ventures. Consumers lose millions of dollars each year responding to ads for phony business opportunities such as those promising $50,000 a year for doing medical billing from a home computer.

Personal selling provides many opportunities for ethical misconduct. *Bribery* occurs when an incentive (usually money or expensive gifts) is offered in exchange for an illicit advantage. Even a bribe that is offered to benefit the organization is usually considered unethical. Because it jeopardizes trust and fairness, it hurts the organization in the long run. As a result, laws have been passed to prevent bribery. The U.S. Foreign Corrupt Practices Act (FCPA) prohibits American companies from making illicit payments to foreign officials in order to obtain or keep business. Under the U.K. Bribery Act, companies can be found guilty of bribery even if the bribery did not take place within the U.K., and company officials without explicit knowledge about the misconduct can still be held accountable. The law applies to any business with operations in the U.K.[45] The U.K. Bribery Act has convinced many multinational organizations to update their ethical codes of conduct to avoid ambiguity in this area.

Fraudulent activity has dramatically increased in the area of direct marketing, in which companies use the telephone and non-personal media to communicate information to customers, who then purchase products via mail, telephone, or the Internet. Each year consumers report billions of dollars in losses resulting from fraud, many of them from direct-marketing scams. About 19 percent are associated with identity theft and 11 percent are associated with third-party and creditor debt collection. Other common types of marketing fraud include those involving prizes, sweepstakes, and lotteries; Internet auctions; credit cards; and shop-at-home and catalog sales.[46]

Managing and Controlling Ethical Issues

Given the conflicting priorities among concerned stakeholders and the nature of most marketing decisions, even the best-designed marketing programs will eventually encounter ethical issues. Since ethical issues can never be completely eliminated, most enlightened firms instead take steps to manage and control ethical issues before they arise. In this section, we look at a number of ways that firms can go about this process.

Regulating Marketing Ethics

Many firms attempt to regulate themselves in an effort to demonstrate ethical responsibility and prevent regulation by federal or state governments. In addition to complying with all relevant laws and regulations, many firms choose to join trade associations that have self-regulatory programs. Although such programs are not a direct outgrowth of laws, many became established to stop or delay the development of laws and regulations that would restrict the associations' business practices. Some trade associations establish

© Susan Van Etten

The Better Business Bureau is the best known self-regulatory association in the U.S. and Canada.

codes of conduct by which their members must abide or risk rebuke or expulsion from the association.

Perhaps the best-known self-regulatory association is the Better Business Bureau. The BBB's 116 local bureaus across the United States and Canada oversee three million businesses and charities, and help resolve problems for millions of consumers each year.[47] Each bureau works to champion good business practices within a community although it usually does not have strong tools for enforcing its rules of business conduct. When a firm violates what the BBB believes to be good business practices, the bureau warns consumers through local newspapers or broadcast media. If the offending organization is a member of the BBB, it may be expelled from the local bureau. The BBB also has a website (www.bbb.org) to help consumers identify businesses that operate in an ethical manner. BBB members who use the site agree to binding arbitration with regard to online privacy issues.

Self-regulatory programs like the BBB have a number of advantages over government regulation. Establishment and implementation of such programs are usually less costly, and their guidelines or codes of conduct are generally more practical and realistic. Furthermore, effective self-regulatory programs reduce the need to expand government bureaucracy. However, self-regulation also has several limitations. Non-member firms are under no obligation to abide by a trade association's industry guidelines or codes. Moreover, most associations lack the tools or authority to enforce their guidelines. Finally, these guidelines are often less strict than the regulations established by government agencies. Still, in many cases, government oversight is essential to ensure the public's trust. *Beyond the Pages 8.3*, for example, discusses how the U.S. government is trying to maintain trust in the banking systems in light of the most recent ethical and legal lapses in the financial sector.

Codes of Conduct

To meet the public's escalating demands for ethical marketing, firms need to develop plans and structures for addressing ethical considerations. Although there are no universal standards that can be applied to organizational ethics programs, most companies develop codes, values, or policies to guide business behavior. It would be very naïve to think that simply having a code of ethics would solve any ethical dilemmas a firm might face. In fact, the majority of firms that experience ethical or legal problems usually have stated ethics codes and programs. Often, the problem is that top management, as

The Consumer Financial Protection Bureau Aims to Build Trust in the Banking System[48]

Financial products are often complex instruments that can be difficult to understand, not only for consumers but for businesses as well. This inability to understand the risks of financial products and lending practices contributed to the 2008–2009 financial meltdown, the massive government bailouts of companies to save them from bankruptcy, and the subsequent recession. To try to prevent similar problems in the future, the United States government has formed the Consumer Financial Protection Bureau (CFPB).

The CFPB became a reality as a component of the Dodd-Frank Act signed into law in July 2010. Established by Harvard Law Professor Elizabeth Warren, the bureau is designed to mimic the independent Consumer Product Safety Commission, which aims to keep unsafe consumer products out of the hands of individuals. Instead of consumer products, however, the CFPB's authority involves financial products and services. The CFPB has rule making authority and supervisory power over the credit market. Its goal is to make financial products and services easy to understand in terms of costs, risks, and product/service comparisons. It also aims to curtail unfair lending and credit card practices, to check the safety of financial products before they are launched into the market, and to require changes to those financial products deemed to be too risky. According to War-ren, the CFPB will work proactively to supervise lenders by regularly checking their books and working together with both federal and state attorney generals and the American people. When necessary, the CFPB will step in to enforce new rules on those not complying.

Although the CFPB sounds like a good idea, critics point out potential problems. Banks are worried that the CFPB might increase costs and inhibit their decision-making authority to serve the market effectively. Critics believe the CFPB will create burdensome regulations, such as capping the interest rates that financial institutions can apply. This could harm borrowers because riskier applicants could be denied loans if rates are capped. Some have criticized Elizabeth Warren for what they perceive as her harsh views toward banks.

The standoff became so great that President Obama placed former attorney general Richard Cordray as the new head of the CFPB. However, the move has done little to appease critics. Some have proposed appointing a board of directors over the agency rather than a single person to keep any one person from gaining too much power. Until the conflict is settled and a director is approved, the powers of the CFPB to enact widespread change in the financial sector might be limited.

---

well as the overall corporate culture, has not integrated these codes, values, and standards into daily operations.

Without ethics training and uniform standards and policies regarding conduct, it is hard for employees to determine what conduct is acceptable within the company. In the absence of such programs and standards, employees will generally make decisions based on their observations of how coworkers and superiors behave.[49] To improve ethics, many organizations have developed codes of conduct (also called *codes of ethics*) that consist of formalized rules and standards that describe what the company expects of its employees. Most large corporations have formal codes of conduct, but codes are not effective unless they are properly implemented. In addition, codes must be periodically revised to identify and eliminate weaknesses in the company's ethical standards and policies.

Most codes address specific ethical risk areas in marketing. For instance, IBM's code of conduct has a bribery policy that prohibits accepting gifts of nominal value if the gift in any way influences IBM's business relationship with the giver. However, employees are allowed to accept promotional premiums or gifts of nominal value if based upon bonus programs (such as with hotels and airlines) or if the gift is routinely offered to all other parties with similar relationships to the gift giver.[50] Codes like IBM's promote ethical

---

EXHIBIT 8.5   **Key Considerations in Developing and Implementing a Code of Ethical Conduct**

---

1. Examine high-risk areas and issues.
2. State values and conduct necessary to comply with laws and regulations. Values are an important buffer in preventing serious misconduct.
3. Identify values that specifically address current ethical issues.
4. Consider values that link the organization to a stakeholder orientation. Attempt to find overlaps among organizational and stakeholder values.
5. Make the code of conduct understandable by providing examples that reflect values.
6. Communicate the code frequently and in language that employees can understand.
7. Revise the code every year with input from a wide variety of internal and external stakeholders.

behavior by reducing opportunities for unethical behavior; however, codes of conduct do not have to be so detailed that they take every situation into account. Instead, the code should provide guidelines that enable employees to achieve organizational objectives in an ethical manner. The American Marketing Association Code of Ethics, for example, does not cover every possible ethical issue, but it provides a useful overview of what marketers believe are sound principles for guiding marketing activities.[51] This code serves as a helpful model for structuring an organization's code of conduct. Exhibit 8.5 lists the key considerations in developing and implementing a code of ethical conduct.

Research has found that corporate codes of ethics often have five to seven core values or principles in addition to more detailed descriptions and examples of appropriate conduct. Six core values are considered to be highly desirable in any code of ethical conduct: (1) trustworthiness, (2) respect, (3) responsibility, (4) fairness, (5) caring, and (6) citizenship.[52] These values will not be effective without distribution, training, and the support of top management in making them a part of the corporate culture and the ethical climate. Employees need specific examples of how these values can be implemented.

Codes of conduct will not resolve every ethical issue encountered in daily operations, but they help employees and managers deal with ethical dilemmas by prescribing or limiting specific activities. Many firms have a code of ethics, but sometimes they do not communicate their code effectively. A code placed on a website or in a training manual is useless if the company doesn't reinforce it on a daily basis. By communicating both the expectations of proper behavior to employees, as well as punishments they face if they violate the rules, codes of conduct curtail opportunities for unethical behavior and thereby improve ethical decision-making.

Ethical Leadership

There is increasing support that ethical cultures emerge from strong leadership. Many agree that the character and success of the most admired companies emanates from their leaders. The reason is simple: Employees look to the leader as a model of acceptable behavior. As a result, if a firm is to maintain ethical behavior, top management must model its policies and standards. In fact, maintaining an ethical culture is near impossible if top management does not support ethical behavior. For example, in an effort to keep earnings high and boost stock prices, many firms have engaged in falsifying revenue reports, sometimes involving the marketing area to overstate sales in a specific quarter. Channel stuffing involves shipping surplus inventory to wholesalers and retailers at an excessive rate, typically before the end of a quarter. The practice may conceal declining demand for a product or inflate financial statement earnings, which misleads investors.[53] Top executives in these firms may encourage the behavior because they hold stock options and can receive bonus packages tied to the company's performance. Thus, higher reported revenues mean larger executive payoffs. Marketing is often seen as the most flexible area to influence sales and earnings.

In the realm of marketing ethics, great leaders (1) create a common goal or vision for the company; (2) obtain buy-in, or support, from significant partners; (3) motivate others to be ethical; (4) use the resources that are available to them; and (5) enjoy their jobs and approach them with an almost contagious tenacity, passion, and commitment.[54] Along with strong ethical leadership, a strong corporate culture in support of ethical behavior can also play a key role in guiding employee behavior. Ninety-four percent of respondents to a survey conducted by business consulting firm LRN said it was very important for them to work for an ethical company, with 82 percent saying they would prefer to be paid less if it meant working in an ethical corporate environment.[55] Additionally, another survey revealed that the most common reason employees give for leaving a company is loss of trust, followed by lack of transparency.[56] Organizational culture, coworkers and supervisors, and the opportunity to engage in unethical behavior influence ethical decision-making. Ethics training can affect all three types of influence. Full awareness of the philosophy of management, rules, and procedures can strengthen both the organizational culture and the ethical stance of peers and supervisors. Such awareness also arms employees against opportunities for unethical behavior and lessens the likelihood of misconduct. If adequately and thoughtfully designed, ethics training can ensure that everyone in the firm (1) recognizes situations that might involve ethical decision-making, (2) understands the values and culture of the firm, and (3) can evaluate the impact of ethical decisions on the firm in the light of its value structure.[57]

Relationship to Marketing and Financial Performance

One of the most powerful arguments for including ethics and social responsibility in the strategic planning process is the evidence of a link between ethics, social responsibility, and financial performance.[58] An ethical climate calls for organizational members to incorporate the interests of all stakeholders, including customers, in their decisions and actions. Hence, employees working in an ethical climate will make an extra effort to better understand the demands and concerns of customers. One study found that ethical climate is associated with employee commitment to quality and intra-firm trust.[59] Employee commitment to the firm, customer loyalty, and profitability have also been linked to increased social responsibility. These findings emphasize the role of an ethical climate in building a strong competitive position. For example, Burgerville, a regional fast food chain from Washington State, realized significant cost savings, decreased employee turnover, and higher sales after it began to cover 90 percent of healthcare costs for all employees who work over 20 hours per week. Burgerville has found that, while initial costs can be high, being ethical and taking care of its workers does pay off in the end.[60]

As employees perceive an improvement in the ethical climate of their firm, their commitment to the achievement of high-quality standards also increases. They become more willing to personally support the quality initiatives of the firm. These employees often discuss quality-related issues with others both inside and outside of the firm, and gain a sense of personal accomplishment from providing quality goods and services. These employees exhibit effort beyond both expectations and requirements in order to supply quality products in their particular job or area of responsibility. Conversely, employees who work in less ethical climates have less commitment to providing such quality. These employees tend to work only for the pay, take longer breaks, and are anxious to leave work every day.

Stakeholder Orientation

A natural progress from a market orientation is to view all stakeholders as important. The degree to which a firm understands and addresses stakeholder demands can be referred to as a stakeholder orientation. This orientation contains three sets of activities: (1) the organization-wide generation of data about stakeholder groups and assessment of the firm's effects on these groups, (2) the distribution of this information throughout the firm, and (3) the organization's responsiveness as a whole to this intelligence.[61] This is very similar to the step involved in a market orientation, but the firm becomes more concerned about all stakeholders, including employees, suppliers, shareholders, regulators, and the community.

Generating data about stakeholders begins with identifying the stakeholders who are relevant to the firm. Relevant stakeholder communities should be analyzed on the basis of the power that each enjoys as well as by the ties between them. Next, the firm should characterize the concerns about the business's conduct that each relevant stakeholder group shares. This information can be derived from formal research, including surveys, focus groups, Internet searches, or press reviews. The responsiveness of the organization to stakeholder intelligence consists of the initiatives that the firm adopts to ensure that it abides by or exceeds stakeholder expectations and has a positive impact on stakeholder issues. Such activities are likely to be specific to a particular stakeholder group (for example, family-friendly work schedules) or to a particular stakeholder issue (for example, pollution-reduction programs). These processes typically involve the participation of the concerned stakeholder groups. Kraft, for example, includes special-interest groups and university representatives in its programs to become sensitized to present and future ethical issues.

A stakeholder orientation can be viewed as a continuum in that firms are likely to adopt the concept to varying degrees. To gauge a given firm's stakeholder orientation, it is necessary to evaluate the extent to which the firm adopts behaviors that typify both the generation and dissemination of stakeholder intelligence and responsiveness to it. A given organization may generate and disseminate more intelligence about certain stakeholder communities than about others and, as a result, may respond to that intelligence differently.

Marketing Financial Performance

A climate of ethics and social responsibility also creates a large measure of trust among a firm's stakeholders and enhances the reputation of the firm in a positive direction. The most important contributing factor to gaining trust is the perception that the firm and its employees will not sacrifice their standards of integrity.[62] In an ethical work climate, employees can reasonably expect to be treated with respect and consideration by their coworkers and superiors. Furthermore, trusting relationships with key external stakeholders can contribute to greater efficiencies and productivity in the supply chain, as well as a stronger sense of loyalty among the firm's customers. Customers want to develop relationships with firms that provide quality products and engage in socially responsible conduct.[63]

Research indicates a strong association between social responsibility and customer loyalty in that customers are likely to keep buying from firms perceived as doing the right thing. Research by the brand and marketing agency BBMG revealed that about three out of four Americans prefer to buy goods and services from firms that are socially responsible and good corporate citizens.[64] Further, a direct association exists between corporate social responsibility and customer satisfaction, profits, and market value.[65] In a survey of consumers, 80 percent indicated that when quality and price are similar among competitors, they would be more likely to buy from the company associated with a particular cause. Young adults aged 18 to 25 are especially likely to take a company's citizenship efforts into account when making not only purchasing but also employment and investment decisions.[66] One explanation for these observations may be that good-citizen firms are responsive to customers' concerns and have a sense of dedication to treating them fairly. By gauging customer satisfaction, continuously improving the quality and safety of products, and by making customer information easily accessible and understandable, ethical and socially responsible firms are more likely to serve customers' needs satisfactorily.

Recognition is growing that the long-term value of conducting business in an ethical and socially responsible manner far outweighs short-term costs.[67] To demonstrate the financial benefits of ethical companies, the Ethisphere Institute compared the stock prices of the World's Most Ethical (WME) companies with companies listed on Standard & Poor's (S&P) 500 index. As Exhibit 8.6 reveals, the stock returns of WME companies surpasses those of the S&P 500.

EXHIBIT 8.6   *Ethisphere*'s 2011 World's Most Ethical Companies versus S&P 500

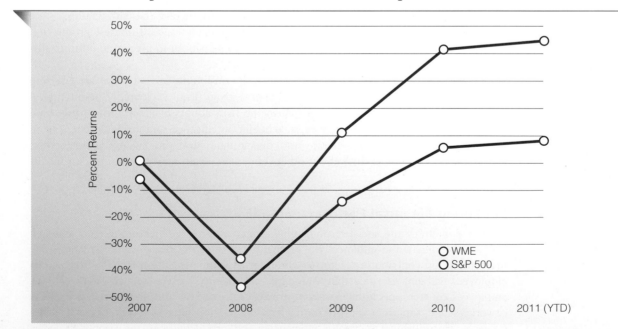

Source: "2011 World's Most Ethical Companies," *Ethisphere*, (http://ethisphere.com/past-wme-honorees/wme2011), accessed May 29, 2012.

Incorporating Ethics and Social Responsibility into Strategic Planning

Companies that fail to incorporate ethics and social responsibility into their organizational culture may pay the price with poor marketing performance and the potential costs of legal violations, civil litigation, and damaging publicity when questionable activities are made public. Because marketing ethics and social responsibility are not always viewed as organizational performance issues, many managers do not believe they need to consider them in the strategic planning process. Individuals also have different ideas as to what is ethical or unethical, leading them to confuse the need for workplace ethics and the right to maintain their own personal values and ethics. Although the concepts are undoubtedly controversial, it is possible—and desirable—to incorporate ethics and social responsibility into the planning process.

Many firms integrate ethics and social responsibility into their strategic planning through ethics compliance programs or integrity initiatives that make legal compliance, ethics, and social responsibility an organization-wide effort. Such programs establish, communicate, and monitor a firm's ethical values and legal requirements through codes of conduct, ethics offices, training programs, and audits. One of the best examples of this process in action occurs at Texas Instruments (TI). As a large multinational firm, TI manufactures computers, calculators, and other high-technology products. Its code of ethics resembles that of many other organizations. The code addresses issues related to policies and procedures; government laws and regulations; relationships with customers, suppliers, and competitors; the acceptance of gifts, travel, and entertainment; political contributions; expense reporting; business payments; conflicts of interest; investment in TI stock; handling of proprietary information and trade secrets; use of TI employees and assets to perform personal work; relationships with government officials and agencies; and the enforcement of the code. TI's code emphasizes that ethical behavior is critical to maintaining long-term success and that each individual is responsible for upholding the integrity of the company. TI's values and ethics statement puts it this way:[68]

> Our reputation at TI depends upon all of the decisions we make and all the actions we take each day. Our values define how we will evaluate our decisions and actions ... and how we will conduct our business. We are working in a difficult and demanding, ever-changing business environment. Together we are building a work environment on the foundation of Integrity, Innovation and Commitment. Together we are moving our company into a new century...one good decision at a time. Our high standards have rewarded us with an enviable reputation in today's marketplace...a reputation of integrity, honesty and trustworthiness. That strong ethical reputation is a vital asset... and each of us shares a personal responsibility to protect, to preserve and to enhance it. Our reputation is a strong but silent partner in all business relationships.

> Integrity is the foundation on which TI is built. There is no other characteristic more essential to a TIer's makeup. It has to be present at all levels. Integrity is expected of managers and individuals when they make commitments. They are expected to stand by their commitments to the best of their ability.

For maximum effectiveness, the marketing plan should include distinct elements of ethics and social responsibility. Marketing strategy and implementation plans should be developed that reflect an understanding of (1) the risks associated with ethical and legal misconduct, (2) the ethical and social consequences of strategic choices, and (3) the values of organizational members and stakeholders. To help ensure success, top managers must demonstrate their commitment to ethical and socially responsible behavior through their actions—words are simply not enough. In the end, a marketing plan that ignores social responsibility or is silent about ethical requirements leaves the guidance of ethical and socially responsible behavior to the work group, which risks ethical breakdowns and damage to the firm.

Lessons from Chapter 8

Marketing ethics and social responsibility:

- have grown in importance over the last few years because many firms have seen their image, reputation, and marketing efforts destroyed by problems in these areas.
- have become necessities in light of stakeholder demands and changes in federal law.
- improve marketing performance and profits.
- are important considerations in the development of marketing strategy.

Social responsibility:

- is a broad concept that relates to an organization's obligation to maximize its positive impact on society while minimizing its negative impact.
- includes the economic responsibility of making a profit to serve shareholders, employees, and the community at large.
- includes the legal responsibility of obeying all laws and regulations.
- includes the ethical responsibility to uphold principles and standards that define acceptable conduct as determined by the public, government regulators, private-interest groups, competitors, and the firm itself.
- includes the philanthropic responsibility to increase the firm's overall positive impact on society, the local community, and the environment.
- includes activities related to sustainability, or programs designed to protect and preserve the natural environment.
- as it relates to sustainability includes green marketing activities and avoiding the deceptive practice of greenwashing.

Marketing ethics:

- includes the principles and standards that guide the behavior of individuals and groups in making marketing decisions.
- requires that both organizations and individuals accept responsibility for their actions and comply with established value systems.
- can lead to violations of public trust when ethical standards are not upheld.
- involves complex and detailed decisions in which correctness may not be so clear cut.

- deals with experiences and decisions made at work, which may be quite different from the ethical decisions made away from work.
- comes into play any time that an activity causes managers, employees, or customers in a target market to feel manipulated or cheated.

Ethical issues in the marketing program:

- include identifiable problems, situations, or opportunities that require an individual or organization to choose from among several actions that must be evaluated as right or wrong.
- come into play any time that an activity causes managers, employees, or customers in a target market to feel manipulated or cheated.
- have the potential to become legal issues if they are not addressed in the strategic planning process.
- include product-related issues such as failure to disclose risks associated with a product, substituting inferior materials or components to reduce costs, and counterfeit products.
- include pricing-related issues such as price gouging, bait-and-switch tactics, price discrimination, price fixing, predatory pricing, and superficial discounting.
- include supply chain-related issues such as sourcing from suppliers who engage in unfair labor practices, sourcing components that damage the natural environment, lack of diversity in the supply chain, and the need to conduct regular supply chain audits.
- include promotion-related issues such as communication that deceives, manipulates, or conceals facts in order to create a false impression; exaggerated claims or statements about a product or firm that cannot be substantiated; ambiguous statements in which claims are so weak that the viewer, reader, or listener must infer the advertiser's intended message; product-labeling issues such as false or misleading claims on a product's package; and selling abuses such as intentionally misleading customers by concealing facts or bribery.

Managing and controlling ethical issues:

- is best done via self-regulatory mechanisms, such as the Better Business Bureau or an industry association, rather than waiting for government regulation to control marketing activities.

- can be handled by establishing a code of conduct (i.e., code of ethics), but only if the code becomes integrated into daily decision making.
- depends to a great extent on the ethical leadership exhibited by top management. Great ethical leaders:
  - create a common goal or vision for the company
  - obtain buy-in, or support, from significant partners
  - motivate others to be ethical
  - use the resources that are available to them; and
  - enjoy their jobs and approach them with an almost contagious tenacity, passion, and commitment.

A code of conduct (code of ethics):

- is not truly effective unless it has the full support of top management.
- should have six core values: (1) trustworthiness, (2) respect, (3) responsibility, fairness, (5) caring, and (6) citizenship.
- will not resolve every ethical issue encountered in daily operations, but it can help employees and managers deal with ethical dilemmas by prescribing or limiting specific activities.

The connection between ethics/social responsibility and marketing performance:

- can cause employees to become more motivated to serve customers, more committed to the firm, more committed to standards of high quality, and more satisfied with their jobs.
- can cause customers to become more loyal to the firm and increase their purchases from the firm.
- can lead to increased trust among the firm's stakeholders. The most important contributing factor to gaining trust is

the perception that the firm and its employees will not sacrifice their standards of integrity.

Stakeholder orientation:

- refers to the degree to which a firm understands and addresses stakeholder demands.
- is composed of three sets of activities: (1) the organization-wide generation of data about stakeholder groups and assessment of the firm's effects on these groups, (2) the distribution of this information throughout the firm, and (3) the organization's responsiveness as a whole to this intelligence.
- consists of the initiatives that the firm adopts to ensure that it abides by or exceeds stakeholder expectations and has a positive impact on stakeholder issues.

The connection between ethics/social responsibility and strategic planning:

- is so strong that firms that fail to incorporate ethics and social responsibility into their organizational cultures may pay the price with poor marketing performance and the potential costs of legal violations, civil litigation, and damaging publicity when questionable events are made public.
- is typically done through ethics compliance programs or integrity initiatives that make legal compliance, ethics, and social responsibility an organization-wide effort.
- should be vested in the marketing plan, which should include distinct elements of ethics and social responsibility.
- is based on an understanding of (1) the risks associated with ethical and legal misconduct, (2) the ethical and social consequences of strategic choices, and (3) the values of organizational members and stakeholders.

Questions for Discussion

1. Why is marketing ethics a strategic consideration in organizational decisions? Who is most important in managing marketing ethics: the individual or the firm's leadership? Explain your answer.
2. Why have we seen more evidence of widespread ethical marketing dilemmas within firms today? Is it necessary to gain the cooperation of marketing

managers to overstate revenue and earnings in a corporation?
3. What is the relationship between marketing ethics and organizational performance? What are the elements of a strong ethical compliance program to support responsible marketing and a successful marketing strategy?

Exercises

1. Visit the Federal Trade Commission website (www.ftc.gov). What is the FTC's current mission? What are the primary areas for which the FTC has responsibility? Review the last two months of press releases from the FTC. Based on these

releases, what appear to be the major marketing ethical issues of concern at this time?
2. Visit the Better Business Bureau website (www.bbb.org). Review the criteria for the BBB Marketplace Torch Awards. What are the most important

marketing activities necessary for a firm to receive this award?

3. Look at several print, broadcast, online, or outdoor advertisements and try to find an ad that you believe is questionable from an ethical perspective. Defend why you believe the ad is ethically questionable.

End Notes

1. "2010 World's Most Ethical Companies—Company Profile: Salesforce.com," *Ethisphere*, Q1, 32–33; Milton Moskowitz and Charles Kapelke, "25 top-paying companies," *CNNMoney*, January 26, 2011 (http://money.cnn.com/galleries/2011/pf/jobs/1101/gallery.best_companies_top_paying.fortune/index.html); "Salesforce.com Named One of the "World's Most Ethical Companies" in 2010 for the Fourth Consecutive Year," Salesforce.com, March 29, 2010 (http://www.salesforce.com/company/news-press/press-releases/2010/03/100329.jsp); Salesforce Foundation Home Page (http://salesforcefoundation.org), accessed May 28, 2012; Salesforce.com website (http://www.salesforce.com/company), accessed May 28, 2012; "Sustainability," Salesforce.com (http://www.salesforce.com/company/sustainability), accessed February 13, 2012; "Corporate Governance," Salesforce.com (http://www.salesforce.com/company/investor/governance), accessed February 13, 2012; "Sustainability at salesforce.com," Salesforce.com (http://www.sfdcstatic.com/assets/pdf/datasheets/DS_salesforcedotcom_Environmental_Policy_Q2FY11.pdf), accessed February 13, 2012; and Eric Martin, "Salesforce.com, Fastenal to Replace Fannie, Freddie in S&P 500," *Bloomberg*, September 9, 2008 (http://www.bloomberg.com/apps/news?pid=newsarchive&sid=abSHUiB Fprac&refer=us).

2. Isabelle Maignan, Tracy L. Gonzalez-Padron, G. Tomas M. Hult, and O.C. Ferrell, "Stakeholder orientation: development and testing of a framework for socially responsible marketing," 90*(4)*, July 2011, pp. 313–338; and "Salesforce.com Named as 'Rising Star' in S&P 500 Carbon Survey," cloudapps (http://www.cloudapps.com/salesforce-carbon-reporting), accessed May 29, 2012.

3. Jeanne Whalen, "Glaxo to Pay U.S. $3 Billion to Settle," *Wall Street Journal*, November 4, 2011 (http://online.wsj.com/article/SB10001424052970203804204577015234100584756.html).

4. Indra Nooyi, "The Responsible Company," *The Economist*, March 31, 2008, p. 132.

5. "The Other Oil Spill," *The Economist*, June 24, 2010 (http://www.economist.com/node/16423833); and Martin Hickman, "Online Protest Drives Nestlé to Environmentally Friendly Palm Oil," *The Independent*, May 19, 2010 (http://www.independent.co.uk/environment/green-living/online-protest-drives-nestl-to-environmentally-friendly-palm-oil-1976443.html).

6. Archie Carroll, "The Pyramid of Corporate Social Responsibility: Toward the Moral Management of Organizational Stakeholders," *Business Horizons*, 34 (July/August 1991), 42.

7. Hadley Malcolm, "Retailers sue Fed, say debit card fees are still too high," *USA Today*, November 23, 2011, 3B; and Richard A. Epstein, "The Dangerous Experiment of the Durbin Amendment," *Regulation*, Spring 2011, pp. 24–29.

8. Thomas Catan, "Google Forks Over Settlement On Rx Ad," *Wall Street Journal*, August 25, 2011 (http://online.wsj.com/article/SB10001424053111904787404576528332418595052.html).

9. "Giving and Volunteering in America," *USA Today*, November 29, 2011, 8D.

10. Lindsay Blakely, "Erasing the Line Between Marketing and Philanthropy," *CBS News*, April 21, 2011 (http://www.cbsnews.com/8301-505143_162-40244368/erasing-the-line-between-marketing-and-philanthropy); and "The Best of 2011," Charlotte Street Computers (http://charlottestreetcomputers.com/the-best-of-2011), accessed May 29, 2012.

11. Box Tops for Education (http://www.boxtops4education.com/Default.aspx), accessed May 29, 2012; and Mike Eiman, "Boosters Compete, Kids Come Out on 'Top,'" *Hanford Sentinel*, January 14, 2012 (http://www.hanfordsentinel.com/news/local/boosters-compete-kids-come-out-on-top/article_36a3ad60-3e51-11e1-b225-001871e3ce6c.html).

12. "Cone LLC Releases the 2010 Cone Cause Evolution Study," Cone (http://www.coneinc.com/cause-grows-consumers-want-more), accessed May 29, 2012.

13. Debbie Thorne McAlister, O.C. Ferrell, and Linda Ferrell, *Business and Society: A Strategic Approach to Social Responsibility*, 3rd ed. (Mason, OH: Cengage, 2008).

14. Patagonia website (http://www.patagonia.com/us/home), accessed May 29, 2012.

15. "Swash+," The Coca-Cola Company (http://www.thecoca-colacompany.com/citizenship/swash.html), accessed May 29, 2012.

16. Christine Birkner, "Green Global Brands," *Marketing News*, September 30, 2011, pp. 12–16.

17. U.S. Green Building Council, "What LEED Is" (http://www.usgbc.org/DisplayPage.aspx?CMSPageID=1988), accessed May 29, 2012.

18. REI, "2010 Stewardship Report" (http://www.rei.com/aboutrei/csr/2010/green-building.html), accessed May 29, 2012.

19. "Welcome to Eco Options: Sustainable Forestry," Home Depot (http://www6.homedepot.com/ecooptions/index.html), accessed February 14, 2012.

20. "The Rainforest Alliance's Better Banana Project," Chiquita (http://www.chiquita.ch/uploads/global/pdf/rainforest-alliance.pdf), accessed February 14, 2012.

21. Traci Watson, "Eco-Friendly Claims Go Unchecked," *USA Today*, June 22, 2009, p. A1.

22. Linda Ferrell and O.C. Ferrell, *Ethical Business* (London: Dorling Kindersley Limited, 2009), 38–39.

23. Paul Keegan, "The trouble with green ratings," *CNNMoney*, July 13, 2011 (http://money.cnn.com/2011/07/12/technology/problem_green_ratings.fortune/index.htm); Bruce Geiselman, "Aisle 7 for Eco Options," *Waste News*, April 30, 2007, p. 35; Federal Trade Commission, *Part 260 – GUIDES FOR THE USE OF ENVIRONMENTAL MARKETING CLAIMS* (http://ftc.gov/bcp/grnrule/guides980427.htm), accessed May 28, 2012; Federal Trade Commission, "FTC Warns 78 Retailers, Including Wal-Mart, Target, and Kmart, to Stop Labeling and Advertising Rayon Textile Products as 'Bamboo,'" February 3, 2010 (http://www.ftc.gov/opa/2010/02/bamboo.shtm); Gwendolyn Bounds, "Misleading Claims on

'Green' Labeling," *Wall Street Journal*, October 26, 2010 (http://online.wsj.com/article/SB1000142405270230346700457557452171008 2414.html); Laura Petrecca and Christine Dugas, "Going truly green might require detective work," *USA Today*, April 22, 2010, pp. 1B–2B; Laura Petrecca and Christina Dugas, "Groups help consumers find 'real' green products," *USA Today*, April 22, 2010, p. 2B; Julie Deardorff, "How to spot greenwashing," *Chicago Tribune*, May 7, 2010 (http://featuresblogs.chicagotribune.com/features_julieshealthclub/2010/05/how-to-spot-greenwashing.html); Greenwashing Index (http://www.greenwashingindex.com), accessed May 28, 2012; and Julie Deardorff, "Eco-friendly claims: when is 'green' really green?" *Chicago Tribune*, May 7, 2010 (http://featuresblogs.chicagotribune.com/features_julieshealthclub/2010/05/ecofriendly-claims-when-is-green-really-green.html).

24. Jon Gertner, "How Do You Solve a Problem like GM, Mary?" *Fast Company*, October 2011, pp. 104–108 and p. 148.

25. Krista Mahr, "Digging Deep for Smarter Heat," *Time*, September 20, 2010, p. 74; and Walmart, "Walmart To Generate Solar Energy At More Than 75 Percent Of Its Stores In California," September 21 (http://walmartstores.com/pressroom/news/10699.aspx), accessed February 14, 2012.

26. Edelman, *2012 Edelman Trust Barometer Global Results* (http://trust.edelman.com/trust-download/global-results), accessed January 25, 2012.

27. Interbrand, "Brand valuation: the financial value of brands," brandchannel (http://www.brandchannel.com/papers_review.asp?sp_id=357), accessed February 14, 2012.

28. "Worth Noting," *Business Ethics*, January/February 1999, 5.

29. Somini Sengupta, "F.T.C. Settles Privacy Issue at Facebook," *New York Times*, November 29, 2011 (http://www.nytimes.com/2011/11/30/technology/facebook-agrees-to-ftc-settlement-on-privacy.html).

30. Barry Newman, "An Ad Professor Huffs Against Puffs, But It's a Quixotic Enterprise," *Wall Street Journal*, January 24, 2003, A1.

31. National Advertising Division, "NAD Finds Verizon Acted Properly in Discontinuing 'Rated #1' Claim Following Comcast Challenge," January 23, 2012 (http://www.narcpartners.org/DocView.aspx?DocumentID=8911&DocType=1).

32. Tim Barnett and Sean Valentine, "Issue Contingencies and Marketers' Recognition of Ethical Issues, Ethical Judgments and Behavioral Intentions," *Journal of Business Research* 57 (2004): pp. 338–346.

33. Shari R. Veil and Michael L. Kent, "Issues Management and Inoculation: Tylenol's Responsible Dosing Advertising," *Public Relations Review* 34 (2008), 399–402.

34. Sean Portnoy, "The Key to Lower Ultrabook Prices? One Word: Plastics," *ZDNet*, May 8, 2012 (http://www.zdnet.com/blog/computers/the-key-to-lower-ultrabook-prices-one-word-plastics/8014).

35. Dirk Rodgers, "Will the FDA Accept RFID for Drug Identification?" *RxTrace*, February 27, 2012 (http://www.rxtrace.com/2012/02/will-the-fda-accept-rfid-for-drug-identification.html).

36. Max Colchester and Christina Passariello, "Dirty Secrets in Soap Prices," *Wall Street Journal*, December 9, 2011 (http://online.wsj.com/article/SB10001424052970203413304577086251676539124.html).

37. Ari Lavaux, "Chocolate's Dark Side," *Weekly Alibi*, February 9–15, 2012, p. 22.

38. Charles Duhigg and David Barboza, "Apple's iPad and the Human Costs for Workers in China," *New York Times*, January 25, 2012 (http://www.nytimes.com/2012/01/26/business/ieconomy-apples-ipad-and-the-human-costs-for-workers-in-china.html?pagewanted=all).

39. Ibid.

40. "Health Care Supply Company Novation Earns Ethics Inside Certification," *Ethisphere*, November 8, 2011 (http://ethisphere.com/leading-health-care-supply-contracting-company-novation-earns-ethics-inside-certification).

41. Ibid.

42. Maxwell Murphy, "Reinforcing the Supply Chain," *Wall Street Journal*, January 11, 2012, B6.

43. Jayne O'Donnell, "Toning Shoe Case Costs Reebok $25M," *USA Today*, September 29, 2011, 1B.

44. Dow Jones Newswires, "FDA, FTC Issue 7 Warning Letters To Firms For HCG Products," *Wall Street Journal*, December 6, 2011 (http://online.wsj.com/article/BT-CO-20111206-708084.html).

45. Julius Melnitzer, "U.K. Enacts 'Far-Reaching' Anti-Bribery Act," *Law Times*, February 13, 2011 (http://www.lawtimesnews.com/201102148245/Headline-News/UK-enacts-far-reaching-anti-bribery-act).

46. Federal Trade Commission, "FTC Releases List of Top Consumer Complaints in 2010; Identity Theft Tops the List Again," March 8, 2011 (http://ftc.gov/opa/2011/03/topcomplaints.shtm).

47. Better Business Bureau, "BBB Structure" (http://www.bbb.org/us/BBB-Structure), accessed May 29, 2012.

48. These facts are from Binyamin Appelbaum, "Former Ohio Attorney General to Head New Consumer Agency," *New York Times*, July 17, 2011 (http://www.huffingtonpost.com/2012/01/04/richard-cordray-obama-recess-appointment-cfpb_n_1183225.html); Drake Bennett and Carter Dougherty, "Elizabeth Warren's Dream Becomes a Real Agency She May Never Get to Lead," *Bloomberg Businessweek*, July 11–July 17, 2011, 58–64; Jennifer Liberto and David Ellis, "Wall Street Reform: What's in the Bill," *CNNMoney*, June 30, 2010 (http://money.cnn.com/2010/06/25/news/economy/whats_in_the_reform_bill/index.htm); and Sudeep Reddy, "Elizabeth Warren's Early Words on a Consumer Financial Protection Bureau," *Wall Street Journal*, September 17, 2010 (http://blogs.wsj.com/economics/2010/09/17/elizabeth-warrens-early-words-on-a-consumer-financial-protection-bureau).

49. O.C. Ferrell, John Fraedrich, and Linda Ferrell, *Business Ethics: Ethical Decision Making and Cases*, 9th ed (Mason, OH: South-Western Cengage Learning, 2013).

50. IBM, *Business Conduct Guidelines* (Armonk, New York: International Business Machines Corp., 2011).

51. American Marketing Association, "Statement of Ethics" (http://www.marketingpower.com/AboutAMA/Pages/Statement%20of%20Ethics.aspx), accessed May 29, 2012.

52. Thorne McAlister, Ferrell, and Ferrell, *Business and Society: A Strategic Approach to Social Responsibility*.

53. Stephen Taub, "SEC Probing Harley Statements," *CFO.com*, July 14, 2005 (http://www.cfo.com/article.cfm/4173321/c_4173841?f=archives&origin=archive).

54. Thomas A. Stewart, Ann Harrington, and Maura Griffin Sol, "America's Most Admired Companies: Why Leadership Matters," *Fortune*, March 3, 1998, 70–71.

55. "LRN Ethics Study: Employee Engagement," LRN, 2007 (http://www.lrn.com/docs/lrn_ethics_study_employee_engagement.pdf), accessed August 7, 2009.

56. Deloitte LLP, *Trust in the Workplace: 2010 Ethics & Workplace Survey*, 2010, (http://www.deloitte.com/assets/Dcom-UnitedStates/Local%20Assets/Documents/us_2010_Ethics_and_

Workplace_Survey_report_071910.pdf), accessed February 14, 2012.

57. Diane E. Kirrane, "Managing Values: A Systematic Approach to Business Ethics," *Training and Development Journal*, 1 (November 1990), 53–60.

58. O.C. Ferrell, Isabelle Maignan, and Terry Loe, "Corporate Ethics + Citizenship = Profits," *The Bottom Line: Good Ethics Is Good Business* (Tampa, FL: University of Tampa, Center for Ethics, 1997).

59. Terry Loe, "The Role of Ethical Climate in Developing Trust, Market Orientation, and Commitment to Quality," unpublished dissertation, University of Memphis, 1996.

60. Sarah Needleman, "Burger Chain's Health-Care Recipe," *Wall Street Journal*, August 31, 2009 (http://online.wsj.com/article/SB125149100886467705.html).

61. Isabelle Maignan and O. C. Ferrell, "Corporate Social Responsibility: Toward a Marketing Conceptualization," *Journal of the Academy of Marketing Science*, 32 (January, 2004), 3–19.

62. Christine Moorman, Gerald Zaltman, and Rohit Deshpande, "The Relationship Between Providers and Users of Market Research: The Dynamics of Trust Within and Between Organizations," *Journal of Marketing Research* 29 (August 1993), 314–328.

63. "Cone LLC Releases the 2010 Cone Cause Evolution Study," Cone, September 15, 2010 (http://www.coneinc.com/cause-grows-consumers-want-more).

64. "BBMG Study: Three-Fourths of U.S. Consumers Reward, Punish Brands Based on Social and Environmental Practices," *CSR Wire*, June 2, 2009 (http://www.csrwire.com/press/press_release/27052-BBMG-Study-Three-Fourths-of-U-S-Consumers-Reward-Punish-Brands-Based-on-Social-and-Environmental-Practices).

65. Marjorie Kelly, "Holy Grail Found: Absolute, Definitive Proof That Responsible Companies Perform Better Financially," *Business Ethics*, Winter 2005 (http://www.business-ethics.com/current_issue/winter_2005_holy_grail_article.html); Xueming Luo and C. B. Bhattacharya, "Corporate Social Responsibility, Customer Satisfaction, and Market Value," *Journal of Marketing* 70 (October 2006); and Isabelle Maignan, O. C. Ferrell, and Linda Ferrell, "A Stakeholder Model for Implementing Social Responsibility in Marketing," *European Journal of Marketing* 39 (September/October 2005): pp. 956–977.

66. "Cone LLC Releases the 2010 Cone Cause Evolution Study."

67. Stefan Ambec and Paul Lanoie, "Does It Pay to Be Green? A Systematic Overview," *Academy of Management Perspective* 22, no. 4 (November 2008): 47; and Mary K. Pratt, "The High Cost of Ethics Compliance," *ComputerWorld*, August 24, 2009 (http://www.computerworld.com/s/article/341268/Ethics_Harder_in_a_Recession_).

68. "The Values and Ethics of TI," Texas Instruments Values and Ethics Statement (http://www.ti.com/values-ethics-at-ti), accessed May 29, 2012. Courtesy of Texas Instruments, Inc.

CHAPTER 9

Marketing Implementation and Control

Introduction

Throughout the history of business, many firms and their top executives have emphasized strategic planning at the expense of strategic implementation. Historically, and even today, this emphasis on planning occurs because many executives believe that strategic planning, by itself, is the key to marketing success. This belief is logical because a firm must have a plan before it can determine where it is going. Although many firms are quite good at devising strategic marketing plans, they are often unprepared to cope with the realities of implementation.

Marketing implementation is the process of executing the marketing strategy by creating and performing specific actions that will ensure the achievement of the firm's marketing objectives. Strategic planning without effective implementation can produce unintended consequences that result in customer dissatisfaction and feelings of frustration within the firm. Likewise, poor implementation will most likely result in the firm's failure to reach its organizational and marketing objectives. Unfortunately, many firms repeatedly experience failures in marketing implementation. Out-of-stock items, overly aggressive salespeople, long checkout lines, malfunctioning websites, and unfriendly or inattentive employees are examples of implementation failure that occur all too frequently today. These and other examples illustrate that even the best-planned marketing strategies are a waste of time without effective implementation to ensure their success.

To track the implementation process, firms must have ways of evaluating and controlling marketing activities, as well as monitoring performance to determine whether marketing goals and objectives have been achieved. As illustrated in *Beyond the Pages 9.1*, implementation, evaluation, and control go hand-in-hand in determining the success or failure of the marketing strategy, and ultimately the entire firm. One of the most important considerations in implementing and controlling marketing activities involves gaining the support of employees. Because a marketing strategy cannot implement itself, all firms depend on employees to carry out marketing activities. As a result, the firm must devise a plan for implementation, just as it devises a plan for marketing strategy.

In this chapter, we examine the critical role of marketing implementation and control in the strategic planning process. First, we discuss a number of important

Beyond the Pages 9.1

Green Mountain Coffee Gets It Done[1]

Green Mountain Coffee Roasters, Inc. is a leader in the specialty coffee industry. The company from Waterbury, VT uses a coordinated multi-channel distribution network that is designed to maximize brand recognition and product availability. Green Mountain roasts high-quality Arabica beans and offers over 100 coffee selections including single-origins, estates, certified organics, Fair Trade Certified™, proprietary blends, and flavored coffees sold under the Green Mountain Coffee Roasters® and Newman's Own® Organics brands. Its products come in a variety of packages including whole bean, fractional packages, premium one-cup coffee pods, Vue Packs, and Keurig® K-Cup® single-serving coffee cartridges. Green Mountain also sells other products including iced coffee, teas, cider, and hot chocolate. The company operates an active e-commerce business at www.GreenMountainCoffee.com.

Most of Green Mountain's revenue is derived from over 8,000 wholesale customer accounts including supermarkets, specialty food stores, convenience stores, food service companies, hotels, restaurants, universities, and office coffee services. One of the company's signature accounts is McDonald's, which sells Green Mountain's organic coffee under the Newman's Own® label. Green Mountain's K-Cup packs are available at roughly 16,000 grocery stores and its Keurig Single Cup Brewing System is available at 20,000 retail locations. The company also estimates that roughly 13 percent of all offices and 188,000 hotel rooms in the U.S. have a Keurig brewer.

In achieving its phenomenal success, Green Mountain pursued three key strategies: boosting market share, expanding into new markets, and making key acquisitions. To increase market share and expand, the company relies on direct relationships with farms, coffee estates, cooperatives, and other parties to ensure a consistent supply and price of 75 different varieties of high quality coffee beans. This, combined with a custom-roasting process, allows Green Mountain to differentiate its coffee offerings. One of Green Mountain's key acquisitions was Keurig—the company that makes its K-Cup® coffee cartridges. While Keurig had been a dominant player in the office coffee service segment, its expansion into the home market under Green Mountain has been extraordinary. Sales of Keurig brewers increased 46 percent in 2011 after triple-digit growth numbers from 2006 to 2010. Green Mountain acquired Tully's—a Seattle-based coffee company in 2009. In 2011, Green Mountain enjoyed a 95 percent revenue growth rate.

One of the major reasons for Green Mountain's success is its overall focus on implementation. The company signed a number of strategic partnerships, including agreements with Dunkin' Donuts, Swiss Miss, Starbucks, and Tazo to make their products available via the patented K-Cup system. Green Mountain also has agreements with Breville, Cuisinart, and Mr. Coffee to make branded single-cup coffee makers that use the K-Cup system. Internally, the company employs roughly 5,600 people, but has a very flat organizational structure. This promotes open communication, passion, and commitment among employees. As a part of the company's evaluation and control system, Green Mountain uses a process called the after-action review—a process adapted from the U.S. Army. The goal of the review is to answer four key questions: What did we set out to do? What happened? Why did it happen? What are we going to do about it? Most of the effort is spent on this last question to ensure that the company learns from both its successes and failures. Employees are empowered to apply these lessons and encouraged to share their views in a "constellation of communication" that ensures a collaborative style of getting things done. Green Mountain has consistently appeared on *Forbes'* list of the "200 Best Small Companies in America," *Fortune's* list of the "100 Fastest-Growing Small Companies in America," and *Business Ethics* magazine's list of the "100 Best Corporate Citizens." In addition, the Society of Human Resource Management has recognized Green Mountain for its socially responsible business practices, including a strong focus on sustainability.

Moving ahead, Green Mountain will continue to focus on innovation and partnerships to maintain its success. Before its patent on K-Cups expired in September 2012, Green Mountain launched its new Vue brewing system that added the ability to brew café beverages, such as lattes and cappuccinos, in addition to coffees, teas, chocolate, and cider. The Vue system also allows more customization than the K-Cup system in terms of strength, temperature, and size. In addition, the new Vue packs are recyclable. The Vue strategy is designed to continue Green Mountain's dominance in the home brewing market as the K-Cup patent expires and competitors launch lower-priced K-Cup competitors into the market.

Long waiting lines are a common symptom that can be tied to problems in strategy, implementation, or both.

strategic issues involved in implementation, including the major components of implementation that must work together in order for a strategy to be executed successfully. Then, we examine the advantages and disadvantages of major marketing implementation approaches. This discussion also describes how internal marketing can be used to motivate employees to implement marketing strategy. Finally, we look at the marketing evaluation and control process.

Strategic Issues in Marketing Implementation

Marketing implementation is critical to the success of any firm because it is responsible for putting the marketing strategy into action. Simply put, implementation refers to the "how" part of the marketing plan. Marketing implementation is a very broad concept, and for that reason it is often misunderstood. Some of this misunderstanding stems from the fact that marketing strategies almost always turn out differently than expected. In fact, all firms have two strategies: their intended strategy and a realized strategy.[2] *Intended marketing strategy* is what the firm wants to happen—it is the firm's planned strategic choices that appear in the marketing plan itself. The *realized marketing strategy*, on the other hand, is the strategy that actually takes place. More often than not, the difference between the intended and the realized strategies is a matter of the implementation of the intended strategy. This is not to say that a firm's realized marketing strategy is necessarily better or worse than the intended marketing strategy, just that it is different in execution and results. Such differences are often the result of internal or external environmental factors that change during implementation.

The Link Between Planning and Implementation

One of the most interesting aspects of marketing implementation is its relationship to the strategic planning process. Many firms assume that planning and implementation are interdependent but separate issues. In reality, planning and implementation intertwine within the marketing planning process. Many of the problems of marketing implementation occur because of its relationship to strategic planning. The three most common issues in this relationship are interdependency, evolution, and separation.

Interdependency   Many firms assume that the planning and implementation process is a one-way street. That is, strategic planning comes first, followed by implementation. Although it is true that the content of the marketing plan determines how it will be implemented, it is also true that how the marketing strategy is to be implemented determines the content of the marketing plan.

Certain marketing strategies will define their implementation by default. For example, a firm such as Southwest Airlines with a strategy of improving customer service may turn to employee training programs as an important part of that strategy's implementation. Through profit sharing, many Southwest employees are also stockholders with a vested interest in the firm's success. Employee training and profit-sharing programs are common in firms that depend on their employees' commitment and enthusiasm to ensure quality customer service. However, employee training, as a tool of implementation, can also dictate the content of the firm's strategy. Perhaps a competitor of Southwest, who is in the process of implementing its own customer service strategy, realizes that it does not possess adequate resources to offer profit sharing and extensive training to its employees. Maybe the company simply lacks the financial resources or the staff required to implement these activities. Consequently, the company will be forced to go back to the planning stage and adjust its customer service strategy. These continual changes in marketing strategy make implementation more difficult. Clearly, a SWOT analysis and strategic thrust conducted with an eye toward what the company can reasonably implement can reduce, but not completely eliminate, this problem.

Evolution   All firms face a simple truth in planning and implementation: Important environmental factors constantly change. As the needs and wants of customers change, as competitors devise new marketing strategies, and as the firm's own internal environment changes, the firm must constantly adapt. In some cases, these changes occur so rapidly that once the firm decides on a marketing strategy, it quickly becomes out-of-date. Because planning and implementation are intertwined, both must constantly evolve to fit the other. The process is never static because environmental changes require shifts in strategy, which require changes in implementation, which require shifts in strategy, and so on.

A related problem is that executives often assume there is only one correct way to implement a given strategy. This is simply not true. Just as strategy often results from trial and error, so does marketing implementation. Firms that are truly customer-oriented must be flexible enough to alter their implementation on the fly to fully embrace customer intimacy and respond to changes in customers' preferences. In the airline industry, for example, competitors quickly alter their pricing strategies when one firm announces a reduction in fares on certain routes. These rapid changes require that firms be flexible in both marketing strategy and implementation.

Separation   The ineffective implementation of marketing strategy is often a self-generated problem that stems from the way that planning and implementation are carried out in most firms. As shown in Exhibit 9.1, middle- or upper-level managers often do strategic planning; however, the responsibility for implementation almost always falls on lower-level managers and frontline employees. Top executives often fall into a trap of believing that a good marketing strategy will implement itself. Because there is distance between executives and the day-to-day activities at the frontline of the firm, they often

EXHIBIT 9.1   **The Separation of Planning and Implementation**

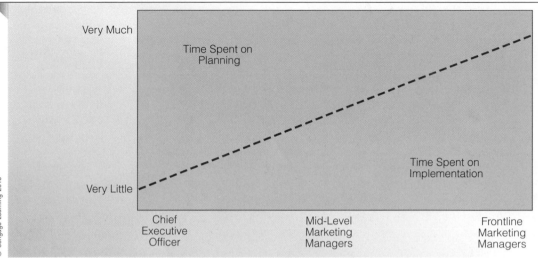

do not understand the unique problems associated with implementing marketing strategy. Conversely, frontline employees—who do understand the challenges and hurdles of implementation—usually have a limited voice in planning the strategy.

Another trap that top executives often fall into is believing that frontline managers and employees will be excited about the marketing strategy and motivated to implement it. However, because they are separated from the planning process, these managers and employees often fail to identify with the firm's goals and objectives, and thus fail to fully understand the marketing strategy.[3] It is unrealistic for top executives to expect frontline managers and employees to be committed to a strategy they had no voice in developing, or to a strategy that they do not understand or feel is inappropriate.[4]

The Elements of Marketing Implementation

Marketing implementation involves a number of interrelated elements and activities, as shown in Exhibit 9.2. These elements must work together for strategy to be implemented effectively. Because we examined marketing strategy issues in previous chapters, we now look briefly at the remaining elements of marketing implementation.

Shared Goals and Values   Shared goals and values among all employees within the firm are the "glue" of successful implementation because they bind the entire organization together as a single, functioning unit. When all employees share the firm's goals and values, all actions will be more closely aligned and directed toward the betterment of the organization. Without a common direction to hold the organization together, different areas of the firm may work toward different outcomes, thus limiting the success of the entire organization. For example, one of the reasons for the tremendous success of the New Belgium Brewery is the fact that all employees have a commitment to make excellent craft beer in ways that conserve environmental resources.[5] Other firms, such as FedEx, Google, and ESPN, are well known for their efforts to ensure that employees share and are committed to corporate goals and values.

Institutionalizing shared goals and values within a firm's culture is a long-term process. The primary means of creating shared goals and values is through employee

EXHIBIT 9.2 **The Elements of Marketing Implementation**

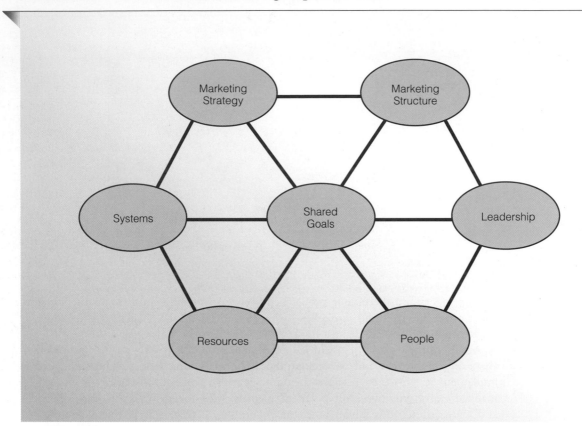

Source: Adapted from Lawrence R. Jaunch and William F. Glueck, *Strategic Management and Business Policy*, 3rd ed. (New York: McGraw-Hill, 1988), 305.

training and socialization programs.[6] Although creating shared goals and values is a difficult process, the rewards are worth the effort. Some experts have argued that creating shared goals and values is the single most important element of implementation because it stimulates organizational commitment where employees become more motivated to implement the marketing strategy, to achieve the firm's goals and objectives, and to serve more fully the needs of the firm's customers.[7]

Marketing Structure Marketing structure refers to the methods of organizing a firm's marketing activities. Marketing structure establishes formal lines of authority, as well as the division of labor within the marketing function. One of the most important decisions that firms make is how to divide and integrate marketing responsibilities. This decision typically comes down to the question of centralization versus decentralization. In a centralized marketing structure, the top of the marketing hierarchy coordinates and manages all marketing activities and decisions. Conversely, in a decentralized marketing structure, the frontline of the firm coordinates and manages marketing activities and decisions. Typically, decentralization means that frontline marketing managers have the responsibility of making day-to-day marketing decisions.

Both centralized and decentralized marketing structures have advantages. Centralized structures are very cost-efficient and effective in ensuring standardization within the marketing program. These advantages can be particularly critical to firms whose competitiveness depends upon maintaining a tight control over marketing activities and expenses.[8] For example, firms employing a strategy of operational excellence, such as Walmart or Dell, may find a centralized structure beneficial to ensuring operational efficiency and consistency. Decentralized marketing structures have the important advantage of placing marketing decisions closer to the frontline where serving customers is the number one priority. By decentralizing marketing decisions, frontline managers can be creative and flexible, allowing them to adapt to changing market conditions.[9] For this reason, firms that employ a strategy of customer intimacy, such as Ritz-Carlton or Nordstrom, may decentralize to ensure that they can respond to customers' needs in a timely manner. The decision to centralize or decentralize marketing activities is a trade-off between reduced costs and enhanced flexibility. However, there is no one correct way to organize the marketing function. The right marketing structure will depend on the specific firm, the nature of its internal and external environments, and its chosen marketing strategy.[10]

Systems and Processes Organizational systems and processes are collections of work activities that absorb a variety of inputs to create information and communication outputs that ensure the consistent day-to-day operation of the firm.[11] Examples include information systems, strategic planning, capital budgeting, procurement, order fulfillment, manufacturing, quality control, and performance measurement. At IBM, for example, research engineers are evaluated on one- and three-year time frames. Employees receive bonuses based on the one-year evaluation, but are awarded rank and salary based on the three-year time frame. This unique system is designed to encourage innovation by minimizing the risk of failure in any single yearly evaluation.[12] As we discussed in Chapter 6, many of these systems and processes are now outsourced to other firms. However, their important role in implementation means that the firm must be very diligent in how these activities are managed.

Resources A firm's resources can include a wide variety of assets that can be brought together during marketing implementation. These assets may be tangible or intangible. Tangible resources include financial resources, manufacturing capacity, facilities, and equipment. Although not quite as obvious, intangible resources such as marketing expertise, customer loyalty, brand equity, corporate goodwill, and external relationships/strategic alliances are equally important. In Chapter 7, we addressed the importance of branding and corporate reputation in the marketing program. These issues are equally important in the implementation of the strategy, especially in leveraging strategic partnerships to ensure that marketing activities are done effectively and efficiently.

Regardless of the type of resource, the amount of resources available can make or break a marketing strategy. However, a critical and honest evaluation of available resources during the planning phase can help ensure that the marketing strategy and marketing implementation are within the realm of possibility. Upon completion of the marketing plan, the analyst or planner must seek the approval of needed resources from top executives. This makes the communication aspects of the actual marketing plan document critical to the success of the strategy. Top executives allocate scarce resources based on the ability of the plan to help the firm reach its goals and objectives.

People (Human Resources) The quality, diversity, and skill of a firm's human resources can also make or break the implementation of the marketing strategy. Consequently, human resource issues have become more important to the marketing function, especially in the areas of employee selection and training, evaluation and compensation policies, and employee motivation, satisfaction, and commitment. In fact, the marketing departments of many firms have taken over the human resources function to ensure that employees have a correct match to required marketing activities.[13] A number of human resource activities are vitally important to marketing implementation:

- **Employee Selection and Training**. One of the most critical aspects of marketing implementation is matching employees' skills and abilities to the marketing tasks to be performed.[14] It is no secret that some people are better at some jobs than others. We all know individuals who are natural salespeople. Some individuals are better at working with people, while others are better at working with tools or computers. The key is to match these employee skills to marketing tasks. A weakening economy and tightening job market in recent years have forced firms to become more demanding in finding the right employee skills to match their required marketing activities.

  Employee diversity is an increasingly important aspect of selection and training practices. As the U.S. population becomes more ethnically diverse, many firms take steps to ensure that the diversity of their employees matches the diversity of their customers. Many firms also face challenges with generational diversity in that most middle and upper managers are baby-boomers (born 1946–1964), whereas most entry-level positions consist of members of Generation X (born 1965–1976) or Generation Y (born after 1976). In many cases, these younger employees have better training, more technological sophistication, and fewer political inclinations than their baby-boomer bosses. Managers must recognize these issues and adapt selection and training practices accordingly.

- **Employee Evaluation and Compensation**. Employee evaluation and compensation are also important to successful marketing implementation. An important decision to be made in this area is the choice between outcome- and behavior-based systems.[15] An outcome-based system evaluates and compensates employees based on measurable, quantitative standards such as sales volume or gross margin. This type of system is fairly easy to use, requires less supervision, and works well when market demand is fairly constant, the selling cycle is relatively short, and all efforts directly affect sales or profits. Conversely, behavior-based systems evaluate and compensate employees based on subjective, qualitative standards such as effort, motivation, teamwork, and friendliness toward customers. This type of system ties directly to customer satisfaction and rewards employees for factors they can control. However, behavior-based systems are expensive and difficult to manage because of their subjective nature and the amount of supervision required. The choice between outcome- and behavior-based systems depends on the firm, and its products, markets, and customers' needs. The important point is to match the employee evaluation and compensation system to the activities that employees must perform in order to implement the marketing strategy.

- **Employee Motivation, Satisfaction, and Commitment**. Other important factors in the implementation of marketing strategy are the extent to which employees have the motivation to implement the strategy, their overall feelings of job satisfaction, and the commitment they feel toward the organization and its goals.[16] For example, one of the major contributors to Google's success is the strong social culture fostered by the company's leaders. Google provides its employees with things such as paid childcare, onsite laundry service, free transportation, gourmet food, onsite haircuts, and time off for personal activities. In return, Google's employees reward the company with exceptionally strong motivation and commitment.[17]

Though factors such as employee motivation, satisfaction, and commitment are critical to successful implementation, they are highly dependent on other elements of implementation, especially training, evaluation/compensation systems, and leadership. Marketing structure and processes can also have an impact on employee behaviors and attitudes. The key is to recognize the importance of these factors to successful marketing implementation and to manage them accordingly.

Leadership The leadership provided by a firm's managers and the behaviors of employees go hand-in-hand in the implementation process. Leadership—often called the art of managing people—includes how managers communicate with employees, as well as how they motivate their people to implement the marketing strategy. As discussed in *Beyond the Pages 9.2*, today's business leaders must be courageous enough to take a long-term view of corporate success—one that often sacrifices short-term gains for the sake of the future.

Leaders have responsibility for establishing the corporate culture necessary for implementation success.[19] A good deal of research has shown that marketing implementation is more successful when leaders create an organizational culture characterized by open communication between employees and managers. In this way, employees are free to discuss their opinions and ideas about the marketing strategy and implementation activities. This type of leadership also creates a climate where managers and employees have full confidence and trust in each other.

Approaches to Marketing Implementation

Whether good or bad, all leaders possess a leadership style, or way of approaching a given task. Managers can use a variety of approaches in implementing marketing strategies and motivating employees to perform implementation activities. In this section, we examine four of these approaches: implementation by command, implementation through change, implementation through consensus, and implementation as organizational cultural.[20]

Implementation by Command

Under this approach, the firm's top executives develop and select the marketing strategies, which are transmitted to lower levels where frontline managers and employees implement them. Implementation by command has two advantages: (1) it makes decision making much easier, and (2) it reduces uncertainty as to what is to be done to implement the marketing strategy. Unfortunately, this approach suffers from several disadvantages. The approach places less emphasis on the feasibility of implementing the marketing strategy. It also divides the firm into strategists and implementers: Executives who develop the marketing strategy are often far removed from the targeted customers it is intended to attract. For these reasons, implementation by command can create employee motivation problems. Many employees do not have motivation to implement strategies in which they have little confidence.

Implementation by command is quite common in franchise systems. For example, McDonald's use of this approach creates a great deal of ongoing tension between the corporate office and its franchisees around the globe. In some cases, the tensions become so hostile that franchisees have flatly refused to implement some corporate strategies, such as the company's dollar menu promotion. Other strategies, such as keeping stores open 24 hours, offering free WiFi, and adding new products such as frozen drinks and McCafé coffee stations, significantly increase costs for franchisees. Rising costs have forced many would be McDonald's franchisees to reconsider the investment.[21]

Implementation Through Change

Implementation through change is similar to the command approach except that it focuses explicitly on implementation. The basic goal of implementation through change is to modify the firm in ways that will ensure the successful implementation of the

The New Rules of CEO Leadership[18]

As we have discussed throughout this text, the rules of the road in marketing have changed in today's economy. Customers now hold most of the power due to increasing access to information, massive product selection and its associated competition, and increasingly mature markets characterized by commoditization. The dynamic nature of today's marketplace has touched all sectors of the global economy. Nowhere is this truer than in the executive suite of today's corporations. Many CEOs struggle with managing their monolithic organizations in an increasingly fast-paced environment.

There is a good reason for the challenges facing today's CEOs: Many of them operate using a set of rules developed in the 1980's and 1990's glory days of corporate expansion and global domination. Many of those rules were developed by the celebrity CEOs of the day such as Jack Welch (GE), Lou Gerstner (IBM), Al Dunlap (Sunbeam), and Roberto Goizueta (Coca-Cola).

Of these, Jack Welch was the iconic leader. Most major corporations adopted his rules for business during the 1980s and 1990s. Welch's rules focused on corporate growth, maximizing market share, and the preeminence of quarterly earnings. However, those rules are ill suited for today's market because the rapid pace of change and increasingly relentless competition force CEOs to take a long-term view of competitiveness. That view is less about market share and stock price and more about making decisions that ensure the viability and long-term survival of the corporation. Today's problems are different than those of 10 to 25 years ago. Consequently, old solutions no longer work.

In order to highlight the importance of the issue, *Fortune* published a set of seven new rules for business that contradict virtually all of the old-school rules advocated by CEOs both past and present. These new rules argue for a dramatic shift away from short-term results in favor of long-term survival:

Old Rules	New Rules	Examples
Big dogs own the street	Agile is best; being big can bite you	Big pharmaceutical companies are losing to smaller biotech firms; the decline of major U.S. automakers such as General Motors; Samsung's rise above Sony
Be #1 or #2 in the market	Find a niche, create something new	Energy drinks are more profitable than traditional soft drinks; the growth of Starbucks from a niche player to a coffee powerhouse
Shareholders rule	The customer is king	Businesses are better at managing earnings rather than the goods and services that produce those earnings; major scandals at firms like Enron and WorldCom
Be lean and mean	Look outside, not inside	Innovation drives today's success (i.e., Apple's iPad); the drive for quality and efficiency only improves *current* processes—it does not promote innovation
Rank your players; go with the A's	Hire passionate people	Employees want purpose and meaning in their work; the growth in hiring employees with passion (Apple, ESPN, Genentech)
Hire a charismatic CEO	Hire a courageous CEO	Today's CEOs must have the fortitude to make decisions that have long-term payoffs, not the quick fixes that are rewarded by Wall Street investors
Admire my might	Admire my soul	Powerful corporations are increasingly targeted by activists on a number of fronts; it is better to be a company with a long-term vision that legitimizes its role in society

Of these rules, hiring a courageous CEO may be the most critical. CEOs who adopt *Fortune*'s new rules for business must be willing to make investments that will not pay off for years—when that CEO is no longer in charge. The old ways of doing business—such as driving down costs through efficiency, growth through mergers and acquisitions, and careful manipulation of financial and accounting decisions—are solutions that simply do not work any longer. Anne Mulcahy, former CEO of Xerox, puts it this way: "You have to change when you're at the top of your game in terms of profit. If you're not nimble, there's no advantage to size. It's like a rock."

Unfortunately, Wall Street gives today's CEOs little incentive to change. A study by Booz Allen found that CEOs become vulnerable to being fired if their company's stock price falls below the S&P 500 by an average of 2 percent. To be courageous in the face of this obstacle, today's CEOs must be willing to take risks and stand up for what they believe is in the long-term interest of their firm.

chosen marketing strategy. For example, the firm's structure can be altered; employees can be transferred, hired, or fired; new technology can be adopted; the employee compensation plan can be changed; or the firm can merge with another firm. Mergers and acquisitions are common today in many industries, particularly in pharmaceuticals. Given the enormous expense of developing new drugs, many pharmaceutical firms have decided that it is easier and less expensive to offer new products or enter new markets by acquiring firms that already possess those capabilities.

The manager who implements through change is more of an architect and politician, skillfully crafting the organization to fit the requirements of the marketing strategy. There are many good historical examples of implementation through change: Lee Iacocca (Chrysler), Fred Smith (FedEx), and Steve Jobs (Apple) come to mind. One of the best success stories, however, is Samsung. Once recognized as a cheap, high-volume supplier of computer chips, circuit boards, and electronic components, Samsung has emerged as a dominant player in the consumer electronics market. The major change at Samsung was a shift in operational focus from production to marketing. Samsung also changed by dropping its 50-plus low-budget brands in favor of a single master Samsung brand. The shift has been so successful that Samsung has been continuously ranked as one of the world's fastest growing brands since 2000. In fact, Samsung is the top electronics manufacturer in the world by revenue and is more successful than Sony, Nokia, and other electronics manufacturers in many different product categories. For example, despite Apple's success, Samsung is actually the top mobile phone company in the world.[22]

Because many business executives are reluctant to give up even a small portion of their control (as is the case with the next two implementation approaches), they often favor implementation through change. The approach achieves a good balance between command and consensus, and its successes are quite evident in business today. However, despite these advantages, implementation through change still suffers from the separation of planning and implementation. By clinging to this power-at-the-top philosophy, employee motivation often remains an issue. Likewise, the changes called for in this approach often take a great deal of time to design and implement (for example, it took Samsung over a decade to reach the top of the electronics market). This can create a situation where the firm becomes stagnant while waiting on the strategy to take hold. As a result, the firm can become vulnerable to changes in the marketing environment.

Implementation Through Consensus

Upper- and lower-level managers work together to evaluate and develop marketing strategies in the consensus approach to implementation. The underlying premise of this approach is that managers from different areas and levels in the firm come together as a team to collaborate and develop the strategy. Each participant has different opinions as well as different perceptions of the marketing environment. The role of the top manager is that of a coordinator, pulling different opinions together to ensure the development of the best overall marketing strategy. Through this collective decision-making process, the firm agrees upon a marketing strategy and reaches a consensus as to the overall direction of the firm.

Implementation through consensus is more advantageous than the first two approaches in that it moves some of the decision-making authority closer to the front-line of the firm. For this reason, this implementation approach is used extensively in service organizations. For example, Royal Caribbean uses a team approach in developing and implementing strategy for any initiative, such as building a new ship, adding a new computer system, or changing the marketing program. CEO Richard Fain then gives the teams milestones to keep them on track.[23] This approach is based on the simple truth that lower-level employees have a unique perspective on the marketing activities necessary to implement the firm's strategy (in the case of Royal Caribbean, the strategy is enhanced amenities and complete customer satisfaction). These employees are also more sensitive to the needs and wants of the firm's customers. In addition, because they are involved in the strategic process, these employees often have a stronger motivation and commitment to the strategy to see that it is properly implemented.

Implementation through consensus tends to work best in complex, uncertain, and highly unstable environments. The collective strategy-making approach works well in this environment because it brings multiple viewpoints to the table. However, implementation through consensus often retains the barrier between strategists and implementers. The end result of this barrier is that the full potential of the firm's human resources is not realized. Thus, for implementation through consensus to be truly effective, managers at all levels must communicate openly about strategy on an ongoing, rather than an occasional, basis.

Implementation as Organizational Culture

Under this approach, marketing strategy and its implementation become extensions of the firm's mission, vision, and organizational culture. In some ways, this approach is similar to implementation through consensus, except that the barrier between strategists and implementers completely dissolves. When personnel see implementation as an extension of the firm's culture, employees at all levels have permission to participate in making decisions that help the firm reach its mission, goals, and objectives.

With a strong organizational culture and an overriding corporate vision, the task of implementing marketing strategy is about 90 percent complete.[24] This occurs because all employees adopt the firm's culture so completely that they instinctively know what their role is in implementing the marketing strategy. At the Ritz-Carlton, for example, the firm's culture is supported and sustained through daily 15-minute meetings among employees—called "line-ups"—where they share stories and educate each other on better ways to serve customers. Ritz-Carlton employees can design their own work procedures and can personally attend to any guest's request.[25] This extreme form of decentralization is often called empowerment. Empowering employees means allowing them to make decisions on how to best perform their jobs. The strong organizational culture and a shared corporate vision ensure that empowered employees make the right decisions.

Although creating a strong culture does not happen overnight, it is absolutely necessary before employees can be empowered to make decisions. Employees must be trained and socialized to accept the firm's mission and to become a part of the firm's culture.[26] Despite the enormous amount of time involved in developing and using this approach to implementation, its rewards of increased effectiveness, efficiency, and increased employee commitment and morale are often well worth the investment.

To summarize, firms and their managers can use any one of these four approaches to implement marketing strategy. Each approach has advantages and disadvantages as outlined in Exhibit 9.3. The choice of an approach will depend heavily on the firm's resources, its current culture, and the manager's own personal preferences. Many managers don't want to give up control over decision making. For these managers,

---

EXHIBIT 9.3 Advantages and Disadvantages of Implementation Approaches

---

Implementation by Command

Basic Premise:	Marketing strategies are developed at the top of the organizational hierarchy and then passed to lower levels where frontline managers and employees are expected to implement them.
Advantages:	Reduces uncertainty and makes decision making easier
	Good when a powerful leader heads the firm
	Good when the strategy is simple to implement
Disadvantages:	Does not consider the feasibility of implementing the strategy
	Divides the firm into strategists and implementers
	Can create employee motivation problems

Implementation Through Change

Basic Premise:	The firm is modified in ways that will ensure the successful implementation of the chosen marketing strategy.
Advantages:	Specifically considers how the strategy will be implemented
	Considers how strategy and implementation affect each other
	Used successfully by a large number of firms
Disadvantages:	Clings to a "power-at-the-top" mentality
	Requires a skilled, persuasive leader
	Changes can take time to design and implement, leaving the firm vulnerable to changes in the marketing environment

Implementation Through Consensus

Basic Premise:	Different areas of the firm come together to "brainstorm" and develop the marketing strategy. Through collective agreement, a consensus is reached as to the overall direction of the firm.
Advantages:	Considers multiple opinions and viewpoints
	Increases firm-wide commitment to the strategy
	Moves some decision making closer to the front line of the firm
	Useful in complex, uncertain, and unstable environments
Disadvantages:	Some managers will not give up their authority
	Can lead to groupthink
	Slows down the strategy development and implementation process
	Requires open horizontal and vertical communication

Implementation as Organizational Cultural

Basic Premise:	Marketing strategy is a part of the overall mission and vision of the firm; therefore, the strategy is embedded in the firm's culture. Top executives manage the firm's culture to ensure that all employees are well versed in the firm's strategy.
Advantages:	Eliminates the barrier between strategists and implementers
	Increases employee commitment to organizational goals
	Allows for the empowerment of employees
	Can make marketing implementation much easier to accomplish
Disadvantages:	Must spend more money on employee selection and training
	Creating the necessary culture can be painful and time-consuming
	Quickly shifting to this approach can cause many internal problems

connecting implementation and culture may be out of the question. Regardless of the approach taken, one of the most important issues that a manager must face is how to deal with the people who have responsibility for implementing the marketing strategy. To examine this issue, we now turn our attention to internal marketing—an increasingly popular approach to marketing implementation.

Internal Marketing and Marketing Implementation

As more firms come to appreciate the importance of employees to marketing implementation, they have become disenchanted with traditional implementation approaches. Several factors have caused this change: U.S. businesses losing out to foreign competitors, high rates of employee turnover and its associated costs, and continuing problems in the implementation of marketing strategy. These problems have led many firms to adopt an internal marketing approach to marketing implementation.

The practice of internal marketing comes from service industries, where it was first used as a means of making all employees aware of the need for customer satisfaction. *Internal marketing* refers to the use of a marketing-like approach to motivate, coordinate, and integrate employees toward the implementation of the firm's marketing strategy. The goals of internal marketing are to: (1) help all employees understand and accept their roles in implementing the marketing strategy, (2) create motivated and customer-oriented employees, and (3) deliver external customer satisfaction.[27] Note that internal marketing explicitly recognizes that external customer satisfaction depends on the actions of the firm's internal customers—its employees.

The Internal Marketing Approach

In the internal marketing approach, every employee has two customers: external and internal. For retail store managers, for example, the people who shop at the store are external customers, whereas the employees who work in the store are the manager's internal customers. In order for implementation to be successful, the store manager must serve the needs of both customer groups. If the internal customers do not receive proper information and training about the strategy and are not motivated to implement it, then it is unlikely that the external customers will be satisfied completely.

This same pattern of internal and external customers takes place throughout all levels of the firm. Even the CEO is responsible for serving the needs of his or her internal and external customers. Thus, unlike traditional implementation approaches where the responsibility for implementation rests with the frontline of the firm, the internal marketing approach places this responsibility on all employees regardless of their level within the firm. In the end, successful marketing implementation comes from an accumulation of individual actions where all employees have responsibility for implementing the marketing strategy. Walmart founder Sam Walton was keenly aware of the importance of internal marketing. He visited Walmart stores on a regular basis, talking with customers and employees about how he could better serve their needs. He felt so strongly about the importance of his associates (his term for store personnel), that he always allowed them the opportunity to voice their concerns about changes in marketing activities. Sam had strong convictions that if he took good care of his associates, they would take good care of Walmart's customers.

The Internal Marketing Process

The process of internal marketing is straightforward and rests on many of the same principles used in traditional external marketing. As shown in Exhibit 9.4, internal marketing is an output of and input to both marketing implementation and the external marketing program. That is, neither the marketing strategy nor its implementation can be designed without a consideration for the internal marketing program.

The product, price, distribution, and promotion elements of the internal marketing program are similar to the elements in the external marketing program. Internal products refer generally to marketing strategies that must be "sold" internally. More specifically, however, internal products refer to any employee tasks, behaviors, attitudes, or values necessary to ensure implementation of the marketing strategy.[28] Implementation of a marketing strategy, particularly a new strategy, typically requires changes on the part of employees. They may have to work harder, change job assignments, or even change their attitudes and expand their abilities. The increased effort and changes that employees must exhibit in implementing the strategy are equivalent to internal prices. Employees pay these prices through what they must do, change, or give up when implementing the marketing strategy.

EXHIBIT 9.4   The Internal Marketing Process

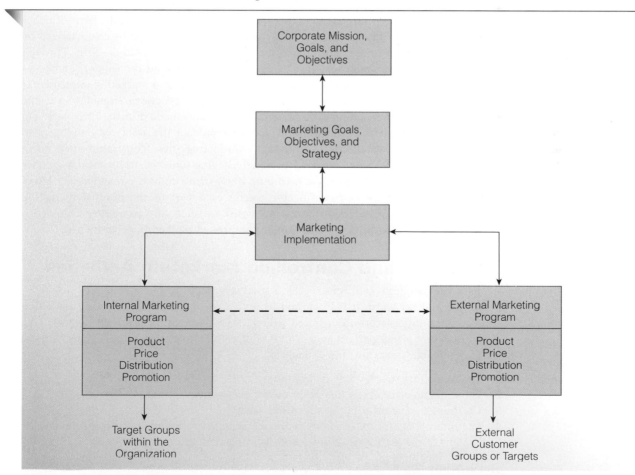

Source: Adapted from Nigel F. Piercy, *Market-Led Strategic Change* (Stoneham, MA: Butterworth-Heinemann, 2008), pp. 496–501.

Internal distribution refers to the internal interactions that disseminate the marketing strategy throughout the firm. Planning sessions, workshops, formal reports, and personal conversations are all examples of internal distribution. Internal distribution also includes employee education, training, and socialization programs designed to assist in the transition to a new marketing strategy. Finally, all communication aimed at informing and persuading employees about the merits of the marketing strategy comprise internal promotion. Internal promotion can take the form of executive speeches, video presentations, blogs, podcasts, or internal company newsletters. Given the growing diversity of today's employees, it is unlikely that any one medium will communicate with all employees successfully. Firms must realize that telling employees important information once in a single format is not good communication. Until the employees "get the strategy," communication has not taken place.

Successfully using an internal marketing approach requires an integration of many factors already discussed in this chapter. First, the recruitment, selection, and training of employees must be considered an important element of marketing implementation, with marketing having input to these human resource and personnel activities as necessary.[29] This ensures that employees will be matched to the marketing tasks to be performed. Second, top executives must be completely committed to the strategy and the overall marketing plan. It is naïve to expect employees to be committed when top executives are not. Simply put, the best-planned strategy in the world cannot succeed if the employees responsible for its implementation do not believe in it or have a commitment to it.[30]

Third, employee compensation programs must be linked to the implementation of the marketing strategy. This means that employees should be rewarded on the basis of behaviors consistent with the marketing strategy. Fourth, the firm should be characterized by open communication among all employees, regardless of their level in the firm. Through open, interactive communication, employees come to understand the support and commitment of top executives, and how their jobs fit into the overall marketing implementation process. Finally, the firm's structure, policies, and processes should match the marketing strategy to ensure that the strategy can be implemented in the first place. On some occasions, the firm's structure and policies constrain the ability of employees to implement the strategy effectively. Although eliminating these constraints may mean that employees should be empowered to creatively fine-tune the strategy or its implementation, empowerment should be used only if the firm's culture can support it. However, if a company uses empowerment correctly as a part of the internal marketing approach, the firm can experience more motivated, satisfied, and committed employees, as well as enhanced customer satisfaction and improved marketing performance.[31]

Evaluating and Controlling Marketing Activities

A marketing strategy can achieve its desired results only if implemented properly. *Properly* is the key word. It is important to remember that a firm's intended marketing strategy often differs from the realized strategy (the one that actually takes place). This also means that actual performance is often different from expectations. Typically, there are four possible causes for this difference:

1. The marketing strategy was inappropriate or unrealistic.
2. The implementation was inappropriate for the strategy.
3. The implementation process was mismanaged.
4. The internal and/or external environments changed substantially between the development of the marketing strategy and its implementation.

To reduce the difference between what actually happened and what the company expected—and to correct any of these four problems—marketing activities must be

---

EXHIBIT 9.5   A Framework for Marketing Control

Formal Controls: Control Activities Initiated by Management

Input controls—actions taken prior to implementation of the strategy

- Employee recruitment, selection, and training processes
- Human resource allocations
- Allocation of financial resources
- Capital outlays
- Research and development expenditures

Process controls—actions taken during implementation of the strategy

- Employee evaluation and compensation systems
- Employee authority and empowerment
- Internal communication programs
- Lines of authority/structure (organizational chart)
- Management commitment to the marketing plan
- Management commitment to employees

Output controls—evaluated after implementation of the strategy

- Formal performance standards (for example, sales, market share, and profitability)
- Marketing audits

Informal Controls: Unwritten Control Activities Initiated by Employees

Employee self-control—control based on personal expectations and goals

- Job satisfaction
- Organizational commitment
- Employee effort
- Commitment to the marketing plan

Social control—small-group control based on group norms and expectations

- Shared organizational values
- Social and behavioral norms in work groups

Cultural control—cultural control based on organizational norms and expectations

- Organizational culture
- Organizational stories, rituals, and legends
- Cultural change

Source: Adapted from Bernard J. Jaworski, "Toward a Theory of Marketing Control: Environmental Context, Control Types, and Consequences," *Journal of Marketing*, 52 (July 1988), pp. 23–39.

evaluated and controlled on an ongoing basis. Although the best way to handle implementation problems is to recognize them in advance, no manager can successfully recognize all of the subtle and unpredictable warning signs of implementation failure.

With that in mind, it is important that the potential for implementation failures be managed strategically by having a system of marketing controls in place that allows the firm to spot potential problems before they cause real trouble. Exhibit 9.5 outlines a framework for marketing control that includes two major types of control: formal controls and informal controls.[32] Although we discuss each type of marketing control separately, most firms use combinations of these control types to monitor strategy implementation.

Formal Marketing Controls

Formal marketing controls are activities, mechanisms, or processes designed by the firm to help ensure the successful implementation of the marketing strategy. The elements of formal control influence the behaviors of employees before and during implementation, and to assess performance outcomes at the completion of the implementation process. These elements are referred to as input, process, and output controls respectively.

Input Controls   Actions taken prior to the implementation of the marketing strategy are input controls. The premise of input control is that the marketing strategy cannot be implemented correctly unless the proper tools and resources are in place for it to succeed. Recruiting, selecting, and training employees are among the most important input controls. Another critical input control deals with financial resources. These control activities include resource allocation decisions (manpower and financial), capital outlays for needed facilities and equipment, and increased expenditures on research and development. Financial resources can make or break a marketing strategy or its implementation. For example, General Motors was quite slow to infuse additional capital into its Saturn division after it was first launched. For years, Saturn was unable to compete effectively due to constrained resources that limited its ability to develop and market new vehicles. A case in point: Saturn did not enter the highly profitable SUV market until 2002—long after its competitors. By the time GM did give Saturn additional resources, it was too late to repair the brand's tarnished image. General Motors later closed the Saturn division as a part of its corporate restructuring.

Process Controls   Process controls include activities that occur during implementation, designed to influence the behavior of employees so they will support the strategy and its objectives. Although the number of process controls is potentially limitless and will vary from one firm to the next, Exhibit 9.5 provides some examples of universal process controls that all firms must employ and manage well.

The process control that stands out above all others is management commitment to the strategy. Several research studies have confirmed that management commitment to the marketing strategy is the single most important determinant of whether the strategy will succeed or fail.[33] This commitment is critical because employees learn to model the behavior of their managers. If management is committed to the marketing strategy, it is more likely that employees will be committed to it as well. Commitment to the marketing strategy also means that managers must be committed to employees and support them in their efforts to implement the strategy.

Another important process control is the system used to evaluate and compensate employees. In general, employees should be evaluated and compensated based on criteria relevant to the marketing strategy.[34] For example, if the strategy requires that salespeople increase their efforts at customer service, they should be rewarded on the basis of this effort, not on other criteria such as sales volume or the number of new accounts created. Further, the degree of authority and empowerment granted to employees is another important process control. Although some degree of empowerment can lead to increased performance, employees given too much authority often become confused and dissatisfied with their jobs.[35] Having good internal communication programs—another type of process control—can help to alleviate these problems.

Output Controls   Output controls ensure that marketing outcomes are in line with anticipated results. The primary means of output control involves setting performance standards against which actual performance can be compared. To ensure an accurate assessment of marketing activities, all performance standards should be based on the firm's marketing objectives. Some performance standards are broad, such as those based on sales, profits, or expenses. We say these are broad standards because many different marketing activities can affect them. Other performance standards are quite specific, such as many customer service standards (e.g., number of customer complaints,

Time-based performance measures are commonly used in evaluating and controlling marketing activities.

repair service within 24 hours, overnight delivery by 10:00 A.M., on-time airline arrivals). In most cases, how the firm performs relative to these specific standards will determine how well it performs relative to broader standards.

But how specific should performance standards be? Standards should reflect the uniqueness of the firm and its resources, as well as the critical activities needed to implement the marketing strategy. In setting performance standards, it is important to remember that employees are always responsible for implementing marketing activities, and ultimately the marketing strategy. For example, if an important part of increasing customer service requires that employees answer the telephone by the second ring, then a performance standard should be set for this activity. Standards for the performance of marketing personnel are typically the most difficult to establish and enforce.

One of the best methods of evaluating whether performance standards have been achieved is to use a marketing audit to examine systematically the firm's marketing objectives, strategy, and performance.[36] The primary purpose of a marketing audit is to identify problems in ongoing marketing activities and to plan the necessary steps to correct these problems. A marketing audit can be long and elaborate, or it can be short and simple. Exhibit 9.6 displays a sample marketing audit. In practice, the elements of the audit must match the elements of the marketing strategy. The marketing audit should also be used to gauge the success of ongoing implementation activities—not just when problems arise.

EXHIBIT 9.6   A Sample Marketing Audit

Marketing Activities

1. In what specific marketing activities is the company currently engaged?

   - Product activities: research, concept testing, test marketing, quality control, etc.
   - Customer service activities: installation, training, maintenance, technical support, complaint handling, etc.
   - Pricing activities: financing, billing, cost control, discounting, etc.
   - Distribution activities: availability, channels used, customer convenience, etc.
   - Promotion activities: media, sales promotion, personal selling, public relations, etc.

2. Are these activities conducted solely by the company, or are some provided by outside contractors (either domestically or offshore)? If outside contractors are used, how are they performing? Should any of these outside activities be brought in-house?

3. What marketing activities do our competitors conduct that we do not offer? What additional marketing activities do customers want, need, or expect?

Standard Procedures for Each Marketing Activity

1. Do written procedures (manuals) exist for each marketing activity? If so, are these procedures (manuals) up to date? Do employees fully understand and follow these procedures (manuals)?

2. What oral or unwritten procedures exist for each marketing activity? Should these procedures be formally included in the written procedures or should they be eliminated?

3. Do marketing personnel regularly interact with other functional areas to establish standard procedures for each activity?

Performance Standards for Each Marketing Activity

1. What specific quantitative standards exist for each activity?
2. What qualitative standards exist for each activity?
3. How does each activity contribute to customer satisfaction within each marketing program element (i.e., product, pricing, distribution, promotion)?
4. How does each activity contribute to marketing goals and objectives?
5. How does each activity contribute to the goals and objectives of the company?

Performance Metrics for Each Marketing Activity

1. What are the internal, profit-based measures for each marketing activity?
2. What are the internal, time-based measures for each marketing activity?
3. How is performance monitored and evaluated internally by management?
4. How is performance monitored and evaluated externally by customers?

Evaluation of Marketing Personnel

1. Are the company's current recruiting, selection, and retention efforts consistent (matched) with the requirements of the marketing activities?

2. What are the nature and content of employee training activities? Are these activities consistent with the requirements of the marketing activities?

3. How are customer-contact personnel supervised, evaluated, and rewarded? Are these procedures consistent with customer requirements?

4. What effect do employee evaluation and reward policies have on employee attitudes, satisfaction, and motivation?

5. Are current levels of employee attitudes, satisfaction, and motivation adequate?

continued

EXHIBIT 9.6 (*continued*)

Evaluation of Customer Support Systems

1. Are the quality and accuracy of customer service materials (e.g., instruction manuals, brochures, letters, etc.) consistent with the image of the company and its products?
2. Are the quality and appearance of physical facilities (e.g., offices, furnishings, layout, store decor, etc.) consistent with the image of the company and its products?
3. Are the quality and appearance of customer service equipment (e.g., repair tools, telephones, computers, delivery vehicles, etc.) consistent with the image of the company and its products?
4. Is the record keeping system accurate? Is the information always readily available when it is needed? What technology could be acquired to enhance record keeping abilities (e.g., bar code scanners, RFID, notebook computers, wireless telephones or smartphones)?

Regardless of the organization of the marketing audit, it should aid the firm in evaluating marketing activities by:

1. Describing current marketing activities and their performance outcomes;
2. Gathering information about changes in the external or internal environments that may affect ongoing marketing activities;
3. Exploring different alternatives for improving the ongoing implementation of marketing activities;
4. Providing a framework to evaluate the attainment of performance standards, as well as marketing goals and objectives.

The information in a marketing audit is often obtained through a series of questionnaires that are given to employees, managers, customers, and/or suppliers. In some cases, outside consultants perform this ongoing evaluation. Using outside auditors has the advantages of being more objective and less time consuming for the firm. However, outside auditors are typically quite expensive. A marketing audit can also be very disruptive, especially if employees are fearful of the scrutiny.

Despite their drawbacks, marketing audits are usually quite beneficial for the firms that use them. They are flexible in that the scope of the audit can be broad (to evaluate the entire marketing strategy) or narrow (to evaluate only a specific element of the marketing program). The results of the audit can be used to reallocate marketing efforts, correct implementation problems, or even to identify new opportunities. The end results of a well-executed marketing audit are usually better marketing performance and increased customer satisfaction.

Informal Marketing Controls

Formal marketing controls are overt in their attempt to influence employee behavior and marketing performance. Informal controls, on the other hand, are more subtle. *Informal marketing controls* are unwritten, employee-based mechanisms that subtly affect the behaviors of employees, both as individuals and in groups.[37] Here, we deal with personal objectives and behaviors, as well as group-based norms and expectations. There are three types of informal control: employee self-control, social control, and cultural control.

Employee Self-Control Through employee self-control, employees manage their own behaviors (and thus the implementation of the marketing strategy) by establishing personal objectives and monitoring their results. The type of personal objectives that employees set depends on how they feel about their jobs. If they have high job satisfaction and a strong commitment to the firm, they are more likely to establish personal objectives that are consistent with the aims of the firm, the marketing strategy, and the firm's goals and objectives. Employee self-control also depends on the rewards employees receive. Some employees prefer the intrinsic rewards of doing a good job rather than the extrinsic rewards of pay and recognition. Intrinsically rewarded employees are likely to exhibit more self-control by managing their behaviors in ways that are consistent with the marketing strategy.

Social Control   Social, or small group, control deals with the standards, norms, and ethics found in workgroups within the firm.[38] The social interaction that occurs within these workgroups can be a powerful motivator of employee behavior. The social and behavioral norms of workgroups provide the "peer pressure" that causes employees to conform to expected standards of performance. If employees fall short of these standards, the group will pressure them to align with group norms. This pressure can be both positive and negative. Positive group influence can encourage employees to increase their effort and performance in ways consistent with the firm's goals and objectives. However, the opposite is also true. If the workgroup's norms encourage slacking or shirking of job responsibilities, employees will feel pressured to conform, or risk being ostracized for good work.

Cultural Control   Cultural control is very similar to social control, only on a much broader scale. Here, we are interested in the behavioral and social norms of the entire firm. One of the most important outcomes of cultural control is the establishment of shared values among all members of the firm. Marketing implementation is most effective and efficient when every employee, guided by the same organizational values or beliefs, has a commitment to the same organizational goals.[39] Companies such as Lockheed Martin and Lexmark have strong organizational cultures that guide employee behavior. Unfortunately, cultural control is very difficult to master, in that it takes a great deal of time to create the appropriate organizational culture to ensure implementation success.

It is important to note that the formal controls employed by the firm affect, to a great extent, the informal controls that occur within an organization. However, the premise of informal control is that some aspects of employee behavior cannot be influenced by formal mechanisms, and therefore must be controlled informally through individual and group actions. *Beyond the Pages 9.3* describes how formal and informal controls overlap to promote risk management principles in today's astute organizations.

Scheduling Marketing Activities

Through good planning and organization, marketing managers can provide purpose, direction, and structure to all marketing activities. However, the manager must understand the problems associated with implementation, understand the coordination of the various components of implementation, and select an overall approach to implementation before actually executing marketing activities. Upon taking these steps, the marketing manager with the responsibility for executing the plan must establish a timetable for the completion of each marketing activity.

Successful implementation requires that employees know the specific activities for which they are responsible and the timetable for completing each activity. Creating a master schedule of marketing activities can be a challenging task because of the wide variety of activities required to execute the plan, the sequential nature of many activities (some take precedence over others and must be performed first), and the fact that time is of the essence in implementing the plan.[41] The basic steps involved in creating a schedule and timeline for implementation include:

Beyond the Pages 9.3

Managing Risk Through Culture[40]

Given the many examples of corporate misconduct and lapses in managerial judgment over the past five to ten years, top executives have become keenly aware of the importance of managing corporate risk. The risks that today's organizations face come in many forms: financial risk, insurance risk, operational risk, product liability risk, strategic risks, reputational risks, etc. As top executives try to better understand the stakes in enterprise risk management, they are beginning to realize that managing risk involves more than making the right decisions in the boardroom. True risk management involves assessing the risk culture of the entire firm.

Experts define risk culture as a system of values and behaviors within an organization that shape risk decisions. An organization's risk culture influences everyone, whether they are aware of it or not. It is this lack of awareness that creates potential problems. Even seemingly small decisions can have implications for corporate risk. The key is to ensure that all employees have a common understanding of risk, and how it is potentially connected to their day-to-day activities.

Sadly, the evidence suggests that most organizations do a poor job of nurturing their risk cultures. While 84 percent of firms include risk management in C-suite discussions, 58 percent of top executives stated that their middle- and lower-level employees had little to no understanding of their company's risk exposure. One-third said that even top managers had no formal risk training. Without training and an open dialogue about risk, organizations cannot ensure that well-informed and consistent decisions about risk occur throughout the firm.

How can an organization inspire a risk culture? Some suggested guidelines include:

- **Set the Tone at the Top and the Middle**. A key axiom of management is that leaders communicate their priorities through what they measure, discuss, praise and criticize. These aspects of "setting the tone" are important because they provide examples for other employees to follow. However, this tone must emanate from all managers, not just those in

the boardroom. The organization and its leaders must have a clearly articulated risk policy, as well as clear penalties for non-compliant behavior.

- **Understand the Difference Between Good and Bad Risk**. Risk management has the potential to stifle an organization's creativity. Thus, it is critical that all employees understand the difference between acceptable risk based on innovation and reckless behavior that jeopardizes the organization. The firm must also encourage and be willing to tolerate mistakes, and then learn from them.

- **Promote Open Communication About Risk**. Creating the proper risk culture requires consistent messages to employees about risk, and the importance of managing risk as a part of daily operations. This means that collaboration is essential in order to mitigate the ambiguity and competitiveness that typically lead to overly risky decisions.

- **Give Employees Incentives to Manage Risk**. Giving proper incentives to manage risk is important. However, it is often more important to eliminate any incentives that reward reckless behavior. This applies to everyone in the organization—from the boardroom to the mailroom.

- **Consider the Risk Cultures of Potential Partners**. To manage risk fully, an organization must ensure that its vendors, suppliers, and strategic partners share its risk tolerances. Risk should always be a consideration in choosing new partners or suppliers. Note that this also applies to the company's most important partners—its employees. Risk should always be a consideration in the hiring process.

Having a strong risk culture means that everyone knows the principles and boundaries within which the organization operates. It means that risk is openly discussed and weighed in all decisions. It ensures that everyone stays on the right path. However, creating this type of culture takes a great deal of patience and time. But then again, the crises that result from poor risk management are often far more costly in terms of time, money, and corporate reputation.

1. **Identify the Specific Activities to Be Performed**. These activities include all marketing program elements contained within the marketing plan. Specific implementation activities, such as employee training, structural changes, or the acquisition of financial resources, should be included as well.

2. **Determine the Time Required to Complete Each Activity**. Some activities require planning and time before they can come to fruition. Others can occur rather quickly after the initiation of the plan.
3. **Determine Which Activities Must Precede Others**. Many marketing activities must be performed in a predetermined sequence (such as creating an advertising campaign from copywriting, to production, to delivery). These activities must be identified and separated from any activities that can be performed concurrently with other activities.
4. **Arrange the Proper Sequence and Timing of All Activities**. In this step, the manager plans the master schedule by sequencing all activities and determining when each activity must occur.
5. **Assign Responsibility**. The manager must assign one or more employees, teams, managers, or departments to each activity and charge them with the responsibility of executing the activity.

A simple, but effective way to create a master implementation schedule is to incorporate all marketing activities into a spreadsheet, like the one shown in Exhibit 9.7. A master schedule such as this can be simple or complex depending on the level of detail

EXHIBIT 9.7   A Hypothetical Three-Month Marketing Implementation Schedule

Month		March				April				May			
Activities	*Week*	1	2	3	4	1	2	3	4	1	2	3	4
Product Activities													
Finalize package changes		•											
Production runs		•	•			•	•			•	•		
Pricing Activities													
Hold 10% off sale at retail							•						
Hold 25% off sale at retail												•	
Distribution Activities													
Shipments to warehouses		•		•		•		•		•		•	
Shipments to retail stores			•		•		•		•		•		•
10% quantity discount to the trade		•	•	•	•	•	•	•	•	•	•	•	•
Promotion Activities													
Website operational		•											
Ongoing sponsorship		•	•	•	•	•	•	•	•	•	•	•	•
Television advertising			•	•			•	•			•	•	
Online advertising		•		•		•		•		•		•	
Mobile coupon					•					•			
In-store displays			•	•		•			•	•			•
Product placement		•	•	•	•	•	•	•	•	•	•	•	•

included within each activity. The master schedule will also be unique to the specific marketing plan tied to it. As a result, a universal template for creating a master schedule does not truly exist.

Although some activities must be performed before others, other activities can be performed concurrently with other activities or later in the implementation process. This requires tight coordination between departments—marketing, production, advertising, sales, and so on—to ensure the completion of all marketing activities on schedule. Pinpointing those activities that can be performed concurrently can greatly reduce the total amount of time needed to execute a given marketing plan. Because scheduling can be a complicated task, most firms use sophisticated project management techniques, such as PERT (program evaluation and review technique), CPM (critical path method), or computerized planning programs, to schedule the timing of marketing activities.

Lessons from Chapter 9

Marketing implementation:

- is critical to the success of any firm because it is responsible for putting the marketing strategy into action.
- has been somewhat ignored throughout the history of business as most firms have emphasized strategic planning rather than strategic implementation.
- is the process of executing the marketing strategy by creating and performing specific actions that will ensure the achievement of the firm's marketing objectives.
- goes hand-in-hand with evaluation and control in determining the success or failure of the marketing strategy, and ultimately for the entire firm.
- is usually the cause for the difference between intended marketing strategy—what the firm wants to happen—and realized marketing strategy—the strategy that actually takes place.
- maintains a relationship with strategic planning that causes three major problems: interdependency, evolution, and separation.

The elements of marketing implementation include:

- Marketing strategy—the firm's planned product, pricing, distribution, and promotion activities.
- Shared goals and values—the glue of implementation that holds the entire firm together as a single, functioning unit.
- Marketing structure—how the firm's marketing activities are organized.
- Systems and processes—collections of work activities that absorb a variety of inputs to create information and communication outputs that ensure the consistent day-to-day operation of the firm.
- Resources—include a wide variety of tangible and intangible assets that can be brought together during marketing implementation.

- People—the quality, diversity, and skill of a firm's human resources. The people element also includes employee selection and training, evaluation and compensation, motivation, satisfaction, and commitment.
- Leadership—how managers communicate with employees, as well as how they motivate their employees to implement the marketing strategy.

Approaches to implementing marketing strategy include:

- Implementation by command—marketing strategies are developed and selected by the firm's top executives, then transmitted to lower levels where frontline managers and employees are expected to implement them.
- Implementation through change—focuses explicitly on implementation by modifying the firm in ways that will ensure the successful implementation of the chosen marketing strategy.
- Implementation through consensus—upper- and lower-level managers from different areas of the firm work together to evaluate and develop marketing strategies.
- Implementation as organizational culture—marketing strategy and implementation are seen as extensions of the firm's mission, vision, and organizational culture. Employees at all levels can participate in making decisions that help the firm reach its mission, goals, and objectives.

Internal marketing:

- refers to the use of a marketing-like approach to motivate, coordinate, and integrate employees toward the implementation of the firm's marketing strategy.
- explicitly recognizes that external customer satisfaction depends on the actions of the firm's internal customers—its employees. If the internal customers are not properly educated about the strategy and motivated to implement

it, then it is unlikely that the external customers will be satisfied completely.

- places the responsibility for implementation on all employees regardless of their level within the firm.
- is based on many of the same principles used in traditional external marketing. The product, price, distribution, and promotion elements of the internal marketing program are similar to the elements in the external marketing program.

In evaluating and controlling marketing activities:

- the firm's intended marketing strategy often differs from the realized strategy for four potential reasons: (1) the marketing strategy was inappropriate or unrealistic, (2) the implementation was inappropriate for the strategy, (3) the implementation process was mismanaged, or (4) the internal and/or external environments changed substantially between the development of the marketing strategy and its implementation.
- it is important that the potential for implementation failures be managed strategically by having a system of marketing controls in place.
- firms design and use formal input, process, and output controls to help ensure the successful implementation of the marketing strategy.

- firms use output controls, or performance standards, extensively to ensure that marketing outcomes are in line with anticipated results.
- employees individually (self-control), in workgroups (social control), and throughout the firm (cultural control) use personal objectives and group-based norms and expectations to informally control their behaviors.

Scheduling marketing activities:

- requires that employees know the specific activities for which they are responsible and the timetable for completing each activity.
- can be a challenging task because of the wide variety of activities required to execute the plan, the sequential nature of many marketing activities, and the fact that time is of the essence in implementing the plan.
- involves five basic steps: (1) identifying the specific activities to be performed, (2) determining the time required to complete each activity, (3) determining which activities must precede others, (4) arranging the proper sequence and timing of all activities, and (5) assigning responsibility to employees, managers, teams, or departments.

Questions for Discussion

1. Forget for a moment that planning the marketing strategy is equally as important as implementing the marketing strategy. What arguments can you make for one being more important than the other? Explain your answers.

2. If you were personally responsible for implementing a particular marketing strategy, which implementation approach would you be most comfortable using, given your personality and personal preferences? Why? Would your chosen approach be universally applicable to any given situation? If not, what would cause you to change or

adapt your approach? Remember, adapting your basic approach means stepping out of your personal comfort zone to match the situation at hand.

3. What do you see as the major stumbling blocks to the successful use of the internal marketing approach? Given the hierarchical structure of employees in most organizations (e.g., CEO, middle management, staff employees), is internal marketing a viable approach for most organizations? Why or why not?

Exercises

1. Find a recent news article about an organization that changed its marketing strategy. What were the reasons for the change? How did the organization approach the development and implementation of the new strategy?

2. One of the best sources for shared goals and values to guide implementation is the firm's own mission or values statement. Find the mission or values statement for the organization you identified in

Exercise 1. Do you see evidence of the mission or values in the way the organization handled its change in marketing strategy? Explain.

3. Think about the unwritten, informal controls in your life. Develop a list of the controls that exist at work, at home, or at school (or substitute another context such as church, social gatherings, or public activities). Are these controls similar or different? Why?

	Controls at Work	Controls at Home	Controls at School
Self Control (personal norms and expectations for behavior)			
Social Control (norms and expectations in small groups)			
Cultural Control (norms and expectations in the entire organization)			

End Notes

1. These facts are from Green Mountain Coffee, 2011 Annual Report (http://investor.gmcr.com/common/download/download.cfm?companyid=GMCR&fileid=540307&filekey=C799E76F-7E06-418D-9BB2-B105A85EE3EA&filename=GMCR_AnnualReport_2011.pdf), accessed June 3, 2012; Green Mountain Coffee Roasters website (http://www.greenmountaincoffee.com), accessed June 3, 2012; Leslie Patton, "Green Mountain's Expiring K-Cup Patents Attract Coffee Rivals," *Bloomberg Businessweek*, November 21, 2011 (http://www.businessweek.com/news/2011-11-21/green-mountain-s-expiring-k-cup-patents-attract-coffee-rivals.html); and Leslie Patton, "Green Mountain Introduces Nestle-Rival Keurig Latte Brewer," *Bloomberg Businessweek*, February 15, 2012 (http://www.businessweek.com/news/2012-02-15/green-mountain-introduces-nestle-rival-keurig-latte-brewer.html).

2. Orville C. Walker, Jr. and Robert W. Ruekert, "Marketing's Role in the Implementation of Business Strategies: A Critical Review and Conceptual Framework," *Journal of Marketing* 51 (July 1987), 15–33.

3. Frank V. Cespedes, *Organizing and Implementing the Marketing Effort* (Reading, MA: Addison-Wesley, 1991), 19.

4. Robert Howard, "Values Make the Company: An Interview with Robert Haas," *Harvard Business Review* 68 (September–October 1990): 132–144.

5. See the New Belgium Brewery website (http://www.newbelgium.com).

6. Michael D. Hartline, James G. Maxham, III, and Daryl O. McKee, "Corridors of Influence in the Dissemination of Customer-Oriented Strategy to Customer Contact Service Employees," *Journal of Marketing* 64 (April 2000), 35–50.

7. Ibid.

8. Cespedes, *Organizing and Implementing the Marketing Effort*, 622–623.

9. Robert W. Ruekert, Orville C. Walker, Jr., and Kenneth J. Roering, "The Organization of Marketing Activities: A Contingency Theory of Structure and Performance," *Journal of Marketing* 49 (Winter 1985), 13–25.

10. Hartline, Maxham, and McKee, "Corridors of Influence."

11. Michael Hammer and James Champy, *Reengineering the Corporation: A Manifesto for Business Revolution* (New York: Harper Business, 1993), 35.

12. Jena McGregor, "How Failure Breeds Success," *BusinessWeek Online*, July 10, 2006 (http://www.businessweek.com/magazine/content/06_28/b3992001.htm?chan=innovation_innovation+%2B+design_the+creative+corporation).

13. Myron Glassman and Bruce McAfee, "Integrating the Personnel and Marketing Functions: The Challenge of the 1990s," *Business Horizons* 35 (May–June 1992), 52–59.

14. Michael D. Hartline and O. C. Ferrell, "Service Quality Implementation: The Effects of Organizational Socialization and Managerial Actions on Customer-Contact Employee Behaviors," *Marketing Science Institute Working Paper Series*, Report No. 93–122 (Cambridge, MA: Marketing Science Institute, 1993).

15. Richard L. Oliver and Erin Anderson, "An Empirical Test of the Consequences of Behavior- and Outcome-Based Sales Control Systems," *Journal of Marketing* 58 (October 1994), 53–67.

16. Hartline, Maxham, and McKee, "Corridors of Influence."

17. Adam Lashinsky, "The Perks of Being a Googler," *Fortune* (CNNMoney.com) (http://money.cnn.com/galleries/2007/fortune/0701/gallery.Google_perks), accessed August 13, 2009; and Dorian Wales, "How to Create the Environment of Organizational Commitment," *Helium* (http://www.helium.com/items/706133-how-to-create-the-environment-of-organizational-commitment), accessed August 13, 2009.

18. These facts are from Ram Charan, "The New (Recovery) Playbook," *Fortune* (CNNMoney.com), August 13, 2009 (http://money.cnn.com/2009/08/11/news/economy/new_rules_recovery.fortune/index.htm); Betsy Morris, "The New Rules," *Fortune*, July 24, 2006, 70–87; and Betsy Morris, "Tearing Up the Jack Welch Playbook," *Fortune* (CNNMoney.com), July 11, 2006 (http://money.cnn.com/2006/07/10/magazines/fortune/rules.fortune/index.htm).

19. W. Chan Kim and Renee Mauborgne, *Blue Ocean Strategy* (Boston, MA: Harvard Business School Press, 2005).

20. The material in this section has been adapted from L. J. Bourgeois III and David R. Brodwin, "Strategic Implementation: Five Approaches to an Elusive Phenomenon," *Strategic Management Journal* 5 (1984), 241–264; and Steven W. Floyd and Bill Wooldridge, "Managing Strategic Consensus: The Foundation of Effective Implementation," *Academy of Management Executive* 6 (November 1992), 27–39.

21. These facts are from Emily Bryson York, "McD's Dollar-Menu Fixation Sparks Revolt," *Advertising Age*, (79) June 2, 2008, 1-2; and Trefis Team, "McDonald's Sales Sizzle But Franchisees Get Fried By Lower Profit Margins," *Forbes*, January 13, 2011 (http://www.forbes.com/sites/greatspeculations/2011/01/13/mcdonalds-sales-sizzle-but-franchisees-get-fried-by-lower-profit-margins).

22. These facts are from "Brand-Led Marketing: Samsung Viewpoint," *Marketing Week*, July 2, 2009, p. 18; Karlene Lukovitz, "Fastest-Growing Brands Are 'Ideal-Driven,'" *Marketing Daily*, January 18, 2012 (http://www.mediapost.com/publications/article/165965/fastest-growing-brands-are-ideal-driven.html); and "What Samsung's Success Means for Apple," *Forbes*, May 9, 2012 (http://www.forbes.com/sites/investor/2012/05/09/what-samsungs-success-means-for-apple).

23. George Bradt, "Royal Caribbean's CEO Exemplifies How to Leverage Milestones," *Forbes*, March 23, 2011 (http://www.forbes.com/sites/georgebradt/2011/03/23/royal-caribbean-cruise-lines-ceo-richard-fain-exemplifies-how-to-leverage-milestones-to-build-ships-and-teams).

24. Bourgeois and Brodwin, "Strategic Implementation: Five Approaches to an Elusive Phenomenon."

25. Carmine Gallo, "Wow Your Customers the Ritz-Carlton Way," *Forbes*, February 23, 2011 (http://www.forbes.com/sites/carminegallo/2011/02/23/wow-your-customers-the-ritz-carlton-way).

26. Hartline, Maxham, and McKee, "Corridors of Influence."

27. This information is from Mohammed Rafiq and Pervaiz K. Ahmed, "Advances in the Internal Marketing Concept: Definition, Synthesis and Extension," *Journal of Services Marketing*, Vol. 14 (2000), 449–463.

28. Ibid.

29. Glassman and McAfee, "Integrating the Personnel and Marketing Functions."

30. Howard, "Values Make the Company."

31. Hartline and Ferrell, "Service Quality Implementation."

32. This section is based on material from Hartline, Maxham, and McKee, "Corridors of Influence"; and Bernard J. Jaworski, "Toward a Theory of Marketing Control: Environmental Context, Control Types, and Consequences," *Journal of Marketing* 52 (July 1988), 23–39.

33. Ibid; and Brian P. Niehoff, Cathy A. Enz, and Richard A. Grover, "The Impact of Top-Management Actions on Employee Attitudes and Perceptions," *Group & Organization Studies* 15 (September 1990), 337–352.

34. Michael D. Hartline and O. C. Ferrell, "The Management of Customer-Contact Service Employees: An Empirical Investigation," *Journal of Marketing* 60 (October 1996): 52–70.

35. Ibid.

36. Ben M. Enis and Stephen J. Garfein, "The Computer-Driven Marketing Audit," *Journal of Management Inquiry* (December 1992), 306–318; and Philip Kotler, William Gregor, and William Rodgers, "The Marketing Audit Comes of Age," *Sloan Management Review* 30 (Winter 1989), 49–62.

37. Jaworski, "Toward a Theory of Marketing Control."

38. Ibid.

39. Hartline, Maxham, and McKee, "Corridors of Influence."

40. These facts are from John Michael Farrell and Angela Hoon, "What's Your Company's Risk Culture," *BusinessWeek Online*, May 12, 2009 (http://www.businessweek.com/managing/content/may2009/ca20090512_720476.htm); Kevin Kelly, "The Key to Risk: It's All About Emotion," *Forbes*, February 23, 2009 (http://www.forbes.com/2009/02/23/risk-culture-crisis-leadership-management_innovation.html); Karen E. Klein, "Using Risk Management to Beat the Downturn," *BusinessWeek Online*, January 9, 2009 (http://www.businessweek.com/smallbiz/content/jan2009/sb2009018_717265.htm); Arvin Maskin, "Creating a Culture of Risk Avoidance," *BusinessWeek Online*, March 6, 2009 (http://www.businessweek.com/managing/content/mar2009/ca2009036_914216.htm); and Max Rudolph, "What Do Risk Officers Worry About?" *Reuters*, May 18, 2012 (http://blogs.reuters.com/great-debate/2012/05/18/what-do-risk-officers-worry-about).

41. Jack R. Meredith and Scott M. Shafer, *Introducing Operations Management* (New York: John Wiley and Sons, Inc., 2003), 458.

CHAPTER **10**

Developing and Maintaining Long-Term Customer Relationships

Introduction

To this point in the text, we have examined the process of strategic planning from its initial stages through the implementation of the marketing plan. At this point, however, we take the opportunity to step back from the process to look at it holistically. Firms often lose sight of the big picture as they rush to complete product development and test marketing, or put the finishing touches on a media campaign. All of the activities involved in developing and implementing the marketing program have one key purpose: to develop and maintain long-term customer relationships. However, as we have seen, implementing a marketing strategy that can effectively satisfy customers' needs and wants has proven difficult in today's rapidly changing business environment. The simple fact is that thorough research, strong competitive advantages, and a well-implemented marketing program are often not enough to guarantee success.

In times past, developing and implementing the "right" marketing strategy was all about creating a large number of transactions with customers in order to maximize the firm's market share. Companies paid scant attention to discovering customers' needs and finding better ways to solve customers' problems. In today's economy, however, that emphasis has shifted to developing strategies that attract and retain customers over the long term. As illustrated in *Beyond the Pages 10.1*, 1-800-Flowers.com does this effectively through a comprehensive understanding of its customers, including their expectations, motivations, and behaviors. With this knowledge in hand, firms like 1-800-Flowers.com can then offer the right marketing program to increase customer satisfaction and retain customers over the long term.

In this chapter, we examine how the marketing program can be leveraged as a whole to deliver quality, value, and satisfaction to customers. We begin by reviewing the strategic issues associated with the customer relationship management process. Developing long-term customer relationships is one of the best ways to insulate the firm against competitive inroads and the rapid pace of environmental change and product commoditization. Next, we address the critical topics of quality and value as we concern ourselves with how the entire

1-800-Flowers.com Focuses on Customers[1]

Customer service. Trust. One-to-one customer interactions. Customer loyalty. These are the foundations of the steady growth of 1-800-Flowers.com for over 20 years. Since the company went online in 1991, CEO Jim McCann has used a laser-like focus on customers to make 1-800-Flowers the number one floral retailer in the world. McCann's company earned $690 million in 2011 and adds roughly 3 million new customers every year. The company also enjoys a very high rate of repeat business.

1-800-Flowers uses the Internet to connect to customers and puts a lot of effort into creating a 360-degree, holistic view of each one. The company collects customer information at every point where it contacts a customer—sales, loyalty programs, surveys, direct mail advertising, sales promotions (contests and sweepstakes), and affiliate programs (with florists, credit card companies, and airlines)—and uses it to create customized communications and product offerings for each of the roughly 40 million customers in its database. 1-800-Flowers uses a sophisticated segmentation system that analyzes transactional behaviors (recency, frequency, monetary) and combines it with gift buying behaviors. This information is then tied to each customer's psychographic profile to create targeted messages for each customer segment. The company then uses a variety of different metrics—financial, customer retention and acquisition, brand awareness, purchase intentions, and customer recommendations—to measure performance.

To increase customer loyalty, 1-800-Flowers launched Fresh Rewards, a point-based loyalty program. Customers earn one point for every dollar they spend, and then receive a Fresh Reward pass via email when they have accumulated 200 points.

There are also higher tiered programs for customers who spend $400 or $800 per year. The program is somewhat unique in that it offers only 1-800-Flowers merchandise as rewards. In addition to increasing customer loyalty, the Fresh Rewards program also allows the company to collect more in-depth information from customers.

To further develop customer relationships, 1-800-Flowers expanded its product mix well beyond floral products. The company now sells traditional gifts such as gift baskets, fruit bouquets, popcorn, cupcakes, cookies, chocolates, and baby gift baskets. Today, 36 percent of the company's sales come from non-floral products. To develop even stronger social links with customers, the company launched applications for multiple smartphones and an online store through Facebook.

For 1-800-Flowers, the key to success has been its ability to integrate and leverage the massive amount of data that it collects from its customers. However, CEO McCann also favors the old-school approach to understanding customers. McCann states that his training as a social worker helps him to understand the importance of solid relationships. True to his background, McCann regularly goes into the field to talk with customers. On key occasions such as Mother's Day and Valentine's Day, McCann and other executives answer the phones, deliver products, and work in the company's retail stores. McCann puts it this way: "Our competitors are all about the sales, we're about relationships. We are helping our customers connect with the important people in their lives through flowers and gifts created and designed for specific relationships, occasions, and sentiments. That's the difference."

marketing program is tied to these issues. Finally, we explore key issues with respect to customer satisfaction, including customer expectations and metrics for tracking customer satisfaction over time.

Managing Customer Relationships

As we briefly mentioned in Chapter 1, creating and maintaining long-term customer relationships requires that organizations see beyond the transactions that occur today to look at the long-term potential of a customer. To do this, the organization must strive to develop a relationship with each customer rather than generate a large number of discrete transactions. Before a relationship can be mutually beneficial to both the firm and the customer, it must provide value to both parties. This is one of the basic requirements of exchange noted in Chapter 1. Creating this value is the goal of *customer relationship management* (CRM), which is defined as a business philosophy aimed at defining and increasing customer value in ways that motivate customers to remain loyal.[2] In essence, CRM is about retaining the right customers. It is important to note that CRM does not focus solely on end customers. Rather, CRM involves a number of different groups:

- **Customers**. The end users of a product, whether they be businesses or individual consumers.
- **Employees**. Firms must manage relationships with their employees if they are to have any hope of fully serving customers' needs. This is especially true in service firms where employees *are* the service in the eyes of customers. Retaining key employees is a vital part of CRM.
- **Supply Chain Partners**. Virtually all firms buy and sell products upstream and/or downstream in the supply chain. This involves the procurement of materials or the sale of finished products to other firms. Either way, maintaining relationships with key supply chain partners is critical to satisfying customers.
- **External Stakeholders**. Relationships with key stakeholders must also be managed effectively. These include investors, government agencies, the media, nonprofit organizations, or facilitating firms that provide goods or services that help a firm achieve its goals.

Delivering good value to customers requires that firms use CRM strategies to effectively manage relationships with each of these groups. This effort includes finding ways to integrate all of these relationships toward the ultimate goal of customer satisfaction.

To fully appreciate the concepts behind customer relationship management, organizations must develop a new perspective on the customer—one that shifts the emphasis from "acquiring customers" to "maintaining clients" as shown in Exhibit 10.1. Although this strategic shift has been underway for some time in business markets, technological

EXHIBIT 10.1   Strategic Shift from Acquiring Customers to Maintaining Clients

Acquiring Customers	Maintaining Clients
Customers are "customers"	Customers are "clients"
Mass marketing	One-to-one marketing
Acquire new customers	Build relationships with current customers
Discrete transactions	Continuous transactions
Increase market share	Increase share of customer
Differentiation based on groups	Differentiation based on individual customers
Segmentation based on homogeneous needs	Segmentation based on heterogeneous needs
Short-term strategic focus	Long-term strategic focus
Standardized products	Mass customization
Lowest-cost provider	Value-based pricing strategy
One-way mass communication	Two-way individualized communication
Competition	Collaboration

advancements allow CRM to be fully embraced in consumer markets as well. Firms that are exceptionally good at developing customer relationships are said to possess "relationship capital"—a key asset that stems from the value generated by the trust, commitment, cooperation, and interdependence among relationship partners. With respect to competitive advantages, many see relationship capital as the most important asset that an organization can possess, as it represents a powerful advantage that can be leveraged to make the most of marketing opportunities.[3]

Developing Relationships in Consumer Markets

Developing long-term customer relationships can be an arduous process. Over the life of the relationship, the firm's goal is to move the customer through a progression of stages, as shown in Exhibit 10.2. The objective of CRM is to move customers from having a simple awareness of the firm and its product offering through levels of increasing relationship intensity, to the point where the customer becomes a true advocate for the firm and/or its products. Note that true CRM attempts to go beyond the creation of satisfied and loyal customers. Ultimately, the firm will possess the highest level of relationship capital when its customers become true believers or sponsors for the company and its products. For example, Harley-Davidson, which is now over 100 years old, is a great example of a firm that enjoys the highest levels of customer advocacy. Harley owners exhibit a cult-like

---

EXHIBIT 10.2   Stages of Customer Relationship Development

Relationship Stage	CRM Goals	Examples
Awareness	Promote customer knowledge and education about the product or company. Prospect for new customers.	Product advertising Personal selling (cold calls) Word of mouth
Initial purchase	Get product or company into customers' evoked set of alternatives. Stimulate interest in the product. Stimulate product trial.	Advertising Product sampling Personal selling
Repeat customer	Fully satisfy customers' needs and wants. Completely meet or exceed customers' expectations or product specifications. Offer incentives to encourage repeat purchase.	Good product quality and value-based pricing Good service before, during, and after the sale Frequent reminders and incentives
Client	Create financial bonds that limit the customer's ability to switch products or suppliers. Acquire more of each individual customer's business. Personalize products to meet evolving customer needs and wants.	Frequent customer cards Frequent-flier programs Broad product offering
Community	Create social bonds that prevent product or supplier switching. Create opportunities for customers to interact with each other in a sense of community.	Membership programs Affinity programs Ongoing personal communication
Advocacy	Create customization or structural bonds that encourage the highest degree of loyalty. Become such a part of the customer's life that he or she is not willing to end the relationship. Think of customers as partners.	Customer events and reunions Long-term contracts Brand-related memorabilia

Harley Davidson enjoys one of the highest levels of customer advocacy around the world.

love for the brand that most other companies do not possess. Other firms, such as Starbucks, Apple, Coca-Cola, and Nike also enjoy a high degree of customer advocacy.[4]

In consumer markets, one of the most viable strategies to build customer relationships is to increase the firm's *share of customer* rather than its market share. This strategy involves abandoning the old notions of acquiring new customers and increasing transactions to focus on more fully serving the needs of current customers. Financial services are a great example of this strategy in action. Most consumers purchase financial services from different firms. They bank at one institution, purchase insurance from a different institution, and handle their investments through another. To counter this fact of life, many companies now offer all of these services under one roof. For example, Regions Financial Corporation offers retail and commercial banking, trust, securities brokerage, mortgage and insurance products to customers in a network of over 1,700 offices in 16 states across the South, Midwest, and

Texas. Regions' commitment to relationships is evident in its product offerings such as "personal banking" and "relationship money market accounts."[5] Rather than focus exclusively on the acquisition of new customers, Regions tries to more fully serve the financial needs of its current customers, thereby acquiring a larger share of each customer's financial business. By creating these types of relationships, customers have little incentive to seek out competitive firms to fulfill their financial services needs. This relationship capital gives Regions an important strategic asset that can be leveraged as it competes with rival banks and financial institutions, both locally and online.

Focusing on share of customer requires an understanding that all customers have different needs; therefore, not all customers have equal value to a firm. The most basic application of this idea is the 80/20 rule: 20 percent of customers provide 80 percent of business profits. Although this idea is not new, advances in technology and data collection techniques now allow firms to profile customers in real-time. In fact, the ability to track customers in detail can allow the firm to increase sales and loyalty among the bottom 80 percent of customers. The goal is to rank the profitability of individual customers to express their lifetime value (LTV) to the firm. Some customers—those that require considerable handholding or that frequently return products—are simply too expensive to keep given the low level of profits they generate. These bottom-tier customers can be "fired" or required to pay very high fees for additional service. Banks and brokerages, for example, slap hefty maintenance fees on small accounts. This allows the firm to spend its resources to more fully develop relationships with its profitable customers.

The firm's top-tier customers (those that fall into the top 20 percent) are the most obvious candidates for retention strategies. These customers are the most loyal and the most profitable, so the firm should take the necessary steps to ensure their continuing satisfaction. Customers that fall just outside of this tier, or second-tier customers, can be encouraged to be better customers or even loyal customers with the right incentives. Exhibit 10.3 outlines strategies that can be used to enhance and maintain customer relationships. The most basic of these strategies is based on financial incentives that encourage increased sales and loyalty. However, financial incentives are easily copied by competitors and are not typically good for retaining customers in the long run. To achieve this ultimate goal, the firm must turn to strategies aimed at closely tying the customer to the firm. These structural connections are the most resilient to competitive action and the most important for maintaining long-term customer relationships.

Developing Relationships in Business Markets

Relationship management in business markets is much like that in consumer markets. The goal is to move business buyers through a sequence of stages, where each stage represents an increasing level of relationship intensity. Although business relationships may not approach the cult-like, emotional involvement found in some consumer markets, businesses could nonetheless become structurally bound to their supply chain partners. These relationships can give both parties an advantage with respect to relationship capital: One firm maintains a loyal and committed customer; the other maintains a loyal and committed supplier. Both parties may also consider each other to be strong partners or advocates within the entire supply chain.

Although our discussion certainly involves generalizations (e.g., some consumer marketers are better at building relationships than many business marketers), relationship development in business markets can be more involving, more complex, and much riskier than relationships in consumer markets. This occurs because business buyers typically have fewer options to choose from; and the financial risks are typically higher. For example, when computer processor maker AMD purchased ATI (a respected maker of graphics chips), the buying and partnering options for AMD, Intel, and other firms in

EXHIBIT 10.3   Strategies for Enhancing and Maintaining Customer Relationships

Increasing Relationship Intensity →			
	Financial Incentives	**Social Bonding**	**Enhanced Customization**	**Structural Bonding**

	Financial Incentives	**Social Bonding**	**Enhanced Customization**	**Structural Bonding**
Strategy	Using financial incentives to increase customer loyalty	Using social and psychological bonds to maintain a clientele	Using intimate customer knowledge to provide one-to-one solutions or mass customization	Creating customized product offerings that create a unique delivery system for each client
Examples	• Volume discounts • Coupons • Frequent-customer programs	• Membership programs • Customer-only events • Community outreach programs	• Customer reminder notifications • Personal recommendations • Personal shopping programs	• Structured, lock-step programs • Automated electronic transactions • Contractual relationships
Used by	• Airlines • Grocery retailers • Music clubs	• Health clubs • Churches • Credit cards	• Auto service centers • Electronic retailers • Department stores • Professional services	• Colleges and universities • Banks • Bundled telecom services
Advantages	• Effective in the short term • Easy to use	• Difficult for competitors to copy • Reduces brand switching	• Promotes strong loyalty and greatly reduces brand switching • Very difficult for competitors to copy customer knowledge	• Ultimate reduction in brand switching • Products become intertwined in customers' lifestyles
Disadvantages	• Easily imitated • Hard to end incentives once started • Can promote continual brand switching	• Social bonds take time to develop • Customer trust is critical and must be maintained at all times	• Can be quite expensive to deliver • Takes time to develop	• Customer resistance • Time-consuming and costly to develop

Sources: Based on Leonard L. Berry and A. Parasuraman. *Marketing Services: Competing Through Quality.* (The Free Press, 1991), 136–148; and Valerie Zeithaml, Mary Jo Bitner, and Dwayne Gremler. *Services Marketing: Integrating Customer Focus Across the Firm.* (New York: McGraw-Hill/Irwin, 2013), 160–166.

the computer industry changed overnight. Intel, not wanting to support its closest competitor, began working with NVIDIA (ATI's major competitor) in producing compatible chipsets for computers. Consequently, Apple's partnership with Intel meant that they also had to turn to NVIDIA for graphics chips. Later, Intel imbedded graphics capabilities into its own chipsets, further changing the partnering options in the industry.[6] The relatively small number of players in this industry means that firms are tightly integrated. This is also important due to the presence of long-term contractual obligations and the sheer dollars involved. These types of business relationships must be built on win–win strategies that focus on cooperation and improving the value of the exchange for both parties, not on strict negotiation strategies where one side wins and the other side loses.

Business relationships have become increasingly complex, as decisions must be made with an eye toward the entire supply chain, not just the two parties involved. In these cases, the relationships that are developed enhance the ability of the entire supply chain to better meet the needs of final customers. Over the past several years, a number of changes have occurred in business relationships, including:

- **A Change in Buyers' and Sellers' Roles**. To build stronger relationships, buyers and sellers have shifted away from competitive negotiation (trying to drive prices up or down) to focus on true collaboration. This represents a major change for many companies.
- **An Increase in Sole Sourcing**. Supplier firms will continue to sell directly to large customers or move to selling through systems suppliers that put together a set of products from various suppliers to deliver a comprehensive solution. The continuing growth in online e-procurement systems is one result of this trend.
- **An Increase in Global Sourcing**. More than ever, buyers and sellers scan the globe in search of suppliers or buyers that represent the best match with their specific needs and requirements. The relationship building process is so costly and complex that only the best potential partners will be pursued.
- **An Increase in Team-Based Buying Decisions**. Increasingly, teams from both buying and supplying firms make purchase decisions. These teams consist of employees from different areas of expertise that are central to the success of both firms. Increasingly, senior management of both firms will be represented on these teams as economic buyers for both sides play a major role in setting goals and objectives.
- **An Increase in Productivity Through Better Integration**. Firms that closely align their buying and selling operations have the capacity to identify and remove any inefficiency in the process. This increased productivity leads to a reduction in both hard and soft costs, thereby enhancing the profitability of both firms. This integration can be extended throughout the supply chain. In the future, only the most efficient supply chains will survive, particularly as more procurement moves into the electronic arena.

These fundamental changes in the structure of most business relationships will lead to dramatic changes in the way that organizations work together. Only those firms willing to make strategic, as opposed to cosmetic, changes in the way they deal with their customers or suppliers are likely to prosper as we move forward in this century.

Quality and Value: The Keys to Developing Customer Relationships

To build relationship capital, a firm must be able to fulfill the needs of its customers better than its competitors. It must also be able to fulfill those needs by offering high-quality goods and services that are a good value relative to the sacrifices customers must make to acquire them. When it comes to developing and maintaining customer relationships, quality is a double-edged sword. If the quality of a good or service is poor, the organization obviously has little chance of satisfying customers or maintaining relationships with them. The adage of "trying something at least once" applies here. A firm may be successful in generating first-time transactions with customers, but poor quality guarantees that repeat purchases will not occur. On the other hand, good quality is not an automatic guarantee of success. Think of it as a necessary but insufficient condition of successful customer relationship management. It is at this point where value becomes critical to maintaining long-term customer relationships.

Understanding the Role of Quality

Quality is a relative term that refers to the degree of superiority of a firm's goods or services. We say that quality is relative because it can only be judged in comparison to competing products, or when compared to an internal standard of excellence. The concept of quality also applies to many different aspects of a firm's product offering. The total product offering of any firm consists of at least three interdependent components, as illustrated in Exhibit 10.4: the core product, supplemental products, and symbolic and experiential attributes.

The Core Product   The heart of the offering, the core product, is the firm's *raison d'etre*, or justification for existence. As shown in Exhibit 10.4, the core can be a tangible good—such as a Chevy Silverado—or an intangible service—such as the Verizon Wireless communication network. Virtually every element of the marketing program has an effect on the quality (or perceived quality) of the core product; however, the firm's product and branding strategies are of utmost importance. Since the core product is the part of the offering that delivers the key benefits desired by customers, the form utility offered by the core product is vital to maintaining its quality. For example, the quality of an entrée in a restaurant depends on the form utility created through the combination of quality raw ingredients and expert preparation. In service offerings, the core product is typically composed of three interrelated dimensions:[7]

- **People**. The interaction among the customer, the firm's employees, and other customers present during service delivery.
- **Processes**. The operational flow of activities or steps in the service delivery process. Processes can be done through technology or face-to-face interaction.
- **Physical Evidence**. Any tangible evidence of the service including written materials, the service facility, people, or equipment. Includes the environment in which the service is delivered.

As a whole, service firms struggle daily with maintaining the quality of their core service offerings. Because services are so people-intensive, effective implementation of the

EXHIBIT 10.4   Components of the Total Product Offering

	Core Product	Supplemental Products	Symbolic and Experiential Attributes
Chevrolet Silverado 1500	Transportation Hauling/towing	Accessories GMAC financing Replacement parts OnStar	"The most dependable, longest-lasting full-size pickup on the road" "Chevy Runs Deep"
Verizon Wireless	Communication	Phone options Rate plan options "Friends and Family" 4G LTE	"Rule the Air" "America's largest and most reliable network"
John Deere Lawn Tractor	Lawn and garden maintenance	Accessories Financing Delivery	John Deere "Green" "Nothing Runs Like a Deere"
Michelin Tires	Tires Safety	Broad availability Installation Financing	"Because a lot is riding on your tires" "A Better Way Forward" The Michelin Man
Waldorf Astoria New York City	Lodging	Mid-Manhattan location on Park Avenue Restaurants Room service	"Peerless service and indulgent comfort" The first "Grand Hotel"

marketing strategy (through shared goals, employee motivation, and employee skills) is a major factor that helps to ensure consistency and quality. The quality of service also depends more on issues such as responsiveness to customer requests, consistent and reliable service over time, and the friendliness and helpfulness of the firm's employees. The quality of tangible goods depends more on issues such as durability, style, ease of use, comfort, or suitability for a specific need.

Whether a good or a service, the firm has little chance of success if its core product is of inferior quality. However, even providing a high quality core product is not enough to ensure customer satisfaction and long-term customer relationships. This occurs because customers expect the core product to be of high quality or at least at a level necessary to meet their needs. When the core product meets this level of expected quality, the customer begins to take it for granted. For example, customers take their telephone service for granted because they expect it to work every time. They only take notice when clarity becomes an issue, or when the service is unavailable. The same thing can be said for a grocery retailer who consistently delivers high quality food and service. Over time, the core product no longer stands out at a level that can maintain the customer relationship in the long term. It is at this point where supplemental products become critical.

Supplemental Products   Supplemental products are goods or services that add value to the core product, thereby differentiating the core product from competing product offerings. In most cases, supplemental products are extra features or benefits that enhance the total product experience; however, they are not necessary for the core product to function correctly. In many product categories, the true difference between competing products or brands lies in the supplemental products provided by the firm. For example, every hotel is capable of delivering the core product—a room with a bed in which to spend the night. Although the quality of the core product varies among hotels, the important differences lie in the supplemental products. Upscale hotels such as Hyatt or Hilton offer many amenities—such as spas, restaurants, health clubs, valet parking, and room service—that budget hotels like Motel 6 or Econolodge do not. Wireless phone service is another example. All wireless firms can fulfill their customers' communication needs; however, customers use supplemental products such as different phone options; rate plans; and freebies like rollover minutes, free roaming, and free long distance to differentiate one product offering from another. In business markets, supplemental services are often the most important factor in developing long-term relationships. Services such as financing, training, installation, and maintenance must be of top quality to ensure that business customers will continue to maintain a relationship with the supplier firm.

It is interesting to note that companies do not market many products with the core product in mind. When was the last time an automaker touted a car or truck on its ability to fulfill your transportation needs (i.e., getting you from Point A to Point B)? Rather, they focus on supplemental product attributes such as special financing, roadside assistance, and warranties. Supplemental products such as these depend heavily on the product, pricing, and distribution elements of the marketing program. For example, in addition to selling a wide range of name brand products, Amazon also offers its own credit card and free "super saver" shipping on many orders of $25 or more, or free shipping with an Amazon Prime membership. These supplemental services, along with 24/7 access and competitive pricing, make Amazon a formidable competitor in many different product categories.

Symbolic and Experiential Attributes   Marketers also use symbolic and experiential differences—such as image, prestige, and brand—to differentiate their products. These features are created primarily through the product and promotional elements of the marketing program. Without a doubt, the most powerful symbolic and experiential attributes are based on branding. In fact, many brands—like Mercedes, iPod, Ritz-Carlton, Coca-Cola, Rolex, Disney World, and Ruth's Chris Steak House—only need their names to get the message across. These brands have immense power in differentiating their products because they can project the entire product offering (core, supplemental, and symbolic/experiential) with one word or phrase. Other types of products don't necessarily rely upon branding, but on their uniqueness to convey their symbolic and experiential nature. Major sporting events, such as the Super Bowl, the NCAA Final Four, or the Tour de France are certainly good examples of this. Even local athletic events, such as high school football games, can have symbolic and experiential qualities if the rivalry is intense.

Delivering Superior Quality

Delivering superior quality day in and day out is one of the most difficult things that any organization can do with regularity. In essence, it is difficult to get everything right—even most of the time. During the 1980s and 1990s, strategic initiatives such as total quality management, ISO 9000, and the advent of the Baldrige Award were quite successful in changing the way businesses thought about quality. As a result, virtually every industry saw dramatic improvements in quality during that time.

Today, however, most businesses struggle with improving the quality of their products, whether they are the core product or supplemental products. As we discussed in Chapter 1, this has happened because: (1) customers have very high expectations about quality, (2) most products today compete in mature markets, and (3) many businesses compete in markets with very little real differentiation among product offerings. As products become further commoditized, it becomes very difficult for marketers to make their products stand out among a crowd of competitors. A great deal of research has been conducted to determine how businesses can improve the quality of their products. These four issues stand out:[8]

- **Understand Customers' Expectations**. It is not surprising that the basis of improving quality is also the starting point for effective customer relationship management. The delivery of superior quality begins with a solid understanding of customers' expectations. This means that marketers must stay in touch with customers by conducting research to better identify their needs and wants. Although this research can include large-scale efforts such as surveys or focus groups, it can also include simple and inexpensive efforts such as customer comment cards or having managers interact in a positive fashion with customers. Advances in technology have greatly improved marketers ability to collect and analyze information from individual customers. New tools such as data warehousing and data mining hold great promise in enabling firms to better understand customers' expectations and needs.
- **Translate Expectations Into Quality Standards**. Firms that can successfully convert customer information into quality standards ensure that they hear the voice of the customer. If customers want better ingredients, friendlier employees, or faster delivery, then standards should be set to match these desires. It is often the case, however, that managers set standards that meet organizational objectives with no consideration for customer expectations. As discussed in *Beyond the Pages 10.2*, this commonly occurs when managers set standards based on productivity, efficiency, or cost reductions rather than quality or customer service. In these cases, the temptation is to focus on internal benchmarks such as cost control or speed rather than customer benchmarks such as quality and satisfaction.

Beyond the Pages 10.2

Customer Service versus Efficiency[9]

As consumers, we are supposed to be living the good life. After all, we have access to an unprecedented variety and assortment of goods and services from around the globe. Everything we need is practically at arm's length and available 24/7. If things are so great, then why do we still suffer from poor service, long wait times, ignored complaints, and the feeling that we are just another number to most firms? In other words, why is customer service so bad? Are we just spoiled or do companies not care anymore?

While we may be spoiled and some companies might not care about service, the truth is that our own demands for convenient, fast, and low priced products are at odds with our demands for better customer service. As firms look to drive down costs and increase speed, they focus more on internal efficiency benchmarks based on costs and time-based measures of performance. This means they focus less on customer-driven benchmarks like quality, value, or satisfaction. This tendency is also driven by human nature: It is much easier to measure costs and time than something as subjective as customer satisfaction. As a result, more and more firms must continuously walk a fine line between service and operational efficiency.

Some companies successfully walk this line (Southwest Airlines is a good example). Others, however, have damaged customer relationships in their attempt to reduce costs. This has been especially true with the recent downturn in the economy. In some cases, firms have been forced to reduce customer service to maintain or improve profitability. Four recent examples are discussed below:

Hertz and Avis

After laying off 4,000 employees in early 2009, Hertz's customers were faced with a shortage of customer service personnel. The company reduced its "instant return" hours at smaller airports, along with reducing the number of personnel at all locations. Avis took a similar route to reduce expenses during the economic downturn. The company cut service, reduced staff, and moved most of their instant return staff to airport counters. The result for customers: longer lines, increased wait time, and declining customer satisfaction. The result wasn't what Hertz and Avis had hoped

for either. Both companies saw many of their most loyal customers move to competing rental companies. In time, both Hertz and Avis reversed their policies and increased the number of agents for their instant return customers.

Home Depot

After years of record growth and profits, Home Depot shifted its strategy to focus on expanding its contractor supply business and increasing efficiency through cost cutting and streamlined operations. Along the way, customer service slipped on the company's list of priorities. Full-time employees were replaced by part-timers, employee incentives for good service were cut, and the employee profit-sharing pool declined from $90 million to $44 million in one year. The end result: Home Depot slipped to dead last in customer satisfaction among major U.S. retailers. More importantly, the company found itself 6 percentage points behind Lowe's, which pursued a strategy that promoted more customer-friendly stores. After launching a major customer service program and abandoning many of its command-and-control practices, Home Depot's customer service improved. The key to the change was redefining employees' roles to focus clearly on customers.

Costco and Sam's Club

While Sam's Club (and its parent company Walmart) is well-known for offering low prices, virtually every customer survey indicates that Costco provides better customer service than Sam's Club. The reason? Costco treats its employees better. In addition to providing better benefit packages, Costco pays its employees $6 to $7 more on average than Sam's Club. While more costly to implement, Costco's treatment of employees pays off in terms of better service to customers. For starters, better pay and benefits usually leads to more satisfied employees. In addition, Costco's employee turnover rate ranges from 6 to 20 percent per year, far lower than Sam's Club rate of 20 to 50 percent each year. This means that Costco's employees are more experienced and better able to serve the company's customers. Increased employee loyalty has another side benefit: Costco's recruiting, hiring, and training costs are lower.

continued

Dell

Dell's strategy and its success have long been tied to internal efficiency. Its business model of selling via phone and Internet is a textbook example of supply chain integration and operational excellence. In recent years, however, Dell has pursued cost cutting with a vengeance. The reason is competition. Virtually all of Dell's competitors match the company on pricing and product availability. Unfortunately, Dell's moves alienated its customers, especially in the company's call center operations, which Dell outsourced to firms in foreign countries. Not surprising, Dell's customer satisfaction ratings, along with its market share, fell dramatically. To turn things around, Dell initiated a $100 million program to improve customer service. The company began by appointing a new director of customer service, who immediately expanded the size of Dell's call centers from 1,000 to 3,000 reps. Dell also invested $1 billion to open new data centers, including 12 global solution centers, which focus on sales, customer service, and technical support.

If business can learn anything from these examples, it's that they can never win the fight between customer service and efficiency. Cost cutting that reduces customer service almost always has to be reinstated once customers start demanding better quality, more attention, and increased value for their money. Customer expectations are simply too high—and competitors too plentiful—for businesses to ignore.

- **Uphold Quality Standards**. The best quality standards are of little use if they are not delivered accurately and consistently. At issue is the ability of managers and employees to deliver quality that is consistent with established standards. Greeting customers by name, answering the phone on the second ring, and delivering a hot pizza within 30 minutes are all examples of quality standards that may, or may not, be achieved. Successfully achieving these standards depends mostly on how well the strategy is implemented. However, it also depends on the ability of the firm to fully fund the quality effort. For example, many retailers—including Walmart—at one time had standards for opening additional checkout lanes when there were more than three people in line. However, these retailers failed to deliver on this standard due to the expense of staffing additional employees to operate the registers.
- **Do Not Overpromise**. It goes without saying that customers will be disappointed if an organization fails to deliver on its promises. The key is to create realistic customer expectations for what can and cannot be delivered. All communication to customers must be honest and realistic with respect to the degree of quality that can be delivered. Intentionally misleading customers by making promises that cannot be kept is a guaranteed recipe for disaster.

Of these four issues, having a thorough understanding of customer expectations is the most critical because it sets the stage for the entire quality improvement effort. Customer expectations are also vital to ensuring customer satisfaction. We will look more closely at customer expectations later in this chapter.

Understanding the Role of Value

Earlier, we stated that quality is a necessary, but insufficient, condition of effective customer relationship management. By this we mean that exceptionally high product quality is of little use to the firm or its customers if the customers cannot afford to pay for it or if the product is too difficult to obtain. In the context of utility (want satisfaction), sacrificing time, place, possession, and psychological utility for the sake of form utility may win product design awards, but it will not always win customers.

Value is critical to maintaining long-term customer relationships because it allows for the necessary balance among the five types of utility and the elements of the marketing program. As a guiding principle of marketing strategy, value is quite useful because it includes the concept of quality, but is broader in scope. It takes into account every marketing program element and can be used to consider explicitly customer perceptions of the marketing program in the strategy development process. Value can also be used as a means of organizing the internal aspects of marketing strategy development.

In Chapter 6, we defined value as a customer's subjective evaluation of benefits relative to costs to determine the worth of a firm's product offering relative to other product offerings. To see how each marketing program element is related to value, we need to break down customer benefits and costs into their component parts, as shown below and in Exhibit 10.5:

$$Perceived\ Value = \frac{(Core\ Product\ Quality + Supplemental\ Product\ Quality + Experiential\ Quality)}{(Monetary\ Costs + Nonmonetary\ Costs)}$$

EXHIBIT 10.5 **Connections Between Value and the Marketing Program**

Value Components	Marketing Program Elements			
	Product Strategy	**Pricing Strategy**	**Distribution Strategy**	**IMC Strategy**
Core Product Quality	Product features Brand name Product design Quality Ease of use Warranties Guarantees	Image Prestige	Availability Exclusivity	Image Prestige Reputation Personal selling
Supplemental Product Quality	Value-added features Accessories Replacement parts Repair services Training Customer service Friendliness of employees	Financing Layaway Image Prestige	Availability Exclusivity Delivery Installation On-site training	Friendliness of employees Personal selling
Experiential Quality	Entertainment Uniqueness Psychological benefits	Image Prestige	Convenience Retail atmosphere Retail décor 24/7 availability Overnight delivery	Image Prestige Reputation Personal selling
Monetary Transactional Costs	Quality Exclusive features	Selling price Delivery charges Installation charges Taxes Licensing fees Registration fees	Delivery charges Installation charges Taxes	Image Prestige Reputation Personal selling
Monetary Life Cycle Costs	Durability Reliability Product design	Maintenance costs Cost of consumables Repair costs Costs of replacement parts	Availability of consumables Availability of replacement parts Speed of repairs	Reputation Personal selling
Nonmonetary Costs	Durability Reliability Minimize opportunity costs	Guarantees Return policy	Convenience Wide availability 24/7 access	Reputation Reinforce purchase decision

Different buyers and target markets have varying perspectives on value. Although monetary cost is certainly a key issue, some buyers place greater importance on other elements of the value equation. To some, good value is about product quality. To these customers, the product element of the marketing program is the most crucial to achieving good value. To others, value hinges on the availability and quality of supplemental products. Here, the firm's product, customer service, pricing, and distribution strategies come together to create value. For other buyers, good value is all about convenience. These customers place greater emphasis on distribution issues such as wide product availability, multiple locations, 24/7 access, or even home delivery to achieve good value. The relationships among marketing program elements must constantly be managed to deliver good value to customers. It is important for managers to remember that any change in one program element will have repercussions for value throughout the entire marketing program.

Core Product, Supplemental Product, and Experiential Quality The relationship between quality and value is most apparent in the quality of the customer benefits depicted in the top portion of the value equation. Here, good value depends on a holistic assessment of the quality of the core product, supplemental products, and experiential attributes. Although each can be judged independently, most customers look at the collective benefits provided by the firm in their assessments of value. Consequently, firms are able to create unique combinations of core, supplemental, and experiential benefits that help drive value perceptions. Consider a hotel stay at the Hyatt versus Motel 6. Despite their obvious differences, both can deliver the same value to different customers at different points in time. The Hyatt may offer better form utility and caché, but Motel 6 may be less expensive and closer to attractions. The overall perception of value is driven by customer needs, expectations, and the sacrifices required in obtaining the benefits provided by each firm.

Monetary and Nonmonetary Costs Customer costs include anything that the customer must give up to obtain the benefits provided by the firm. The most obvious cost is the monetary cost of the product, which comes in two forms: transactional costs and life cycle costs. *Transactional costs* include the immediate financial outlay or commitment that must be made to purchase the product. Other than the purchase price of the product, examples of these costs include sales taxes, usage taxes, licensing fees, registration fees, and delivery or installation charges. For example, appliance or furniture retailers can increase value by offering free delivery or installation when their competitors charge for these services. *Life cycle costs* include any additional costs that customers will incur over the life of the product, such as the costs of consumable supplies, maintenance, and repairs. Hyundai and Kia, for example, offer long-term warranties on their cars, vans, and SUVs that significantly reduce life cycle costs for their customers. Product quality, warranties, and the availability of repair services all play into the equation when customers judge monetary costs. Firms that have the capability to reduce transactional or life cycle costs can often provide a better value than their competitors.

Nonmonetary costs are not quite as obvious as monetary costs, and customers sometimes ignore them. Two such costs include the time and effort customers expend to find and purchase goods and services. These costs are closely related to a firm's distribution activities. To reduce time and effort, the firm must increase product availability, thereby making it more convenient for customers to purchase the firm's products. The growth in nonstore and electronic retailing is a direct result of firms taking steps to reduce the time and effort required to purchase their products, thereby reducing customers' nonmonetary costs. The sheer number of products that customers can have delivered directly to their homes is a testament to the growing importance of customers' time.

Offering good basic warranties or extended warranties for an additional charge can reduce risk, another nonmonetary cost. Retailers reduce risk by maintaining liberal return and exchange policies. Personal safety and security risks come into play when customers purchase products that are potentially dangerous. Common examples include tobacco products, alcohol, firearms, and exotic products like skydiving, bungee jumping, and dangerous pets. The final nonmonetary cost, opportunity costs, is harder for the firm to control. Customers incur opportunity costs because they forgo alternative products in making a purchase. Some firms attempt to reduce opportunity costs by promoting their products as being the best or by promising good service after the sale. To anticipate opportunity costs, marketers must consider all potential competitors, including total budget competitors that offer customers alternatives for spending their money.

Competing on Value

After breaking down value into its component parts, we can better understand how a firm's marketing strategy can be designed to optimize customer value. By altering each element of the marketing program, the firm can enhance value by increasing core, supplemental, or experiential quality and/or reducing monetary or nonmonetary costs. This effort must be based on a thorough understanding of customers' needs and wants, as well as an appreciation for how the firm's customers define value.

In consumer markets, retailers offer good examples of how value can be delivered by altering one or more parts of the value equation. Convenience stores offer value to customers by reducing nonmonetary costs (time and effort) and increasing monetary prices. These high-priced (in dollars) stores stay in business because customers value their time and effort more than money in many situations. Online retailers offer a similar mix of value by reducing time and effort costs, and in some cases by reducing monetary costs through free shipping or by not collecting sales taxes. Customers who want the best quality may be willing to spend large sums of money and/or spend more time searching because they consider their nonmonetary costs to be less important. These consumers are likely to shop at retailers such as Macy's, Nordstrom, or Saks rather than discount chains. Finally, specialty stores, like Victoria's Secret or Banana Republic, offer an attractive mix of value in terms of quality clothing, fashionable styling, excellent service, and attractive décor, albeit at higher monetary prices.

Those in business markets often define value in terms of product specifications, availability, and conformity to a delivery schedule, rather than in terms of price or convenience. Business customers must ensure that the products purchased will work right the first time, with minimal disruption to ongoing operations. In some cases, products have value not only because of their features or quality, but because the buying firm has a long-standing relationship with the supplying firm. Business buyers tend to become loyal to suppliers that consistently meet their expectations, solve their problems, and cause them no headaches. All of this is not to say that monetary considerations are not important. In fact, unlike most consumers, business buyers are keenly aware of total transactional and life cycle costs as they seek to reduce the total lifetime expenditure associated with a particular purchase. Business customers will quite often pay more in up-front costs if the total lifetime cost can be reduced.

Obviously, different market segments will have different perceptions of good value. The key is for the marketer to understand the different value requirements of each segment and adapt the marketing program accordingly. From a strategic perspective, it is important to remember that each marketing program element is vital to delivering value. Strategic decisions about one element alone can change perceived value for better or worse. If a decision lowers overall value, the firm should consider modifying other marketing program elements to offset this decrease. For example, an increase in price may have to be offset by an increase in customer benefits to maintain the value ratio.

Customer Satisfaction: The Key to Customer Retention

In the final part of this chapter, we look at customer satisfaction and the role it plays in maintaining long-term customer relationships. To maintain and manage customer satisfaction from a strategic point of view, managers must understand customer expectations and the differences between satisfaction, quality, and value. They must also make customer satisfaction measurement a long-term, continuous commitment of the entire organization.

Understanding Customer Expectations

Although customer satisfaction can be conceived in a number of ways, it is typically defined as the degree to which a product meets or exceeds the customer's expectations about that product. Obviously, the key to this definition lies in understanding customer expectations and how they are formed. Marketing researchers have discovered that customers can hold many different types of expectations as shown in Exhibit 10.6. Customer expectations can vary based on the situation. For example, expectations are likely to be very high (i.e., closer to the ideal end of the range) in situations where personal needs are very high. In highly involving situations such as weddings, birthdays, or funerals, customers will demand a great deal from the firm. Expectations also tend to be higher when customers have many alternatives for meeting their needs. This connection between expectations and alternatives is one reason that serving customers in highly commoditized markets is so challenging. Other situations can cause customer expectations to be lower (i.e., closer to the tolerable end of the range), such as when the purchase is not involving, or when the monetary or nonmonetary prices are low.

EXHIBIT 10.6 **Range of Customer Expectations**

Type of Expectation	Descriptive Example	Typical Situations	Expectation Range
Ideal Expectations	"Everyone says this is the best MP3 player on the market. I want to get my sister something special for her birthday."	Highly involving purchases Special occasions Unique events	*High (Desired)*
Normative Expectations	"As expensive as this MP3 player is, it ought to hold a lot of music and come with several included accessories."	Shopping comparisons Value judgments	
Experience-Based Expectations	"I bought this brand of MP3 player last time and it served me very well."	Frequent purchase situations Brand loyalty	
Minimum Tolerable Expectations	"I know it's not the best MP3 player out there. I only bought it because it was inexpensive."	Price-driven purchases Low-involvement purchases	*Low (Adequate)*

Sources: Adapted from James H. Myers, *Measuring Customer Satisfaction* (Chicago: American Marketing Association, 1999); and Valarie A. Zeithaml, Leonard L. Berry, and A. Parasuraman, "The Nature of Determinants of Customer Expectations of Service," *Journal of the Academy of Marketing Science,* 21 (January 1993), pp. 1–12.

Customers can also become more tolerable of weak or poor performance when they have fewer product alternatives, or when the poor performance is beyond the control of the firm (e.g., bad weather, excessively high demand, natural disasters).

The Zone of Tolerance   The difference between the upper and lower end of the range of possible customer expectations is an important strategic consideration in managing customer satisfaction. Marketers often refer to the upper end of expectations as desired performance expectations (what customers want) and the lower end of the range as adequate performance expectations (what customers are willing to accept). As shown in Exhibit 10.7, the extent of the difference between desired and adequate performance is called the zone of tolerance.[10] The width of the zone of tolerance represents the degree to which customers recognize and are willing to accept variability in performance (i.e., quality, value, or some other measurable aspect of the marketing program). Performance can fall above the zone of tolerance, within the zone of tolerance, or below it:

- **Customer delight**—occurs when actual performance exceeds the desired performance expectation. This level of performance is rare and quite surprising when it occurs. Therefore, customers find it to be memorable.

EXHIBIT 10.7   The Zone of Tolerance

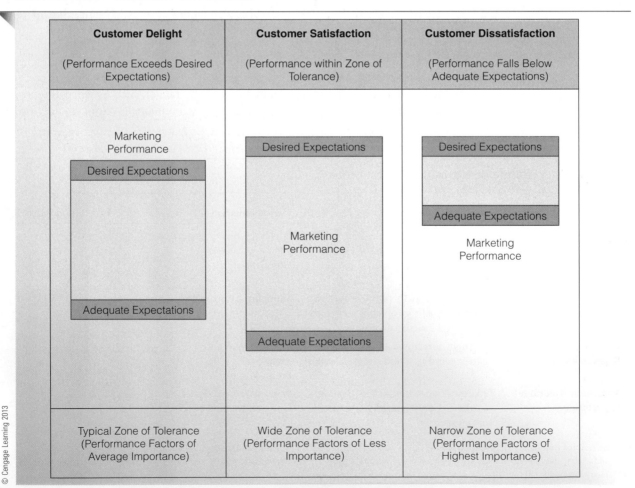

- **Customer satisfaction**—occurs when actual performance falls within the zone of tolerance. Satisfaction levels vary based on where performance falls within the zone (high or low).
- **Customer dissatisfaction**—occurs when actual performance falls below the adequate performance expectation. Depending upon the severity of the performance level, customers may go beyond dissatisfaction to become frustrated or even angry. This too can be very memorable for customers.

We addressed these three issues in Chapter 5 as being a consequence of the buying process. Now, with the marketing plan developed and implemented, we can think of these issues in a strategic sense by considering the zone of tolerance as a moving target. If the zone is narrow, the difference between what customers want and what they are willing to accept is also narrow. This means that the marketer will have a relatively more difficult time matching performance to customer expectations. Hence, customer satisfaction is harder to achieve when the zone of tolerance is narrow. Conversely, customer satisfaction is relatively easier to achieve when the zone of tolerance is wide. In these instances, the marketer's hurdle is lower and the satisfaction targets are easier to hit. Delighting the customer by exceeding desired expectations is an exceedingly difficult task for any marketer. And, causing customer dissatisfaction by failing to meet even adequate expectations is a situation that should be avoided at all times.

Customers will typically hold different expectation levels and zones of tolerance for different factors of performance. In a restaurant, for example, customers might have a narrow zone of tolerance for food quality, an even narrower zone of tolerance for service quality, an average zone of tolerance for wait time, and a relatively wide zone of tolerance for cleanliness. From the marketer's point of view, two issues are important. First, the firm must clearly understand the relevant performance factors about which customers will hold performance expectations. Customers can have expectations for just about anything, though there are typically only a few factors that are critical for most customers. Many firms look first at factors dealing with product strategy; however, critical performance factors can cut across the entire marketing program. Second, the firm must track expectations and performance over time. Tracking performance levels vis-à-vis expectations and the zone of tolerance is a useful diagnostic tool for both strategic planning and the management of customer satisfaction. The approach is also useful for tracking the effectiveness of performance improvements, and in assessing the performance of new goods or services. In the end, tracking both expectations and performance is an important way to ensure that customer satisfaction remains stable or improves over time. Declining customer satisfaction suggests a need for immediate corrective action.

Managing Customer Expectations   Many marketers ask two key questions as they work toward managing customer expectations: (1) Why are customer expectations unrealistic? and (2) Should we strive to delight our customers by consistently exceeding their desired expectations? Although it is true that customers are more demanding today than ever (especially American consumers), their expectations are typically not that unrealistic. Most customers are looking for the basics of performance—things that a firm is supposed to do or has promised to do.[11] For example, flights should take off and land on time, meals in a restaurant should taste good and be prepared as ordered, new cars should be hassle free throughout the warranty period, and your soft drink should be cold and fresh. On these and other basic factors of performance, it is essentially impossible for the firm to exceed customer expectations. These basic factors represent the bare minimum: If the firm wants to exceed expectations, it has to go above and beyond the call of duty. *Beyond the Pages 10.3* explains how exceeding customer expectations is an important component of customer loyalty.

Beyond the Pages 10.3

Satisfied, But Not Loyal[12]

Generally speaking, American consumers are a satisfied lot. At least that's what survey after survey reveals. Sure there are ups and downs, and some industries or firms fair better than others, but the general tendency is a positive one. Despite this good news, however, a recent survey indicated that roughly 30 percent of satisfied customers would switch to a new company if given a good reason to do so. This begs the question: Why will satisfied customers leave a firm for a competitor? The answer is that customer satisfaction is not the same thing as customer loyalty.

Customer satisfaction by itself tells a firm very little about where it stands with customers. There are two issues at work: relative satisfaction and customer expectations. Relative satisfaction tells a firm where it ranks against the competition. For example, Outback Steakhouse's satisfaction rating of 81 says little about the firm and its products until that score is compared with Red Lobster (83), Olive Garden (80), Applebee's (77), and Chili's (76). Similarly, Apple might consider its most recent satisfaction score of 83 to be somewhat low until that score is compared to LG (75), Nokia (75), Motorola (73), Samsung (71), and RIM (Blackberry) (69). Comparisons like these are important because customers make similar comparisons when making purchase decisions. A customer may be satisfied with a specific product or company, but will switch if they believe they will be better satisfied (via higher quality, a better user experience, or a better value) by another firm. For this reason, satisfied customers are not necessarily loyal customers.

To increase loyalty, firms must look at the second issue: customer expectations. Customer expectations are key because they serve as the anchor points for customer satisfaction. Research suggests that firms that simply meet customer expectations do little to create loyalty. Thus, while customers may have no complaints, the firm's products probably do not stand out in any meaningful way. In other words, loyalty comes from providing products that exceed customer expectations. Loyalty can be especially strong in situations where customers believe the firm's performance is better than can be expected from a competitor. In this situation, the customer has little incentive to switch.

Most firms do a good job of tracking customer satisfaction over time. However, many do a rather poor job in tracking customer expectations. A recent survey found that 47 percent of customers believe that company executives do not understand their expectations or what they experience in day-to-day contact with their firms. Another 41 percent don't believe that companies take their complaints seriously. Further, half of customers who do complain will leave the firm if their complaints are not resolved. The other half may stay, but they spread negative word-of-mouth either in person or via online forums. Across all industries, 17 percent of customer interactions result in a lost customer.

As we have seen, to promote genuine loyalty to the firm, executives must have a full understanding of their customers' expectations. Then, the firm must set out to deliver on those expectations and create value beyond the norm for the industry. Some tips on how to make this happen include:

- **Seek Out Negative Feedback**. In addition to carefully considering customer complaints, firms must look outside to gather information from dissatisfied customers who do not complain. This can be done via websites, blogs, message boards, and third-party rating services.
- **Manage from the Outside In**. This involves leveraging customer information (both positive and negative) to improve business practices. Firms must take what customers tell them and use it to improve the customer experience.
- **Recognize That One Size Does Not Fit All**. Different customers have different preferred avenues to meeting their expectations. For example, some customers prefer high automation, or even self-service, with respect to the customer experience. Young customers are a good example. Others prefer a personal, customized experience. Older customers, for instance, prefer to bank with live tellers than use automation.
- **Put Service Over Personalization**. The majority of customers—78 percent—place more importance on good service than personalized service. This means that firms must be able to address customers' needs on the first try. Simply knowing the customer's name is not enough.

Research shows that about 33 percent of a firm's customers feel loyal to the firm and show their loyalty by making most of their purchases in a category with

continued

the firm. Unfortunately, the same research shows that only 20 percent of the firm's customers are profitable, and that most of the company's profitable customers are not loyal. To get past this enigma, executives must ask three questions about their customers: (1) Which loyal customers are good for our business? (2) How do we retain these customers? and (3) How do we get more customers like them? Customers who do not meet this profile are simply not worth having as customers. In the end, most executives will discover that even some of their most satisfied and loyal customers are not worth the effort.

The second question about delighting the customer is a bit more controversial. Firms should always strive to exceed adequate expectations. After all, this is the basic delineation between satisfaction and dissatisfaction. The tougher question is whether the firm should try to exceed desired expectations. The answer depends on several issues. One is the time and expense involved in delighting customers. If delighting a customer does not translate into stronger customer loyalty or long-term customer retention, then it is not likely to be worth the effort. It may also not be a good investment if delighting one customer lowers performance for other customers. Another issue is whether continually delighting customers raises their expectations over time. To be effective, customer delight should be both surprising and rare, not a daily event. Firms should look for small ways to delight customers without elevating expectations beyond what can reasonably be delivered. Finally, the firm must be aware of whether its initiatives to delight the customer can be copied by competitors. If customer delight is easily copied, it ceases to be a key means of differentiation for the firm.

Satisfaction versus Quality versus Value

Now that we better understand customer expectations, let's look at how satisfaction differs from quality and value. The answer is not so obvious because the concepts overlap to some extent. Since customer satisfaction is defined relative to customer expectations, it becomes difficult to separate satisfaction from quality and value because customers can hold expectations about quality or value or both. In fact, customers can hold expectations about any part of the product offering, including seemingly minor issues such as parking availability, crowding, or room temperature in addition to major issues like quality and value.

Toyota typically scores well in both customer and third-party ratings of customer satisfaction.

To solve this dilemma, think of each concept not in terms of what it is, but in terms of its size. The most narrowly defined concept is quality, which customers judge on an attribute-by-attribute basis. Consider a meal at a restaurant. The quality of that meal stems from specific attributes: the quality of the food, the drink, the atmosphere, and the service are each important. We could even go so far as to judge the quality of the ingredients in the food. In fact, many restaurants, like Ruth's Chris Steakhouse, promote themselves based on the quality of their ingredients. When the customer considers the broader issue of value, they begin to include things other than quality: the price of the meal, the time and effort required getting to the restaurant, parking availability, and opportunity costs. In this case, even the best meal in a great restaurant can be viewed as a poor value if the price is too high in terms of monetary or nonmonetary costs.

When a customer considers satisfaction, he or she will typically respond based on his or her expectations of the item in question. If the quality of the food is not what the customer expected, then the customer will be dissatisfied with the food. Similarly, if the value of the meal is not what the customer expected, the customer will be dissatisfied with the value. Note that these are independent judgments. It is entirely possible for a customer to be satisfied with the quality of the meal, but dissatisfied with its value. The opposite is also true.

However, most customers do not make independent judgments about satisfaction. Instead, customers generally think of satisfaction based on the totality of their experience without overtly considering issues like quality or value. We are not saying that customers do not judge quality or value. Rather, we are saying that customers think of satisfaction in more abstract terms than they do quality or value. This happens because customers' expectations—hence their satisfaction—can be based on any number of factors, *even factors that have nothing to do with quality or value*. Continuing with our restaurant example, it is entirely possible for a customer to receive the absolute best quality and value, yet still be dissatisfied with the experience. The weather, other customers, a bad date, and a bad mood are just a few examples of non-quality and non-value factors that can affect customers' expectations and cloud their satisfaction judgments.

Customer Satisfaction and Customer Retention

Customer satisfaction is the key to customer retention. Fully satisfied customers are more likely to become loyal customers, or even advocates for the firm and its products. Satisfied customers are less likely to explore alternative suppliers and they are less price sensitive. Therefore, satisfied customers are less likely to switch to competitors. Satisfied customers are also more likely to spread positive word-of-mouth about the firm and its products. However, the way that customers think about satisfaction creates some interesting challenges for marketers. It is one thing to strive for the best in terms of quality and value, but how can a firm control the uncontrollable factors that affect customer satisfaction? Certainly, marketers cannot control the weather or the fact that their customers are in a bad mood. However, there are several things that marketers can do manage customer satisfaction and leverage it in their marketing efforts:

- **Understand What Can Go Wrong.** Managers, particularly those on the frontline, must understand that an endless number of things can and will go wrong in meeting customers' expectations. Even the best strategies will not work in the face of customers who are in a bad mood. Although some factors are simply uncontrollable, managers should be aware of these factors and be ready to respond if possible.
- **Focus on Controllable Issues.** The key is to keep an eye on the uncontrollable factors, but focus more on things that can be controlled. Core product quality, customer service, atmosphere, experiences, pricing, convenience, distribution, and

promotion must all be managed in an effort to increase share of customer and maintain loyal relationships. It is especially important that the core product be of high quality. Without that, the firm stands little chance of creating customer satisfaction or long-term customer relationships.

- **Manage Customer Expectations**. As we have seen, managing customer expectations is more than promising only what you can deliver. To manage expectations well, the firm must educate customers on how to be satisfied by the firm and its products. These efforts can include in-depth product training, educating customers on how to get the best service from the company, telling customers about product availability and delivery schedules, and giving customers tips and hints for improving quality and service. For example, the U.S. Postal Service routinely reminds customers to mail early during the busy holiday season in November and December. This simple reminder is valuable in managing customers' expectations regarding mail delivery times.
- **Offer Satisfaction Guarantees**. Companies that care about customer satisfaction back up their offerings by guaranteeing customer satisfaction or product quality. Exhibit 10.8 provides several examples of customer satisfaction guarantees. Guarantees offer a number of benefits. For the firm, a guarantee can serve as a

---

EXHIBIT 10.8   Examples of Customer Satisfaction Guarantees

Hampton Inn

Friendly Service, clean rooms, comfortable surroundings, every time. If you're not satisfied, we don't expect you to pay. That's our commitment & your guarantee. That's 100% Hampton.

L.L.Bean

Our products are guaranteed to give 100% satisfaction in every way. Return anything purchased from us at any time if it proves otherwise. We do not want you to have anything from L.L.Bean that is not completely satisfactory.

FedEx Express

FedEx offers a money-back guarantee for every U.S. shipment. You may request a refund or credit of your shipping charges if we miss our published (or quoted, as in the case of FedEx SameDay®) delivery time by even 60 seconds. This guarantee applies to all U.S. shipments, commercial and residential, to all 50 states.

Xerox

If you are not totally satisfied with any Xerox-brand Equipment delivered under this Agreement, Xerox will, at your request, replace it without charge with an identical model or, at Xerox's option, with Xerox Equipment with comparable features and capabilities. This Guarantee applies only to Xerox-brand Equipment that has been continuously maintained by Xerox under this Agreement or a Xerox maintenance agreement.

Midas

Purchase a Midas lifetime guaranteed muffler, brake pads or shoes, shocks or struts and you will never, ever need to buy a replacement part as long as you own your car.

Eddie Bauer

Every item we sell will give you complete satisfaction or you may return it for a full refund.

Publix Supermarkets

The philosophy of pleasing our customers was established from the beginning by our founder, George W. Jenkins. The purpose of his guarantee remains to satisfy the customer: "We will never knowingly disappoint you. If for any reason your purchase does not give you complete satisfaction, the full purchase price will be cheerfully refunded immediately upon request."

corporate vision, creed, or goal that all employees can strive to meet. A good guarantee is also a viable marketing tool that can be used to differentiate the firm's product offering. For customers, guarantees reduce the risk of buying from the firm and give the customer a point of leverage if they have a complaint.

- **Make It Easy for Customers to Complain**. Over 90 percent of dissatisfied customers never complain—they just go elsewhere to meet their needs. To counter this customer defection, marketers must make it easy for customers to complain. Whether by mail, phone, email, or in person, firms that care about customer satisfaction will make customer complaints an important part of their ongoing research efforts. However, tracking complaints is not enough. The firm must also be willing to listen and act to rectify customers' problems. Complaining customers are much more likely to buy again if the firm handles their complaints effectively and swiftly.

- **Create Relationship Programs**. As we discussed earlier, firms can use relationship strategies to increase customer loyalty. Today, loyalty or membership programs are everywhere: banks, restaurants, supermarkets, and even bookstores. The idea behind all of these programs is to create financial, social, customization, and/or structural bonds that link customers to the firm.

- **Make Customer Satisfaction Measurement an Ongoing Priority**. If you don't know what customers want, need, or expect, everything else is a waste of time. A permanent, ongoing program to measure customer satisfaction is one of the most important foundations of customer relationship management.

Customer Satisfaction Measurement

There are a number of different methods for measuring customer satisfaction. The simplest method involves the direct measurement of performance across various factors using simple rating scales. For example, a customer might be asked to rate the quality of housekeeping services in a hotel using a 10-point scale from ranging from poor to excellent. While this method is simple and allows the firm to track satisfaction, it is not diagnostic in the sense that it permits the firm to determine *how* satisfaction varies over time. To do this, the firm can measure both expectations and performance at the same time. Exhibit 10.9 illustrates how this might be done for a hypothetical health club.

The ongoing measurement of customer satisfaction has changed dramatically over the last decade. Although most firms track their customer satisfaction ratings over time, firms that are serious about customer relationship management have adopted more robust means of tracking satisfaction based on actual customer behavior. Advances in technology, which allow firms to track the behaviors of individual customers over time, provide the basis for these new metrics. Some of these new metrics include:[13]

- **Lifetime Value of a Customer (LTV).** The net present value of the revenue stream generated by a specific customer over a period of time. LTV recognizes that some customers are worth more than others. Companies can better leverage their customer satisfaction programs by focusing on valuable customers and giving poor service or charging hefty fees to customers with low LTV profiles to encourage them to leave.

- **Average Order Value (AOV).** A customer's purchase dollars divided by the number of orders over a period of time. The AOV will increase over time as customer satisfaction increases and customers become more loyal. E-commerce companies use AOV quite often to pinpoint customers that need extra incentives or reminders to stimulate purchases.

EXHIBIT 10.9 **Measuring Expectations and Performance for a Hypothetical Health Club**

When it comes to....	The Lowest Adequate Level of Service I Expect Is:		The Highest Desired Level of Service I Expect Is:		The Actual Performance of This Health Club Is:	
	Low	High	Low	High	Low	High
The quality and variety of exercise equipment provided	1 2 3 4 5		1 2 3 4 5		1 2 3 4 5	
The amount of time I have to wait for a specific piece of exercise equipment	1 2 3 4 5		1 2 3 4 5		1 2 3 4 5	
The quality and variety of exercise classes offered	1 2 3 4 5		1 2 3 4 5		1 2 3 4 5	
The availability of specific exercise classes	1 2 3 4 5		1 2 3 4 5		1 2 3 4 5	
The availability of facilities, such as racquetball or basketball courts, the running track, or the pool	1 2 3 4 5		1 2 3 4 5		1 2 3 4 5	
Having a clean, attractive, and inviting facility	1 2 3 4 5		1 2 3 4 5		1 2 3 4 5	
Having a comfortable atmosphere (temperature, lighting, music)	1 2 3 4 5		1 2 3 4 5		1 2 3 4 5	
The overall helpfulness and friendliness of the staff	1 2 3 4 5		1 2 3 4 5		1 2 3 4 5	
Having convenient hours of operation	1 2 3 4 5		1 2 3 4 5		1 2 3 4 5	
Having plenty of available parking	1 2 3 4 5		1 2 3 4 5		1 2 3 4 5	

© Cengage Learning 2013

- **Customer Acquisition/Retention Costs**. It is typically less expensive to retain current customers than to acquire new customers. As long as this holds true, a company is better off keeping its current customers satisfied.
- **Customer Conversion Rate**. The percentage of visitors or potential customers that actually buy. Low conversion rates are not necessarily a cause for concern if the number of prospects is high.
- **Customer Retention Rate**. The percentage of customers who are repeat purchasers. This number should remain stable or increase over time. A declining retention rate is a cause for immediate concern.
- **Customer Attrition Rate**. The percentage of customers who do not repurchase (sometimes called the churn rate). This number should remain stable or decline over time. An increasing attrition rate is a cause for immediate concern.
- **Customer Recovery Rate**. The percentage of customers who leave the firm (through attrition) that can be lured back using various offers or incentives. Companies that sell products via subscriptions (e.g., record and movie clubs, magazines, satellite radio or television) frequently offer special incentives to lure back former customers.
- **Referrals**. Dollars generated from customers referred to the firm by current customers. A declining referral rate is a cause for concern.
- **Social Communication**. Companies can track satisfaction by monitoring customers' online commentary. The number of blogs, newsgroups, chat rooms, and general websites where customers praise and complain about companies is staggering.

Firms also have another research method at their disposal: the focus group. Long used as a means of understanding customer requirements during product development, companies use focus groups more often to measure customer satisfaction. Focus groups allow firms to more fully explore the subtleties of satisfaction, including its emotional and psychological underpinnings. By better understanding the roots of customer satisfaction, marketers should be better able to develop marketing strategies that can meet customers' needs.

Lessons from Chapter 10

The "right" marketing strategy:

- is not necessarily about creating a large number of customer transactions in order to maximize market share.
- is one that attracts and retains customers over the long term.
- considers customers' needs, wants, and expectations in order to ensure customer satisfaction and customer retention.
- develops long-term relationships with customers in order to insulate the firm against competitive inroads and the rapid pace of environmental change.

Customer relationship management:

- requires that firms look beyond current transactions to examine the long-term potential of a customer.
- is based on creating mutually beneficial relationships where each party provides value to the other party.
- is a business philosophy aimed at defining and increasing customer value in ways that motivate customers to remain loyal to the firm.
- is about retaining the right customers.
- involves a number of stakeholders in addition to customers including employees, supply chain partners, and external stakeholders such as government agencies, investors, the media, nonprofits, and facilitating firms.
- shifts the firm's marketing emphasis from "acquiring customers" to "maintaining clients."
- involves the creation of relationship capital—the ability to build and maintain relationships with customers, suppliers, and partners based on trust, commitment, cooperation, and interdependence.

CRM in consumer markets:

- is a long-term process with the goal of moving consumers through a series of stages ranging from simple awareness, through levels of increasing relationship intensity, to the point where consumers become true advocates for the firm and its products.
- attempts to go beyond the creation of satisfied and loyal customers to create true believers and sponsors for the company.
- is usually based on strategies that increase share of customer rather than market share.

- abandons old notions of acquiring new customers and increasing transactions to focus more on fully serving the needs of current customers.
- is based on the precept that all customers have different needs; therefore, not all customers have equal value to the firm.
- involves estimating the worth of individual customers to express their lifetime value (LTV) to the firm. Some customers are simply too expensive to keep given the low level of profits they generate.
- not only involves strategies to retain top-tier customers; it also involves finding ways to encourage second-tier customers to be even better customers.
- involves the use of four types of relationship strategies: financial incentives, social bonding, enhanced customization, and structural bonding.

CRM in business markets:

- also involves moving buyers through a sequence of stages, where each stage represents an increasing level of relationship intensity.
- is based more on creating structural bonds with customers or supply-chain partners.
- creates win–win scenarios where both parties build relationship capital; one firm maintains a loyal and committed customer, the other maintains a loyal and committed supplier.
- is typically more involving, more complex, and much riskier due to the nature of business buying, the presence of long-term contractual obligations, and the sheer dollars involved in many business purchases.
- leads to many changes in the way that companies conduct business, including a change in buyers' and sellers' roles; as well as increases in sole sourcing, global sourcing, team-based buying decisions, and productivity through better integration of operations.

As one of the keys to customer relationship management, quality:

- is a relative term that refers to the degree of superiority of a firm's goods or services.
- is a double-edged sword: good quality can successfully generate first-time transactions, but poor quality guarantees that repeat purchases will not occur.

- is not an automatic guarantee of success—it is a necessary but insufficient condition of customer relationship management.
- is affected by every element in the marketing program. However, the firm's product and branding strategies are of utmost importance.
- depends heavily on the form utility offered by the core product. In service offerings, the core product is typically based on a combination of people, processes, and physical evidence.
- is often taken for granted in the core product because customers expect the core product to be of high quality, or at least at a level necessary to meet their needs.
- is critical in supplemental products that add value to the core product. In most cases, these supplemental products, not the core product, are responsible for product differentiation.
- is often found in the symbolic and experiential attributes of a product. Characteristics such as image, prestige, or brand have immense power in differentiating product offerings.
- is hard to maintain with regularity because: (1) customers have very high expectations about quality, (2) most products today compete in mature markets, and (3) many businesses compete in markets with very little real differentiation among product offerings.
- is difficult to continuously improve over time. Delivering superior quality involves understanding customers' expectations, translating expectations into quality standards, upholding quality standards, and avoiding the tendency to overpromise.

As one of the keys to customer relationship management, value:

- is critical to maintaining long-term customer relationships because it allows for the necessary balance among the five types of utility and the elements of the marketing program.
- is a useful guiding principle of marketing strategy because it takes into account every marketing program element and can be used to consider explicitly customer perceptions of the marketing program in the strategy development process.
- is defined as a customer's subjective evaluation of benefits relative to costs to determine the worth of a firm's product offering relative to other product offerings.
- breaks down into customer benefits (e.g., core product quality, supplemental product quality, experiential quality) and customer costs (monetary and nonmonetary costs).
- can vary across different situations or points in time depending on a customer's expectations and needs.
- depends on much more than the selling price of a product. Value perceptions are also affected by

transaction costs (taxes, fees, other charges), life-cycle costs (maintenance, repairs, consumables), and non-monetary costs (time, effort, risk, opportunity costs).
- can be altered by changing one or more parts of the marketing program. If a change lowers overall value, the firm should consider modifying other marketing program elements to offset this decrease.

Customer expectations:

- are at the core of customer satisfaction.
- can be described as ideal (essentially perfect performance), normative ("should be" or "ought to be" performance), experience-based (based on past experiences), or minimum tolerable (lowest acceptable performance).
- can be examined strategically by considering the zone of tolerance between desired performance expectations and adequate performance expectations. The zone of tolerance represents the degree to which customers recognize and are willing to accept variability in performance.
- as measured against the zone of tolerance can lead to three outcomes:
  - customer delight—actual performance exceeds desired expectations
  - customer satisfaction—actual performance falls within the zone of tolerance
  - customer dissatisfaction—actual performance falls below adequate expectations
- are typically not unrealistic. Customers are looking for the basics of performance—things that the firm is supposed to do or has promised to do.
- can be increased over time if the firm is not mindful of its initiatives aimed at delighting customers on a continuous basis.

Customer satisfaction:

- is defined as the degree to which a product meets or exceeds the customer's expectations about that product.
- is typically judged by customers within the context of the total experience, not just with respect to quality and value. Customer satisfaction can also include any number of factors that have nothing to do with quality or value.
- is the key to customer retention. Fully satisfied customers are:
  - more likely to become loyal customers or even advocates for the firm;
  - less likely to explore alternative suppliers;
  - less price sensitive;
  - less likely to switch to competitors;
  - more likely to spread good word-of-mouth about the firm and its products.

- creates some interesting challenges for marketers. Some of the steps that marketers can take to manage customer satisfaction include:
  - understand what can go wrong;
  - focus on controllable issues;
  - manage customer expectations;
  - offer satisfaction guarantees;
  - make it easy for customers to complain;
  - create relationship programs;
  - make customer satisfaction measurement an ongoing priority.

- can be measured using simple rating scales to directly measure performance across various factors in the marketing program.
- can be tracked diagnostically by measuring both expectations and performance at the same time.
- is now tracked using a number of new metrics based on actual customer behavior, including lifetime value of a customer; average order value; customer acquisition/retention costs; customer conversion, retention, attrition, and recovery rates; referrals; and social communication.

Questions for Discussion

1. One of the common uses of customer relationship management (CRM) in consumer markets is to rank customers on profitability or lifetime value measures. Highly profitable customers get special attention, while unprofitable customers get poor service or are often "fired." What are the ethical and social issues involved in these practices? Could CRM be misused? How and why?
2. Given the commoditized nature of many markets today, does customer relationship management—and its associated focus on quality, value, and

satisfaction—make sense? If price is the only true means of differentiation in a commoditized market, why should a firm care about quality? Explain.
3. Of the two types of customer expectations, adequate performance expectations fluctuate the most. Describe situations that might cause adequate expectations to increase, thereby narrowing the width of the zone of tolerance. What might a firm do in these situations to achieve its satisfaction targets?

Exercises

1. Visit 1to1 Media (www.1to1media.com) to learn more about customer relationship management. You can register for free access to useful tools, articles, discussions, and webinars about CRM and its use in a number of different industries.
2. Think about all of the organizations with which you maintain an ongoing relationship (banks, doctors, schools, accountants, mechanics, etc.). Would you consider yourself to be unprofitable for any of these organizations? Why? How might each of

these organizations fire you as a customer? What would you do if they did?
3. J.D. Power and Associates (www.jdpower.com) is a well-known research company specializing in the measurement of product quality and customer satisfaction. Explore their website to look at their customer satisfaction ratings for a number of industries. What role will third-party firms like J.D. Power play in the future given the increasing use of internal customer satisfaction metrics?

End Notes

1. These facts are from the 1-800-Flowers corporate website (http://investor.1800flowers.com), accessed June 19, 2012; 1-800-Flowers 2011 Annual Report (http://investor.1800flowers.com/common/download/download.cfm?companyid=FLWS&fileid=530260&filekey=4E7020C3-23D7-4C6E-A021-62867BE40DA4&filename=FLWS_2011_annual_FINAL.pdf), accessed June 19, 2012; Barbara Ortutay, "Flower Shop Launches First Facebook Store," *BusinessWeek Online*, July 29, 2009 (http://www.businessweek.com/ap/tech/D99O5K680.htm); and Rebecca Reisner, "Mixing Up the Bouquet at 1-800-Flowers.com," *BusinessWeek Online*, April 7,

2009 (http://www.businessweek.com/managing/content/apr2009/ca2009047_439174.htm).

2. Jill Dyché, *The CRM Handbook*. (Boston, MA: Addison-Wesley, 2002), 4–5.

3. "Relationships Rule," *Business 2.0*, May 2000, 303–319.

4. G.B. Kumar, "Being Customer Focused: The Customer Advocacy Imperative," Cisco Blog (http://www.cisco.com/web/IN/about/leadership/gbkumar_customer.html), accessed June 19, 2012.

5. This information is taken from the Regions website (http://www.regions.com).

6. Cliff Edwards, "AMD + ATI: Imperfect Together?" *BusinessWeek Online*, July 25, 2006 (http://www.businessweek.com/technology/content/jul2006/tc20060725_893757.htm).

7. Adapted from Valarie Zeithaml, Mary Jo Bitner, and Dwayne Gremler, *Services Marketing*, 6th edition (Boston: McGraw-Hill/Irwin, 2013), pp. 25–27.

8. This material is adapted from Valarie A. Zeithaml, A. Parasuraman, and Leonard L. Berry, *Delivering Quality Service: Balancing Customer Perceptions and Expectations* (New York: The Free Press, 2001).

9. These facts are from M. Joy Hayes, "Bad Customer Service? Blame the Bosses' Bad Policies," *Daily Finance*, May 25, 2012 (http://www.dailyfinance.com/2012/05/25/bad-customer-service-blame-the-bosses-bad-policies); Brian Hindo, "Satisfaction Not Guaranteed," *BusinessWeek Online*, June 19, 2006 (http://www.businessweek.com/magazine/content/06_25/b3989041.htm); Jena McGregor, "Marvin Ellison: Home Depot's Mr. Fixit?" *BusinessWeek Online*, May 7, 2009 (http://www.businessweek.com/magazine/content/09_20/b4131054579392.htm); Jena McGregor, Aili McConnon, and David Kiley, "Customer Service in a Shrinking Economy," *BusinessWeek Online*, February 19, 2009 (http://www.businessweek.com/magazine/content/09_09/b4121026559235.htm); Erica Ogg, "A Modest Proposal to Fix Dell's Customer Service," *CNET News*, May 9, 2008 (http://news.cnet.com/8301-10784_3-9939821-7.html); Aaron Ricadela, "Dell Will Spend $1 Billion on Data Centers, Customer Labs," *BusinessWeek*, April 7, 2011 (http://www.businessweek.com/news/2011-04-07/dell-will-spend-1-billion-on-data-centers-customer-labs.html); and Harold L. Sirkin, "Serving Customers in a Downturn," *BusinessWeek*, July 31, 2009 (http://www.businessweek.com/managing/content/jul2009/ca20090731_913928.htm).

10. Information in this section is based on James H. Myers, *Measuring Customer Satisfaction* (Chicago: American Marketing Association, 1999); and Valarie A. Zeithaml, Leonard L. Berry, and A. Parasuraman, "The Nature and Determinants of Customer Expectations of Service," *Journal of the Academy of Marketing Science*, 21 (January 1993), 1–12.

11. A. Parasuraman, Leonard L. Berry, and Valarie A. Zeithaml, "Understanding Customer Expectations of Service," *Sloan Management Review*, 32 (Spring 1991), 42.

12. These facts are from the American Customer Satisfaction Index Scores by Industry (http://www.theacsi.org/index.php?option=com_content&view=article&id=18&Itemid=115), accessed June 19, 2012; Andrea J. Ayers, "Executives Have No Idea What Customers Want," *Forbes*, March 10, 2009 (http://www.forbes.com/2009/03/10/consumers-executives-disconnect-leadership-managing-convergys.html); Kevin P. Coyne, "The Customer Satisfaction Survey Snag," *BusinessWeek Online*, June 19, 2009 (http://www.businessweek.com/managing/content/jun2009/ca20090619_272945.htm); and Timothy Keiningham and Lerzan Aksoy, "When Customer Loyalty Is a Bad Thing," *BusinessWeek Online*, May 8, 2009 (http://www.businessweek.com/managing/content/may2009/ca2009058_567988.htm).

13. Adapted from Judy Strauss, Adel El-Ansary, and Raymond Frost, *E-Marketing*, 3rd ed. (Upper Saddle River, NJ: Prentice Hall, 2003), 435–437.

CASE 1

USA Today: Innovation in an Evolving Industry*

Synopsis: As the entire newspaper industry sits on the brink of collapse, Gannett and *USA Today* work to avoid disaster and transform the nation's most read newspaper into tomorrow's best resource for news and information. This case reviews the history of *USA Today*, including its continued use of innovation to stay on top of the technological and sociocultural shifts that are rapidly changing the newspaper industry. In the face of continual competition across a variety of media sources, the future of *USA Today* depends on its ability to continually push the envelope of innovation and offer value-added, proprietary content to ensure continued differentiation and the future of the *USA Today* brand.

Themes: Product strategy, innovation, target marketing, distribution strategy, changing technology, changing sociocultural patterns, customer relationships, competition, differentiation, strategic focus, SWOT analysis

USA Today, subtitled "The Nation's Newspaper," debuted in 1982 as America's first national general-interest daily newspaper. The paper was the brainchild of Allen H. Neuharth, who until 1989 was Chairman of Gannett Co., Inc., a diversified international news, information, and communications company—now worth $4.7 billion. Gannett is a global information juggernaut that publishes 82 daily and 700 nondaily newspapers and affiliated websites, operates 23 broadcast television stations reaching 18.2 percent of the U.S. population, and is engaged in marketing, commercial printing, newswire services, data services, news programming, information and search websites, and several other content delivery services. Gannett is currently the largest U.S. newspaper group in terms of circulation. Its newspapers, including *USA Today*, have a combined circulation of 11.6 million readers every weekday and 12 million readers every Sunday. Gannett's total online audience is roughly 52 million unique visitors per month—nearly a quarter of the total U.S. Internet audience.

When *USA Today* debuted in 1982, it achieved rapid success due to its innovative format. No other media source had considered a national newspaper written in shorter pieces and sprinkled with eye-catching, colorful photos, graphs, and charts. Designed to address the needs of a sound-byte generation, readers found *USA Today*'s content refreshing and more engaging than other papers. Circulation grew rapidly from roughly 350,000 in 1982 to approximately 5.9 million daily print and online readers today. *USA Today* remains the number one print newspaper, with over 1.8 million daily papers in circulation, and *USA Today*'s website, USAToday.com, is one of the Internet's top sites

*Harper Baird, University of New Mexico, prepared the updated version of this case with assistance from Celeste Wood, Robyn Watson, and Kevin Mihaly, Florida State University. This case is intended for classroom discussion rather than to illustrate effective or ineffective handling of an administrative situation.

for news and information. However, as newspapers struggle to stay relevant amidst technical and cultural changes, *USA Today* must continue to deliver innovative content and continuously improve their marketing strategies.

The History and Growth of *USA Today*

In February 1980, Allen Neuharth met with "Project NN" task force members to discuss his vision for producing and marketing a unique nationally distributed daily newspaper. Satellite technology had recently solved the problem of limited geographical distribution, so Neuharth was ready to take advantage of two trends in the reading public: (1) an increasingly short attention span among a generation nurtured on television, and (2) a growing hunger for more information. Neuharth believed that readers faced a time crunch in a world where so much information is available, but there is so little time to absorb it. His vision for *USA Today* positioned the paper as an information source that would provide more news about more subjects in less time.

Research suggested that *USA Today* should target achievement-oriented men in professional and managerial positions who were heavy newspaper readers and frequent travelers. While the *New York Times* targeted the nation's intellectual elite, thinkers, and policy makers, and the *Wall Street Journal* targeted business leaders, *USA Today* was targeted to Middle America—young, well-educated Americans who were on the move and cared about current events.

By early 1982, a team of news, advertising, and production personnel from the staffs of Gannett's daily newspapers developed, edited, published, and tested several different prototypes. Gannett sent three different 40-page prototype versions of *USA Today* to almost 5,000 professional people. Along with each prototype, they sent readers a response card that asked what they liked best and least about the proposed paper, and whether they would buy it. Although the content of each prototype was similar, the layout and graphics presentations differed. For example, one prototype included a section called "Agenda" that included comics and a calendar of meetings to be held by various professional organizations. According to marketplace feedback, readers liked the prototypes. The Gannett Board of Directors unanimously approved the paper's launch. On April 20, 1982, Gannett announced that the first copies of *USA Today* would be available in the Washington and Baltimore areas.

USA Today Launches

On September 15, 1982, 155,000 copies of the newspaper's first edition hit the newsstands. On page one, founder Neuharth wrote a short summary of *USA Today*'s mission statement, explaining that he wanted to make *USA Today* enlightening and enjoyable to the public, informative to national leaders, and attractive to advertisers. The first issue sold out. A little over a month following its debut, *USA Today*'s circulation hit 362,879—double the original year-end projection. In April 1983, just seven months after its introduction, the newspaper's circulation topped the 1 million mark. Case Exhibit 1.1 illustrates *USA Today*'s growth in circulation over time. The typical reader turned out to be a professional, usually a manager, about 40 years old, well educated, with an income of about $60,000 a year. The typical reader was also a news or sports junkie.

Compared to other newspapers, *USA Today* was truly unique. Designed for the TV generation, the paper was laid out for easy access and quick comprehension by time-pressed readers. Examples of this formatting included extensive use of briefs, columns, secondary headlines, subheads, breakouts, at-a-glance boxes, and informational graphics. These techniques captured the most salient points of a story and presented them in a

CASE EXHIBIT 1.1 **Growth in *USA Today*'s Circulation**

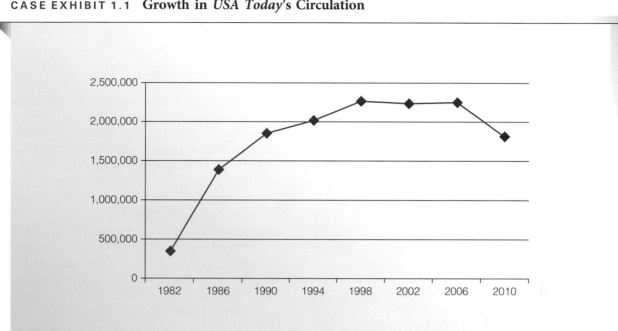

Source: Based on information from "USA TODAY Timeline," *USA Today* Media Kit (http://www.usatoday.com/marketing/media_kit/pressroom/timeline.html), accessed July 10, 2012.

format that readers appreciated. Gannett's research had shown that readers got most of their information from such snippets and that they were just as interested in sports, movie reviews, and health information as they were in traditional news. Each issue presented four sections: News, Money, Life, and Sports. The paper's motto fit its design: "An economy of words. A wealth of information."

Because *USA Today* was untraditional, its critics were numerous and fierce. In their view, the paper was loaded with gimmicks—tight, short stories; no jumps from page to page, except for the cover story (stories that jump to another page are one of newspaper readers' major complaints); splashy, colorful graphics everywhere; a distinctive, casual writing style; a colorful national weather map; a round-up of news items from each state, one paragraph each; summary boxes; little charts and statistics-laden sports coverage; and a focus on celebrity and sports, with more detailed sports stories than almost any other paper in the nation. There was no foreign staff and little coverage of the world outside the United States. *USA Today* was quickly derided for its shallowness by journalists and labeled "McPaper"—junk-food journalism or the fast food of the newspaper business—due to its terse, brash writing style and its short coverage of complex issues. Even within Gannett, Neuharth met with bitter resistance from some senior executives. Nevertheless, readers admired the paper for its focus on brevity and clarity, short sentences, and short words.

Clearly, the newspaper filled a gap in the market, satisfying several unmet needs and wants. *USA Today*'s success came from listening to its readers and giving them what they wanted. The paper communicates with readers on a personal level very quickly (many of the short, fact-filled stories are under 250 words), clearly, and directly, in an upbeat and positive way. The color is riveting and gives the paper a contemporary look, and so is the space-defying number of stories, factoids, larger than usual pictures, bar graphs, and charts, all squeezed onto each page without seeming too crowded. Instead of confusion, readers get neatness and order. The paper's dependably consistent organization enables readers to go directly to any one of *USA Today*'s major sections. As a result, it takes an average of only 25 minutes for a reader to peruse the paper.

Marketing Program Innovation

In spite of its critics, *USA Today*'s circulation surpassed 1.4 million by late 1985 as the paper expanded to 56 pages in length. The cover price had also increased to 50 cents, double its original price of 25 cents per issue. By this time, *USA Today* had become the second-largest paper in the country, with a circulation topped only by the *Wall Street Journal*. Although Neuharth had predicted that *USA Today* would quickly turn a profit, it took about five years to move into profitability, with the newspaper losing an estimated $600 million during its first decade. By 1993, however, *USA Today*'s profits were approximately $5 million. One year later profits doubled to about $10 million.

During its early growth, the paper unearthed a class of newspaper readers few others had stumbled upon: the business traveler. Airline deregulation had led to a large general price decline for airline tickets, inducing a swell in business travel. On-the-road business travelers wished to keep abreast of both world and national news as well as what was going on in their home state and how their local sports teams were doing. *USA Today* rushed in to fill the void, but in doing so quickly entered direct competition with the *Wall Street Journal*. By this time, hard-line newspapers, including the *New York Times*, began adding color; shorter, more tightly written stories; and beefed up circulation campaigns to compete with "The Nation's Newspaper." The *Wall Street Journal* followed suit by introducing two new sections—Money & Investing and Marketplace—to broaden the paper's coverage of media, marketing, technology, and personal investing. In the face of this competition, as well as an awareness of changing reader needs, *USA Today* responded through innovation of its own.

Product Innovation   To stay ahead of the imitative competition, *USA Today* decided to become a more serious newspaper with improved journalism. The shift from primarily soft news to hard news began with the space shuttle *Challenger* disaster in 1986. By 1991, editors began focusing much more sharply on hard news rather than soft features, and by 1994, under president and publisher Tom Curley, there was a massive drive to upgrade the paper to be a more serious, more responsible news-oriented product.

Gannett also incorporated less traditional value-added features to keep readers interested. The paper added 1-800 and 1-900 "hot-line" numbers that readers could call for expert information on financial planning, college admissions, minority business development, taxes, and other subjects. Thousands of readers responded to reader-opinion polls and write-in surveys on political and current event issues. Editorial pages were also redesigned to provide more room for guest columnists and to encourage debate. Gannett also initiated a high school "Academic All Star" program that was later expanded to include colleges and universities. The increasing ubiquity of the Internet in the late 1990s also resulted in some changes in content. For instance, the Money section began to focus more on technology issues and to look at business through an ecommerce perspective.

The first major redesign in *USA Today*'s history occurred in 2000 as the paper moved from a 54-inch to a 50-inch width. The goal of the redesign was to make the paper easier to read and cleaner in design. The pages were slimmer and easier to handle, especially in tight spaces like airplanes, trains, buses, and subways, and the paper fit more readily into briefcases, reflecting what Gannett had learned from focus groups.

Promotional Innovation *USA Today* also innovated in its promotional activities. Historically, the paper had limited its promotion to outdoor advertising and television. However, in the late 1980s Neuharth undertook a "BusCapade" promotion tour, traveling to all 50 states to talk with people about *USA Today*. Neuharth succeeded in raising public awareness of his paper, which was credited for *USA Today*'s move into profitability. Encouraged by his success, Neuharth forged ahead with a "JetCapade" campaign where he and a small news team traveled to 30 countries in seven months, stimulating global demand for the paper. During a visit to the troops of Operation Desert Storm in the Persian Gulf in 1991, General Norman Schwarzkopf expressed a need for news from home. *USA Today* arranged for delivery of 18,000 copies per day. The overseas success of *USA Today* led to the publication of *USA Today International*, which is now available in more than 60 countries in Western Europe, the Middle East, North Africa, and Asia.

Early on, *USA Today* faced a challenge in selling ad space because advertisers were not convinced that it would pay to advertise in the paper. Gannett's first strategy for enlisting advertisers was the Partnership Plan, which provided six months of free space to those who purchased six months of paid advertising. *USA Today* also began to accept regional advertising across a wide variety of categories such as travel, retail, tourism, and economic development. Color advertisements could arrive as late as 6:00 P.M. the day before publication, giving local advertisers increased flexibility. The paper also moved aggressively into "blue-chip circulation," where bulk quantities of *USA Today* are sold at discounted prices to hotels, airlines, and restaurants, and are provided free of charge to customers.

USA Today pulled off another promotional first in 1999 when it broke one of the most sacred practices of daily newspapers and began offering advertising space on the front page (one-inch strips across the entire width of the bottom of the page). This highly sought after front-page position was sold through one-year contracts for $1 million to $1.2 million each, with each advertiser taking one day a week. As *USA Today* continued to prosper, advertisers became attracted to the paper's large volume of readers. To help cope with advertiser demand, the paper implemented the technology to allow advertisers to transmit copy electronically 24 hours per day.

Distribution Innovation Fast delivery has always been important to *USA Today*. By the late-1990s, the paper was earning kudos for its ability to deliver timely news, thanks to its late deadlines. For instance, in many parts of the country *USA Today* could print later sports scores than local or regional papers. In hard news, *USA Today* was able to offer more up-to-date coverage by rolling the presses over four hours earlier than the *Wall Street Journal* and almost three hours later than the *New York Times*. The paper added print sites around the world in a move to further speed up distribution. An innovative readership program was also added that brought *USA Today* to more than 160 college campuses around the nation. Likewise, technological advances allowed the paper's production to become totally digital. A new computer-to-plate technology was implemented to give newsrooms later deadlines and readers earlier delivery times.

USA Today Moves Online

A decade after *USA Today*'s launch, Gannett found itself in the enviable position of owning one of America's most successful newspapers. *USA Today* was the most widely read newspaper in the country, with daily readership of over 3.7 million (readership numbers are higher than paid circulation numbers due to the passing of copies to other readers). In an era when nearly all major national media were suffering declines in readership or viewing audience, *USA Today* continued to grow. Rising distribution and promotion costs, however, were beginning to make the newspaper slightly unprofitable.

To reverse this trend, *USA Today* created several spin-offs, including its first special interest publication, *Baseball Weekly*. During its first month of operation, *Baseball Weekly*'s circulation reached 250,000 copies. *Baseball Weekly* was eventually expanded to include a variety of sports coverage and was renamed *Sports Weekly*. At the end of 2007, *Sports Weekly* was ranked the highest sports magazine in newsstand sales. Due to the success of the *Sports Weekly* format, *USA Today* launched a similar magazine in March 2009. *USA Today*'s *Open Air* magazine was geared toward the "busy, well-informed, affluent customer" and designed to inspire "millions of readers to find adventure and its rewards in their everyday lives." According to *USA Today*, "*Open Air* offers a compelling new look at the possibilities for adventure that surround us each day—from regular activities like improving your golf game with a stretch the pros use, or finding the best gear for your next softball tournament, to once-in-a-lifetime opportunities like a six-day hike into the spectacular Rio Grande Gorge in New Mexico." However, rather than marketing the publication as a stand-alone product, *Open Air* was used to increase demand in the print sector and made available four times a year in Friday editions of *USA Today*. Also, venturing into news media, *USA Today* joined with CNN to produce a football TV program and launched SkyRadio to provide live radio on commercial airline flights.

The major spin-off, in terms of current success and future potential, was *USA Today Online*, which the company introduced on April 17, 1995. The online version was seen as a natural companion to the print version of *USA Today*, given the paper's worldwide distribution. The first version was available through CompuServe's Mosaic browser and required special software, a CompuServe Network connection, and a monthly subscription of $14.95 plus $3.95 per hour. By June of 1995, *USA Today Online* converted to a free service that worked with any web browser and Internet service provider. The "online" was later dropped in favor of USAToday.com.

Like its print sister, USAToday.com is bright, upbeat, and full of nugget-sized news stories. The online version allows readers to receive up-to-the-moment news that incorporates colorful visuals and crisp audio. It provides one of the most extensive sites on the Internet, featuring thousands of pages of up-to-the-minute news, sports, business and technology news, four-day weather forecasts, and travel information available 24 hours a day, seven days a week.

Another revenue generator, launched in 1998 in response to frequent reader requests for archived material, was the pay-per-view archives service (http://archives.usatoday.com). The *USA Today* Archives section allows readers to do a free, unlimited search of the paper's articles that have appeared since April 1987. Articles may be downloaded for $3.95 per story or as a part of the site's daily, monthly, and yearly access plans.

USA Today Provides to On-Demand News and Information

USAToday.com has evolved from an online news media source to an on-demand, information-rich community. This movement toward online media was the result of rising newsprint costs, which, in fact, forced virtually all newspaper firms to add online news to increase readership and cut distribution expenses. In addition, to align with the advancing pace of communication and technology, CEO Craig Dubow announced his commitment to "getting news and information into the hands of consumers faster than ever before." To aid the company in this initiative, USAToday.com added blogs, RSS (really simple syndication), and podcasts to ensure that its news stayed relevant to busy and mobile readers. Gannett also purchased interest in a company with unique technology that aggregated news on the Internet and categorized the information into 300,000 topics. Other acquisitions included PointRoll, a service that allowed Internet advertisers to expand their online space. One innovative way Gannett leveraged this service was to help advertisers to direct consumers to local merchants. When a user rolled their cursor over an ad, the ad expanded to reveal information about the closest retailer.

Also, in an effort to become the one-stop shop for all types of information, USAToday.com began providing readers and site visitors with the opportunity to search for their unique interests and connect with like-minded individuals. For instance, in the first quarter of 2008, USAToday.com introduced "Network Journalism," a site that combines professionally created content from *USA Today* writers, with consumer-generated content, comments, and recommendations, as well as instant message news alerts and advanced search functions. The company also created online communities with discussion forums, polls, and other interactive content. Today, USAToday.com's online community groups continue to expand, with forums targeting individuals interested in topics such as MMA (Mixed Martial Arts), cars ("Open Road"), and video gaming.

In addition, USAToday.com launched nearly 200,000 unique online topics pages available via links threaded in the story pages or through a stand-alone topics section. According to Jeff Webber, publisher of USAToday.com, "*USA Today* has always focused on what America is talking about and provides the content that fuels the nation's conversation. Our new topics pages go in-depth into subjects ranging from Sarah Palin to Starbucks; Barack Obama to Bono; and American Idol to the iPhone, all the things that make America tick." The topics page categories include Brands; Culture; Events and Awards; Health and Wellness; Legislation and Acts; Natural and Physical Sciences; Organizations; People; Places, Geography; and Religion and Beliefs.

Brand Extensions and Partnerships

A key part of *USA Today*'s marketing strategy is forming partnerships to expand their reach. In 2008, *USA Today* began to look beyond the scope of daily news media and ventured into brand extensions by way of retail locations and television. As an attempt to capture more share of customer (rather than market share), *USA Today* opened three *USA Today* Travel Zone retail locations in airport terminals in late 2008. These retail shops carry all products travelers expect to find, including reading materials, sundries, travel accessories, and other convenience items. To align with the current look and feel of the paper its customers recognize, sections of the store are clearly identified and utilize colors representing *USA Today*'s signature sections: News (blue), Money (green), Sports (red), and Life (purple).

Also in 2008, the company launched *USA Today Live*—a television service designed to extend the company's reach beyond current concentrated efforts and target business professionals and travelers. By partnering with Fuse, the national music television network Versus, and MOJO HD on a variety of series-based programming, *USA Today Live* introduced new audiences to the *USA Today* brand. The programming partnerships included: "City Limits Fishing," a six-part weekly series on Versus that highlighted places where anglers regularly catch limits of fish in not so far-off, exotic destinations; "10 Great Reasons," an eight-part weekly series on Fuse designed to "pay tribute to acts, genres, rumors and stories about our musical guilty pleasures and why we love them so, but may be just a tad embarrassed to admit;" as well as "Gotta Get Gold," a 10-part series on MOJO HD that focused on what it takes to train and to compete at the highest levels in athletics.

In January 2011, *USA Today* acquired Reviewed.com, a company that tests and rates consumer electronics such as cameras, camcorders, and HD televisions. *USA Today* also worked with Learning.com in 2012 to give teachers and students better access to digital teaching resources and educational content. Other recent partnerships include Major League Baseball, Doritos, Seat Geek, and National Geographic. These brand extensions are part of *USA Today*'s strategy to develop an "integrated consumer media strategy" and add more value to their products.

USA Today—Today and Tomorrow

Looking at the total national newspaper market, *USA Today* has been quite successful. It has seen more than 30 years of continuous growth and is one of the most widely read newspapers in the United States. Together, *USA Today* and USAToday.com have over 5.3 million daily readers, including over 1.8 million paid subscribers. Although the newspaper's print circulation has declined, *USA Today* still has the largest print circulation with over 1.8 million copies daily and 3.2 million daily readers. The paper also boasts the highest volume of newsstand sales at 425,000 papers per day. Although *USA Today* still has the most print newspapers in circulation, its 116,000 digital subscriptions lag behind both the *Wall Street Journal*'s 552,000 and the *New York Times*' 807,000 digital subscriptions. This has led to *USA Today* losing its lead as the most widely read newspaper to the *Wall Street Journal*.

Although the newspaper's digital subscription rates are low, *USA Today*'s online audience has increased to almost 24 million unique visitors per month. During 2011, USAToday.com saw double-digit growth in unique visitors, visits, and page views per month. In October 2011, the site had its best month on record in nearly five years. Engagement on the site also increased, with the average time spent on the site per visitor increasing 34 percent.

In addition to declines in print media, *USA Today* also faces fierce competition in online information distribution through television and magazine sites, blogs, and podcasts. Internet-based companies like Yahoo! and Google have now moved into the advertising market. The multitude of choices for both consumers and advertisers means that *USA Today* will have to work harder at innovation, finding a way to differentiate its products from the sea of competition. This will be a challenging task given the continuing decline in newspaper readership and the growing consumer demand for free online news.

As *USA Today* looks ahead, a number of issues must be considered. The following sections describe some of the key issues that the company faces as it plans for its future.

USA Today's Customers

The overwhelming majority of *USA Today*'s circulation is within the United States. Most *USA Today* readers work in middle- to upper-management positions and are often purchasing decision makers for their offices and households, as well as technological junkies and sports fans. They also participate in a wide range of leisure activities such as attending movies and traveling. The print newspaper's readers are 69 percent male and 31 percent female, with a median age of 50 and a median household income of $91,683. For USAToday.com, the audience is balanced between men (51 percent) and women (49 percent), but with a much lower median age (30 years) and median household income ($47,500). Home ownership is also much lower for USAToday.com's audience (49 percent) than for the newspaper's readers (80 percent).

Important players in the purchase process are subscribers, single-copy buyers, and third-party sponsors, often referred to as blue-chip buyers. *USA Today*'s most loyal customers are print subscribers, who buy Sunday or daily newspapers delivered directly to their home or office at 13- to 52-week intervals for $195 per year. Single-copy buyers tend to purchase the paper out of daily routine (heavy users) or on occasion based on specific newsworthy events (light users). Single-copy editions of *USA Today* are distributed via newsstand retailers, large grocery store chains, bookstores, and coin-operated vending machines. Twenty percent of paid copies are purchased by third parties, which distribute complimentary copies to end users to add value to their own goods or services. For example, hotels, restaurants, banks, college campuses, airports and other service organizations offer customers the opportunity to enjoy a copy of *USA Today* during breakfast or while waiting in the lobby. *USA Today* content is also available in electronic formats from USAToday.com, mobile devices, and e-mail updates. The e-edition costs $99 per year. The availability of *USA Today* via electronic distribution may deter some consumers from purchasing the print product.

Competition

Gannett has competitors from several fields, including other national newspapers such as the *Wall Street Journal* and the *New York Times*, cable networks, nationally syndicated terrestrial and satellite radio providers such as Sirius/XM, Internet sites such as Yahoo! and Google, and blogs such as the Huffington Post.

The **Wall Street Journal** *USA Today*'s biggest newspaper competitor is the *Wall Street Journal*, owned by Dow Jones & Co. Inc. The *Wall Street Journal* targets influential business readers as its primary audience. The company's product lines include newspapers, newswires, magazines, websites, indexes, television, and radio. The *Journal's* website, www.wsj.com, adds over 1,000 news stories per day and includes price information on over 30,000 stocks and funds worldwide. The *Wall Street Journal* has strategic alliances with other information companies, including CNBC, Reuters, and SmartMoney.

Total print and digital circulation for the *Wall Street Journal* version is 2.12 million, which includes 1.56 million print subscriptions and over 552,000 paid digital subscriptions. The large number of paid subscribers gives the *Wall Street Journal* the widest circulation of any newspaper, beating *USA Today* by over 310,000. Fifty-six percent of the print newspaper's readers are employed as top management, and 88 percent are college graduates. The average household income is $257,100 and the average net worth is $2.6 million. Eighty-two percent of print readers are male, and the average reader is 57 years old. The *Wall Street Journal* charges a fee of $9.65 per week (about $502 per year) for a combined digital and print subscription and $4.99 per week (about $260 per year) for a digital only subscription.

Dow Jones has made several improvements to the *Journal* in an attempt to make it more competitive. It added a Weekend Edition in 2005, designed to help advertisers reach the paper's audience at home on the weekends. The *Wall Street Journal* also implemented compact 48-inch width and new design. The newspaper followed *USA Today*'s lead and added ads to the front page, showing that this practice is becoming more common as newspapers look for ways to increase revenue.

The **New York Times** In addition to the *New York Times*, the New York Times Co. owns other newspapers and related websites, two New York City radio stations, nine television stations serving seven states, and search engine About.com, which they acquired in 2005 for $410 million. The newspaper's target market is the intellectual elite. As explained in their press kit, "The *New York Times*—Influential people read it because influential people read it." Like *USA Today* and the *Wall Street Journal*, the *New York Times* is available both in print and online at www.nytimes.com.

Total circulation for the *New York Times* is 1.58 million, which includes 779,000 print subscriptions and 807,000 digital subscriptions. *New York Times* readers are 52 percent male, 65 percent college graduates, 40 percent professional/managerial, and have a median age of 49. The average household income is $99,645. Print subscriptions (which include full digital access) for customers outside of the New York City area cost $200 to $400 per year depending on the frequency of delivery. Digital subscriptions (which include unlimited access to NYTimes.com) are available for smartphones ($195 per year), tablets ($260 per year), or both ($455 per year).

The company has recently made changes in an attempt to be more profitable. The *New York Times* raised its home-delivery rates and reduced the number of pages in its stock section. Additionally, the paper has implemented cost-savings policies including staff reductions, reducing the width of its print version. From 2011–2012, the *New York Times* saw a 73 percent increase in its circulation due to an increase in paid digital subscriptions.

Other Media Competitors   *USA Today* also faces competition for audience attention and advertising dollars from companies outside its industry, including network and cable television, television news websites, and Internet news aggregators. As shown in Case Exhibit 1.2, national newspapers fare poorly in terms of regular use when compared to other media options.

More and more Americans, especially younger people, are turning to new sources of media consumption. Internet information providers or news aggregators are another source of competition for *USA Today*. Over one billion people globally have access to the Internet at home or work. Most Internet information providers make their money through subscriptions, advertising, or both. It is important to note that the Internet as a communications and advertising medium is no longer tied to desktop computers. Virtually all major Internet providers and content developers now make their content available via handheld devices, including *USA Today*.

Economic Woes

USA Today and other newspapers have been struggling with falling revenues and increased costs for several years. Both print and online advertising revenues have been falling steadily, declining by over 51 percent since 2005. Classified advertising has been hit particularly hard, declining by over 71 percent in just six years, most likely due to sites like Craigslist, which host ads for free (see Case Exhibit 1.3). Although advertising revenues had been falling before the recession, 2008 and 2009 saw steep declines triggered by a soft ad market, particularly in the automotive, retail, and employment sectors. In fact, 2008 and 2009 were the worst years ever for the U.S. newspaper industry. Although advertising revenues continue to decline today, the rate

CASE EXHIBIT 1.2   Sources of News for U.S. Adults

	Use All the Time or Occasionally	Use Rarely or Never
Local TV News	76%	23%
Network TV News	66%	32%
Cable TV News	60%	38%
Local Newspapers	69%	30%
National Newspapers	25%	73%
Weekly News Magazines	25%	72%
Online News Aggregators	49%	48%
Cable TV Websites	36%	61%
National Newspaper Websites	36%	61%

Source: Based on information from "Troubles for Traditional Media—Both Print and Television," Harris Interactive, October 28, 2010 (http://www.harrisinteractive.com/NewsRoom/HarrisPolls/tabid/447/mid/1508/articleId/604/ctl/ReadCustom%20Default/Default.aspx).

CASE EXHIBIT 1.3 **Annual Advertising Expenditures in Newspapers**

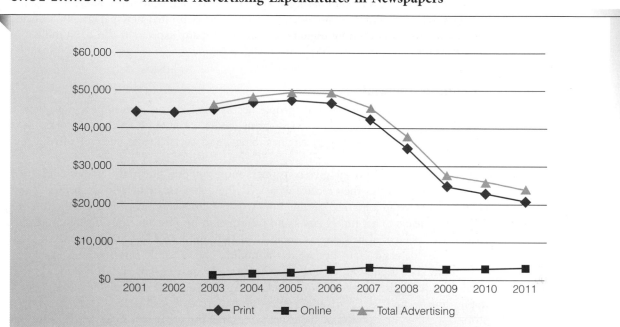

Source: Based on Newspaper Association of America, March 2012 (http://www.naa.org/Trends-and-Numbers/Advertising-Expenditures/Annual-All-Categories.aspx).

of decline has slowed in recent years, with total newspaper advertising down 7.3 percent in 2011.

In addition, the high cost of newsprint is also a problem for newspapers. The average cost per ton of newsprint consumed increased by 13 percent in 2011, but the effects of price increases were partially offset by a decline in print newspaper consumption. In attempt to mitigate the print cost increases, Gannett continues to moderate newsprint consumption and expenses through press web-width reductions and the use of lighter-weight and recycled papers.

These costs have forced numerous newspapers to close, reduce publication days, lay off employees, reduce salaries, or adopt an online-online format. Gannet has started to focus on diminishing its newspapers' reliance on print sales. In August 2010, *USA Today* restructured their newsroom to adjust to changes in the economy and the newspaper industry. The company made major changes to the circulation, finance, and news divisions, and created ten new executive positions and cut 9 percent of its staff. The remaining staff was broken up into "content rings" instead of the News, Sports, Money, and Life sections. In addition, in 2012 Gannett named media industry veteran Larry Kramer as CEO of *USA Today*. Kramer is responsible for implementing a corporate strategy focused on digital media, starting with a planned relaunch of *USAToday*'s online, mobile, and tablet products.

To respond to rising costs and the loss of adverting revenue, *USA Today* and other newspapers are attempting to find new ways to generate revenue through their pricing strategies. After years of offering online news for free, a growing number of newspapers, including *USA Today* and other Gannett newspapers, have implemented metered pay walls, which give readers online access to a few free stories before requiring them to sign up for a digital subscription. Readers are limited to 5 to 15 free stories a month and can have digital access by purchasing at least a Sunday print subscription. Gannett is also raising single-copy prices by as much as a third for its printed newspapers. By reducing their print costs and pushing digital media, the company expects to add $100 million in annual profit.

Changing Technology

Technology has changed the way people access information. Consumers now have a variety of ways to get the latest news—print media, 24-hour television networks, news websites, mobile devices, search engines, blogs, and social media sites all provide up-to-the-minute news.

Not only does technology give consumers more options, but it also allows consumers to customize the news they receive at a level they were never able to do before. These changes have led to a marked decline in newspaper circulation as people use the Internet and other means to get timely news and information. In just one year, digital circulation rose to 14.2 percent of newspapers' total circulation, up from 8.66 percent in March 2011.

As the demand for update-to-the-minute news and information expanded, USAToday.com capitalized on the growth of mobile devices. For smartphone and tablet users (including the Amazon Kindle and the Apple iPad), the company created multiple applications. The *USA Today* applications provide readers with access to the latest news stories, weather, and photos at the exact same time the paper hits newsstands. The apps also feature interactive polls, and users can share News, Money, Sports, Life, Tech, and Travel articles via e-mail, text message, Facebook, or Twitter. Both *USA Today*'s iPhone and iPad applications lead the news category; the iPhone application reaches 1.4 million monthly visitors and has over 4.7 million downloads, while the iPad application reaches 1.1 million monthly visitors and has over 2.8 million downloads.

In addition, *USA Today* offers several other mobile apps, including games and trivia. The company partnered with Hampton Hotels to offer the AutoPilot application, targeting business and travel consumer groups. The AutoPilot app offers users the ability to easily track trip and flight itineraries, utilize GPS capabilities in real time, get "up to the minute delay information for more than 16,000 airports, 1,400 airlines and 100,000 daily flights," monitor departing and arriving flight information, and access current and future weather conditions. The company's mobile strategy appears to be working; USAToday.com mobile traffic increased 154 percent in 2011, with the iPad generating almost half the traffic.

USA Today is also taking advantage of the rise of social media sites. In 2011, social media referrals to USAToday.com increased 61 percent, with Facebook, Twitter, and Stumble Upon driving the majority of referrals. In a move to provide more customizable content and take advantage of the popularity of Facebook, *USA Today* launched the USA Today + Me Social News app in January 2012. This app suggests select *USA Today* news articles to Facebook users based on personal interests as well as what their friends have read and recommended. This may be a key innovation for the company as more and more people spend time on Facebook. The apps make it convenient for customers to access news and add a social aspect to reading the news.

Overall, technology may have initiated the decline of the newspaper industry, but it also offers *USA Today* opportunities to maintain and even expand its readership. Technology allows *USA Today* and other newspapers to deliver news in more cost-efficient, customizable, direct, and useful ways than will ever be possible using newsprint. In particular, mobile technology has allowed *USA Today* to literally execute Dubow's vision of "getting news and information into the hands of consumers faster than ever before."

Cultural Shifts

The decline of the *USA Today* and other print newspapers is part of a wider cultural trend. People are increasingly getting their news from the Internet. Research by the Pew Research Center shows that 41 percent of people cite the Internet as one of their main sources of news, compared to 31 percent who cite newspapers. This trend reflects both the growth of the Internet and the gradual decline in newspapers' readership.

This trend is even stronger among younger people. Sixty-five percent of 18- to 29-year-olds cite the Internet as one of their main sources of news, making it the most popular source of information. To take advantage of this trend, newspapers are attempting to attract new and younger readers, offering more interactive and social components. The transition is a difficult one, however, because there are significant differences between the interests of current newspaper readers (mostly Baby Boomers) and younger consumers. Baby Boomers are most interested in major news stories and local news coverage, while younger readers are more interested in sports, entertainment, and comics.

Evolving to Meet the Future

Although increasing digital options for news and information have some industry observers bemoaning the death of newspapers, some feel that newspapers will thrive if they develop a healthy online presence and adapt to evolving media consumption patterns. New technologies, shifts in readership, and increased printing costs present challenges to *USA Today* as well as opportunities to expand their reach to new customers and mediums. For over 30 years, the newspaper has met the needs of its customers in new and unexpected ways. In the face of competition in both print and digital markets, the future of *USA Today* depends on its ability to continue to innovate and adapt its marketing strategies to changing needs of the market. To remain successful, *USA Today* must continue to use a value-added strategy to further enhance distribution of its proprietary content and ensure continued product differentiation.

Questions for Discussion

1. What opportunities in the marketing environment did Gannett seize in launching *USA Today*? How did the company learn about and respond to these opportunities? Answer these same questions for USAToday.com.
2. How has a continuous strategy of marketing innovation proved successful for *USA Today* and USAToday.com? Do you believe that *USA Today* is well positioned for the future? Explain.
3. What are the SWOT implications for *USA Today* as it looks toward its future? What strengths and opportunities can *USA Today* leverage as it looks for a competitive advantage in the distribution of news and information?
4. Based on *USA Today*'s experiences with print and online news, evaluate the long-term potential of printed news and the newspaper publishing industry. Do you believe printed newspapers will continue to survive despite digital competition?

Sources

The facts of this case are from American Free Press, "US Papers Decline Despite Online Growth: Report," March 6, 2012 (http://www.turkishpress.com/news.asp?id=379507); Tim Arango, "Drop in Newspaper Circulation Accelerates to Pass 7%," NYTimes.com, April 27, 2009 (http://www.nytimes.com/2009/04/28/business/media/28paper.html?_r=2); Dow Jones, Inc. Fact Sheet (http://www.dj.com/djcom/Fact Sheets/DowJones.htm), accessed July 10, 2012; Rick Edmonds, "Why USA Today's Declines Led to Radical Restructuring," *Poynter*, March 4, 2011 (http://www.poynter.org/latest-news/business-news/the-biz-blog/105382/why-usa-todays-declines-led-to-radical-restructuring); "Electronic Paper," *Wikipedia* (http://en.wikipedia.org/wiki/Electronic_paper), accessed July 10, 2012; Gannett Company, Inc., 2008 Annual Report (http://media.corporate-ir.net/media_files/irol/84/84662/08GCIAnnualReport.pdf), accessed October 19, 2009; Paul Gillin, "Some Innovative Papers Find Ways to Diversify," *Newspaper Death Watch*, March 21, 2012 (http://newspaperdeathwatch.com); Harris Interactive, "Troubles for Traditional Media - Both Print and Television," October, 28, 2010 (http://www.harrisinteractive.com/NewsRoom/HarrisPolls/tabid/447/mid/1508/articleId/604/ctl/ReadCustom%20Default/Default.aspx); Peter Johnson, "Internet News Supplements Papers, TV," *USA Today*, July 31, 2006, p. 5D; K. Jurgensen, "Quick Response; Paper Chase: *USA Today* Editor Sees Shifts in How Information is Generated and Delivered to Readers," *Advertising Age*, February 14, 2000, p. S6; K. Jurgensen, "*USA Today*'s New Look Designed for Readers," *USA Today*, April 3, 2000, p. 1A; "Larry Kramer Named Publisher Of USA Today," *Huffington Post*, May 14, 2012 (http://www.huffingtonpost.com/2012/05/15/larry-kramer-usa-today-publisher_n_1517611.html); P. Long, "After Long Career, *USA Today* Founder Al Neuharth is Ready for More," *Knight-Ridder/Tribune Business News*, April 28, 1999; Neal Lulofs, "The Top U.S. Newspapers for March 2012," *Audit Bureau of Circulations* (http://accessabc.wordpress.com/2012/05/01/the-top-u-s-newspapers-for-march-2012), accessed May 15, 2012; "Media Kit," *Wall Street Journal* (http://www.wsjmediakit.com), accessed May 18, 2012; "Media Trends Track," Television Bureau of Advertising (http://www.tvb.org/media comparisons/02_A_Consumers_Continue.asp?mod=R), accessed September 1, 2006; J. McCartney, "*USA Today* Grows Up," *American Journalism Review*, September 1997, 19; Douglas McIntyre, "USA Today Ad Revenue in Free Fall, a Nightmare for the Future of Print," BloggingStocks.com, June 18, 2008 (http://www.bloggingstocks.com/2008/06/18/usa-today-ad-revenue-in-free-fall-a-nightmare-for-the-future-of); B. Miller, "*USA Today*, Gannett to Launch *USA Today Live*," *Television & Cable*, February 8, 2000; "Newspaper Closings Raise Fears About Industry," USAToday.com, March 19, 2009 (http://www.usatoday.com/money/media/2009-03-17-newspapers-downturn_N.htm); Ryan Nakashima, "Newspapers Erect Pay Walls in Hunt for New Revenue," Associated Press, April 3, 2012 (http://www.dispatch.com/content/stories/business/2012/04/03/newspapers-erect-pay-walls-in-hunt-for-new-revenue.html); Newspaper Association of America, "Trends & Numbers," March 14, 2012 (http://www.naa.org/Trends-and-Numbers/Advertising-Expenditures/Annual-All-Categories.aspx); *New York Times* Revenue and Circulation Data, New York Times, Inc. (http://www.nytco.com/excel/1208adrev/ad-circ-other-rev.xls), accessed October 19, 2009; Shira Ovide, "USA Today Likely to Fall To No. 2 in Circulation," *Wall Street Journal.com*, October 10, 2009 (http://online.wsj.com/article/SB125513318195777441.html); Eric Sass, "Newspaper Revenues Plunge 28% in Q1, Online Falling Too," *MediaDaily* News.com, May 28, 2009 (http://www.mediapost.com/publications/?fa=Articles.showArticle&art_aid=106948); Erick Schonfeld, "The Wounded U.S. Newspaper Industry Lost $7.5 Billion in Advertising Revenues Last Year," *TechCrunch*, March 29, 2009 (http://www.techcrunch.com/2009/03/29/the-wounded-us-newspaper-industry-lost-75-billion-in-advertising-rev enues-last-year); "The New York Times Media Kit" (http://nytmarketing.whsites.net/mediakit), accessed May 18, 2012; The Pew Research Center, "Internet Gains on Television as Public's Main News Source," January 4, 2011 (http://www.ris.org/uploadi/editor/1296476726689.pdf); *USA Today* Corporate website (http://www.usatoday.com), accessed May 15, 2011; "*USA Today* and Gannett Partner with MobileVoiceControl to Bring Voice-Driven Mobile Search to Blackberry," TMCnet, May 23, 2006 (http://www.tmcnet.com/usubmit/2006/05/23/1658295.htm); "*USA Today* No Longer a Newspaper," *Advertising Age*, September 9, 2002, p. 18; *USA Today* Press Kit: Audience (http://www.usatoday.com/marketing/media_kit/pressroom/audience.html), accessed October 19, 2009; "*USA Today* Sells Page One Advertising Space," *PR Newswire*, May 5, 1999, p. 351; *USA Today*, "Snapshot," August 22, 2006, p. 1; and Andrew Vanacore, "USA Today to Post 17 Percent Drop in Circulation," *BusinessWeek Online*, October 9, 2009 (http://www.business week.com/ap/financialnews/D9B7OR2O0.htm).

CASE 2

Apple's Winning Marketing Strategy*

Synopsis: Few companies have been able to master the arts of product innovation, a "cool" brand image, and customer evangelism like Apple. After nearly collapsing under a cloud of bankruptcy in the mid-1990s, late Apple CEO Steve Jobs was able to save the company he created through product innovation, a masterful marketing program, and an entrepreneurial corporate culture. This case reviews Apple's history and remarkable comeback with an eye toward the marketing strategies that created the company's success. The case also examines many of the challenges faced by a company that continually pushes the boundaries of marketing practice to stay on top of the consumer electronics and computer industries.

Themes: Product innovation, marketing program, prestige pricing, competition, changing technology, differentiation, customer loyalty, foreign sourcing, intellectual property, privacy issues, corporate culture, sustainability

Few companies can boast that they have fans that sleep outside its doors to be the first to snag its latest products, but such is the case with Apple, Inc. In 2011, Apple surpassed Google to become the most valuable global brand, with an estimated value of $153 billion. Headquartered in Cupertino, California, Apple has transformed itself from a company near bankruptcy in 1997 (with a stock price of $3.30) to the world's most valuable company in 2012 (with a stock price of more than $600).

Many companies have tried to copy Apple's strategies, but none have reached the iconic status of Apple and its products. Some believe that Apple's success stems from a combination of several factors, including the leadership qualities of late CEO Steve Jobs, a corporate culture of enthusiasm and innovation, and the revolutionary products for which Apple has become known. While every organization must acquire resources and develop a business strategy to pursue its objectives, Apple has excelled in both leadership and operations. One of the company's most important resources is its employees, and the company has effectively recruited, trained, and compensated employees to create loyalty. Another resource is suppliers, and Apple has created a highly efficient and effective supply chain with most of its production in China. Apple has also mastered core research and development skills that have allowed the company to translate its technological capabilities into products that consumers want and are willing to pay a premium price to obtain. The capstone of Apple's strategy is its retail stores that have become a role model for its competitors,

---

*Jennifer Sawayda and Harper Baird, University of New Mexico, prepared this case under the direction of O.C. Ferrell for classroom discussion rather than to illustrate effective or ineffective handling of an administrative situation.

both in and out of the electronics industry. Such factors have allowed Apple to revolutionize the technology and retail industries.

The History of Apple, Inc.

When Apple Computer was founded in 1976, it would have been unrecognizable to its diehard fans of today. Apple's first product, the Apple I, was essentially a computer kit that lacked a graphic user interface, keyboard, or display (users had to provide their own). Co-founders Steve Jobs and Steve Wozniak released the Apple I for $666.66. Jobs and Wozniak continued to create innovative products, and because the duo designed Apple's computers from the user's point of view, its products seemed to resonate with consumers. A few years later, Apple had more than $1 million in sales. The company was off to a promising start.

Yet, Apple's initial success did not last. Its downturn started during the 1980s with a series of product flops and CEO changes. Steve Jobs was ousted in 1985 due to internal conflicts within the company. By the mid-1990s, the company was approaching bankruptcy. Dell Computer founder Michael Dell commented about Apple's future, saying, "I'd shut it down and give the money back to the shareholders."

The return of Steve Jobs in 1997 instituted major changes for Apple. The company successfully adopted a market orientation in which it was able to gather intelligence about customers' current and future needs for certain features—even before the customers themselves knew they needed them. Apple expanded into the electronics industry and began to release innovative products that resonated deeply with customers. For instance, the creation of the iPod and iTunes met customer needs for an efficient way to manage and listen to a variety of music on the go. This ability of Apple to recognize strategic windows of opportunity and act upon them before the competition remains with the company today.

In 2007, Jobs announced that Apple Computer, Inc. would be re-named Apple, Inc. Some perceived this renaming to be a shift away from computers toward consumer electronics. However, a more appropriate viewpoint would be to say that Apple was reinventing its stance toward computers. With the introduction of the iPad in 2010, Apple began to take market share away from top competitors in the computer industry. Sales of desktops, laptops, and netbooks began to decline after the iPad was introduced. Now almost three years since the iPad's introduction, its sales continue to skyrocket. Apple owns a commanding 70-plus percent of the worldwide tablet market.

Although the Apple products of today are high in demand, this was not always the case. Apple went through its share of product failures in its past. Several of these failures can be attributed to a failure to accurately predict consumer behavior. For instance, even though Apple products are generally premium priced, the Apple Lisa and Cube were judged as too expensive for the mass market. In addition, the Apple Newton (a precursor to the iPad) was a great product that was well ahead of its time. Thanks to its innovative products and marketing strategies, Apple has grown into one of the most admired and successful brands in the world. To millions of consumers, the Apple brand embodies quality, prestige, and innovation.

Apple's Products

While introducing new products is expensive and risky, Apple has reinvented the concept of a new product. While many Apple products provide a function that was already on the market, Apple's products are different, distinctive, and are often viewed as superior to the competition. After introducing new products such as the iPod, iPhone, and iPad, Apple has changed the products' features, quality, and/or aesthetics on a regular basis to create a perception that consumers have to have the latest model. For example, with each new version of the iPad, Apple offered new features and benefits that effectively made the older models obsolete. Few companies have been able to exploit the concept of product modification as effectively as Apple.

Today, Apple has honed its ability to produce iconic products that consumers desire. The company's product strategy is based on innovative designs, ease-of-use, and seamless integration. Apple has not only created highly successful products, but also whet consumers' appetites for yet-to-be-released and rumored products. For example, rumors continue to swirl that Apple will release a mini iPad and an Apple-branded television in the near future.

Mac Computers

Apple first made a name for itself in the personal computer industry, and even though it has since expanded into the consumer electronics industry, its Macintosh computers remain a strong asset to the company's product mix. Many computer owners identify themselves as either Mac or PC users. Major differences between Macs and PCs lie with their processors and interfaces. Mac enthusiasts often prefer the superior video and graphic software as well as the look and feel of Macs. MacBook laptops also tend to last longer than the average 2-year life span of PC-based laptops. For these reasons, Macs are priced much higher than competitors. Apple sells two types of Macs: desktop and laptop computers. Desktop Macs include the iMac, Mac Pro, and Mac Mini, while its laptops include the MacBook Pro and MacBook Air. The Air proved to be so popular with consumers that a variety of PC manufacturers created an entire line of copycat "ultrabook" laptops running the Windows operating system.

iPod and iTunes

In 2001, Apple launched the iPod—a portable music player that forever changed the music industry. The company also introduced iTunes, a type of "jukebox" software that allows users to upload songs from CDs onto their Macs and then organize and manage their personalized music libraries. Two years later, Apple introduced the iTunes Store, in which users could download millions of their favorite songs for $0.99 each. The average price later increased to $1.29 per song. Both the iPod and iTunes became market leaders in their respective industries. Apple has sold more than 300 million iPods since its introduction, and users have downloaded approximately 16 billion songs from iTunes. However, iPod sales have declined in recent years as consumers have begun to favor the iPhone instead. Still, the iPod remains a popular music device and has largely supplanted traditional CDs. The current Apple iPod product line includes the iPod touch, iPod nano, iPod shuffle, and iPod classic. Apple also sells the Apple TV, a device that essentially allows any television to connect to the iTunes store. Users can rent or purchase movies, or stream their own content wirelessly to any connected television.

iPhone

The Apple iPhone debuted in 2007 and quickly became a favorite among mobile phone users. The iPhone combined smartphone technology with a straightforward operating system, an easy-to-use touch screen, iPod features, and a simple design. Each new generation is highly anticipated by Apple fans eager to use the iPhone's newest features. For example, the iPhone 4s includes a built-in "personal assistant" called Siri. Siri recognizes voice commands and can answer with the appropriate response. The iPhone has been a resounding success: Apple has sold almost 200 million of the devices since its launch.

iPad

In April 2010, Apple introduced the iPad, a tablet computer designed for simple interaction with electronic media and the Internet. Sometimes described as a large iPod touch, the iPad targets the product gap between smartphones and netbooks. It has a 9.7-inch touch screen, accelerometers, ambient light sensors, speakers, a microphone, and GPS capabilities. Newer generations included technology upgrades and 2-way cameras for video calling. The iPad has been incredibly popular, with almost 60 million sold to date. In fact, Best Buy has reported that their laptop sales plunged by 50 percent after the iPad was introduced.

The App Store

The App Store was launched in 2008 to provide applications for Apple's mobile devices. In its first year, the App Store had 1.5 million downloads and then continued to grow rapidly. By early 2012, the App Store reached 25 billion downloads largely fueled by the growth of the iPhone, iPod touch, and iPad. The App Store makes downloading applications easier, which encourages more purchases. The average iPhone user has 48 apps compared to 35 apps for Android users and 15 apps for BlackBerry users. Almost 70 percent of all apps on the App Store cost less than $2.00. Independent developers can distribute their original apps through the App Store, and Apple shares profits with them. The App Store generated over $15 billion in revenue in 2011.

Apple's Marketing Program

In addition to its revolutionary products, Apple's success in pricing, promotion, and distribution have also contributed to its popularity. Marketing is such an important part of Apple that former CEO John Sculley once commented that Apple was, first and foremost, a marketing company. Apple has a clear sense of who its customers are and what the brand represents, which helps it to align its pricing, promotion, and distribution with the its overall goals.

Pricing

Apple products are traditionally priced high compared to competitors. For example, Apple's iPad retails for approximately $500 while Google's Nexus 7 and Amazon's Kindle Fire retail for $200. Apple's MacBook laptops cost well over $1,000, while most PC laptops are hundreds of dollars less. Most of Apple's profit comes from the high margins on its hardware devices. Yet, rather than dissuading consumers from adopting the products, the high price point provides Apple with a prestige image. Apple also stresses the convenience of its products as well as the revolutionary new capabilities they have to offer. Thus, it attempts to create value for customers, prompting them to pay more for Apple than for its competitors.

Promotion

Apple encourages demand for its products through several types of promotion, including word-of-mouth marketing. The company relies on hit products and high-impact rollouts (often after months of rumors) to stimulate emotional buying.

The company positions itself as the technology provider for creative people. Like Apple's products, its advertisements are often simple, artistic, and instantly recognizable. For example, several brightly colored iPod commercials featured the silhouettes of dancers wearing the company's iconic white ear buds. Apple's ads sometimes directly attack its competitors, as in the "I'm a Mac" television campaign. The ads pitted a cool, young

Mac character against a PC portrayed as a goofy businessman. Apple also supports "evangelism" of its products, even employing a chief evangelist to spread awareness about Apple and spur demand. Corporate evangelists refer to people who extensively promote a corporation's products, acting as both employees and loyal customers. Successful evangelists spread enthusiasm about a company among consumers. These consumers in turn convince other people about the value of the product. Through product evangelism, Apple has created a "Mac cult"—loyal customers eager to share their enthusiasm about the company with others.

Apple's promotion strategy has led to a perception that Apple products are part of a consumer's identity. When asked why they would want to buy an iPad, over 42 percent of consumers responded that it has a cool factor. However, Apple products still remain a niche product; 95 percent of consumers do not consider Macs when buying new computers.

Distribution

Apple distributes its products to consumers via retailers, the company's online store, and Apple Stores. Apple Stores have enhanced the brand and changed Apple's distribution strategies. Originally created to give Apple more control over product displays and customer experiences, the Apple Store model was a huge success and grew faster than any other retailer in history. It currently has over 360 locations worldwide.

Apple Stores differentiate themselves significantly from other retailers; in fact, Apple took the concept of retail in an entirely new direction. Apple Stores are a place where customers can both shop and play. Everything in the store is carefully planned to align with the company's image, from the glass-and-steel design reminiscent of the company's technology to the stations where customers can try out Apple products. Customer service is also important to the Apple Store image. Employees are expected to speak with customers within two minutes of them entering the store. Each employee has received extensive training and often receives greater compensation than those at other retail stores to encourage better customer service.

Apple executives constantly look for ways to improve stores, enhance customer service, and increase the time that customers spend in-store. In 2011, the company installed iPad stations within its stores. The iPads feature a customer service app designed to answer customer questions. If the customer requires additional assistance, he or she can press a help button on the app. The app changes the customer service experience because rather than the customer seeking out the sales representative, the representative comes straight to the customer.

Apple's Corporate Culture

In addition to its highly effective marketing program, Apple's corporate culture is an important part of its marketing success. Many people attribute Apple's success to Steve Jobs' remarkable leadership abilities, Apple's highly skilled employees, and its strong corporate culture. Apple markets itself as a fast-paced, innovative, and collaborative environment committed toward doing things "the right way." The organization has a flat structure, lacking the layers of bureaucracy of other corporations. Apple also emphasizes that it does not adhere to normal work environments in which employees are at their stations from 9:00 A.M. to 5:00 P.M. By offering both challenges and benefits to applicants, Apple hopes to attract those who fit best with its corporate culture.

Successful evangelism can only occur with dedicated, enthusiastic employees who are willing to spread the word about Apple. When Jobs returned to Apple in 1997, he instituted two cultural changes: he encouraged debate on ideas, and he created a vision that employees could believe in. By implementing these two changes, employees felt that their input was important and that they were a part of something bigger than themselves.

Additionally, in order to maintain its competitive advantage, Apple also fosters a culture of secrecy. Secrecy is also necessary to prevent damage to sales of existing products because if consumers learn about a future upgrade, they may delay their purchases. Certain places at Apple are off-limits to most employees, and employees are not allowed to discuss their work unless everyone in the room knows about the project. This lack of transparency challenges traditional conceptions of what makes a company successful. However, employees say that they remain passionate about their work and are part of a unique experience.

Apple's Marketing Challenges

Although Apple has consistently won first place as the World's Most Admired Company, it has experienced several ethical issues within recent years. These issues could have a profound effect on the company's future success. Apple's sterling reputation could easily be damaged by serious misconduct or a failure to address risks appropriately.

Competition

Apple faces competition on a variety of fronts. Although a diverse product mix mitigates the risk of any one product failing, it also increases Apple's number of competitors. Rivals include Hewlett-Packard, Dell, Acer, and Toshiba for computers; Samsung, HTC, and Google for smartphones; Microsoft, Amazon, and Samsung for tablets; and Microsoft, Google, and Amazon for cloud storage services. Despite Apple's lead in many of these areas, rivals are striving to catch up. Amazon, for example, represents a formidable competitor in the mobile device arena. Its Kindle Fire, a 7-inch Android-based tablet, offers a full array of apps, e-books, music, movies, cloud services, and more at a budget-friendly $199 price—a full $300 less than the cheapest iPad. Amazon is expected to launch its own smartphone in the near future as well. A slate of other competitors, such as Asus, Acer, and Samsung, also offer Android-based tablets at prices lower than the iPad. Microsoft has also launched Surface, a Windows 8-based tablet, which looks to be very competitive with the iPad.

Google is also a strong competitor to Apple's offerings in terms of operating systems, music, books, and cloud services. The company's Android operating system enjoys a much larger installed base of users thanks to the multitude of smartphone and tablet manufacturers that use the system. For example, the Samsung Galaxy S line of smartphones, which uses the Android operating system, is considered to be on par with the iPhone in many ways. One of the major benefits of the Android system over Apple's iOS is its more open approach. This allows manufacturers like Samsung and HTC to release new devices at a much faster pace than Apple's yearly refreshes. In the future, Apple may need to re-examine whether its closed system is the best way to compete.

Customer Privacy

Privacy is another major concern for Apple. In 2011, Apple and Google disclosed that certain features of their smartphones collect data about the phone's location. Many consumers and government officials saw this as an infringement of user privacy. The companies announced that users have the option to disable these features on their phones.

However, this was not entirely true for Apple as some of its phones continued to collect location information even after users had disabled the feature. Apple attributed this to a glitch that it remedied with a software update. Both Google and Apple defend their data-collection practices, but many government officials disagree. The government is considering passing legislation on mobile privacy, actions which could have profound effects on Apple and other mobile device manufacturers.

Product Quality

Apple's image hinges upon product quality, so mistakes can create serious marketing problems. Because several new products are introduced every year, mistakes can become hard to detect before product introduction. After Apple introduced the iPhone 4, consumers complained of reception problems caused by antenna interference that occurred when users held the phone a certain way. Public relations experts criticized Apple for appearing to minimize the problem rather than reacting quickly to remedy it. After *Consumer Reports* would not endorse the iPhone 4, Apple provided free bumpers and cases for a certain period of time that resolved the reception problems. Although the issue did not stop millions of consumers from purchasing the iPhone 4, it did create lingering doubts about Apple's ability to consistently raise the bar on product quality.

Intellectual Property

With the many products Apple releases each year, it makes sense for it to protect its technology from theft. Apple is serious about keeping its proprietary information a secret to prevent other companies from stealing its ideas. This confidentiality has led to many patent and copyright lawsuits from Apple to other technology firms, including Franklin Computer Corporation, Microsoft, Cisco Systems, Samsung, and HTC. Apple is also the target of lawsuits. Kodak filed a lawsuit against Apple and Research in Motion alleging that the companies infringed on its patent on digital-imaging technology. In response, Apple countersued Kodak by claiming it violated Apple's patents. Unfortunately for Apple, a U.S. International Trade Commission judge ruled in Kodak's favor in Apple's lawsuit. However, the issue still stands regarding whether Apple infringed on Kodak's patents. Kodak is seeking $1 billion in licensing revenue. Additionally, Proview Electronics filed a lawsuit alleging that Apple fraudulently acquired the iPad trademark by creating a fake company to purchase the trademark and not disclosing their intent. Apple eventually settled the suit for $60 million.

Apple's aggressiveness regarding patent protection has led it to file lawsuits against some powerful companies. For example, the company filed a patent infringement lawsuit against Samsung, claiming that Samsung had copied the designs of its iPhone and iPad for its own products. In 2012, Apple won a landmark verdict against Samsung. The jury awarded Apple just over $1 billion in damages after it found Samsung guilty of copying some of the iPhone's features in its own line of smartphones. Apple also filed a lawsuit against HTC Corporation, a Taiwanese smartphone manufacturer that makes phones for Google's Android products. Apple accused HTC of replicating a range of cellphone features protected under Apple's patents. Apple won the lawsuit, and HTC was banned from selling products that infringed on Apple's patents within the United States.

Although the outcomes of some of these lawsuits have provided technology companies with more extensive intellectual property protections, they also bring attention to the legitimacy of Apple's claims. Is Apple pursuing companies that it honestly believes infringed on its patents, or is it simply trying to cast its competitors in a bad light so it can become the major player in the market? Although it might seem that Apple is being too aggressive, companies that do not set boundaries and protect their property can easily have it copied by their competitors, who can then use it to gain market share.

Supply Chain Management

Many of Apple's product components are manufactured in countries with low labor costs. This means that the potential for issues to arise is high due to varying labor standards and less direct oversight. As a result, Apple makes each of its suppliers sign a supplier code of conduct and performs factory audits to ensure compliance. To emphasize its commitment toward responsible supplier conduct, Apple releases an annual Supplier Responsibility Progress Report that explains expectations for suppliers, the results of its audits, and corrective actions the company will take against factories where violations have occurred. In addition, Apple says that it has trained over one million workers about their rights, increased the number of suppliers they audit by 80 percent, and allowed outside organizations to evaluate its labor practices.

Despite these measures, Apple has faced scrutiny for its manufacturing processes. Over 50 percent of the suppliers audited by Apple have violated at least one part of its supplier code of conduct every year since 2007. Suppliers claim that Apple's manufacturing standards are hard to achieve because suppliers are allowed slim profit margins. In contrast, competitors like Hewlett-Packard allow suppliers to keep more profits if they improve worker conditions. Apple's focus on the bottom line can cause suppliers to find other ways to cut costs, usually by requiring employees to work longer hours and using less expensive but more dangerous chemicals.

In this environment, mistakes and safety issues become more common. According to the company's own audits, 62 percent of Apple's suppliers did not comply with working-hours limits, 35 percent failed to meet Apple's standards to prevent worker injuries, and 32 percent do not follow hazardous-substance management practices. Other problems with Apple's supply chain have included underage workers, falsified records, overcrowded worker dormitories, and other labor violations. Apple claims that suppliers who violate company policies have 90 days to address the problem, but fewer than 15 suppliers have been dropped for violations since 2007.

Several high-profile events at Apple factories generated even more criticism of its supply chain. In January 2010, over 135 workers fell ill after using a poisonous chemical to clean iPhone screens. In 2011, aluminum dust and improper ventilation caused two explosions that killed 4 people and injured 77. Additionally, over a dozen workers have committed suicide at Apple supplier factories. Much of the media attention has focused on the conditions at Foxconn, Apple's largest supplier with a consistent background of labor violations and the site of one of the explosions and several of the suicides. Foxconn continues to assert that it is in compliance with all regulations, despite the reports.

Apple claims that it is significantly improving supplier conditions and becoming more transparent about its labor processes. However, the continuing issues with its supply chain may indicate that it values profit more than employee welfare. Some blame Apple's culture of innovation and the need to release new or improved products each year, which requires suppliers to work quickly at the expense of safety standards. However, the Foxconn factory is one of only a few facilities in the world with the capacity to build iPods and iPads, which makes it difficult for Apple to switch suppliers. Additionally, inconsistent international labor standards and high competition mean that virtually every major electronic producer faces similar manufacturing issues. As media and consumer scrutiny increase, Apple must continue to address its supply chain management issues. However, as one current Apple executive told the *New York Times*, "Customers care more about a new iPhone than working conditions in China."

Sustainability

Apple has taken steps to become a greener company, such as reducing its environmental impact at its facilities. However, the company admits that the majority of its emissions (97 percent) come from the life cycle of its products. Apple's success hinges on constantly developing and launching new products, which leads to planned obsolescence—pushing people to replace or upgrade their technology whenever Apple comes out with an updated version. Since Apple annually releases upgraded products, this could result in older technology being tossed aside.

Apple takes different approaches to this environmental problem. The company builds its products with materials that are suitable for recycling, it builds its products to last, and it recycles responsibly. To encourage its customers to recycle, Apple created an in-store recycling program where customers can trade in old products and receive various discounts. However, despite this recycling program, many consumers feel that tossing out their old products is more convenient, particularly if they have no value. E-waste will remain a significant issue as long as consumers continue to throw away their old electronics.

Apple has also publicly stated its achievements in reducing toxic chemicals within its products. The company eliminated cathode-ray tubes—which contain lead—from its products and constructs iPods with light-emitting diodes (LEDs) rather than fluorescent lamps (which contain mercury). The company also eliminated the use of two toxic chemicals, polyvinyl chloride and brominated flame retardants, from its products.

Apple's Impact on the Practice of Marketing

No company has mastered the concept of product differentiation better than Apple. While products such as the iPod and iPhone provided functions and benefits similar to competing products, Apple's technology and user-friendly interface provided a consumer perception of a completely new product. Apple retail stores and service help create a total product that was unlike any available in the marketplace. The Apple brand name became a cultural icon with loyal followers that were devoted to Apple's products. Cultural branding results in consumers exhibiting almost cult-like loyalty to products. Companies such as Coca-Cola, Harley Davidson, and Nike are examples of companies with strong cultural branding. The product becomes a part of their self-concept and image when interacting with others. Once a product becomes so important to an individual, they are less sensitive to price and quickly adopt new products that are brought to the market. Few companies have been able to develop cultural branding and a cult-like following like Apple.

Apple's corporate culture of innovation and creative marketing has had a profound impact on the practice of marketing among consumer electronics firms and other industries. For example, the iPhone popularized the concept of mobile marketing. The iPhone's easy-to-use features and applications allowed consumers to shop from home or in-store. This innovation provided new opportunities for retailers to introduce their own iPhone apps and create customized marketing messages delivered over mobile devices. Brands are utilizing Apple's platform to create product awareness and/or generate repeat business. Apple's advances in mobile marketing have not only changed the way that customers interact with mobile devices but also enhanced customer relationships between businesses and consumers.

Additionally, many companies are seizing upon the opportunity to learn from Apple. Due to the immense success of Apple stores, other companies are attempting to imitate its retail model. Microsoft and Sony opened some of their own stores. Other companies now use Apple products to enhance their businesses. For instance, some pharmaceutical and car salespeople have adopted the iPad to aid in business transactions, and some restaurants even use the iPad to show menu items.

The Future of Apple

Over the last decade, Apple has excelled at keeping pace with the quickly evolving computer and electronics industries. Its diversification, collaborative corporate culture, and product evangelism propelled it to heights that could not have been envisioned when Jobs and Wozniak sold their first computer kit in 1976. The death of Steve Jobs in 2011, however, concerned some people about the future of Apple. To customers, employees, and investors, Jobs appeared to be a savior who brought the company back from near bankruptcy and who was the driving force behind its innovative products. However, his entrepreneurial spirit remains embedded in Apple's culture, and the company remains focused on innovation under the leadership of CEO Tim Cook. The company shows no signs of stopping its momentum, while consumers have shown no signs of reducing their admiration for Apple.

On the other hand, Apple will face many challenges in the future. Not only has it been criticized for violations in its supply chain, but it has also been questioned about why it offshores most of its production. Since Apple makes such high profits and reportedly received tax breaks earlier in its history, some politicians have suggested that Apple bring production jobs back to the United States. As concerns over high unemployment continue, Apple may experience increasing pressure from stakeholders to create more manufacturing opportunities in the United States. The question, however, is whether consumers will continue to pay more to quench their thirst for the latest iPods, iPhones, and iPads.

Questions for Discussion

1. How has Apple developed extreme loyalty among consumers that has resulted in an almost cult-like following?
2. Describe the role of Apple stores as an important part of its marketing strategy.
3. What will Apple need to do to maintain product innovation and customer loyalty?

Sources

The facts of this case are from Chloe Albanesius, "Apple unveils updated iPod Nano, Touch," *PC Magazine*, October 4, 2011 (http://www.pcmag.com/article2/0,2817,2394061,00.asp); Jim Aley, "The Beginning," *Business-Week*, Special Issue on Steve Jobs, October 2011, pp. 20–26; "Apple begins counting down to 25 billion App Store downloads," *AppleInsider*, February 17, 2012 (http://www.appleinsider.com/articles/12/02/17/apple_be gins_counting_down_to_25_billion_app_store_downloads.html); "Apple chronology," *CNN Money*, January 6, 1998 (http://money.cnn.com/1998/01/06/technology/apple_chrono); "Apple's 25% Solution," *Seeking Alpha*, November 7, 2011 (http://seekingalpha.com/article/305849-apple-s-25-solution); Peter Burrows, "The Wilderness," *BusinessWeek*, Special Issue on Steve Jobs, October 2011, pp. 28–34; Ben Camm-Jones, "Apple disputes Kodak's patent ownership claims," *Macworld*, January 23, 2012 (http://www.macworld.co.uk/apple-business/news/?newsid=3331817&pagtype=allchandate); Amanda Cantrell, "Apple's remarkable comeback Story," *CNN Money*, March 29, 2006 (http://money.cnn.com/2006/03/29/technology/apple_anniversary/?cnn=ye); Neal Colgrass, "Apple *Can* Bring Those Jobs Back," *Newser*, February 13, 2012 (http://www.newser.com/story/139577/apple-can-bring-those-jobs-back.html); Brandon Davenport, "A brief history of Apple's iPad," *Okay Geek*, April 30, 2011 (http://www.okaygeek.com/blog/a-brief-history-of-apples-ipad-infographic.html); Alan Deutschman, "The once and future Steve Jobs," *Salon*, October 11, 2000 (http://www.salon.com/technology/books/

2000/10/11/jobs_excerpt); Charles Duhigg and Keith Bradsher, "How the US Lost Out on iPhone Work," *CNBC*, January 22, 2012 (http://www.cnbc.com/id/46090589/How_the_US_Lost_Out_on_iPhone_Work); Kit Eaton and Noah Robischon, "The iPad's Biggest Innovation: Its $500 Price," *Fast Company*, January 27, 2010 (http://www.fastcompany.com/article/apples-tablet-introduced?page=0%2C0); Paul Elias, "Samsung Ordered to Pay Apple $1.05B in Patent Case," *BusinessWeek*, August 25, 2012 (http://www.businessweek.com/ap/2012-08-24/verdict-reached-in-epic-apple-vs-dot-samsung-case); "The evangelist's evangelist," Creating Customer Evangelists (http://www.creatingcustomerevangelists.com/resources/evangelists/guy_kawasaki.asp), accessed June 6, 2011; *Form 10K Annual Report*, October 26, 2011 (http://investor.apple.com/secfiling.cfm?filingID=1193125-11-282113&CIK=320193); "Former Apple evangelist on company's history," *CNET News*, March 29, 2006 (http://news.cnet.com/1606-2_3-6055676.html); Bryan Gardiner, "Learning from Failure: Apple's Most Notorious Flops," *Wired*, January 24, 2008 (http://www.wired.com/gadgets/mac/multimedia/2008/01/gallery_apple_flops?slide=1&slideView=8); Jefferson Graham, "At Apple stores, iPads at your service," *USA Today*, May 23, 2011, 1B; "A genius departs," *The Economist*, October 14–18, 2011, pp. 81–82; David Goldman, "Apple's iPod Dilemma," *CNN Money*, July 29, 2011 (http://money.cnn.com/2011/07/29/technology/apple_ipod_sales/index.htm); "A History of App Stores: Apple, Google, and Everyone Else," WebpageFX, August 15, 2011 (http://www.webpagefx.com/blog/internet/history-of-app-stores-infographic); "In China, Human Costs Are Built Into an iPad," *New York Times*, January 25, 2012; "The iPhone 4 antenna class-action settlement: What it means for consumers," *Consumer Reports*, February 23, 2012 (http://news.consumerreports.org/electronics/2012/02/the-iphone-4-antenna-class-action-settlement-what-it-means-for-consumers.html); Yukari Iwatani Kane and Ian Sherr, "Apple: Samsung Copied Design," *Wall Street Journal*, April 19, 2011 (http://online.wsj.com/article/SB10001424052748703916004576271210109389154.html); Rimma Kats, "What impact did Apple's Steve Jobs have on mobile advertising, marketing and content?" *Mobile Marketing*, August 26, 2011 (http://www.mobilemarketer.com/cms/news/manufacturers/10807.html); Kevin Kelleher, "Amazon versus Apple? Not so fast," *CNN Money*, October 12, 2011 (http://tech.fortune.cnn.com/2011/10/12/amazon-versus-apple); Ryan Kim, "Apple App Store developers look to next level," *San Francisco Chronicle*, February 9, 2009 (http://www.sfgate.com/business/article/Apple-App-Store-developers-look-to-next-level-3251564.php); Adam Lashinsky, "The Secrets Apple Keeps," *Fortune*, February 6, 2012, pp. 85–94; "Learn more about Siri," Apple (http://www.apple.com/iphone/features/siri-faq.html), accessed January 19, 2012; Scott Martin, "Apple invites review of labor practices in overseas factories," *USA Today*, January 16, 2012, 3B; Scott Martin, "How Apple rewrote the rules of retailing," *USA Today*, May 19, 2011, 1B; Declan McCullagh, "Apple wins patent victory over HTC, which faces looming import ban," *CNET News*, December 19, 2011 (http://news.cnet.com/8301-13579_3-57345291-37/apple-wins-patent-victory-over-htc-which-faces-looming-import-ban); Donald Melanson, "Apple: 16 billion iTunes songs downloaded, 300 million iPods sold," *Engadget*, October 4, 2011 (http://www.engadget.com/2011/10/04/apple-16-billion-itunes-songs-downloaded-300-million-ipods-sol); Nilofer Merchant, "Apple's Startup Culture," *BusinessWeek*, June 24, 2010 (http://www.businessweek.com/innovate/content/jun2010/id20100610_525759.htm); Chris Morrison, "Insanely Great Marketing," *CBS MoneyWatch*, August 10, 2009 (http://www.cbsnews.com/8301-505125_162-51330244/insanely-great-marketing); Michael Muchmore, "Apple iCloud vs. Amazon Cloud Player vs. Google Music Beta," *PC Magazine*, June 6, 2011 (http://www.pcmag.com/article2/0,2817,2386491,00.asp); Ian Sherr and Spencer E. Ante, "Fight Over iPad Name Spills Into U.S. Court," *Wall Street Journal*, February 24, 2012 (http://online.wsj.com/article/SB10001424052970203918304577240790926896520.html); Brad Stone, "The Omnivore," *BusinessWeek*, October 3–9, 2011, 58–65; Peter Svensson, "iPhone Sales Propel Apple to Massive Q1 Earnings," *Huffington Post*, January 24, 2012 (http://www.huffingtonpost.com/2012/01/24/iphone-sales-apple_n_1229379.html); I.B. Times, "Apple Wins Patent Lawsuit, Forcing Sales Ban on Rival HTC," *Fox News*, December 20, 2011 (http://www.foxbusiness.com/technology/2011/12/20/apple-wins-patent-lawsuit-forcing-sales-ban-on-rival-htc); Darby Tober, "Introduction to Macs for PC Users," University of Texas, 2005 (http://www.ischool.utexas.edu/technology/tutorials/start/pctomac/differences.html), accessed February 2, 2012; Jessica E. Vascellaro and Owen Fletcher, "Apple Navigates China Maze," *Wall Street Journal*, January 15, 2012, B1–B2; Martyn Williams, "Timeline: iTunes Store at 10 Billion," *ComputerWorld*, February 24, 2010 (http://www.computerworld.com/s/article/9162018/Timeline_iTunes_Store_at_10_billion); "World's Most Admired Companies 2011: Apple," *CNN Money* (http://money.cnn.com/magazines/fortune/mostadmired/2011/snapshots/670.html), accessed July 12, 2012; Stu Woo and Jeffrey A. Trachtenberg, "Amazon Fights the iPad With 'Fire'," *Wall Street Journal*, September 29, 2011, B1, B10; and Alberto Zanco, "Apple Inc.: A success built on distribution & design" (http://www.slideshare.net/Nanor/distribution-policy-apple-presentation), accessed February 21, 2012.

CASE **3**

Monsanto Balances the Interests of Multiple Stakeholders*

Synopsis: This case focuses on Monsanto's desire to balance the many significant benefits that its products bring to society (and the company's resulting profits) with the interests of a variety of stakeholders. The case examines Monsanto's history as it shifted from a chemical company to one focused on biotechnology. Monsanto's development of genetically modified seeds and bovine growth hormone are discussed, along with the safety and environmental concerns expressed by a number of Monsanto's stakeholders around the world. Some of Monsanto's ethical and patent-enforcement issues are addressed, along with the company's major corporate responsibility initiatives. The case concludes by examining the challenges and opportunities that Monsanto may face in the future.

Themes: Ethics and social responsibility, sustainability, product strategy, product liability, corporate affairs, stakeholder relationships, product labeling, government regulation, legal environment, global marketing

The Monsanto Company is the world's largest seed company, with sales over $11.5 billion. It specializes in biotechnology, or the genetic manipulation of organisms. Monsanto scientists have spent the last few decades modifying crops, often by inserting new genes or adapting existing genes within plant seeds, to meet certain objectives such as higher yield or insect resistance. Monsanto products can survive weeks of drought, ward off weeds, and kill invasive insects. Monsanto's genetically modified seeds have increased the quantity and availability of crops, helping farmers worldwide increase food production and revenues.

Today, 90 percent of the world's genetically modified seeds are sold by Monsanto or by companies that use Monsanto genes. Monsanto also holds a 70 to 100 percent market share on certain crops. Yet, stakeholders as diverse as governments, farmers, activists, and advocacy groups have criticized Monsanto. Monsanto supporters say the company creates solutions to world hunger by generating higher crop yields and hardier plants. Critics accuse the multinational giant of trying to take over the world's food supply and destroying biodiversity. Because biotechnology is relatively new, critics also express concerns about the possibility of negative health and environmental effects from biotech food. However, such criticisms have not deterred Monsanto from becoming one of the world's most successful companies.

---

*Jennifer Sawayda, University of New Mexico, prepared this case under the direction of O.C. Ferrell and Jennifer Jackson for classroom discussion rather than to illustrate effective or ineffective handling of an administrative situation.

Monsanto's History: From Chemicals to Food

The original Monsanto was very different from the current company. It was started by John F. Queeny in 1901 in St. Louis and was named after his wife, Olga Monsanto Queeny. The company's first product was the artificial sweetener saccharine, sold to Coca-Cola. Monsanto followed by selling Coca-Cola caffeine extract and vanillin, an artificial vanilla flavoring. At the start of World War I, company leaders realized the growth opportunities in the industrial chemicals industry and renamed the company The Monsanto Chemical Company. The company began specializing in plastics, its own agricultural chemicals, and synthetic rubber. Due to its expanding product lines, Monsanto's name was changed to the "Monsanto Company" in 1964. By this time, Monsanto was producing such diverse products as petroleum, fibers, and packaging. A few years later, Monsanto created its first Roundup herbicide, a successful product that would propel the company even more into the limelight.

During the 1970s, however, Monsanto hit a major legal snare. The company had produced a chemical known as Agent Orange that was used during the Vietnam War to quickly deforest the thick Vietnamese jungle. Agent Orange contained dioxin, a chemical that caused a legal nightmare for Monsanto. Dioxin was found to be extremely carcinogenic, and in 1979, a lawsuit was filed against Monsanto on behalf of hundreds of veterans who claimed they were harmed by the chemical. Monsanto and several other manufacturers agreed to settle for $180 million. The repercussions of dioxin would continue to plague the company for decades.

In 1981, Monsanto's leaders determined that biotechnology would be the company's new strategic focus. Monsanto's quest for biotechnology continued for over a decade, and in 1994 Monsanto introduced the first biotech product to win regulatory approval. Soon the company was selling soybean, cotton, and canola seeds that were engineered to be tolerant to Monsanto's Roundup herbicide. Many other herbicides killed the good plants as well as the bad ones. Roundup Ready seeds allowed farmers to use the herbicide to eliminate weeds while sparing the crop.

In 1997, Monsanto spun off its chemical business as Solutia, and in 2000 the company entered into a merger and changed its name to the Pharmacia Corporation. Two years later, a new Monsanto, focused entirely on agriculture, broke off from Pharmacia, and the companies became two separate legal entities. The company before 2000 is often referred to as "old Monsanto," while today's company is known as "new Monsanto."

The emergence of new Monsanto was tainted by some disturbing news that the company had been covering up decades of environmental pollution. For nearly 40 years, the Monsanto Company had released toxic waste into a creek in Anniston, Alabama. It had also disposed of polychlorinated biphenyls (PCBs), a highly toxic chemical, in open-pit landfills in the area. The results were catastrophic. Fish in the creek were deformed, and the population had elevated PCB levels that shocked environmental health experts. A paper trail showed that Monsanto leaders had known about the pollution since the 1960s but had not stopped production. Once the cover-up was discovered, thousands of plaintiffs from the area filed a lawsuit against the company. In 2003, Monsanto and Solutia agreed to pay $700 million to more than 20,000 Anniston-area residents.

When current CEO Hugh Grant took over in 2003, scandals and stakeholder uncertainty had tarnished the company's reputation. The price of Monsanto's stock had fallen almost 50 percent, down to $8 a share. The company had lost $1.7 billion the previous year. Grant knew the company was fragile; yet through a strategic focus on genetically modified foods, the company has recovered and is now prospering. Monsanto became so successful with its genetically modified seeds that it acquired Seminis, Inc., a leader in the fruit and vegetable seed industry. The acquisition transformed Monsanto into a global leader in the seed industry. Today, Monsanto employs more than 21,000 people in 160 countries and has been recognized as a top employer in Argentina, Mexico, India, and Brazil.

The Seeds of Change: Monsanto's Emphasis on Biotechnology

Although the original Monsanto made a name for itself by manufacturing chemicals, the new Monsanto took quite a different turn. After switching its emphasis from chemicals to food, today's Monsanto owes its more than $11.5 billion in sales to biotechnology, specifically to the sale of genetically modified plant seeds. These seeds have revolutionized the agriculture industry.

Throughout history, weeds, insects, and drought have been the banes of the farmer's existence. In the past century, herbicides and pesticides were invented to ward off pests. Yet applying these chemicals to an entire crop was both costly and time-consuming. Monsanto scientists, through their work in biotechnology, were able to implant seeds with genes to make the plants themselves kill bugs. They also created seeds containing the Roundup herbicide, an herbicide that kills weeds but spares the crop.

Since then, Monsanto has used technology to create many valuable products, such as drought-tolerant seeds for dry areas like Africa. The company uses this technological prowess as a form of marketing. Monsanto's laboratory in St. Louis allows farmers to tour the facility and see how the seeds are selected. One of the technologies that farmers are shown is a technology known as the corn chipper, a machine that picks up seeds and takes genetic material from them. That material is then analyzed to see how well the seed will do if planted. The "best" seeds are the ones Monsanto sells for planting. Impressing farmers with its technology and the promise of better yields is one way that Monsanto promotes its products to potential customers.

Although genetically modified seeds are widely accepted today, their introduction in the 1990s unleashed a stream of criticism. Monsanto was nicknamed "Mutanto," and genetically modified produce was called "Frankenfood." Critics believed that influencing the genes of edible plants could result in negative health consequences, a fear that remains to this day. Others worried about the health effects on beneficial insects and plants. Could pollinating genetically modified plants have an effect on nearby insects and non-genetically modified plants? CEO Hugh Grant decided to curtail the tide of criticism by focusing biotechnology on products that would not be directly placed on the dinner plate, but instead on products like animal feed and corn syrup. In this way, Grant was able to reduce some of the opposition. Today, the company invests largely in four crops: corn, cotton, soybeans, and canola.

Thus far, the dire predictions of critics have not occurred. Monsanto owes approximately 60 percent of its revenue to its work in genetically modified seeds, and today, more than half of U.S. crops, including most soybeans and 70 percent of corn, are genetically modified. Farmers who purchase genetically modified seeds can now grow more crops on less land and with less left to chance. For example, in 1970 the average corn harvest yielded approximately 70 bushels per acre. With the introduction of biotech crops, the average corn harvest has increased to roughly 150 bushels per acre. Monsanto predicts even higher yields in the future, possibly up to 300 bushels per acre by 2030. "As agricultural productivity increases, farmers are able to produce more food, feed, fuel, and fiber on the same amount of land, helping to ensure that agriculture can meet humanity's needs in the future," said Monsanto CEO Hugh Grant, concerning Monsanto technology.

As a result of higher yields, the revenues of farmers in developing countries have increased. According to company statistics, the cotton yield of Indian farmers rose by

50 percent, doubling their income in one year. Additionally, the company claims that its insect-protected corn has raised the income level in the Philippines to above poverty level. Critics argue that these numbers are inflated; they say the cost of genetically modified seeds is dramatically higher than that of traditional seeds, and therefore they actually reduce farmers' take-home profits. An increase in the rate of suicides among Indian farmers within the last decade has partially been attributed to allegations that many Indian farmers go into debt because they must buy Monsanto seeds year after year. Monsanto denies these allegations and claims the suicides stemmed from a variety of different factors unrelated to their seed products.

Despite Monsanto's assurances, many countries do not support genetically modified crops. Attempts to introduce them into Europe have elicited extreme consumer backlash. The European Union has banned most Monsanto crops except for one variety of corn, and consumers have gone so far as to destroy fields of genetically modified crops and arrange sit-ins. Greenpeace has fought Monsanto for years, especially in the company's efforts to promote genetically modified crops in developing countries. This animosity toward Monsanto's products is generated by two main concerns: worries about the safety of genetically modified food and concerns about potential environmental effects.

Safety Concerns About Genetically Modified Food

Of great concern for many stakeholders are the moral and safety implications of genetically modified food. Many skeptics see biotech crops as unnatural, with Monsanto scientists essentially "playing God" by controlling what goes into the seed. Also, because genetically modified crops are relatively new, critics maintain that the health implications of biotech food may not be known for years to come. They also contend that effective standards have not been created to determine the safety of biotech crops. Some geneticists believe the splicing of these genes into seeds could create small changes that might negatively impact the health of humans and animals that eat them. Although the FDA has declared biotech crops safe, critics say they have not been around long enough to gauge their long-term effects.

One major health concern is that a lack of appropriate regulation could allow allergens to creep into the products. Another concern is toxicity, particularly considering that many Monsanto seeds are equipped with a gene to allow them to produce their own Roundup herbicide. Could ingesting this herbicide, even in small amounts, cause detrimental effects on consumers? Some stakeholders say yes and point to statistics on glyphosate, Roundup's chief ingredient, for support. According to an ecology center fact sheet, glyphosate exposure is the third most commonly reported illness among California agriculture workers, and glyphosate residues can last for a year. Yet the EPA lists glyphosate as having a low skin and oral toxicity, and a study from the New York Medical College states that Roundup does not create a health risk for humans.

Despite consumer concerns, the FDA has proclaimed that genetically modified food is safe to consume. As a result, it also has determined that Americans do not need to know when they are consuming genetically modified products. Thus, this information is not placed on labels in the United States, although other countries, most notably Great Britain and the European Union, do require genetically modified food products to state this fact in their labeling.

Safety Concerns About Bovine Growth Hormone

Monsanto has also come under scrutiny for a synthetic hormone that it previously owned called Posilac, the brand name of a drug that contains recombinant bovine growth hormone (rBST). This hormone is a supplement to the naturally occurring hormone BST in cows. Posilac causes cows to produce more milk, a boon to dairy farmers but a cause of concern to many stakeholders who fear that Posilac may cause health problems in cows and in the humans who drink their milk. After numerous tests, the FDA has found that milk from Posilac-treated cows is no different in terms of safety than milk from rBST-free cows. Yet these assurances have done little to alleviate stakeholder fears, especially because some studies maintain that rBST increases health problems in cows. Public outcry from concerned consumers has become so loud that many grocery stores and restaurants have stopped purchasing rBST-treated milk. Starbucks, Kroger, Ben & Jerry's, and even Walmart have responded to consumer demand by only using or selling rBST-free milk, which has put a damper on Monsanto's profits from Posilac.

In the past few years, certain groups, including Monsanto, have fought back against the popularity of rBST-free milk. They maintain that consumers are being misled by implications that rBST-free milk is safer than rBST-treated milk. In 2006, a Pennsylvania senator and agriculture secretary tried to ban milk that was labeled as rBST-free, but stakeholder outrage prevented the law from being enforced. Instead, tighter restrictions on labels have been initiated. All rBST-free milk must now contain the following FDA claim: "No significant difference has been shown between milk derived from rBST-treated and non-rBST-treated cows." Monsanto stated that it has no problem with milk labels listed as rBST-free as long as the label contains the claim of the FDA. Monsanto has since sold its Posilac business to Eli Lilly.

Concerns About the Environmental Effects of Monsanto's Products

Some studies have supported the premise that Roundup herbicide, which is used in conjunction with the Roundup Ready seeds, can be harmful to birds, insects, and particularly amphibians. Such studies have revealed that small concentrations of Roundup may be deadly to tadpoles, which is a major concern, as frog and toad species are rapidly disappearing around the globe. Other studies suggest that Roundup might have a detrimental effect on human cells, especially embryonic, umbilical, and placental cells. Monsanto has countered these claims by questioning the methodology used in the studies, and the EPA maintains that glyphosate is not dangerous at recommended doses.

Another concern with genetically modified seeds in general is the threat of environmental contamination. Bumblebees, insects, and wind can carry a crop's seeds to other areas, sometimes to fields containing non-genetically modified crops. Many organic farmers have complained that genetically modified seeds from nearby farms have "contaminated" their crops. This environmental contamination could pose a serious threat. Some scientists fear that genetically modified seeds that are spread to native plants may cause those plants to adopt the genetically modified trait, thus creating new genetic variations of those plants that could negatively influence (through genetic advantages) the surrounding ecosystem. The topic has taken on particular significance in Mexico. For eleven years, Mexico had a moratorium on genetically modified corn. It lifted the moratorium in 2005, enabling Monsanto to begin testing its genetically modified corn in northern Mexico a few years later. Monsanto is seeking authorization to begin the precommercial stage in Mexico, which would allow the company to expand its growing area to approximately 500 acres. However, consumers are putting up a fight. Believing that genetically modified corn could contaminate their over 60 maize varieties, Mexicans have staged protests and formed groups to try and keep genetically modified corn out of the country.

Monsanto has not been silent on these issues and has acted to address some of these concerns. The company maintains that the environmental impact of everything it creates has been studied by the EPA and approved. Monsanto officials claim that the glyphosate in Roundup does not usually end up in ground water and cites a study, which revealed that less than 1 percent of glyphosate, contaminates ground water through runoff. The company also claims that when it does contaminate ground water, it is soluble and will not have much effect on aquatic species. Stakeholders are left to make their own decisions regarding these issues.

Crop Resistance to Pesticides and Herbicides

Another environmental problem that has emerged is the possibility of weed and insect resistance to the herbicides and pesticides on Monsanto crops. Critics fear that continual use of the chemicals could result in "super weeds" and "super bugs," much like the overuse of antibiotics in humans has resulted in drug-resistant bacteria. The company's Roundup line, in particular, has come under attack. Monsanto points out, and rightly so, that Roundup herbicide has been used for 30 years, largely without resistance issues. However, genetically modified plants labeled "Roundup Ready" are genetically engineered to withstand large doses of the herbicide. As Roundup has been used more frequently and exclusively, significant numbers of Roundup-resistant weeds have been found in the United States and Australia.

To combat "super bugs," the government requires farmers using Monsanto's products to create "refuges" in which they plant 20 percent of their fields with a non-genetically modified crop. The theory is that this allows nonresistant bugs to mate with those that are resistant, preventing a new race of super bugs. To prevent resistance to the Roundup herbicide, farmers are supposed to vary herbicide use and practice crop rotation. However, because Roundup is so easy to use, particularly in conjunction with Roundup Ready seeds, many farmers do not take the time to take these preventative measures. When they do rotate their crops, some will rotate one Roundup Ready crop with another type of Roundup Ready crop, which does little to solve the problem. This is of particular concern in Latin America, Africa, and Asia, where farmers may not be as informed of the risks of herbicide and pesticide overuse.

Monsanto Addresses Ethical and Legal Issues

In addition to concerns over the safety of genetically modified seeds and environmental issues, Monsanto has had to deal with concerns about organizational conduct. Organizations face significant risks from strategies and from employees striving for high performance standards. Such pressure sometimes encourages employees to engage in illegal or unethical conduct. All firms have these concerns, and in the case of Monsanto, bribes and patents have resulted in legal, ethical, and reputational consequences.

Bribery Issues

Bribery presents a dilemma to multinational corporations because different countries have different perspectives on it. Although it is illegal in the United States, other countries allow it. Monsanto faced such a problem with Indonesia, and its actions resulted in the company being fined a large sum.

In 2002, a Monsanto manager instructed an Indonesian consulting firm to pay a bribe of $50,000 to an official in the country's environment ministry. The bribe was to bypass an environmental study. It was later revealed that such bribery was not an isolated event; the company had paid off many officials between 1997 and 2002. Monsanto became aware of the problem after discovering irregularities at its Indonesian subsidiary in 2001. As a result, the company launched an internal investigation and reported the bribery to the U.S. Department of Justice (DOJ) and the Securities and Exchange

Commission (SEC). Monsanto accepted full responsibility for its employees' behavior and agreed to pay $1 million to the Department of Justice and $500,000 to the SEC. It also agreed to three years of close monitoring of its activities by American authorities. The incident showed that although Monsanto has not been immune to scandals, it has been willing to work with authorities to correct them.

Patent Issues

Like most businesses, Monsanto needs to patent its products. A problem arises, however, when it comes to patenting seeds. As bioengineered creations of the Monsanto Company, Monsanto's seeds are protected under patent law. Under the terms of the patent, farmers using Monsanto seeds are not allowed to harvest seeds from the plants for use in upcoming seasons. Instead, they must purchase new Monsanto seeds each season. By issuing new seeds each year, Monsanto ensures it will secure a profit as well as maintain control over its intellectual property.

Unfortunately, this is a new concept for most farmers. Throughout agricultural history, farmers have collected and saved seeds from previous harvests to plant the following year's crops. Critics argue that requiring farmers to suddenly purchase new seeds year after year puts an undue financial burden on them and gives Monsanto too much power. However, the law protects Monsanto's right to have exclusive control over its creations, and farmers must abide by these laws. When they are found guilty of using Monsanto seeds from previous seasons, either deliberately or out of ignorance, the farmers are often fined.

Because it is fairly easy for farmers to violate the patent, Monsanto has found it necessary to employ investigators to look into suspected violations. The resulting investigations are a source of contention between Monsanto and accused farmers. According to Monsanto, investigators approach the farmers suspected of patent infringement and ask them questions. The investigators must practice transparency with the farmers and tell them why they are there and who they represent. If suspicions still exist after the initial interview, investigators may pull the farmer's records (after assuring the farmer they will do so in a respectful manner). Sometimes they bring in a sampling team, with the farmer's permission, to test the farmer's fields. If found guilty, the farmer often pays a fine to Monsanto.

Some farmers, on the other hand, tell a different story about Monsanto and its seed investigators, calling the investigators the "seed police" and even referring to them with such harsh words as "Gestapo" or "mafia." They have claimed that Monsanto investigators have used unethical practices to get them to cooperate. Monsanto is also not limiting its investigations to farmers. It filed a lawsuit against DuPont, the world's second-largest seed maker, for combining DuPont technology with Roundup Ready. Monsanto won the lawsuit, but was countersued by DuPont for anticompetitive practices. Accusations of anticompetitive practices have garnered the attention of federal antitrust lawyers. With increased pressure coming from different areas, Monsanto agreed to allow patents to expire on its seeds starting in 2014. This will allow other companies to create less expensive knockoffs of Monsanto seeds. However, Monsanto announced that it would continue to strictly enforce patents for new versions of its products, such as Roundup Ready 2 soybeans.

Legal Issues

Many major companies have government and legal forces to deal with, and Monsanto is no exception. Recently, the government has begun to more closely examine Monsanto's practices. This is a bit ironic considering it was a legal decision that helped pave the way for Monsanto's success in the seed industry. In 1980, the Supreme Court for the first time allowed living organisms to be patented, giving Monsanto the ability to patent its seeds.

Despite this legal victory, Monsanto has now come under the attention of the American Antitrust Institute for alleged anticompetitive activities. The institute wrote a paper suggesting that Monsanto is hindering competition, exerting too much power over the transgenic seed industry, and limiting seed innovation. When Monsanto acquired DeKalb and Delta Land and Pine, it had to get the approval of antitrust authorities. Still, it gained approval after agreeing to certain concessions.

However, Monsanto may be walking a fine line with the Department of Justice (DOJ) and could soon become a target for antitrust litigation. Monsanto's competitor DuPont even complained to the DOJ about Monsanto's so-called anticompetitive practices. DuPont has filed a lawsuit claiming that Monsanto is using its power and licenses to block its products. As a result of complaints, the Department of Justice has begun a civil investigation into Monsanto's practices. If the DOJ agrees that Monsanto's practices are anticompetitive, resulting decisions could affect how Monsanto does business.

Corporate Responsibility at Monsanto

It is a common expectation today for multinational companies to take actions to advance the interests and well being of the people in the countries in which they do business. Monsanto is no exception. The company has given millions of dollars in programs to help improve communities in developing countries.

In addition, as an agricultural company, Monsanto must address the grim reality facing the world in the future: The world's population is increasing at a fast rate, and the amount of available land and water for agriculture is decreasing. Some experts believe that our planet will have to produce more food in the next 50 years to feed the world's population than it has grown in the past 10,000 years, requiring us to double our food output. As a multinational corporation dedicated to agriculture, Monsanto is expected to address these problems. The company has also developed a three-tiered commitment policy: (1) produce more yield in crops, (2) conserve more resources, and (3) improve the lives of farmers. The company hopes to achieve these goals by taking initiatives in sustainable agriculture and philanthropy.

Sustainable Agriculture

Agriculture intersects the toughest challenges we all face on the planet. Together, we must meet the needs for increased food, fiber and energy while protecting the environment. In short, the world needs to produce more and conserve smarter.

This quote by Monsanto CEO Hugh Grant demonstrates the challenges agriculture is facing today, along with Monsanto's goals to meet these challenges. For instance, Monsanto is quick to point out that its biotech products added more than 100 million tons to worldwide agriculture production within a ten-year period, which they estimate has increased farmer's incomes by $33.8 billion. Monsanto has also created partnerships between nonprofit organizations across the world to enrich the lives of farmers in developing countries. Two regions on which Monsanto is focusing are India and Africa.

The need for better agriculture is apparent in India, where the population is expected to reach 1.3 billion by 2017. Biotech crops have helped to improve the size of yields in India, allowing some biotech farmers to increase their yields by 50 percent. Monsanto estimates that cotton farmers in India using biotech crops earn approximately $176 more in revenues per acre than their non-biotech contemporaries. In 2009, Monsanto launched Project SHARE, a sustainable yield initiative done in conjunction with the non-profit Indian Society of Agribusiness, to try and improve the lives of 10,000 cotton farmers in 1,100 villages.

In Africa, Monsanto has helped many farmers prosper and thrive through difficult periods. For instance, Monsanto has partnered with the African Agricultural Technology Foundation, scientists, and philanthropists to embark on the Water Efficient Maize for Africa (WEMA) initiative. During this five-year project, Monsanto will help to develop drought-tolerant maize seeds and provide them to small-scale African farmers royalty-free.

Not all view Monsanto's presence in Africa as an outreach in corporate responsibility. Some see it as another way for Monsanto to improve the bottom line. Critics see the company as trying to take control of African agriculture and destroy African agricultural practices that have lasted for thousands of years. Yet despite this criticism, there is no denying that Monsanto has positively affected African farmers' lives, along with increasing the company's profits for its shareholders. As CEO Hugh Grant writes, "This initiative isn't simply altruistic; we see it as a unique business proposition that rewards farmers and shareowners."

Philanthropy

In 1964, the Monsanto Company established the Monsanto Fund, which today funds many of the company's projects in Africa. One recipient of the Monsanto Fund included Africare, which received a $400,000 grant from Monsanto to fund a two-year food security project. The Monsanto Company also supports youth programs. In the first decade of the twenty-first century, the company donated nearly $1.5 million in scholarships to students who want to pursue agriculture-related degrees. The company also supports 4-H programs and the program Farm Safety 4 Just Kids, a program which helps teach rural children about safety while working on farms. Additionally, Monsanto donated $4 million in seeds to Haiti after the massive 2010 earthquake.

The Future of Monsanto

Monsanto has many challenges that it needs to address, including lingering concerns over the safety and environmental impact of its products. India, a major buyer of genetically modified seeds, instituted a moratorium for a type of genetically modified eggplant and filed a lawsuit against Monsanto citing safety concerns. The company needs to enforce its code of ethics effectively to avoid organizational misconduct (like bribery) in the future. Monsanto is also facing competition from other companies. For instance, Chinese companies are becoming formidable rivals for Monsanto as their weed killer is eating up some of Monsanto's Roundup profits. As a result, Monsanto was forced to lower the prices of Roundup and announced plans to restructure the Roundup area of the business.

Perhaps even more serious is the growing resistance to Monsanto seeds and herbicides. After many years on the market, Monsanto's Roundup herbicide and genetically modified seeds have begun to lead to super weeds and superbugs. If enough of these pests proliferate, the products may no longer be useful in killing them. Recent studies have shown that 11 super weeds in more than 25 states have developed a resistance against Roundup. Additionally, some farms in Iowa appear to have western corn rootworms (a major corn pest) that have developed a resistance to a type of genetically modified crop. Although Monsanto claims these superbugs are "isolated cases," the possibility that this resistance could spread is a serious threat. As a result, Monsanto is looking into a new RNA technology that will make these crops deadly for bugs to consume. Monsanto must be careful not to underestimate this problem but take proactive steps to prevent it from becoming a crisis.

Yet despite these challenges, Monsanto has numerous opportunities to thrive in the future. The company is currently working on new innovations that could increase its competitive edge, as well as provide enormous benefits to farmers worldwide. For instance, after a plunge in Roundup sales, Monsanto's profits are bouncing back once more. The company is also preparing several biotech products for commercialization.

Although Monsanto has made some mistakes in the past, it is trying to portray itself as a socially responsible company dedicated to improving agriculture. As noted, the company still has some problems. The predictions from Monsanto critics about biotech food have not yet come true, but that has not eradicated the fears of stakeholders. With the increasing popularity of organic food, staunch criticism from opponents, and the possibility of superbugs and super weeds, Monsanto will need to continue working with stakeholders to promote its technological innovations and to eliminate fears concerning its industry.

Questions for Discussion

1. If you were Monsanto's CEO, how would you best balance the conflicting needs of the variety of stakeholder groups that Monsanto must successfully engage?
2. Companies, like Monsanto, that can offer technology to improve human lives are often said to have a moral obligation to society. How can Monsanto best fulfill this moral obligation while also protecting society and the environment from the potential negative consequences of its products?
3. Monsanto has developed a differentiated, patent-protected product that produces superior yields when compared to traditional seeds. How has this successful marketing strategy been impacted by the potential negative side effects and the potential negative environmental impact of genetically modified seeds?
4. What can Monsanto do to alleviate stakeholder concerns? How could these actions be woven into the marketing strategy for the company's products?

Sources

The facts of this case are from Donald L. Barlett and James B. Steele, "Monsanto's Harvest of Fear," *Vanity Fair*, May 5, 2008 (http://www.vanityfair.com/politics/features/2008/05/monsanto200805); Ian Berry, "Monsanto's Seeds Sow a Profit," *Wall Street Journal*, January 7, 2011, B3; Rina Chadran, "Debate over GM eggplant consumes India," *Reuters*, February 16, 2010 (http://www.reuters.com/article/2010/02/16/us-india-food-idUS TRE61F0RS20100216); Environmental Protection Agency, "R.E.D. Facts," September 1993 (http://www.epa.gov/oppsrrd1/REDs/factsheets/0178fact.pdf), accessed April 20, 2012; "Even Small Doses of Popular Weed Killer Fatal to Frogs, Scientist Finds," *Science Daily*, August 5, 2005 (http://www.sciencedaily.com/releases/2005/08/050804053212.htm); Crystal Gammon, "Weed-Whacking Herbicide Proves Deadly to Human Cells," *Scientific American*, June 23, 2009 (http://www.scientificamerican.com/article.cfm?id=weed-whacking-herbicide-p&page=3); Ellen Gibson, "Monsanto," *BusinessWeek*, December 22, 2008, p. 51; "GMOs Under a Microscope," Science & Technology in Congress, October 1999 (http://www.aaas.org/gr/stc/Archive/1996-2003/stc99-10.pdf), accessed April 20, 2012; Jean Guerrero, "Altered Corn Advances Slowly in Mexico," *Wall Street Journal*, December 9, 2010, B8; Michael Grunwald, "Monsanto Hid Decades of Pollution," *Washington Post*, January 1, 2002, p. A1; Brian Hindo, "Monsanto: Winning the Ground War," *BusinessWeek*, December 5, 2007 (http://www.businessweek.com/stories/2007-12-05/monsanto-winning-the-ground-war); Jack Kaskey, "Monsanto Will Let Bio-Crop Patent Expire," *BusinessWeek*, January 20, 2010 (http://www.businessweek.com/stories/2010-01-20/monsanto-will-let-bio-crop-patents-expire); Jack Kaskey, "Attack of the Superweed," *BusinessWeek*, September 8, 2011 (http://www.businessweek.com/magazine/attack-of-the-superweed-09082011.html); Scott Kilman, "Monsanto's Net Profit Declines by 45%," *Wall Street Journal*, July 1, 2010, B7; Scott

Kilman, "Monsanto Corn Plant Losing Bug Resistance," *Wall Street Journal*, August 29, 2011, B1; Andrew Martin, "Fighting on a Battlefield the Size of a Milk Label," *New York Times*, March 9, 2008 (http://www.nytimes.com/2008/03/09/business/09feed.html); John W. Miller, "Monsanto Loses Case In Europe Over Seeds," *Wall Street Journal*, July 7, 2010, B1; "Monsanto Company—Company Profile, Information, Business Description, History, Background Information on Monsanto Company," Reference for Business: Encyclopedia of Small Business website (http://www.referenceforbusiness.com/history2/92/Monsanto-Company.html), accessed July 15, 2012; "Monsanto Co. (MON)," Yahoo Finance! (http://finance.yahoo.com/q/is?s=MON+Income+Statement&annual), accessed July 15, 2012; "Monsanto Fined $1.5M for Bribery," *BBC News*, January 7, 2005 (http://news.bbc.co.uk/2/hi/business/4153635.stm); "Monsanto Mania: The Seed of Profits," *iStockAnalyst*, January 17, 2008 (http://www.istockanalyst.com/article/viewarticle.aspx?articleid=1235584&zoneid=Home); "Monsanto Sells Cow Hormone to Eli Lilly," *The Chicago Tribune*, August 21, 2008 (http://articles.chicagotribune.com/2008-08-21/business/0808201398_1_posilac-monsanto-cow-hormone); Monsanto website (http://www.monsanto.com), accessed July 15, 2012; Claire Oxborrow, Becky Price, and Peter Riley, "Breaking Free," *Ecologist*, 38(9) (November 2008), pp. 35–36; Andrew Pollack, "So What's the Problem with Roundup?" Ecology Center, January 14, 2003 (http://www.ecologycenter.org/factsheets/roundup.html); Andrew Pollack, "Widely Used Crop Herbicide Is Losing Weed Resistance," *New York Times*, January 14, 2003 (http://www.nytimes.com/2003/01/14/business/widely-used-crop-herbicide-is-losing-weed-resistance.html); William Pentland, "India Sues Monsanto Over Genetically-Modified Eggplant," *Forbes*, August 12, 2011 (http://www.forbes.com/sites/williampentland/2011/08/12/india-sues-monsanto-over-genetically-modified-eggplant); Michael Pollan, "Playing God in the Garden," *New York Times Magazine*, October 25, 1998 (http://www.michaelpollan.com/article.php?id=73); "Report on Animal Welfare Aspects of the Use of Bovine Sematotrophin," *Report of the Scientific Committee on Animal Health and Animal Welfare*, March 10, 1999 (http://ec.europa.eu/food/fs/sc/scah/out21_en.pdf); "$700 Million Settlement in Alabama PCB Lawsuit," *New York Times*, August 21, 2003 (http://www.nytimes.com/2003/08/21/business/700-million-settlement-in-alabama-pcb-lawsuit.html); "The Parable of the Sower," *The Economist*, November 19, 2009 (http://www.economist.com/node/14904184); "The Pros and Cons of Genetically Modified Seeds," *Wall Street Journal*, March 15, 2010 (http://online.wsj.com/article/SB126862629333762259.html); and G. M. Williams, R. Kroes, and I. C. Monro, "Safety Evaluation and Risk Assessment of the Herbicide Roundup and Its Active Ingredient, Glyphosate, for Humans," NCBI, April 2000 (http://www.ncbi.nlm.nih.gov/pubmed/10854122), accessed July 15, 2012.

New Belgium Brewing (A): Gaining Competitive Advantage Through Socially Responsible Marketing*

Synopsis: From its roots in a Fort Collins, Colorado, basement, New Belgium Brewing has always aimed for business goals loftier than profitability. The company's tremendous growth to become the nation's third-largest craft brewery and ninth-largest overall has been guided by a steadfast branding strategy based on customer intimacy, social responsibility, and whimsy. The company's products, especially Fat Tire Amber Ale, have always appealed to beer connoisseurs who appreciate New Belgium's focus on sustainability as much as the company's world-class brews. Despite its growth and success, New Belgium has managed to stay true to its core values and brand authenticity—the keys to its marketing advantage in the highly competitive craft brewing industry.

Themes: Customer intimacy, competitive advantage, social responsibility, sustainability, branding strategy, product strategy, distribution strategy, marketing implementation, customer relationships

L arge corporations and well-known brand names come to mind when most of us think about successful businesses. However, the success of small- and medium-sized businesses can be just as noteworthy, while often having a greater impact on local communities and neighborhoods. One such business is the New Belgium Brewing Company, Inc., based in Fort Collins, Colorado. The New Belgium brand has become known for two things: its high-quality, Belgian-style beers and its commitment toward sustainability. Its socially responsible initiatives have contributed greatly to New Belgium's success. In fact, New Belgium's business model has been so successful that it is increasingly easy to find its beers around the country as more consumers embrace what the company stands for. Studies have shown that the stock prices of ethically and socially responsible companies as a whole outperform those on the S&P 500 index. Although New Belgium is not a public company and thus does not offer publically owned stock, it seems to follow this trend of success. The company has become the seventh-largest brewery in the nation and the third-largest brewery in the "craft beer" segment.

---

*O.C. Ferrell, University of New Mexico, prepared this case for classroom discussion rather than to illustrate effective of ineffective handling of an administrative situation. Jennifer Sawayda, University of New Mexico, provided editorial assistance.

History of the New Belgium Brewing Company

The idea for the New Belgium Brewing Company (NBB) began with a bicycling trip through Belgium—home to some of the world's finest ales, many of which have been brewed for centuries in that country's monasteries. As Jeff Lebesch, an American electrical engineer, cruised around that country on his fat-tired mountain bike, he wondered whether he could produce such high quality beers back home in Colorado. After acquiring the special strain of yeast used to brew Belgian-style ales, Lebesch returned home and began to experiment in his Colorado basement. When his beers earned thumbs up from friends, Lebesch decided to market them.

New Belgium Brewing (NBB) opened for business in 1991 as a tiny basement operation in Lebesch's home in Fort Collins. Lebesch's wife at the time, Kim Jordan, became the firm's marketing director. They named their first brew Fat Tire Amber Ale in honor of Lebesch's bike ride through Belgium. Initially, getting New Belgium beer onto store shelves was not easy. Jordan often delivered the beer to stores in the back of her Toyota station wagon. However, New Belgium beers quickly developed a small but devoted customer base, first in Fort Collins and then throughout Colorado. The brewery soon outgrew the couple's basement and moved into an old railroad depot before settling into its present custom-built facility in 1995. The brewery includes two brew houses, four quality assurance labs, a wastewater treatment facility, a canning and bottling line, and numerous technological innovations for which New Belgium has become nationally recognized as a "paradigm of environmental efficiencies."

Under the leadership of Kim Jordan, who has since become CEO, New Belgium Brewing Company currently offers a variety of permanent and seasonal ales and pilsners. The company's standard line includes Sunshine Wheat, Blue Paddle, 1554 (a black ale), and the original Fat Tire Amber Ale, still the firm's bestseller. Some customers even refer to the company as the Fat Tire Brewery. The brewery also has its Explore Series, consisting of Shift, Ranger IPA, Belgo IPA, Abby, and Trippel, as well as seasonal ales Dig and Snow Day. The firm also started a Lips of Faith program, where small batch brews like La Folie, Biere de Mars, and Abbey Grand Cru are created for internal celebrations or landmark events. Additionally, New Belgium is working in "collabeeration" with Elysian Brewing Company, in which each company will be able to use the other's brew houses, though they remain independent businesses. Through this partnership, they hope to create better efficiency and experimentation along with taking collaborative strides toward the future of American craft beer making. One collabeeration resulting from this partnership is Ranger IPA and Kick from NBB's Explore and Lips of Faith programs.

Although still a small brewery when compared to many beer companies, like fellow Coloradan Coors, NBB has consistently experienced strong growth with estimated sales of more than $100 million. (Since New Belgium is a private firm, detailed sales and revenue numbers are not available.) The company sells more than 700,000 barrels of beer per year and has many opportunities for continued growth. For instance, while total beer consumption has decreased 2 percent by volume, the craft brewing industry has grown by 16.4 percent.

NBB's most effective form of advertising has always been its customers' word of mouth, especially in the early days. Indeed, before New Belgium beers were widely distributed throughout Colorado, one liquor-store owner in Telluride is purported to have offered people gas money if they would stop by and pick up New Belgium beer on their way through Fort Collins. Although New Belgium has expanded distribution to a good portion of the U.S. market, the brewery receives numerous e-mails and phone calls every day inquiring when its beers will be available in other parts of the country.

NBB joined Facebook in November 2007 and started activity marketing through social media in 2009. NBB actively coordinates its marketing campaigns through both Facebook (with over 300,000 fans) and Twitter (with over 100,000 followers), as well as a NBB Pandora radio station, a NBB Instagram channel, live streaming video of special events called the Beer Stream, and NBB's YouTube channel. Currently, New Belgium's products are distributed in 28 states plus the District of Columbia (see Case Exhibit 4.1). Beer connoisseurs that appreciate the high quality of NBB's products, as well as the company's environmental and ethical business practices, have driven this growth. For example, when the company began distribution in Minnesota, the beers were so popular that a liquor store had to open early and make other accommodations for the large amount of customers. The store sold 400 cases of Fat Tire in the first hour it was open.

With expanding distribution, NBB recognized a need to increase its opportunities for reaching its far-flung customers. It consulted with Dr. Douglas Holt, an Oxford professor and cultural branding expert. After studying the company, Holt, together with former Marketing Director Greg Owsley, drafted a 70-page "manifesto" describing the brand's attributes, character, cultural relevancy, and promise. In particular, Holt identified in New Belgium an ethos of pursuing creative activities simply for the joy of doing them well and in harmony with the natural environment. With the brand defined, New Belgium worked with New York advertising agency Amalgamated to create a $10 million advertising campaign for New Belgium. The campaign would target high-end beer drinkers, men ages 25 to 44, and highlight the brewery's down-to-earth image. (This process is discussed in the New Belgium Brewing (B) case).

CASE EXHIBIT 4.1 New Belgium's Distribution Territories

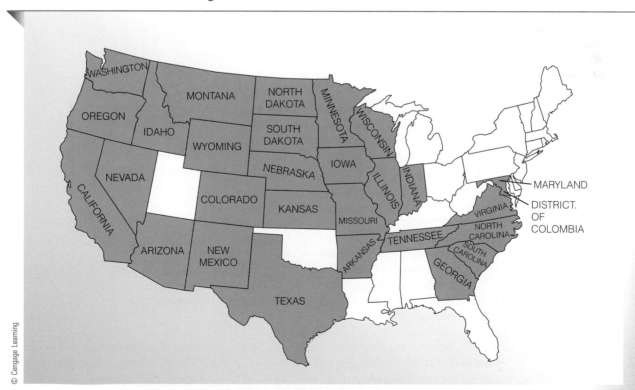

Source: Based on the New Belgium Brewing website (http://www.newbelgium.com/culture/faq.aspx), accessed July 16, 2012.

New Belgium Embraces Social Responsibility

According to New Belgium, the company maintains a fundamental focus on the ethical culture of the brand. Although consumer suspicion of business is at an all-time high, those in good standing—as opposed to those trading on hype—are eyed with icon-like adoration. Today, businesses that fully embrace citizenship in the communities they serve can forge enduring bonds with customers. At New Belgium, the synergy between branding and corporate citizenship occurred naturally as the firm's ethical culture (in the form of core values and beliefs) and was in place long before NBB had a marketing department.

Back in early 1991, when New Belgium was just a fledgling home-brewed business, Jeff and Kim took a hike into Rocky Mountain National Park. Armed with a pen and a notebook, they took their first stab at what the company's core purpose would be. If they were going forward with this venture, what were their aspirations beyond profitability? What was at the heart of their dream? What they wrote down that spring day, give or take a little editing, was the core values and beliefs you can read on the NBB website today. More importantly, ask just about any New Belgium employee and he or she can list for you many, if not all, of these shared values and can inform you which are the most personally poignant. For NBB, branding strategies are as rooted in its company values as in its other business practices. For instance, as a way to live out its values, the company adopted a triple bottom line (TBL) approach to business. TBL incorporates economic, social, and environmental factors into its business strategies. In other words, the company looks at its impact upon profits, people, and the planet rather than simply on the bottom line. New Belgium's dedication to quality, the environment, and its employees and customers is expressed in its mission statement and core values:

Mission Statement:

To operate a profitable brewery which makes our love and talent manifest.

Company Core Values and Beliefs:

1. Remembering that we are incredibly lucky to create something fine that enhances people's lives while surpassing our consumers' expectations.
2. Producing world-class beers
3. Promoting beer culture and the responsible enjoyment of beer
4. Kindling social, environmental, and cultural change as a business role model
5. Environmental stewardship: minimizing resource consumption, maximizing energy efficiency, and recycling
6. Cultivating potential through learning, participative management, and the pursuit of opportunities
7. Balancing the myriad needs of the company, staff, and their families
8. Trusting each other and committing ourselves to authentic relationships, communications, and promises
9. Continuous, innovative quality and efficiency improvements
10. Having Fun

Employees believe that these statements help communicate to customers and other stakeholders what New Belgium, as a company, is about. These simple values developed roughly 20 years ago are just as meaningful to the company and its customers today, even though there has been much growth.

Responsibilities to the Environment

New Belgium's marketing strategy involves linking the quality of its products, as well as its brand, with the company's philosophy of environmental friendliness. From leading-edge environmental gadgets and high-tech industry advancements to employee-ownership programs and a strong belief in giving back to the community, New Belgium demonstrates its desire to create a living, learning community.

NBB strives for cost-efficient energy-saving alternatives for conducting its business and reducing its impact on the environment. In staying true to the company's core values and beliefs, the brewery's employee–owners unanimously agreed to invest in a wind turbine, making New Belgium the first fully wind-powered brewery in the United States. NBB has also invested in the following energy-saving technologies:

- A smart grid installation that allows NBB to communicate with its electricity provider to conserve energy. For example, the smart grid will alert NBB to non-essential operational functions, allowing the company to turn them off and save power.
- The installation of a 20 kW photovoltaic array on top of the packaging hall. The array produces 3 percent of the company's electricity.
- A brew kettle, the second of its kind installed in the nation, which heats wort sheets instead of the whole kettle at once. This kettle heating method conserves energy more than standard kettles do.
- Sun tubes, which provide natural daytime lighting throughout the brew house all year long.
- A system to capture its wastewater and extract methane from it. This can contribute up to 15 percent of the brewery's power needs while reducing the strain on the local municipal water treatment facility.
- A steam condenser that captures and reuses the hot water that boils the barley and hops in the production process to start the next brew. The steam is redirected to heat the floor tiles and de-ice the loading docks in cold weather.

New Belgium also takes pride in reducing waste through recycling and creative reuse strategies. The company strives to recycle as many supplies as possible, including cardboard boxes, keg caps, office materials, and the amber glass used in bottling. The brewery also stores spent barley and hop grains in an on-premise silo and invites local farmers to pick up the grains, free of charge, to feed their pigs. Going further down the road to producing products for the food chain, NBB is working with partners to take the same bacteria that create methane from NBB wastewater and convert them into a harvestable, high-protein fish food. NBB also buys recycled products when it can, and even encourages its employees to reduce air pollution by using alternative transportation. Reduce, Reuse, Recycle—the three R's of environmental stewardship—are taken seriously at NBB. Case Exhibit 4.2 depicts New Belgium's recycling efforts.

Additionally, New Belgium has been a long-time participant in green building techniques. With each expansion of the facility, it has incorporated new technologies and learned a few lessons along the way. In 2002, NBB agreed to participate in the United States Green Building Council's Leadership in Energy and Environment Design for Existing Buildings (LEED-EB) pilot program. From sun tubes and day lighting throughout the facility to reusing heat in the brew house, NBB continues to search for new ways to close loops and conserve resources.

New Belgium has made significant achievements in sustainability, particularly compared to other companies in the industry. For one, New Belgium uses only 3.9 gallons of water to make 1 gallon of beer, which is 20 percent less than most companies. The company is attempting to create a closed-loop system for their wastewater with its own Process Water Treatment Plant, in which microbes are used to clean the wastewater. New Belgium recycles over 95 percent of its waste, and today 100 percent of its

CASE EXHIBIT 4.2   New Belgium's Recycling Efforts

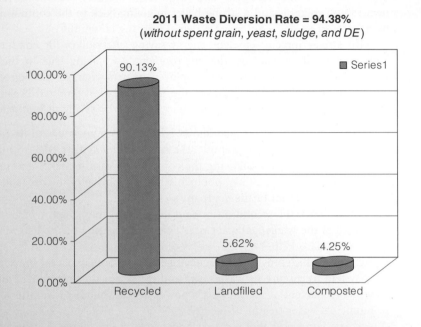

2011 Waste Diversion Rate = 94.38%
(*without spent grain, yeast, sludge, and DE*)

Source: Based on New Belgium Brewing Company, 2011 Waste Diversion Report (http://www.newbelgium.com/files/sustainability/2011%20NBB%20Waste%20Diverion%20Report.pdf), accessed July 16, 2012.

electricity comes from renewables. Despite these achievements, New Belgium has no intention of halting its sustainability efforts. The company recently expanded its canning capacity by six times with a new canning line that injects less carbon dioxide into each can. In addition to reducing carbon dioxide emissions into the atmosphere, the cans are also more sustainable than glass bottles. By 2015, the company hopes to reduce the amount of water used to make beer by 10 percent through better production processes and decrease its carbon footprint by 25 percent per barrel. To encourage sustainability throughout the supply chain, NBB adopted Sustainable Purchasing Guidelines. The Guidelines allow them to pinpoint eco-friendly suppliers and work with them closely to create sustainability throughout the entire value chain.

Responsibilities to Society

Beyond its use of environmentally friendly technologies and innovations, New Belgium also strives to improve communities and enhance people's lives through corporate giving, event sponsorship, and philanthropic involvement. Since its inception, NBB has donated more than $2.5 million to philanthropic causes through its Stewardship Grants program. For every barrel of beer sold the prior year, NBB donates $1 to philanthropic causes within their distribution territories. The donations are divided between states in proportion to their percentage of overall sales. This is the company's way of staying local and giving back to the communities that support and purchase NBB products. NBB also participates in "1% For the Planet," a philanthropic network to which the company donates 1 percent of its profits.

Funding decisions are made by New Belgium's Philanthropy Committee, which is comprised of employees throughout the brewery, including owners, employee owners, area leaders, and production workers. New Belgium looks for nonprofit organizations that demonstrate creativity, diversity, and an innovative approach to their mission and objectives. The Philanthropy Committee also looks for groups that involve the community to reach their goals. The breakdown of NBB's Stewardship Grant awards is shown in Case Exhibit 4.3.

Additionally, NBB maintains a community bulletin board in its facility, where it posts an array of community involvement activities and proposals. This community board allows tourists and employees to see the different ways they can help out the community, and it gives nonprofit organizations a chance to make their needs known. Organizations can even apply for grants through the NBB website, which has a link designated for this purpose. The company donates to causes with a particular emphasis on water conservation, sensible transportation and bike advocacy, sustainable agriculture, and youth environmental education, among other areas.

NBB also sponsors a number of events, with a special focus on those that involve "human-powered" sports that cause minimal damage to the natural environment. Through event sponsorships, such as the Tour de Fat, NBB supports various environmental, social, and cycling nonprofit organizations. In the Tour de Fat, one participant hands over his or her car keys and vehicle title in exchange for an NBB commuter bike and trailer. The participant is then filmed for the world to see as he or she promotes sustainable transportation over driving. In 2011, Tour de Fat traveled to 13 cities, with more than 69,000 attendees and 41,000 cyclists in the parades. New Belgium also partners with nonprofit organizations to support Skinny Dip for a Cause, a campaign where

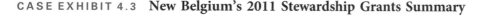

CASE EXHIBIT 4.3   New Belgium's 2011 Stewardship Grants Summary

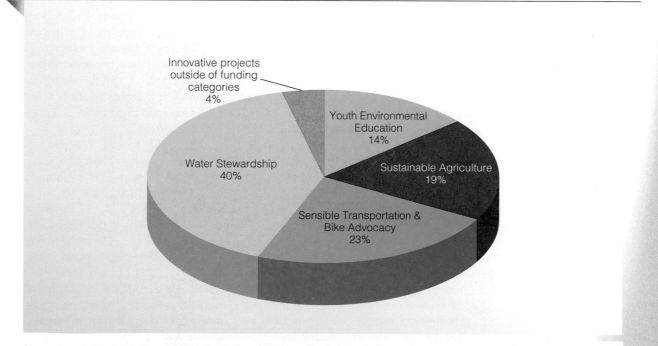

Source: New Belgium Brewing Company, 2011 Stewardship Grants Program Summary (http://www.newbelgium.com/Files/Local_Grants_Program_2011_summary.pdf), accessed July 17, 2012.

skinny-dipping is used to raise awareness of water issues and conservation. In the course of one year, New Belgium can be found at anywhere from 150 to 200 festivals and events across the nation.

Responsibilities to Employees

Recognizing employees' role in the company's success, New Belgium provides many generous benefits for its over 400 employees. In addition to the usual paid health and dental insurance and retirement plans, employees get a catered lunch every month to celebrate employees' birthdays as well as a free massage once a year, and they can bring their children and dogs to work. Employees who stay with the company for five years earn an all-expenses paid trip to Belgium to "study beer culture." Employees are also reimbursed for one hour of paid time off for every two hours of volunteer work that they perform. Perhaps most importantly, employees can also earn stock in the privately held corporation, which grants them a vote in company decisions. Employees currently own about 43 percent of company stock. Open book management also allows employees to see the financial costs and performance of the company. Employees are provided with financial training so they can understand the books and ask questions about the numbers.

New Belgium also wishes to get its employees involved not only in the company but in its sustainability efforts as well. To help their own sustainability efforts, employees are given a fat-tired cruiser bike after one year's employment so they can ride to work instead of drive. An onsite recycling center is also provided for employees. Other company perks include inexpensive yoga classes, free beer at quitting time, and a climbing wall. To ensure that workers' voices are heard, NBB has a democratically elected group of co-workers called POSSE. POSSE acts as a liaison between the board, managers, and employees.

Responsibility Breeds Success

New Belgium Brewing's efforts to live up to its own high standards have paid off with a very loyal following—in fact, the company recently expanded the number of tours it offers of its facilities due to such high demand. The company has also been the recipient of numerous awards. Past awards for NBB include the Business Ethics Magazine's Business Ethics Award for its "dedication to environmental excellence in every part of its innovative brewing process," its inclusion in the *Wall Street Journal*'s 15 best small workplaces, and the awards for best mid-sized brewing company of the year and best mid-sized brewmaster at the Great American Beer Festival. New Belgium has taken home medals for three different brews: Abbey Belgian Style Ale, Blue Paddle Pilsner, and La Folie specialty ale.

According to David Edgar, director of the Institute for Brewing Studies, "They've created a very positive image for their company in the beer-consuming public with smart decision-making." Although some members of society do not believe that a company whose major product is alcohol can be socially responsible, New Belgium has set out to prove that for those who make a choice to drink responsibly, the company can do everything possible to contribute to society. New Belgium also promotes the responsible appreciation of beer through its participation in and support of the culinary arts. For instance, it frequently hosts New Belgium Beer Dinners, in which every course of the meal is served with a complementary culinary treat.

Although New Belgium has made great strides in creating a socially responsible brand image, its work is not done. New Belgium must continually reexamine its ethical, social, and environmental responsibilities. In 2004, New Belgium received the Environmental Protection Agency's regional Environmental Achievement Award. It was both an honor and a motivator for the company to continue its socially responsible goals. After all, there are still many ways for NBB to improve as a corporate citizen. For example, although all electric power comes from renewable sources, the plant is still heated in part by using natural gas. There will always be a need for more public dialogue on avoiding alcohol abuse.

Additionally, continued expansion requires longer distances to travel for distributing the product, which increases the use of fossil fuels. As a way to deal with these longer distances, New Belgium announced it would open a second brewery in Asheville, North Carolina to expand NBB's capacity and place the product closer to markets in the eastern United States. The new $175 million facility, which will create 154 jobs and expand the company's capacity by 400,000 barrels per year, will be supported by a $1 million grant from the One North Carolina fund.

NBB executives acknowledge that as its annual sales increase, so do the challenges to remain on a human scale and to continue to be culturally authentic. How to boldly grow the brand while maintaining its humble feel has always been a challenge. Additionally, reducing waste to an even greater extent will take lots of work on behalf of both managers and employees, creating the need for a collaborative process that will require the dedication of both parties toward sustainability.

New Belgium also faces increased competition from other craft breweries. It still remains behind Boston Beer Co. (maker of Sam Adams beer) and Sierra Nevada in market share. Like New Belgium, Boston Beer Co. and Sierra Nevada have plans to expand, with Boston Beer allocating $35 million for capital investment projects at breweries in Massachusetts, Pennsylvania, and Ohio in 2012. New Belgium must also compete against craft beer alternatives released by traditional breweries, such as MillerCoor's New Moon Belgian White. New Belgium must constantly engage in environmental scanning and competitive analysis to compete in this increasingly competitive environment.

Every six-pack of New Belgium Beer displays the phrase "In this box is our labor of love. We feel incredibly lucky to be creating something fine that enhances people's lives." Although Jeff Lebesch and Kim Jordan are divorced and Lebesch has left the company to focus on other interests, the founders of New Belgium hope this statement captures the spirit of the company. According to employee Dave Kemp, NBB's social responsibilities give the company a competitive advantage because consumers want to believe in and feel good about the products they purchase. NBB's most important asset is its image—a corporate brand that stands for quality, responsibility, and concern for society. Defining itself as more than a beer company, the brewer also sees itself as a caring organization that is concerned for all stakeholders.

Questions for Discussion

1. What environmental issues does the New Belgium Brewing Company work to address? How has NBB taken a strategic approach to addressing these issues? Why do you think the company has taken such a strong stance toward sustainability?

2. Do you agree that New Belgium's focus on social responsibility provides a key competitive advantage for the company? Why or why not?

3. What are the challenges associated with combining the need for growth with the need to maintain customer intimacy and social responsibility? Does NBB risk losing focus on its core beliefs if it grows too quickly? Explain.

4. Some segments of society contend that companies that sell alcoholic beverages and tobacco products cannot be socially responsible organizations because of the nature of their primary products. Do you believe that New Belgium's actions and initiatives are indicative of a socially responsible corporation? Why or why not?

Sources

The facts of this case are from Peter Asmus, "Goodbye Coal, Hello Wind," *Business Ethics*, 13 (July/August 1999), pp. 10–11; "A Tour of the New Belgium Brewery—Act One," LiveGreen blog, April 9, 2007 (http://www.livegreensd.com/2007/04/tour-of-new-belgium-brewery-act-one.html); Robert Baun, "What's in a Name? Ask the Makers of Fat Tire," [Fort Collins] *Coloradoan.com*, October 8, 2000, pp. E1, E3; "Breweries Industry Profile," First Research, April 30, 2012 (http://www.firstresearch.com/industry-research/Breweries.html); "COL-LABEERATIONS," Elysian Brewing Company (http://www.elysianbrewing.com/beer/collabeerations.html), accessed July 16, 2012; *Corporate Sustainability Report*, New Belgium Brewing website (http://www.newbel gium.com/culture/alternatively_empowered/sustainable-business-story.aspx), accessed July 16, 2012; Robert F. Dwyer and John F. Tanner, Jr., *Business Marketing* (Irwin McGraw-Hill, 1999), p. 104; Julie Gordon, "Lebesch Balances Interests in Business, Community," *Coloradoan.com*, February 26, 2003; Mike Esterl, "Craft Brewers Tap Big Expansion," *Wall Street Journal*, December 28, 2011 (http://online.wsj.com/article/SB10001424052970203686204577114291721661070.html); Del I. Hawkins, Roger J. Best, and Kenneth A. Coney, *Consumer Behavior: Building Marketing Strategy*, 8th ed. (Irwin McGraw-Hill, 2001); David Kemp, Tour Connoisseur, New Belgium Brewing Company, personal interview by Nikole Haiar, November 21, 2000; Dick Kreck, "Strange Brewing Standing Out," *Denver Post*, June 2, 2010 (http://www.denverpost.com/lifestyles/ci_15198853); Devin Leonard, "New Belgium and the Battle of the Microbrews," *BusinessWeek*, December 1, 2011 (http://www.businessweek.com/magazine/new-belgium-and-the-battle-of-the-microbrews-12012011.html); Karlene Lukovitz, "New Belgium Brewing Gets 'Hopped Up,'" *Marketing Daily*, February 3, 2010 (http://www.mediapost.com/publications/?fa=Articles.showArticle&art_aid=121806); Norman Miller, "Craft Beer Industry Continues to Grow," *PJ Star*, March 26, 2012 (http://www.pjstar.com/community/blogs/beer-nut/x140148153/Craft-Beer-industry-continues-to-grow); New Belgium Brewing, *New Belgium Brewing: Follow Your Folly*, May 9, 2007 (http://www.newbelgium.com/Files/NBB_student-info-packet.pdf); "New Belgium Brewing Announces Asheville as Site for Second Brewery," *Denver Post*, April 5, 2012 (http://marketwire.den verpost.com/client/denver_post/release.jsp?actionFor=1595119); "New Belgium Brewing Company, Inc.," *BusinessWeek* (http://investing.businessweek.com/research/stocks/private/snapshot.asp?privcapId=919332), accessed July 16, 2012; New Belgium Brewing website (http://www.newbelgium.com), accessed July 16, 2012; "New Belgium Brewing Wins Ethics Award," *Denver Business Journal*, January 2, 2003 (http://www.bizjournals.com/denver/stories/2002/12/30/daily21.html); Greg Owsley, "The Necessity For Aligning Brand with Corporate Ethics," in Sheb L. True, Linda Ferrell, O.C. Ferrell, *Fulfilling Our Obligation, Perspectives on Teaching Business Ethics* (Atlanta, GA: Kennesaw State University Press, 2005), pp. 128–132; Steve Raabe, "New Belgium Brewing Turns to Cans," *Denver Post*, May 15, 2008 (http://www.denverpost.com/breakingnews/ci_9262005); Steve Raabe, "Plans Brewing for New Belgium Facility on East Coast," *Denver Post*, December 22, 2011 (http://www.denverpost.com/business/ci_19597528); Kelly K. Spors, "Top Small Workplaces 2008," *Wall Street Journal*, February 22, 2009 (http://online.wsj.com/article/SB122347733961315417.html); "The 2011 World's Most Ethical Companies," *Ethisphere*, Q1 2011, 37–43; and "Tour de New Belgium," Brew Public, November 23, 2010 (http://brewpublic.com/places-to-drink-beer/tour-de-new-belgium).

New Belgium Brewing (B): Developing a Brand Personality*

Synopsis: This case, a follow up to New Belgium (A), discusses how New Belgium Brewing expanded its branding and communication strategy from a focus on word of mouth and event sponsorship to include television advertising, web-based communication, and social media. The development of New Belgium's "Brand Manifesto" is reviewed, along with the company's decisions regarding media selection, messaging components, and advertising production. Despite the company's continued growth in terms of both distribution and promotional complexity, New Belgium has remained focused on its core values of customer intimacy, sustainability, whimsy, and fun.

Themes: Integrated marketing communication, branding strategy, positioning, advertising, customer intimacy, distribution strategy, sustainability, marketing implementation, customer relationships

T he idea for the New Belgium Brewing Company began with a bicycling trip through Belgium. Belgium is arguably home to many of the world's finest ales, some of which have been brewed for centuries in that country's monasteries and small artisan breweries. As Jeff Lebesch, an American electrical engineer by trade and a home brewer by hobby, cruised around that country on his fat-tired mountain bike, he wondered whether he could produce such high quality beers back home in Colorado. After acquiring the special strain of yeast used to brew Belgian-style ales, Lebesch returned home and began to experiment in his Colorado basement. When his beers earned thumbs up from friends, Lebesch decided to market them.

The New Belgium Brewing Company (NBB) opened for business in 1991 as a tiny basement operation in Lebesch's home in Fort Collins. Lebesch's wife at the time, Kim Jordan, handled all the marketing, sales, and deliveries from her station wagon. NBB beers quickly developed a small but devoted customer base, first in Fort Collins and then throughout Colorado. The brewery soon outgrew the couple's basement and moved into an old railroad depot before settling into its present custom-built facility in 1995. The company's standard product line has grown to include Sunshine Wheat, Blue Paddle Pilsner, 1554 (a black ale), and the original Fat Tire Amber Ale, still the firm's bestseller. Today, NBB is America's third largest craft brewer; with Sam Adams (owned by Boston Beer Company) number one and Sierra Nevada number two. The craft beer market accounts for more than 5.5 percent of the total U.S. beer market. However, it is

*© Bryan Simpson, New Belgium Brewing, 500 Linden Street, Fort Collins, CO 80524. All rights reserved. This case was prepared for classroom discussion rather than to illustrate effective or ineffective handling of an administrative situation. Jennifer Sawayda, University of New Mexico, provided editorial assistance.

CASE EXHIBIT 5.1   **Craft Beer's Share of the U.S. Beer Market**

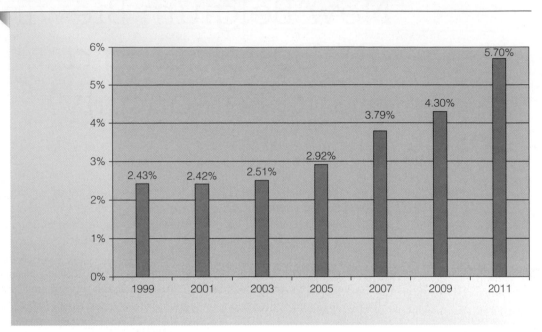

Source: Brewers Association, Boulder, Colorado.

the fastest-growing segment of the U.S. alcoholic beverage market. Case Exhibit 5.1 illustrates that craft beer's overall market share has increased more than 100 percent between 1999 and 2011, with market share rising rapidly since 2005.

New Belgium's Initial Marketing Strategy

When a company grows as rapidly as NBB, the tendency is not to mess with a good thing. This applies to the beer portfolio, the culture, and the marketing process. For many years, NBB, best known for Fat Tire Amber Ale, thrived on word-of-mouth communication to sell the brand. In fact, for the first four years of its existence, NBB's marketing consisted of traveling to beer festivals and handing out free samples. Relational marketing, done barstool to barstool, launched the advent of its Ranger Team—a sales staff who acts as brand stewards throughout the U.S. distribution network. Each ranger has his or her own Facebook page as a way to enhance relationship marketing with the company's customers.

When Greg Owsley was hired as marketing director in 1996, NBB became more focused and proactive in its marketing efforts. Festivals and sponsorships, coupled with print media in alternative weeklies, increased brand sales to over 100,000 barrels annually by 1998. (Ten years later this number hit nearly 500,000 barrels, while today NBB sells more than 700,000 barrels of beer annually.) Owsley and his team introduced such signature NBB events as the multicity philanthropic bike festival, Tour de Fat. They launched an educational "Beerstream" in the form of a traveling slide show and beer tasting in an old Airstream trailer. NBB developed engaging contests like "What's Your Folly?" to invite consumers to pitch their Beerdream (an adventure enhanced by NBB beers) to win immortal fame on an NBB postcoaster (mailable postcard and coaster). All events, sponsorships, and interactive games were bolstered by strategic purchase of print media advertising.

In 2003, as NBB expanded into northern California, it became evident that new avenues would have to be considered to effectively reach the increasingly far-flung consumer base. For the first time, NBB looked to a more formalized and systematic approach to analyzing its audience. A consulting firm conducted research in Colorado and in other markets and suggested a mind-share approach to branding. However, Owsley rejected the consulting firm's suggestion and continued researching branding's foremost progressive thinkers, eventually coming across the works of Douglas Holt.

Developing a Brand Manifesto

Holt, then of Harvard Business School and currently with Oxford, is the leading proponent of "cultural branding"—a philosophy of branding that tries to speak to tensions within society. Owsley contacted Holt after reading some of his published work online. The two agreed to meet, and Holt was hired as a consultant in September 2003. Holt came to NBB on several occasions to study the brand and immerse himself in the brewery's unique culture. This process led to the creation of a brand manifesto—a 70-page document, coauthored over many months by Owsley and Holt, describing the brand's attributes, character, cultural relevancy, and potential. This opened the door to a relationship with Amalgamated Inc., a young upstart advertising agency in New York. In discussing the brand with the agency, NBB's creative team collaborated with Amalgamated to flesh out the brand's cultural contributions and messaging components.

Developing the Ad Campaign

Working with the manifesto as a guide, Amalgamated explored a wide array of possibilities within a somewhat restrictive budget. Television, with its low cost per viewer and wide reach, quickly rose as the preferred option. It also seemed more authentic to embrace the medium where consumers expected to see advertising interwoven with entertainment.

Creating a television campaign for a craft brewer provided a litany of challenges and opportunities. The "Big Three" brewers—Anheuser-Bush, Coors, and Miller—had long dominated mainstream televised beer advertising in the United States. Boston Brewing's foray into television several years back presented an interesting case study. The makers of Sam Adams started a campaign with founder Jim Koch delivering a folksy voice-over that positioned Sam Adams as a beer of the highest quality. Over time, this morphed into televised spots that looked more and more like the positioning of America's Big Three brewers.

NBB understood at the inception that the power of television could work to bolster or undermine the brand with equal efficacy. If the spots did not ring true to the NBB character, they could alienate the core consumers who had helped build the company to this point. Within the ethos of NBB, Holt unearthed a mindset where a highly creative activity or avocation is pursued for the intrinsic value of doing it, as well as performed in a balanced manner with nature. It is the cultural counterpoint to the "urban professional." The mindset personified is the mountain local who eschews a high-dollar job in Denver to pursue a simpler existence. It is the unsigned musician who writes songs just to entertain her friends. It is the amateur bread maker who bakes experimental breads and then hand delivers them on his bike. It is the juxtaposition of traditional American values that often compels workers into a position of compromising their true selves in order to exist within a modern technopoly—those people who live their lives in a way that emphasizes experience for the sake of experience rather than for the sake of profit.

With these shared attributes in mind, the audience for NBB's commercials would likely be the professional who follows the traditional route of existing within a capitalist economy but still has artistic leanings and desires. These are the executives, lawyers, and accountants who live in Kansas or Missouri but come to Colorado for a ski week every year to indulge in the mountain lifestyle. These are folks who look at the mountain local and envy his dedication but could never fathom making that career sacrifice. The cultural tension then can be seen as the compromise between living the life one wants with balancing the economic needs of existing within a technopoly. NBB beers could be positioned as a manifestation of that lifestyle. It would be possible to pop a cap off a Fat Tire in Springfield, Missouri, and travel metaphorically to the Colorado mountains and the mountain local's life.

With this understanding, Amalgamated developed a series of storyboards for the commercials featuring the "Tinkerer," a character who discovers an old cruiser bike that has been customized, modernized, and ultimately left for scrap. The Tinkerer then proceeds to strip the cruiser bike back down to its bare elements. The original boards featured three complete narratives with a potential fourth when Amalgamated flew to NBB to present its material at the company's monthly staff meeting. True to a culture based on employee ownership and ownership mentality, every NBB employee was offered the opportunity to weigh in on the storyboards.

The NBB team reacted positively to the presentation with the exception of Amalgamated's suggested tagline: "Follow Your Folly … Ours Is Beer." Several people suggested that folly had too negative a connotation or undermined the science and technology it took to produce such consistently high quality beers. The debate built steam over several weeks, with the creative team suggesting that a word like *folly* had fallen so far from the vernacular that it was ripe for reinterpretation and a fresh new definition. Following one's folly also aptly alluded to the ideal of offbeat endeavors versus the traditional "follow the money" thinking that created the social tensions inherent to potential consumers' lives. After a healthy volley of e-mails from nearly every NBB department, the creative team won out and "Follow Your Folly" became the campaign's tagline.

Advertising Production

At this stage in the process, a search for the right director for the commercials ensued. Amalgamated reviewed dozens of highlight reels and passed the most likely candidates along to NBB. Much of the work represented had great visual power with big budget, 70-millimeter sheen. In the end NBB went with Jake Scott, who suggested shooting the spots on grittier 16-millimeter film stock and giving the work a timeless feel influenced by the photography of the 1960s documentarian William Eggelston. Scott flew to the brewery to learn about NBB and then jumped into a car and scouted locations throughout Colorado. He sent still photos from a variety of locales, and ultimately the group committed to shooting in and around Hotchkiss and Paonia. After reviewing a tape of locals for potential casting shots outside bike shops in Fort Collins and Boulder, Scott decided on Boulder craftsman Charles Srbecky to play the Tinkerer. Srbecky, formerly of the Czech Republic, was an atypical choice with tousled hair, weathered features, and a maturity not seen in contemporary U.S. beer advertising.

In September 2004, members of NBB, Amalgamated, and the production company RSA out of Los Angeles met in Hotchkiss and commenced shooting over a three-day period. Much of the talent and crew came from surrounding Colorado communities. The production quickly took on a collaborative and improvisational feel reflective of NBB's culture. Although great attention was paid to fulfilling the promise of Amalgamated's storyboards, spontaneous opportunities were embraced as they arose. This led to no fewer than nine potential spots coming out of the three-day shoot.

Amalgamated returned to New York to begin postproduction of the spots with NBB's input. Choosing a musical bed quickly developed into the next creative challenge. Editors at Whitehouse Post in New York tried a variety of genres, from progressive to country alternative, and landed on an artist in the category of "Freak Folk" by the name of Devendra Banhart. Banhart's tunes added a haunting sense of cheerful nostalgia to the works. With the 16-millimeter film stock giving a mid-1970s feel buoyed by Banhart's acoustic tunes, the campaign took a far more muted and poignant tone than the ubiquitous mainstream beer advertising seen elsewhere. The NBB product appeared only in the final five seconds of film between the tag lines, "Follow Your Folly ... Ours Is Beer." Quick to embrace the latent talents of their own crew, NBB allowed brewery employees to compose a reggae-like score for one of the 15-second spots—a playful little film called *Joust*.

Maintaining a Local Touch

Even as NBB decided to speak to a wider audience through television, the roots-style marketing that launched the company could not be abandoned. It became even more important to speak to the insiders who helped build the brand in the same authentic and personal tone they had come to know and embrace. Rather than redirect energies from event sponsorship to media, events became an even greater opportunity to maintain that vital dialogue. Rather than test the spots on focus groups, NBB turned to insiders in the bike community and friends of the brewery with some personal history and knowledge of the brand. The theory was that television would reach those faraway outposts where Ranger sales staff penetration was difficult and not cost-effective. In mature markets, the personal touch would be redoubled.

The spots first aired in Arizona in January 2005, with a summer campaign to follow throughout the rest of the Western United States. After viewing the NBB spots at a brewing industry conference in March 2005, Miller SAB vice president of marketing, Bob Mikulay, had this to say:

> At its heart, the basic proposition of beer has to be about fun. The small brewers have always done this well ... often with great irreverence, quirkiness or just plain silliness ... but always with a strong, instinctive understanding of the unique personality of their brands. And we need them to keep it coming ... and even step it up a bit. In fact, I was encouraged to see New Belgium actually taking their brand of fun into a television spot.
>
> Now humility will probably prevent Kim [Kim Jordan, CEO of New Belgium] from saying this later ... but I believe that's a truly great piece of advertising. Is there anybody who doesn't now have a very good idea about what Fat Tire is all about? So the specialty and other small brewers are showing every sign that they are ready to fulfill their role in the industry better than ever.

In the end, NBB's first television-based advertising campaign—approached with a great deal of inner reflection—mirrored well the craft brewer's personality. In a sea of loud, flashy beer advertising aimed seemingly at a youthful demographic, NBB positioned itself as whimsical, thoughtful, and reflective. The bicycling imagery shot in Colorado gave a palpable sense of place to the brand among viewers on the coasts and in the plains. The iconic cruiser bike itself harkened the idea of creative play. The act of rescuing the bike from bad technology and neglect can be read as metaphor for NBB's efforts to recycle and reuse materials to the point of 98 percent diversion of their waste stream. The Tinkerer himself pays homage to the bicycle tour that NBB's founder Jeff Lebesch took through Belgium that inspired his home-brewing shift toward Belgian-based beers. Even the texture of the film and the musical tone capture the ideals of whimsy and joy inherent to NBB's philosophy of brewing and quality of life. At a time when marketers were seeking ever-more insidious means to cut through the clutter, NBB chose to redefine a category in a very traditional medium where ads are acceptable and the rare good ones can still be groundbreaking, thoughtful, and effective.

This is the only major television advertising campaign that NBB has launched to date. While the campaign was deemed very successful and sales increases in major markets were attributed to the campaign, the company believed that it had accomplished its advertising objectives. The advertising helped reinforce the brand manifesto developed by Greg Owsley and Doug Holt. The fun, folly, and whimsical image of the NBB brand was strengthened through the advertisements. Unlike its much larger domestic brand competitors, NBB did not continue television advertising but believed that its brand image and culture were well suited for social media.

New Media and Consistent Messaging

Over the years, New Belgium has used a variety of media to promote its products and establish brand recognition. Although the medium may change, New Belgium's principles and brand image have remained the same. To reach audiences more efficiently and effectively, NBB has launched a series of web and print campaigns to promote NBB's sustainability practices. NBB's interactive website (www.newbelgium.com) provides visitors with an in-depth understanding of the company's activities, goals, and values. When users first log on to the site, they are asked to provide their birthday to make sure they are 21 or older. Once on the site, visitors can choose from the topics of Beers, Events, Community, and Culture. The Community tab connects users to New Belgium's blog, whereas the Culture tab displays NBB's philosophy and provides access to its goals and progress in sustainability. A recent edition to the Beer section is an interactive flavor wheel. Visitors can click on one of the beers on the "wheel" and get information on its flavor, ingredients, and food that can be paired with that particular beer. The website also contains a Video section containing videos of NBB events, news clips, and testimonials from New Belgium employees about their "joy ride" with the company. These sections serve not only to help consumers understand the company but also to create relationships between consumers and the brand.

Today, New Belgium uses new forms of media to promote its brand while still maintaining its overall branding philosophy. Although the company has not ruled out new television advertisements, NBB has focused on other forms of "new media" such as social networking sites and digital videos to attract new consumers to the brand. Traditional media often supplements these digital marketing initiatives. When NBB released its Ranger IPA ale, the company placed advertisements in *Wired* and *Rolling Stone*. It also created a digital marketing campaign incorporating its own microsite and Facebook to encourage the information to go viral. The microsite featured a video of the NBB sales force dressed in tan-and-olive ranger uniforms performing a hip-hop number to promote the product, with the tagline "To Protect. To Pour. To Partake." Rather than riding horses, however, these rangers rode bicycles to link the campaign to the brand. The microsite also included a "Ranger Yourself?" function that allowed users to paste a photo of their face to the body of a ranger and post the picture to their Facebook walls. According to NBB director of public relations Bryan Simpson, the intent was to create a hip identity for the product and brand as a whole. Digital videos have been an important part of NBB's marketing strategy to reach consumers from various parts of the nation. Many of its videos can be viewed on the company's YouTube channel (www.youtube.com/user/nbbfilms).

NBB also uses a range of other digital networking tools to promote its products. For instance, the firm has abandoned its newsletter in exchange for a blog, to which viewers can subscribe and receive news articles and feeds. NBB is jumping on the mobile marketing bandwagon by releasing mobile apps available for both Apple and Android devices. The apps allow users to post photos of their beers and friends in a photo gallery, link to Facebook and Twitter, locate their favorite beers, and alert friends to when its time to "clock out" and have a beer. NBB also posts photos in the mobile photo-sharing site Instagram. Additionally, NBB has been very active on its Twitter account. Called "beer tweets," consumers can post their comments and thoughts about New Belgium on Twitter. The Twitter team responds to NBB's more than 85,000 followers in what web developer, Kurt Herrman, calls "a two-way street" of communication.

New Belgium is widely popular on Facebook as well. Although it is the third largest craft brewer, NBB has more fans (over 300,000) than both Boston Brewing Company's Sam Adams and Sierra Nevada. Facebook has been such an important digital marketing tool for NBB that the firm decided to monetize just how much its Facebook fans are worth to the company—and was pleasantly surprised at the results. After conducting a study, NBB found that its Facebook fans contribute $50.7 million in sales annually—about half of the company's annual sales. NBB has become experts at using digital media tools effectively to both attract and understand its customer base.

Although New Belgium may vary the types of media it utilizes, the company's goals to be a truly sustainable brand have remained the same. Its message is, and always has been, that consumers can be environmentally conscious and still have fun. Some people scoff at the idea that a company that sells alcohol can be a socially responsible brand, but with each new social and environmental initiative, New Belgium seeks to prove its critics wrong.

Sustainable Branding Principles

NBB has always remained committed to its initial mission of being a fun, socially and environmentally responsible company. For instance, to learn more about the consumption habits and desires of its consumers, NBB developed and distributed a survey to 612 beer drinkers. The results indicate that 39 percent of beer consumers will make extra efforts to buy from and support sustainable companies. Larger studies outside NBB suggest that as many as 60 million consumers frequently support businesses that broadcast their sustainable practices.

Studies also reveal that environmentally conscious consumers are on the lookout for deceptive business practices, such as greenwashing and spin doctoring, or as former NBB Marketing Director Greg Owsley put it, "casual dating between core values and brand [that] leaves both short of their optimal potential." Because NBB has focused on sustainable business practices since the company's inception, the authenticity of NBB's environmentally conscious actions and messaging is solid. However, the challenge for NBB, and for other sustainable companies as well, is to convince the public of the genuineness of these claims, particularly because the public is often inundated with deceptive claims from businesses that want to appear "green." To help businesses take a genuine approach to sustainability and communicate this approach to the public, NBB has adopted five principles that it calls its Sustainable Branding Strategy:

- **Walk before talk.** This principle is perhaps the most apparent, but certainly no less challenging, as it requires the business to live up to its sustainable claims. The business must practice sustainability before promoting its environmentally friendly practices.
- **Admit the flaws.** Even NBB admits that its sustainable business practices are far from perfect. Instead of covering up flaws in their sustainability plans, businesses should

own up to them. Intelligent green consumers are likely to investigate a company's green claims, and they will undoubtedly find areas that need improving. Preparing responses about how to address these flaws will convince consumers that the company recognizes the problems in their plan and will take a proactive stance to address them.

- **Provide the smile.** Green businesses should be optimistic, seeking to make their customers feel good about making a positive difference by being green rather than causing them to feel pessimistic and guilty about their actions.

- **Go slow to go fast.** Be empathetic to the customer by not bogging them down with all the company's core values at once. The purpose is communication: Make sure the customer clearly understands these values, which requires the company to go slow rather than throwing everything at the consumer.

- **Make ripples.** Starting out as a small company, NBB could not immediately expect its marketing efforts to take hold all at once. Companies must have a clear purpose and show commitment to the cause. Cause-based marketing is particularly useful because it convinces the company's public that its advertisements are not just to promote its brand, but to create a positive difference as well. Of course, the public must be able to trust that a company's cause-based marketing is sincere, which requires the previous steps to convince consumers of the company's sustainable authenticity.

New Belgium has strived to live out these principles, even when it means admitting mistakes. For instance, in 2005 an ex-employee accused NBB of greenwashing, or exaggerating its green marketing claims. He alleged that NBB's claims of being "100 percent wind-powered" was misleading because the company still uses electricity and gas in its operations while purchasing energy-saving credits. While NBB initially dismissed the employee's claims, it later admitted that it was in the wrong and modified its "100 percent wind-powered" statements. The company also began releasing sustainability reports, which are available on its website, to allow consumers to see both the company's progress in sustainability and where the company still needs improvement. In so doing, New Belgium has followed its first two principles, *admit the flaws* and *walk the talk*, while increasing transparency in its operations.

Kim Jordon and NBB employees are quick to point out that New Belgium Brewing has been a long but joyful ride. The company has made much progress since it first began as a small basement brewery. "For me brand is absolutely everything we are. It's the people here. It's how we interact with one another. And then there's the other piece of that creativity, obviously, which is designing beers," Kim Jordan said. The company consists of highly creative and innovative people to expand New Belgium's sphere of influence as a role model. Although Greg Owsley has since left the company, talented individuals such as Jenn Vervier, the Director of Strategic Development and Sustainability at New Belgium, are taking a leadership role in moving the company forward. New Belgium desires to spread its values of sustainability, quality, and folly among its stakeholders.

Although New Belgium is a much larger company than it was when it started more than two decades ago, its mission and core values have remained the same. As the company plans to create a second brewery in Asheville, NC, the challenges of remaining authentic, true to the company culture, and customer focused will remain. Even as the company will continue to grow, product offerings will continue to diversify, and marketing strategies will consistently evolve, New Belgium remains an example of a company that continues to have a strong, stable brand image—one that consumers continue to trust.

Questions for Discussion

1. New Belgium has effectively used integrated marketing communications over the last 20 years. Evaluate the use of one major advertising campaign to fortify and enhance the company's brand image.

2. NBB seemed to agonize over the use of the word "folly" in its advertising campaign. What do you make of the company's struggle with this decision? Also, how do you personally feel about their use of the word?

3. New Belgium's focus on sustainability, whimsy, and fun is clearly rooted in its Colorado-based culture and the ethos of its founders and employees. As New Belgium's distribution continues to expand away from that locale, how can the company make its branding and messaging resonate with consumers in different parts of the country?

4. Currently, New Belgium has been much more successful using social media than competitors Boston Brewing Co. and Sierra Nevada. Evaluate how social media has contributed to the firm's marketing strategy, and make suggestions for the use of social media in the future.

Sources

The facts of this case are from Cotton Delo, "New Belgium Toasts to Its Facebook Fans," *Advertising Age*, February 13, 2012 (http://adage.com/article/news/belgium-toasts-facebook-fans/232681); Janet Forgrieve from *Rocky Mountain News*, "Sales of Craft Beer Make Biggest Jump in Decade," HighBeam Research, August 23, 2006 (http://www.highbeam.com/doc/1G1-149883191.html); Jeremy Mullman, "Craft Beer Steps into Wine Country," *Advertising Age*, June 19, 2006 (http://adage.com/article/news/craft-beer-steps-wine-country/109958); New Belgium Brewing Company website (http://www.newbelgium.com), accessed July 17, 2012; New Belgium Brewing Facebook Page (https://www.facebook.com/newbelgium), accessed July 17, 2012; "New Belgium Brewing Launches Follow Your Folly Campaign Integrating Web And Print," *PRWeb*, February 20, 2007 (http://www.prweb.com/releases/2007/02/prweb506247.htm); "New Belgium Brewing Selects Backbone to Handle Media," New Belgium Brewing Social Media Release, September 10, 2008 (http://www.pitchengine.com/newbelgiumbrewing/new-belgium-brewing-selects-backbone-to-handle-media); New Belgium Brewing Twitter Site (https://twitter.com/newbelgium), accessed July 17, 2012; "New Belgium New Expansion," Probrewer.com, May 30, 2006 (http://www.probrewer.com/news/news-002935.php); Ciara O'Rourke, "Brewer Learns Lesson About Green Marketing," *New York Times*, February 3, 2009 (http://green.blogs.nytimes.com/2009/02/03/brewer-learns-lesson-about-green-marketing); Greg Owsley, "Sustainable Branding: Five Steps to Gaining the Approval of the Environmentally-Conscious Consumer," *Advertising Age*, June 25, 2007 (http://adage.com/article/cmo-strategy/brand-veneer-reflect-a-real-soul/118654); and Greg Owsley, "The Necessity for Aligning Brand with Corporate Ethics," in Sheb True, Linda Ferrell, and O.C. Ferrell, eds., *Fulfilling Our Obligation* (Kennesaw, GA: Kennesaw State University Press, 2005).

CASE **6**

Mattel Confronts Its Marketing Challenges*

Synopsis: As a global leader in toy manufacturing and marketing, Mattel faces a number of potential threats to its ongoing operations. Like most firms that market products for children, Mattel is ever mindful of its social and ethical obligations and the target on its corporate back. This case summarizes many of the challenges that Mattel has faced over the past decade, including tough competition, changing consumer preferences and lifestyles, lawsuits, product liability issues, global sourcing, and declining sales. Mattel's social responsibility imperative is discussed along with the company's reactions to its challenges and its prospects for the future.

Themes: Environmental threats, competition, social responsibility, marketing ethics, product/branding strategy, intellectual property, global marketing, product liability, global manufacturing/sourcing, marketing control

I
t all started in a California garage workshop when Ruth and Elliot Handler and Matt Matson founded Mattel in 1945. The company started out making picture frames, but the founders soon recognized the profitability of the toy industry and switched their emphasis to toys. Mattel became a publicly owned company in 1960, with sales exceeding $100 million by 1965. Over the next forty years, Mattel went on to become the world's largest toy company in terms of revenue. Today, Mattel, Inc. is a global leader in designing and manufacturing toys and family products. Well-known for brands such as Barbie, Fisher-Price, Disney, Hot Wheels, Matchbox, Tyco, Cabbage Patch Kids, and board games, the company boasts nearly $5.9 billion in annual revenue. Headquartered in El Segundo, California, with offices across the world, Mattel markets its products in over 150 nations.

In spite of its overall success, Mattel has had its share of losses over its history. During the mid to late 1990s, Mattel lost millions to declining sales and bad business acquisitions. In January 1997, Jill Barad took over as Mattel's CEO. Barad's management-style was characterized as strict and her tenure at the helm proved challenging for many employees. While Barad had been successful in building the Barbie brand to $2 billion by the end of the 20th century, growth slowed in the early 2000s. Declining sales at outlets such as Toys "R" Us marked the start of some difficulties for the retailer, responsibilities for which Barad accepted and resigned in 2000.

Robert Eckert replaced Barad as CEO. Aiming to turn things around, Eckert sold unprofitable units and cut hundreds of jobs. In 2000, under Eckert, Mattel was granted

---

*Debbie Thorne, Texas State University, John Fraedrich, Southern Illinois University-Carbondale, O.C. Ferrell, University of New Mexico, and Jennifer Jackson, University of New Mexico, prepared this case with the editorial assistance of Jennifer Sawayda. This case is meant for classroom discussion and is not meant to illustrate either effective or ineffective handling of an administrative situation.

371

the highly sought-after licensing agreement for products related to the *Harry Potter* series of books and movies. The company continued to flourish and build its reputation, even earning the Corporate Responsibility Award from UNICEF in 2003. Mattel released its first Annual Corporate Responsibility Report the following year. In 2011, Mattel was recognized as one of *Fortune* magazine's "100 Best Companies to Work For" for the fourth consecutive year.

Mattel's Core Products

Barbie

Among its many lines of popular toy products, Mattel is famous for owning top girls' brands. In 1959, Mattel introduced a product that would change its future forever: the Barbie doll. After seeing her daughter's fascination with cutout paper dolls, Ruth suggested that a three-dimensional doll should be produced so that young girls could live out their dreams and fantasies. This doll was named "Barbie," the nickname of Ruth and Elliot Handler's daughter. The first Barbie doll sported open-toed shoes, a ponytail, sunglasses, earrings, and a zebra-striped bathing suit. Fashions and accessories were also available for the doll. Although buyers at the annual Toy Fair in New York took no interest in the Barbie doll, little girls of the time certainly did. The intense demand seen at the retail stores was insufficiently met for several years. Mattel just could not produce the Barbie dolls fast enough. Today, Barbie is Mattel's flagship brand and its number one seller—routinely accounting for approximately half of Mattel's profits. This makes Barbie the best-selling fashion doll in most global markets. The Barbie line today includes dolls, accessories, Barbie software, and a broad assortment of licensed products such as books, apparel, food, home furnishings, home electronics, and movies.

Although Barbie remains a blockbuster by any standard, Barbie's popularity has slipped over the past twenty years. There are two major reasons for Barbie's slump. First, the changing lifestyles of today's young girls are a concern for Mattel. Many young girls prefer to spend time with music, movies, or the Internet than play with traditional toys like dolls. Second, Barbie has suffered at the hands of new and innovative competition, including the Bratz doll line that gained significant market share during the early 2000s. The dolls, which featured contemporary, ethnic designs and skimpy clothes, were a stark contrast to Barbie and an immediate hit with young girls. By 2005, four years after the brand's debut, Bratz sales were at $2 billion. By 2009, Barbie's worldwide sales had fallen by 15 percent. In an attempt to recover, Mattel introduced the new line of My Scene dolls aimed at "tweens." These dolls are trendier, look younger, and are considered to be more hip for this age group who is on the cusp of outgrowing playing with dolls. A website (www.myscene.com) engages girls in a variety of fun, engaging, and promotional activities.

American Girl

In 1998, to supplement the Barbie line, Mattel acquired Pleasant Company and its American Girl collection for $700 million. Originally, American Girl products were sold exclusively through catalogs. Mattel extended that base by opening American Girl Place shops in major metropolitan areas including New York, Chicago, Los Angeles, Atlanta, Dallas, Boston, Denver, Miami, and Minneapolis. The New York store features three floors of dolls, accessories, and books in the heart of the 5th Avenue shopping district. The store also offers a café where girls can dine with their dolls and a stage production where young actors bring American Girl stories to life. The American Girls brand includes several book series, accessories, clothing for dolls and girls, and a magazine that ranks in the top 10 American children's magazines.

The American Girl collection is wildly popular with girls in the 7- to 12-year-old demographic. The dolls have a wholesome and educational image that offsets Barbie's image. This move by Mattel represented a long-term strategy to reduce reliance on traditional products and to take away the stigma surrounding the "perfect image" of Barbie. Each American Girl doll lives during a specific time in American history, and all have stories that describe the hardships they face while maturing into young adults. For example, Felicity's stories describe life in 1774 just prior to the Revolutionary War. Likewise, Josephina lives in New Mexico in 1824 during the rapid growth of the American West.

Hot Wheels

Hot Wheels roared into the toy world in 1968. More than thirty years later, the brand is hotter than ever and includes high-end collectibles, NASCAR (National Association for Stock Car Auto Racing) and Formula One models for adults, high-performance cars, track sets, and play sets for children of all ages. The brand is connected with racing circuits worldwide. More than 15 million boys aged 5 to 15 are avid collectors, each owning forty-one cars on average. Two Hot Wheels cars are sold every second of every day. The brand began with cars designed to run on a track and has evolved into a "lifestyle" brand with licensed Hot Wheels shirts, caps, lunch boxes, backpacks, and more. Together, Hot Wheels and Barbie generate 45 percent of Mattel's revenue and 65 percent of its profits.

Fisher-Price

Acquired in 1993 as a wholly owned subsidiary, Fisher-Price is the umbrella brand for all of Mattel's infant and preschool lines. The brand is trusted by parents around the world and appears on everything from children's software to eyewear, and books to bicycles. Some of the more classic products include the Rock-a-Stack, Power Wheels vehicles, and Little People play sets. Through licensing agreements, the brand also develops character-based toys such as *Sesame Street*'s Elmo, Disney's Winnie the Pooh, and Nickelodeon's Dora the Explorer.

Fisher-Price has built a trust with parents by creating products that are educational, safe, and useful. For example, during recent years, the brand has earned high regard for innovative car seats and nursery monitors. Fisher-Price keeps pace with the interests of today's families through innovative learning toys and award-winning products. One example is the Computer Cool School, a kid-friendly keyboard with a tablet and stylus, which turns a standard Windows-based computer into an interactive classroom for kids ages 3 to 6. The product was awarded the "Best Toy of 2008" by both *Parents Magazine* and *Family Fun Magazine*.

Cabbage Patch Kids

Since the introduction of mass-produced Cabbage Patch Kids in 1982, more than 90 million dolls have been sold worldwide. In 1994, Mattel took over selling these beloved dolls after purchasing production rights from Hasbro. In 1996, Mattel created a new line of Cabbage Patch doll, called Snacktime Kids, which was expected to meet with immense success. The Snacktime Kids had moving mouths that enabled children to "feed" them plastic snacks. However, the product backfired. The toy had no on/off switch and reports of children getting their fingers or hair caught in the dolls' mouths surfaced during the 1996 holiday season. Mattel voluntarily pulled the dolls from store shelves by January 1997, and offered consumers a cash refund of $40 on returned dolls. The U.S. Consumer Product Safety Commission applauded Mattel's handling of the Snacktime

Kids situation. Mattel effectively managed a situation that could easily have created bad publicity or a crisis situation. In 2001, Toys "R" Us took over the Cabbage Patch brand from Mattel.

Mattel's Commitment to Ethics and Social Responsibility

Mattel's core products and business environment create many challenging issues. Because the company's products are designed primarily for children, it must be sensitive to social concerns about children's rights. It must also be aware that the international environment often complicates business transactions. Different legal systems and cultural expectations about business can create ethical conflicts. Finally, the use of technology may present ethical dilemmas, especially regarding consumer privacy. Mattel has recognized these potential issues and taken steps to strengthen its commitment to business ethics. The company also purports to take a stand on social responsibility, encouraging its employees and consumers to do the same.

Privacy and Marketing Technology

One issue Mattel has tried to address repeatedly is that of privacy and online technology. Advances in technology have created special marketing issues for Mattel. The company recognizes that, because it markets to children, it must communicate with parents regarding its corporate marketing strategy. Mattel has taken steps to inform both children and adults about its philosophy regarding Internet-based marketing tools, such as the Hot Wheels website. This website contains a lengthy online privacy policy, part of which is excerpted below:

> Mattel, Inc. and its family of companies ("Mattel") are committed to protecting your online privacy when visiting a website operated by us. We do not collect and keep any personal information online from you unless you volunteer it and you are 13 or older. We also do not collect and keep personal information online from children under the age of 13 without consent of a parent or legal guardian, except in limited circumstances authorized by law and described in this policy.....[1]

By assuring parents that their children's privacy will be respected, Mattel demonstrates that it takes its responsibility of marketing to children seriously.

Expectations of Mattel's Business Partners

Mattel, Inc. also makes a serious commitment to business ethics in its dealings with other industries. In late 1997, the company completed its first full ethics audit of each of its manufacturing sites as well as the facilities of its primary contractors. The audit revealed that the company was not using any child labor or forced labor, a problem plaguing other overseas manufacturers. However, several contractors were found to be in violation of Mattel's safety and human rights standards and were asked to change their operations or risk losing Mattel's business. The company now conducts an independent monitoring council audit in manufacturing facilities every three years.

In an effort to continue its strong record on human rights and related ethical standards, Mattel instituted a code of conduct entitled Global Manufacturing Principles in 1997. One of these principles requires all Mattel-owned and contracted manufacturing facilities to favor business partners committed to ethical standards comparable with

[1]Mattel, Inc., Online Privacy Policy (http://corporate.mattel.com/privacy-policy.aspx), accessed July 17, 2012.

those of Mattel. Other principles relate to safety, wages, and adherence to local laws. Mattel's audits and subsequent code of conduct were designed as preventative, not punitive measures. The company is dedicated to creating and encouraging responsible business practices throughout the world.

Mattel also claims to be committed to its workforce. As one company consultant noted, "Mattel is committed to improving the skill level of workers… [so that they] will experience increased opportunities and productivity." This statement reflects Mattel's concern for relationships between and with employees and business partners. The company's code is a signal to potential partners, customers, and other stakeholders that Mattel has made a commitment to fostering and upholding ethical values.

Legal and Ethical Business Practices

Mattel prefers to partner with businesses similarly committed to high ethical standards. At a minimum, partners must comply with the local and national laws of the countries in which they operate. In addition, all partners must respect the intellectual property of the company, and support Mattel in the protection of assets such as patents, trademarks, or copyrights. They are also responsible for product safety and quality, protecting the environment, customs, evaluation and monitoring, and compliance.

Mattel's business partners must have high standards for product safety and quality, adhering to practices that meet Mattel's safety and quality standards. Also, because of the global nature of Mattel's business and its history of leadership in this area, the company insists that business partners strictly adhere to local and international customs laws. Partners must also comply with all import and export regulations. To assist in compliance with standards, Mattel insists that all manufacturing facilities provide the following:

- Full access for on-site inspections by Mattel or parties designated by Mattel
- Full access to those records that will enable Mattel to determine compliance with its principles
- An annual statement of compliance with Mattel's Global Manufacturing Principles, signed by an officer of the manufacturer or manufacturing facility

With the creation of the Mattel Independent Monitoring Council (MIMCO), Mattel became the first global consumer products company to apply such a system to facilities and core contractors worldwide. The company seeks to maintain an independent monitoring system that provides checks and balances to help ensure that standards are met.

If certain aspects of Mattel's manufacturing Principles are not being met, Mattel will try to work with them to help them fix their problems. New partners will not be hired unless they meet Mattel's standards. If corrective action is advised but not taken, Mattel will terminate its relationship with the partner in question. Overall, Mattel is committed to both business success and ethical standards, and it recognizes that it is part of a continuous improvement process.

Mattel Children's Foundation

Mattel takes its social responsibilities very seriously. Through the Mattel Children's Foundation, established in 1978, the company promotes philanthropy and community involvement among its employees and makes charitable investments to better the lives of children in need. Funding priorities have included building a new Mattel Children's Hospital at the University of California, Los Angeles (UCLA), sustaining the Mattel Family Learning Program, and promoting giving among Mattel employees. In November 1998, Mattel donated a multiyear, $25 million gift to the UCLA Children's Hospital. The gift was meant to support the existing hospital and provide for a new state-of-the-art facility. In honor of Mattel's donation, the hospital was renamed Mattel Children's Hospital at UCLA.

The Mattel Family Learning Program utilizes computerized learning labs as a way to advance children's basic skills. Now numbering more than eighty throughout the United States, Hong Kong, Canada, and Mexico, the labs offer software and technology designed to help children with special needs or limited English proficiency.

Mattel employees are also encouraged to participate in a wide range of volunteer activities as part of "Mattel Volunteers: Happy to Help." Employees serving on boards of local nonprofit organizations or helping with ongoing nonprofit programs are eligible to apply for volunteer grants supporting their organizations. Mattel employees contributing to higher education or to nonprofit organizations serving children in need are eligible to have their personal donations matched dollar for dollar up to $5,000 annually.

Global Manufacturing Principles

As a U.S.-based multinational company owning and operating facilities and contracting worldwide, Mattel's Global Manufacturing Principles reflect not only its need to conduct manufacturing responsibly, but to respect the cultural, ethical, and philosophical differences of the countries in which it operates. These Principles set uniform standards across Mattel manufacturers and attempt to benefit both employees and consumers.

Mattel's principles cover issues such as wages, work hours, child labor, forced labor, discrimination, freedom of association, and working conditions. Workers must be paid at least minimum wage or a wage that meets local industry standards (whichever is greater). No one under the age of 16 or the local age limit (whichever is higher) may be allowed to work for Mattel facilities. Mattel refuses to work with facilities that use forced or prison labor, or to use these types of labor itself. Additionally, Mattel does not tolerate discrimination. The company states that an individual should be hired and employed based on his or her ability—not on individual characteristics or beliefs. Mattel recognizes all employees' rights to choose to associate with organizations or associations without interference. Regarding working conditions, all Mattel facilities and its business partners must provide safe working environments for their employees.

Mattel Faces Product Recalls

Despite Mattel's best efforts, not all overseas manufacturers have faithfully adhered to its high standards. Mattel has come under scrutiny over its sale of unsafe products. In September 2007, Mattel announced recalls of toys containing lead paint. The problem surfaced when a European retailer discovered lead paint on a toy. An estimated 10 million individual toys produced in China were affected. Mattel quickly stopped production at Lee Der, the company officially producing the recalled toys, after it was discovered that Lee Der had purchased lead-tainted paint to be used on the toys. Mattel blamed the fiasco on the manufacturers' desire to save money in the face of increasing prices. "In the last three or five years, you've seen labor prices more than double, raw material prices double or triple," CEO Eckert said in an interview, "and I think that there's a lot of pressure on guys that are working at the margin to try to save money."

The situation began when Early Light Industrial Co., a subcontractor for Mattel owned by Hong Kong toy tycoon Choi Chee Ming, subcontracted the painting of parts of *Cars* toys to another China-based vendor. The vendor, named Hong Li Da, decided to source paint from a non-authorized third-party supplier—a violation of Mattel's requirement to use paint supplied directly by Early Light. The products were found to contain "impermissible levels of lead." On August 2, 2007, it was announced that another of

Early Light's subcontractors, Lee Der Industrial Co., used the same lead paint found on *Cars* products. China immediately suspended the company's export license. Afterward, Mattel pinpointed three paint suppliers working for Lee Der—Dongxin, Zhongxin, and Mingdai. This paint was used by Lee Der to produce Mattel's line of Fisher-Price products. It is said that Lee Der purchased the paint from Mingdai due to an intimate friendship between the two company's owners. On August 11, 2007, Zhang Shuhong, operator of Lee Der, hung himself after paying his 5,000 staff members.

Later that month, Mattel was forced to recall several more toys because of powerful magnets in the toys that could come loose and pose a choking hazard for young children. If more than one magnet is swallowed, the magnets can attract each other inside the child's stomach, causing potentially fatal complications. Over 21 million Mattel toys were recalled in all, and parents filed several lawsuits claiming that these Mattel products harmed their children.

Mattel's Response

At first, Mattel blamed Chinese subcontractors for the huge toy recalls, but the company later accepted a portion of the blame for its troubles, while maintaining that Chinese manufacturers were largely at fault. The Chinese view the situation quite differently. As reported by the state-run Xinhua news agency, the spokesman for China's General Administration of Quality Supervision and Inspection and Quarantine said, "Mattel should improve its product design and supervision over product quality. Chinese original equipment manufacturers were doing the job just as importers requested, and the toys conformed to the U.S. regulations and standards at the time of the production." Mattel also faced criticism from many of its consumers, who believed Mattel was denying culpability by placing much of the blame on China. Mattel was later awarded the 2007 "Bad Product" Award by Consumers International.

Many critics asked how this crisis occurred under the watch of a company praised for its ethics and high safety standards. Although Mattel had investigated its contractors, it did not audit the entire supply chain, including subcontractors. These oversights left room for these violations to occur. Mattel has also moved to enforce a rule that subcontractors cannot hire suppliers two or three tiers down. In a statement, Mattel says it has spent more than 50,000 hours investigating its vendors and testing its toys. Mattel also announced a three-point plan. This plan aims to tighten Mattel's control of production, discover and prevent the unauthorized use of subcontractors, and test the products itself rather than depending on contractors.

The Chinese Government's Response

Chinese officials eventually did admit the government's failure to properly protect the public. The Chinese government promised to tighten supervision of exported products, but effective supervision is challenging in such a large country that is so burdened with corruption. In January 2008, the Chinese government launched a four-month-long nationwide product quality campaign, offering intensive training courses to domestic toy manufacturers to help them brush up on their knowledge of international product standards and safety awareness. As a result of the crackdown, the State Administration for Quality Supervision and Inspection and Quarantine (AQSIQ) announced that it had revoked the licenses of more than 600 Chinese toy makers. As of 2008, the State Administration for Commerce and Industry (SACI) released a report claiming that 87.5 percent of China's newly manufactured toys met quality requirements. While this represents an improvement, the temptation to cut corners remains strong in a country that uses price, not quality, as its main competitive advantage. Where there is demand, there will be people trying to turn a quick profit.

Mattel's Intellectual Property Fight with Bratz

In 2004, Mattel became embroiled in a bitter intellectual property rights battle with former employee Carter Bryant and MGA Entertainment Inc. over rights to MGA's popular Bratz dolls. Carter Bryant, an on-again/off-again Mattel employee, designed the Bratz dolls and pitched them to MGA. A few months after the pitch, Bryant left Mattel to work at MGA, which began producing Bratz in 2001. In 2002, Mattel launched an investigation into whether Bryant had designed the Bratz dolls while employed with Mattel. After two years of investigation, Mattel sued Bryant. A year later MGA fired off a suit of its own, claiming that Mattel was creating Barbie dolls with looks similar to those of Bratz in an effort to eliminate the competition. Mattel answered by expanding its own suit to include MGA and its CEO, Isaac Larian.

Four years after the initial suit was filed, Bryant settled with Mattel under an undisclosed set of terms. In July 2008, a jury deemed MGA and its CEO liable for what it termed "intentional interference" regarding Bryant's contract with Mattel. In August 2008, Mattel received damages in the range of $100 million. Although Mattel first requested damages of $1.8 billion, the company is pleased with the principle behind the victory.

In December 2008, Mattel appeared to win another victory when a California judge banned MGA from issuing or selling any more Bratz dolls. However, the tide soon turned on Mattel's victory. In July 2010, the Ninth U.S. Circuit Court of Appeals threw out the ruling. Eventually, the case came down to whether Mattel owned Bryant's ideas under the contract he had with the company. In April 2011, a California federal jury rejected Mattel's claims to ownership. In another blow to Mattel, the jury also ruled that the company had stolen trade secrets from MGA. According to the allegations, Mattel employees used fake business cards to get into MGA showrooms during toy fairs. Mattel was ordered to pay $85 million in liabilities, plus an additional $225 million in damages and legal fees. MGA CEO Isaac Larian has also announced that he will file an antitrust case against Mattel. Mattel continues to claim that Bryant violated his contract when he was working for the company.

Mattel Looks Toward the Future

Like all major companies, Mattel has weathered its share of storms. The company has faced a series of difficult and potentially crippling challenges, including the recent verdict against the company in the Bratz lawsuit. During the wave of toy recalls, some analysts suggested that the company's reputation was battered beyond repair. Mattel, however, has refused to go quietly. Although the company admits to poorly handling recent affairs, it is attempting to rectify its mistakes and to prevent future mistakes as well. The company appears to be dedicated to shoring up its ethical defenses to protect both itself and its customers. Mattel's experiences should teach all companies that threats could materialize within the marketing environment in spite of the best-laid plans to prevent such issues from occurring.

With the economic future of the United States uncertain, Mattel may be in for slow growth for some time to come. Today, Mattel faces many market opportunities and threats including the rate at which children are growing up and leaving toys, the role of technology in consumer products, and purchasing power and consumer needs in global markets. The continuing lifestyle shift of American youth is of particular concern for Mattel. The phenomenal success of gaming systems, portable media devices, smartphones, and social networking sites among today's youth is a testament to this shift. Children and teens are also more active in extracurricular activities (i.e., sports, music, and volunteerism) than ever before. Consequently, these young consumers have less time to spend with traditional toys.

Despite these concerns, Mattel has a lot to offer both children and investors. Barbie remains the number one doll in the United States and worldwide. And Barbie.com, the number one website for girls, routinely gets over 50 million visits per month. Furthermore, all of Mattel's core brands are instantly recognizable around the world. Hence, the ability to leverage one or all of these brands is high. A few remaining issues include Mattel's reliance on major retailers, such as Walmart, Target, Toys "R" Us, and Amazon (which lessens Mattel's pricing power), volatile oil prices (oil is used to make plastics), and increasing competition on a global scale. However, analysts believe Mattel has a great growth potential with technology-based toys, especially in international markets, in spite of changing demographic and socioeconomic trends.

For a company that began with two friends making picture frames, Mattel has demonstrated marketing dexterity and longevity. The next few years, however, will test the firm's resolve. Mattel is hard at work restoring goodwill and faith in its brands, even as it continues to be plagued with residual distrust over the lead paint scandal and its alleged theft of trade secrets. Reputations are hard won and easily lost, but Mattel appears to be steadfast in its commitment to restoring its reputation.

Questions for Discussion

1. Do manufacturers of products for children have special obligations to consumers and society? If so, what are these responsibilities?
2. How effective has Mattel been at encouraging ethical and legal conduct by its manufacturers? What changes and additions would you make to the company's global manufacturing principles?
3. To what extent is Mattel responsible for issues related to its production of toys in China? How might Mattel have avoided these issues?

Sources

American Girl website (http://www.americangirl.com), accessed July 18, 2012; Lisa Bannon and Carita Vitzthum, "One-Toy-Fits-All: How Industry Learned to Love the Global Kid," *Wall Street Journal*, April 30, 2003 (http://online.wsj.com/article/SB105156578439799000.html); David Barboza and Louise Story, "Toymaking in China, Mattel's Way," *New York Times*, July 26, 2007 (http://www.nytimes.com/2007/07/26/business/26toy.html?pagewanted=all); David Barboza, "Scandal and Suicide in China: A Dark Side of Toys," *New York Times*, August 23, 2007 (http://www.nytimes.com/2007/08/23/business/worldbusiness/23suicide.html?pagewanted=all); "Bratz loses battle of the dolls," *BBC News*, December 5, 2008 (http://news.bbc.co.uk/2/hi/business/7767270.stm); Nicholas Casey, "Mattel Prevails Over MGA in Bratz-Doll Trial," *Wall Street Journal*, July 18, 2008, pp. B18-B19; Nicholas Casey, "Mattel to Get Up to $100 Million in Bratz Case," *Wall Street Journal*, August 27, 2008 (http://online.wsj.com/article/SB121978263398273857.html); Andrea Chang, "Mattel must pay MGA $310 million in Bratz case," *Los Angeles Times*, August 5, 2011 (http://articles.latimes.com/2011/aug/05/business/la-fi-mattel-bratz-20110805); Shu-Ching Jean Chen, "A Blow to Hong Kong's Toy King," *Forbes*, August 15, 2007 (http://www.forbes.com/2007/08/15/mattel-china-choi-face-markets-cx_jc_0815autofacescan01.html); Miranda Hitti, "9 Million Mattel Toys Recalled," *WebMD*, August 14, 2007 (http://children.webmd.com/news/20070814/9_million_mattel_toys_recalled); Hot Wheels website, Mattel, Inc. (http://www.hotwheels.com), accessed July 18, 2012; "Independent Monitoring Council Completes Audits of Mattel Manufacturing Facilities in Indonesia, Malaysia and Thailand," *PR Newswire*, November 15, 2002 (http://www.prnewswire.com/news-releases/independent-monitoring-council-completes-audits-of-mattel-manufacturing-facilities-in-indonesia-malaysia-and-thailand-76850522.html); "International Bad Product Awards 2007," Consumers International (http://www.consumersinternational.org/media/105567/international%20bad%20products%20awards%20-%20press%20briefing.pdf), accessed December 3, 2008; Gina Keating, "MGA 'still accessing' impact of Bratz ruling: CEO," *Reuters*, December 4, 2008 (http://www.reuters.com/article/2008/12/05/us-mattel-larian-idUSTRE4B405820081205); "Mattel and U.S. Consumer Product Safety Commission Announce Voluntary Refund Program for Cabbage Patch Kids & Snacktime Kids Dolls," U.S. Consumer Product Safety Commission,

Office of Information and Public Affairs, Release No. 97-055, May 9, 2005 (http://www.cpsc.gov/cpscpub/prerel/prhtml97/97055.html); Mattel Annual Reports 1998–2011, 2008 (http://investor.shareholder.com/mattel/annuals.cfm), accessed July 18, 2012; "Mattel awarded $100M in doll lawsuit," *USA Today*, August 27, 2008, p. B1; Mattel corporate website (http://corporate.mattel.com), accessed July 18, 2012; "Mattel History," Mattel, Inc. (http://corporate.mattel.com/about-us/history/default.aspx), accessed July 18, 2012; "Mattel, Inc., Launches Global Code of Conduct Intended to Improve Workplace, Workers' Standard of Living," *PR Newswire*, November 20, 1997 (http://www2.prnewswire.com/cgi-bin/stories.pl?ACCT=104&STORY=/www/story/11-20-97/364032&EDATE=); "Mattel, Inc. Online Privacy Policy," Mattel, Inc., June 2008 (http://service.mattel.com/us/privacy.asp), accessed July 18, 2012; "Mattel Recalls Batman™ and One Piece™ Magnetic Action Figure Sets Due to Magnets Coming Loose," U.S. Consumer Product Safety Commission, Office of Information and Public Affairs, August 14, 2007 (http://service.mattel.com/us/recall/J1944CPSC.pdf); "Mattel to Sell Learning Company," *Chief Marketer Network*, October 2, 2000 (http://directmag.com/news/marketing_mattel_sell_learning); Benjamin B. Olshin, "China, Culture, and Product Recalls," *Specialized Research + Reports*, August 20, 2007 (http://www.s2r.biz/s2rpapers/papers-Chinese_Product.pdf); "100 Best Companies to Work For 2011," *CNN Money* (http://money.cnn.com/magazines/fortune/bestcompanies/2011/full_list); Laura Smith-Spark, "Chinese Product Scares Prompt US Fears," *BBC News*, July 10 2007 (http://news.bbc.co.uk/2/hi/americas/6275758.stm); "The United States Has Not Restricted Imports Under the China Safeguard," *United States Government Accountability Office*, September 2005 (http://www.gao.gov/new.items/d051056.pdf), accessed July 18, 2012; "Third toy recall by Mattel in five weeks," *Business Standard*, September 6, 2007 (http://www.business-standard.com/india/storypage.php?autono=297057); Karen Weise and James E. Ellis, "Mattel: Must Pay for Stealing Bratz Secrets," *BusinessWeek*, August 11 2011 (http://mobile.businessweek.com/magazine/briefs-08112011.html); and Ann Zimmerman, "Mattel Loses in Bratz Spat," *Wall Street Journal*, April 22, 2011 (http://online.wsj.com/article/SB10001424052748703983704576276984087591872.html).

Mistine: Direct Selling in the Thai Cosmetics Market*

Synopsis: This case summarizes the growth of Better Way (Thailand) and its highly successful Mistine brand of cosmetics. From its meager beginnings in 1991, Mistine has risen to become the dominant brand in Thailand's direct selling cosmetics market. The brand's value-based positioning (high quality at affordable prices), along with successful target marketing and a tightly integrated marketing program, has kept the company at the top of the market despite strong competition. Mistine's success has allowed Better Way to expand its efforts into other countries, most notably in Asia, Europe, the Middle East, and Africa. Better Way is now looking to further expand its operations, perhaps into Western countries and China.

Themes: Direct selling, global marketing, branding strategy, value, positioning, distribution strategy, integrated marketing communication, marketing implementation

Under the principle "to create a better way of life" for Thai people, Dr. Amornthep Deerojanawong, Thailand's king of direct selling, in partnership with Boonyakiat Chokwatana, founded Better Way (Thailand) in 1988. In 1991, the company launched its Mistine brand and began its rapid ascent as a key player in Thailand's direct selling cosmetics industry. Mistine started with fewer than 10 employees and 100 products at a time when the Thai people were not familiar with the direct selling model for cosmetics. Direct selling is the marketing of products to consumers through face-to-face sales presentations at home or in the workplace. Based on Mistine's success, direct selling now accounts for over 60 percent of the market and is the preferred method of selling and distributing cosmetics in Thailand. Mistine and Better Way quickly became the leader in the Thai direct selling cosmetics market—a position it has held since 1997. The company's distribution warehouses, among the largest in Asia, handle more than 7,000 products under the Mistine umbrella. These warehouses distribute products to approximately 1 million Mistine sales representatives around the globe and more than 1 million customers in Mistine's membership program.

---

*This case has been compiled and developed by Jennifer Sawayda, University of New Mexico, based on information supplied by Ekachai Wangprapa, Nuntiya Ittiwattanakorn, Rawadee Mekwichai, and Supishsha Sajja-manochai (Thammasat University, Thailand) with additional information from a project conducted in MIM XXI, Thammasat University, 2012. The case was developed under the direction of O.C. Ferrell and Linda Ferrell, University of New Mexico, for classroom discussion rather than to illustrate effective or ineffective handling of an administrative situation.

Mistine's Marketing Program

Mistine spends approximately 10 percent of its revenue on marketing and plans to increase its marketing budget as the company continues to grow. Company executives believe that Mistine's double-digit growth will continue over the next few years. Their main concerns are primarily related to political situations in the countries where it does business, to the worldwide volatility of oil prices (oil is a key ingredient in many cosmetics), and to natural disasters, such as flooding and typhoons, that can disrupt the company's operations.

To attain its status as a leading direct seller in the cosmetics industry, Mistine worked to develop a highly efficient and effective marketing program. The company must regularly evaluate each component of its marketing program in order to maintain its competitive positioning against very strong competitors.

Mistine's Product Mix

Cosmetics under the Mistine brand are divided into five categories and target markets: Body Care, Personal Care, Makeup, Fragrance, and Skin Care. An experienced production team develops hundreds of new and unique products each year. At least two to three new products are launched each month. Customers can be sure that they will receive only the highest quality, "value-for-money" products. Manufacturers who are certified by ISO 9001 and 9002 produce all of Mistine's cosmetics. To ensure quality, Mistine and its manufacturers adhere to Good Manufacturing Principles espoused by the U.S. Food and Drug Administration. Every Mistine product is thoroughly inspected and tested before being delivered to the warehouse. In addition, every Mistine product comes with a satisfaction guarantee that if for any reason a customer is unsatisfied with his or her purchase, Mistine will replace the product or offer a full refund without condition.

To combat its key competitors, Mistine positions itself as an Asian company that produces products that are developed and formulated especially for Asian woman. Mistine products are created to blend well with Asian complexions and skin tones. They are also made to better suit the warmer and more humid climate of the Asian region, so that the product stays on longer and looks fresher throughout the day.

Mistine's products are popular among Thai housewives, factory workers, teenagers, and consumers with a monthly household income of $200 or less. Yet as Mistine has gained prominence, it has also begun to reach out to higher-income professionals with new product offerings. In 2010, Mistine introduced Blemish Balm (BB) cosmetics through a partnership with Korean firm *Klomar Korea Co., Ltd.* Since its introduction, the BB line has become one of Mistine's most popular cosmetic lines. The cosmetics industry in Thailand has exhibited a growing trend toward Korean cosmetics, particularly among teenagers. Thai men and women view Korean actresses and movie stars as being among the most beautiful women in Asia, and teenagers and younger people view Korean models and actresses as the ultimate in Asian beauty. Mistine is therefore collaborating with Korean firms to develop more Korean-type cosmetics for the Thai market.

Mistine's parent company Better Way has also introduced an entirely new line of products under its own name, Faris by Naris. Faris by Naris products are imported from Japan, another country highly admired for its quality cosmetics. Unlike the Mistine brand, Faris by Naris products are sold using a premium pricing strategy. This shift toward more prestigious products implies that Mistine is looking to expand its target market to women in the middle to upper classes.

Mistine's Pricing Strategy

Mistine's core market, which accounts for 70 to 80 percent of sales, includes housewives with a high school diploma, an occupational certificate level or high occupational certificate level of education, and a monthly household income of about $125 to $200 (U.S.). The company also targets professional women who earn $200 to $300 (U.S.) per month. While Mistine has traditionally priced its cosmetics to focus more upon the middle- to lower-income market, the company is expanding its emphasis to women making above average incomes at more than $480 (U.S.) per month. Mistine hopes to increase its number of sales to middle- and upper-class markets from 25 percent to 50 percent of sales. Furthermore, Mistine wants to fully leverage its product quality, popularity, and market-leading position.

As a result, the company has started to increase prices. Historically, 80 percent of Mistine's sales were for products that cost an average of $3 (U.S.) each. By boosting the average price to $6 (U.S.), Mistine estimated the average order would increase from $27 (U.S.) to $45 (U.S.). Wage increases mandated by Thai law will also significantly impact Mistine's pricing strategy. Since 20 percent of production costs go toward wages, wage increases are increasing Mistine's prices by approximately 6 to 10 percent annually.

Mistine's Distribution Strategy

Mistine was the first domestic cosmetics company to use the direct selling model in Thailand. The company continues to sell the majority of products through direct sales but has also expanded into retail and e-commerce. Although the company does not own its own stores, Mistine's products can be found in Tesco Lotus, Boots, Lotus Express, and 7-11 convenience stores. Consumers can also purchase Mistine products through the company's Internet site or through its Mistine catalogue. An advanced computer system tracks sales, and Mistine's fleet of trucks can deliver the product within one week of ordering. Mistine has also built a distribution center near the Suvarnabhumi Airport, which will make it easier to export to other countries.

Mistine has also extended its reach globally. Although international markets comprise only 2 to 3 percent of Mistine's sales revenue, the potential for increased global sales is enormous. In addition to Thailand, Mistine's products are sold in many Asian, European, Middle Eastern, and African markets, including countries such as Ghana, Iran, South Africa, and the Democratic Republic of the Congo. The Association of Southeast Asian Nations (ASEAN) trade agreement will help to increase Mistine's global reach into other Southeast Asian countries. ASEAN is a trade agreement between Thailand, Cambodia, Myanmar, the Philippines, Malaysia, Singapore, Indonesia, Brunei, Laos, and Vietnam. As part of the agreement, tariffs between member states have been reduced or eliminated. This increases the opportunities for companies such as Mistine to expand their distribution. Additionally, in 2010, ASEAN members developed an agreement with China called ACFTA (ASEAN–China Free Trade Area) for free trade between the nations. This creates a lucrative opportunity for Mistine to tap into the world's largest market of consumers. In anticipation of these increased growth opportunities, Mistine plans to build a new plant in Vietnam within the next few years.

Mistine's Promotion Strategy

Direct selling companies normally depend on word of mouth to develop brand awareness, recruit salespeople, and encourage product purchases. Better Way decided to do things differently by being the first direct selling company in the world to use mass media advertising. The company's continuous advertising campaigns build its brand image and position Mistine in customers' minds. In addition, Better Way also developed many advertising campaigns to recruit salespeople.

When the company first started, Dr. Deerojanawong used his credibility to advertise Mistine during interviews with the media and at seminars with educational institutions. People applied as district managers with the company mainly because of his reputation. He was certain that the district managers would be able to establish a large network of salespeople. To increase knowledge about the company, however, Mistine wanted to reach greater audiences. This eventually led it to move into television advertising.

"Mistine is here!" was launched as the company's first television campaign with the objectives to communicate to the public that Mistine is a direct selling cosmetics business and to create a brand character of beauty for Mistine's products. Using the message "Mistine is here!" was an effective way for the public to envision a salesperson coming to visit them with Mistine products. After only two months, the campaign generated an incredible buzz as it increased brand awareness from 10 percent to roughly 70 percent. As Mistine continues to globalize, "Mistine is here!" has been translated into Burmese with plans to translate the slogan into Bahasa Indonesia and Tagalog. The company also markets itself as "The Asian brand for Asian women" as a way to promote the fact that its products are made to complement Asian skin tones.

Mistine's second advertising campaign was designed to assist district managers in their efforts to recruit new salespeople. This campaign consisted of two advertisements. The message of the first ad was that it was possible to buy a car by becoming a Mistine salesperson. Within three months, a total of 30,000 people applied and sales rose by 100 percent. The message of the second ad was that it was possible to buy a house by becoming a Mistine salesperson. Again, the company succeeded in creating stronger brand awareness through this campaign.

Based on this success, the company decided that the next step was to increase its customers' confidence in Mistine products, as well as generate more product trial. As such, "If you're not satisfied, we will give you your money back" was the concept for the third campaign. This campaign was not only successful in stimulating product trial, but it also created a great deal of brand switching from competitors' products to Mistine products. In the end, there were few cases of product dissatisfaction or customers requesting their money back.

Mistine has remained a first mover in the direct selling market by launching advertising campaigns featuring popular actresses, actors, and bands as Mistine brand ambassadors. Many of these celebrities have been featured on Channel 7 or RS Entertainment, Thai television channels with soap operas popular among Mistine's core market. Mistine has become an expert at choosing celebrities that resonate with these target markets. To take advantage of the favorable impression of Korean cosmetics (especially among teenagers), Mistine used a famous Korean band to promote its BB Powder. The company has also created its own Facebook page to extend its worldwide reach.

Due to its extensive marketing campaigns, the Mistine brand is one of the best-known brands in Thailand. In 2011, the brand won a Superbrands award as the "brand most accepted by Thai consumers." This high level of brand awareness has helped propel Mistine to a market leadership position in the Thai cosmetics industry.

Mistine's Direct Selling Operation

Mistine's single-level marketing approach to its direct sales operations is simple and efficient. It is also suitable to the Thai culture and lifestyle. The company recruits district managers who in turn recruit as many salespeople as he/she can handle.

Each day the salespeople make their rounds to meet customers and prospective customers. Once a sale is confirmed, the salesperson submits a purchase order. Each salesperson earns a full 25 to 30 percent commission without having to share his or her earnings with others. The more sales a salesperson makes, the more income he or she receives. Each district manager earns a fixed salary plus commission based on sales generated by the salespersons under his or her responsibility. In addition, to increase morale, mobility, and efficiency, the company provides a car to each of its district managers and pays for their gas.

In the direct selling business, the length of a selling period is critical and shapes the operation of the business. A selling period starts when the product catalog is sent to the sales force. The selling period ends when the sales force submits purchase orders to the company. Normally, direct selling companies use a three-week selling period, totaling 18 periods within a year. Although Mistine used this approach, the company found that most salespeople did not begin selling products to customers until the last week of the selling period. As such, most of the customers' purchase orders were generated from sales during the third week of the selling period. Accordingly, Mistine's management decided to reduce the selling period to two weeks, resulting in 26 selling periods per year.

The change was a challenge for Mistine's operations. Because as many as 20,000 purchase orders are submitted to the company each day, the company was forced to implement an efficient mail traffic management plan to control and balance the workload. Within a two-week selling period, personnel had only 10 days to work. If order processing was not completed each day, sales personnel would not be able to deliver the products as promised. After some time, the new operating plan worked smoothly and was a resounding success. Sales increased, and salespeople became more active in selling products. The impressive sales were not only a result of reducing the distribution cycle but were also due to the positive attitude created throughout the company. The company's pledge—"We will make Mistine No. 1"—was successful in motivating salespeople and office personnel to adapt to the changes and cooperate with the company's direction.

Mistine welcomes anyone, male or female, with free time, who would like to earn money, make new friends, and develop self-confidence. Salespeople can plan their own schedule and movement in order to reach target sales and obtain rewards. Mistine's turnover rate for salespeople once averaged 200 percent per year because most salespeople sell Mistine products as a second job. However, the company was able to reduce turnover by 30 percent through simple improvements in order processing and fulfillment that streamlined many of the mundane, time-consuming tasks for salespeople. One example is the "Mistine Corporate Solution," a strategic alliance with DTAC, a major Thai telecommunications provider. The system greatly increases efficiency and productivity by enabling salespeople to call the 24-hour Mistine Call Center for free when using the DTAC network. This innovative alliance not only made Mistine sales reps happier, it also cut Better Way's phone expenses by $25,000 (U.S.) per month.

With the belief that salespeople can live without Mistine, but Mistine cannot live without its salespeople, Mistine has launched several programs to maximize employee loyalty. The company provides life insurance with coverage of $50,000 (U.S.) to each salesperson. Nonmonetary rewards and recognition incentives for salespeople include crystal trophies, photos in the Hall of Fame, and prizes such as a gold necklace for achieving target objectives. Salespeople also have a chance to earn extra for surpassing sales goals.

Mistine's Key Competitors

Cosmetics are the number one product sold through direct selling channels in Thailand. The total direct selling market is more than $1.5 billion (U.S.) per year. Of that amount, the cosmetics market accounts for roughly 60 percent of all products sold via direct selling channels. In terms of direct selling market share, the top four cosmetics companies are Mistine, Avon, Giffarine, and Amway. However, domestic brands and Asian competitors have begun to challenge the top four for dominancy. Price, quality, and attractive packages are the three most important criteria for Thai consumers when buying cosmetics.

Avon   Founded in 1978, AVON Cosmetics (Thailand) Co., Ltd., is the 22nd branch of AVON Products Inc, USA. It was the first company in Thailand to use a single-level marketing direct selling approach for Thai consumers. With the company's motto—*The Company for Women*—Avon targets teenagers and working women. Avon cosmetics are truly high-quality products for which the brand is recognized throughout the world. As such, it is not difficult for Avon Thailand to sell its products and gain the confidence of consumers. The company has a team of representatives known as Avon Members who are headquartered in Bangkok and visit all the customers in their areas of responsibility. The Members not only sell products, they also provide beauty tips, customer service, and ensure that customers are satisfied with the products.

Giffarine   Giffarine Skyline Unity Co., Ltd., was founded in 1966 by a team of Thai doctors and pharmacists. The company's medical roots translate into its positioning today: Giffarine's products are developed and tested with the highest standards of quality. However, like Mistine, the company also focuses on affordable pricing. Giffarine's portfolio includes a wide range of cosmetics, body treatments, household items, diet supplements, and health food products. Giffarine's success can be attributed to several factors. In addition to product quality, the company places a great deal of emphasis on social responsibility and ethics in the treatment of both customers and employees. Giffarine is also a master of multilevel marketing, which extends to how it structures its sales force. Its partnership with the website YouCanDo.net increased the online presence of Giffarine's sales representatives. Giffarine also announced it would launch a direct-selling channel to better target the Thai population.

Amway   Established in May 1988, Amway (Thailand) Co., Ltd., sells various consumer products in addition to cosmetics, using a multilevel marketing approach. The company's most popular products include health products, herbal products, air purifiers, and water purifiers. Amway offers nutritional supplements under the Nutrilite brand and cosmetics products under the Artistry brand, both of which have high brand awareness among Thai consumers. The company has received ISO 14001 certification for environmental management systems and ISO 9001 certification for quality service standards. The company has also received awards for promoting social and environmental causes along with outstanding industrial relations and employee welfare. Unlike Mistine, Amway owns shops in Thailand. These shops exist to provide inventory for salespeople to sell to consumers. Although Amway products are more expensive, they are also perceived to be of high quality.

New Competitors   As the cosmetics industry within Thailand grows, domestic competitors are challenging Mistine's market dominancy. U*Star is a cosmetic firm established in 2002 through a collaboration between a cosmetics firm and the entertainment company GMM Grammy Music Records. The company is certified by ISO 9001 and Good Manufacturing Principles. Its distribution channels include direct selling and company-owned retail stores. The SSUP Company owns the cosmetic brands Cute Press and Oriental Princess. Established in 1976, Cute Press is sold in more than 150 retail stores. Oriental Press is sold mainly through retail channels and targets upper-class consumers. Consumer products company Aim Star also sells cosmetics as one of its product lines. It is the first Thai direct selling company to become successful in America. Mistine also faces competition from other Asian brands. Korean brands are perceived as more prestigious than domestic brands and are growing throughout the region. This is based on the fact that Korean movie stars and models are viewed as among the most beautiful Asian women.

Strategic Assessment of Mistine

In less than 30 years, Mistine has grown to be the market leader in the Thai cosmetics industry. Its then revolutionary idea to market its products through direct selling channels was a hit with Thai consumers, spurring competitors to adopt similar channels of distribution. Mistine's influence has caused the direct selling industry in Thailand to flourish. The company has succeeded in forming strengths that are hard for rivals to replicate and has become adept at seizing upon marketing opportunities.

On the other hand, the increase in competition, both domestically and internationally, means that Mistine cannot remain idle. Rather, the company must constantly adapt to ensure that it retains its competitive advantages and market leadership position. Doing so requires Mistine to continually reassess its strategies and competitiveness. Case Exhibit 7.1 provides a SWOT analysis of Mistine's competitive position.

CASE EXHIBIT 7.1   SWOT Analysis for Mistine

Strengths

- Wide variety of products
- High brand awareness
- Highest market share in domestic market
- Short selling period
- Affordable prices
- Strong corporate social responsibility program
- Certifications for quality and environmental standards
- Expertise at recruiting effective ambassadors
- Different channels makes products more accessible to consumers
- Strong partnerships with foreign companies

Weaknesses

- Quality perceptions
- High employee turnover rate
- Large dependence on direct selling channel
- Failure to capitalize on e-commerce channels
- Multiple channels of distribution might potentially alienate sales force

Opportunities

- High growth rate in the cosmetics industry and direct selling market
- Popularity of Korean and Japanese cosmetic trends
- Removal of tariffs through ACFTA
- Expanding purchasing power in developing countries

Threats

- Growing competition from domestic brands
- Potential for increased competition from new foreign entrants
- Flooding and other natural disasters
- Economic or political uncertainty
- New minimum wage law
- Rising commodity costs

Mistine's Strengths

Mistine has high brand awareness and a loyal following among Thai consumers. The company is skilled at being able to meet its customer needs while leveraging ways to be more efficient. For instance, its expertise at recruiting celebrities to be brand ambassadors and its recognition of emerging trends (i.e., the growing popularity of Japanese and Korean cosmetics) are effective ways to spread awareness of Mistine among its target markets. The short selling period and the quick time it takes to deliver the products to customers enables Mistine to create more efficient direct selling operations and increase customer satisfaction.

Mistine has also created strong partnerships with other countries, which could expand its global reach and perhaps decrease its production costs. For instance, Mistine is working with a dealer in Ghana to sell its products in the country and has created a joint venture with a firm in Burma to build a second factory there. Mistine is also eyeing Indonesia as a potential prospect and has been in talks with a domestic business to sell cosmetics. However, Mistine will likely not use the "Mistine" name in Indonesia as Indonesian consumers are unfamiliar with the brand name. The company has already made lucrative partnerships with firms in Japan and Korea to collaborate on projects and import cosmetic products.

Mistine has become adept at using the marketing mix to create competitive advantages. Affordable prices and multiple distribution channels make Mistine products accessible to a wide variety of stakeholders. Consumers can trust that Mistine products adhere to high quality standards. Mistine has also created a corporate social responsibility (CSR) program. The company founded the Dr. Amornthep Deerojanawong Foundation to give back to the community and provide relief for flooding victims. These CSR initiatives serve to create stronger relationships with Thai consumers as well as enhance the reputation of the Mistine brand.

Mistine's Weaknesses

Like all major companies, Mistine also has several weaknesses it must address to compete in the cosmetics market. Some of these weaknesses involve the very elements that Mistine has used to gain a competitive advantage. For instance, its low prices have made Mistine products accessible to a wide variety of stakeholders, but they have also added to the perception that Mistine products might be of lower quality. Mistine's emphasis on the lower- and middle-classes has contributed to the idea that Mistine is a brand for those with lower incomes. This is becoming a challenge as Mistine tries to extend its reach to consumers with higher incomes. Better Way is trying to counter this perception of lower quality by raising prices (partially to offset the increase in labor wages) and investing in products with a more favorable perception, such as BB Powder and the brand Faris by Naris. However, price increases could backfire if they alienate the company's core market of lower-income consumers. Mistine's target market is more price-sensitive and may decide to switch brands if prices are raised too high.

The high salesperson turnover rate is also a problem for Mistine, although its initiatives have successfully reduced the turnover rate by 30 percent. Many distributors work at Mistine as a second job and are thus less committed to staying with the company. Higher turnover rates increase costs for Mistine because it must spend more resources to train new salespeople. The company's dependence on its sales force to sell products further increases this risk. Perhaps to reduce this risk and compete against its established rivals, Mistine has adopted other distribution channels, including retail outlets and ecommerce. While this may turn out to be a significant strength for Mistine, it could also alienate its sales force. Salespeople may feel that by adopting other distribution channels, Mistine is taking sales away from them. Mistine must work hard to balance the benefits that come with adopting multiple distribution channels with the needs and morale of its sales force.

As social networking and digital communication become more important channels for direct selling, Mistine recognizes that it must use digital communication to keep up with these changing technological trends. The company created its own Facebook page and allows consumers to order products through its website. However, consumers have pointed out that the Mistine website is not satisfactorily equipped to handle orders. For instance, the main website (www.mistine.co.th) does not immediately allow consumers to order products. Instead, it has a section entitled "How to Order." Users who click on "Online Purchase" will be redirected to the Better Way website (www.bworder.com) to make their purchases. The use of two different sites could be confusing for customers. Because the professional class tends to rely more upon the Internet, Mistine should work to make its website more user-friendly as it expands into higher income markets.

Mistine's Market Opportunities

Mistine has significant opportunities for growth in both the domestic and international markets. Direct selling is growing rapidly in other countries; the industry grew 30 percent in China in 2011. The purchasing power of consumers in countries such as China is increasing as well. This will likely increase the demand for cosmetics and other fashion items. The trend toward Korean and Japanese cosmetics and the popularity of Mistine's BB Powder provides the company with an opportunity to enhance its brand image of quality.

Perhaps one of Mistine's most notable opportunities are the ASEAN and ACFTA trade agreements. These agreements give domestic companies a significant advantage over foreign brands such as Amway and Avon. As a Southeast Asian company, Mistine can take advantage of reduced trade barriers to export its products to other countries in the region. By leveraging its inclusion in ASEAN and its partnerships in other countries, Mistine has the chance to gain a profound competitive edge over its foreign rivals.

Mistine's Market Threats

In spite of its strengths and opportunities, Mistine faces many threats in the future. The growing competition from domestic cosmetic brands will force Mistine to watch its rivals SSUP, Aim Star, and U*Star closely, particularly as they too will be able to benefit from the ACFTA trade agreement. Additionally, while these trade agreements provide Mistine with an opportunity to enter foreign Asian markets more easily, it also provides foreign brands with greater ease of entry into the Thai market. Hence, Mistine may have more foreign competitors with which to contend. Korean and Japanese cosmetics brands could become a major threat due to the growing popularity of these brands among Thai consumers.

As Mistine expands internationally, it will also likely run into trade barriers. Some of the countries in which it wants to expand have obstacles that Mistine will need to overcome if it wants to succeed. For instance, many African countries have poor infrastructure, which may hinder distribution. Iran, another country in which Mistine wants to expand, has a high inflation rate. Mistine also faces barriers in its own home country with political uncertainty, the threat of natural disasters such as flooding, and higher production costs. The government-mandated wage increases will force Mistine to increase how it compensates its work force, which will likely translate into increased prices for Mistine products that could dissuade price-sensitive customers. Mistine must make the decision on whether to pass these increases onto consumers through higher-priced products or find alternative ways to reduce its production costs.

Mistine's Future

Mistine successfully conquered Thailand's direct selling cosmetics market within a very short period of time. The company's success is based on Dr. Deerojanawong's clear vision and determination. Since his death in 2000, his son Danai has been at the helm of Better Way. Danai's contribution to the Better Way vision has been to take the Mistine brand into the modern era via an aggressive strategy of expansion into foreign markets. Considering the relationship of Thailand to its neighboring countries, its geographic proximity, and Thailand's position in Asia, foreign markets are an extremely interesting prospect for Mistine. The company opened manufacturing sites in the Philippines and Vietnam, and has successfully offered products for sale in Cambodia, Laos, Myanmar, and several Middle Eastern and African countries. These successes are due to Mistine's affordable prices that match the income of the people in these countries. Moreover, Mistine's advertising campaigns use popular actresses who are also well known to people in these countries.

However, Mistine faces many challenges as it continues to grow. For instance, the firm missed its 2011 growth targets because of massive flooding in Thailand. Such natural disasters may reoccur, causing consumers to forgo cosmetic purchases to focus on more immediate needs. Mistine must keep this mind when setting growth targets and sales goals.

Danai knows that there will be many bumps on the road ahead, with strong competitors at Mistine's doorstep. In looking ahead to the next 10 years, Danai is considering the best ways to take Mistine further into the global arena. How can Mistine leverage its current strengths to take advantage of global opportunities? How can the company maintain its number one position in Thailand while it simultaneously looks outside its borders, particularly in China, Russia, and even Western nations? Should Mistine invest in more technological innovations such as mobile apps to target the more technologically savvy professional market? As Danai considers these issues, his father's words—"Face what you fear!"—echo in his mind.

Questions for Discussion

1. Based on the SWOT analysis provided in the case, what are the two or three factors that Mistine should stress in its strategic planning as it looks to continue its growth and dominance in the Thai market? How can Mistine match its strengths with its market opportunities to create competitive advantages moving forward?
2. How can Better Way stay on top in Thailand while it looks to expand internationally?
3. What specific marketing program initiatives would you recommend over the next five years?

Sources

Aim Star Network website (http://www.aimstarnetwork.com/th), accessed July 23, 2012; "Aim Star News," Aim Star Network (http://www.aimstarnetwork.com/th/massmedias/default2554-2011.html), accessed July 23, 2012; "Amway," *Siamturakij*, January 2010 (http://www.siamturakij.com/home/news/display_news.php?news_id=413342493); "Asean Mutual Recognition Arrangement of Product Registration Approval for Cosmetics," The Seventeenth Meeting of the Asean Free Trade Area (AFTA) Council, 2003; ASTV Manager, "Mistine Top 8 Months Total Loss. Auxiliary Partners Grew 11% Year-End," Manager Online, September 7, 2011 (http://www.manager.co.th/business/viewnews.aspx?NewsID=9540000113722); ASTV Manager Journal, "Mistine, finding partners to boost sales," *Daily News*, September 7, 2011 (http://mgr.manager.co.th/Daily/ViewNews.aspx?NewsID=9540000113691); Avon Thailand website (http://www.avon.co.th), accessed July 23, 2012; "Better Way Internet Order" (http://www.bworder.com), accessed July 23, 2012; Better Way (Thailand) Company website (http://www.mistine.co.th), accessed July 23, 2012; "Big Five Direct Sellers," *Business Thailand*, October 12, 2001 (http://www.businessthai.in.th); "Branding for Direct Selling," *Business Thailand*, December 12, 2003 (http://www.businessthai.in.th); "Cosmetic for the Asian Woman," Health-Fitness-Beauty.com (http://www.health-fitness-beauty.com/Cosmetic_for_the_Asian_Woman.htm), accessed July 23, 2012; "Cosmetics and Toiletries in Thailand," *Euromonitor International*, July 2009 (http://www.euromonitor.com/Cosmetics_And_Toiletries_in_Thailand), accessed October 16, 2009; "Danai good roll through family Direct sales mogul," *Positioning*, November 2005 (http://www.positioningmag.com/magazine/details.aspx?id=41548), accessed July 23, 2012; Anuwat Dharamadhaj, "How Direct Selling is Regulated and Managed in Different Markets in Thailand," Asian Symposium on Direct Selling, 2003; "Direct Sale: Market Analysis," *Ta-Lad-vi-kod*, 14 (311), 2012, pp. 1–15; "Direct-Sales intense war in 2012," *Talad Vi Kro*, January 1–15, 2012 (http://www.taladvikrao.com/311news/directsale01.html); "Direct Sale War," *Manager Online*, November 24, 2011 (http://www.gotomanager.com/news/details.aspx?id=42915); "Direct Sale War," *Siam-Rad*, June 7–8, 2010 (http://www.brandage.com/Asset/BrandAge-Siamrath/75.pdf); "Direct Selling," *Marketeer*, 43 (September 2003), p. 62; "Direct Selling War," *Bangkok Business News*, March 24, 2003 (http://www.bangkokbiznews.com); Euromonitor International, *Direct Selling in Thailand*, February 2012 (http://www.euromonitor.com/direct-selling-in-thailand/report), accessed July 23, 2012; Giffarine Thailand website (http://www.giffarinethailand.com/th), accessed July 23, 2012; "Global Networks, 'Dream Big' Danai D. Robert and Family," *Bangkokbiznews.com*, January 21, 2009 (http://www.bangkokbiznews.com); "Group Chronology," SSUP Group (http://www.ssup.co.th/index.php?page=Group-Chronology), accessed July 23, 2012; Sujintana Hemtasilpa, "Mobile Phones, Appliances Join Growing Mistine Cosmetics Lineup in Thailand," *Bangkok Post*, October 2004 (http://findarticles.com), accessed October 16, 2009; "History," *Amber Way, Thailand*, 2008 (https://www.amwayshopping.com/amwayshopping-frontend/shopping/contentPage?id=177), accessed October 19, 2009; Industrial Research Institute Co., Ltd., *Health & Beauty Care Marketing in Thailand 2009*, NNA Japan Co., Ltd., 2009; Jaturong Kobkaew, *King of Direct Sales* (Bangkok: Thai Public Relations and Publishing, 2002); "Mistine Cosmetics" (http://www.mistinecosmetics.com), accessed July 23, 2012; "Mistine entering into multi-channel Modern Trade," Pracachat.net, October 2, 2010 (http://www.prachachat.net/news_detail.php?newsid=1285937922&grpid=00&catid=no); "Mistine Sale 2011," *Leader Time*, 9 (191), 2012, pp. 16–31; "Mistine to target A investment up 10%," *Krungthep Turakit* (http://www.krungthebturakit.co.th), accessed March 29, 2012; "Move: Artistry Essentials," *Marketeer* (http://www.marketeer.co.th/inside_detail.php?inside_id=7507), accessed July 23, 2012; "New trend media use for Direct Sale," *Ta-Lad-vi-kod*, 14 (312), 2012, pp. 16–31; Katherine B. Ponder, "Direct Selling's Billion-Dollar Markets," *Direct Selling News*, March 1, 2011 (http://directsellingnews.com/index.php/view/direct_sellings_billion_dollar_markets/P1); Achara Pongvutitham, "Better Way has big plans for Mistine in Asean markets," *The Nation*, January 20, 2012 (http://www.nationmultimedia.com/business/Better-Way-has-big-plans-for-Mistine-in-Asean-mark-30174717.html); Research Projects from the Competitive Strategies in Marketing Course, MIM XXI 2012, Thammasat University (Rachchakrit M., Tippawan Y., Tuangploi C., Yuji Y., Maxime H., Vitantonio S., Preawphan Lertnaitum, Sasipim Tansatru, Teerapath Pongsapas, Thai Boontae, Noemie Frachon, Kong Teerachutimanant, Nattamon Coo-iead, Nawatta Kimwong, Sureeyapat Sereeumnuoi, Yodyuth Chaisuwan, Ratanawalee Indraphuag, Sarun Vatjanajaroenrat, Vichak Jirisant, Vimolyos Sawadsaringkarn, Mike Heijstek, Pichaya Choochuenchaimongkol, Pimpatr Wongnongtoey, Ponglada Paniangwet, Poramin Tanwattana, Saifon Hanchaikul, Pimpichcha Pongpornsakul, Poomphatt Visavavetmethee, Saranya Wattanatrakulchat, Thitiched Mungkiatskul, Emmanuel Froim, Pitch Laosrisakdakul, Supachot Wangchinda, Supreecha Mahagittilarb, Tanita Watprasong, Caroline Wisniewski, Kittikarn Tantanasarid, Patcharapan Vanadurongwan, Pattrawan Muongrattana, Piyapoj Rojanasopondist, Polwat Luengsupabul, Korntheap Kangwanpiboon, Atthasit, Dutsadee, Jiarawut, Kritika, Natchar, Nopphatsorn Sribooneak, Patarinee Bovonratwet, Patcharapa Wannasumrerng, Suparat Kosolsuk, Arunnee T., Eakthana C., Manisa W., Sarat B., and Sawika S.); Kwanchai Rungfapaisarn, "Direct sales firms satisfied with 2010 performance amid negative factors," *The Nation*, January 8, 2011 (http://www.nationmultimedia.com/2011/01/08/business/Directsales-firms-satisfied-with-2010-performance–30145912.html); Kwanchai Rungfapaisarn, "Bright Future Awaits Thai Cosmetics Industry," *The Nation*, March 26, 2011 (http://www.nationmultimedia.com/2011/03/26/business/Bright-future-awaits-Thai-cosmetics-industry-30151799.html); Kwanchai Rungfapaisarn, "Mistine supplier aims to double sales in five years," *The Nation*, September 8, 2011 (http://www.nationmultimedia.com/2011/09/08/business/Mistine-supplier-aims-to-double-sales-in-five-year-30164754.html); Kwanchai Rungfapaisarn, "Thai cosmetics firm eyes foreign markets," Asia News Network, March 29, 2012 (http://www.asianewsnet.net/home/news.php?sec=2&id=29110); Thomas Schmid, "Article: Cosmetics Firm Debuts Thailand's Longest TV Commercial," *HighBeam Research*, September 1, 2002 (http://www.highbeam.com/doc/1G1-106646831.html); "Success Story," nationejobs.com (http://www.nationejobs.com/content/worklife/worklife/template.php?conno=522), accessed July 23, 2012; "Successful and Prestigious Award," *Amber Way, Thailand*, 2008 (https://www.amwayshopping.com/amwayshopping-frontend/shopping/contentPage?id=178), accessed October 19,

2009; "Surgery strategies cosmetics counters j brand VS brand application in consumer theory," *Manager Weekly 360˚*, September 15, 2011 (http://www.manager.co.th/mgrweekly/viewnews.aspx?NewsID=9540000117344); "Thailand based Better Way invests in Logistics," Global Supply Chain Council, April 16, 2010 (http://www.supplychains.com/en/art/3583); "Thailand Direct Selling," Competitive Strategies in Marketing, Thammasat University, Thailand, 2004; "Thailand Top Direct Sale 2008" (http://guru.google.co.th/guru/thread?tid=52886fdbc6e4cae8), accessed July 23, 2012; "The Top Sale 2011," *Leader Time Magazine*, 12 (134), 2012; "'Together as One'—A New Joint Venture Between Mistine and DTAC," *Newswit.com*, November 23, 2003 (http://www.newswit.com/enews/2003-11-24/1700-together-as-one—a-new-joint-venture-between); Nalin Viboonchart, "Better Way shifts focus to boost revenue," *The Nation*, August 22, 2009 (http://www.nationmultimedia.com/home/2009/08/22/business/Better-Way-shifts-focus-to-boost-revenue-30110418.html); and Ara Wilson, "The Empire of Direct Sales and the Making of Thai Entrepreneurs," *Critiques of Anthropology*, 19 (1999), pp. 402–22.

CASE **8**

BP Struggles to Repair Its Tarnished Reputation*

Synopsis: In the wake of the *Deepwater Horizon* disaster in the Gulf of Mexico, BP faces a monumental task in reestablishing its sustainability-based branding strategy and repairing its tarnished reputation. This case examines the history of BP, its efforts to rebrand the company to focus on sustainability, and its environmental and ethical lapses preceding the *Deepwater Horizon* accident. BP had realized the need to become more environmentally responsible and was the first energy company to recognize the presence of global warming and launch initiatives to produce cleaner forms of energy. Unfortunately, the company's questionable safety and environmental record effectively undermined its branding initiatives. To move beyond the Gulf oil spill, BP must find ways to repair its damaged reputation through a commitment to integrity and an authentic concern for both the environment and the company's many stakeholders.

Themes: Ethics and social responsibility, sustainability, corporate branding and positioning, corporate affairs, stakeholder engagement, strategic thrust

BP has experienced a lot of ups and downs over its hundred-year history—from nearly bankrupting its founder William D'Arcy to becoming one of the world's largest energy companies. BP has also experienced its fair share of controversies regarding business practices, environmental damage, hazards to workers, and greenhouse gases. For some time, BP has attempted to turn a page in its history book toward a more environmentally friendly future through investments in renewable energy and ethics initiatives. British Petroleum changed its name to BP and then tried to rebrand itself as Beyond Petroleum. This rebranding was a signal to stakeholders that it was focused on sustainability and the need to move beyond nonrenewable energy sources.

Changes in demand patterns for energy products require that firms respond to the value desired by a target market. BP was trying to position its products as not just commodities, but as differentiated products that support sustainability and other social responsibility concerns. One of the key concerns when such claims are made involves maintaining a product that is authentic and trustworthy. By using the Beyond Petroleum positioning, BP presented itself as being committed to investing in renewable energy, which has gained a great deal of popularity among consumers and other members of society concerned about the planet's future. A marketing strategy has to be

---

*O.C. Ferrell and Jennifer Sawayda, University of New Mexico, developed this case for classroom discussion rather than to illustrate effective or ineffective handling of an administrative situation.

built on a solid foundation of supportable claims about the true nature of the product. However, BP's efforts backfired on April 20, 2010 when the explosion of the *Deepwater Horizon* oil rig, operated under the oversight of BP, created one of the greatest offshore oil disasters in history.

This case provides an opportunity to observe the past efforts of BP to improve its image, along with how these efforts were eclipsed by the oil spill. Certain disasters resulting from company negligence are detailed in this analysis, and although BP made efforts to establish itself as a socially responsible company, the recent oil spill crisis undid many of BP's marketing initiatives. While BP has experienced other disasters related to its social responsibility, before the 2010 oil spill, BP was garnering a better reputation as a socially responsible oil company. It became the first oil company to recognize the presence of global warming and to launch initiatives to produce cleaner forms of energy. This one disaster has tainted BP's brand image, causing the company to lose billions of dollars and the reputation it worked so hard to build.

The History of BP

BP was founded more than a century ago by William D'Arcy, a wealthy British gentleman who had invested all his savings in the quest for oil in the Middle East. While experts and scientists had encouraged D'Arcy to pursue the venture, after more than six years of drilling, both his patience and finances were running low. Finally, in 1908, the drillers had reached almost 1,200 feet when a fountain of oil spewed out. After long years of disappointment, the Anglo-Persian Oil Company, what would become BP, was born. The company quickly opened trade on the stock market, and D'Arcy, who had lost nearly his entire net worth, became rich.

A naphtha field in Iran, located around 130 miles from the mouth of the Persian Gulf, was the first place where the Anglo-Persian Oil Company established a refinery. (Naphtha refers to any sort of petroleum product; in this case, the Anglo-Persian Oil Company was pumping crude oil.) George Reynolds, D'Arcy's head manager for all the miners, quickly discovered that navigating this rugged land could take months. To facilitate transportation of the oil, BP started building a pipeline through the area, and many of the necessary supplies had to be shipped from the United States. The huge scope of the undertaking drew workers from across the world—all of which were seeking work in helping to build the largest refinery in the world.

By 1914, BP was about to go bankrupt again. The company had a lot of oil, but demand for that oil was low. The automobile had not become a mass-market product yet, and companies in the New World and Europe had first-mover advantages in the industrial oils market. An even worse problem was the strong smell of Persian oil, which eliminated it from the heating and kerosene lamp markets.

Winston Churchill, who was at the time the British First Lord of the Admiralty, changed all that. He felt that the British navy, which was the envy of the world, needed a reliable and dedicated source of oil. Oil executives had been courting the navy for some years, but until Churchill, commanders had been reluctant to abandon coal. Churchill was adamant that only Anglo-Persian, because it was a British-owned company, could adequately protect British interests. Parliament overwhelmingly agreed and soon was a major shareholder in the oil company. Thus began the debate over the repercussions of involving politics in the oil industry, a debate that only became louder throughout World War II, the Persian Gulf War, and the Iraq War.

The twentieth century saw enormous growth in the oil industry, along with massive power shifts in the Middle East. In 1969, Muammar al-Gaddafi led a coup in Libya, promptly demanding a tax increase on all oil exports. Gaddafi eventually nationalized BP's share of an oil operation in Libya. This move led other oil-rich countries in the Middle East, including Iran, Saudi Arabia, Abu Dhabi, and Qatar, to eventually nationalize. The effect on BP was massive—between 1975 and 1983, the oil production in the Middle East fell from 140 million to 500,000 barrels.

In order to survive, BP had to find new places to drill for oil. The Forties Field off the coast of Scotland, capable of producing 400,000 barrels of crude oil a day, and Prudhoe Bay in Alaska, where BP had tapped its largest oil field yet in 1969, were the two great hopes for BP's future at this time. However, transportation of the oil was a problem. The remoteness of BP's best sites would challenge not only BP's engineering capabilities, but also more importantly its commitment to the environment. The Forties Field pipeline would eventually become the largest deep-water pipeline ever constructed, a project that required special attention due to the harsh weather. The Trans-Alaska pipeline system would become the largest civil engineering project in North America, measuring nearly 746 miles long. The company performed extensive research to identify any potential environmental risks, making sure the pipeline included long above-water stretches to ensure that the warm oil transporting through it wouldn't melt the permafrost. BP also had to take steps to ensure that habitat disruption would be minimal. The company tried to assure concerned stakeholders that the environment was a serious matter to them, which they would address with an intense level of focus and commitment.

Questions About BP's Ethical and Social Conduct

Unfortunately, BP's actions have not always coincided with its words. The company's promises to act as a responsible environmental steward have been marred by numerous instances of questionable behavior. As the company's operating environment became more complex and chaotic, BP often lost sight of its responsibilities to the environment, employees, society, and shareholders.

In March 2005, a huge explosion occurred at a BP-owned oil refinery in Texas that killed 15 employees and injured another 170 people. The company was found guilty by the Southern District of Texas for a one-count felony for violating the Clean Air Act and ordered to pay $50 million in criminal fines. The explosion was the result of a leak of hydrocarbon liquid and vapor, which then ignited. BP admitted that it had ignored several procedures required by the Clean Air Act for ensuring mechanical integrity and a safe startup between 1999 until the explosion in 2005. The BP case was the first prosecution under a section of the Clean Air Act, which was created to help prevent injuries from such accidental leaks of explosive substances.

The company was also charged with violating the Clean Water Act when Alaskan oil pipelines leaked crude oil into the tundra and the frozen lake. The leaks occurred in March and August of 2006, after BP failed to respond to numerous red flags. One of these flags was the dangerous corrosion of the pipes that went unchecked for more than a decade before the Clean Water Act violation. A contract worker discovered the first pipeline leak in March of 2006. This leak resulted in more than 200,000 gallons of crude oil spilling onto the fragile tundra and a nearby frozen lake and was the largest spill to ever occur on the North Slope. A second 1,000-gallon leak occurred shortly after the first, in August of 2006. Although it was small, the second leak led to the shutdown of oil production in the east side of Prudhoe Bay until BP could guarantee that the pipelines were fit for use. The fines resulting from these infractions included $12 million in criminal fines, $4 million in payments to the National Fish and Wildlife Foundation, and $4 million in criminal restitution to the state of Alaska. BP would later pay an additional $25 million for violating clean-water and clean-air laws. Regular routine cleaning of the pipes is simple and would have prevented the 2006 oil leaks in Alaska. Nevertheless, in October 2007, BP recorded yet another spill near Prudhoe Bay. This time it was 2,000 gallons of toxic methanol, a deicing agent that spilled onto the tundra and killed many plants and animals.

In the Northern District of Illinois, BP was charged with conspiring to violate the Commodity Exchange Act and also to commit mail fraud and wire fraud. The fraud involved purchasing more than the available supply of TET propane, and then selling it to other market participants at a price inflated well above market value. BP was forced to pay large fines for this market manipulation. The company had to pay $100 million in criminal penalties, $25 million to the U.S. Postal Inspection Consumer Fraud Fund, and restitution of $53 million. Additionally, BP had to pay a civil penalty of $125 million to the Commodity Futures Trading Commission. Furthermore, four former employees were indicted in February 2004 for conspiring to manipulate the propane market at an artificially high price. The estimated loss to consumers who paid over market value exceeded $53 million dollars. The violation resulted in a 20-count indictment by a federal grand jury in Chicago.

BP Tries to Repair Its Image Through Branding and Sustainability

BP's environmental, legal, and ethical transgressions demonstrate that the company has a history of disregarding the well being of stakeholders. The mistakes of BP and similar companies have caused many types of stakeholders to become more wary, especially after decades of repeated violations and misconduct across many different industries. Being an energy company, however, BP also finds itself in the midst of a key debate over the future of the world's energy supply and such key issues as global warming and greenhouse gas emissions. In this regard, BP has taken major steps toward repairing its tattered image.

One way BP worked to repair its damaged image was by changing its name from British Petroleum to simply BP and increasing alternative energy offerings in its product mix. John Browne, former BP chief executive proclaimed "we are all citizens of one world, and we must take shared responsibility for its future and for its sustainable development." BP was the first global energy firm to publicly announce its recognition of the problem of climate change. While its primary product is still petroleum, BP accepts that global warming is human-made, and it has begun to seek alternative revenue streams in wind farms and other lower-emissions energy sources.

To adapt to a changing world, BP launched its Alternative Energy business in 2005. While still a small part of its overall company, BP sees "going green" as an increasingly important part of its business which it will expand as it becomes more profitable to do so. The company has invested $4 billion in alternative energy and plans to double that amount by 2015.

Wind   BP has invested significantly in wind energy through the creation of wind farms across the nation. In the U.S., BP-operated wind farms have a total capacity of 1,955 MW. In 2010, BP Wind Energy, in partnership with Ridgeline Energy, LLC, launched the Goshen North Wind Farm in Idaho, the state's largest wind farm to date. The farm can generate up to 124.5 MW of wind energy, enough to power 37,000 American homes. The company also extended its strategic partnership with Sempra U.S. Gas & Power to develop two wind farms in Pennsylvania and Kansas with a combined power of 560 megawatts (MW). BP currently operates 13 wind farms across the nation, with more underway.

Solar   BP has installed 4 MW of solar panels at Walmart stores and helped develop a 32 MW solar installation on eastern Long Island, enough to power approximately 5,000 households. BP has also developed two of the largest solar power plants in the world in Spain, projects that will supply some energy to up to a million homes. However, according to its website, BP's solar energy projects have not generated enough of a return to continue expansion in solar energy projects. The company has therefore decided to exit this sector.

Biofuels   BP became the single largest foreign stockholder in a Brazilian bioethanol company when it purchased a 50 percent stake in Tropical Energia S.A. In 2011, BP acquired the remaining 50 percent stake in Tropical Energia S.A. as well as an 83 percent stake in Brazilian ethanol producer Companhia Nacional de Acucar e Alcool. The company sees these acquisitions as a crucial step toward becoming a leader in Brazil's ethanol market. BP has also been working with DuPont to develop biobutanol, a biofuel with higher energy content than bioethanol.

BP's push into the biofuel energy sector prompted the creation of a special purpose entity (SPE) with Verenium Corporation, a leader in the development of cellulosic ethanol, a fuel that is still in its infancy but that many hope will be the future of biofuels. Cellulosic ethanol is a renewable fuel produced from grasses and nonedible plant parts, such as sugarcane waste, rice straw, switch grass, and wood chips. Although at this point it is much more difficult and energy-intensive to produce than corn or sugarcane ethanol, many believe that, as the technology improves, cellulosic ethanol will provide such benefits as greater per-acre yields and lower environmental impact. Another potential benefit is that cellulosic ethanol will not affect commodity or food prices, since it uses only waste products.

In 2010, BP bought Verenium Corp.'s cellulosic biofuels business for $98.3 million. According to the CEO of BP Biofuels, BP remains dedicated to becoming a leader in the cellulosic biofuel industry. If all goes as planned, BP's investment will help stimulate the development and production of cellulosic ethanol over other types of liquid fuels.

Carbon Sequestration and Storage   Carbon sequestration and storage (CCS) involves capturing greenhouse gas emissions from smokestacks and other sources of the pollutant and pumping the gases deep underground to empty oil or gas fields or aquifers. BP has been researching CCS since 2000 and opened the Salah Gas Field in Algeria for experimentation in 2004. BP captures and stores up to 1 million tons of carbon dioxide per year at Salah, which is equivalent to removing 250,000 cars from the road. Over 3 million tons of CO_2 have already been stored underground at the site. While questions remain about the long-term effectiveness of CCS (no one knows for sure if the CO_2 stays underground, or whether it eventually leaks out), many energy companies such as BP see it as a promising technology.

Other Energy-Saving Measures   Beyond alternative energy sources, BP is also looking to save energy through better planning and implementation of its many operations around the world. The BP Zhuhai (BPZ) PTA plant is setting an example by using more efficient forms of energy. This development of more efficient, cleaner energy and the reduction of CO_2 emissions is an increasing priority in China. BPZ is working to set new standards and make a greater contribution in this area. A sequence of heat recovery projects has allowed the plant to optimize the use of steam as a way to reduce liquefied petroleum gas (LPG) consumption significantly. This has saved energy and reduced emissions. Additionally, by reducing fuel consumption, BPZ also has reduced the road safety and operational risks associated with delivery and unloading of LPG. The BP Zhuhai plant has been so successful that a second plant was added in 2008. In 2011, BP announced it would open another plant at the site with a capacity of 1.25 million tons.

BP has also unveiled a carbon offset program called BP Target Neutral, a not-for-profit organization. BP Target Neutral was established to help individuals and businesses calculate their carbon footprint and advise them on ways they could reduce their impact. BP also provides carbon offsets for stakeholders to purchase. Carbon offsets are ways that stakeholders can "offset" the carbon they emit by supporting projects that reduce carbon emissions (e.g. a wind farm project). Participants provide payments to BP Target Neutral, which in turn invests the money in carbon reduction projects. Both FedEx and the British Olympic Association have participated in the BP Target Neutral program.

In addition to its Alternative Energy program, BP has implemented environmental awareness programs in Britain to help stakeholders understand the impacts of global warming and the importance of sustainability issues. BP Educational Service (BPES) initiated the distribution of the Carbon Footprint Toolkit, an award-winning program designed to help high school students understand the effects of climate change and their own carbon footprint. Developed in conjunction with teachers and BP's experts, the toolkit enables students to examine their school's carbon footprint and to help develop carbon reduction plans for their schools. The Carbon Footprint Toolkit was originally developed as a response to teachers' demands that came out of a series of "green" workshops that BP held. The toolkit received a prestigious award for e-learning at the International Visual Communications Association (IVCA) awards in 2007.

BP Establishes a Code of Conduct

To help deal with BP's growing reputation for ethical misconduct, BP's Ethics and Compliance team organized the creation, publication, and distribution of a company code of conduct in 2005, entitled "Our Commitment to Integrity." The code was distributed to BP employees around the globe and is also publicly available online at the BP website. Given the multinational nature of the BP business, the code seeks to unite its diverse employees behind a set of universal standards of behavior. The cross-functional team that drafted the code of conduct faced many major challenges, like how to agree upon and communicate consistent standards for all BP employees regardless of location, culture, and language. The code of conduct was the largest mass communications exercise ever attempted at BP.

To ensure that BP employees are familiar with the code, the company holds awareness meetings to help employees understand its contents. Perhaps the most important role of the code is that it put BP's ethical and legal expectations in writing for the first time. BP's intension was to give clear guidelines for individuals covering five key areas: health, safety, security, and the environment; employees; business partners; government and communities; and company assets and financial integrity.

It is now clear that BP's code of conduct was not equipped to prevent the worst environmental disaster along the Gulf Coast. Regardless of the degree of comprehensiveness, ethical codes should always reflect upper management's desire for compliance with values, rules, and policies. Most importantly, legal staff has to be called upon to ensure that the code correctly assesses key areas of risk. The BP code of conduct was not designed to resolve every legal and ethical issue encountered in daily operations, but the code should have helped employees and managers deal with ethical dilemmas in high-risk areas by prescribing or limiting specific activities.

The Worst Oil Spill in U.S. History

Despite BP's efforts to repair its image, safety violations continued at its facilities. In early 2010, U.S. regulators fined the oil giant $3 million for safety problems at an Ohio factory. The Occupational Safety and Health Administration (OSHA) found that workers might be exposed to injury or death should explosive or flammable chemicals be released at the factory. This violation was not an isolated event. Just four months earlier, OSHA had fined BP a record $87 million for not correcting safety problems that were identified after the 2005 explosion at its Texas refinery. These instances of safety violations culminated with the explosion at the *Deepwater Horizon* oil rig in April 2010.

The Explosion

It all started with an opportunity to tap into a new, highly profitable oil reservoir. The reservoir was dubbed "Macondo," after the doomed town in Gabriel Garcia Marquez's novel *One Hundred Years of Solitude*. To tap the reservoir, BP hired an oil rig from Transocean, Ltd. By April, the project was behind schedule, but BP was convinced it would lead to success. Then on April 20, 2010, an explosion rocked the rig, killing 11 employees. The burning rig sank two days later.

The situation quickly worsened because the well, located nearly a mile below the surface, was damaged in the explosion. Thousands of gallons of crude oil gushed into the Gulf of Mexico. BP sent submarine robots to the seabed in an attempt to activate the switch-off valve on the well. The entire process soon became a public relations nightmare, with BP sending out conflicting messages. One company official informed Fox News that BP had successfully activated part of a failed blowout preventer, which was slowing the oil flow. The announcement turned out to be false. BP's underwater robot did in fact trigger a device, but the device did not stop the oil flow.

The primary event that caused the explosion is unknown. However, investigations have suggested that BP's actions made the well more vulnerable. One investigation implies that BP cut short procedures and quality testing of the pipe—tests that are meant to detect gas in the well. Some experts hypothesize that one of the final actions in installing the pipe—which involved cementing the steel pipe in place—was the catalyst for the explosion. A government panel investigating the crisis also concluded that BP, Transocean, and Halliburton—some of the major firms involved in the drilling—failed to adequately consider risks or communicate with one another on major decisions involving the well.

One of the many criticisms levied against BP is its decision to use a less costly well design that some Congressional investigators have deemed "risky." Installation of this design is easier and costs are lower. However, it also provides a better path for gas to rise outside of the pipe. While this did not cause the explosion, investigators believe it may have contributed to the well's vulnerability. Although BP did not break any laws by using such a design, it ignored safer alternatives that might have prevented, or at least hindered, the accident.

The next few months unleashed a series of failed efforts by BP to stop the flow. Oil washed up on the coasts of Louisiana, Texas, Alabama, Mississippi, and Florida, disrupting the livelihoods of fishermen and others who depended on the Gulf for income. A constant stream of finger pointing took place among the administration and the public as everyone tried to decide who bore the most blame for the tragedy. With all eyes on BP, company actions were scrutinized, and often criticized, throughout the duration of the disaster.

Failure to Manage Risks

The main question on everyone's mind after the disaster was how BP could have overlooked the risks association with the *Deepwater Horizon*. The ocean rig did have safety systems in place, but these systems were not as safe as they could have been. For instance, the rig did not have a remote-control shut-off switch that would have been used as a last resort in a major oil leak disaster. However, neither Transocean (the rig's owner) nor BP were breaking any laws by not having one; the Minerals Management Service (MMS), a federal agency charged with oversight of the nation's offshore oil-and-gas industry, did not require such a device as long as the rig had a backup control system that could shut off the well in case of an emergency. Some suggest that this represented a lapse in regulatory oversight on the government's part.

Yet this cannot explain other lapses in BP's risk management strategy. Some suggest that BP cut corners in risk management to save time and money. For example, records reveal that nearly three of every four incidents that caused federal investigations into safety on deep-sea drilling rigs in the Gulf of Mexico were owned by Transocean. As the biggest client of Transocean in the Gulf of Mexico, BP had a responsibility to properly oversee that appropriate precautions were taken to prevent a disaster. Later investigations also revealed that BP's disaster recovery plan was inadequate. The plan contained several inaccuracies. For instance, one of the wildlife experts who were listed as emergency responders had been dead since 2005. The plan also estimated that should a spill occur, the company would be able to recover about 500,000 barrels of oil per day. In reality, it took BP months to contain the leak, at a spill rate of much less than what was listed in the contingency plan. The inaccuracies in BP's disaster recovery plan highlight how unprepared the company was for a disaster like the *Deepwater Horizon* spill.

Repercussions of the Disaster

The BP oil spill has had and will continue to have wide-ranging repercussions for both BP and the oil industry. The financial toll on BP alone is extensive. BP share prices plunged over 50 percent after the accident. More than two years after the crisis, BP's shares remained 33 percent lower than they had been before the spill. BP was also held liable for cleanup costs and damages. Under current legislation, the most BP would have to pay for economic damage would be $75 million, as mandated by the Oil Pollution Act of 1990. However, BP chose to go beyond what was required by law. Estimates place cleanup costs at $40 billion.

The Justice Department has launched a civil lawsuit against BP, Transocean, Cameron International, Halliburton, and other companies, alleging that they knowingly took risks and disregarded safety rules. To successfully prosecute, the government must show that the disaster resulted from a deliberate flouting of the law or from negligence. If nothing else, BP may be charged with violating the federal Clean Water Act (constituting a civil, not criminal, charge). If found guilty, BP could pay up to $4,300 per barrel of oil released during the spill.

One of the most immediate consequences of the disaster was the resignation of BP CEO Tony Hayward. Despite an impressive track record, including a net profit of $6.08 billion in the first quarter of 2010 and a seemingly dedicated attempt to "turn things around" at BP, Hayward became the face of the worst oil spill in U.S. history—and perhaps the scapegoat as well. Experts believe that it was Hayward's verbal blunders, his lack of visible empathy, and failed crisis management that triggered his downfall. For instance, his comments on how he wanted "his life back" and his attendance of a yacht race made him appear unsympathetic to the Gulf crisis. With the heavy criticism Hayward had generated, the company felt that he would not be able to restore BP's credibility.

The Long Road to Recovery

After years of re-branding initiatives aimed at sustainability, it took only a few months for BP's hard work to unravel. It took several wide-scale efforts to contain the oil leaking into the Gulf. In the interim, thousands of marine animals died in the oily waters, white sand beaches turned to black, and hundreds of people that depended upon the Gulf of Mexico lost part of their income. In August 2010—over one hundred days after the disaster began—BP plugged the leak and dug relief wells to effectively "kill the well." However, the damage done to stakeholders was not over. More than 640 miles of shorelines across several states were "tarred" with oil.

To compensate stakeholders that depend on the Gulf, BP set aside a $20 billion escrow fund. A government-appointed administrator oversaw the claims. As always, though, compensating the right people for the right amounts is tricky. For example, how far from the coast should a claimant be in order to have an effective claim? What about the many workers without sufficient documentation to prove they worked in the Gulf? Although the escrow fund will serve to compensate some individuals, others will likely receive little or no compensation.

Several investigations have been subsequently launched to determine where the blame lies. After performing an internal investigation of the incident, BP admitted fault but placed much of the blame on its contractors Transocean and Halliburton. A report by the National Commission came to a different conclusion. While it places some of the responsibility on Transocean and Halliburton, the panel found that lapses in management and oversight on BP's part contributed to the disaster. The commission also placed some blame on the government, stating that the administration was too slow to respond and then created a liability by overreacting. The panel's findings have led some to call for massive overhauls in oil industry regulation.

Another investigation sheds additional light on why the oil spill became such a large-scale environmental disaster. Engineers discovered that the blowout preventer was indeed faulty. Instead of sealing the pipe completely, the blowout preventer blades got stuck in the pipe, leaving enough space for oil to leak out. BP filed lawsuits against the manufacturer of the blowout preventer, Cameron International Corp. Cameron settled with BP for $250 million.

Perhaps the best news for BP was that the oil began biodegrading faster than expected due to bacteria, which fed on the methane in the crude. Although nature seems to be bouncing back, scientists have detected evidence of oil across several thousand square miles of seafloor. BP's own recovery does not seem to be running so smoothly either. With its role in the disaster along with its public relations blunders, the company's reputation has undergone a severe blow. BP has virtually become synonymous with oil spill in the minds of many stakeholders. Even with a renewed focus on energy-saving technologies, BP's marketing efforts might be viewed as little more than an attempt to regain credibility without any serious dedication to the environment. The company will need to work doubly hard to convince stakeholders that its marketing messages are authentic and sincere.

Yet efforts are already underway. After the ousting of BP CEO Tony Hayward, American Bob Dudley took over operations. While BP originally appeared to downplay the catastrophe, Dudley freely admitted that the incident was a serious "catastrophe" and that the company was committed to the cleanup. BP hired former Federal Emergency Management Agency chief James Lee Witt and his public safety and crisis management consulting firm to help manage the incident and establish plans for long-term recovery. BP also created a safety organization that has been given authority to stop operations whenever danger is detected.

Although BP faces a $40 billion cleanup bill, a slew of negative publicity, and a 2010 loss of $4.9 billion, the company is striving to rebuild its reputation. In addition to a new safety division at BP, CEO Dudley has appointed a board member with knowledge of process safety. The company is intent on attaining growth and will pay smaller dividends in order to spend more on oil exploration. Dudley also promised to make BP into the safest offshore energy operator in the business. Unfortunately, a day after this announcement, a U.K. safety regulator reprimanded BP for safety issues on three of its North Sea rigs—which draws BP's commitment into question.

Implications for BP's Marketing Strategy

BP's "Beyond Petroleum" positioning backfired due to the *Deepwater Horizon* environmental disaster. A firm can spend many years building a reputation, and it can be tarnished in a single day through an event that destroys the confidence of customers and other stakeholders. In this case, BP became the target of almost every group on the Gulf Coast negatively impacted by the environmental effects of the oil spill. BP's attempt to move its product away from being a commodity like those of its competitors failed. In fact, about the only strategy available for BP was to apologize and try to compensate the victims of the disaster. One of the worst things that can happen is to make claims of being a sustainable company and then be involved in a disaster that is just the opposite. A priority for BP's future marketing strategies, at least for its consumer products, is to restore its reputation as much as possible and build a foundation for more realistic and authentic marketing activities to build strong relationships and trust with consumers.

Another area where BP the marketing strategy has to be improved is its public relations activities with various stakeholders such as regulators, local government entities, business communities, and those who earn their living directly from the Gulf Coast environment. The company has taken action by investing heavily in advertising about the recovery from the disaster and the restored Gulf Coast beaches and hospitality industry. As BP does a good job with its public relations and compensation programs, it is attempting to create the groundwork for developing better relationships with customers in the future.

From the beginning, BP proved it was able to overcome significant obstacles. It went from near bankruptcy to being one of the largest energy companies worldwide. BP has worked hard to overcome its negative image through sustainability marketing initiatives and social responsibility. However, BP's emphasis on environmental responsibility backfired after the *Deepwater Horizon* disaster. Although it made great strides in repositioning its brand, it failed to properly manage its brand as a socially responsible company.

The damage to BP's Beyond Petroleum marketing strategy is not easy to repair. The development of trust is based on a firm's commitment to integrity, transparency, and a concern for all stakeholders. In the future, BP needs to develop a marketing strategy that is seen as authentic in the face of the socially responsible corporation that it claims to be.

Questions for Discussion

1. Analyze BP's efforts to improve sustainability and its reputation prior to the *Deepwater Horizon* disaster. Was the company on the right track? Why or why not?
2. Because most BP products can be viewed as commodities, do you think consumers will avoid purchasing from BP because of its track record and the *Deepwater Horizon* disaster? Why or why not?

3.   How can BP prove to its stakeholders that it is serious about social responsibility, sustainability, and ethics, and that its efforts are not just a public relations ploy? What strategic issues would you focus on in trying to repair the company's reputation?

Sources

"Alternative Energy Brochure," BP (http://www.bp.com/liveassets/bp_internet/alternative_energy/alternative_energy_english_new/STAGING/local_assets/downloads_pdfs/AE_Brochure_2010A4.pdf), accessed July 25, 2012; Jeffrey Ball, "BP Spill's Next Major Phase: Wrangling Over Toll on Gulf," *Wall Street Journal*, April 13, 2011 (http://online.wsj.com/article/SB10001424052748704013604576248531530234442.html); Jeffrey Ball, "Strong Evidence Emerges of BP Oil on Seafloor," *Wall Street Journal*, December 9, 2010, A20; Jeffrey Ball, Stephen Power, and Russell Gold, "Oil Agency Draws Fire," *Wall Street Journal*, May 4, 2010, A1; Joel K. Bourne, Jr., "The Deep Dilemma," *National Geographic*, October 2010, p. 40; BP Alternative Energy website (http://www.bp.com/modularhome.do?categoryId=7040&contentId=7051376), accessed April 17, 2012; "BP and Sempra U.S. Gas & Power Announce Plans to Further Expand Strategic Relationship in Wind Business," BP Alternative Energy, January 10, 2012 (http://www.bp.com/genericarticle.do?categoryId=9024973&contentId= 7072928); BP Sustainability Review, 2008 (http://www.bp.com/liveassets/bp_internet/globalbp/STAGING/global_assets/e_s_assets/e_s_assets_2008/downloads/bp_sustainability_review_2008.pdf), accessed July 25, 2012; BP Target Neutral website (http://www.bptargetneutral.com), accessed July 25, 2012; "BP to Expand Activities in Biofuels, Buying Out Remaining Shares in Brazil's Tropical Bioenergia S.A.," BP Alternative Energy, September 14, 2011 (http://www.bp.com/genericarticle.do?categoryId=9024973&contentId=7070981); "BP Zhuhai Leaps Forward for Further Success," BP (http://www.bp.com/genericarticle.do?categoryId=9004958&contentId=7070454), accessed April 17, 2012; "BP's Spill Contingency Plans Vastly Inadequate," *CBS News*, June 9, 2010 (http://www.cbsnews.com/stories/2010/06/09/national/main6563631.shtml); "British Petroleum to Pay More than $370 Million in Environmental Crimes, Fraud Cases," *PR Newswire*, October 25, 2007 (http://www.prnewswire.com/news-releases/british-petroleum-to-pay-more-than-370-million-in-environmental-crimes-fraud-cases-58927382.html); John M. Broder, "Blunders Abounded Before Gulf Spill, Panel Says," *New York Times*, January 5, 2011 (http://www.nytimes.com/2011/01/06/science/earth/06spill.html?_r=2&ref=gulfofmexico2010); John Browne, "Breaking Ranks," *Stanford Business*, 1997 (http://www.gsb.stanford.edu/community/bmag/sbsm0997/feature_ranks.html), accessed July 25, 2012; Ben Casselman, "Rig Owner Had Rising Tally of Accidents," *Wall Street Journal*, May 10, 2010 (http://online.wsj.com/article/SB100014 2405274870430780 4575234471807539054.html); Ben Casselman and Russell Gold, "BP Decisions Set Stage for Disaster," *Wall Street Journal*, May 27, 2010 (http://online.wsj.com/article/SB100014240527487040 26204575266560930780190.html); Guy Chazan, "BP Comeback Is Sidetracked in Artic," *Wall Street Journal*, April 19, 2011, B5; Guy Chazan, "BP Dividend Takes Back Seat to Growth," *Wall Street Journal*, November 3, 2010, B1–B2; Guy Chazan, "BP Faces Fine Over Safety at Ohio Refinery," *Wall Street Journal*, March 9, 2010, A4; Guy Chazan, "BP Feels Shareholder Heat After String of Setbacks," *Wall Street Journal*, September 7, 2011, B1; Guy Chazan, "BP's Worsening Spill Crisis Undermines CEO's Reforms," *Wall Street Journal*, May 3, 2010, A1; "Day 64: Latest oil disaster developments," *CNN*, June 22, 2010 (http://news.blogs.cnn.com/2010/06/22/day-64-latest-oil-disaster-developments/?iref=allsearch); Peter Elkind, David Whitford, Doris Burke, "'An Accident Waiting to Happen'," *Fortune*, February 7, 2011, 107–132; Jeff Fick and Alexis Flynn, "BP Expands Biofuels Business in Brazil," *Wall Street Journal*, March 14, 2011 (http://online.wsj.com/article/SB10001424052748703597804576194 820019691968.html); Darcey Frey, "How Green Is BP?" *New York Times*, December 8, 2002, (http://www.nytimes.com/2002/12/08/magazine/how-green-is-bp.html?page wanted=all&src=pm); Tom Fowler, "BP Spill Saga Far From Over," *Wall Street Journal*, March 5, 2012, A3; Tom Fowler, "Cameron Will Pay BP To Settle Spill Claims," *Wall Street Journal*, December 17–18, 2011, B4; Tom Fowler, "U.S. Readies Attack on BP," *Wall Street Journal*, February 24, 2012, A2; Russell Gold, "BP Sues Maker of Blowout Preventer," *Wall Street Journal*, April 21, 2011, B1; Angel Gonzalez and Brian Baskin, "'Static Kill' Begins, Raising New Hopes," *Wall Street Journal*, August 4, 2010 (http://online.wsj.com/article/SB100014240527487035456045754072516644 4386.html); Russell Gold and Tom McGinty, "BP Relied on Cheaper Wells," *Wall Street Journal*, June 19, 2010 (http://online.wsj.com/article/SB10001424052748704289504 575313010283981200.html); James Herron, "BP Rapped Over North Sea Rig Safety," *Wall Street Journal*, February 2, 2011 (http://online.wsj.com/article/SB10001424052748703960804576119631110061702.html); "History of BP," BP International website (http://www.bp.com/multipleimagesection.do?categoryId=2010123&contentId=7059226), accessed July 25, 2012; Siobhan Hughes, "BP Deposits $3 Billion in Spill Fund," *Wall Street Journal*, August 9, 2010 (http://online.wsj.com/article/SB1000142405274870438850457541928162043 6778.html); Neil King Jr., "BP-Claims Chief Faces Knotty Task," *Wall Street Journal*, July 17–18, 2010, A5; Kevin Johnson and Rick Jervis, "Justice Dept. sues BP, others," *USA Today*, December 16, 2010, 3A; Amy Judd, "British Petroleum Ordered to Pay $180 Million in Settlement Case," *NowPublic*, February 19, 2009 (http://www.nowpublic.com/environment/british-petroleum-ordered-pay-180-million-settlement-case); Monica

Langley, "U.S. Drills Deep Into BP As Spill Drama Drags On," *Wall Street Journal*, July 21, 2010, A1, A14; David Leonhardt, "Spillonomics: Underestimating Risk," *New York Times*, May 31, 2010 (http://www.nytimes.com/2010/06/06/magazine/06fob-wwln-t.html); Bruce Orwall, Monica Langley, and James Herron, "Embattled BP Chief to Exit," *Wall Street Journal*, July 26, 2010, A1, A6; Greg Palast, "British Petroleum's 'Smart Pig'," *Greg Palast: Journalism and Film*, August 9, 2006 (http://www.gregpalast.com/british-petroleums-smart-pig); Jim Polson, "BP Oil Is Biodegrading, Easing Threat to East Coast," *BusinessWeek*, July 28, 2010 (http://www.businessweek.com/news/2010-07-28/bp-oil-is-biodegrading-easing-threat-to-east-coast.html); Stephen Power and Ben Casselman, "White House Probe Blames BP, Industry in Gulf Blast," *Wall Street Journal*, January 6, 2011, A2; Stephen Power and Tennille Tracy, "Spill Panel Finds U.S. Was Slow To React," *Wall Street Journal*, October 7, 2011, A6; Paul Sonne, "Hayward Fell Short of Modern CEO Demands," *Wall Street Journal*, July 26, 2010, A7; Cassandra Sweet, "BP Will Pay Fine In Spills," *Wall Street Journal*, May 4, 2011, B3; Brian Swint and Alex Morales, "BP Plc Buys Verenium Corp.'s Cellulosic Biofuels Unit for $98.3 Million," *Bloomberg*, July 15, 2010 (http://www.bloomberg.com/news/2010-07-15/bp-plc-buys-verenium-corp-s-cellulosic-biofuels-unit-for-98-3-million.html); Vivienne Walt, "Can BP Ever Rebuild Its Reputation?" *TIME*, July 19, 2010 (http://www.time.com/time/business/article/0,8599,2004701-2,00.html); and Harry R. Weber and Greg Bluestein, "Dudley: Time for 'Scaleback' in BP Cleanup," *TIME*, July 30, 2010 (http://www.time.com/time/business/article/0,8599,2007638,00.html).

Chevrolet: 100 Years of Product Innovation*

Synopsis: This case examines Chevrolet's history of product innovation, branding strategy, and successful product mix in connection with its relationship to parent General Motors and its rivalry with Ford. Chevrolet has a long history of success in developing and marketing cars, trucks, and SUVs that are practical, sporty, and affordable. The brand's relationship with General Motors is both a strength and a weakness, especially in the aftermath of the federal government's financial bailout of General Motors in 2008. Government demands for improved fuel economy and ever changing customer needs and preferences will be constant challenges as Chevrolet looks toward its next 100 years.

Themes: Product innovation, product mix, branding, product strategy, competition, corporate reputation, evolving technology, customer loyalty, government regulation, international marketing

General Motor's (GM) Chevrolet brand celebrated its 100th anniversary in 2011. Throughout its history, Chevrolet has launched many different vehicle models, some of them widely successful and others deleted from the product mix shortly after introduction. Over the years, the company has transitioned from an American icon into a worldwide brand known for quality and durability. Despite numerous successes and failures in its history, including the recent bankruptcy and bailout of parent company GM, Chevrolet is still going strong after a century of product innovation.

A History of Product Innovation

Ironically, Chevrolet exists because of its top competitor, Ford Motor Company. William Durant founded Chevrolet in 1911 to compete head on with Ford's popular Model T. Durant had formed General Motors in 1908 but was ousted from the company three years later. To compete against Ford's single model of vehicle, Durant realized that GM would need to create several different models. He applied this idea to his new company, Chevrolet. The brand was named after Louis Chevrolet, a top racer who was hired to design the first Chevrolet. Chevrolet's initial model cost $2,000. This was a high-priced vehicle at the time, which Durant disliked because he wanted to compete directly against

---

*Jennifer Sawayda, University of New Mexico, prepared this case under the direction of O.C. Ferrell for classroom discussion rather than to illustrate effective or ineffective handling of an administrative situation.

Ford on price. A disagreement between the two men resulted in Chevrolet leaving the company, but the name of the brand stuck. In 1915, Chevrolet released a less expensive model priced at $490, the same price as a Ford Model T. The company was acquired by General Motors in 1918 after Durant gained controlling shares in both companies, and Chevrolet went on to become one of GM's most popular brands. Durant once again became GM's president but was ousted a final time in 1920.

With the Chevrolet brand, GM was able to give Ford a run for its money. In 1912, Chevrolet sold 2,999 vehicles, a mere 1 percent market share in the United States. By 1920, Chevrolet was selling over 100,000 vehicles, and in 1927, it surpassed Ford in number of cars sold. Five years later, one-third of cars sold in America were Chevrolets, although the Great Depression significantly weakened company sales. Over the ensuing decades, Chevrolet attempted to position its products as cutting-edge, equipping its vehicles with innovative technologies and even forming a joint venture with competitor Toyota in 1984 to learn more about Toyota's famous production system (in turn, Toyota was able to gain entry into the U.S. market). The partnership, called New United Motor Manufacturing Inc., lasted until 2010.

From its beginning with namesake Louis Chevrolet, the company had a penchant for racing. Chevrolet continued courting racecar drivers as endorsers, and racing greats Junior Johnson, Mark Donohue, Tony DeLorenzo, Dale Earnhardt, and Jeff Gordon all won races driving Chevrolet models. More recently, the Chevrolet Cruze, one of the company's most popular models, won the Driver's Championship and Manufacturer's Championship in the 2010 World Touring Car Championship races. Chevrolet's association with racecar driving has established many of its models as sporty, high-quality vehicles. Chevrolet also provided engines for the 2012 Indy Racing League. By reentering the Indy Racing League, Chevrolet has reinforced its racing heritage and brand image.

Chevrolet's Product Mix

Over the last 100 years, the Chevrolet brand has been associated with almost every type of vehicle on the road. The company has developed large trucks; delivery vans; full-size, mid-size, compact, and sub-compact automobiles; sports cars; and even racecars. This broad portfolio of products falls under the Chevrolet brand because of the strong brand equity that Chevrolet has developed over the last century. A vehicle's brand provides many intangible attributes related to quality, design, utility, and self-image for the buyer. It is not uncommon for consumers to have extreme brand loyalty to either Chevrolet or Ford, especially in the purchase of light trucks. Therefore, most of the vehicles sold under the Chevrolet brand name start with a competitive advantage over many other existing brands of vehicles. This is why General Motors uses the Chevrolet brand name on a broader diversity of their vehicles than any other brand. For instance, Cadillac, Buick, and GMC have much narrower portfolios of vehicles and more distinct brand images. Consequently, the Chevrolet brand is an asset to the launch of a new vehicle such as the Volt, an electric vehicle.

Over the years Chevrolet has had many models, and not all of those models are discussed in this case. Case Exhibit 9.1 shows the entire portfolio of Chevrolet vehicle models sold in the United States. Here, we look at a number of models that represents the diversity of the Chevrolet product mix that exists today.

Chevrolet is credited with being the first carmaker to create the idea of planned product obsolescence. Based on this concept, Chevrolet introduces a new car model each year, a type of product modification. This marketing strategy allowed Chevrolet to overtake Ford in sales. Many consumers look forward to each new model and are often encouraged to trade in cars every year.

CASE EXHIBIT 9.1   **Chevrolet Models Sold within the United States**

Cars	SUVs/Crossovers	Trucks/Vans	Electric Vehicles
Sonic	Equinox	Colorado	Volt
Cruze	Traverse	Avalanche	
Malibu	Tahoe	Silverado	
Corvette	Suburban	Express	
Camaro			
Impala			
Spark			

Source: Based on Chevrolet website (http://www.chevrolet.com), accessed July 25, 2012.

Like all established companies, Chevrolet vehicles underwent several successes and failures. Some vehicles that Chevrolet thought would succeed failed miserably. The 1962 Chevy Corvair was a popular Chevy vehicle until Ralph Nader published *Unsafe at Any Speed*, which pointed out safety issues with the Corvair's steering. The car was eventually deleted from Chevrolet's product mix. The Chevy Vega was another product failure after complaints of the car's poor quality and product recalls created negative publicity. On the other hand, many Chevrolet vehicles became immensely popular, and some, such as the sporty Corvette, still exist today. The following vehicles helped cement Chevrolet's reputation as an icon.

Chevy Corvette

The Chevy Corvette is one of Chevrolet's most important milestones. The Corvette, first revealed at a car show in 1953, was GM's initial foray into the sports car world. Despite initial enthusiasm for the Corvette, the first ones were not very popular. The introduction of the small-block V8 engine in 1955 changed that. GM engineer Zora Arkus-Duntov began to work with the engine to turn the Corvette into a racing vehicle. One year later, Arkus-Duntov raced the revamped Corvette at the Pikes Peak Hill Climb race. Arkus-Duntov won the race for his class and set a new record for stock cars. The 1957 Corvette achieved a reputation for speed, achieving 60 miles per hour (mph) in 5.7 seconds. The Corvette had embarked upon its reputation as "America's sports car."

Chevrolet attempted to position the Corvette as a combination of sportiness and luxury. For instance, one of its early taglines was "looks like a sports car…feels like a sports car…performs like a sports car…how come it's a luxury car?" The Corvette has gone through six generations, with each successive model undergoing additional modifications in quality and style.

The Corvette has attracted many fans over the years, both on and off the racetrack. Corvette owners have included Alan Shepard (astronaut), Johnny Carson, Jeff Gordon, Jay Leno, and Vice President Joe Biden. The Corvette's fame has made it into a prestigious product with models selling from $50,000 to over $100,000. To celebrate its 100th birthday in 2012, Chevrolet announced the release of the Corvette Centennial edition, available only in carbon flash metallic.

Although the Corvette is still going strong, it has likely reached the maturity stage due to product innovations on newer Chevrolet models and changing customer tastes. The maturity stage occurs when growth begins to slow. In the case of the Corvette, the average owner is in his or her fifties, which means that younger people are not purchasing them as much, perhaps because they perceive the Corvette as the car that their parents or grandparents drove. In 2009, Corvette sales were the lowest they had been since 1961, and Corvette sales had decreased 48.3 percent since the year before. Some speculated that interest in sports cars was waning. However, this does not necessarily mean the Corvette is going away anytime soon. Whereas it looked as if the model might be declining in 2009, Corvette sales reached a 19-month high in 2011. Loyal fans and the Corvette's reputation as America's sports car could keep the Corvette going strong for many more years.

Chevrolet Camaro

The Camaro is the story of a car model that would not be conquered. GM released the Camaro in 1967 to directly compete against the Ford Mustang. The competitive intent behind the Camaro was soon clear; when asked what the name of the small sportster meant, product managers stated that it was the name of an animal that ate mustangs. The model has gone through five generations and many ups and downs in popularity over its 35-year run. Toward the turn of the century, it became clear that GM was considering discontinuing the Camaro, as new lineups did not have significant changes in design from previous ones. In 2002, the Camaro line was officially discontinued. Eight years later, due to the pressure from dedicated fans, GM resurrected the Camaro with the release of the 2010 model. The new Camaro blended design elements from the 1960s with modern features, including Bluetooth connectivity, USB connectivity, and OnStar. It also took advantage of car lovers' demands for speed. The car went on to win the 2010 World Car Design of the Year award. In fact, the Camaro was attributed to keeping the sports car industry from floundering. The recently released car sold well even in the midst of a recession, with sales of over 60,000 vehicles.

When the new Camaro was announced in 2009, demand was so high that GM strived to create enough supply. Enthusiasts were paying $500 to $2,500 above the sticker price. Although demand has stabilized somewhat, the Camaro seems to be in the growth stage of the product life cycle. In 2009, when convertible sales were at a low, the Chevy Camaro sold well. Two years later it was outselling the Ford Mustang. Resurrecting the Camaro appears to be a smart move on Chevrolet's part, but fierce competition and rapidly changing consumer tastes will require the company to continually modify its product in order to maintain its competitive advantage.

Chevrolet Impala

The Chevrolet Impala was introduced in 1958 and went on to become one of Chevrolet's best-known brand names. As a full-size family sedan, the Impala is one of Chevrolet's larger car models. The Impala experienced extreme growth during the 1960s. Its 1963 model, with its small-block V8 engine and front bucket seats, is now considered to be a collector's item. The Impala's best-selling year occurred in 1965 with sales of 1 million vehicles. Its popularity continued throughout the 1970s, and it was named the best-selling car in 1973.

The Chevy Impala has undergone ten generations of new models. Its 1994–1996 models have also become collector's items largely due to their luxurious design and strong horsepower. The Impala is a common sight in the NASCAR races after it replaced the Monte Carlo, a car model discontinued by GM. However, the Impala has encountered a number of challenges during its long life span. The Impala began losing sales to midsized cars in the 1980s and continues to contend with its smaller rivals to this day. In addition, a suspension problem in Impala vehicles sold in 2007 and 2008 caused a class-action lawsuit to be filed against GM.

Despite these challenges, the Impala remains an industry leader in its segment. The Impala sold over 170,000 vehicles in 2010, an improvement of almost 4 percent from the year before. The amount of space the Impala offers and its better fuel efficiency gives it a competitive advantage. Yet its 2012 model received lackluster reviews and was criticized for using "cheap interior materials and construction." Whether consumers perceive the vehicle similarly will largely determine if sales of the newest Chevy Impala will grow or stagnate.

Chevrolet Cruze

The 2010 Chevrolet Cruze was a risk that paid off for Chevrolet. This five-seat sedan designed to replace the unpopular Chevy Cobalt jumped almost immediately from the introductory to the growth stage. The success of the Cruze shocked industry experts. Within its first year of sales, the Cruze ranked as the tenth most popular vehicle within the United States. In June 2011, it became the nation's best-selling car.

The Cruze was released as a global vehicle. It was introduced in Europe in 2009 and has since expanded to the United States, India, China, Mexico, and Russia. Approximately 270,000 vehicles have been sold in over 60 countries. The sedan combines safety, technology, speed, and greater fuel efficiency, sporting 10 airbags and a 1.8-liter four-cylinder engine. The 2012 version of the Cruze, the Cruze Eco, can get 42 miles per gallon (mpg) on the highway, currently the highest mileage for traditional gas powered vehicles within the United States. Improved fuel economy is particularly important in light of impending federal legislation mandating that vehicles get better mileage.

To promote the Cruze, Chevrolet released a series of advertisements voiced by actor Tim Allen that tell viewers to "get used to more" while touting the Cruze's technological advances and price tag of $17,000. The company chose to take an adversarial approach to the competition; its "Dear Corolla" advertisements subtly criticize the Toyota Corolla for not offering the latest technology in its vehicles. Such an approach recognizes the highly competitive industry the Chevy Cruze occupies.

In spite of its initial success, analysts believe that the Ford Focus or Hyundai Sonata could easily supplant the Cruze. In many ways, the increasingly competitive nature of the auto industry has shortened the life cycles of many vehicle brands; whereas vehicles such as the Corvette have experienced long periods of growth, a competitive environment and increased government regulation could significantly shorten the Cruze's growth period to a small number of years. It remains to be seen whether Chevrolet will be able to maintain the Cruze's competitive advantage over the long-term or quickly lose it to better-adapted rivals.

Chevrolet Silverado

Chevrolet's pickup trucks are even more popular than its cars. After introducing its first truck in 1918, sales of Chevrolet pickup trucks surpassed car sales in 1989. Chevrolet positions its trucks as strong and durable, using the successful ad slogan "Like a Rock" in all its truck commercials for a decade. Its most popular truck is the Silverado. According to *USA Today*, sales of the Silverado surpass the gross domestic product of several countries. Successive models of the Silverado have been manufactured to ensure a smoother ride, increase towing capacity, and improve fuel economy. For instance, the newer Silverado HD increased fuel efficiency by 11 percent. Improvements to the Chevrolet Silverado pickup have resounded with consumers.

The Silverado is available as three different types of pickup truck: light duty, heavy duty, and hybrid. Chevrolet's heavy duty (HD) Silverado pickup truck won automobile magazine *Motor Trend*'s Truck of the Year award for its ability to tow 21,700 pounds, its reduced vibrations, and its smoother ride. The ability to haul or tow large loads seemed to gain importance during the recession. For those who love big trucks but hate the large amounts of emissions they generate, the Silverado HD comes equipped with a new system that reduces nitrogen-oxide emissions.

Chevrolet is trying to discover the right blend between America's love for big trucks (the two best-selling vehicles in 2011 were trucks) and being environmentally friendly. As a result, it began manufacturing a hybrid Silverado. The hybrid Silverado has many of the same characteristics of a traditional Silverado, including high torque and horsepower, yet it can get 20 mpg in the city and 23 mpg on the highway (versus 15 mpg in the city and 20 mpg on the highway for the light duty Silverado). By making the Silverado greener, Chevrolet is not only preparing itself for tougher emissions regulations, but also appealing to the market's demand for less-polluting trucks.

Chevrolet SUVs/Crossover Vehicles

SUVs, or sports-utility vehicles, became a hit during the 1990s as they provided owners with a sense of prestige and power. To meet this demand, GM created several SUV lines such as the Hummer. However, because SUVs require so much fuel, rising gas prices and greater concern for the environment contributed to their decline. As a result, GM discontinued its Hummer line along with several of its Chevrolet SUVs, including the Trailblazer.

Although SUVs seemed to be on the decline, they appear to be gaining in popularity once more. In 2008, when fuel prices were high, many consumers began switching to hybrid vehicles and smaller cars with greater fuel efficiency. However, when gas prices dropped to under $4 a gallon, SUVs made a comeback—with some slight modifications. Auto companies such as GM began manufacturing SUVs with better fuel efficiency. The safety of SUVs has also improved. Thanks to the addition of stability control within SUV models, studies indicate that drivers of SUVs are less likely to die in a crash than those driving smaller cars; the death rate for SUV drivers dropped 66 percent after newer models were introduced.

This is good news for Chevrolet's SUVs, which include the Suburban and the Tahoe. First emerging in 1936, the Suburban is the oldest surviving vehicle model in the United States. Today the Suburban appears to be in the growth stage as a favorite among families and was nominated by Kelley Blue Book as one of the Top 10 Family Cars for 2011. One likely reason is due to its safety features, which include six airbags and traction control. In contrast, the Tahoe is targeted more toward those who need lots of space and who travel in more rugged terrain. The Tahoe has been one of the most popular SUV models since the 1990s. To attract eco-conscious consumers, Chevrolet also has a hybrid Tahoe model that gets 20 mpg in the city and 23 mpg on the highway.

Chevrolet also combines features of smaller cars with those of SUVs through its crossover vehicles. One of its most recent successes is the Chevrolet Traverse. Released in 2008, the Chevrolet Traverse is targeted toward families. Kelly Blue Book also nominated it as one of the Top 10 Family Cars for 2011. The Traverse can seat eight and received high scores in crash safety from the National Highway Traffic Safety Administration. Sales of the Traverse grew 17 percent in 2010 from the previous year. The Chevrolet Equinox crossover vehicle is unique as it is powered by hydrogen fuel cells, making it more fuel-efficient than its contemporaries. Combined with its spacious interior, the advantages of the Equinox led to its nomination by Auto Press to the highest place on its list of Affordable Compact SUVs for 2012.

Chevrolet Volt

Chevrolet's product mix would not be complete without venturing into the electric vehicle industry. Its Chevrolet Volt, unleashed in 2010, runs on a battery but also uses gasoline once the electrical charge is depleted. The Volt's battery allows the vehicle to travel 35 miles on electricity; it can then travel 37 more miles using gas.

Initial views of the Volt seemed positive. In 2011, it was named as the winner of the World's Green Car award. However, the Volt may take longer than anticipated to go from the introductory to the growth stage of the product life cycle. GM's plans to sell 10,000 Volts in 2011 were too optimistic; only approximately 8,000 Chevrolet Volts were sold. Many Chevrolet dealers were hesitant to sell the Volt due to a perceived lack of local demand. Such obstacles are not uncommon with new products, as both dealers and consumers need to learn more about the product before making a commitment to purchase it. The high price tag of $41,000 also increases the risk of purchase. While the current interest in electric vehicles is high, demand may take longer to catch up due to the high level of perceived purchase risk.

The Volt faced a more serious challenge when its lithium-ion battery proved to be problematic in crashes. The battery caught on fire after three government crash tests, but the fires themselves would not occur until days or weeks after the crashes. Further investigations revealed that the coolant line got damaged during the crash tests. Coolant leaked onto the battery wires, eventually causing a fire.

After these safety issues came to light, GM took quick action to address the problem. It created a plan to increase the reinforcement surrounding the battery pack and issued a voluntary recall on the more than 7,000 Volts already sold as well as the more than 4,000 in its showrooms. It also provided loaner cars for consumers to use until their Volts were modified and offered to buy Volts back from customers who no longer wanted them. Although this quick action might have saved the Volt from an early demise, the initial safety challenges could still have a significant effect on demand.

The safety issues have also provided threats and opportunities for the Chevy Volt's prime competitor, the Nissan Leaf. Although both the Leaf and the Volt are electric vehicles, they are positioned differently. The Nissan is a truly electric car, whereas the Volt will run on gasoline if needed. GM's VP of marketing saw this as a major advantage, using it to position the Volt as "a car first and electric second" and claimed that the Volt can give drivers the peace of mind that they will not become stranded if they use up the electricity reserves. However, the recent battery fires have reduced faith in the Volt and cast doubt on the electric vehicle industry as a whole. Nissan was quick to respond to these safety concerns by detailing the triple layer safety structure of its batteries. In 2011, the Nissan Leaf appeared to be taking the lead in the number of vehicles sold, but the Volt was catching up. With analysts predicting that only one will win in grabbing the majority of the U.S. market share, the stakes are high.

Chevrolet's Branding Strategy

Although the Chevrolet brand has evolved over the years, it maintains many of the same themes that it started out with a century ago: a quality vehicle with deep roots in America's past. When Durant first envisioned Chevrolet, his desire was to create a low-priced vehicle that could compete head on with Ford. Therefore, one of its first slogans, "Quality at low cost" comes as no surprise. As Chevrolet vehicles became more popular with Americans, minus a dip during the Great Depression, the company wanted to firmly entrench the brand as a key part of American culture. It found part of this solution by associating itself with American sporting events. In 1935, Chevrolet started sponsoring the All-American Soap Box Derby, which it would continue to support for the next decade. Chevrolet vehicles driven by drivers such as Jeff Gordon and Jimmie Johnson would go on to become a common sight in racing circuits.

On the promotional side, Chevrolet adopted a patriotic theme with taglines such as "America's Best Seller, America's Best Buy" and "Baseball, hot dogs, apple pie and Chevrolet." One of its most popular taglines "Like a Rock" began in 1991 to describe its Chevrolet pickup truck. The tagline imbued the brand with a sense of strength and durability. Chevrolet would continue its American theme with its "An American Revolution" tagline adopted in 1994 and its most recent "Chevy Runs Deep."

The Chevrolet brand resonates with consumers, so much so that the company's marketers must exert caution when implementing changes. For instance, in 2010 GM decided the company would stop using the popular American nickname Chevy and only use Chevrolet in corporate communications and advertising. Although American consumers were encouraged to still use the popular nickname, employees were not to use Chevy internally. The reasoning behind this was that international buyers of Chevrolet tended to get "Chevy" and "Chevrolet" confused, believing that they were different cars. However, consumer backlash and managerial changes convinced GM to drop this plan.

Changing the tagline to "Chevy Runs Deep" has not been free from criticism either. Chevrolet fans did not feel that the slogan was as strong as previous ones, and others were unsure about what it meant. This confusion caused GM to begin overhauling its marketing to clear up the confusion. According to Chevrolet's marketing director, the tagline is meant to have an emotional impact while tying Chevrolet to its American heritage.

While Chevrolet modifies its taglines to fit certain countries, many of its taglines are used for multiple countries to create strong brand cohesiveness. Globally, the company positions its vehicles along four values: durability, value, practicality, and friendliness. In South Africa, Chevrolet commercials have emphasized familial values as well as excitement. Taglines include "Captiva. Made for Memories." and "Where Will Chevrolet Take You?" Although Chevrolet has adopted more of a global brand strategy, it still customizes its branding to appeal to certain markets.

General Motors' Rivalry with Ford

General Motors is one of the "Big Three" carmakers in the United States, along with Ford and Chrysler. Although Ford and Chrysler are formidable competitors to Chevrolet, most view Ford as being the more serious rival. Ford and Chevy vehicles are both considered to be practical and affordable cars, and although Chevy is generally viewed as being sportier than Ford, Ford's sports vehicles like the Mustang are direct competitors to Chevy's sports cars. While Chrysler came onto the scene later during the 1920s, Ford and Chevrolet are closer in age and have been competing since the inception of Chevrolet.

This highly competitive rivalry has challenged many of Chevrolet's branding strategies. For instance, Ford is also deeply entrenched in American culture. Many view the Model T as the first American car, although it would be more accurate to say it was the first one produced for the masses. The unproven statement by founder Henry Ford regarding the Model T, "You can paint it any color, so long as it's black," is remembered nearly a century later. Ford also claims that its Ford Aerospace engineers and technicians helped place a man on the moon by helping to design and provide services for NASA's Mission Control Center. Supporters of Ford are more likely to view Ford as a greater part of America's heritage than Chevrolet.

From the beginning, Ford has also made a name for itself in racing history, starting with founder Henry Ford's 1901 win against professional driver Alexander Winton in a vehicle he manufactured himself. Ever since racing has become an important part of Ford's DNA. The car company has had a notable presence in the Indy 500, Formula One, and NASCAR series, with drivers like Tom Kendall, Jacques Villeneuve, John Force, and even Paul Newman choosing to race Ford vehicles. Creating solid connections to America's past is an important part of Ford's branding strategy.

Ford and General Motors also take very different approaches toward marketing. While Chevrolet's tagline "Chevy Runs Deep" is an attempt to position the brand as a critical part of America's heritage, Ford's tagline "Ford. Drive One." and its previous taglines of "Bold Moves" and "Have You Driven a Ford Lately?" evoke a more exclusive image than Chevrolet. Ford and GM also differ in how they brand their vehicles. Ford takes a family branding approach to its vehicles, placing the Ford name along with the brand of the vehicle on the car. General Motors, however, has embraced invisible brand architecture, beginning in 2009. Prior to this time, GM was placing its "Mark of Excellence" logo on its vehicles to connect them with the parent company. But in 2009, GM expressed its intention of allowing its vehicles to stand on its own. New Chevrolet vehicles will not have any visible affiliation with GM, nor will GM's other brands. This branding strategy has both advantages and disadvantages. Family branding informs consumers when the same company offers a slate of different vehicles. If the consumer has a favorable impression of the company or even an individual model, then he or she is likely to carry that perception over to another company model. On the other hand, family branding risks contaminating the entire family if one product in the mix is perceived to be inferior. In the case of GM, the company's bankruptcy and subsequent bailout had the ability to contaminate its four brands of vehicles, in spite of their individual merits. By adopting invisible brand architecture, GM is reducing the risk of brand contamination.

International Marketing

Chevrolet sells over 4 million vehicles in more than 140 countries and accounts for roughly 70 percent of all GM sales in foreign markets. While Chevrolet has tried to create a consistent brand image across the world, its products differ by market. For instance, South Africa Chevrolet's product line includes the Chevrolet Spark, Aveo, Lumina, Optra, Cruze, Orlando, and Sonic. In Brazil, Chevrolet's product line includes the Camaro as well as the Chevrolet Captiva, Prisma, S10, Meriva, Zafira, and Astra. The different models appeal to the differing tastes of Chevrolet's various target markets.

Although for years Chevrolet has portrayed itself as an American brand, in reality the brand has become truly globalized. In fact, marketers at Chevrolet are now trying to embed the Chevrolet brand into other cultures just as they set off to make it a core part of American culture. In an attempt to create greater brand awareness, GM has decided to rebrand Daewoo—a South Korean brand that GM acquired in the early 2000s—as Chevrolet. Despite the fact that sales of Daewoo vehicles have increased in recent years, GM recognizes that many South Koreans lack awareness of the Chevrolet brand. It hopes that recasting Daewoo as Chevrolet will increase awareness and allow Chevrolet to compete against its competitors.

Chevrolet's sales are still highest in the United States, followed by Brazil. However, China is not far behind. China is now the third largest market for Chevrolet and is the largest market in the world for vehicles. Chevrolet sells a variety of vehicles in China, including the Volt, Camaro, Captiva, Aveo, Sail, and Spark. GM has entered into several joint ventures with Chinese companies in order to sell Chevrolet vehicles within the country. China is also a lucrative market for electric vehicles (EVs), and Chevrolet is optimistic about how the Chevy Volt will fare. Yet the company also faces many challenges in its plans to introduce EVs into China. The Chinese government has mandated that foreign EV automakers enter into joint ventures with domestic companies to produce EVs in China. Such joint ventures offer many advantages but also require Chevrolet to share some of its trade secrets with its partners. For this reason, GM has decided to import the Chevy Volt, forgoing certain benefits rather than share the Volt's technologies.

Another challenge for Chevrolet relates to customization. Customizing vehicles to different markets takes time, and GM managers want to increase production and decrease the commercialization process. This has led GM to consider a new design for its vehicles that incorporates "global core architecture." Such a move would enable GM brands to create a more standardized design with slight adaptations for different markets. This would likely save GM both time and money, but because cultural tastes can significantly differ, a globalized design is not without risks. It is uncertain whether Chevrolet can create a standardized vehicle that will be accepted by several different cultures.

Challenges and Recovery

After nearly a century in business, Chevrolet faced its greatest threat with GM's bankruptcy in 2008. The company required a massive $50 billion government bailout, and although GM has rebounded, its reputation will take a while to recover. According to GM CEO Dan Akerson, the company "failed because we failed to innovate." Ford, the only one of the Big Three automakers that did not accept a government bailout, took a combative approach against its competitors in its advertising. The company filmed one ad of a customer who had just bought a new Ford pickup truck as saying, "I wasn't going to buy another car that was bailed out by our government. I was going to buy from a manufacturer that's standing on their own: win, lose, or draw." Although the commercial was later pulled from the air (Ford stated that it had run its course), this viewpoint represented the sentiments of many Americans who felt that GM and Chrysler had overextended themselves and then depended upon taxpayers to bail them out for their mistakes.

Despite these dark times for GM, CEO Akerson stated that he viewed Chevrolet as an innovation powerhouse and believed the brand would bring GM back from the brink of collapse. The recovery, however, has been painful for GM. The company dropped half its brands from its product mix, including Pontiac, Hummer, Saturn, and Saab. Although this gives customers fewer vehicle brands from which to choose, it might benefit Chevrolet in the long run as GM can now focus more upon modifying its remaining brands.

Such modifications will be important as environmental conditions in the market continue to change. For instance, new and impending regulations require automakers to create vehicles that are more fuel efficient. By 2025, vehicles must be able to reach 54.5 miles per gallon. Such changes will be costly and demand that GM take action now. Thus, new Chevrolet vehicles are likely to be lighter and possess more energy saving technologies. Such modifications are essential to ensuring that Chevrolet meets both consumer demands and the regulatory demands of the government.

The Chevrolet brand is a model to which marketers aspire. Unlike so many other brands, it has lasted for a century due to its innovative product modifications and ability to rebound from failures. It must continue to seize market opportunities, constantly modify its products, and adapt its brand to changing customer tastes. Successfully meeting these criteria could enable the Chevrolet brand to succeed for another century.

Questions for Discussion

1. Evaluate the diversity of vehicle types and sizes that are sold under the Chevrolet brand name. What strengths and weaknesses are evident in Chevy's product mix?

2. How has Chevrolet strategically managed its brand and reputation over the last 100 years? What opportunities and threats will affect Chevy's branding and reputation in the future?

3. What specific marketing strategies would you recommend that might help Chevrolet last another 100 years? How important is Chevy's legacy of innovation to the brand's future?

Sources

AutolineDetroit, "Chevy Cruze: The Most Important Car in GM History," YouTube, September 16, 2010 (http://www.youtube.com/watch?v=87WlQU23WgY); Keith Barry, "Ground Control: Celebrating Astronauts and their Corvettes," *Wired*, May 9, 2011 (http://www.wired.com/autopia/2011/05/astronauts-chevrolet-cor vette); Jim Bernardin, "About Old Chevy Ads," February 7, 2008 (http://oldchevyads.blogspot.com/2008/02/63-corvette-magazine_1336.html); Henry Biggs, "Top 10: Muscle Cars," MSN, March 2, 2006 (http://cars.uk.msn.com/news/articles.aspx?cp-documentid=147864031); Keith Bradsher, "G.M. Plans to Develop Electric Cars With China," *New York Times*, September 20, 2011 (http://www.nytimes.com/2011/09/21/business/global/gm-plans-to-develop-electric-cars-with-chinese-automaker.html); Dave Caldwell, "Monte Carlo Off the Track," *New York Times*, November 25, 2007 (http://www.nytimes.com/2007/11/25/automobiles/25MONTE.html); "Chevrolet" (http://www.superbrands.com/za/pdfs/CHEV.pdf), accessed July 27, 2012; "Chevrolet Camaro History," Edmunds (http://www.edmunds.com/chevrolet/camaro/history.html), accessed July 27, 2012; "Chevrolet Camaro—World Car Design of the Year 2010," AUSmotive.com, April 8, 2010 (http://www.ausmotive.com/2010/04/08/chevrolet-camaro-world-car-design-of-the-year-2010.html); Chevrolet China (http://www.chevrolet.com.cn/brandsite), accessed July 27, 2012; "Chevrolet Corvette History," Edmunds (http://www.edmunds.com/chevrolet/corvette/history.html), accessed July 27, 2012; "Chevrolet Equinox Review," *US News & World Report*, February 27, 2012 (http://usnews.rankingsandreviews.com/cars-trucks/Chevrolet_Equinox); "Chevrolet Impala Review," Edmunds (http://www.edmunds.com/chevrolet/impala), accessed July 27, 2012; Chevrolet South Africa, "Chevrolet Captiva Gold Commercial," YouTube, June 14, 2011 (http://www.youtube.com/watch?v=uogbShJddNY); Chevrolet South Africa, "Chevrolet TV Commercial," YouTube, July 30, 2010 (http://www.youtube.com/watch?v=BmswxNKGG9w&NR=1&feature=endscreen); "Chevrolet Suburban Review," Edmunds (http://www.edmunds.com/chevrolet/suburban), accessed July 27, 2012; "Chevrolet Suburban and Traverse Named Top 10 Family Cars by Kelley Blue Book's kbb.com," General Motors, February 24, 2011 (http://media.gm.com/content/media/us/en/chevrolet/news.detail.html/content/Pages/news/us/en/2011/Feb/0224_Chevrolet); "Chevrolet Tahoe Review," Edmunds (http://www.edmunds.com/chevrolet/tahoe), accessed July 27, 2012; "Chevrolet Turns 100," *Automobile*, November 2011, 53–97; Chevrolet website (http://www.chevrolet.com), accessed July 27, 2012; "Chevrolet Volt," Chevrolet (http://www.chevrolet.com/volt-electric-car), accessed July 27, 2012; Bill Connell, "Astronauts and Corvettes," Corvette Blog, September 2, 2007 (http://www.corvetteblog.com/2007/09/celebrity-corvettes-astronauts-and-corvettes); Kevin Cool, "Heavy Metal," *Stanford Magazine*, September/October 2004 (http://alumni.stanford.edu/get/page/magazine/article/?article_id=35646), accessed December 21, 2011; "Corvette Drops to 50-Year Sales Low as Sports Cars Sputter, Reports Edmunds' AutoObserver.com," Edmunds, January 21, 2010 (http://www.edmunds.com/about/press/corvette-drops-to-50-year-sales-low-as-sports-cars-sputter-reports-edmunds-autoobservercom.html); Matt Davis, "2011 World Car Awards: How close it was," *Auto Blog*, April 27, 2011 (http://www.autoblog.com/2011/04/27/2011-world-car-awards-how-close-it-was); Lindsey Fisher, "Corvette Sales Reach 19-Month Record High in April," *Corvette Online*, May 5, 2011 (http://www.corvetteonline.com/news/corvette-sales-reach-19-month-record-high-in-april); "From 0 to 100," *The Economist*, October 29, 2011, 76; Burton W. Fulsom, "Billy Durant and the Founding of General Motors," Mackinac Center for Public Policy, September 8, 1998 (http://www.mackinac.org/article.aspx?ID=651); Jon Gertner, "How Do You Solve a Problem like GM, Mary?" *Fast Company*, October 2011, pp. 104–108, 148; "GM rebrands GM Daewoo as Chevrolet in S. Korea," *Reuters*, January 19, 2011 (http://www.reuters.com/article/2011/01/20/gmdaewoo-chevy-idUSTOE70I05A20110120); Allyson Harwood, "2011 Motor Trend Truck Of The Year: Chevrolet Silverado HD," *Motor Trend*, December 12, 2010 (http://www.motortrend.com/oftheyear/truck/1102_2011_motor_trend_truck_of_the_year_chevrolet_silverado_hd/viewall.html#ixzz1hCvSvs7t); James R. Healy, "100 Years of Chevy," *USA Today*, October 31, 2011, 1B, 2B; James Healey "2012 Chevy Cruze Eco: Mileage gain, no pain," *USA Today*, May 27, 2011 (http://www.usatoday.com/money/autos/reviews/healey/2011-05-26-chevrolet-cruze-eco-test-drive_n.htm); Jim Henry, "Nissan Says Batteries for the Nissan Leaf Can Take a Licking,"

Forbes, December 22, 2011 (http://www.forbes.com/sites/jimhenry/2011/12/22/nissan-says-batteries-for-the-nis san-leaf-can-take-a-licking); "Heritage," Ford website (http://corporate.ford.com/our-company/heritage), accessed July 27, 2012; Dan Ikenson, "Ford Pulling Anti-Bailout Ad Shows Ongoing Ripples From Washington," *Forbes*, September 27, 2011 (http://www.forbes.com/sites/beltway/2011/09/27/ford-pulling-anti-bailout-ad-shows-ongoing-rip ples-from-washington); Cheryl Jensen, "Forecast Says China Provides Opportunities and Competi-tion," *New York Times*, August 23, 2010 (http://wheels.blogs.nytimes.com/2010/04/23/forecast-says-china-pro vides-opportu nities-and-competition); Bradley Johnson, "From 'See the USA in your Chevrolet' to 'Like a Rock,' Chevy Ads Run Deep," *Advertising Age*, October 31, 2011 (http://adage.com/article/special-report-chevy-100/100-years-chev rolet-advertising-a-timeline/230636/#2000); Soyoung Kim, "GM bans use of 'Chevy' brand name internally," *Reuters*, June 10, 2010 (http://www.reuters.com/article/2010/06/10/gm-chevy-idUSN1024152620100610); Jeremy Korzeniewski, "Tagline shuffle: 'Bold Moves' out, 'Ford. Drive One' in," *AutoBlog*, March 19, 2008 (http://www.autoblog.com/2008/03/19/tagline-shuffle-bold-moves-out-ford-drive-one-in); Jeremy Korzeniewski, "Report: New slogan 'Chevy Runs Deep' coming this fall [w/poll]," *AutoBlog*, Octo-ber 25, 2010 (http://www.autoblog.com/2010/10/25/report-new-slogan-chevy-runs-deep-coming-this-fall-w-poll); Charles Krome, "2011 Chevrolet Impala: The Same As Ever," *Autobytel*, February 15, 2011 (http://www.auto bytel.com/chevrolet/impala/2011/car-buying-guides/2011-chevrolet-impala-same-as-it-ever-was-104636); Katie LaBarre, "2012 Suburban Safety," *US News*, March 7, 2012 (http://usnews.rankingsandreviews.com/cars-trucks/Chevrolet_Suburban/Safety); Katie LaBarre, "Chevrolet Tahoe Review," *US News & World Report*, February 3, 2012 (http://usnews.rankingsandre views.com/cars-trucks/Chevrolet_Tahoe); Joann Muller, "Ford Looks Hypo-critical In New Anti-Bailout Commercial," *Forbes*, September 19, 2011 (http://www.forbes.com/sites/joannmul ler/2011/09/19/ford-looks-hypocritical-in-new-anti-bailout-commercial); Joann Muller, "The best-selling vehicles of 2011," *MSNBC*, November 9, 2011 (http://www.msnbc.msn.com/id/45165770/ns/business-forbes_com/t/best-selling-vehicles); Dan Neil, "Brand-New and Almost Out of Date," *Wall Street Journal*, July 31, 2010 (http://online.wsj.com/article/SB10001424052748703578104575397271724890814.html); "New Chevrolet Corvette Reviews, Specs, & Pricing," *Motor Trend* (http://www.motortrend.com/new_cars/04/chevrolet/corvette), accessed July 27, 2012; Jayne O'Donnell, "Chevrolet races to meet demand for 2010 Camaro," *USA Today*, June 29, 2009 (http://www.usatoday.com/money/autos/2009-06-28-camaro-chevrolet-2010_N.htm); Jayne O'Donnell and Rachel Roubein, "SUVs safer than ever, but small cars still perilous," *USA Today*, June 9, 2011 (http://www.usatoday.com/money/autos/2011-06-09-suv-crash-death-rates-drop_n.htm); "100 Years of Icons," Chevrolet Culture, (http://www.chevrolet.com/culture/article/iconicchevys), accessed July 27, 2012; Mike Ramsey and Sharon Terlep, "Americans Embrace SUVs Again," *Wall Street Journal*, December 2, 2011 (http://online.wsj.com/article/SB10001424052970204012004577072132855087336.html); Aaron Robinson, "2008 Chevrolet Equi-nox Fuel Cell," *Car and Driver*, September 2006 (http://www.caranddriver.com/news/2008-chevrolet-equinox-fuel-cell-car-news), accessed July 27, 2012; Norihiko Shirouzu, "China Spooks Auto Makers," *Wall Street Jour-nal*, September 16, 2010 (http://online.wsj.com/article/SB10001424052748704394704575495480368918268.html); Chris Shunk, "Video: Chevrolet Cruze ads ramps up," *AutoBlog*, September 8, 2010 (http://www.autoblog.com/2010/09/08/video-chevrolet-cruze-ads-ramp-up/#continued); Chuck Squatriglia, "Feds OK GM's Fix for Volt Battery Pack," *Wired*, January 5, 2012 (http://www.wired.com/autopia/2012/01/feds-ok-gms-redesign-of-volt-battery-pack); Jonathon Stempel, "GM says bankruptcy excuses it from Impala repairs," *Reuters*, August 19, 2011 (http://www.reuters.com/article/2011/08/19/gm-impala-lawsuit-idUSN1E77I0Z820110819); Alex Taylor III, "Chevy Volt vs. Nissan Leaf: Who's winning?" *CNNMoney*, September 15, 2011 (http://tech.fortune.cnn.com/2011/09/15/chevy-volt-vs-nissan-leaf-whos-winning); "Ten Chevrolet Trucks That Built a Global Brand," General Motors, November 22, 2011 (http://media.gm.com/content/media/us/en/chevrolet/news.detail.html/con tent/Pages/news/us/en/2011/Nov/1121_truckhistory); Sharon Terlep, "The Secrets of the GM Diet," *Wall Street Journal*, August 5, 2011 (http://online.wsj.com/article/SB10001424053111903454504576487822808431928.html); Sharon Terlep, "Slow Sales Dogged Volt Before Fires," *Wall Street Journal*, December 5, 2011 (http://online.wsj.com/article/SB10001424052970204903804577078692310067200.html); "The 2012 Chevrolet Cruze," Chevro-let (http://www.chevrolet.com/cruze-compact-car), accessed July 27, 2012; "The Model T," Showroom of Auto-motive History (http://www.hfmgv.org/exhibits/showroom/1908/model.t.html), accessed July 27, 2012; "The Top 10 Moments in Chevrolet Motor Sports," Chevrolet (http://www.chevrolet.com/culture/article/chevy-rac ing-history.html), accessed July 27, 2012; David Thomas, "Chevy drops ad campaign 'Like a Rock'," *AutoBlog*, August 8, 2004 (http://www.autoblog.com/2004/08/08/chevy-drops-ad-campaign-like-a-rock); Chrissie Thomp-son, "Chevrolet Cruze's success shocks the auto industry," *USA Today*, November 6, 2011 (http://content.usa today.com/commu nities/driveon/post/2011/11/chevrolet-cruze-general-motors-gm-big-sales/1); "2010 Chevrolet Camaro Preview," JDPower.com (http://www.jdpower.com/content/detail.htm?jdpaArticleId=759), accessed July 27, 2012; "2012 Chevrolet Impala," Edmunds (http://www.edmunds.com/chevrolet/impala/2012), accessed July 27, 2012; Peter Valdes-Dapena, "GM dumps Chevy for Chevrolet," *CNN Money*, June 10, 2010 (http://money.cnn.com/2010/06/10/autos/gm_no_chevy/index.htm); David Welch, "GM Looking to Reboot Chevrolet Advertising Campaign After a Slow Start," *Bloomberg*, August 31, 2011 (http://www.bloomberg.com/news/2011-08-31/gm-looking-to-reboot-chevrolet-advertising-campaign-after-a-slow-start.html); "What Marketers Can Learn From Ford," Branding Strategy Insider, August 13, 2010 (http://www.brandingstrategyinsider.com/2010/

08/what-marketers-can-learn-from-ford.html); Chris Woodyard, "General Motors to remove its 'Mark of Excellence' logos from new cars," *USA Today*, August 26, 2009 (http://content.usatoday.com/communities/driveon/post/2009/08/68497806/1); Chris Woodyard, "Sales shockers: Chevrolet Camaro whipping Ford Mustang," *USA Today*, April 4, 2011 (http://content.usatoday.com/communities/driveon/post/2011/04/sales-shockers-chevrolet-camaro-whipping-ford-mustang/1); Chris Woodyard, "Chevrolet Volt outsells Nissan Leaf," *USA Today*, December 4, 2011 (http://con tent.usatoday.com/communities/driveon/post/2011/12/electric-wars-chevrolt-volt-outsells-nissan-leaf-last-month/1); and Chris Woodyard, "Volt loses some potential buyers," *USA Today*, December 8, 2011, 1A.

CASE **10**

Wyndham Worldwide Adopts a Stakeholder Orientation Marketing Strategy*

Synopsis: From its founding in 1981, Wyndham Worldwide has emerged as a global powerhouse in the lodging, timeshare, and rental industry. Along the way, Wyndham struggled through several mergers and acquisitions and an inconsistent branding strategy. After struggling through the recession of 2008, Wyndham moved quickly to reinvigorate its core brands and launch new lodging concepts, all with a laser focus on a stakeholder orientation marketing strategy. This case briefly reviews Wyndham's history and challenges that the company faced in becoming the powerful brand that it is today. Wyndham's multifaceted stakeholder orientation marketing strategy is also reviewed with consideration for how Wyndham's brands have become synonymous with quality, ethical leadership, customer satisfaction, and sustainability.

Themes: Stakeholder orientation, marketing strategy, branding strategy, ethics, sustainability, social responsibility, corporate reputation, customer satisfaction, international marketing

Wyndham Worldwide, headquartered in Parsippany, New Jersey, is a leading global provider of travel-related services, including lodging, timeshare exchange, and rentals. The company can be broken down into three components: Wyndham Hotel Group, Wyndham Vacation Ownership, and Wyndham Exchange & Rentals. Each of these parts is comprised of different companies and brands that are well known in their own right. Despite the many services the organization offers, Wyndham Worldwide is best known for its hotel chains. Wyndham Hotel Group consists of more than 7,200 franchised hotels, including well-known brands such as Days Inn, Howard Johnson, Super 8, Ramada, and Planet Hollywood. Case Exhibit 10.1 provides an overview of Wyndham's product mix.

Since Wyndham Worldwide became an independent company in 2006, the company has achieved a solid reputation for quality and strong stakeholder management. Many different stakeholders view Wyndham Worldwide as a company that truly cares about

---

*Harper Baird and Jennifer Sawayda, University of New Mexico, developed this case, with assistance from Chandani Bhasin and Cassondra Lopez, under the direction of O.C. Ferrell and Linda Ferrell, University of New Mexico. The case is intended for classroom discussion rather than to illustrate effective or ineffective handling of an administrative situation.

CASE EXHIBIT 10.1   Wyndham's Product Mix

Wyndham Hotel Group	Wyndham Exchange & Rentals	Wyndham Vacation Ownership
Wyndham Hotels and Resorts	Wyndham Vacation Rentals	Club Wyndham
Wyndham Grand Collection	Landal Greenparks	Wyndham Vacation Resorts Asia Pacific
Wyndham Garden	cottages4you	WorldMark
TRYP	Canvas Holidays	
Wingate	James Villa Holidays	
Hawthorn Suites	Hoseasons	
Microtel Inns & Suites	RCI	
Dream Hotels	The Registry Collections	
Planet Hollywood		
Ramada Worldwide		
Night Hotels		
Baymont Inns & Suites		
Days Inn		
Super 8		
Howard Johnson		
Travelodge		
Knights Inn		

Source: Wyndham Worldwide website, (http://www.wyndhamworldwide.com/about-wyndham-worldwide/our-brands), accessed August 31, 2012.

their needs and concerns. The company's stakeholder initiatives and strong ethics and compliance programs are role models for practices within the hotel and resort industry.

History and Background

Trammel Crow founded Wyndham Hotel Corporation in 1981. The company grew rapidly and merged with Patriot American Hospitality, Inc. in 1998. The newly merged company was renamed Wyndham International, Inc. The new Wyndham embarked upon an aggressive acquisition strategy by acquiring other hotels and companies. However, the organization made the common mistake of growing too rapidly, acquiring massive debt in the process. Patriot American sought a $1 billion bailout from private investor groups. The company underwent an extensive restructuring process, in which Patriot became a wholly owned subsidiary of Wyndham International.

In 2005, Cendant Corp. bought the Wyndham hotel brand. The stock price of Cendant had remained stagnant since its merger with CUC International in 1997—a company that was later implicated in one of the largest accounting frauds of its time. Unfortunately for Cendant, the acquisition of Wyndham did not do much to raise its stock price. One year later, Cendant spun off its lodging, vacation exchange, and rental businesses to create Wyndham Worldwide and the Cendant name was officially retired.

Despite these changes, Wyndham Worldwide continued to face challenges. For instance, its hotel brands had earned a reputation for inconsistency. Each hotel seemed to differ from the other, making it difficult for Wyndham to establish a solid brand identity. CEO Stephen Holmes blamed its identity crisis on ineffective marketing by previous investors. Holmes believed the key to success was to create a consistent look for the brand and hired designer Michael Graves to redesign its hotels. Then the recession hit. With hotel demand decreasing, Wyndham posted a quarterly loss of $1.36 billion in 2009 and was forced to sell more shares to raise needed funds. However, the CEO for its hotel division, Eric Danziger, continued to work to create a more consistent brand image for Wyndham hotels. In creating its new image, the company also began expanding its international reach by acquiring hotel brands in major international cities. Today, Wyndham Worldwide is located on six continents and employs 25,000 people globally.

Wyndham's Branding Strategy

For some time, many people considered the quality of service and benefits at Wyndham hotels to be inconsistent. Hotel Group CEO Eric Danziger believed that past marketing initiatives conflicted with one another to muddle the company's brand identity. As part of the company's redesign, Wyndham sought to create a solid identity for each hotel chain that captured the feel of the chain's history and purpose. The company's goal was to create a "customer-centric lifestyle experience that will be relevant to guests across all tiers."

As part of its new brand strategy, each Wyndham hotel chain was redesigned with customers in mind. For instance, the Howard Johnson hotel chain's longer history prompted Wyndham to create an "iconic" atmosphere for these hotels that target leisure travelers and families. The experiential benefits of the Howard Johnson chain therefore include a family friendly environment and the ability to stay in a classic hotel at a reasonable price. On the other hand, Wyndham's more upscale hotel chains offer a completely different experience. Its Night Hotel in New York City claims to be "for the traveler who revels in all things after dark." The hotel tries to imbue a "sexy" feel with a chic eatery and bar as well as dark-colored furnishings. Wyndham's TRYP hotels are located in some of the world's largest cities in Europe, South America, and North America. The hotels are designed to fit in with the local environment and thus range from modernistic to historical designs. The hotels are meant to be an extension of the city in which they are located, enabling visitors to experience the excitement of the city even before leaving the hotel's doors. Wyndham hoped that the new identities for each hotel chain combined with consistent marketing would help solidify the brand and attract more customers.

Wyndham's Focus on Stakeholder Orientation

Wyndham Worldwide's vision is "to be the world's premier branded-hotel operating company." To help it achieve this goal, the company has adopted a stakeholder orientation marketing strategy to address the demands of a wide range of primary and secondary stakeholders. Stakeholder orientation in marketing involves activities and processes that create value through relationships with multiple stakeholders such as customers, suppliers, employees, shareholders, regulators, and the local community. Wyndham relies on their primary stakeholders for their continued success.

In order to satisfy relevant stakeholders, Wyndham gathers information, both formally and informally, to ascertain relevant issues of concern. However, a stakeholder orientation is not complete unless it includes activities that address specific stakeholder issues that reach or exceed expectations. This has led Wyndham to develop a number of initiatives, including benefits to its loyal customers and employees, community programs, and environmentally friendly practices. Wyndham gauges its stakeholder orientation through feedback from stakeholders and generation of data from across the organization, which then results in the assessment of the firm's effect on these groups.

Wyndham is aware that a stakeholder orientation is connected to market share performance, financial performance, reputation, and employee commitment. The company works "to maintain social responsibility, as a way of living, working and playing that fully encompasses the vision and values that Wyndham Worldwide has incorporated." A climate of ethics and social responsibility creates a large measure of trust among a firm's stakeholders. Wyndham Worldwide has therefore adopted five core values of corporate social responsibility including integrity, respect, individual opportunity and accountability, improving customer lives, and community support. These values guide how Wyndham interacts with its stakeholders.

Relationships with Customers

When customers consider the Wyndham brand, they most likely think of upscale hotel chains that cater to wealthy vacationers and businesspeople. In reality, Wyndham targets travelers from across all segments of the price spectrum. Hotels carrying the Wyndham name tend to be luxury chains—Wyndham Hotels and Resorts, Wyndham Garden, and Wyndham Grand Collection. However, Wyndham also owns the budget hotel chains Howard Johnson, Days Inn, Super 8, Travelodge, and others. The diversity in hotel chains enables Wyndham to target a wide range of travelers. This strategy allows Wyndham to avoid brand confusion by omitting the Wyndham name from its budget hotels.

Wyndham offers its customers many different benefits to increase customer loyalty. For instance, Wyndham's Rewards program awards points and air miles to customers for staying at more than 6,000 hotels and resorts worldwide. Those customers with enough points can receive free nights at Wyndham hotels. Wyndham's ByRequest program provides a more personalized benefits package; members get free Internet access, expedited check-in, and—after three nights—a snack and drink, extra items such as higher quality pillows, and the option to have the room personalized to the customer's preferences.

In addition, Wyndham strives to encourage travel among businesswomen and make their stays more comfortable. Since 1995 Wyndham has run Women on Their Way, a program that specifically targets female business travelers. The program's website offers advice and special packages for businesswomen planning their trips. Wyndham also prides itself on being one of the first chains to conduct research on the woman traveler when it was still an underserved area. Wyndham claims that its research and feedback from its female travelers prompted the hotel chain to offer improved amenities in the hotel rooms, such as full-length mirrors, coffee pots, and healthier menu options. The company has its own female advisory board and periodically conducts surveys and research in what it sees as an important market for future success.

Wyndham has great faith in its hotels' abilities to meet and exceed customer expectations. In addition to being the first hotel company to implement fully online customer service satisfaction tracking, each of the company's 7,200 hotels' websites displays ratings and feedback from TripAdvisor, a travel website where customers can share their opinions. Because 40 to 60 percent of Wyndham's customers refer to TripAdvisor, this move shows that Wyndham understands the importance of customers' experiences.

Relationships with Employees

The corporate culture at Wyndham Worldwide focuses extensively on employee well being. The company considers its employees to be crucial to its success. For this reason, Wyndham offers a range of employee benefits, including health and welfare, retirement planning, employee discounts, education assistance, employee assistance, adoption reimbursement, flexible work arrangements, and domestic partner benefits. Wyndham also has several unique programs for employees:

- University Relations, which provides students with information regarding internship and job opportunities at Wyndham.
- The Be Well program, which aims to improve the holistic health of employees and advocates for exercise, lifestyle management, emotional wellness, financial health, and the quality of the work environment through programs such as weight management and stress reduction.
- The Count On Me! Service Promise, which holds employees accountable to one another in fulfilling Wyndham's core service values of responding to customer needs, being respectful, and delivering a great experience.

Wyndham Worldwide also realizes that one of the best benefits it can offer its employees is knowledge. The company believes its employees have the chance to embark on long-term careers in the hospitality industry, and Wyndham wants to cultivate these skills. In so doing, Wyndham not only helps its employees learn the necessary skills but also creates benefits for the company as well, because more skilled employees translate into better service for customers. Wyndham created the Employee Value Proposition (see Case Exhibit 10.2) to summarize the benefits of employment with the company.

Relationships with Shareholders

As a publicly traded company, Wyndham must create value for its shareholders, which the company has achieved in recent years. Wyndham Worldwide's stock price has steadily increased, and the company outperformed the hotel industry in 2011, with its stock price increasing 26 percent. Its Hotel Group is the leading franchiser of hotels, its Exchange & Rentals Group is the leading timeshare exchange and rental company, and its Vacation Ownership Group is the leading timeshare developer. Its high cash flows

---

CASE EXHIBIT 10.2   The Three Es of Wyndham's Employee Value Proposition

Experience *(expand know-how)*
- On the job assignments
- Job rotation and job shadowing
- Development of a personal career development plan
- Interaction with cross-functional, cross-business unit and project teams

Exposure *(expand network)*
- Interaction with senior leadership
- Personal feedback through self-appraisals
- Frequent "lunch-and-learns" and informational sessions
- One-on-one coaching

Education *(expand knowledge)*
- Wyndham Worldwide University's learning and development programs
- Research and study opportunities
- Online course offerings
- Tuition reimbursement program

Source: "Employee Value Proposition," Wyndham Worldwide, http://www.wyndhamworldwide.com/careers_at_wyndham/evp.html, accessed July 28, 2012.

and diversity of products and services makes it uniquely positioned in the lodging industry.

Although the lodging industry lagged in the years following the recession, it is expected to grow over the coming years. The slowly strengthening U.S. economy, increases in corporate and government hotel bookings, and expansion into international markets will drive room rates higher. However, unstable global economic conditions may continue to hinder growth. Going forward, Wyndham must be certain to carefully survey its competition. Four large competitors that represent potential threats to Wyndham include Marriot Hotels, Starwood Resorts, Wynn Resorts, and MGM Mirage. All of these hotels are widely admired and score high on brand awareness. To improve its competitive position and thus its value to shareholders, Wyndham will need to identify, monitor, and react to threats and opportunities in a rapidly changing business environment.

Relationships with Communities

One of Wyndham Worldwide's corporate values is to support its communities. The company states that, "As a large company, we provide employment that helps out the communities in which we operate. But the Wyndham philosophy is that is not enough. We need to give back to our communities to improve the world around us." This led the company to create several ethical and philanthropic programs.

Wyndham is committed to protecting the human rights of the people within the company's "sphere of influence." The company adopted a Human Rights Policy Statement in 2007 and focuses on the ethical treatment of all workers. Wyndham aims to provide a safe working environment, rejects all forms of forced labor (especially child labor), and supports the rights of employees to form unions.

Wyndham Worldwide has a number of philanthropic programs to address the needs of its stakeholders. The biggest program is Wishes by Wyndham, which works to support charities that help women and children through donations, volunteerism, fundraising, and raising awareness. Under Wishes by Wyndham, the company has adopted three charities:

- The SeriousFun Children's Network, an organization that provides free programs to children with serious medical illnesses.
- The Christel House, a learning center for children founded by Wyndham employee and board member Christel DeHann, who realized that helping people by providing food and clothing was only a temporary solution to the much bigger problem of poverty.
- The Starlight Children's Foundation, which provides entertainment and educational activities to children with illnesses.

In addition to its corporate support of these programs, Wyndham strongly encourages its employees to contribute toward its philanthropic endeavors and gets its customers involved by giving them a chance to donate their rewards points to charity.

Relationship with the Environment

Wyndham Worldwide recognizes that its work practices have an immense impact on the environment. The company believes that using more eco-friendly products and reducing its environmental impact will not only help the environment but also save it money in the form of energy savings—contributing to the financial performance of the company. It therefore aims to reduce its negative impact and support sustainable initiatives. Wyndham Worldwide emphasizes the following goals:

- Educate and influence internal and external stakeholders on environmental issues
- Reduce energy consumption and track performance
- Reduce water and energy usage and recycle
- Improve air quality
- Minimize waste by recycling and reusing materials
- Implement sustainable procurement practices
- Participate in local community environmental activities

Just as Wyndham has teams devoted to ethics and compliance, it also has a team committed toward improving the company's sustainability. The company also collaborates with a variety of institutions to increase green practices in the hotel and leisure industry.

Thus far, more than 300 Wyndham facilities have received green certification. To become a greener company in every aspect of its operations, Wyndham Worldwide sets individual goals for each of its hotel brands. These goals target important subjects such as energy conservation, water conservation, recycle-reuse, education, and innovation. Some of Wyndham's major energy conservation initiatives include replacing incandescent lights with energy efficient bulbs, upgrading to more energy-efficient appliances, and using the ENERGY STAR® tracking system to measure energy use. Although many of these devices are expensive, most of them pay for themselves in a few years. Afterward, the company gets the increased benefit of energy savings. For example, Wyndham has installed an energy-saving DECTRON system in the hotel pools of its Hawthorne Suites by Wyndham. This device saved Wyndham an estimated $20,000 over two years.

Wyndham attempts to conserve water through a variety of initiatives, including the EarthSmart® linen and towel program; low flow faucets, toilets, and other appliances; the Ozone Laundry System; drip irrigation and drought resistant landscaping; and EPA WaterSense® certified products. Although some of these initiatives appear small in nature, the company has advanced significantly in water conservation. For instance, low-flow fixtures have reduced water consumption at Wyndham's Vacation Ownership by 20 percent.

Wyndham uses several recycled products (including pens, key cards, coffee cups, and laundry bags) throughout its hotels to reduce its impact on the environment. One unique way in which Wyndham has reused materials is in its employee uniforms. At some Wyndham Hotel & Resorts, the uniforms of front-desk staff consist of recycled 2-liter plastic bottles. By making genuine attempts to recycle and reuse materials, Wyndham has been able to reduce the amount of construction waste that ends up in landfills by 88 percent at its New Jersey headquarters.

Wyndham views the education of consumers on sustainability as a key driving force in achieving environmental success. In order to achieve its educational goals, Wyndham Worldwide takes steps such as educating guests and employees regarding environmental certification programs, green technologies, and ways to protect their natural environment. The Wyndham Worldwide green website (www.wyndhamgreen.com) educates consumers by outlining important facts regarding energy conservation, removal/cleanup guidelines for compact fluorescent light bulbs, consumer product rebates, and tax incentives and rebates offered by state governments. Additionally, the website educates consumers by outlining important facts regarding education, green reading, air quality, and green kids. Wyndham Worldwide's Green Program for Kids has been developed and designed around educating kids about the environment, communities, and the planet. In addition, the company's Global Best Practices guide educates businesses about environmentally friendly initiatives.

Wyndham's Ethics and Compliance Programs

To maintain a strong corporate culture, Wyndham has implemented an extensive compliance program to reinforce ethics throughout the organization. A climate of ethics and social responsibility creates a large measure of trust among a firm's stakeholders. The company has drafted a thorough Code of Business Conduct that has received top scores from the Ethisphere Institute for its comprehensiveness and availability to stakeholders.

Codes of conduct have several purposes. For employees, the code of conduct (or code of ethics) helps them to become familiar with the company's expectations for them. It also provides an essential reference for employees when faced with difficult decisions. Research suggests that employees in organizations with ethical codes of conduct are less accepting of potential misconduct toward stakeholders. For stakeholders in general, a code expresses the company's commitment to corporate social responsibility and ethical conduct. In addition, a code of conduct is an important way to share information about stakeholder issues. Therefore, the clarity and comprehensiveness of a company's code of conduct is an important signal of a company's dedication toward ethics, compliance, and stakeholder relationships. Wyndham received high scores for the company's values and commitments within its Code of Business Conduct, its coverage of risk topics, and the code's availability to stakeholders.

In addition to its strong code of conduct, Wyndham has created an Ethics and Compliance Program, a Compliance Governance Board, and a Compliance and Ethics Leadership Team. The audit committee on Wyndham's Board of Directors is also involved with the Ethics and Compliance Program and receives quarterly updates on the program's progress. The program is designed and directed by the Compliance Governance Board, which is made up of the company's CEO, Chief Financial Officer, Chief Human Resources Officer, and the General Counsel. The Compliance and Ethics Leadership Team helps to keep the company on its ethical course. They receive updates regarding the Ethics and Compliance program, collect feedback, assess the company's global risks, and train employees. All of these different positions and programs demonstrate an ethical tone at the top. In other words, Wyndham Worldwide believes that ethical programs must start with ethical leaders to be successfully implemented throughout the organization.

Wyndham Worldwide's efforts have not gone unnoticed. The company has received many awards regarding its ethical initiatives. Recently, *Newsweek* magazine ranked Wyndham Worldwide as one of the 100 Greenest Big Companies and ranked it in the top 10 of its Media, Travel and Entertainment category. Additional awards include the following:

- The Lodging Hospitality Chain Leadership Award
- *Fortune* magazine's World's Most Admired Companies for 2010
- ConEdison Green Pioneer Award
- DiversityInc.'s 2010 Top 50 Companies for Diversity
- *PINK* magazine's 15 Top Companies for Women
- *Ethisphere*'s World's Most Ethical Companies

Wyndham Worldwide's numerous initiatives in sustainability and corporate responsibility are key factors in enhancing Wyndham's reputation and contributing to future success.

Wyndham's Future

Wyndham has achieved great success with its stakeholder orientation marketing strategy. The company's ability to adapt its marketing strategies to suit its various chains has provided it with unique advantages that make it a formidable competitor to rival hotel companies.

Wyndham's hotel brands are at different levels of the life cycle. The company's Night and TRYP brands, for example, are in the introductory and growth stages, while its Howard Johnson, Super 8, and Days Inn chains are mature brands. However, despite heavy marketing to promote awareness of its newer brands, Wyndham has not neglected its more mature brands. For example, the company has worked hard to portray Howard Johnson as an iconic brand and continues to offer benefits packages to encourage families to stay at the chain. Wyndham makes sure to adjust its marketing strategies to suit both the brand's image and its stage in the product life cycle.

One opportunity for Wyndham that could prove profitable is expansion into emerging economies. Approximately 10 percent of Wyndham Worldwide hotels are in emerging markets such as India and China. With property prices at a low and a rising middle class in these countries, the disposable income makes these countries increasingly lucrative markets to capture. The company seized this advantage with the announcement that it will open seven additional hotels in India. Entering emerging markets will create new marketing challenges, and Wyndham must continue to adapt its brand strategies to new groups of stakeholders.

The company has demonstrated its concern for a variety of stakeholders by embracing a stakeholder orientation and focusing on competitive advantage. Although Wyndham seems to be on the right track, it still faces a variety of risks and competitive threats in the hospitality industry. Since these issues are inevitable in large corporations, Wyndham must ensure that it has plans in place to address these risks. Additionally, Wyndham must avoid complacency in its continued efforts to integrate its corporate culture into its global operations. Now more than ever, Wyndham should leverage its competitive advantage in ethics and social responsibility to enhance its reputation. As consumers become increasingly concerned with value and a quality experience, Wyndham's strong stakeholder relationships and reputation will likely prove a valuable asset that gives it a competitive edge over its rivals.

Questions for Discussion

1. How does Wyndham's stakeholder orientation create a strategic marketing advantage?
2. How do Wyndham's diverse brands contribute to customer satisfaction and marketing performance?
3. Do the awards and recognition that Wyndham has received for social responsibility and ethics contribute to its financial performance? If so, how?

Sources

The information for this case came from publically available information on the Wyndham Worldwide website (http://www.wyndhamworldwide.com) and the following additional sources: "About RCI," RCI (http://www.rci.com/RCI/prelogin/aboutUs.do), accessed July 28, 2012; "About Us," SeriousFun Children's Network (http://www.seriousfunnetwork.org/About), accessed July 28, 2012; "About Us," Christel House (http://www.christel-house.org/about-us), accessed July 28, 2012; Bloomberg News, "Wyndham Posts $1.36 Billion Loss," *New York Times*, February 13, 2009 (http://www.nytimes.com/2009/02/14/business/14wyndham.html?ref=wyndhamworldwidecorporation); "Cendant buys Wyndham hotel brand for $100m," *IndUS Business Journal*, October 15, 2005 (http://www.indusbusinessjournal.com/ME2/dirmod.asp?sid=&nm=&type=Publishing&mod=Publications%3A%3AArticle&mid=8F3A7027421841978F18BE895F87F791&tier=4&id=217E6E851DF84383B6141F0B73912F24); "Cendant Corporation Announces Filing of Wyndham Worldwide Corporation Registration Statement," Wyndham Worldwide, May 11, 2006 (http://www.wyndhamworldwide.com/investors/show_release.cfm?id=53); "Court Approves RCI Settlement," *Timesharing Today*, Issue #109, January/February 2010, 1; Barbara De Lollis, "Wyndham hotels embrace TripAdvisor reviews," *USA Today*, March 6, 2012 (http://travel.usatoday.com/hotels/post/2012/03/wyndham-hotels-tripadvisor-reviews-social-media/640578/1); Ethisphere Magazine, "The 2011 World's Most Ethical Companies," *Ethisphere*, Q1 2011, 37–43; O.C. Ferrell, John Fraedrich, and Linda Ferrell, *Business Ethics: Ethical Decision Making and Cases,*

8th ed. (Mason, OH: South-Western Cengage Learning, 2011), 248; G. Tomas M Hult, Jeannette A. Mena, O.C. Ferrell, and Linda Ferrell, "Stakeholder marketing: a definition and conceptual framework," *AMS Review*, Spring 2011, Vol. 1 (1), pp. 44–65; Susan Knox, "The RCI Christel House Charity Golf Event 2011–Escaping Poverty is not easy unless you are taught how," *Perspective*, March 29, 2011 (http://www.theperspectivemagazine.com/the-rci-christel-house-charity-golf-event-2011-%e2%80%93-escaping-poverty-is-not-easy-unless-you-are-taught-how-014653); Isabelle Maignan, Tracy L. Gonzales-Padron, G. Tomas M. Hult, and O.C. Ferrell, "Stakeholder orientation: development and testing of a framework for socially responsible culture," *Journal of Strategic Marketing*, 2011, Vol. 19, pp. 313–338; Joseph A McKinney, Tisha L. Emerson, and Mitchell J. Neubert, "The Effects of Ethical Codes on Ethical Perceptions of Actions toward Stakeholders," *Journal of Business Ethics*, (2010) 97:505–516; Night Hotel New York (http://www.nighthotelny.com/index.html), accessed July 28, 2012; "PwC Releases 2012 Lodging Industry Forecast" (http://www.hotelnewsnow.com/articles.aspx/7367/PwC-US-releases-2012-Lodging-Industry-Forecast), accessed July 28, 2012; Christopher Sindik, "50 Asian Companies & the World's Most Ethical Companies," *Ethisphere*, Q1 2011, 15–17; Tess Stynes, "Wyndham Profit Rises on Improved Demand," *Wall Street Journal*, February 9, 2011 (http://online.wsj.com/article/SB10001424052748703310104576134783753550522.html); TRYP by Wyndham (http://www.tryphotels.com/en/index.html), accessed July 28, 2012; "Who We Are," Starlight Children's Foundation (http://www.starlight.org/whoweare), accessed July 28, 2012; Women on Their Way (http://www.womenontheirway.com/about), accessed July 28, 2012; Wyndham Green (http://www.wyndhamgreen.com), accessed July 28, 2012; "Wyndham Hotel Group," Starlight Children's Foundation (http://www.starlight.org/wyndham), accessed July 28, 2012; "Wyndham is Tops for Customer Service," *Breaking Travel News*, May 10, 2004 (http://www.breakingtravelnews.com/news/article/btn20040510083409820); "Wyndham to open seven hotels in India," *Business Today*, April 5, 2011 (http://businesstoday.intoday.in/story/wyndham-hotel-group-part-of-wyndham-worldwide-to-open-seven-hotels-in-india-under-the-ramada-and-days-inn-brands/1/14497.html); "Wyndham Worldwide Corporation (WYN): Historical Prices," Yahoo! Finance (http://finance.yahoo.com/q/hp?s=WYN&a=06&b=19&c=2006&d=04&e=1&f=2011&g=m), accessed July 28, 2012; "Wyndham Worldwide Named to Fortune Magazine's Most Admired Companies List," Wyndham Worldwide, March 9, 2010 (http://www.wyndhamworldwide.com/media/press-releases/press-release?wwprdid=666); Roger Yu, "New spinoff Wyndham hopes to re-establish hotels with fresh look," *USA Today*, August 2, 2006 (http://www.usatoday.com/money/biztravel/2006-08-01-wyndham-usat_x.htm); and Roger Yu, "Travel Q&A: Wyndham CEO Eric Danziger," *USA Today*, January 29, 2009 (http://www.usatoday.com/travel/hotels/2009-01-29-qa-eric-danzinger_N.htm).

CASE **11**

NASCAR: Can't Keep a Good Brand Down*

Synopsis: This case discusses NASCAR's successful branding strategy and how it became one of the top sports in America. The history of NASCAR is reviewed, followed by an overview of NASCAR's marketing and branding strategies. Despite its unparalleled success, NASCAR has faced a number of challenges and criticisms over the past decade, most notably the loss of revenue stemming from the 2008 recession. The case examines many of the challenges that NASCAR must address if it is to sustain its branding juggernaut and retain its top spot in the motorsports arena.

Themes: Branding strategy, branding alliances, brand image, pricing strategy, integrated marketing communication, sports marketing, differentiation, social responsibility

In the past 60 years, the National Association for Stock Car Auto Racing, better known as NASCAR, has become the top auto-racing series in the United States and the number one spectator sport in America. It has also become well known for its branding alliances, with drivers sporting everything from coffee to deodorant logos on their cars and jumpsuits. The sport is currently comprised of three national series: the NASCAR Nationwide Series, the NASCAR Sprint Cup Series, and the NASCAR Camping World Cup Series, along with some regional and international series. Although primarily a U.S. sport, NASCAR has held races in Mexico, Canada, Australia, and Japan. It currently sanctions over 1,500 races on 100 tracks in 39 U.S. states and Canada.

NASCAR's popularity soared over the past ten years, partially due to extensive media coverage. Drivers like Jeff Gordon and Dale Earnhardt, Jr., have become heroes of the auto racing industry, and many NASCAR drivers have made appearances in movies and television. NASCAR's growth has been so dramatic that it is now second only to the National Football League (NFL) in popularity. Despite its immense success, the sport has had to overcome challenges in its 60-year history and will likely have to face many more because of declining attendance and other difficulties such as diversity, safety, and its impact on the environment. Still, its strong brand image and brand alliances with other companies will likely keep the sport afloat through these tough times.

*Timothy Aurand, Northern Illinois University, and Kimberly Judson, Illinois State University, prepared this case for classroom discussion rather than to illustrate effective or ineffective handling of an administrative situation. A student team including Joe Izral, Rhonda McCormick, Alex Mbuthia, Jamie Scott, and Felix Villa contributed to the development of this case.

NASCAR's History

NASCAR began with the vision of one man, a worker at an automobile dealership named William Henry France. France was already in love with auto racing when he moved to Daytona Beach, Florida, during the 1930s. Daytona Beach was the perfect place for auto racing enthusiasts like France, as the beach's open expanses and flat ground offered a perfect area for races. In fact, by the time of NASCAR's founding over a decade later, automobile racing had become popular in places like Florida, Alabama, and North Carolina. Many sources give bootleggers the credit for promoting auto racing during the '20s and '30s, as moonshine cars had to be built to go fast in order to evade the law. The popular idea of bootleggers racing from the law is etched in racing mythology as one of the precursors of stock car racing, although in reality its influence on stock car racing is likely overemphasized. Auto racing continued to increase in popularity in the early decades of the twentieth century.

France recognized the potential popularity and profitability that auto racing offered. Yet at the time, this lucrative movement lacked what it needed to become a professional sport, including promoters, racetracks, rules, or respectability on the part of the racers. Therefore, in 1947 France met with owners, drivers, and mechanics at the Streamline Hotel to launch his idea of creating a professional sport out of stock car racing. Over the next few days, they worked on the details for the organization. The first race of the newly formed organization—held on February 15, 1948—was won by stock car racer Red Byron. A few days later on February 21, NASCAR was officially incorporated, with France serving as president and CEO. What is today known as the NASCAR Sprint Cup Series was created in 1949.

Racing fans flocked to the tracks, and soon NASCAR names like Lee Petty, the Flock brothers, and Fireball Roberts became household names among NASCAR enthusiasts. Originally, many of the races were held on simple makeshift tracks, but in 1959 France opened Daytona International Speedway, which offered a paved racetrack. The 2.5-mile racetrack provided an enclosure and more accommodations for spectators. Ten years later, France opened the Talladega Superspeedway in Alabama, a 2.7-mile racetrack that is the largest oval track in the world. France would serve as NASCAR president and CEO until 1972, when his son William France, Jr., took over. NASCAR continues to remain largely under the control of the France family to this day, a source of some contention among NASCAR fans and critics.

In the late 1960s and 1970s, NASCAR tracks began to emerge outside of the Southeast. Tracks were built in Delaware and Pennsylvania. Since then, NASCAR has tried to become more of a national sport, building racetracks in many U.S. states.

Early Corporate Sponsors of NASCAR

NASCAR's growth really took off when it partnered with automakers Ford, General Motors (GM), and Chrysler in the 1950s. The automakers hoped their support of NASCAR would boost their own sales. The marketing phrase "Win on Sunday, Sell on Monday" became popular with the automakers as it was believed that success in the races meant greater success for their companies. In 1971, the R.J. Reynolds Tobacco Company's Winston brand became a sponsor of NASCAR. During that time period, NASCAR also formed limited sponsorships with Union 76, Goodyear Tires, and Pepsi. Anheuser-Busch began to sponsor NASCAR's Budweiser Late Model Sportsman Series in 1984. NASCAR would soon become famous for its branding partnerships, and the support of major sponsors and brands has contributed to NASCAR's well-known image.

NASCAR's Jump in Attendance

NASCAR began to experience unprecedented growth in the 1990s, coming a long way from its 1.4 million attendees in 1976. To help with this growth, it launched its first website in 1995, which offered up-to-date news on NASCAR activities and even had a NASCAR community where members could chat online and post opinions and videos. In five years, NASCAR attendance increased by 57 percent to over 6.3 million. Its television viewership grew 48 percent between 1993 and 2002, and by 2006 about 6 percent of U.S. households watched NASCAR races on television, compared to less than 2 percent for its competitor, the Indy Racing League. New, younger NASCAR stars such as Ryan Newman, Kyle Petty, and Kurt Busch began emerging, which helped attract the youth market to the sport. Women also began racing for NASCAR, including drivers Tina Gordon, Deborah Renshaw, and Kelly Sutton, the only NASCAR driver with multiple sclerosis. Consequently, female NASCAR fans grew to roughly 40 percent of its fan base.

Today NASCAR has approximately 75 million fans and has the second-highest television ratings for regular season sports. NASCAR fans are believed to be the most brand-loyal of any sport, and one estimate claims that fans spend over $2 billion in licensed product sales. For this reason, NASCAR has attracted the attention of numerous *Fortune* 500 companies. Currently, NASCAR is broadcast in over 150 countries in over 30 languages.

NASCAR's Branding Strategy

Early on, NASCAR worked hard to promote its brand name. It has been largely successful in its endeavors by integrating multiple marketing initiatives into a well-organized branding strategy. Part of this strategy dealt with partnering and co-branding with other companies. Driver jumpsuits and racecars are filled with the logos of various companies that NASCAR has formed brand alliances with. At the same time, NASCAR has successfully differentiated its own brand and, through the launch of campaigns, has effectively marketed its brand throughout the world.

Television Broadens NASCAR's Reach

Before the mid-1970s, the only way to watch a NASCAR racing event was to attend a race in person. During the mid- to late-1970s, NASCAR began to receive sporadic television coverage, and in 1979 the Daytona 500 was the first NASCAR event televised in its entirety. NASCAR started to rely on television as a branding medium, and by 1989 all races on the Winston Cup schedule were televised (later changed to the NASCAR Nextel Cup and then the Sprint Cup). This did not mean that television did not introduce some problems for NASCAR. Each track negotiated its own television contract, which meant that each race could potentially be shown on a different network. This hindered NASCAR's exposure and presented a problem that NASCAR was not able to overcome until the turn of the century.

In 2001, NASCAR took a proactive stance by signing a comprehensive television contract with FOX and NBC that was worth $2.4 billion and enabled the televising of all the NASCAR races that season. Just four years later, another contract was signed for $4.48 billion, providing broadcasts in a total of 167 countries including Thailand, Pakistan, New Zealand, and Venezuela. Such media coverage has, in part, accounted for NASCAR's large fan base.

Co-Branding Enhances Profits and Brand Image

NASCAR also recognized the benefits of co-branding relationships. It realized that a successful branding alliance can give the companies involved a greater competitive advantage. In the early 1970s, NASCAR was primarily sponsored by R.J. Reynolds Tobacco

Company. Today, NASCAR has marketing and sponsorship deals with a wide range of *Fortune* 500 companies such as Sunoco, Coca-Cola, Allstate, DuPont, Gillette, and UPS. In 2004, Sprint Nextel replaced R.J. Reynolds as the series' sponsor, with Nextel paying NASCAR $70 million annually for the title rights. The former Busch Grand National Series, which had been sponsored by Anheuser-Busch since 1984, became the Nationwide Series in 2007.

NASCAR takes its sponsorship deals very seriously. A sponsor may spend several million dollars for a race team and then spend just as much on promotional events. It is not a task to be taken lightly. Brian France even has a team that runs seminars to help sponsors get the greatest advantage out of their sponsorships. Of course, the relationship between NASCAR and its sponsors changes over time as their needs change and the economy ebbs and flows. During the economic downturn in 2008 and 2009, NASCAR lost several sponsors due to financial reasons.

One potential weakness of NASCAR's co-branding is that some experts feel that the sport is becoming flooded with sponsorships. It has about 50 league sponsors and numerous team sponsors. This creates a cluttered environment of signage at the racetracks. Sponsorship has also increased in price within the last few decades, which means sponsors are now expecting more from drivers. Drivers are now expected not only to race well but also to show up for marketing functions and appear early on the morning of the race to sign autographs and answer questions. The pressure is on to win races, not only for the glory of the driver and for NASCAR but to retain the sponsor as well. New teams, even when legendary racecar drivers own them, also have a hard time attracting sponsors, despite the teams' talent. NASCAR driver Jeff Gordon, for example, had a difficult time finding sponsors for his new team featuring novice driver Jim Johnson despite Gordon's legendary status.

Sponsors find that co-branding with NASCAR is extremely profitable, saving them from having to promote themselves through traditional media. And, because NASCAR fans are some of the most brand-loyal consumers to be had, NASCAR-sponsored products have benefitted from sizable sales and market share increases. As a result of its co-branding alliances, NASCAR itself offers a plethora of consumer products either as brand extensions or through a direct relationship with other firms. Currently, NASCAR has licensing and merchandising rights for watches, clothes, chairs, tables, grills, hats, clocks, flags, door mats, blankets, auto accessories, sunglasses, and even food products.

Differentiation Seeks New Audiences

In spite of its various brand partnerships, NASCAR has worked hard to differentiate its brand from other companies, particularly from competing racing circuits. This often takes place in the form of well-coordinated marketing campaigns, such as the lavish campaign NASCAR launched to celebrate its 50th anniversary. One of the strongest differentiating factors for NASCAR is the experience of the race. NASCAR fans like the constant, unpredictable, and even dangerous action. Crashes, live entertainment, and danger all make up the NASCAR experience.

With only a single driver per racecar, NASCAR also offers a human touch in the bargain. The driver provides a face and personality to fans, allowing them to strongly identify with NASCAR. Additionally, NASCAR lets several drivers share the spotlight throughout the race. From an owner's perspective, it is more efficient to manage the public relations opportunities of one driver as opposed to an entire team of athletes.

A similar dynamic can be observed in advertising and sponsorship during the competition. Within the NASCAR culture, a large amount of sponsorship signage around the track and on the drivers' cars has historically been acceptable and is perceived to be part of the NASCAR experience. Although clutter is an issue that sponsoring organizations must consider, it does not appear to be viewed as negatively by the NASCAR fan base as it is viewed in professional golf and tennis, which are more conservative and traditional sports.

NASCAR also differentiates its sport through connections cultivated within the media and Hollywood. Brian France, CEO of NASCAR, realizes that to remain successful, NASCAR must continuously attract new fans. He understands that to attract and retain a young fan base year after year, the promotional strategy requires the support of Hollywood and films such as *Talladega Nights*. The film features strategic brand placement that includes the official NASCAR logo and the logos of many corporate sponsors.

NASCAR has also attempted to further differentiate itself in order to attract other, more diverse market segments. In recent years, NASCAR has made it a priority to create awareness among diverse ethnic groups and among women. Called the "Drive for Diversity," this program gives minority and female drivers the opportunity to compete with a NASCAR team. Since the program began in 2004, 31 minority and female drivers have competed, winning a total of 34 races.

NASCAR is also pursuing the Hispanic market in the United States, Mexico, and Latin America. In addition to holding races in Mexico, NASCAR routinely creates Hispanic-themed promotions before races held near large Hispanic communities, such as in southern California. Additionally, Columbian NASCAR racer Juan Pablo Montoya is also garnering attention from different segments of the population. Montoya, formerly a Formula 1 and Indy Car racer, won the Nationwide Series race in Mexico City in 2007. Since then, he has had continued success, including finishing second at the 2008 Talladega 500. NASCAR hopes Montoya's success will portray it as a diversified sports venue as well as attract more Hispanic fans. This integration of racers, sponsors, and fans from the United States, Latin America, and South America seeks to expand NASCAR's popularity and audience over different countries, which separates it from other sports mainly geared toward American audiences.

Due to lower TV ratings and competition from other sports venues, NASCAR attempted to generate greater fan interest in the Sprint Cup Series by implementing the Chase for the Cup in 2004. The format was later changed in 2007 and again in 2011. After 26 regular season races, the top 10 drivers, plus two wild card drivers, advance to contend for the Cup championship. Prior to the Chase format, the overall champion was usually determined well in advance of the end of the season. This presented a problem for NASCAR since the timing coincided with the start of football season each fall. With these changes, each of the 12 drivers who contend for the Cup has a legitimate chance of winning. NASCAR's Chase for the Cup turned out to be so popular that the Professional Golfers' Association adopted a similar format.

Innovative co-branding relationships have also helped differentiate the NASCAR brand and catapult it into new markets. The partnership between NASCAR and Harlequin (romance novels) launched in 2006 created awareness among women who may not have even been otherwise exposed to the sport. It also provided a way for NASCAR to tap into emotional branding strategies. Another effort to attract women and younger people to NASCAR includes a joint venture between the rock band Three Doors Down and Dale Earnhardt, Jr., in which he participated in a music video and the band members drove his car in a race. Additionally, the partnership between The Cartoon Network and NASCAR emphasizes sponsorship diversification directed at the younger consumer.

NASCAR's Brand Equity and Brand Loyalty

NASCAR's brand equity is the value that is added to a product or service by having the NASCAR brand attached to the offering. As a result, many companies choose to sport the NASCAR logo on their products. A 2005 study by James Madison University revealed that fans appreciate the sponsorship associated with NASCAR. Approximately 93 percent feel that corporate sponsors are "very important" to NASCAR, and 51 percent said that when they buy a NASCAR product, they feel as if they are supporting the sport. A full 40 percent of fans would switch to a product that sponsored NASCAR. Numbers like these account for the over $2 billion fans spend on NASCAR-licensed products. A whopping 47 percent of fans claimed they appreciate a sponsor's brand more because it sponsors NASCAR, giving companies a major incentive to sponsor NASCAR. Finally, unlike some sports figures who are seen as endorsing products just for the money, 57 percent of fans believe that NASCAR drivers use the products they endorse, which further increases the respectability of the drivers in their fans' eyes.

Despite all the efforts made by NASCAR to engage the customer, fan interest has begun to decline in the past few years. This situation was exacerbated during the 2008 recession. The median income of NASCAR fans is below that of the national average, making it harder for fans to afford to attend the races. In addition to lowering the cost of tickets, NASCAR also cut the costs of food at its events. To show that it cares about its fans, NASCAR reimbursed the difference to fans at Daytona who had bought tickets before NASCAR began offering lower ticket offerings. NASCAR is clearly making significant efforts to maintain its brand equity and its loyal fan base.

NASCAR fans are loyal for several reasons. One reason is the sense of community NASCAR fans feel when engaged in the sport. NASCAR's brand is embodied in its drivers. When fans feel connected to the drivers, a bond is created that promotes the sport's brand image. NASCAR recognizes the sense of community that fans experience as a competitive advantage. Thus, a major link on NASCAR's website is "Community," where fans can become members of an online community devoted to NASCAR. The area allows fans to meet, discuss, and establish emotional bonds. Thus, a strong sense of community is a driving force behind NASCAR. NASCAR also cashes in on brand loyalty by using loyal fans as brand ambassadors and by establishing an emotional component with the brand.

NASCAR's Challenges

Despite NASCAR's immense success, the road has not always been an easy one. As with all major companies, the organization has had its share of criticisms and challenges. As NASCAR looks toward its future, a number of significant challenges remain.

Ownership and Structure

One major criticism involves the control the France family has over NASCAR. A descendent of William France has been CEO of NASCAR ever since the sport was founded in 1948. In 1972, William France's son Bill France, Jr., took over as CEO of the company, and in 2003 his grandson followed suit. The family continues to be the majority stockholder of the company, allowing them to call many of the shots. Indeed, even those within NASCAR refer to the sport as a "benevolent dictatorship." Some argue that this gives the France family too much power. For instance, William France was known for replacing drivers that would try to unionize. So far, business decisions made by the France family have seemed to work out well for the sport. Many of the marketing strategies and changes the France CEOs have implemented have served to effectively promote

NASCAR and attract an increased fan base. Still, some view dictatorial style of the France family with concern because it depends largely upon the leadership abilities and business savvy of a few.

Safety Concerns

Another major issue involves vehicle safety. Critics claim that NASCAR often does not implement safety precautions until after a disaster has happened, even if those safety features have been around for years. Its own drivers have expressed concerns over the lack of appropriate medical care received after a crash. NASCAR drivers who have died in crashes include Adam Petty, Tony Roper, Kenny Irwin, and perhaps most publicized, Dale Earnhardt. Earnhardt's death in 2001 was perhaps the most influential in convincing NASCAR to implement more safety features. After Earnhardt's death, NASCAR made it mandatory for drivers to wear a head-and-neck support system, known as HANS, with a seat-belt restraint system. Cars were also equipped with a fire-suppressant system and equipment that measures the forces placed on driver's heads in a crash.

One of NASCAR's most visible safety initiatives is the Research and Design Center in Concord, NC where the Car of Tomorrow was designed for the Sprint Cup Series. The new car, which became mandatory for all Sprint Cup teams in 2008, extended safety measures and set standard tolerances that brought greater equality to the sport. Before the Car of Tomorrow debuted, dominant teams were able to produce cars specifically tailored for each racetrack. NASCAR inspects each car using a coordinate measuring machine to ensure that all teams have cars within required specifications. NASCAR continued this trend by introducing a similar car for its Nationwide Series in 2010.

Since 2005, Steel And Foam Energy Reduction (SAFER) barriers have been installed in all of NASCAR's tracks. Developed by the Midwest Roadside Safety Facility at the University of Nebraska, SAFER barriers absorb energy among vehicle impact and distribute the energy among the wall without forcing the vehicle back into traffic. This technology offers hope that fewer cars will be involved in a single accident incident, thus decreasing the probability of endangering other drivers.

A more controversial safety measure is the use of restrictor plates, a piece of equipment used on superspeedways like the Daytona and Talladega racetracks to reduce speeds of the cars. Drivers have accused NASCAR of trying to manipulate the races with these, but NASCAR insists they are a necessary safety measure. Critics argue that restrictor plates only make superspeedway races boring.

Some drivers, including Dale Earnhardt, Jr. and Jeff Burton, have been recruited by Chevrolet to promote safety on and off the track to young children, teens, and caretakers. Working with the National Highway Traffic Safety Administration (NHTSA) and the National SAFE KIDS Campaign, they have successfully aired public announcements regarding using safety belts and child seats properly. This is a positive initiative because NASCAR is one of the highest sports viewed among teens, second only to the NFL.

Environmental Impact

Environmentalists have cited NASCAR for its lack of environmental responsibility. NASCAR estimates that it uses 6,000 gallons of fuel during a race weekend, which comes out to about 216,000 gallons for one season. It also used leaded gasoline for years after the Environmental Protection Agency (EPA) asked it to quit. Because a law makes NASCAR exempt from the EPA's regulation on gasoline, NASCAR is under no obligation to comply. Yet the pressures to go green have caught up with NASCAR, and in the past few years it has instituted many changes to improve its environmental footprint. NASCAR eventually partnered with the EPA and its fuel supplier Sunoco to phase in unleaded gasoline in 2006 and switch to unleaded gasoline in 2007. In an attempt to carry its green efforts further, NASCAR hired Mike Lynch in 2008 to head the company's new green initiative. NASCAR recently advocated a 15% ethanol-blended gasoline made with American grown corn. This position has paved the way for the ethanol industry to be in sponsorship with NASCAR, and opened opportunities to connect the NASCAR brand with American farmers who supply the corn. This connection allows for new waves of support for the sport in general.

Another big step slated for 2013 is the move to fuel injected engines versus carburetors. Fuel injection systems create higher fuel efficiency while increasing power within engines. According to CEO Brian France, "fuel injection excites the manufacturers, it excites technology companies." France expects car manufacturers to increase their support of their respective teams once the switch is made.

Off the track, NASCAR has taken several initiatives to create a "greener" environment reflecting greater social responsibility. NASCAR has agreed to plant ten trees for every green flag dropped in the Sprint Cup Series races. In 2011, NASCAR planted 110 trees at Daytona Beach International Airport alone. NASCAR has also implemented a recycling program at all of its tracks. Such co-sponsors of this movement are Coca-Cola, UPS, Coors Light, and Office Depot.

Diversity

NASCAR has also been criticized for its lack of its driver diversity. The majority of NASCAR drivers are white males, which has caused concern among some minority fans. There are still few women in the NASCAR driver populace, even though 40 percent of NASCAR fans are women. Sexual discrimination allegations have also been a problem. In 2008, NASCAR official Mauricia Grant won a $225 million lawsuit for racial discrimination (Grant is African-American), sexual discrimination, and wrongful termination. Additionally, NASCAR has not had many African-American drivers. In 2006, Bill Lester became the first African-American driver in almost 20 years to qualify for a race in NASCAR's top series. According to Lester, many African-Americans are secret NASCAR fans, but are not comfortable coming to the races because they cannot identify with the drivers. Indeed, only a few African-American drivers have participated in the Cup series in its history. In an effort to attract minority and female fans, NASCAR launched the "Drive for Diversity" program in 2004. "Drive for Diversity" is an academy style program where participants learn racing skills in the developmental series: NASCAR K&N Pro Series and NASCAR Whelen All-American Series.

NASCAR has also tried to recruit interesting and recognizable drivers to attract new fans. Most notably, female driver Danica Patrick has been racing full-time since her debut in the Sprint Cup at the Daytona 500 in February 2012. Patrick's participation in NASCAR is important not only for diversity reasons, but also for branding. Danica Patrick is 233 percent more recognizable than the average NASCAR driver, and her activities generate far more media buzz, TV ratings, and race attendance than any other driver. In addition to the success of Juan Pablo Montoya, African-American Michael Cherry won an event at the Tri-County Speedway in Hudson, NC in 2010. By winning this race, Cherry has opened the door for other African-Americans to become interested in joining NASCAR.

Financial Concerns

The impact of the 2008 recession introduced new challenges for NASCAR. One major problem was the financial situation of NASCAR's sponsors and partners. The "Big Three" automakers, GM (through Chevrolet), Ford, and Chrysler, experienced extreme financial setbacks. Additionally, other NASCAR sponsors felt the crunch and did not renew their NASCAR contracts, some of which total $15 million. Economic woes have also affected NASCAR fans. In the onset of the recession, NASCAR experienced a decrease in attendance and a significant drop in television ratings. The downturn in attendance during the NASCAR race at the Atlanta Motor Speedway in 2009 shocked some racers, as the stands were only two-thirds full. NASCAR was forced to respond by laying off some workers in order to cut costs.

As the economic issues lingered into 2010 and 2011, NASCAR continued to face problems. In 2010, for example, the Daytona 500 experienced its lowest television ratings since 1991. In addition to decreased viewership, attendance also declined at many races that were once consistent sellouts. The Bristol Motor Speedway, for example, enjoyed a 55-race sellout streak until March 2010. The prolonged recession and high gas prices made it difficult for fans to afford a weekend at the races. The average ticket price for a NASCAR race is around $91, compared to $72 for the NFL, $49 for the NHL, $48 for the NBA, and $25 for MLB. In 2010, many of the major tracks reduced ticket prices. However, the cuts did not improve attendance. A 2012 report showed that sales revenue for major tracks fell 25 to 60 percent between 2008 and 2011. Speedway Motorsports, which operates eight racetracks, posted a $1.5 million loss in April 2011, in large part due to falling attendance.

The economic downturn was especially hard on NASCAR because of its revenue sources, as depicted in Case Exhibit 11.1. Sponsorship alone is worth over $1.5 billion annually to NASCAR. Despite the scare, however, there are signs of life on the economic front. Sponsorship revenues increased 10 percent in 2011. Additional sponsors have joined NASCAR, and most long-time sponsors have decided to remain—though many have chosen to sponsor

---

CASE EXHIBIT 11.1   NASCAR's Revenue Sources

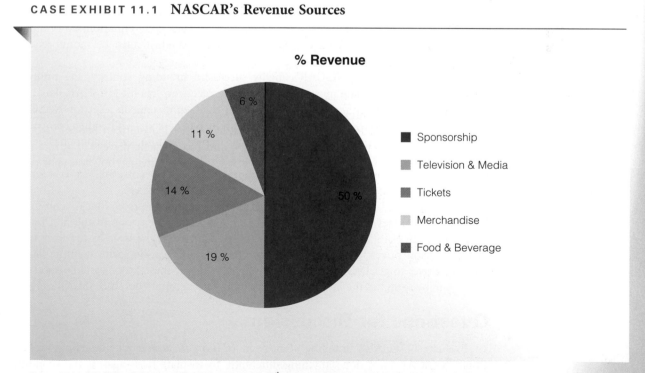

% Revenue

- Sponsorship
- Television & Media
- Tickets
- Merchandise
- Food & Beverage

Source: Richard K. Miller, "Chapter 36 " in *Sports Marketing*, 15th edition (Richard K. Miller & Associates, 2012), pp. 265–271.

only selected races rather than the entire season. Additionally, after three years of declining viewership, NASCAR ratings saw an increase in 2011 for the Sprint Cup Series on FOX. Nielsen ratings showed a 9.7 percent jump to 8.6 million viewers, up from 7.8 million viewers in 2010. More importantly, the ratings showed a 19 percent rating boost in their target market of 18- to 34-year-old males, a coveted target audience.

The improvement in NASCAR's fortunes can be credited to a number of factors. First, the lack of competition with other viewing options in 2011 and more exciting races than in past years helped to increase viewership. At the tracks, NASCAR has worked to improve the fan experience by better understanding fans' needs. Towards this end, the NASCAR Fan Council has been developed as a pre-qualified online community of 12,000 passionate fans who provide feedback on every race and channel ideas and opinions that would improve the racing experience. In addition, NASCAR CEO Brian France signaled a bid to simplify the points structure in all three series in order to place greater emphasis on race victories, thereby, increasing the enthusiasm for the sport. To make the races more exciting, NASCAR relaxed its code of conduct for drivers to promote more heated rivalries between drivers and racing teams. Likewise, NASCAR started enforcing double-file restarts to promote rivalry and bumping on the track. Finally, NASCAR has also continued to lower ticket prices in an effort to woo fans back to the tracks.

Conclusion

Branding has evolved to represent the personality of a company, and NASCAR is a shining example of an organization that successfully embraces the branding mantra. Throughout its 60-plus years of existence, NASCAR has developed and implemented a branding strategy that encompasses a wide range of marketing initiatives. Brands are built on powerful emotional connections through an extremely wide variety of touch points. NASCAR delivers these connections through event marketing, emotional branding, brand communities, customer understanding, drivers, differentiation, co-branding, and the understanding that once a brand has been created, it must be monitored and allowed to continuously evolve.

However, in spite of NASCAR's highly successful branding strategy, the future of NASCAR is uncertain. The most recent economic recession has hit NASCAR hard. The majority of sports are suffering as sponsors pull their endorsements. Yet for NASCAR, which depends so much on its brand alliances and partnerships with other companies, the pullout of sponsors has had an even greater impact. Automaker support has been a crucial component to NASCAR's success, and as the financial situation of key automakers remains in doubt, so does their funding of NASCAR events. Still, experts foresee that manufacturers will continue to play a major part in NASCAR.

The lower attendance at NASCAR events is also borne of the recession. As consumers strive to save money, discretionary spending on entertainment is one of the first budget items to be cut. NASCAR has taken a proactive stance toward the issue by lowering ticket and concession prices, changing the racing structure, and working with communities to offer incentives to get fans to travel to the events. Whether these actions will be successful remains to be seen, but the intense brand loyalty of fans certainly lies in NASCAR's favor.

Questions for Discussion

1. Evaluate NASCAR's branding strategy in relation to its overall marketing strategy. Could NASCAR have done anything differently to insulate itself against the economic downturn?

2. Conduct a strategic SWOT analysis for NASCAR at this point in its history. What opportunities are available for NASCAR to take advantage of given its many significant strengths?

3. What strategies do you recommend to counter the criticisms leveled against NASCAR? Should the company become more involved in sustainability initiatives? If so, how might that be tied in with NASCAR's branding strategies?

4. What strategies can you offer to move NASCAR to the next level in its evolution? How can the company maintain, or even increase, its sponsor and fan base?

Sources

The facts of this case are from Ken Belson, "Reacting to Its Stalled Popularity, NASCAR Checked Under the Hood," *New York Times*, February 23, 2012 (http://www.nytimes.com/2012/02/24/sports/autoracing/nascar-takes-steps-to-regain-its-following.html?pagewanted=all); Viv Bernstein, "NASCAR Remains Low on Its Main Fuel," *New York Times*, February 25, 2012 (http://www.nytimes.com/2012/02/26/sports/daytona-500-nascars-sponsors-still-cautious.html?_r=2); Viv Bernstein, "Driver's Seat Elusive for Black Racers," *New York Times*, May 19, 2012 (http://www.nytimes.com/2012/05/20/sports/autoracing/nascar-stuggles-with-diversity-as-drivers-seat-eludes-black-racers.html?pagewanted=all); Matthew T. Bodie (2011), "NASCAR Green: The Problem of Sustainability in Corporations and Corporate Law," *Wake Forest Law Review*, Vol. 46, Issue 3, pp. 491–522; "Bootlegging Roots," *All About Racin'* (http://nascarfans.wetpaint.com/page/Bootlegging+Roots); David Caraviello, "NASCAR Ticket Prices Can Be a Source of Contention," NASCAR.com, October 25, 2008 (http://www.nascar.com/2008/news/opinion/10/25/inside.line.dcaraviello.ticket.prices/index.html); Liz Clarke, "In Wake of Lower TV Ratings and Sagging Attendance, NASCAR Looks for Some Fast Buzz," *The Washington Post*, May 31, 2009 (http://www.washingtonpost.com/wp-dyn/content/article/2009/05/30/AR2009053001696.html); Larry DeGaris, "NASCAR Fans Have Unparalleled Awareness of Sport's Sponsors, New Study Finds," James Madison University, February 7, 2005 (www.jmu.edu/kinesiology/pdfs/NASCAR.pdf); "Fan Loyalty to NASCAR Sponsors," *Marketing at 200 MPH* (http://it.darden.virginia.edu/itpreview/Nascar/128/html/fanloyal.htm), accessed July 27, 2012; Mark Finney, "Like the Cars, Fuel Goes Fast in NASCAR," *azcentral.com*, January 2, 2006 "Former NASCAR Official Files $225 Million Lawsuit," NASCAR.com, June 11, 2008 (http://www.nascar.com/2008/news/headlines/cup/06/10/former.official.lawsuit/index.html); Jenna Fryer, "NASCAR to Begin Phasing in Unleaded Fuel," *USA Today*, June 19, 2006 (http://www.usatoday.com/sports/motor/nascar/2006-06-19-unleaded-fuel_x.htm); Jack Gage, "NASCAR's Trouble At The Track," *Forbes*, February 9, 2009 (http://www.forbes.com/2009/02/09/nascar-france-advertising-business-sportsmoney_0209_nascar.html); Sean Gregory, "NASCAR: A Once Hot Sport Tries to Restart Its Engine," *Time*, April 26, 2010 (http://www.time.com/time/magazine/article/0,9171,1982299,00.html); Sean Gregory and Steve Goldberg, "Daytona Drag: NASCAR Tries To Outrace the Recession," *Time*, February 12, 2009 (http://www.time.com/time/business/article/0,8599,1879136-2,00.html); "Growth of the Sport," *All About Racin'* (http://nascarfans.wetpaint.com/page/The+Growth+of+the+Sport), accessed July 28, 2012; Ed Hinton, "Drive for Diversity Shifts Out of Neutral,"*ESPN*, January 21, 2009 (http://sports.espn.go.com/rpm/nascar/cup/columns/story?columnist=hinton_ed&id=3850027); "History of NASCAR," NASCAR.com, March 8, 2010 (http://www.nascar.com/news/features/history); Godwin Kelly, "How NASCAR, ISC Prospered with France Jr. at the Helm," *The Daytona Beach News-Journal*, June 5, 2007 (http://www.news-journalonline.com/special/billfrancejr/newHEAD08060507.htm); Godwin Kelly, "Despite Economy, NASCAR Rallying Revenue, Fan Base," *The Daytona Beach News Journal*, July 6, 2011 (http://www.news-journalonline.com/columns/motorsports/2011/07/06/despite-economy-nascar-rallying-revenue-fan-base.html); Ben Klayman, "NASCAR Expects Lower Attendance in 2009," *Reuters*, February 11, 2009 (http://www.reuters.com/article/reutersEdge/idUSTRE51B03J20090212); Lee, J. W., Bernthal, M. J., Whisenant, W. A., & Mullane, S. (2010), "NASCAR: Checkered Flags Are Not All That Are Being Waved," *Sport Marketing Quarterly*, 19 (3), pp. 170–179; Tim Lemke, "Future Starts Now for NASCAR; Tweaks Designed to Halt Decline in Attendance and Ratings," *The Washington Times*, February 8, 2007 (http://www.highbeam.com/doc/1G1-159039606.html); "Lester Hopes He Inspires More Blacks into NASCAR," *ESPN*, March 18, 2006 (http://sports.espn.go.com/rpm/news/story?seriesId=2&id=2373984); "NASCAR Drive for Diversity Initiative Moves Forward in 2009 with An Expanded Driver Lineup," *Auto Racing Daily*, January 23, 2009 (http://www.autoracingdaily.com/news/nascar/nascar-drive-for-diversity-initiative-moves-forward-in-2009-with-an-expande); "NASCAR History," *All About Racin'* (http://nascarfans.wetpaint.com/page/NASCAR+History), accessed July 28, 2012; "NASCAR 101," NASCAR.com (http://www.nascar.com/kyn), accessed July 28, 2012; "NASCAR Racing Series," NASCAR.com, April 28, 2008 (http://www.nascar.com/news/features/nascar.series/index.html); "NASCAR's Sponsorship Revenue Up By 10 Percent," NASCAR.com, December 8, 2010 (http://www.nascar.com/news/101208/nascar-sponsorship-up-2011/index.html); "NASCAR's TV Ratings Rise After Three-Year Decline," NASCAR.com, June 14, 2011 (http://www.nascar.com/news/110614/ratings-increase-2011/index.html); Nate Ryan, "Pinch on Automakers Could Leave NASCAR 'Truly Hurting,'" *USA Today*, December 21, 2008 (http://www.usatoday.com/sports/motor/nascar/2008-12-21-cover-automakers_N.htm); Nate Ryan, "Lower Prices, Promotions Don't Stop NASCAR Attendance Drop," *USA Today*, May 7, 2010 (http://www.usatoday.com/sports/motor/nascar/2010-05-06-nascar-attendance_N.htm); Nate Ryan, "Did NASCAR Go Too Far in Promoting Driver Safety?" *USA Today*, February 20, 2011 (http://www.usatoday.com/sports/motor/nascar/2011-02-18-safety_N.htm); Lee Spencer, "Can NASCAR Up the Pace in 2012?" *Fox Sports*, January 27, 2012 (http://msn.foxsports.com/nascar/story/nascar-state-of-the-sport-address-brian-france-mike-helton-robin-pemberton-2012-means-bigger-changes-012612); Lee Spencer, "What NASCAR Fans Can Expect in 2012," *Fox Sports*, February 7, 2012 (http://msn.foxsports.com/nascar/story/nascar-daytona-500-nascar-sheds-light-on-technical-and-rules-changes-as-2012-season-nears-020612); "Talladega Reduces Ticket Prices for Cup Series Races," NASCAR.com, January 8, 2009 (http://www.nascar.com/2009/news/headlines/cup/01/08/talladega.reduces.ticket.prices/index.html); "Toyota Racing President Expects NASCAR Cutbacks," NASCAR.com, January 14, 2009 (http://www.nascar.com/2009/news/headlines/cup/01/14/toyota.expected.cutbacks/index.html?eref=/rss/news/headlines/cup); Steve Waid, "Despite Great Competition, NASCAR Must Still Deal With An Ongoing Problem," *Motorsports Unplugged*, December 18, 2011 (http://motorsportsunplugged.com/?p=5315); and Nolan Weidner, "NASCAR Thriving with Some Variety; Five Years Later, the Organization's Drive for Diversity is Bearing Fruit," *The Post-Standard* (Syracuse, NY), August 13, 2005, p. D1.

CASE 12

IndyCar: Seeking a Return to Motorsports' Fast Lane*

Synopsis: Auto racing is the fastest growing spectator sport in the United States. Unfortunately, open-wheel racing has experienced a period of decline while other forms of auto racing—most notably NASCAR—have grown. After years of damaging competition, the Indy Racing League and Champ Car (CART) have finally reunified. New sponsors, new business opportunities, and a new television contract are positive signs for IndyCar, but the league remains a distant third to NASCAR in terms of popularity in the motorsports market. In addition, the death of driver Dan Wheldon in 2011 casts serious doubts on the safety of IndyCar racing. IndyCar must address this issue and several other concerns in order to strengthen its standing in the American motorsports market, continue the task of reconnecting with former fans, and build connections with new fans and sponsors.

Themes: Competition, market segmentation, product and branding strategy, sports and event marketing, sponsorship, global marketing, corporate governance, marketing implementation

The origins of IndyCar can be traced back to the formation of Championship Auto Racing Teams (CART) in 1978. Several automobile racing team owners created CART as a sanctioning body for open-wheel racing in the United States. Open-wheel racing refers to cars whose wheels are located outside the body of the car rather than underneath the body or fenders as found on streetcars. Also, they have an open cockpit, also called a pod, with the engine housed at the rear of the vehicle. The sport had been sanctioned since the mid-1950s by the United States Auto Club (USAC), but many racing teams were dissatisfied with USAC's administration and promotion of open-wheel racing. Consequently, CART was founded when 18 of the 21 team owners left USAC to form the new league.

Growth and Division of U.S. Open-Wheel Racing

For the first 17 years of its existence, CART dominated auto racing in the United States, and open-wheel racing enjoyed greater notoriety than other forms of racing, including stock-car racing. However, not everyone associated with open-wheel racing in the United States welcomed the success enjoyed by CART. One person with major concerns about the direction of CART was Anton H. "Tony" George, President of the Indianapolis

*Don Roy, Middle Tennessee State University, prepared this case for classroom discussion rather than to illustrate effective or ineffective handling of an administrative situation.

Motor Speedway. George's family had founded the Indianapolis 500 and developed it into the premier American auto race and an event of worldwide significance. George was concerned that CART was beginning to lose sight of the interests of American open-wheel racing by holding events in foreign countries, putting too much emphasis on racing at road courses instead of oval tracks, and focusing too much on promoting top foreign drivers as CART stars.

In 1994, George announced that he was creating a new open-wheel league that would compete with CART beginning in 1996 called the Indy Racing League (IRL) (the forerunner to today's IndyCar). The new league was divisive to open-wheel racing in the United States, as team owners were forced to decide whether to remain with CART or move to the new IRL. Only IRL members would be allowed to race in the Indianapolis 500. CART teams responded by planning their own event on the same day as the Indianapolis 500. CART held the U.S. 500 at the Michigan International Speedway on Memorial Day weekend, 1996, and drew over 100,000 spectators to the event. The rift between CART and the IRL moved to the courts when lawsuits were filed over use of the terms "IndyCar" and "Indy car," which CART had licensed from the Indianapolis Motor Speedway for several years. The result of the lawsuit was that neither party could use the terms until December 31, 2002.

The IRL-CART feud distracted both leagues and stock car racing solidified its standing as the favorite motor sport in the United States. A 2001 ESPN Sports Poll survey found that 56 percent of American auto racing fans said stock car racing was their favorite type of racing, with open-wheel racing third at 9 percent (drag racing was second at 12 percent). The diminished appeal of open-wheel racing contributed to additional problems with sponsor relationships. Three major partners left CART, including Honda and Toyota, which provided engines and technical support to CART and its teams. In addition, FedEx discontinued its title sponsor relationship with CART after the 2002 season. During the same time, the IRL struggled to find corporate partners as a weakened economy and a fragmented market for open-wheel racing made both the IRL and CART less attractive to sponsors.

The IRL experienced ups and downs in the years following the split. Interest in IRL as measured by television ratings took a noticeable dip between 2002–2004, with 25 percent fewer viewers watching races in 2004 than just two years earlier. The declining television audience was a factor in the IRL's inability to sell naming rights for its series. The IRL went without a title sponsor for the series from 2002 through 2009. In contrast, NASCAR signed a blockbuster deal with Nextel that called for more $700 million over 10 years beginning in 2004. Industry experts believed that the most the IRL could command for its title sponsorship as long as it competed with CART was about $50 million over 10 years.

In response to declining interest in the IRL, marketing initiatives were taken to reverse the trend. The IRL beefed up its marketing staff. The league did not even have a dedicated marketing staff until 2001. In 2005, the IRL launched a new ad campaign that targeted 18- to 34-year-old males. The focus of the ads was different, too. Instead of focusing on the cutting-edge technology found in IRL cars, as had been done in previous ad campaigns, the focus shifted to drivers and the drama created on the track. The campaign was part of a broader strategy to expand the association of IRL beyond a sport for middle-aged Midwestern males. The idea was to position the brand has hip and young.

In support of this effort, two developments can be noted. First, the IRL followed a trend observed in NASCAR and got several celebrities involved in the sport through team ownership. Among the celebrities involved with the IRL are talk show host David Letterman, NBA star Carmelo Anthony, former NFL quarterback Jim Harbaugh, and actor Patrick Dempsey. Another celebrity involved with the IRL is rock star Gene Simmons. He is a partner in Simmons Abramson Marketing, who was hired to help the

IRL devise new marketing strategies. The firm's entertainment marketing savvy was tapped to help the IRL connect with fans on an emotional level through its drivers, whom Simmons referred to as "rock stars in rocket ships."

Second, driver personalities began to give the IRL some visibility. The emergence of Danica Patrick as a star in the IRL broadened the appeal of the league and assisted its efforts to reach young males. In 2005, Patrick was a 23-year-old IRL rookie, who finished fourth in the Indianapolis 500. The combination of the novelty of a female driver and her captivating looks and personality made her the darling of American sports that year. Patrick's effect on the IRL was very noticeable; the IRL reported gains in event attendance, merchandise sales, website traffic, and television ratings during Patrick's rookie season. Patrick has drawn the interest of many companies that have hired her as a product endorser, including Motorola, Go Daddy, Boost Mobile, and XM Radio. In addition, she appeared in photo shoots in *FHM* and the 2008 and 2009 *Sports Illustrated* swimsuit issues. Another driver that has gained notoriety is Helio Castroneves, a Brazilian driver who won the Indianapolis 500 in 2001, 2002, and 2009. He enhanced his celebrity status by appearing on the popular television show *Dancing with the Stars* in 2007, winning the competition.

The Motorsports Market

Although many forms of motorsports exist, competition for IndyCar can be narrowed to two properties: Formula 1 and NASCAR. Each competitor is discussed below.

Formula 1

Formula 1 is an open-wheel series that has the greatest global reach in terms of race venues and races exclusively on road courses. Formula 1's 20-race schedule includes eight races in Europe as well as races in Australia, Bahrain, Brazil, Canada, China, India, Japan, Malaysia, Singapore, South Korea, United Arab Emirates, and United States. A Formula 1 race is known as a Grand Prix, with each race taking on the name of the country hosting a particular race (e.g., Grand Prix of Spain). Formula 1 was the first racing league in the Western hemisphere to stage an event in the lucrative Chinese market. Formula 1's drivers have an international flavor. Most hail from European countries, although there are also drivers from Australia, Brazil, and Japan. The winner of the Formula 1 season series is referred to as the "Formula 1 World Driver Champion" further reinforcing Formula 1 as a global racing league.

NASCAR

The clear leader in the U.S. motorsports market is NASCAR (National Association of Stock Car Auto Racing). It was founded in the early 1950s, approximately the same time period when USAC was founded. NASCAR fields three racing circuits in the United States: The Sprint Cup Series, the Nationwide Series, and the Camping World Truck Series. The Sprint Cup Series is NASCAR's premier circuit. Its 36 races are held primarily on oval tracks and exclusively in U.S. markets. Like IndyCar, NASCAR has a strong regional following, with the southeast U.S. being a long-time hotbed for the league. NASCAR was predominantly a southern U.S. sport until the 1990s as exposure provided by cable television and the emergence of strong driver personalities such as Dale Earnhardt and Jeff Gordon led to an explosion in NASCAR's popularity. The league has become even more popular as it has focused on marketing drivers, especially young drivers often referred to as NASCAR's "Young Guns." League and sponsor promotion of drivers such as Dale Earnhardt, Jr., Jimmie Johnson, Ryan Newman, and

Kasey Kahne has vaulted NASCAR to a level of popularity in the U.S. second only to the National Football League.

Today, NASCAR towers over IndyCar in the United States in terms of sponsor support and audiences. NASCAR has sought to expand to become a truly national sport, adding races in Chicago, southern California, and Texas while eliminating races in smaller markets such as Rockingham, North Carolina. Future expansion plans include adding events in the Pacific Northwest and the New York City area. The average television audience for NASCAR races in 2011 averaged approximately 5 percent of U.S. households, compared to less than 2 percent for IndyCar. As a result of NASCAR's popularity growth, it was able to negotiate a lucrative, multi-billion dollar contract with Fox and ESPN, while IndyCar struggled to secure a favorable television deal.

Reunification

Many racing observers believe that open-wheel racing could have been as popular as NASCAR is today. In the 1980s and early 1990s it was CART that enjoyed greater popularity and television ratings. The split in open-wheel racing that led to the formation of the IRL was a setback to open-wheel racing in general. The split resulted in a dilution of competition quality, sponsor dollars, and fan support. Many experts believed a reunification of open-wheel racing was the only way to compete against NASCAR.

The long awaited reunification of U.S. open-wheel racing occurred before the beginning of the 2008 season. Champ Car's operations (CART had changed ownership and its name in 2007) were on the verge of ceasing following the cancellation of its final event in 2007 and uncertainty whether a 2008 schedule would be run. Tony George's IRL bought the assets of Champ Car for a mere $10 million and provided a $30 million capital investment for equipment and incentives to bring Champ Car teams into the IRL fold.

After reunification, the IRL rebranded as IndyCar, and its reunified open-wheel racing circuit was branded the IndyCar Series. Decisions had to be made about the markets and racing courses that the IndyCar Series would target following the merger of Champ Car and IRL. The 2012 schedule included 16 races—less than one-half the number of NASCAR Sprint Cup Series races (see Case Exhibit 12.1). One change has been an increase in the number of street and road course races. The IndyCar Series added street races in markets that had been very successful for CART/Champ Car: Long Beach, California, and Toronto, Ontario. Road/street races make up 11 of the 16 races on the IndyCar Series schedule. In contrast, only two of the 36 races in the NASCAR Sprint Cup Series are held on road courses. This characteristic of IndyCar's schedule is drastically different than the product of the old IRL, which ran on oval tracks exclusively between 1996 and 2008.

In addition to the influence of Champ Car's strategy of more street/road courses, another feature of Champ Car that IndyCar sought to leverage was the positioning of races as entertainment events. The race itself is only one piece of the product. Champ Car used the term "Festival of Speed" to position its events. In addition to the race, fans can often partake in such activities as kids' zones, beach volleyball, wine tasting, or live concerts. One description of this approach is "We throw a party and a race breaks out. We don't want people to come out and sit in metal grandstands for three hours and get sweaty and get sunburned and go home. We want stuff going on everywhere." The festival concept has been a success. Street races in Long Beach and Toronto annually draw more than 150,000 people over the course of a three-day race schedule.

Another positive development for the IndyCar Series was a new television broadcast partner. ABC has televised the Indianapolis 500 for 45 years, and IndyCar will continue that relationship. For most of the other races on the schedule (at least 13 per season), IndyCar broke ties with ESPN and signed a 10-year, $67 million contract with

CASE EXHIBIT 12.1   2012 IndyCar Series Racing Schedule

Date	Race
March 25	Honda Grand Prix of St. Petersburg (St. Petersburg, FL)
April 1	Honda Indy Grand Prix of Alabama (Birmingham, AL)
April 15	Toyota Grand Prix Long Beach (Long Beach, CA)
April 29	Sao Paulo Indy 300 (Brazil)
May 27	Indianapolis 500 (Indianapolis, IN)
June 3	Chevrolet Detroit Belle Isle Grand Prix (Detroit, MI)
June 9	Firestone 550, Fort Worth (Fort Worth, TX)
June 16	Milwaukee IndyFest (Milwaukee, WI)
June 23	Iowa Corn Indy 250 (Newton, IA)
July 8	Honda Indy Toronto (Canada)
July 22	Edmonton Indy (Canada)
Aug. 5	Honda Indy 200 at Mid-Ohio (Lexington, OH)
Aug. 19	IndyQingdao 600 (China)*
Aug. 26	Indy Grand Prix of Sonoma (Sonoma, CA)
Sept. 2	Grand Prix of Baltimore (Baltimore, MD)
Sept. 15	Auto Club Speedway (Fontana, CA)

*Race was cancelled June 2012; no race scheduled in its place.
Source: IZOD IndyCar Series—2012 Schedule, IndyCar website, http://www.indycar.com/schedule, accessed July 29, 2012.

VERSUS—rebranded in 2011 as the NBC Sports Network. While the NBC Sports Network has a smaller audience than ESPN, it covers fewer sports and plans to give the IndyCar Series more coverage (at least 10 hours per week during the racing season) than ESPN did when it owned the broadcast rights. The expanded coverage has helped IndyCar move beyond merely broadcasting races to tell the story of its drivers and the series.

Steps Forward, Backward

Both optimism and uncertainty existed as IndyCar moved beyond reunification. A primary concern for IndyCar following reunification was top leadership. Tony George resigned his top positions with both IndyCar and the Indianapolis Motor Speedway in July 2009. His role in causing the split in open-wheel racing was never forgotten, and many people within the industry believed a reunified league would benefit from a new leader. In 2010, Randy Bernard joined IndyCar as CEO following a highly successful tenure leading Professional Bull Riders. Bernard created excitement around PBR events and marketed riders' personalities. He had similar priorities for IndyCar. Bernard wanted to raise the profile of IndyCar drivers, to make them "bigger than life." More elaborate driver introductions were produced at races to spotlight drivers, and the league invested in an office responsible for placing IndyCar and drivers in television and movies. Bernard's commitment to marketing was apparent in the successes IndyCar had signing new sponsors and moving into new markets in the United States (Baltimore) as well as Brazil and China. Bernard's efforts to grow IndyCar showed signs of paying off, as average viewership of televised races increased from 1.1 million in 2010 to 1.3 million in 2011. Also, average attendance rose from 88,805 per race in 2010 to 97,852 in 2011.

New Business Opportunities

Optimism also existed in new business opportunities IndyCar was realizing. One area where IndyCar has made important gains is sponsorships. New marketing agreements have been signed with Coca-Cola, Orbitz, and The National Guard. A partnership with Mattel brought Hot Wheels-branded IndyCars to retail stores and IndyCar Series events, promoting drivers and the Series schedule by including it on product packaging. In 2010, the IndyCar Series landed a title sponsor for the first time since 2001 when IZOD began a six-year deal for the IZOD IndyCar Series. IZOD immediately realized benefits of its IndyCar sponsorship. Using a variety of performance metrics including brand familiarity and digital impressions, IZOD concluded that the first year of the sponsorship in 2010 delivered a 350 percent return on investment. IZOD focused its marketing efforts on advertising, in-store displays, and special events. In particular, IZOD felt it had achieved desired impacts among a key demographic: 25- to 35-year-old males.

Signs of sponsorship growth were seen in 2011. All five sponsors whose deals were up for renewal re-signed with IndyCar: Firestone, Peak Performance Motor Oil, The National Guard, Philips, and Honda. Also, new sponsorship deals were signed with the Boy Scouts of America, MGM Resorts, Green Fuel Technologies, Las Vegas Convention and Visitors Authority, and Trim Nutrition. Sponsorship categories that the league hoped to fill included financial services, health and wellness, green energy, alcohol, and technology. In 2012, IndyCar added new sponsors, a sign that the league may be heading in the right direction. Discover became the official credit card of IndyCar, a category sponsorship that had been vacant since 2006. Fuzzy Vodka also signed on as a sponsor. A partnership with hat retailer Lids put IndyCar merchandise in the company's 1,000-plus stores and turned over management of IndyCar's online merchandise sales to Lids. Also, Chevrolet and Lotus, a British firm, joined Honda as engine suppliers in 2012. The addition of these engine manufacturers, coupled with Firestone's decision to renew its partnership as the official tire supplier, were positive developments that strengthened IndyCar's relationships with its equipment providers.

Another step forward for IndyCar is increasing its presence beyond tracks and race broadcasts. IndyCar will be prominently featured in the DreamWorks movie "Turbo." It is a story of a snail that dreams of being fast enough to win the Indianapolis 500. The movie will be released in 2013 and feature the Indianapolis Motor Speedway as well as several IndyCar teams, drivers, and sponsors. IndyCar stands to reap great benefits from the exposure that a DreamWorks movie can provide; an estimated $100 million will be spent by the studio to promote "Turbo." Also, a weekly television series "INDY-CAR 36" follows a driver at the track and away from it over a 36-hour period that gives fans a more intimate view of some of the personalities of IndyCar.

Global Expansion?

IndyCar executives see potential benefits in global expansion, although not all car owners are bullish on adding more races outside of North America. CEO Randy Bernard wants to increase the current IndyCar Series schedule from 16 to 20 races. Among his desires are scheduling two races each in Brazil and China. The league would gain large sanctioning fees, the payment made by a race promoter to stage a race. Great fan interest in markets like Brazil and China means that fees for international TV rights IndyCar receives would increase by staging races in lucrative markets. Cities in emerging markets eager to showcase their locations would welcome IndyCar. And, holding races outside of North America expands the potential pool of sponsors for the league and racing teams.

However, not all teams share the enthusiasm for global expansion. Established teams with sponsors whose base of operations is primarily North America say that global expansion hurts exposure for their sponsors and television ratings as races are broadcast either live in early-morning hours or rebroadcast after the outcome is known. The consensus among car owners is that while an international presence is beneficial to the IndyCar Series, its efforts must focus on growing the business in North America. Adding a race in Canada is appealing to IndyCar because of the success of races in Toronto and Edmonton. Vancouver, Calgary, and Quebec City have been mentioned as possible additions to future IndyCar schedules.

Fan Engagement

Another marketing priority for IndyCar has been to enhance engagement with fans, both at and away from the tracks. Developing a consistent presentation for all events has enhanced the fan experience at IndyCar Series races. The IZOD IndyCar Fan Village debuted in 2011 and included involvement from several sponsors in the form of pavilions that gave fans opportunities to interact with sponsors' products, play games, and visit exhibits. The decision to go with a league-operated experience was made because of an inconsistent presence of interactive areas for fans—some race venues had many exhibits while others had few interactive opportunities. A key feature of the IZOD IndyCar Fan Village is that admission requires fans to be a member of IndyCar Nation. Membership is free; the purpose of the membership requirement is to enable IndyCar to collect more data about fans that attend races.

Improving the fan experience has not been limited to efforts at the tracks. A redesign of the IndyCar.com website connected fans with content on the league's social media sites (Facebook, Twitter, YouTube, and Flickr) as well as bloggers from other sites writing about IndyCar. Also, the profile of sponsors was elevated as league partners were featured on the website. IndyCar uses social networking to engage fans beyond providing news and information. The league partnered with Cie Games, a gaming company that created the Facebook game "Car Town." The game has more than eight million players. IndyCar's presence in "Car Town" includes cars that players buy and a pit-stop challenge with an Indianapolis 500 theme. IndyCar and Cie Games shared revenue from IndyCar-related purchases made by "Car Town" players.

Like NASCAR, IndyCar is challenged to get young people interested in the sport. Among the steps taken to target youth have been lowering the age to enter the garage area to as young as 9 years old. Also, the Indianapolis Motor Speedway offered children 12 and under a free general admission ticket to the race with a paid adult ticket. Creating value by offering interactive, entertaining experiences at races at customer-friendly prices has potential strategic benefits for IndyCar. Michael Andretti, a former IRL driver and now IndyCar team owner, believes the cost advantage of attending IndyCar races compared to NASCAR gives the league an upper hand in a difficult economic environment.

Lingering Concerns

Despite the positive developments for IndyCar, the long-term future is unclear. One concern is the mix of racetracks and target markets. The 2012 schedule has twice as many road/street races than oval track races. IndyCar touts the mix of races as challenging to drivers, forcing them to master a variety of tracks in order to win the IndyCar season championship. Critics fear fewer oval tracks will take the IndyCar series away from its roots. Also, oval track racing is more popular with fans in the United States as evidenced by NASCAR's popularity.

The trend toward scheduling more races outside the United States is another concern. While only four of the 16 markets on the 2012 schedule were outside the U.S. (two in Canada and one each in Brazil and China), some observers feel that IndyCar is not doing enough to market itself in the U.S. nor adequately promoting American drivers.

The IndyCar driver roster has a more global flavor to it than NASCAR, with drivers hailing from Brazil, Canada, England, France, New Zealand, Spain, and Switzerland, in addition to American drivers. The strong Midwestern U.S. influence of IndyCar seems to be at odds with the globalization of auto racing in general and the desires of IndyCar leadership in particular.

Another challenge faced by IndyCar has been to bring stability to its schedule. American markets such as Cincinnati and Nashville were dropped as IndyCar seeks to find the best locations and tracks for its events. Financial problems of race promoters created headaches for IndyCar to meet its planned race schedule. In 2012, the first-ever IndyCar race in China had to be canceled when the race promoter could not meet the financial requirements to hold the race. As a result, the season was reduced to 15 races. Also, promoters of the Baltimore Grand Prix faced serious financial problems that threatened the two-year-old event. Luckily, a new promoter was signed to bring in financial stability.

Maintaining continuity in drivers has been an issue facing Indy racing for years as successful drivers have left to pursue more lucrative opportunities in NASCAR. Tony Stewart, Sam Hornish, Jr., and Robby Gordon all left for NASCAR in recent years, and the most popular IndyCar driver in two decades, Danica Patrick, left IndyCar to compete in NASCAR in 2012. Marketing top drivers can be an effective strategy, but those efforts can be negated if a driver leaves for another series. Despite only winning one race in seven years, Patrick had brought great interest to the league with a combination of attractiveness and determination. Her popularity brought Patrick many endorsement deals, making her very appealing to sponsors seeking to reach the large audience that NASCAR has. Despite Danica Patrick's popularity and visibility as the face of IndyCar, some insiders believe that her departure will actually benefit the league. Patrick's presence overshadowed other drivers like four-time IndyCar Series champion Dario Franchitti. Now, the league can be more diverse in its marketing of drivers and personalities.

Problems with schedules, race promoters, and marketing drivers paled in comparison to the situation IndyCar was forced to deal with on October 16, 2011, at the season-ending race in Las Vegas. IndyCar invested heavily in the race, taking the unusual step of renting the track and handling all promotions and race operations. A crowd of 70,000 was anticipated, including 50,000 tickets that were given away to fans that supported other IndyCar races during the season. A massive marketing blitz included more than 1,600 ads on radio, TV, and billboards. Randy Bernard issued a $5 million challenge to any driver from NASCAR or Formula 1 that entered and won the race. No drivers accepted the challenge, so Bernard sought to build excitement by offering a fan a chance to split $5 million with driver Dan Wheldon, the 2011 Indianapolis 500 winner. Go Daddy sponsored Wheldon as part of a special promotion, the Go Daddy IndyCar Challenge. To add intrigue to the promotion, Wheldon would start the race from the back of the field. The promotion had the desired effect as thousands of people entered online for a chance at the prize money. However, the excitement and buzz created for the race was replaced with grief and loss; Dan Wheldon was killed in a horrific crash just 11 laps into the race.

Dan Wheldon's death called into question the safety of racing on oval tracks, which were built for stock car racing such as NASCAR. IndyCars reach speeds of more than 220 miles per hour, significantly faster than stock cars. Many people in the racing industry said that IndyCar should discontinue racing on ovals. The decision is complicated by the fact that American auto racing fans prefer racing on oval tracks. One executive said of IndyCar: "the cars have to adapt to run these oval tracks, or I don't think the sport has a very bright future." The Wheldon tragedy brought scrutiny to the IndyCar Series and the safety of its drivers. In the days following Wheldon's death, CEO Randy Bernard said that IndyCar was "in crisis, and we have to get answers."

Conclusion

Auto racing has been the fastest growing spectator sport in the United States in recent years. Unfortunately, open-wheel racing has experienced a period of decline while other forms of auto racing have grown. IndyCar is a distant second to NASCAR in terms of popularity. The league must strengthen its standing in the American motorsports market. With the two major open-wheel leagues reunified, IndyCar must reconnect with fans and sponsors as well as build new relationships. And, it must ensure the safety of its greatest marketing asset—the IndyCar drivers.

Questions for Discussion

1. Identify the external factors that have impacted and continue to impact IndyCar and its marketing efforts. Which factors appear to be IndyCar's greatest opportunities and threats?
2. What are IndyCar's greatest strengths? Which weaknesses would you recommend IndyCar attempt to convert into strengths? How might these weaknesses be converted?
3. What advantages does IndyCar possess over NASCAR? How should these advantages be used by IndyCar to compete with NASCAR?
4. What can IndyCar learn from NASCAR's success? Are there elements of NASCAR's marketing strategy that IndyCar could adopt?
5. What steps should IndyCar take to move beyond the death of Dan Wheldon and reassure both fans and drivers about the safety of IndyCar racing?

Sources

The facts of this case are from "Andretti Has Eye on Regaining Market Share," *Street & Smith's Sports Business Journal*, May 18, 2009 (http://m.sportsbusinessdaily.com/Journal/Issues/2009/05/20090518/SBJ-In-Depth/Andretti-Has-Eye-On-Regaining-Market-Share.aspx); Steve Ballard, "Championship Auto Racing Teams' Board Votes to Accept Buyout," *The Indianapolis Star*, December 16, 2003 (http://www.highbeam.com/doc/1G1-119497409.html); Theresa Bradley, "Racing League Gears Hip Events at Youth," *Knight Ridder Tribune Business News*, March 23, 2006, p. 1; "Celebrities Who Are Revved Up Over Racing," *Street & Smith's Sports Business Journal*, May 22, 2006, p. 27; Tony Fabrizio, "Racer Danica Patrick Embraces Celebrity Exposure," *Tampa Tribune*, February 27, 2009 (http://www2.tbo.com/sports/breaking-news-sports/2009/feb/27/racer-danica-patrick-embraces-celebrity-exposure-ar-115990); Shawn Fenner, "IRL Sees Significance of Selling Product to U.S. Market," *Richmond Times-Dispatch*, June 23, 2009 (http://www2.timesdispatch.com/sports/2009/jun/23/irlf23_20090622-214806-ar-39355); "Helio Castroneves Heading Back to Dancing With the Stars," *Autoweek*, July 27, 2012 (http://www.autoweek.com/article/20120727/INDYCAR/120729846); Reggie Hayes, "What's Next for IndyCar?" *Fort Wayne News-Sentinel*, July 1, 2009; "Hot Wheels Announces Partnership with the IndyCar Series, Indianapolis 500," *Entertainment Newsweekly*, April 24, 2009, p. 140; "IndyCar Renews Toronto Race through '14, Looks to Add More Canadian Races," *Sports Business Daily*, May 15, 2012 (http://www.sportsbusinessdaily.com/Daily/Issues/2012/05/15/Leagues-and-Governing-Bodies/Indy-Car.aspx); "IndyCar CEO Randy Bernard Breaks His Silence, Says Now is Time to be Leader," *Sports Business Daily*, October 26, 2011 (http://www.sportsbusinessdaily.com/Daily/Issues/2011/10/26/Leagues-and-Governing-Bodies/IndyCar.aspx?hl=IndyCar&sc=0); "IndyCar CEO Randy Bernard is Optimistic Race in Vegas will Create more Fans," October 14, 2011 (http://www.sportsbusinessdaily.com/Daily/Issues/2011/10/14/Events-and-Attractions/IndyCar.aspx?hl=IndyCar&sc=0); Terry Lefton, "Ad Sales Encouraging as IRL Launches Season," *Street & Smith's Sports Business Journal*, March 30, 2009, p. 8; Tripp Mickle, "IndyCar Offering Deal to Eventually Replace Sponsor Izod," *Sports Business Journal*, June 11, 2012, p. 1; Tripp Mickle, "IndyCar's China Race in Doubt over Fee," *Sports Business Journal*, June 11, 2012, p. 8; Tripp Mickle, "IndyCar Turbocharged over Animated Film," *Sports Business Journal*, March 12, 2012, p. 3; Tripp Mickle, "IndyCar Moves beyond Tragedy, Targets Growth," *Sports Business Journal*, February 13, 2012, p. 6; Tripp Mickle, "Final-Race Fatality Overshadows Season of Growth in Ratings and Attendance for IndyCar," *Sports Business Journal*, October 31, 2011, p. 7; Tripp Mickle, "IndyCar Faces Push-Back on Global Plans," *Sports Business Journal*, October 10, 2011, p. 6; Tripp Mickle, "5 Keys to IndyCar's Growth," *Sports Business Journal*, May 16, 2011, p. 17; Tripp Mickle, "IndyCar Moves into Facebook's 'Car Town'," *Sports Business Journal*, April 11, 2011, p. 9; Tripp Mickle, "Versus Boosts IndyCar Coverage with Expanded Live Race Windows and Shoulder Programming,"

Sports Business Journal, March 21, 2011, p. 5; Tripp Mickle, "It Takes a Village, and IndyCar is Planning One," *Sports Business Journal*, March 7, 2011, p. 6; Tripp Mickle, "Izod: 350% Return in First Year of IndyCar Deal," *Sports Business Journal*, November 15, 2010 (http://www.sportsbusinessdaily.com/Journal/Issues/2010/11/20101115/This-Weeks-Issue/Izod-350-Return-In-First-Year-Of-Indycar-Deal.aspx?hl=IndyCar&sc=0); John Oreovicz, "Brazil, Bama on 2010 IndyCar Schedule," *ESPN Racing*, July 31, 2009 (http://espn.go.com/rpm/blog/_/name/oreovicz_john/id/4370121/brazil-bama-2010-indycar-schedule); John Ourand, "Early IRL Numbers Small, But Please Versus," *Street & Smith's Sports Business Journal*, May 18, 2009, p. 18; John Ourand, "IRL to Get at Least 7 Hours Weekly on Versus," *Street & Smith's Sports Business Journal*, February 23, 2009, p. 7; Nate Ryan, "Dan Wheldon's Death Raises Questions for IndyCar Circuit," *USA Today*, October 18, 2011 (http://www.usatoday.com/sports/motor/indycar/story/2011-10-17/indycar-faces-questions-about-future-after-death-of-dan-wheldon/50807480/1?csp=ip); Michael Smith, "New IndyCar Site Geared to Help Fans Make Connections," *Sports Business Journal*, March 15, 2010 (http://www.sportsbusinessdaily.com/Journal/Issues/2010/03/20100315/This-Weeks-News/New-Indycar-Site-Geared-To-Help-Fans-Make-Connections.aspx?hl=IndyCar&sc=0); Michael Smith, "United Series Begins Long Trek of Rebuilding," *Street & Smith's Sports Business Journal*, March 3, 2008, p. 5; Alan Snel, "Kiss Rocker Lends Voice to Indy Races," *Knight Ridder Tribune Business News*, April 1, 2006, p. 1; J.K. Wall, "Indy Racing League Sets Sights on Marketing Dollars, *Knight Ridder Tribune Business News*, May 27, 2004, p. 1; Scott Warfield, "Danica Patrick Provides Sizzle to IRL," *Street & Smith's Sports Business Journal*, May 23, 2005, p. 1; Scott Warfield, "IRL in Line to Court Young Males," *Street & Smith's Sports Business Journal*, November 29, 2004, p. 4; "Wheldon's Death Puts Spotlight on IndyCar for Wrong Reasons," *Sports Business Daily*, October 18, 2011 (http://www.sportsbusinessdaily.com/Daily/Issues/2011/10/18/Leagues-and-Governing-Bodies/IndyCar.aspx?hl=IndyCar&sc=0); and Jeff Wolf, "George's Ouster Clouds IRL's Future," *Las Vegas Review-Journal*, July 3, 2009 (http://article.wn.com/view/2009/07/03/JEFF_WOLF_Georges_ouster_clouds_IRLs_future).

CASE 13

Zappos: Delivering Happiness*

Synopsis: This case examines Zappos' unique marketing strategy and corporate culture, both of which focus on delivering happiness to the company's varied stakeholders. Despite a few stumbles along the way, Zappos has been a role model of success since its founding in 1999. The company survived the dot-com collapse because its charismatic CEO, Tony Hsieh, created a corporate culture that put its customers and employees ahead of financial success. The case looks at Zappos' business model and how it influences the company's relationships with customers, employees, the environment, and its communities. The case also discusses some of the challenges the company faces and how it plans to move into the future.

Themes: Marketing strategy, ecommerce, branding, long-term customer relationships, customer satisfaction, corporate culture, employee relations, social responsibility, customer loyalty, corporate reputation

C an a company focused on happiness be successful? Zappos, an online retailer, is proving that it can. The company's revenue grew from $1.6 million in 2000 to $1.64 billion in 2010. Tony Hsieh, Zappos' CEO says, "It's a brand about happiness, whether to customers or employees or even vendors." Zappos' zany corporate culture and focus on customer satisfaction has made it both successful and a model for other companies.

The History of Zappos

Nick Swinmurn founded Zappos in 1999 after a fruitless day spent shopping for shoes in San Francisco. After looking online, Swinmurn decided to quit his job and start a shoe website that offered the best selection and best service. Originally called ShoeSite.com, the company started as a middleman, transferring orders between customers and suppliers but not holding any inventory. The website was soon renamed Zappos, after the Spanish word for shoes (zapatos).

In 2000, entrepreneur Tony Hsieh became the company's CEO. Hsieh, 26 at the time, was an early investor in Zappos, having made $265 million selling his startup company to Microsoft in 1998. Hsieh wasn't initially sold on the idea of an Internet shoe store. He

*Harper Baird, Bernadette Gallegos, and Beau Shelton developed this case under the direction of O.C. Ferrell and Linda Ferrell, University of New Mexico. It is intended for classroom discussion rather than to illustrate effective or ineffective handling of administrative situation.

told Inc. Magazine, "It sounded like the poster child of bad Internet ideas...but I got sucked in." After becoming CEO, Hsieh made an unconventional decision to keep Zappos going, even selling his San Francisco loft to pay for a new warehouse and once setting his salary at just $24.

Zappos struggled its first few years, making sales but not generating a profit. The dotcom crash forced Zappos to lay off half its staff, but the company recovered. By the end of 2002, Zappos had sales of $32 million but was still not profitable. In 2003, the company decided that in order to offer the best customer service, it had to control the entire value chain—from order to fulfillment to delivery—and began holding its own inventory. Zappos moved to Las Vegas in 2004 to take advantage of a larger pool of experienced call center employees. The company generated its first profit in 2007 after reaching $840 million in annual sales. Zappos also started to be recognized for its unique work environment and approach to customer service.

In 2010, Amazon bought the company for $1.2 billion. Although Hsieh had rejected an offer from Amazon in 2005, he believed that this buyout would be better for the company than management from the current board of directors or an outside investor. Hsieh said, "With Amazon, it seemed that Zappos could continue to build its culture, brand, and business. We would be free to be ourselves." Amazon agreed to let Zappos operate independently and to keep Hsieh as CEO (at his current $36,000 annual salary). Hsieh made $214 million from the merger, and Amazon set aside $40 million for distribution to Zappos employees. After the merger, the company restructured into 10 separate companies organized under the Zappos Family.

Zappos' Business Model and Operating Philosophy

Zappos has ten core values that guide every activity at the company and form the heart of the company's business model and culture:

- Deliver WOW through service.
- Embrace and drive change.
- Create fun and a little weirdness.
- Be adventurous, creative and open-minded.
- Pursue growth and learning.
- Build open and honest relationships with communication.
- Build a positive team and family spirit.
- Do more with less.
- Be passionate and determined.
- Be humble.

Zappos' core values differ from those of other companies in a couple of ways. In addition to being untraditional, the core values create a framework for the company's actions. This is exemplified in the company's commitment to their customers' and employees' well-being and satisfaction.

Zappos' Customer-Focused Business Model

The Zappos business model is built around developing long-term customer relationships. Zappos does not compete on price because it believes that customers will want to buy from the store with the best service and selection. The company strives to create a unique and addicting shopping experience, offering a wide selection of shoes, apparel, accessories, and home products, free shipping to the customer, free shipping and full refunds on returns, and great customer service.

Shopping and Shipping   Zappos strives to make the shopping experience enjoyable. The website is streamlined for an easy shopping experience. Products are grouped in specialized segments, with some (like outdoor products) on their own mini-sites. Customers can view each product from multiple angles thanks to photographs taken at the company's studio, and Zappos employees make short videos highlighting the product's features. Zappos analyzes how customers navigate the site to improve features, adapt search results, and plan inventory.

This spirit of simplicity, innovation, and great service extends to Zappos' inventory and distribution systems as well. Zappos has one of the few live inventory systems on the web. If the Zappos website displays an item, it is in stock. Once the company sells out of an item, the listing is removed from the website. This helps to reduce customer frustration. Its inventory and shipping systems are linked directly to the website via a central database, and all its information systems are developed in-house and customized to the company's needs. Their warehouses operate around the clock, which allows them to get a product to the customer faster. Fast shipping creates an instant gratification that is similar to shopping in a physical store.

Most companies have a negative view toward returns, but Zappos' mentality is the complete opposite. It sees returns as the ability to maintain customer relationships and to increase its profits. Zappos offers a 100% Satisfaction Guaranteed Return Policy. If a customer is not satisfied with a purchase, he or she can return it within 365 days for a full refund. The customer can print a pre-paid shipping label that allows all domestic customers to return the product for free. This return policy encourages customers to order several styles or different sizes and return the items that do not work out.

While this strategy seems expensive, it actually works to Zappos' advantage. The average industry merchandise return rate is 35 percent, but Zappos' most profitable customers tend to return 50 percent of what they purchase. The customers who have the higher return percentages are the most profitable because they have experienced Zappos' customer service and return policy, which create loyalty to the company. These customers are likely to make purchases more often and to spend more on each purchase. Craig Adkins, who is the vice president of services and operations, stated that this is exactly what has made Zappos so successful, saying, "Since it costs the same to ship a $300 pair of pumps as it does a $30 pair of sandals, the Zappos policy of winning over shoppers with its returns policy has helped to bring in high profit margins on many of its orders."

Customer Service   What really makes the Zappos business model unique is the company's focus on customer service. The company has established a method of serving customers and handling their issues that is distinctive from the rest of the industry. Zappos believes great customer service is an opportunity to make the customer happy. Customers are encouraged to call Zappos with any questions. The number is displayed on every page of the website. Hsieh says, "…At Zappos, we want people to call us. We believe that forming personal, emotional connections with our customers is the best way to provide great service." Customer service representatives also actively use social media sites such as Facebook and Twitter to respond to customer issues.

Another key aspect of Zappos' customer service model is that nothing is scripted. Employees have free reign in their decision-making and are expected to spend as much time as they need to "wow" customers. They help customers shop, even on their competitors' websites, encourage them to buy multiple sizes or colors to try (since return shipping is free), and do anything it takes to make the shopping experience memorable.

Zappos' customer service representatives try to develop relationships with their customers and make them happy. Stories about great customer service include customer support calls that last for hours, sending flowers to customers on their birthdays, and surprise upgrades to faster shipping. Some extreme cases have included Zappos hand-delivering shoes to customers who have lost luggage and to a groom who forgot the shoes for his wedding. Zappos has even sent pizzas to the homes of customers who have tweeted to the company about being hungry.

Zappos believes that great customer experiences encourage customers to use the store again. In addition, Zappos' long-term strategy is based on the idea that great customer service will help them expand into other categories. While around 80 percent of Zappos' orders come from shoes, the markets for housewares and apparel are much larger. The company says it will expand into any area that it is passionate about and that meet their customers' needs.

The company also considers word-of-mouth marketing to be the best way to reach new customers. CFO/COO Alfred Lin says, "The customer is more powerful than paid advertising." With over 75 percent of purchases made by repeat customers, it is evident that Zappos' mission to "provide the best customer service possible" is working well for the company.

Corporate Culture and Work Environment

The corporate culture at Zappos sets it apart from nearly every other company. As Amazon's CEO, Jeff Bezos, says, "I've seen a lot of companies, and I have never seen a company with a culture like Zappos." Zappos' unorthodox culture is the work of CEO Tony Hsieh, an innovative and successful entrepreneur. Hsieh built the culture on the idea that if you can attract talented people and employees enjoy their work, great service and brand power will naturally develop.

Zappos is famous for its relaxed and wacky atmosphere. Employee antics include Nerf ball wars, office parades, ugly sweater days, and donut-eating contests. The headquarters features an employee nap room, a wellness center, and an open mic in the cafeteria. Other quirky activities include forcing employees to wear a "reply-all" hat when they accidentally send a company-wide e-mail. This environment isn't just fun; it's also strategic. According to Zappos, "When you combine a little weirdness with making sure everyone is also having fun at work, it ends up being a win-win for everyone: Employees are more engaged in the work that they do, and the company as a whole becomes more innovative."

Hiring and Training   The key to creating a zany work environment lies in hiring the right people. The job application features a crossword puzzle about Zappos and asks employees questions about which superhero they'd like to be and how lucky they are. They may also check how potential employees treat people like their shuttle driver. Zappos is looking for people with a sense of humor who can work hard and play hard. Potential employees go through both cultural and technical interviews to make sure they will fit with the company. However, even Hsieh admits that finding great employees is tough. "One of the biggest enemies to culture is hyper-growth. You're trying to fill seats with warm bodies, and you end up making compromises," says Hsieh.

All new employees then attend a five-week training program, which includes two weeks on the phones providing customer service and a week fulfilling orders in a warehouse. To make sure that new employees feel committed to a future with the company, Zappos offers $2,000 to leave the company after the training (less than 1 percent of new employees take the deal). Even after the initial training is over, employees take 200 hours of classes—with the company, covering everything from the basics of business to advanced Twitter use—and read at least nine business books a year.

Benefits   Another aspect of Zappos that is unique is the benefits that it provides to its employees. The company has an extensive health plan, where it pays 100 percent of employee's medical benefits and on average 85 percent of medical expenses for employees' dependents. The company also provides employees with dental, vision, and life insurance. Other benefits include a flexible spending account, pre-paid legal services, a 40 percent employee discount, free lunches and snacks, paid volunteer time, life coaching, and a car pool program.

Along with the extensive benefits package, Zappos has developed a compensation model for its "Customer Loyalty Team" (call center representatives) that incentivizes employee development. All employees are paid $11 per hour for the first 90 days. After 90 days, the employee moves to $13 per hour. To move beyond $13 an hour, employees must demonstrate growth and learning by completing specific skill set courses that allow employees to specialize in certain areas of the call center. Although the reasoning for Zappos' compensation model is to motivate employees and promote personal growth, the $13 base pay is less than the national hourly average of $15.92 earned by call center representatives. Zappos says, "While the Zappos Family tends to pay on the low-average to average side of the scale, the relaxed environment and potential for advancement both add value that cannot be counted on a paycheck."

Work-Life Integration   One of Zappos' core values is "Build a positive team and family spirit," so the company expects employees to socialize with each other both in and out of the office. In fact, managers spend 10 to 20 percent of their time bonding with team members outside of work. Zappos outings include hiking trips, going to the movies, and hanging out at bars. Hsieh says that this increases efficiency by improving communication, building trust, and creating friendships.

Along with creating friendships, employees are encouraged to support each other. Any employee can give another employee a $50 reward for great work. Zappos employees compile an annual "culture book" comprised of essays on the Zappos culture and reviews of the company. The culture book helps employees to think about the meaning of their work and is available unedited to the public.

This positive work environment comes with the expectation that employees will work hard. Employees are evaluated on how well they embody the core values and inspire others. Zappos will fire people who are doing great work if they don't fit with the culture of the company. Hsieh says, "We definitely don't want anyone to feel that they're entitled to employment for life. It's more about us creating an environment and growth opportunities for our employees such that they want to be employees for life."

Transparency   As with its customers, the foundation of Zappos' relationships with its employees is trust and transparency. The company wants its employees, like its customers, to actively discuss any issues or concerns that may come up. Hsieh does not have an office; he sits in an open cubicle among the rest of the employees. He believes that "the best way to have an open-door policy is not to have a door in the first place." Zappos' management is very open with employees by regularly discussing issues on the company blog. Employees receive detailed information about the company's performance and are encouraged to share information about the company. Zappos believes that employees should develop open and honest relationships with all stakeholders with the hope that this will assist in maintaining the company's reputation. Hsieh uses Facebook and Twitter to share information with employees and customers (he has over 2.6 million followers).

Despite the benefits of transparency, it can also be painful at times. In October 2008, Sequoia Capital, a venture capital firm and controlling investor in Zappos, told the company to "cut expenses as much as possible and get to profitability and cash flow positive as soon as possible." As a result, Hsieh had to make a difficult decision and lay off 8 percent, or 124, of Zappos' employees. Hsieh strived to handle the layoffs in a respectful and kind manner. He sent an e-mail notifying employees of the layoff and was honest and upfront about the reasons behind the decisions, even discussing the move on Twitter and his blog. Employees who were laid off received generous severance packages, including six months of paid COBRA health insurance coverage. Because of the company's honesty and transparency, employees and customers were more understanding of the tough decision Hsieh and Zappos had to make. Although some companies may hesitate to open themselves to public criticism, Zappos feels it has nothing to hide. In fact, most of the public posts on Zappos' social media sites are praise from customers.

Corporate Social Responsibility Zappos also takes an unconventional approach to corporate social responsibility and philanthropy. Many companies have CSR programs that are dedicated to a certain area or cause such as education, but Zappos prefers to support a variety of programs based on the needs of communities and the interests of employees.

Zappos is involved in a variety of philanthropic efforts. Programs include donating shoes and gifts, giving gift cards to elementary school students, and participating in LIVESTRONG Day (wearing yellow to create awareness about cancer). Zappos donates money to organizations such as the Shade Tree, a non-profit that provides shelter to women and children, and the Nevada Childhood Cancer Foundation.

Zappos recently started a campaign to improve the company's impact on the environment. A group of employees created the initiative, which is known as Zappos Leading Environmental Awareness for the Future (L.E.A.F.). The campaign focuses on several environmental efforts, including a new recycling program, community gardens, and getting LEED certification for the company. L.E.A.F.'s most recent effort was Zappos Recycles Day, an event to raise awareness on recycling and other ways the company can reduce its carbon footprint. Like the rest of the company, L.E.A.F. is very open with its progress posted on its Twitter account and blog.

Another area on the company's blog is a section on "Eco-friendly Products." Here, the company highlights new products that are organic or were manufactured using environmentally friendly procedures. The postings also list ways that customers can live more sustainable lifestyles, including tips on how to throw an eco-friendly party.

Zappos' Marketing Challenges

Like any company, Zappos has faced some challenging business and ethical issues in the past. When these issues occur, Zappos attempts to handle situations in a professional and efficient manner. However, the transparency at Zappos makes some business and ethical issues more complex as the company strives to solve problems while keeping its stakeholders informed.

Merger with Amazon

In 2009, Zappos was acquired by ecommerce giant Amazon.com. Many Zappos customers were confused by the unexpected move and expressed concerns about the future of the company's culture and customer service. Most CEOs would not have felt any obligation to address customer concerns over the merger, but Tony Hsieh valued the support of Zappos' employees and customers.

Shortly after the acquisition, Hsieh issued a statement about why he sold Zappos to Amazon. In the statement, Hsieh discussed the disagreement between Zappos and Sequoia Capital over management styles and company focus. Specifically, Hsieh said, "The board's attitude was that my 'social experiments' might make for good PR but that they didn't move the overall business forward. The board wanted me, or whoever was CEO, to spend less time on worrying about employee happiness and more time selling shoes." Hsieh and Alfred Lin, Zappos' CFO and COO, were the only two members on the board committed to preserving Zappos' culture. The board could fire Hsieh and hire a new CEO who would focus more on profits.

Hsieh decided that the best way to resolve these issues was to buy out the board, but he could not do this on his own. After meeting with Amazon CEO Jeff Bezos, Hsieh committed to a full acquisition, as long as Zappos could operate independently and continue to focus on building its culture and customer service. Many customers were concerned that Amazon was not a good fit for Zappos, but Hsieh addressed those concerns, saying, "Amazon wants to do what is best for its customers—even, it seemed to me, at the expense of short-term financial performance. Zappos has the same goal. We just have a different philosophy about how to do it." Although consumers were not pleased with the acquisition, they at least understood why it occurred. Moreover, Hsieh's commitment to his beliefs and management style resonated with customers and employees.

More than Shoes Campaign

To bring awareness to the fact that Zappos sells more than just shoes, Zappos created a marketing campaign in 2011 that was designed to catch people's attention. The company released several advertisements that featured people who appeared to be naked doing daily activities such as running, hailing a cab, and driving a scooter. The creative advertisements had certain parts of models' bodies blocked off with a box that said "more than shoes." The campaign received criticism from several groups because of its sexual nature. However, the catch with these ads was that the subjects of the ads were not actually nude; they wore bathing suits or small shorts that were later covered by the box. Because of the negative attention, Zappos pulled the ads and released an apology that explained the production process.

Technical Difficulties

In October 2011, Zappos experienced some technical difficulties that resulted in delays and problems in customers' orders and shipments. Zappos upgraded one of its processing systems, and in the process many orders were deleted or delayed. Some orders had the incorrect shipping information, and products were shipped to the wrong location. Although this upset several customers, Zappos handled the problems and reassured customers that it would get their merchandise as soon as possible. The company also offered different perks, depending on the circumstances of each customer experience.

Another problem Zappos encountered was that every item from 6pm.com, one of its websites, was priced at $49.95 for six hours in 2010. The company had to shut down the website for a few hours to solve the problem. Zappos honored all the orders from the pricing mistake, which resulted in a $1.6 million loss.

In January 2012, hackers broke into Zappos' computer system, and the company had to respond to the theft of 24 million customers' critical personal information. The stolen data included customers' names, e-mail addresses, shipping and billing addresses, phone numbers, and the last four digits of their credit cards. Zappos immediately addressed the situation by sending an e-mail to customers notifying them of the security breach. Zappos assured customers the servers containing their full credit card information were not hacked. Zappos' next move was to disconnect its call center, reasoning that the expected number of calls would overload its system.

While Zappos has a reputation for delivering customer service that is unmatched by any competitor, some customers were unhappy with how Zappos handled the hacking. Many customers were upset by their information being hacked, but the situation was made worse by Zappos' action of disconnecting its call center. Although this situation caused problems for Zappos and blemished its customer service record, the company believes that it can restore its reputation.

The Future of Zappos

Zappos remains committed to serving its customers and employees. So far, the company has retained its unique culture and continues to expand into new product categories. In a recent interview, Hsieh talked about the growth of Zappos and how he believes that expanding into the clothing and merchandise market will help the company to grow. Hsieh says that "the sky is the limit" for Zappos, and that growing and expanding into many different types of businesses is Zappos' future. During his interview, Hsieh states, "Although Zappos is a long way from becoming a company that is similar to Virgin, it does consider Virgin a role model in how Zappos wants to shape itself." (Virgin Group Limited is a successful U.K. conglomerate.) As Zappos expands, it will have to work harder to hire the right people, avoid technical issues, and maintain its quirky culture.

Leadership is a key factor in the success of any company, and for Zappos, having Tony Hsieh as a leader is a strong indicator for future success. Hsieh has expressed that he will do whatever it takes to make his employees, customers, and vendors happy. The future for any company looks bright when its leadership is committed to such strong values. However, Zappos needs to make sure that it continues to focus on its stakeholders and its long-term vision with or without Hsieh.

Ultimately, Zappos intends to continue to deliver happiness to its stakeholders. Hsieh says,

> "At Zappos, our higher purpose is delivering happiness. Whether it's the happiness our customers receive when they get a new pair of shoes or the perfect piece of clothing, or the happiness they get when dealing with a friendly customer rep over the phone, or the happiness our employees feel about being a part of a culture that celebrates their individuality, these are all ways we bring happiness to people's lives."

Zappos' success and innovative business model have caught the attention of many other companies. The company has appeared on several prestigious lists including *Fortune*'s "Best Companies to Work For," *Fast Company*'s "50 Most Innovative Companies," *BusinessWeek*'s "Top 25 Customer Service Champs," and *Ethisphere*'s "World's Most Ethical Companies." Zappos' business model is so successful that the company offers tours and workshops, which cost $5,000 for two days at the company's headquarters. The company also created Zappos Insights, an online service that allows subscribers to learn more about Zappos' business practices through blogs and videos. These programs have high profit potential for the company because they are built on what Zappos already does best. As the company continues to gain recognition for its efforts in creating a vibrant and transparent corporate culture and business model, Zappos' success among its varied stakeholders looks promising.

Questions for Discussion

1. How would you define Zappos' target market, and how would you describe its strategy to serve this market?
2. Has Zappos' emphasis on customer satisfaction contributed to its profitability? Explain.
3. Has Zappos developed long-term customer relationships that provide a competitive advantage in the purchase of shoes and other products?

Sources

Scott Adams, "Refreshing Honesty on Why Zappos Sold to Amazon," *Tech Dirt*, June 7, 2010 (http://www.techdirt.com/articles/20100607/0014299706.shtml); Peter Bernard, "Zappos Hacking Could Cause Consumer Problems Later," *The Tampa Tribune*, January 16, 2012 (http://www2.tbo.com/news/breaking-news/2012/jan/16/zappos-hacking-could-cause-consumer-problems-later-ar-348177); David Burkus, "The Tale of Two Cultures: Why Culture Trumps Core Values in Building Ethical Organizations," *The Journal of Value Based Leadership*, Winter/Spring 2011 (http://www.valuesbasedleadershipjournal.com/issues/vol4issue1/tale_2culture.php), accessed July 29, 2012; Brian Cantor, "How Zappos Escaped Outrage over Customer Service Problems," *Customer Management*, October 11, 2011 (http://www.customermanagementiq.com/operations/articles/how-zappos-escaped-outrage-over-customer-service-p); Max Chafkin, "How I Did It: Tony Hsieh, CEO, Zappos.com," *Inc.*, September 1, 2006 (http://www.inc.com/magazine/20060901/hidi-hsieh.html); Max Chafkin, "The Zappos Way of Managing," *Inc.*, May 1, 2009 (http://www.inc.com/magazine/20090501/the-zappos-way-of-managing.html); Andria Cheng, "Zappos, under Amazon, keeps its independent streak," *MarketWatch*, June 11, 2010 (http://www.marketwatch.com/story/zappos-under-amazon-keeps-its-independent-streak-2010-06-11); Michael Dart and Robin Lewis, "Break the Rules the Way Zappos and Amazon Do," *BusinessWeek*, May 2, 2011, p. 2; Eric Engleman, "Q&A: Zappos CEO Tony Hsieh on Life Under Amazon, Future Plans," *Puget Sound Business Journal*, September 29, 2010 (http://www.bizjournals.com/seattle/blog/techflash/2010/09/qa_zappos_ceo_tony_hsieh_on_life_under_amazon_and_moving_beyond_shoes.html); Cheryl Fernandez, "Zappos Customer Loyalty Team - Pay, Benefits, and Growth Opportunities," YouTube, October 26, 2010 (http://www.youtube.com/watch?v=OB3Qog5Jhq4); Ed Frauenheim, "Jungle Survival," *Workforce Management*, September 14, 2009, Vol. 88 (Issue 10), pp. 18–23; Carmine Gallo, "Delivering Happiness the Zappos Way," *BusinessWeek*, May 13, 2009 (http://www.businessweek.com/smallbiz/content/may2009/sb20090512_831040.htm); "Henderson-Based Zappos Earns Honors for Ethics," *Las Vegas Sun*, April 14, 2009 (http://www.lasvegassun.com/news/2009/apr/13/henderson-based-zappos-earns-honors-ethics); Tony Hsieh, "Zappos: Where Company Culture is #1," YouTube, May 26, 2010 (http://www.youtube.com/watch?v=bsLTh9Gity4); Tony Hsieh and Max Chafkin, "Why I Sold Zappos," *Inc.*, June 2010, pp. 100–104; John R. Karman III, "Zappos Plans to Add 5,000 Full-Time Jobs in Bullitt County," *Business First*, October 28, 2011 (http://www.bizjournals.com/louisville/print-edition/2011/10/28/zappos-plans-to-add-5000-full-time.html); Aneel Karnani, "The Case Against Corporate Social Responsibility," *MIT Sloan Management Review*, August 22, 2010 (http://sloanreview.mit.edu/executive-adviser/2010-3/5231/the-case-against-corporate-social-responsibility); Elizabeth C. Kitchen, "Zappos.com Hack Affects 24 Million Customers," *Yahoo Voices*, January 16, 2012 (http://voices.yahoo.com/zapposcom-hack-affects-24-million-customers-10842473.html); Sara Lacy, "Amazon-Zappos: Not the Usual Silicon Valley M&A," *BusinessWeek*, July 30, 2009 (http://www.businessweek.com/technology/content/jul2009/tc20090730_169311.htm); Greg Lamm, "Zappos Up-Front with Challenges of New Ordering System," *Puget Sound Business Journal*, October 8, 2011 (http://www.bizjournals.com/seattle/blog/techflash/2011/10/zappos-up-front-with-challenges.html); Jeffrey M. O'Brien, "Zappos Knows How to Kick It," *Fortune*, February 2, 2009, Vol. 159 Issue 2, pp. 54-60; Joyce Routson, "Hsieh of Zappos Takes Happiness Seriously," *Stanford Center for Social Innovation*, November 4, 2010 (http://csi.gsb.stanford.edu/hsieh-zappos-takes-happiness-seriously); Aman Singh, "At Zappos, Getting Fired For Not Contributing to Company Culture," *Forbes*, November 23, 2010 (http://www.forbes.com/sites/csr/2010/11/23/at-zappos-getting-fired-for-not-contributing-to-company-culture); "Tony Hsieh: Redefining Zappos' Business Model," *BusinessWeek*, May 27, 2010 (http://www.businessweek.com/magazine/content/10_23/b4181088591033.htm); "2011 World's Most Ethical Companies," *Ethisphere*, 2012 (http://ethisphere.com/2011-worlds-most-ethical-companies), accessed July 29, 2012; United States Bureau of Labor Statistics, Occupational Employment and Wages: Customer Service Representatives, May 2011 (http://www.bls.gov/oes/current/oes434051.htm), accessed July 29, 2012; William Wei, "The Future of Zappos: From Shoes to Clothing to a Zappos Airline," *Business Insider*,

October 22, 2010, (http://www.businessinsider.com/zappos-shoes-clothing-airline-2010-10); Samantha White-horne, "Cultural Lessons from the Leaders at Zappos.com," *American Society of Association Executives*, August 2009 (http://www.asaecenter.org/Resources/ANowDetail.cfm?ItemNumber=43360), accessed July 29, 2012; "Whitewater Rafting? 12 Unusual Perks," *CNN Money* (http://money.cnn.com/galleries/2012/pf/jobs/1201/gallery.best-companies-unusual-perks.fortune/3.html), accessed July 29, 2012; Marcie Young and Erin E. Clack, "Zappos Milestone: Focus on Apparel," *Footwear News*, May 4, 2009 (http://about.zappos.com/press-center/media-coverage/zappos-milestone-focus-apparel); Masha Zager, "Zappos Delivers Service…With Shoes on the Side," *Apparel Magazine*, January 2009, Vol. 50 Issue 5, pp. 10–13; and "Zappos gives up lunch to Give Back to Community," *Zappos Blogs: Zappos Family*, September 9, 2008 (http://blogs.zappos.com/blogs/inside-zappos/2008/09/09/zappos-gives-up-lunch-to-give-back-to-community).

CASE **14**

Sigma Marketing: Strategic Marketing Adaptation*

Synopsis: This case reviews the growth of a small, family-owned business, from a regional provider of generic printing services to a global provider of specialty advertising products. Throughout its history, Sigma Marketing has exhibited the uncanny ability to understand market opportunities and to adapt its strategic focus accordingly. As its marketing environment changes, Sigma Marketing gathers information from existing and potential customers to develop the most effective marketing strategy possible. Even in the face of changing technology, communication, and advertising methods, Sigma Marketing has managed to reinvent its mindset and strategies in order to remain successful.

Themes: Changing marketing environments, market opportunities, strategic focus, product strategy, direct marketing, promotion, personal selling, implementation, customer relationships, family-owned business

In 1967, Don Sapit purchased a small printing company in Streator, Illinois, as a hands-off personal investment that would later grow into what is today a successful specialty advertising business located in Orange Park (Jacksonville), Florida. Sigma Marketing has a unique identity that has evolved over the past 45 years from a small-town printing company to a marketing services company with a diverse, multinational clientele. Sigma's marketing history is an excellent example of the strategic shift from a production orientation to a market orientation.

Don Sapit was president of Weston Laboratories, a small research facility in Ottawa, 80 miles southwest of Chicago, when he had an opportunity to acquire Dayne Printing Company. Sapit had been a Dayne client for several years. When Dayne was on the verge of bankruptcy, Don bought the company as an investment while still focusing most of his day-to-day efforts on Weston Labs. The managers of Dayne at the time were willing to stay on and handle the operations with little outside help. Don felt that with the increased volume that Weston would provide, the operation could become profitable within a 12-month period. To enhance the corporate image, the name was changed to Sigma Press, Inc. A new sales manager was hired to focus on the sales aspect of the business, while Sapit took the position of absentee owner. Over the next few years, their efforts provided only minimal increases in sales volume. The business survived, but made little progress—typical

*Mike Sapit, President, Sigma Marketing (http://www.sigmamktg.com), with assistance from O.C. Ferrell and Jennifer Sawayda, University of New Mexico, prepared this case for classroom discussion rather than to illustrate effective or ineffective handling of an administrative situation.

results for an absentee-owned business. In addition, Sigma mainly focused on the production process and selling generic printing services.

In spite of the slow progress, Sapit saw the potential for turning Sigma into a quality-oriented printing business that could make substantial gains against its local competition. The area served by the shop covered a radius of approximately 30 miles around the city of Streator and had a number of major manufacturing plants that were potential users of substantial quantities of printing. Unfortunately, most of these plants were headquartered in other cities and did not have authority for local purchasing of anything beyond the basic necessities required for daily plant operations. Although Sigma could do custom printing, the small firm did not have a unique niche other than its quality and service.

The Desk Calendar: A Strategic Opportunity

In seeking alternatives to improve sales, Sapit and Sigma's staff developed an advertising desk pad calendar for distribution as a customer gift. Its purpose was to keep the Sigma name, phone number, and list of services in front of the customer as a constant reminder of its existence. It was freely offered to any customer thought to have sufficient volume potential to justify the expense of the calendar and its distribution costs. At the time, Sigma thought of the calendar as a promotional tool for its own business and did not consider the calendar as a product that could potentially differentiate the company and give it a competitive edge.

One of the customers that received the calendar, Oak State Products, an Archway Cookie Bakery, asked whether Sigma could produce similar calendars for them with the Archway advertisement printed at the top. Sigma filled this initial order, and it proved popular with Archway's customers. The next year, Archway asked whether the calendars could be produced with a color photo of the plant in the ad space. This version was so well received that Oak State recommended the use of the calendar as a marketing tool to other Archway Bakeries around the country. Sigma recognized that the opportunity for a new marketing strategy was developing. The small printer with a generic product identified an opportunity to expand its market beyond its small geographic service area.

The sales volume realized from the calendar was not substantial, but Sapit saw in it a good possibility for a totally new marketing strategy, removed from the limitations imposed by Sigma's present sales territory. Furthermore, he conceived a direct marketing effort that would permit sales penetration into a much larger geographical area than was practical to serve with Sigma's limited sales staff.

At this time, Weston Laboratories was sold and Sapit was forced to make a decision to leave the company due to philosophical differences with the new owners. Although Sigma was starting to show potential for very modest profitability and good growth, it was still just barely able to support itself. After a family council meeting in 1971, the decision was made to "tough it out." Sapit chose to enter the Sigma operation on a full-time basis and to prove that it really could become a first-class operation based on a new marketing strategy.

After coming aboard full time, Sapit assumed all marketing and management responsibilities himself. Previously, sales representatives had been making calls on a hit-or-miss basis with no real continuity. Sapit developed a general marketing strategy, which included defining specific sales territories, and developing target markets and sales prospect databases. He also implemented a scheduled mailing program as part of the strategy. On the commercial printing side, a sample "job of the month" was sent to customers and prospects at regular intervals. On the calendar side, direct mail materials promoting the desk calendar to specific target markets were utilized. At that time, direct mail promotion of printing services was relatively unheard of in the printing industry. Most of Sigma's competitors performed custom printing based on the needs and projects that the customer desired, and did not promote specific products.

The advertising desk calendar was marketed on the theme of "constant exposure advertising." It was given the product name "Salesbuilder," which moved Sigma into the specialty advertising business. Each customer was offered a standard calendar format with an individual ad imprint customized to fit the needs of the company's business. The imprint could contain line drawings, photos, product lists, or any special information necessary to convey the company's message to customers. Sigma's willingness to encourage attractive and creative designs received immediate attention and acceptance by customers. It set the company apart from the competition, which allowed only "four lines of block type, not to exceed 32 letters." In effect, Sigma was at the forefront of a new specialty-advertising product.

Within a year of Sapit's entry into the business, total volume was up 50 percent; even more important, the response to the calendar marketing effort was starting to show real promise. As a result, Sigma was experiencing the need for additional capital to finance the growth. Capital was obtained through the private sale of one-third of the company to Sapit's friend and colleague, who was a local attorney. The new investor was not involved in the daily operations of the business, but served as corporate secretary, legal counsel, board member, and advisor. The cash raised from the stock was used to help fund the day-to-day operations and expand accounts receivable resulting from the increased volume.

By late 1972, Sigma's commercial printing sales were gaining at a modest rate of increase, but calendar sales were increasing at a rate of 40 percent per year. It was becoming apparent that larger manufacturing facilities would be required in the immediate future or the sales efforts would have to be scaled back. The company purchased a more visible and accessible 5-acre site in Ottawa, Illinois, and constructed a new facility with a focus on improved production as well as image. Sapit decided to capitalize on the new visibility and image by changing the strategic emphasis of the business.

Sigma Expands Its Strategy

Over the next few years, Sigma's strategy was oriented toward building a reputation for producing the most creative and highest quality printing in its service area, which had a 35- to 40-mile radius around Ottawa. Sapit anticipated that this new direction would give his firm a solid reputation as a quality printer, one that fully justified the higher prices it charged. Several of the larger local companies obtained permission from their corporate offices to procure their printing locally. The downstate division of Carson Pirie Scott & Company, a large department store chain, chose Sigma for the production of its catalogs. The new marketing strategy paid off, and total sales volume had increased 220 percent by 1976.

Calendar sales increased slowly but steadily. Management wanted growth, but in an orderly and controlled manner. Management also wanted its growth to be more profitable than the industry average of approximately 5 percent on sales. It was becoming obvious that to be successful in the printing business, Sigma needed to specialize. After long and deliberate discussion during 1976, company management wrote a three-year corporate plan.

The corporate plan emphasized marketing, which at this time was considered unique for a small commercial printer. The marketing plan focused a major share of the sales and marketing effort on building a market for the "Salesbuilder" desk calendar. The target market consisted primarily of smaller corporate accounts; while the marketing program emphasized a quality product and advertising with an internal sales staff, direct marketing distribution, and a superior price point. Space advertising in sales and marketing-oriented publications created substantial numbers of inquiries, but sales levels did not follow. Direct mail, primarily to manufacturers, produced a much higher response and return on investment. Sigma had created a unique product that was very flexible in terms of unique designs, advertising messages, photographic techniques, and other special requirements. In short, "Salesbuilder" became a highly effective marketing tool.

Within the next few calendar seasons, large accounts such as Serta Mattress, Domino Sugar, and Borden, Inc., were added to the list of satisfied customers. Reorder rates were very high, usually in the 88 to 90 percent range. Quantities ordered by individual companies tended to increase annually for three or four years and then level off. Total calendar sales had increased at a rate of approximately 40 percent per year during the 1976–1980 period, during which time commercial printing sales increased at a rate of about 15 percent annually.

A Strategic Shift

Because of the success of the new strategy, production capacity was being taxed. In 1979–1980, major capital commitments were made to add a new high-speed two-color press and to purchase, redesign, and rebuild a specialized collating machine to further automate calendar assembly, previously assembled by hand. This opened the way to mass marketing of the "Salesbuilder" calendar line. Direct mail techniques were improved to allow selection of prospects by SIC number and sales volume. A toll-free 1-800 number encouraged direct response by interested parties. Whenever possible, Sigma responded to inquiries by sending a sample calendar that contained advertising ideas related to the respondent's line of business. The sample would be followed up with a personal phone call within two to three weeks. Calendar sales continued to improve until, by 1983, they represented 50 percent of total sales and approximately 75 percent of net profit.

In spite of the success of the calendar marketing programs and attractive profit levels, Sapit was disturbed by trends in the printing industry that pointed toward a diminishing market and increased competition for the commercial segment, particularly in Sigma's local Rust Belt area. Rapid development of new technology and high-speed equipment had caused industry-wide investments in new equipment well beyond immediate need, creating excess capacity. The result was cost cutting and reduced margins.

Sigma's management had for some time been considering selling the commercial portion of its business in favor of becoming an exclusive marketer of calendar products. Through its membership in the Printing Industry of Illinois, a buyer was found for the plant, equipment, and the goodwill of the commercial portion of the business. The buyer agreed to enter into a long-term contract to handle the majority of calendar production for Sigma, using the same plant and staff that had been handling the production for the previous 10 years. The sale was completed in June 1983. This signaled the strategic move from a company based on production to one based on marketing.

Sigma's management now found itself free of the daily problems of production and plant management and able to commit all its efforts to creating and marketing new calendar products. Sapit had a long-standing personal desire to move the business to the Sun Belt for the better weather and, more importantly, for the better business climate. In May 1985, Sigma's corporate offices were moved to Orange Park, Florida. Concurrently, Sapit's son, Mike, a graduate of Illinois State University in graphic arts management, joined the business.

Strategic Refinements

To take advantage of Sigma's marketing expertise, the company took actions to expand its product line to include several additional personalized calendar items. The new items included a year-at-a-glance wall planning calendar, desk diary, pocket diary, and a smaller version of the original desk calendar.

Sigma had built its calendar business on products that were basically "off-the-shelf" formats that could be imprinted with the customer's advertising message. In the late 1980s and into the 1990s, Sigma began to see a growing demand for products that were totally customized not only in graphic design but in product specifications as well. Sigma's management saw a market for a new line of "super customized" calendars targeted to medium-to-large corporations with a substantial customer base. These companies were service oriented with large advertising budgets, thus creating the potential for very large orders. The market was relatively small in terms of number of companies, but very large with respect to total sales potential. It would require a totally different marketing approach than previously utilized.

Test advertisements for custom-designed calendars were run in *Advertising Age* and in several marketing trade journals. These advertisements appealed to larger corporate accounts. In addition, the Sigma sales staff became much more aggressive in searching out individual accounts that appeared to have high potential as customized calendar customers. Prospects were researched, and contacted by phone and mail, to determine the individual with the responsibility to specify and authorize this type of purchase. Unsolicited samples of several different customized products were sent via FedEx in order to attract attention. Each prospect was followed up by a phone call within a few days to confirm interest and provide additional information.

The goal was to establish Sigma as a publisher of high quality, creatively designed custom calendars. Initial response to the new marketing strategy was good, with indications that the blue chip companies could, in fact, be reached through this approach. To reach its growth goals, Sigma felt it had to be successful in this marketing strategy. This type of highly customized product design was very demanding on the creative staff. Because only 10 to 15 new accounts of this type could be handled each year, it was important that creative time be spent on high-potential accounts. The new strategy was successful in landing substantial orders from Nabisco, Fidelity Investments, and FedEx. Realizing that these blue chip companies were consumers, Sigma focused the entire organization on meeting five customer needs: (1) flexibility, (2) production of a quality product consistent with the client's image and marketing goals, (3) personal service and attention from beginning to end, (4) fair pricing, and (5) timely, efficient fulfillment.

Sigma's Total Service Package

With the blue chip accounts, Sigma realized that it had to be able to offer its products on a turnkey, or concept-through-fulfillment, basis. Many of these corporations wanted to use a calendar program, but were not able to devote staff, time, or expertise to such a project. Sigma offered the solution—handling the entire calendar promotion, including conception, design, production, and delivery—so that customers could devote their time to more productive efforts, confident that their calendar program was running smoothly and efficiently. They dubbed this the "Total Service Package."

In order to provide total service effectively, Sigma installed new computer equipment and programs to enable comprehensive order fulfillment for a variety of programs. Special shipping manifest programs were developed to simplify the handling of large quantities of drop shipments. From established customer lists or those generated through Sigma's direct order programs, calendars could be shipped to as many as 20,000 locations for a single account. This was particularly helpful to accounts that had dealers or customers scattered across the country.

The business grew rapidly from 1985 to 1990, and by 1991, Don and Mike Sapit saw a new opportunity to expand the business again. After carefully analyzing the characteristics of its buyers and their buying decisions, Sigma found new market opportunities.

During its first 15 years in the promotional calendar business, Sigma focused on large companies that usually distributed their promotional calendars through their sales forces to customers. These companies usually supplied Sigma with the basic idea for their calendar promotion, including an imprint or art design for the firm's individualized calendar.

With its own computer order tracking and manifest system in place, Sigma was able to offer its customers and prospects an efficient and cost-saving order and distribution system. With a customer-supplied list, Sigma began marketing the calendars directly to the customer's distributors. Flyers and samples were produced and mailed by Sigma. Orders were then returned directly to Sigma. This process allowed individual distributors or a single branch to include its own imprint on the calendar. A customer list may have over 10,000 names, and a single order may consist of over 1,000 different imprints. Because each customer has its own requirements, a staff member dedicated to personalized service is assigned to each customer. Sigma learned how its customers made decisions about specialty advertising purchases such as promotional calendars and then developed a program to satisfy the needs of purchasing agents and buyers in large organizations. The strategy was very successful, and during the 1990s, the company added prime accounts such as Milwaukee Electric Tool Corporation, Hoffman LaRoche, Inc., International Paper Company, and Nabisco Brands, Inc.

An Emphasis on Implementation

After focusing on the "Total Service Package" approach as its primary marketing strategy, Sigma experienced a large increase in corporate clientele with very specialized product and service requirements. The "Salesbuilder" orders that were the foundation of the business became secondary to "programs"—larger corporate accounts with networks of dealers, franchises, or sales representatives to place orders—as well as multiple products and services offered as part of their calendar promotion. Sigma's reputation was bolstered by strong clientele references and testimonials. Companies were drawn to the custom calendar vendor known for high-quality products and a staff with tremendous flexibility and creativity. In an effort to distance itself from competitors, Sigma improved on the "Total Service Package," which had become an important part of its marketing strategy. Customers were surveyed before and after they received the product, and large corporate account contacts received a visit from their account representative early in the year to review the previous year's program and begin laying groundwork on the upcoming promotion. In addition, international promotions and shipping became important aspects of several large accounts. Account representatives began developing large corporate accounts by promoting multiple products, while some promotional items beyond calendars were produced in an effort to maintain exclusivity with a client.

The company continued to add to its list of satisfied customers such prime accounts as Unisource, xpedx, Volvo Cars, Volvo Trucks, Ditch Witch, and Enterprise Leasing. Mega-accounts also came on board, such as Yellow Freight Systems (including all of its subsidiaries) and CNH, the parent company that brought along the business of its multiple operating divisions including Case IH/Case Construction and New Holland Agricultural/New Holland Construction.

After many instances of being asked by corporate clients to include additional advertising products as companion pieces to their calendar program, management began to consider the viability of becoming an ASI (Advertising Specialty Institute) dealer distributor. The annual cost was acceptable, considering the cost savings to be realized in purchasing specialty items and specialized printing products wholesale through ASI vendors. Sigma became an ASI distributor in March of 2000, providing new and useful resources to enhance the calendar programs and meet specific needs of established customers. The ASI resources opened up new markets for additional business from many of their existing customers, without the need to aggressively sell the specialty promotions segment of business and without diluting the focus on calendar programs.

Customer demand led to changes and the expansion of the sales and administrative areas, as well as the graphics department. A stronger focus on the service aspect of the business was a strategic move for the sales and administrative areas, resulting in the creation of a dedicated customer service department. Sigma also saw tremendous growth in its graphics capabilities—a response to the major technical changes in the printing industry itself, as well as the needs of its customers.

Despite the additional staff and resources, the demand from program accounts was so great that the company was in danger of overselling its production capabilities. Recognizing that possibility, Sigma became more selective in its marketing efforts for program accounts. The company also began to reevaluate the potential of smaller, easy-to-produce and profitable "Salesbuilder" calendar orders as a product to be marketed on their corporate e-commerce website, suitable for smaller companies that could not support a completely customized program.

Linking Technology to the Marketing Program

In the late 1980s and early 1990s, Sigma offered limited in-house design/layout services. Prior to desktop publishing, type was set, paste-ups were created, and film was shot manually on a camera. Graphic needs beyond the company's capabilities were outsourced to service bureaus. Even though Sigma's capabilities were limited, very few of its customers had complex needs or technologically capable marketing departments.

With the onset of the digital age, Sigma's technology was forced to change. Sigma's pre-press capabilities were transformed over a 10-year period. Graphics workstations became an integral part of the business, with increasing storage capacity and applications to handle larger and more complex files. In the mid 1990s, a digital image setter replaced the old camera and film technology. That evolved in less than 10 years to a direct-to-plate workflow with color management, digital color proofing, and multiplatform capability. Photos are now almost completely digital—scanning is becoming a thing of the past—and many customers have their own in-house design and graphics staff that work closely with Sigma's graphics department. The sophisticated technology created the need for advanced training and continued education and upgrades. Sigma's management has maintained a commitment to stay in the forefront of graphics technology through strong staffing and investment in equipment and software applications.

The mid-1990s also ushered in the company's Internet presence and online capabilities. A corporate identity on the Internet is absolutely essential in today's marketplace, and Sigma has taken the additional steps to utilize the Internet for e-commerce, namely product promotion and ordering capabilities. Many of the company's larger clients demand online ordering and communications with their networks in order to maintain their accounts.

Upgrading technology on the administrative side has allowed the company to better serve its customers. A centralized file and information system has integrated many previously separate functions and increased flexibility among the staff. Sigma is now online with several transportation companies, making package tracking an easy task. The company has added many features with the improved technology, such as direct invoicing, credit card sales, digital faxing, and proofing online or via e-mail.

Sigma's Current and Future Marketing Strategy

During Sigma's expansion period, Don began to turn over the daily operations of the business to his son Mike. In early 1996, the transition was complete, with Mike in full charge of the business. Don has retired but remains chairman of the board, acting in an advisory capacity. Stock was purchased back from Don's attorney/colleague who had invested in the company many years ago, and Sigma issued stock to key employees, creating a greater sense of ownership and commitment to the business. A major concern was to develop personnel strategies and a succession plan in the event of Mike's death or disability. Key employees with long tenure will soon be considering retirement, and the skills held by management and key employees would need to be taught and transferred to newer employees. In 2007, a succession plan was developed for the company to ensure its continuation.

In 2009, Jeff Sapit joined Sigma as marketing production manager, the third-generation of his family to become involved in the business. Jeff has a different educational background focusing more on management and marketing. While his father Mike Sapit's college education was in graphic arts—and initially he was much more concerned with operations and production—Jeff brings a perspective to the firm that differs from both his father and grandfather. Mike's goal is to allow his son considerable freedom in contributing to the strategic plans on Sigma. Mike wants to allow Jeff to apply his education and experience in developing new products and expanding Sigma's markets.

Annual marketing meetings have been scheduled each year since 1991 for staff members to meet and review the past year, addressing and solving both internal and external problems. The meetings encourage teamwork, foster company loyalty, and increase employee's knowledge about Sigma's status in the marketplace. In addition to the business meetings, the company has also conducted a number of pleasure trips for employees (sometimes with their spouses and/or families) to promote stronger personal relationships and interaction. The employees have visited a number of resort complexes and major cities, and even sailed together on a cruise ship to the Caribbean. These events have contributed to a strong sense of community and teamwork among the employees. Sigma has constructed a diverse team of people with a wide range of skills, each playing a key role in the overall success of the company. Sapit believes that the knowledge and skills of his employees are an important part of what gives Sigma its edge.

One of Sigma's many strengths is the ability to understand market opportunities and to develop and continue to adapt its strategic focus. This ability has enabled the company to maintain a 90 percent repeat customer rate. As the environment changes, Sigma gathers information from existing and potential customers to develop the most effective marketing strategy. For example, as more companies become concerned about sustainability issues, particularly renewable resources, Sigma has responded. In 2008, Sigma became a Chain-of-Custody (CoC) certified company with the Forest Stewardship Council (FSC)—a designation that ensures the integrity of the paper supply chain (forest to mill) by certifying that the paper used by Sigma comes from responsibly managed forests. The following year, the company became certified with the Sustainable Forestry Initiative (SFI) and the Program for the Endorsement of Forest Certification (PEFC). Chain-of-Custody certification is a response to the demands of Sigma's customers and the company's own desires to reduce their environmental impact.

In the future, there will be new challenges, including the changing environment related to technology, communication, and methods of advertising. So far, potential competitors like Google or other specialty advertising methods have not replaced the printed calendar. However, Sigma's team is aware that the industry is constantly changing, and that to survive, the company must adapt.

The latest recession led to changes for both Sigma and its competitors. Sigma's rivals consist mainly of other specialty advertising companies. Many of these companies began outsourcing certain functions during the recession, which has enabled them to expand into selling other customized products such as pens. Businesses also began to desire more economical customized products during the recession. All of these factors created a more competitive environment, leading Sigma to develop cost-effective products for their customers. This allowed the company to maintain existing customers and even bring back customers that had purchased from its new competitors. Sigma changed its sales focus from a custom calendar company to a customer calendar "solutions" company. This change has allowed the firm to tap into an asset that does not equate to a price tag but that offers clients exceptional value. It also emphasizes Sigma's ability to develop solutions to meet customers' unique specialty advertising needs.

Another adaptation has led to a new opportunity for maximizing resources and increasing revenue. While much of Sigma's printing and bindery work is done at its partner production facilities in Ottawa, Illinois, Sigma has recently purchased and installed several pieces of equipment in its corporate office in Orange Park, Florida, to aid in the production of promotional materials and specific calendar projects with smaller quantities. This equipment consists of color digital laser production printers and small bindery equipment, such as a cutter, folder, punch, and other binding equipment. By producing most of its calendar promotional materials (such as brochures, flyers, order forms, and envelopes for direct mail) in its Orange Park office, as well as some of the actual calendar products or components themselves, Sigma is able to realize substantial savings in production costs. Sigma is also able to better control the quality and timely distribution of materials produced in-house.

With the expansion of its internal production capabilities has come the opportunity to more fully utilize this new equipment and to increase production. Plans are underway to sell other color digital printing and graphic design services to Sigma's established calendar customers as well as the local business market. By targeting specific customers who have regular projects that are well suited for Sigma's equipment (such as newsletters, brochures, flyers, reports, business cards, booklets, and postcards), Sigma hopes to maximize the production value of the equipment and staff, particularly during the time of year when calendar production is paused. This is a swing back to Sigma's commercial printing roots with a twist: using digital technology and targeting a specific market with compatible printing needs.

Additionally, Sigma's ASI sales have been expanded over the past couple of years to new markets as well as to select calendar customers. One of Sigma's new sales reps brought specific expertise in the local school markets, and the company was able to dovetail on this expertise by focusing its ASI efforts to that client base. Those efforts brought Sigma increased experience and sales in the apparel market, which it was then able to use in expanding services offered to other corporate clients. In 2011, one of Sigma's mid-sized calendar program clients, E-ONE, awarded Sigma an additional contract for managing its corporate web store and supplying promotional items and corporate apparel for its Welcome Center store, as well as for awards, dealer promotions, trade shows, and conference support. The expanded ASI-related sales, along with the digital printing services, should give Sigma the cushion it needs to continue its corporate calendar promotions as a more integrated product line.

Conclusion

Throughout its history, Sigma Marketing has exhibited the uncanny ability to understand market opportunities and to adapt its strategic focus accordingly. As its marketing environment changes, Sigma Marketing gathers information from existing and potential customers to develop the most effective marketing strategy possible. Even in the face of changing technology, communication, and advertising methods, Sigma Marketing has managed to reinvent its mindset and strategies in order to remain successful. Sigma's long-held philosophy is "always be prepared." In the words of Mike Sapit, "The future is bright."

Questions for Discussion

1. Discuss potential key changes in technology, communications, and competition that Sigma will face in the future. Which will have the most impact on Sigma's future marketing strategies?
2. Prepare a SWOT analysis for long-term strategic planning at Sigma Marketing.
3. Suggest some possible strategic initiatives that Sigma could pursue to continue its growth.

Sources

The facts of this case are from the personal knowledge of the author; Sigma Marketing website (http://www. sigmamktg.com), accessed August 9, 2012; and "Up Close with Mike Sapit, President of Sigma Marketing," *HPxpressions*, pp. 14–15.

CASE **15**

Netflix Fights to Stay Ahead of a Rapidly Changing Market*

Synopsis: In the face of changing technology and shifting customer preferences with respect to movie distribution, video rental giant Blockbuster fell to its competition. Meanwhile, Netflix has grown to become the top rent-by-mail and video streaming company, while other strong competitors have emerged to dominate movie distribution via kiosks (Redbox) and online (Apple, Amazon, Hulu, and others). Looking to the future, Netflix's survival depends on its ability to adapt to and adopt new technology and marketing practices—issues Blockbuster failed to navigate due to its reactive, rather than proactive, stance toward a rapidly changing market. Netflix faces an uncertain future as the DVD rental sector approaches the end of its life cycle. However, the company is poised to dominate the video streaming sector for the foreseeable future. The problem is, the future changes rapidly in this industry.

Themes: Changing technology, changing consumer preferences, competition, competitive advantage, product strategy, product life cycle, services marketing, pricing strategy, distribution strategy, non-store retailing, customer relationships, value, implementation

Technology has played a leading role in the evolution of the movie and rental industry. Several of the major movie production companies have now opted to bypass the theatre experience and instead promote a selection of their movies directly to the home viewing audience via on-demand services, broadband downloads, or online streaming. Through increasing disintermediation (bypassing theaters and rental chains), movie studios stand to increase profit margins dramatically. Today there are at least 20 major competitors in the sales and rental industry that compete with Netflix. These include major retail firms such as Walmart, Target, Best Buy, Amazon, and Time Warner. In the rental sector, Netflix faces intense competition from Redbox, and a variety of online-only services such as Apple, Amazon, Google, and Hulu.

Netflix's History

CEO Reed Hastings told *Fortune* he got the idea for the DVD-by-mail service after paying a $40 late fee for *Apollo 13* in 1997. Although VHS was the popular format at the time, Hastings heard that DVDs were on the way, and he knew there was a big market waiting to be tapped. At first he and fellow software executive Marc Randolph attempted

*Kelsey Reddick, Florida State University, Jacqueline Trent, University of New Mexico, and Jennifer Sawayda, University of New Mexico, prepared this case under the direction of Michael Hartline and O.C. Ferrell. This case is for classroom discussion, rather than to illustrate either effective or ineffective handling of an administrative situation.

a rent-by-mail service that didn't require a subscription, but it was very unpopular. The company launched the subscription service on September 23, 1999 with a free trial for the first month and found that 80 percent of customers renewed after the trial ended. Netflix turned its first profit in 2003 in the same quarter that it reached one million subscribers. Hastings said the company was named Netflix because they saw the industry's future moving from the DVD format to Internet streaming in the long run. Netflix introduced streaming services in 2007 after reaching more than 6.3 million members.

Intense competition from Netflix was a main reason that Blockbuster dropped its late-fee program in 2005 (a shift that led to a $400 million loss in revenue for Blockbuster). In 2006, Hastings set a goal of reaching 20 million subscribers by 2012—a goal they would exceed. Their launch in Canada in September 2010 helped them reach the 20 million subscriber goal sooner than expected. Quarterly sales topped $320 million in late 2008, followed by $394 million during the first quarter of 2009. Even more impressive, Netflix managed to increase sales at a time when the entire movie rental industry experienced an 8 percent sales decline. Today, with more than 23 million members, Netflix touts itself as the world's largest online entertainment subscription service, with operations in the United States, Canada, Ireland, the United Kingdom, and the Caribbean.

Early Strategy

Netflix built its success around online movie rentals with expedited delivery of DVDs. DVDs were first introduced to the United States in March of 1996. In August of 1997, few American households owned DVD players as they cost more than $1,000 at the time. In addition, few movie titles were available on DVD. However, Hastings and Randolph successfully predicted that the format would quickly replace the comparatively low quality, bulky, and cumbersome VHS format among American consumers. A key factor in Netflix's strategy was that the DVD's compact size made the U.S. Postal Service a viable delivery method. It experimented with 200 different mailing packages in order to perfect the packages for disc safety, shipping cost, and reliability. On April 14, 1998, Netflix officially opened for business with 30 employees and 925 titles—the majority of DVDs in print at the time. Initially, Netflix offered a seven-day rental for $4 plus $2 in shipping, with per item prices decreasing with each additional title. They offered no-hassle "time-extensions" rather than punitive and costly "late-fees," which had been the industry standard and a big revenue generator.

During the initial period, when demand was low, Netflix formed strategic relationships that were important in expanding the DVD market and ensuring its early success. The company forged cross-promotional agreements with DVD hardware manufacturers and studios, offering free Netflix rentals with purchases of DVD players from manufacturers such as Toshiba, Hewlett-Packard, Pioneer, Sony, and Apple to help get DVD players in American homes. It also teamed with studios to promote high profile films and with online movie information/review providers to funnel movie-interested Internet traffic directly to Netflix. The company also enjoyed significant positive publicity in 1998 when it offered videos of President Bill Clinton's grand jury testimony for 2 cents, plus $2 shipping and handling.

In September of 1999, Hastings announced that Netflix had achieved economies of scale and could now offer subscription services. A few months later in early 2000, it dropped the pay-per-title model entirely and began to market itself as an unlimited subscription service, completely free of due dates, late fees, shipping charges, and per-title fees. At that time, Netflix charged $19.99 per month for 3 DVDs at a time and added its less expensive one- and two-DVD options a short time later.

Bob Pisano, a former MGM executive and sitting president of the Screen Actors Guild, joined the Board of Directors of Netflix in April 2000. Pisano cultivated relationships with the studios, and in December, Netflix signed revenue sharing agreements with Warner Home Video and Columbia Tri-Star. This enabled Netflix to consistently and more profitably fill the short-lived new release demand peak. Agreements with other studios would soon follow.

Optimizing Distribution

In February 2002, Netflix reached the milestone of 500,000 subscribers. It made its initial public offering in March, raising $82.5 million on 5.5 million shares. On June 20, 2002, Netflix announced the opening of ten additional warehouses throughout the country. The company situated its warehouses to supply as many customers as possible with overnight first-class DVD delivery because its per-capita subscription rates were much higher in markets with overnight delivery. As competitors entered the market over the next couple of years, Netflix was already refining its processes and opening more distribution centers to better serve its expanding subscriber base more profitably and quickly.

The location of these distribution centers has always remained a mystery. Netflix employees sign confidentiality agreements when hired, and the exterior of the warehouses themselves are non-descript and are designed expressly to camouflage the building's function. Although Netflix was concerned with trade secrets early on, former Vice President of Communications Steve Swasey explained in 2009 that Netflix was already so ahead of the competition that it was not worried about industrial espionage. Rather, it is more worried about the possible disruption of processes when customers show up and expect to be able to drop off the DVDs directly at the warehouse, rather than through the U.S. Postal Service.

In February 2003, Netflix hit one million subscribers. Customers appreciated the low-cost subscription fees, the ease of returning DVDs, and the elimination of late fees. In June 2003, Netflix was awarded a patent for its preference tracking software and by mid-summer possessed a library of 15,000 titles.

Taking Down a Giant

Entrepreneur David Cook opened Blockbuster, formerly the dominant movie-rental company, in 1985. Noting the opportunities in the rental market, investor Warne Huizenga invested $18 million in the startup and helped the company expand from 130 stores to more than 1,500 in about three years. When former Walmart CEO Bill Fields took over in March of 1996, Blockbuster was repositioned as a retail establishment. This vision, as well as Fields' tenure, was short-lived. John Antioco, Fields' successor who took over in mid-1997, refocused the company on video and game rentals; this strengthened and solidified the firm's strategy and allowed Blockbuster to successfully navigate the transition from VHS to DVDs in the late 1990s through the early 2000s.

The home entertainment business continued to evolve, and Blockbuster's revised mission was to be "the complete resource for movies and games." Recognizing the growing threat posed by Netflix, Blockbuster began to experiment with a non-subscription online rental service with a postal delivery component in the United Kingdom. Most of Blockbuster's success during this period was attributed to its successful positioning as the market leader, combined with strong growth trends in the gaming industry. In 2004, Blockbuster finally entered the online movie rental business in a bid to compete more directly with increasingly competitive Netflix. However, Blockbuster continued its focus on its bricks-and-mortar stores by offering online renters the option of two free in-store rentals each month, designed to cater to impulse home entertainment demand. The mix of in-store rentals and Blockbuster's new online offering was considered a competitive advantage over Netflix.

Antioco unexpectedly left Blockbuster in 2007, and was replaced by James Keys, previously the "turnaround artist" for 7-Eleven. When Keyes began as CEO, Blockbuster was facing serious difficulties: its stock price had fallen more than 83 percent in the years between 2002 and 2007, and it had made the strategic decision to close nearly 300 stores in both 2007 and 2008. Netflix had quickly become one of Blockbuster's most serious competitors. Due to competition from Netflix, Blockbuster chose to drop its late fees; this resulted in an astounding $400 million loss for Blockbuster, as well as legal problems. Even as the movie rental industry began to lose its growth trajectory and move into the decline phase, Netflix enjoyed strong growth. Netflix's advantages over Blockbuster's offerings included renters' access to an unlimited number of movies upon subscribing; convenient, automatic, and free shipping once a movie is returned via the postal service; extremely fast turnaround; and a broad distribution network.

In the end, Blockbuster failed to adapt to the changing market and declared bankruptcy in September 2010 after facing $1 billion in debt. That same year, Netflix reached 20 million members, up 63 percent from 2009, and launched services in Canada.

Netflix Changes Its Business Model

Netflix CEO Reed Hastings correctly anticipated the new technology entering the home entertainment industry. A study from IHS Screen Digest suggested that by 2012, online movie streaming in the U.S. would exceed both DVD and Blu-ray use. Hastings expected that Netflix's DVD subscriptions would decline steadily over each quarter as new technology diffused into consumers' homes. At that point, Hastings made a strategic decision that he would later regret.

In the third quarter of 2011, Netflix attempted to move its DVD-by-mail business into a new subsidiary called Qwikster that would focus solely on DVD-by-mail services. This move would free Netflix to focus on the streaming side of the operation. While this supported Hastings' vision of an all-streaming future, it led to a price increase of 60 percent and took away the convenient and valued one-stop shopping experience for subscribers that used both DVD-by-mail and streaming.

Netflix suddenly announced the decision to split the services in July 2011. Ironically, in the past, Netflix had used focus groups to research how the market might respond to a particular decision. This time, however, Netflix relied on data showing that 75 percent of consumers preferred streaming. While this data is likely true, it failed to account for how consumers would react to the change. In addition to splitting into two companies, Netflix announced a price increase for one of its most popular subscription packages. Instead of paying $9.99 per month to receive movies either via streaming or DVD-by-mail service, interchangeably, customers would now pay $7.99 per month for each service. Netflix implemented the price adjustment and started the process of spinning off Qwikster in August 2011.

The customer backlash was swift and dramatic. Customers were angry at what they perceived to be a drastic price increase. The outrage worsened after e-mails were sent to Netflix subscribers containing an apology from Hastings for not explaining the reasoning behind raising prices. The e-mail also announced the splitting of the two companies. Rather than placating customers, many became angrier. They did not like the idea of moving between two websites—Qwikster for DVDs and Netflix for streaming. The company lost 405,000 paid subscribers in a matter of weeks. Investors doubted the move, and Netflix's stock price plummeted by 26 percent in a single day following the release of the third quarter financial report.

Qwikster was given the boot after only three weeks as Netflix finally acknowledged that the change would be inconvenient for customers. Yet, the blunder cost Netflix its status as a Wall Street darling. The company traded at almost $300 per share before the Qwikster announcement. By the third quarter of 2012, it traded in the $50 to $60 range. Although Netflix chose to stay as one company, it maintained the price increase for its subscription package, forcing customers who only want to pay $7.99 per month to choose either DVDs or streaming. Despite the Qwikster failure, the price increase has led to modest success for the company. In the third quarter of 2012, Netflix reported a 1.7 percent decrease in paid subscriptions and an 11.9 percent increase in revenue per customer. This resulted in a net increase in revenue of 10 percent and a 15.4 percent increase in profit margin.

Netflix seems to be recovering somewhat from this debacle, finishing 2011 with earnings above expectations. Yet the company received another blow when it settled a class action lawsuit over consumer privacy issues. The lawsuit claimed that Netflix was retaining records of subscribers DVD and streaming videos two years after subscribers cancelled. According to the lawsuit, this violated a provision of the Video Protection Privacy Act stating that personally identifiable information must be deleted after one year of cancellation. Netflix reached a $9 million settlement without admitting guilt.

Intense Competition in the Movie Rental Industry

In the movie rental industry, many companies have come and gone since the 1980s. Netflix has always been the number one DVD-by-mail rental company, but as the market continues to evolve and streaming becomes the preferred format, the company finds itself in an ever-changing market. The onset of competitors in both the DVD rental industry and the online streaming industry has created new challenges for Netflix to address.

Redbox

Whether you are getting gas at 7-Eleven, buying groceries at Walmart, or picking up a prescription from Walgreens, your favorite movie or video game may be available for a few dollars at a Redbox kiosk. Each kiosk holds 630 discs, with about 200 different movie titles. Customers pay around $1.00 per day (now $1.20)—$2.00 for video games—and can return movies to any Redbox kiosk anywhere in the country. Customers can even reserve movies online before visiting a kiosk. Since its initial launch with just 12 kiosks, Redbox has grown to roughly 36,000 kiosks nationwide. That level of penetration maximizes convenience for customers, who now rent movies while they are out doing other things. The company claims that 68 percent of the U.S. population lives within a 5-minute drive of a Redbox kiosk.

Surprisingly, the idea for Redbox began as a new business venture for McDonald's in 2002. At that time, McDonald's was experimenting with vending machines to sell a variety of different items. After the concept proved to be a success, Redbox was sold to Coinstar—a Bellevue, Washington, company that also operates coin-counting machines and gift card dispensers. Soon after, Coinstar developed deals with Walmart, Kroger, Winn-Dixie, Walgreens, Kangaroo (gas stations), and other national outlets to place Redbox kiosks in high-traffic locations. As it turned out, the timing couldn't have been better. As a consequence of the most recent economic recession, customers who began to reconsider their $15 per month Netflix plans or $5 DVD rentals from Blockbuster suddenly saw the $1 Redbox rentals as a bargain.

Redbox has achieved phenomenal sales growth in a very short time: from 200 million cumulative rentals in 2008, to 500 million in 2009, to 1.5 billion total rentals in 2012. These numbers are startling when compared to the 43.9 percent decline in DVD sales from 2009 to 2012. Further evidence of success can be found in the penetration of Redbox into mainstream America. The Redbox mobile apps have been downloaded 4.7 million times on Android and 6.5 million times on iPhone.

After Blockbuster declared bankruptcy in 2010, NCR acquired the company's Blockbuster Express kiosks. NCR then sold Blockbuster Express to Redbox for $100 million in 2012. Meanwhile, to remain competitive with streaming, Redbox announced a partnership with Verizon in February 2012 to create on-demand video streaming. While the two companies have offered limited details on their partnership, the new subscription service will surely leverage Verizon's relationships with various content providers.

Interestingly, when Redbox announced a 20 percent price increase from $1.00 to $1.20, the company experienced a far different outcome than Netflix experienced. Redbox handled the announcement more smoothly than Netflix, stating that the change was necessary due to new regulations on debit card fees passed in the Dodd–Frank Wall Street Reform and Consumer Protection Act (consumers pay using their credit or debit cards). The regulations increased the cost of using a debit card for small purchases. However, Redbox actually raised its prices higher than what was needed to offset the debit card cost increase. Yet, by positioning it as a necessary move, Redbox avoided consumer backlash. Indeed, whereas Redbox's stock increased 36 percent in a one-year period, Netflix's decreased by 43 percent during the same time.

Fully Digital Competitors

If trends in the movie rental industry continue, digital downloads will replace DVDs as the de facto standard for movie rentals. While Netflix clearly recognizes this trend and is making changes to establish a competitive advantage, so are many of its competitors. Recently, the market has become crowded with offerings from Apple, Amazon, Hulu, YouTube, and Google Play.

A number of well-known firms offer downloadable movie rentals. Apple, for example, offers thousands of titles in both standard and high-definition formats via its iTunes store. Apple's key advantage is that iTunes works seamlessly with the millions of iPods, iPhones, iPads, and Apple TV's that have sold in recent years. What Apple is missing, however, is an easy way to connect its handheld devices to older televisions—many of which do not have wireless connectivity or even HDMI ports.

Amazon offers more than 13,000 titles for rent via its Instant Video service. Amazon's original advantage was its partnership with Roku's Digital Video player that allows consumers to wirelessly stream Amazon movies to their televisions. The Roku, starting at $49, now supports Hulu Plus, Netflix, Amazon Instant Video, HBO GO, and more. Amazon Prime Instant Video can now be streamed via Internet, Kindle Fire, Roku, PlayStation 3, and on connected TVs and Blu-ray players. With the addition of their subscription service Amazon Prime, which provides members with free two-day shipping for $79 annually, customers can also enjoy a portion of the Amazon Instant Video catalog. In February 2012, Amazon signed a deal with Viacom to add 2,000 new titles to Amazon Prime Instant Video, including programs from Nickelodeon, Comedy Central, and MTV.

In 2007, NBCUniversal, Fox Entertainment Group, and Disney-ABC Television Group joined forces on a new venture called Hulu (www.hulu.com), which has experienced a steady growth since its inception. Hulu is an ad-supported, web-based service that provides access to movies and traditional broadcast shows such as *Grey's Anatomy*, *The Office*, *Glee*, and *30 Rock* free of charge. Hulu also offers a video menu exceeding 350 content companies, including such names as ABC, NBC, FOX, MGM, and Sony. The company launched Hulu Plus, an ad-supported subscription service, in November 2010 for $7.99 a month. Unlike its free online service, Hulu Plus allows users to watch programs on connected TVs and Blu-ray players, gaming consoles, set-top boxes like Roku, mobile phones, and computers with limited advertising. While Hulu.com typically offers the five most recent episodes of a series in standard definition, Hulu Plus generally offers all episodes in the current season, in high definition when available.

In April 2012, Paramount Films added 500 films to the YouTube and Google Play rental service, which now sits at 9,000 titles. Paramount joined Disney, Sony, Warner Brothers, and NBCUniversal in partnerships with the YouTube, with 20th Century Fox as the only major studio that hasn't signed on. All six major film studios currently sell films though Apple's iTunes. Google has started talks with film studios to begin selling movies through Google Play, a new one-stop entertainment shop. With Google Play, users can rent high definition movies, accessible via any Android device or through the Web. Users can also purchase music, download Android apps, and purchase e-books to read on a tablet, phone, e-reader, or the Web. Google Play stores all music purchases and up to 20,000 songs from the purchaser's iTunes, Windows Media Player, or folders with the help of the Google Play Music Manager.

While Netflix might have had first-mover advantages, other companies seem to be catching up in terms of their digital product offerings. Netflix will need to constantly innovate in order to remain one step ahead of the competition.

Analyzing Netflix's Marketing Strategy

Netflix's target market includes consumers with Internet access and a penchant for movies. Netflix has been moving away from its DVD-by-mail service—although it is still an important part of its strategy—and emphasizing its streaming services. Its website promotes its streaming services for $7.99 per month, while its DVD services seem more secondary. Netflix currently has 26 million subscribers for streaming in the United States, Canada, the United Kingdom, Ireland, and Latin America.

Many analysts now consider Netflix's multi-platform streaming capability to be one of its major competitive advantages. Netflix streaming can take place on televisions, iPhones, iPads, Xboxes, or online. The process is seamless, meaning that a consumer can easily move from one platform to another. None of Netflix's competitors yet have this capability. A 2011 study jointly conducted by CBS, The Nielsen Company, and The Cambridge Group found that two segments, amounting to 40 million U.S. households, have high demand for multi-platform streaming content. The demand for multiple-platform streaming continues to grow, making this a high potential growth segment for Netflix.

Netflix continues to expand the content it offers to subscribers. While Netflix must wait a certain period for new DVD releases, it has developed lucrative partnerships with movie studios and content providers. In 2011, Starz announced that it would no longer license its programming to Netflix starting in 2012. However, the news was offset somewhat with the announcement that DreamWorks would begin licensing its films and shows to Netflix in 2013, replacing DreamWorks' current deal with HBO. According to financial reports, the cost of the licenses to acquire and deliver its content totaled $1.8 billion in 2011. Considering the rising cost of content licensing and the ability of original cable television programming to attract subscribers, Netflix is now adding original programming to its streaming offerings. Unlike with Qwikster, however, Netflix has returned to its policy of performing market research. Netflix conducted an experiment adding an original program to its streaming service. The program received enough views for Netflix to declare the experiment a success and commit to more programs. In 2012, Netflix plans to spend $75 to $100 million on original programming to attract new subscribers.

While competition for Netflix has been increasing, Netflix is showing that it will not give up market share without a fight. According to a recent consumer satisfaction survey, Netflix rates higher than video-on-demand and premium broadcast channels because of its comparatively low cost and viewing flexibility. Although the company only has about

30 percent market share in physical rentals, it has 61 percent of the online streaming market share. In 2012, Netflix overcame Apple in the online video market and now earns 44 percent of online video revenue in the United States. The cost and multi-platform flexibility benefit that Netflix offers is significant enough to affect consumer decisions.

Netflix's Future

As Netflix looks toward the future, the decline of the DVD will continue to present a challenge. Although Qwikster was an instant flop, the company will eventually have to phase out its DVD-by-mail business when it is no longer profitable. The continued growth of streaming options, from Amazon Instant Video to Google Play, and rental kiosk giant Redbox offer increases in movie-renting convenience for consumers. However, Netflix continues to maintain its competitive edge with significant market share in online videos, streaming, and video rentals. Its decision to develop its own original content demonstrates its willingness to embrace market opportunities.

The backlash that Netflix experienced after its price increase and failed plan to split the company shows that the company must carefully evaluate its marketing strategy. Failing to accurately predict consumer reaction could lead to future debacles. Netflix will also have to foster various content provider relationships and proactively search for newer, better opportunities. The heart of this challenge is simple in concept but difficult to execute in practice: Will Netflix remain innovative enough to compete in such a highly saturated market?

Questions for Discussion

1. What role will Redbox play in the development of Netflix's strategic plans? How threatening is Redbox to Netflix's future?
2. How will new competition from digital content providers force Netflix to alter its strategy?
3. What new opportunities do you see in the movie streaming business, or the entertainment industry as a whole?
4. Do you think Netflix will remain the dominant force in both streaming and movie rentals? Why or why not?
5. What could Netflix have done differently to ensure Qwikster's success?

Sources

The facts of this case are from Alyssa Abkowitz, "Secrets of My Success: CEO Reed Hastings," *CNNMoney*, January 28, 2009 (http://money.cnn.com/2009/01/27/news/newsmakers/hastings_netflix.fortune); Thomas K. Arnold, "Economic Downturn May Be Behind a Rise in DVD Rentals," *USA Today*, May 4, 2009 (http://www.usatoday.com/life/movies/dvd/2009-05-04-rentals-recession_N.htm); Claire Atkinson, "Disney-Hulu Puts Focus on CBS," *Broadcasting and Cable*, May 4, 2009, p. 3; Lauren Barack, "Blockbuster Pushes Fast Forward: CEO James Keyes has a Vision for His Company—and It's Not Going Back to the Videotape," *On Wall Street*, September 1, 2007, p. 1; Brook Barnes and Brian Stelter, "Netflix Secures Streaming Deal with DreamWorks," *New York Times*, September 25, 2011 (http://www.nytimes.com/2011/09/26/business/media/netflix-secures-streaming-deal-with-dreamworks.html?_r=1&pagewanted=all); Eric Berte, "Blockbuster Cuts Losses Despite Lower Revenue," *Fox Business*, August 13, 2009 (http://www.foxbusiness.com/story/markets/industries/retail/blockbuster-cuts-losses-despite-lower-revenue); Tim Beyers, "Why I Bought Netflix," *Daily Finance*, September 26, 2011 (http://www.dailyfinance.com/2011/09/26/why-i-bought-netflix-); Christopher Borrelli, "How Netflix Gets Your Movies to Your Mailbox So Fast," *Chicago Tribune*, August 4, 2009 (http://articles.chicagotribune.com/2009-08-04/entertainment/0908030313_1_dvd-by-mail-warehouse-trade-secrets); Cliff Edward and Ronald Grover, "Can Netflix Regain Lost Ground?" *BusinessWeek*, October 19, 2011 (http://www.business week.com/magazine/can-netflix-regain-lost-ground-10192011.html); "Facts about Redbox," Redbox website (http://www.redbox.com/facts), accessed August 7, 2012; David Goldman, "Verizon and Redbox Team Up to Battle Netflix," *CNNMoney*, February 6, 2012 (http://money.cnn.com/2012/02/06/technology/verizon_redbox/ index.htm?iid=HP_River); Rob Golum, "Netflix Rises 5% After Report On Market Share: Los Angeles Makeover," *Bloomberg*, June 19, 2012 (http://www.bloomberg.com/news/2012-01-19/netflix-rises-5-after-report-on-market-share-los-angeles-mover.html); Jefferson Graham, "Netflix Looks to Future But Still Going Strong with DVD Rentals," *USA Today*, July 1, 2009 (http://www.usatoday.com/tech/products/2009-06-30-netflix-future_N.htm); Peter Grant, "Telecommunications; Outside the Box: As Broadband Connections Proliferate, So Do the Opportunities for Niche Video-Content Providers," *Wall Street Journal*, December 19, 2005, p. R11; Dan Graziano, "Online Movie Streaming In U.S. to Top DVDs for the First Time in 2012," *Boy Genius Report*, March 26, 2012 (http://www.bgr.com/2012/03/26/online-movie-streaming-in-u-s-to-top-dvds-for-the-first-time-in-2012); Todd Haselton, "Upset Investors File Class Action Lawsuit Against Netflix," *Boy Genius Report*, January 17, 2012 (http://www.bgr.com/2012/01/17/upset-investors-file-class-action-lawsuit-against-netflix); Bruce Horovitz, "McDonald's Wades Deeper into DVDs," *USA Today*, May 23, 2004 (http://www.usatoday.com/money/industries/retail/2004-05-23-mcdvd_x.htm); Richard Hull, "Content Goes Hollywood: How the Film Industry Is Struggling with Digital Content," *EContent*, October 2004, p. 22; Lauren Indvik, "Soon You May Be Able to Buy, Not Just Rent, Movies from Google," *Mashable*, March 23, 2012 (http://mashable.com/2012/03/23/google-selling-films); Lauren Indvik, "500 Paramount Films Coming to YouTube," *Mashable*, April 4, 2012 (http://mashable.com/2012/04/04/paramount-youtube-rentals); *International Directory of Company Histories*, Vol. 58 (St. James Press, 2004); "Investor Relations," Netflix website (http://ir.netflix.com), accessed August 7, 2012; Kevin Kelleher, "The Rise of Redbox Should Spook Netflix," *CNNMoney*, February 10, 2012 (http://tech.fortune.cnn.com/2012/02/10/the-rise-of-redbox-should-spook-netflix); Brent Lang, "Netflix CEO Reed Hastings: 'We Expect DVD Subscribers to Decline Forever,'" *Reuters*, January 25, 2012 (http://www.reuters.com/article/2012/01/26/idUS257021289720120126); David Lieberman, "DVD Kiosks Like Redbox Have Rivals Seeing Red," *USA Today*, August 13, 2009 (http://www.usatoday.com/money/media/2009-08-11-rental-dvd-redbox_N.htm); Michael Liedtke, "Blockbuster to Stream Video Rentals on Samsung TVs," *USA Today*, July 14, 2009 (http://www.usatoday.com/tech/news/2009-07-14-blockbuster-samsung_N.htm); Michael Liedtke, "Netflix Class Action Settlement: Service Pays $9 Million After Allegations Of Privacy Violations," *The Huffington Post*, February 10, 2012 (http://www.huffingtonpost.com/2012/02/11/netflix-class-action-settlement_n_1270230.html); Michael Liedtke, "Netflix Users Watched a Billion Hours Last Month," *USA Today*, July 4, 2012 (http://www.usatoday.com/tech/news/story/2012-07-03/netflix-online-video/56009322/1); Katie Marsal, "Viacom Deal Brings MTV, Comedy Central, Nickelodeon Shows to Amazon Prime," *AppleInsider*, February 8, 2012 (http://www.appleinsider.com/articles/12/02/08/viacom_deal_brings_mtv_comedy_central_nickelodeon_shows_to_amazon_prime.html); Anna Wilde Mathews, "E-Commerce (A Special Report): Selling Strategies—Stop, Thief! Movie Studios Hope to Slow Widespread Online Piracy Before It Takes Off; They're Convinced They Can," *Wall Street Journal*, April 28, 2003, p. R6; Jessica Mintz, "Redbox's Machines Take on Netflix's Red Envelopes," *USA Today*, June 22, 2009 (http://www.usatoday.com/tech/news/2009-06-22-redbox_N.htm); Timothy J. Mullaney, "Netflix," *BusinessWeek*, May 25, 2006 (http://www.businessweek.com/smallbiz/content/may2006/sb20060525_268860.htm); Timothy J. Mullaney, "The Mail-Order Movie House That Clobbered Blockbuster," *BusinessWeek*, June 5, 2006, pp. 56–57; *Netflix, Inc.*, Hoovers Company Capsules (http://www.hoovers.com/company/Netflix_Inc/rffkhti-1.html), accessed August 9, 2012; "Netflix To Rise On 61% Online Streaming Share," *Seeking Alpha*, May 14, 2012 (http://seekingalpha.com/article/585631-netflix-to-rise-on-61-online-streaming-share); Netflix website (http://www.netflix.com), accessed August 9, 2012; Jeffrey O'Brien, "The Netflix Effect," *Wired*, December 2002 (http://www.wired.com/wired/archive/10.12/netflix.html?pg=1&topic=&topic_set=), accessed August 7, 2012; Terrence O'Brien, "Redbox Snatches Up NCR's Entertainment Division, Swallows Blockbuster Express Business," *Engadget*, February 6, 2012 (http://www.engadget.com/2012/02/06/redbox-snatches-up-ncrs-entertainment-division-future-of-block); Annika Olson and Eddie Yoon, "Netflix Will Rebound Faster than You Think," *Harvard Business Review*, January 26, 2012 (http://blogs.hbr.org/cs/2012/01/netflix_will_rebound_faster_th.html); "Online Movies: The Future, Today," *Screen Digest*, March 22, 2012 (http://www.screendigest.com/reports/2012222a/2012_03_online_movies_the_future_today/view.html?start_ser=vi); Julianne Pepitone, "Netflix Tops Apple in Online Video Sales," *CNNMoney*, June 1, 2012 (http://money.cnn.com/2012/06/01/technology/netflix-online-video-revenue/index.htm); Redbox website (http://www.redbox.com), accessed August 9, 2012; Lisa Richwine, "Mobster Show Gives Netflix an Idea It Can't Refuse, *Reuters*, April 24, 2012 (http://www.reuters.com/article/2012/04/24/us-netflix-programs-idUSBRE83N1GQ20120424); Lisa Richwine, "RPT-HBO Nixes Idea of Netflix Partnership," *Reuters*, July 25, 2012 (http://www.reuters.com/article/2012/07/25/netflix-hbo-idUSL2E8IP10020120725?type=companyNews); Greg Sandoval, "YouTube Wants to Offer Film Rentals," *CNET News*, September 2, 2009 (http://news.cnet.com/8301-1023_3-10337004-93.html); Greg Sandoval, "Redbox Pays $100 Million for NCR's Blockbuster Express," *CNET News*, February 6, 2012 (http://news.cnet.com/8301-31001_3-57372197-261/redbox-pays-$100-million-for-ncrs-blockbuster-express); Amy Schien, *Hulu, LLC*, Hoovers Company Capsules (http://www.hoovers.com/company/Hulu_LLC/rhscyci-1-1NJHW5.html), accessed August 9, 2012; Mike Snider, "Netflix Axes Qwikster; Kills Plan to Split in Two," *USA Today*,

October 10, 2011 (http://www.usatoday.com/tech/news/story/2011-10-10/netflix-axes-qwikster/50723084/1); Mike Snider, "Blu-ray Grows, But DVD Slide Nips Home Video Sales," *USA Today*, January 9, 2012 (http://www.usatoday.com/tech/news/story/2012-01-10/blu-ray-sales-2011/52473310/1); and John Young, "Starz Says It Won't Renew Netflix Streaming Contract, as 1,000 Movies Hang in the Balance," *Entertainment Weekly*, September 1, 2011 (http://insidemovies.ew.com/2011/09/01/netflix-starz-streaming).

CASE 16
Gillette: Why Innovation May Not Be Enough*

Synopsis: Gillette has long been known for innovation in both product development and marketing strategy. In the highly competitive, but mature, razor and blade market, Gillette holds a commanding worldwide market share. The peak of its innovation occurred in 2006 with the introduction of the Fusion 5-bladed razor. Today, innovation in razors and blades is thwarted by a lack of new technology and increasing consumer reluctance to pay for the "latest and greatest" in shaving technology. Gillette must decide how to put the razor wars behind them and maintain or increase its share of the global razor market.

Themes: Product leadership, product innovation, pricing strategy, integrated marketing communication, segmentation, competition, sports marketing, global marketing, strategic focus

S ince its inception in 1901, Gillette has always prided itself on providing the best shaving care products for men and women. In fact, the company was so visionary that it didn't have any serious competition until 1962, when Wilkinson Sword introduced its stainless steel blade. Since that time, the Wilkinson Sword-Schick Company has evolved into Gillette's primary competitor. Through the years, Gillette has strived to stay on the cutting edge of shaving technology in a market that thrives on innovation. This focus led to a game of one-upsmanship with Schick as each company introduced 3-bladed (Gillette's Mach3), 4-bladed (Schick's Quattro), and 5-bladed (Gillette's Fusion) razors in rapid succession. Now, under the ownership and guidance of Procter & Gamble, Gillette faces a saturated U.S. market that fluctuates only when newer, more innovative products are introduced. However, many analysts believe that Gillette and Schick have reached the end of truly meaningful product innovation. Given this, Gillette faces the challenge of further expanding its already dominant 66 percent share of the $12.8 billion global market. And in a market that thrives on innovation, Gillette must determine how to balance the continued investment of resources in research and development, searching for "the next big thing" in the global shaving market, and capturing more consumers who have become increasingly sensitive to the high prices associated with innovative shaving technology.

---

*Michael D. Hartline, Florida State University, prepared this case for classroom discussion rather than to illustrate effective or ineffective handling of an administrative situation. Editorial assistance was provided by MBA students Leanne Davis, Brent Scherz, Matthew Cagiolosi, Daniel Breiding, Nicole Dyche, Colin Roddy, and Ryan Wach.

The History of Innovation at Gillette

Born in Fond du Lac, Wisconsin in 1855, King Camp Gillette learned from an early age the importance of self-sufficiency, innovation, and invention. After his family's home was destroyed in the Chicago Fire of 1871, Gillette left home at 16 years of age to become a traveling salesman. His experiences in his position led him to William Painter, the inventor of the disposable Crown Cork bottle cap, who assured him that a successful invention was one that was purchased over and over again by a satisfied customer. In 1895, after several years of considering and rejecting possible inventions, Gillette suddenly had a brilliant idea while shaving one morning. It was an entirely new razor and blade that flashed in his mind—a razor with a safe, inexpensive, and disposable blade. According to reports, Gillette's idea wasn't immediately successful, as technical experts said it would be impossible to produce steel that was hard, thin, and inexpensive enough for commercial development of the disposable razor blade. However, in 1901, with the technical partnership of MIT graduate William Nickerson, Gillette produced the original Gillette safety razor and blade, establishing the foundation for the Gillette Safety Razor Company.

Since 1901, the Gillette Company has led the personal care and grooming industry through manufacturing efficiency and exceptional marketing. By offering "consumers high-quality shaving products that would satisfy basic grooming needs at a fair price," Gillette effectively captured more than half of the entire razor and blades market across the globe. In fact, in the 1920s Gillette said the following of his razor product: "There is no other article for individual use so universally known or widely distributed. In my travels, I have found it in the most northern town in Norway and in the heart of the Sahara Desert."

Gillette's success in this market carried the company through economic droughts in the 1920s and 1930s, as well as allowed it to weather the storm brought on by World War II. Encouraged by the successful development of his razor products, Gillette felt inclined to challenge his entrepreneurial spirit with the acquisition of two unrelated ventures: the Toni Company, maker of do-it-yourself home permanent-wave kits, and the Paper Mate Pen company, producer of retractable, refillable ballpoint pens. Although seemingly profitable at first, both acquisitions proved to be unsuccessful as sales and revenue waned due to declining demand and innovative competitors, such as Bic's low-priced disposable (nonrefillable) pens from France. As a result, Gillette's unblemished track record for success became tarnished as net profits slumped to $1.33 per share in 1964.

Despite this fact, Gillette reigned as a visionary monopoly in the personal shaving market until 1962, when English firm Wilkinson Sword introduced its stainless-steel blade. Distracted by its experimental ventures with the Toni Company and Paper Mate, Gillette neglected to foresee the impact this small company could have on its core business of razors and blades and began to lose a substantial portion of market share. Although Gillette retained 70 percent of the market at the time, the arrival of Wilkinson Sword's stainless-steel blade initiated a transition in niche markets. For the first time, Gillette executives were unsure how to respond. Should they introduce their own stainless-steel blade or ignore the rival and hope that its market niche would remain small? Fortunately for Gillette, Wilkinson Sword lacked the resources necessary to exploit the niche markets it had penetrated and where it competed with Gillette. Eventually, Wilkinson Sword sold much of its blade business to Gillette. Unfortunately, by this time Gillette had already begun to feel the impact of competition as its market share had dipped to an all-time low of 49 percent.

To revive Gillette's market share and bounce back from unsuccessful product ventures into do-it-yourself permanent-wave kits and refillable ballpoint pens, Gillette's new CEO Vincent Ziegler spearheaded an acquisition and product development campaign. Ziegler was often described as aggressive, marketing oriented, and ambitious for the company, believing in diversification through the acquisition of companies in other business segments. Under Ziegler's leadership, Gillette purchased the following companies: Braun AG (German manufacturer of small appliances), S.T. Dupont (French maker of luxury lighters), Eve of Roma (high-fashion perfume), Buxton Leather goods, Welcome Wagon, Inc., Sterilon hospital razors, and Jafra Cosmetics (home sales). Unfortunately, four of these acquisitions proved to be unprofitable or unsuitable and were divested, and the other three yielded low profits by Gillette's standards. These ill ventures exposed the company to competitive pressures, especially in the form of Bic's disposable razors and lighters. In addition, Bic's 19-cent disposable stick pens particularly affected the Paper Mate line of refillable pens and drove Paper Mate's share of the retail ballpoint pen market from more than 50 percent down to 13 percent. In 1975, Gillette retaliated with the introduction of its new Write Brothers line of disposable pens and salvaged a good portion of the lost market share with heavy price promotions.

Despite these pressures, Gillette experienced moderate successes under the leadership of Ziegler with the introduction of Cricket disposable lighters and Soft & Dri antiperspirant (until the industry experienced a sharp decline in sales of the spray product due to the belief that aerosols destroy the ozone layer.) Furthermore, the introduction of the Trac II razor was deemed a "great success" and thus continued Gillette's dominance in this market. Other successful product developments came under the leadership of Colman Mockler, Gillette's next CEO, whose strategy was to cut costs and invest more money into advertising and product development. Under Mockler, Gillette experienced some of its greatest successes including memorable innovations such as the Atra razor, the Good News! disposable razor, and the Daisy razor for women. After these product additions, Gillette held roughly 75 percent of the global market in razors and blades, including a majority of the U.S. shaving market (razors, blades, and the leading shaving cream). By the end of 1980, Gillette's sales rose above $2 billion for the first time in the company's history.

The foundation of this success was the introduction of new products for the razor and blade market developed in Gillette's home laboratories. As previously mentioned, Gillette's Atra-Plus shaving system, which featured a refillable Atra cartridge with a lubricating strip, overtook the Trac II as the number one selling razor. In addition, to directly compete with Bic and other razor companies, Gillette updated its Good News! line to include a disposable razor with a lubricating strip. Furthermore, in the personal care segment, Gillette made several introductions, including Aapri facial care products, Dry Idea deodorant, Bare Elegance body lotion, Mink Difference hair spray, White Rain hair care products, and Silkience shampoo and moisturizers. These additions had mixed results and left Gillette still searching for the keys to success in this business segment. In the writing instruments segment, Gillette achieved moderate success with the development of Eraser Mate erasable, disposable pens. Also, the steady sales of Paper Mate pens and Liquid Paper correction fluids helped to maintain company performance.

The Razor Wars

By 1990, Gillette found itself in the interesting position of cannibalizing its own successful products with the launch of the Sensor razor. The Sensor soared in sales globally and quickly dominated the market, only to be succeeded by the Sensor Excel in 1993. This was not the first competing product produced by Gillette; however, it represented the first product that was able to effectively shift consumer demand and sales away from the Atra and Trac II—Gillette's leading products. A similar effect occurred in the women's razor market with the development of the Sensor for Women in 1992 and the Sensor Excel for Women in 1996. As to be expected, the continued success of the Sensor family of shaving systems led to the gradual decline of the Atra and Trac II twin-blade shaving systems. However, despite this decline, the Atra and Trac II razors continued to hold decent market share positions worldwide. In addition, holding steady since 1976, Gillette's Good News! brand maintained its position as the best-selling disposable razor in its product category worldwide.

Gillette's internal competition heated up with the introduction of the Mach3 razor in 1998. Touting three thin blades designed to provide a closer shave with fewer strokes and less irritation, the Mach3 became Gillette's most successful new product ever as sales rose to $1 billion in the first 18 months. Recognized for its innovative design (blades on tiny springs), the Mach3 was named winner of the American Marketing Association's Grand Edison Award for the best new product of 1998. Similar to the marketing strategy employed for the Sensor and Sensor Excel products, Gillette sequentially produced the Mach3 Turbo for men and the Venus system for women in an attempt to further expand the reach of Mach3 technology and market share.

In 2003, the razor wars got ugly as Gillette faced a new, more threatening competitor: Schick and the Quattro—the world's first four-bladed razor. Before Schick introduced the Quattro to the market, Gillette sued Energizer holdings and its Schick division, arguing that the Quattro illegally used the same "progressive geometry" technology as the Mach3. However, despite the lawsuit, Schick was allowed to launch the Quattro. To combat the suit, Schick countersued Gillette, claiming that Gillette's advertisements stating "the world's best shave" and "the best a man can get" were misleading. While Gillette and Schick engaged in a legal ping-pong match, consumer preferences and purchases were changing. In addition to Schick's Quattro for men, its Intuition for women began to encroach upon Gillette's hold of the women's shaving market. Schick's total share of the U.S. market had risen 2.9 percent to 17 percent, while Gillette's total share of the razor and blades market had fallen 4.3 percent to 63 percent.

To fight back, Gillette aggressively established a two-fold plan of attack for recapturing market share. This strategy included converting consumers to higher-priced razors and blades, such as the Sensor, Sensor Excel, and Mach3 lines, from the single- and twin-blade razors, and geographically expanding into the areas of Romania and the former Yugoslavia, the Soviet Union, and the Czech Republic. At the forefront of Gillette's strategy sat its secret weapon: the Fusion—the world's first 5 (+1) blade razor, introduced in 2006. Using a unique 5-blade design with a single blade on the back of the cartridge for use in trimming moustaches and side burns, the Fusion exploded off the shelves and sold more than 4 billion razors within the first two months. Furthermore, the Fusion razor represented the first product introduction since Proctor & Gamble finalized its purchase of The Gillette Company and its subsidiaries, including Braun, Duracell, and Oral-B.

Although the Fusion represented a victory for Gillette and P&G, the hype surrounding its initial success was quickly fleeting. Other than being more expensive than the Mach3 (each cartridge costing 75 cents to $1 more than the Mach3 cartridge,) critics questioned why five blades were needed to get the best shave when Gillette had touted its three-bladed Mach3 as "the best a man can get" since the late 1990s. In addition, *Consumer Reports* concluded that there were no additional performance benefits provided by the 5-bladed Fusion, especially when compared to the Mach3. However, what was the most concerning for Gillette was the fact that sales reports indicated that the razors were outselling the cartridge refills. This translated to a consumer perception akin to a "novelty" product with a lack of staying power and product loyalty. Further, from a financial standpoint, Gillette feared not reaching the sales potential for the product combination, because it is well known that razor manufacturers earn most of their profits from blade refills, not the initial razor purchase. Despite these concerns, the Fusion line continued to be a successful revenue generator for Gillette and P&G.

The Quest for Continued Innovation

Rather than continue the razor wars by producing a six- or seven-blade razor, Gillette focused on releasing complementary products, enhancing its existing product lines and expanding its intensely successful marketing strategy. To complement its already successful razor and blades division, Gillette sought to expand its product portfolio inside the shower doors to create the full "shower experience." For example, the launch of Gillette Hair Care and Body Wash for men, as well as its Clinical Strength deodorant, represented the most significant Gillette brand extensions outside of the razor and blades division, and aimed to reinforce the brand's standing as the world's leading male-grooming authority. "We've earned the trust of the more than 600 million men who start their day with a Gillette razor," said Chip Bergh, Group President, Global Personal Care, Procter & Gamble. "By offering superior deodorant, body washes, and shampoos, we are able to reward that trust by giving guys what they want and need in other areas of their grooming routines."

Because razors and blades are in the maturity stage of their product life cycle, focusing on these complementary products allows the company to increase its share of customer. Defined, share of customer refers to the percentage of each customer's needs in a particular area met by the firm and is exploited when a company with brand loyalty effectively capitalizes on that preference to market other products. Gillette's ability to increase its share of customer is greatly enhanced due to the resources available at Proctor & Gamble. According to Clayton C. Daley, Jr., vice chairman and chief financial officer of P&G, "One of the objectives of the Gillette integration has been to leverage the strengths and technologies of both companies to develop new products. We're generating revenue synergies by combining our superior science and male-grooming expertise to introduce these adjacent Gillette-branded products."

In addition to complementary products, Gillette's primary focus has been on the extension of its core business and the marketing programs that support it. Going beyond simple brand advertising, many of the initiatives and activities introduced by Gillette created a synergy between product development and marketing strategy. For example, building off the success of the Fusion and Fusion Power razor and blades, Gillette released the Fusion Power Phantom (Stealth in the United Kingdom) in February 2007. The Phantom razor featured a redesigned handle and a darker color scheme than the original Fusion Power. In addition, in February 2008, Gillette released another revision, the Fusion Power Phenom, redesigned with a metallic blue and silver satin chrome handles color scheme. In 2009, Gillette launched the gaming-inspired Fusion Power Gamer razor at the EA SPORTS Champions of Gaming Tournament.

Despite these advances in shaving technology, Gillette's market research indicated that most men still experienced discomfort during and after shaving. In response, Gillette released the Gillette Fusion ProGlide shaving system in 2010. The ProGlide and ProGlide Power were built on the original Fusion platform and included new innovations such as 15 percent thinner and finer blades, a blade stabilizer, comfort guard, a 25 percent larger lubrastrip, a microcomb, a redesigned precision trimmer, and a redesigned handle. Gillette's testing with consumers showed that the Fusion ProGlide family was preferred 2-to-1 over the Gillette Fusion, which was already the world's best-selling razor. The ProGlide family was also named Best Razor of 2011 by *Men's Health* magazine. Chip Bergh speaks to the motivation and results of their efforts, "By taking the world's number one selling razor and making it better—dramatically better—we are defining a new standard for the more than 600 million men around the world who trust their faces to Gillette." These strategies of innovation and global expansion enabled Gillette and its products to grow market share every year from 2006 to 2011, selling nearly 100 million razors and blades in 75 countries.

In January 2012, Gillette launched the Fusion ProGlide Styler in conjunction with a new "Masters of Style" campaign. The campaign focused on three celebrities known for their facial hair styles, namely André 3000 Benjamin (a musician), Adrian Brody (an actor), and Gael García Bernal (an actor). The ProGlide Styler was designed to simplify facial hair styling; a complex process involving trimmers, scissors, and razors. P&G combined the best attributes of its Gillette and Braun brands to develop a single, three function product that trims, edges, and shaves. P&G also developed a new ProGlide Clear Shave Gel to accompany the 3-in-1 styling tool.

While Gillette's bread-and-butter has always been male consumers, the company has also made great strides in appealing to the needs of women. In 2010, Gillette won the Most Profitable Solution to a Business Problem—Gold Award for its women's Venus razor. In the past, most women's razors were simply pink-colored men's razors. Gillette changed the game by tackling women's shaving issues head-on. The Venus was the first wet-shaving product designed specifically for women, and was considered to be the first shaving product that actually improved the daily shaving experience for billions of women around the world.

Marketing Strategies

Gillette's lethal combination of marketing and product development stemmed from the fact that when it came to blades and razors, Gillette was not content with merely having an innovative product. The company virtually turned its marketing into a quantitative science, pouring time and resources into marketing plans that were almost military in their precision and implementation. Gillette's stellar marketing strategies date back to the Sensor and Senor Excel products and can be attributed, in large part, to the success of its current market position and yearly sales volume. Focused heavily on male-dominated sports marketing activities, Gillette's marketing program includes the following major elements:

- Gillette Stadium, home to the NFL's New England Patriots and soccer's New England Revolution, seats nearly 70,000 fans and has hosted numerous MSL Cup, World Cup, and NFL championships. Gillette's sponsorship of the stadium allows it to reach a worldwide audience, as both soccer and the NFL are tremendously popular in Latin America and European countries. This is important because 60 percent of Gillette's sales are generated outside the United States. Given the importance of the stadium sponsorship, Gillette extended its naming rights until 2031.
- Gillette Young Guns, which is aimed at fans of NASCAR, the NFL, and MLB, is designed to drive sales for Gillette's premium razors and shave care products. The Young Guns campaign, which includes noted athletes such as Denny Hamlin, Kyle Busch, Matt Ryan, Ray Rice, Carlos Gonzalez, and Evan Longoria, promotes the fast and furious life of men though television, print, online, public relations, and event marketing tactics.
- Team Gillette is the company's tie-in with the Olympic games. For the 2012 Summer Games in London, Team Gillette consisted of 24 world-class athletes from 18 countries, including U.S. athletes Ryan Lochte (swimming) and Tyson Gay (track and field). Interestingly, four of the 24 athletes were from Brazil, a country where Gillette is making a strong push to promote advanced shaving technology.
- Gillette began its social media presence in 2007 when it launched on Facebook. However, the company did not take social media seriously until 2011. Gillette now actively coordinates its marketing campaigns with Facebook and Twitter. Their U.S. Facebook page has over 1.3 million likes. Gillette also maintains active Facebook

pages for India (over 900,000 likes), Argentina (over 40,000 likes) and the Venus shaver (over 900,000 likes). All of Gillette's Facebook pages feature instructional videos, photos, and sweepstakes. Gillette has over 21,000 followers of its U.S. Twitter feed and over 4,000 following its Brazil feed.

One of the major reasons that Gillette focuses on sports in its marketing efforts is that sport resonates with consumers all around the globe. In virtually every worldwide market, Gillette is the dominant brand in both men's and women's shaving. Given that dominance, and the always present need for shaving equipment and supplies, it is vital that Gillette maintain top of mind awareness in every market that it enters. The company feels that sports marketing and sponsorship are the best ways to meet this need.

Global Expansion

P&G discovered that the best way to gain an understanding of customer needs around the world is to perform R&D where the end product will be sold. A case in point is the Indian market. In 2005, before Gillette was acquired by P&G, it set out to market a new razor for Indian men. Many Indian men shave only a couple of times a week, often with a basin. To test its new razor, Gillette conducted product testing with Indian students at the Massachusetts Institute of Technology (MIT), who responded with rave reviews. However, the students shaved with running water, something not readily available in the Indian market. Consequently, the product launch failed. Later, however, after a product redesign and local market testing, Gillette launched the Gillette Guard to unprecedented demand among Indian men. Within three months of the launch, Gillette Guard became the best selling razor in India. It now holds a 50 percent market share. The success of the Gillette Guard also promoted sales of Gillette's other brands, most notably the Mach3.

Today, P&G invests about $2 billion a year in R&D—60 percent more than its closest competitor. Much of that R&D effort occurs in nations other than the U.S. For instance, P&G recently opened the Beijing Innovation Center (BJIC) in China—a $70 million home for P&G's regional R&D efforts. P&G has poured $1 billion into China for R&D purposes and plans to spend another $1 billion within the next five years. P&G now has 25 R&D centers around the globe aimed at creating product innovations to serve the needs of customers regionally. The success has been evident as P&G has made product launches globally in untapped markets that have allowed their share of the razors and blades market to reach 70 percent. Shipments of both the Fusion and Mach3 have been increasing in global markets at a fast pace.

Pricing Strategy

Since 2007, Gillette has acknowledged that product quality and efficient marketing are the core value propositions that set the pace for the success of Gillette's product lines. "If you have a significantly and demonstrably superior product or service, it really is quite meaningful," said Benson P. Shapiro, a marketing consultant in Concord, Massachusetts. However, "If you don't put it into language that gives a promise of something better, people won't try it." Gillette learned this first hand during the economic recession that began in 2008. Despite the company's stellar marketing efforts, U.S. unit sales of Gillette's blade cartridges fell roughly 10 percent every month from 2008 through 2009. When combined with the fact that Gillette consistently raised prices to offset higher production costs, it became clear that U.S. consumers had slowed their purchases of Gillette's razor products. This was especially evident when compared to the sales of private-label disposable razors, which increased 19 percent over the same time frame.

Still, Gillette's solid gains in foreign markets offset some of the decline in the U.S. market.

Approximately 1.3 billion men worldwide shave with a razor blade. Within the United States, 94 million men ages 15 years and older remove hair in some fashion. Of these, 85 percent prefer to wet shave with a razor blade. The average American male begins to shave between the ages of 14 and 16 and continues to shave for the majority of his life. In addition, 100 million women in the United States, ages 13 years and older, remove hair in some fashion. Of these women, 94 percent prefer to shave with a razor blade. On average, men in the United States shave 5.33 times per week, or 24 times a month, and spend approximately $20 to $25 per month for razors, blades, and shave preparations.

These statistics point to a potential vulnerability in Gillette's pricing strategy. The retail price of a Fusion ProGlide razor for men and an eight-pack of replacement cartridges is almost $39.00. Step up to Fusion ProGlide Power and the price increases to almost $44.00. Gillette claims that the ProGlide cartridge will last up to 5 weeks with daily use. Although the veracity of this claim is up for debate, evidence shows that most men and women like less expensive three-blade razors just as well. A 2006 *Consumer Reports* test showed that 18 of 26 men who tested the Fusion razor would not switch from their regular three-blade razor. Reviews for the Fusion ProGlide razor on Amazon.com are mixed, with a four-star average. A price comparison of various brands in the men's and women's wet-shaving market is shown in Case Exhibit 16.1.

Gillette's own research shows that men try to reduce the cost of shaving by cleaning their razors with toothbrushes or in the dishwasher to make the blades last longer. The high cost of shaving has led to a number of start-ups that are attempting to shake up the market. For example, the Dollar Shave Club (www.dollarshaveclub.com) signed up 12,000 customers in its first 48 hours of operating online. Customers can choose from three service offerings: The Humble Twin ($1.00 per month, plus $2 shipping and handling, for 5 twin-blade cartridges), The 4X ($6.00 per month for 4 four-bladed cartridges), or The Executive ($9.00 per month for 3 six-bladed cartridges). The company explains its service this way:

> *Like most good ideas, The Dollar Shave Club started with two guys who were pissed off about something and decided to do something about it.*
>
> *We got tired of spending $15-$20 every time we bought razor blades. We asked ourselves, did we really need all this fancy technology in our shave: a vibrating handle, LED guide-lights, 8-blades, and grip that could steady a 9-iron? The answer was a defiant "No"!*
>
> *We felt like we'd been over-marketed to. "Big Shave" companies keep telling us we need more expensive equipment, but why? Shaving should be simple. It sure used to be. Look at old photos of your father & grandfather. They didn't have extreme shave gear, and they look pretty handsome, don't they?*
>
> *So... we teamed up with one of the world's leading blade manufacturers and created signature 2, 4, and 6 blade razors. They've got everything you need in a shave: stainless steel blades, lubrication bars, and pivoting heads.*
>
> ***But we didn't stop there...*** *We thought: You know what also sucks... forgetting to pick up razor blades at the store and then making excuses about why we look like we slept in a motel last night. Razor blades are one of the most regular purchases we make. Someone should just send us our blades once a month.*

CASE EXHIBIT 16.1   Wet-Shaving Products and Prices

Brand		Initial Price of Razor	Price of Replacement Cartridges
Men's Products			
Gillette	Mach3	$8.59	12 for $25.99
	Mach3 Turbo	$9.99	8 for $22.99
	Fusion	$9.99	4 for $13.49
			8 for $24.99
	Fusion Power	$11.49	4 for $15.99
			8 for $26.99
	Fusion ProGlide	$9.99	8 for $28.99
	Fusion ProGlide Power	$11.99	8 for $31.99
Schick	Hydro 5	$9.49	4 for $11.99
	Hydro 5 Power Select	$11.49	4 for $12.49
	Hydro 3	$8.99	4 for $8.99
	Quattro	$9.99	4 for $10.29
			8 for $18.99
	Quattro Titanium	$9.99	4 for $10.99
			8 for $20.99
Bic	Comfort 3	4 for $3.89	
		8 for $6.99	
	Comfort 3 Advanced	4 for $5.99	
		6 for $7.99	
Women's Products			
Gillette	Venus	$5.99	4 for $9.99
			8 for $19.99
	Venus Divine	$8.99	8 for $19.99
	Venus Breeze	$9.99	4 for $12.99
	Venus Vibrance	$11.99	4 for $16.49
	Venus Embrace	$10.99	4 for $14.99
			8 for $28.49
Schick	Hydro Silk	$11.49	4 for $16.99
	Quattro for Women	$9.49	4 for $11.49
			8 for $21.99
	Silk Effects Plus	$5.99	5 for $8.99
	Intuition Plus Renewing Moisture	$9.89	6 for $20.99
	Intuition Plus Sensitive Care	$9.89	3 for $11.49
Bic	Soleil Triple Blade	4 for $6.49	
	Soleil Twilight	4 for $6.49	

Sources: Lowest posted prices at Drugstore.com (http://www.drugstore.com) and CVS.com (http://www.cvs.com), accessed July 31, 2012.

And just like that, the Dollar Shave Club was born! *For as little as $1/month, a great shave delivered right to your door. No more superfluous shave tech. No more stubble in the status meeting. Just a great shave for a low-commitment.*

The Dollar Shave Club has been so successful that it has raised over $1 million in seed money from venture capital firms. A similar company, RazWar.com, has launched in Belgium with similar funding from venture capitalists. Another company is planned in the U.K. Not to be outdone, Amazon offers Gillette Mach3 Cartridges for $2.06 each if customers agree to regular shipments. ProGlide cartridges are also available for $3.44 each. Gillette responded with new advertising focusing on the value and long-lasting attributes of the ProGlide system. However, early signs show that Gillette's U.S. market share has dipped as much as 2 percent over the last year. With the trend in online razor purchases, it is clear that Gillette and P&G will face significant pressure on their premium pricing strategy as more consumers learn about other options.

Looking Toward the Future

To succeed in the future and effectively win the razor wars and beyond, Gillette must find new ways to innovatively out-produce or out-market the competition. In essence, the challenge for Gillette is to push the envelope without creating innovations that are seen as trivial. This requires massive expenditures on R&D that lead to products capable of recouping their investments. As Gillette looks to future technological innovations, the company must be concerned about broad consumer acceptance and whether its research investment can be recovered in a reasonable time frame.

Similarly, when considering possible increased global expansion, Gillette must consider the roles that culture, religion, and Western influences play in shaving behavior. For example, internationally, 15 percent of the world's male population does not shave due to discomfort from shaving; 7 percent do not shave for religious reasons; and 3 percent simply do not care to shave. Being aware of these behavioral and cultural characteristics will allow Gillette to effectively segment and target those they will be most successful in transforming into customers. Similarly, although some women in European countries choose not to shave for cultural reasons, others now prefer to engage in the activity as they increasingly embrace Western lifestyles. For example, younger generations of European women are being influenced by American movies and television that depict women with sleek underarms and legs. By fostering adoption of the shaving lifestyle, Gillette can effectively capitalize on this trend. In fact, if European women embraced hair elimination at the same pace as American women, total blade sales would increase by hundreds of millions each year.

In many ways, Gillette and Procter & Gamble are in an enviable position. Gillette's products dominate the global wet-shaving market. The company continues to grow, although slowly, in every worldwide market. Still, many industry analysts wonder if Gillette has reached the end of its historical innovation in wet-shaving technology. Thus far, Schick has not responded to the Fusion ProGlide with a breakthrough innovation of its own; however, it did respond by creating its own 5-bladed razor called the Hydro. Given that the wet-shaving market is mature, Gillette must depend on innovation to perpetuate its dominance (whether in product design or marketing), as well as create an appeal that entices customers to try and purchase its products. By aligning that appeal with what customers value, Gillette has the potential to establish a position of long-term product maturity and market dominance. In that position, it won't matter how many blades a competitor puts on a razor.

Questions for Discussion

1. Evaluate product innovation at Gillette throughout its history. Has Gillette been a victim of its own success? Has product innovation in the wet-shaving market come to an end? Explain.
2. What do you make of the razor wars, first between Gillette and Schick, and now with online competitors? Does Gillette face a serious threat from competitive inroads? Explain.
3. What actions would you recommend over the next five years that could help Gillette maintain its worldwide dominance in the shaving market? What specific marketing program decisions would you recommend? Should Gillette be worried about its pricing strategy? Explain.

Sources

The facts of this case are from Gen Abelson, "Gillette Sharpens Its Focus on Women," *The Boston Globe*, January 4, 2009 (http://www.boston.com/business/articles/2009/01/04/gillette_sharpens_its_focus_on_women/?page=3); "A Competitive Edge in a Cutthroat Market," *BusinessWeek*, November 22, 2005 (http://www.businessweek.com/stories/2005-11-22/a-competitive-edge-in-a-cutthroat-market); Afrooz Family, "Vibrating Gillette Razors," MadPhysics.com, April 2, 2006 (http://www.madphysics.com/ask/vibrating_gillette_razors.htm); Amazon Health & Personal Care site, Razors & Razor Blades (http://www.amazon.com/gp/search/ref=sr_nr_scat_3778671_ln?rh=n%3A3778671%2Ck%3Aproglide&keywords=proglide&ie=UTF8&qid=1343756422&scn=3778671&h=d7a8338 4670cd528cea154d8c574dc96d235e4e5), accessed July 31, 2012; Ellen Byron, "Gillette Sharpens its Pitch for Expensive Razor," *Wall Street Journal*, October 6, 2008 (http://online.wsj.com/article/SB122325275682206367.html); Mercedes M. Cardona, "Gillette's Mach3 Captures Top Prize at Edison Awards," *Advertising Age*, March 22, 1999, p. 54; Scott Cendrowski, "How long does a razor really last? Gillette comes clean," *CNNMoney*, June 7, 2012 (http://management.fortune.cnn.com/2012/06/07/gillette-razor-lifespan); "Cutting Edge: Moore's Law for Razor Blades," *The Economist*, March 16, 2006, p. 8; CVS website, Personal Care, Shaving (http://www.cvs.com/shop/Personal-Care/Shaving/_/N-3tZ54aZ2k?pt=CATEGORY), accessed July 31, 2012; Derrick Daye and Brad Van Auken, "5 Reasons Gillette Is The Best A Brand Can Get," *Branding Strategy Insider*, June 23, 2009 (http://www.brandingstrategyinsider.com/2009/06/5-reasons-gillette-is-the-best-a-brand-can-get.html); Dollar Shave Club, About Us (http://www.dollarshaveclub.com/about-us), accessed July 31, 2012; Drugstore.com website, Personal Care, Shaving & Hair Removal (http://www.drugstore.com/personal-care/shaving-and-hair-removal/qxg180638-0), accessed July 31, 2012; Gillette Corporate website (http://www.gillette.com), accessed July 31, 2012; "Gillette's Edge," *BusinessWeek*, January 19, 1998, pp. 70–77; "Gillette Launches New Facial Hair Styling Tool with Three Masters of Style," *BusinessWire*, January 18, 2012 (http://www.businesswire.com/news/home/20120118005270/en/Gillette-Launches-Facial-Hair-Styling-Tool-Masters); "Gillette Reaches Agreement to Sell White Rain Brand, St. Paul Manufacturing Center," Gillette News Release, March 23, 2000 (http://www.thefreelibrary.com/Gillette+Reaches+Agreement+to+Sell+White+Rain+Brand,+St.+Paul...-a060583068); "Gillette Reaches Definitive Agreement to Sell Stationery Products Business," Gillette News Release, August 22, 2000 (http://www.thefreelibrary.com/Gillette+Reaches+Definitive+Agreement+to+Sell+Stationery+Products...-a064460868); "Gillette Rings in New Era as World's Leading Male Grooming Brand," *Reuters*, July 11, 2008 (http://www.reuters.com/article/pressRelease/idUS119120+11-Jul-2008+BW20080711); Emily Glazer, "A David and Gillette Story," *Wall Street Journal*, April 12, 2012 (http://online.wsj.com/article/SB10001424052702303624004577338103789934144.html); Jeff Gluck, "Only Two NASCAR Drivers Make The Cut For New Gillette 'Young Guns' Class," *SB Nation*, January 8, 2011 (http://www.sbnation.com/nascar/2011/1/8/1922795/gillette-young-guns-denny-hamlin-kyle-busch-matt-ryan-ray-rice-evan-longoria-carlos-gonzalez-2011); Vijay Govindarajan, "P&G Innovates on Razor-Thin Margins," *Harvard Business Review Blog Network*, April 16, 2012 (http://blogs.hbr.org/cs/2012/04/how_pg_innovates_on_razor_thin.html); "History of Gillette Razors," The Executive Shaving Company (http://www.executive-shaving.co.uk/gillette-history.php); Jeremy Kahn, "Gillette Loses Face," *Fortune*, November 8, 1999, pp. 147–152; Mark Maremount, "Gillette's New Strategy Is to Sharpen Pitch to Women," *Wall Street Journal*, May 11, 1998, p. B1; Mark Maremount, "Gillette to Shut 14 of Its Plants, Lay Off 4,700," *Wall Street Journal*, September 29, 1998, p. A3; Mark Maremount, "Gillette to Unveil Women's Version of Mach3 Razor," *Wall Street Journal*, December 2, 1999, p. B14; Jack Neff, "Gillette Shaves Prices as It's Nicked by Rivals Both New and Old," *Advertising Age*, April 9, 2012 (http://adage.com/article/news/gillette-shaves-prices-nicked-rivals/234019); Molly Prior, "Fighting for the Edge in Shaving (Blade Wars: Shaving Report)," March 8, 2004 (http://www.accessmylibrary.com/article-1G1-114404714/fighting-edge-shaving-blade.html); Proctor & Gamble News Releases website (http://news.pg.com/news_releases), accessed July 31, 2012; Proctor & Gamble 2011 Annual Report (http://www.pg.com/annualreport2011/index.shtml), accessed July 31, 2012; RazWar website (http://www.razwar.com), accessed July 31, 2012; Jennifer Reingold, "Can P&G Make Money Where People Earn $2 a Day?" *CNNMoney*, January 6, 2011 (http://features.blogs.fortune.cnn.com/2011/01/06/can-pg-make-money-in-places-where-people-earn-2-a-day); Christina Rexrode, "As US Slows, P&G Turns to Developing Markets," *Inquirer Business*, February 2, 2012 (http://business.inquirer.net/42663/as-us-slows-pg-turns-to-developing-markets); Glenn Rifkin, "Mach3: Anatomy of Gillette's Latest Global Launch," *Strategy + Business*, April 1, 1999 (http://www.strategy-business.com/article/16651?gko=927cc); Mike Sandoval, "The Benefits of Traditional Wet Shaving," *Shaving 101*, October 14, 2010 (http://www.shaving101.com/index.php/education/double-edge-shaving/164-money-magazine-got-it-wrong.html); "Shaving Stats for Men," Razor-Gator.com (http://www.razor-gator.com/ShavingFacts/shaving_stats_for_men.htm), accessed July 31, 2012; E. B. Solomont, "Schick Cuts into Gillette's Market Share," *St. Louis Business Journal*, April 20, 2012 (http://www.bizjournals.com/stlouis/print-edition/2012/04/20/schick-cuts-into-gillettes-market-share.html?page=all); William Symonds, "Gillette's Five-Blade Wonder," *BusinessWeek*, September 15, 2005 (http://www.businessweek.com/bwdaily/dnflash/sep2005/nf20050915_1654_db035.htm); and "The Power of Fusion," *Consumer Reports Health* (subscription required for access), July 2006 (http://www.consumerreports.org/health/healthy-living/beauty-personal-care/skincare/shaving/gillette-fusion-razor-7-06/overview/0607_fusion-razor_ov.htm), accessed July 31, 2012.

IKEA Slowly Expands Its U.S. Market Presence*

Synopsis: IKEA is known around the world for its stylish, quality, and low-cost furniture and home furnishings. The company's success is based on a strategy of operational excellence in production, supply chain operations, and marketing. IKEA—wildly popular in Europe—has leveraged its brand reputation to penetrate markets in other countries. However, its penetration of the U.S. market has been hampered by a weakened economy and the inconsistency between the traditional U.S furniture market and IKEA's low-cost operating philosophy. IKEA must find a balance between its operational excellence strategy and U.S. consumers' demands for customization, good service, convenience, and quality.

Themes: Operational excellence, target marketing, product design, branding strategy, positioning, global marketing, pricing strategy, supply chain strategy, retailing, implementation, customer relationships, SWOT analysis, strategic focus

When 17-year-old Ingvar Kamprad founded IKEA in 1943, he could not have imagined that his company would become one of the world's most popular and iconic brands or the world's largest home furnishings retailer. The IKEA name is a combination of Kamprad's initials (IK) and the first letters of the farm (Elmtaryd) and village (Agunnaryd) in southern Sweden where he grew up. From the beginning, IKEA was founded on different principles—namely, frugality and low cost. Most furniture companies offer personalized service and advice in lavish showrooms where salespeople compete for sales commissions. Kamprad, however, recognized that customers are willing to trade off typical amenities to save money. Today, the no-frills frugality is the cornerstone of the IKEA caché and one of the reasons for its immense popularity.

IKEA operates under a unique corporate structure. When Kamprad founded the company, he wanted to create an independent organization that would be sustainable for the long term. Since 1982, the Stichting INGKA Foundation, a Netherlands-based charitable foundation, has owned the IKEA Group. Many estimates peg the foundation as one of the world's wealthiest charities—worth an estimated $36 billion. INGKA Holding B.V., also based in the Netherlands, is the parent company for all IKEA Group companies. The IKEA Group includes IKEA of Sweden (which designs and develops all IKEA products), Swedspan (which makes environmentally friendly wood panels), Swedwood (which makes all IKEA furniture), the sales companies that operate IKEA stores, and all purchasing and supply chain functions. This type of ownership is unique in that the foundation is a nonprofit organization designed to promote innovation in architectural

---

*Christin Copeland and Michael D. Hartline, Florida State University, prepared this case for classroom discussion rather than to illustrate effective or ineffective handling of an administrative situation.

and interior design. Some criticize IKEA's ownership as an arrangement that leverages the uniqueness of Dutch law to avoid taxes and prevent a hostile takeover attempt.

Today, IKEA is Sweden's best-known export. The company had 2011 worldwide sales totaling EUR 25.2 billion and an average annual growth rate of almost 7 percent. Roughly 79 percent of IKEA's sales come from operations in Europe, with North America and Russia/Asia/Australia contributing 14 percent and 7 percent, respectively. The company has 131,000 employees and more than 325 IKEA stores in 38 countries, with 287 stores in 26 countries belonging to the IKEA Group. The remaining stores are owned and operated by franchisees. The first U.S. IKEA store opened in Philadelphia in 1985. Today, there are 38 U.S. stores, with 11 stores in Canada. IKEA had originally planned to have 50 stores operating in the United States by 2010, but the 2008–2009 worldwide economic recession slowed IKEA's plans.

The IKEA Concept

The backbone of IKEA's success is "The IKEA Concept," which serves as both the company's vision and core operating philosophy:

> *The IKEA Concept: Provide functional, well-designed furniture at prices so low that as many people as possible will be able to afford them. Creating a better everyday life for the many people.*

The IKEA Concept guides every aspect of how the company's products are designed, manufactured, transported, sold, and assembled. To transform the IKEA Concept into reality, the company provides stylish, functional, low-cost home furnishings that customers must assemble themselves. Furniture products are shipped in flat packs to save money on manufacturing and distribution, which IKEA then passes on to customers in the form of lower prices at retail. To compensate for the customer having to "do it yourself," IKEA offers other services that make this proposition a little more attractive. These extra services include in-store child-care and play areas, restaurants, and longer store hours. To help visitors prepare for this experience, IKEA provides its customers with pencils, paper, tape measures, store guides, catalogs, strollers, and shopping bags. IKEA even offers delivery for the bulky items that customers cannot carry themselves. For those who want to carry their own bulky furniture home, IKEA rents carracks for convenience. IKEA stores are designed as a circle so that everything can be seen no matter in what direction the customer is headed. The aisles are wide to reduce traffic congestion that could occur when customers stop to look at different showrooms and displays.

Production

IKEA's key objective regarding production is to establish and maintain long-term supplier relationships. When designing new products, IKEA actually begins with a target retail price in mind, and then works with thousands of suppliers in over 50 countries to find the lowest cost way to manufacture that product. Its oldest suppliers are Swedish; however, other major suppliers are located in China (22 percent), Poland (18 percent), Italy (8 percent), and Germany (4 percent). IKEA accounts for approximately 10 percent of the furniture market in each country where its products are manufactured.

One strategy that IKEA has implemented is to place its trading offices in countries around the world to localize operations. This gives IKEA leverage to increase production capacity (that is, labor hours and purchasing materials) when needed. The strategy also allows IKEA to closely monitor manufacturing performance. Producing high-quality products at the lowest possible cost drives IKEA's production mentality. In addition to local trading offices, IKEA also manages production through long-term contractual relation-ships based on bulk buying. Committing to high-volume purchases over a longer time frame allows IKEA to dramatically cut costs. Additionally, IKEA is in a position to offer its suppliers financial assistance if necessary. This optimization is key to achieving the low-cost business model that IKEA wants to maintain.

Cost consciousness dominates all aspects of IKEA's operations. In land acquisition, IKEA locates stores on property just outside of target cities. In production, the remnants of fabric and wood used for products are used to create more products. IKEA uses natural colors to cut production costs and increase social responsibility to the environment through the manufacturing process. Across its distribution centers, flat packages are used to efficiently transport the large bulk of products from suppliers to IKEA stores. The use of flat packages lowers warehousing and distribution costs and the environmental impact throughout the supply chain.

IKEA's production goals also include a strong sustainability component. The company has partnered with the World Wildlife Federation and the Forestry Stewardship Council to ensure that raw materials (primarily wood and cotton) come from responsibly managed and sustainable sources. IKEA helps educate cotton farmers in India, China, Pakistan, and Turkey to use sustainable methods, such as reducing water, pesticides, and fertilizers. Currently, 16 percent of wood materials and 24 percent of cotton materials come from sustainable sources. In addition, IKEA has a goal to obtain 100 percent of its energy from renewable resources. The company operates its own wind turbines and solar systems to power both stores and distribution centers. Today, 51 percent of IKEA's energy comes from sustainable sources.

Marketing

IKEA's marketing program has four focal areas: product design, catalogs, advertising, and public relations/promotions. IKEA's product designs are arguably the most important part of its brand image. Customers love the clean lines, frugal styling, and caché that ownership affords. IKEA admits that creating stylish and inexpensive products is a challenging task. To fulfill its vision, the company's full-time and freelance designers work closely with in-house production teams to pair the appropriate materials with the least costly suppliers. Though the work is tedious, IKEA is well known for its product innovation.

IKEA's main marketing focus is its printed catalog, where the company spends the majority of its annual marketing budget. The 300- to 400-page catalog is produced in 59 different editions in 30 languages. In 2012, 211 million copies were put into circulation. New for 2013, the IKEA catalog featured special symbols that are readable by IKEA's iPhone and Android apps. When users scan the symbols, they are presented with an augmented reality experience that allows customers to see the company's products more in depth. The apps also offer 3D models of products and how-to videos. A similar experience is available online where customers can view products and download free programs to help redesign kitchens, bathrooms, and bedrooms. The website also provides information about each store's local events and promotions, services, and product specials. Because the website offers limited online purchasing capabilities, customers are often forced to visit the stores to buy products. Approximately 30 percent of IKEA's product line is available for online purchase.

In addition to the catalog, IKEA also uses television, radio, and Internet-based communication to reach its target customers. The company's advertising is intended to increase both brand awareness and store traffic. Some of the company's advertising is controversial, especially ads that portray gay customers or sexually suggestive storylines. IKEA has even taken its advertising to the streets in Italy (with a graffiti campaign) and in Paris (where a complete IKEA furnished apartment was installed in the Paris underground). Advertising, however, is not a major focus of IKEA's promotional efforts. The company prefers to rely on word-of-mouth communication. This is reflected in its use of social media. For example, IKEA's Facebook pages provide up-to-date information on company activities, sales, and local store events. IKEA's U.S. Facebook page boasts over 1 million fans, while its international pages have several hundred thousand fans each. Several thousand fans typically follow each local store page.

Local store events are another key marketing focus for IKEA. The San Diego, California, store offers birthday parties for children on the first Tuesday of every month. The Atlanta, Georgia, store features activities such as culinary tasting events, face painting, college student activities, and fundraising events for local charities. In a unique promotion prior to the grand opening of the Atlanta store, IKEA managers invited locals to apply for the post of Ambassador of Kul (Swedish for "fun"). The five winners of an essay contest received $2,000 in vouchers, had to live in the store for three days, sleep in the bedding department, and participate in contests. Finally, the entire IKEA family holds "Antibureaucracy Weeks" on a regular basis. These are times when executives work on the shop floor or stockroom, operate cash registers, and even load trucks and cars for IKEA customers. This simple step goes a long way in upholding the IKEA culture and maintaining employee morale.

IKEA's marketing program is designed to be thrifty but still effective. In fact, all of IKEA's marketing activities are designed to maintain a downward pressure on operating expenses. For example, in most stores, IKEA does not accept checks—only cash or credit cards, including its own "IKEA Card." This helps to reduce IKEA's accounts receivable and eliminates the need to maintain an expensive collections operation. With policies like these, it is not surprising the company's operating margin of 10 percent is among the best in the home furnishings industry. And, despite its low cost and price model, IKEA aims to cut prices by an average of 2 to 3 percent every year.

The Future of IKEA's U.S. Expansion

IKEA considers the United States an important part of its plans for global expansion. The U.S. standard of living is higher than most countries; however, most American consumers actively buy into the cost-conscious mentality. The value of the U.S. dollar is stable and not prone to wide exchange rate fluctuations. The United States has very high Internet usage, and IKEA's sustainability efforts are welcomed by a wide margin of the consuming public. Another factor that makes the United States favorable to IKEA is its melting pot of cultures. The IKEA Concept can appeal to the different lifestyles and ways of life found in the United States.

Despite these advantages, IKEA must address two key issues regarding U.S. expansion. The first is the need to adapt to the preferences of U.S. consumers. American consumers are very demanding and tend to reward marketers that go out of their way to address individual tastes and needs. Further expansion into the U.S. market will require IKEA to adapt its offerings and stores to local tastes—a marketing strategy that is much more expensive to deliver and contrary to IKEA's cost-conscious operating philosophy. IKEA's franchised structure is well suited to this task. This allows IKEA to get closer to customers by hiring local employees that represent the same values, cultures, and lifestyles of the local area. Another adaptation issue involves IKEA's promotional strategy, which must be tailored to U.S. standards. For example, most of IKEA's television commercials are considered too "edgy" for American viewers.

The second key issue is quality. Although American consumers are increasingly value-driven, they also demand quality products. In this regard, IKEA's low-cost, do-it-yourself concept misses the mark for many potential furniture consumers. Many Americans view self-assembled furniture as being lower in quality, and similar to the types of furniture one might buy at Walmart or Target. The particleboard construction often used in these products has tarnished consumers' perceptions of do-it-yourself furniture.

Facing these challenges, IKEA's U.S. expansion has moved slowly. The company opened only three U.S. stores from 2009 to 2012 and does not plan to open any new U.S. stores in 2013. IKEA's low-cost, do-it-yourself marketing strategy is not a perfect match for U.S. tastes in furniture retailing, nor does the company have the financial resources and marketing experience to roll out a large number of products and stores simultaneously. The most recent economic conditions have not helped either. As the company looks toward further expansion into the U.S. market, it must consider a number of relevant issues in both its internal and external environments.

IKEA's Strengths

Low Cost Structure   IKEA's low cost structure has been the very essence of its success. Being that low cost measures are ingrained into IKEA's corporate DNA, the company does not have a hard time tailoring its operations around this business model. This model also pairs nicely with customers who appreciate IKEA's operating style. Furthermore, IKEA's low cost structure has kept the company profitable while competitors, such as Pier 1 in the United States, are struggling. Despite the state of the economy, IKEA has continued to see positive revenue growth. IKEA has continued to use every possible avenue to maintain its low cost structure and competitiveness without compromising customer value.

Corporate Culture   IKEA values antibureaucracy in its operations, and strongly follows worker and environmental protection rules. These tenets are codified in the company's code of conduct know as "The IKEA Way." The company's culture is based on the core values of togetherness, cost consciousness, respect, and simplicity. Kamprad once said, "Work should always be fun for all colleagues. We all only have one life; a third of life is work. Without desire and fun, work becomes hell." To ensure the company culture is upheld, the company looks for very specific traits in potential employees. IKEA's managers look for people who "display a desire to learn, motivation to do things better, common sense, and the ability to lead by example." The company believes in keeping employees happy by engaging in activities throughout the year that promote well being and job satisfaction. These are all reasons that IKEA has been ranked in *Fortune* magazine's annual list of "100 Best Companies to Work For" on many occasions.

Do-It-Yourself Approach   IKEA maintains its low-cost business model by creating a different furniture shopping experience. IKEA supplies customers with all possible materials needed to complete their shopping when they enter the store (that is, measuring tape, paper, and pencils). The floor has showrooms displaying IKEA furniture with multiple accessories that will accentuate the style. With this approach, customers do not have to be bothered with salespeople who work on commission. Customers can pick and choose among the different options of accessories that they would like to use with furniture. Many customers appreciate the feeling of accomplishment that comes from doing things for themselves. For those customer who do not like the DIY approach, IKEA offers assembly services and home delivery options.

Added Amenities   Although IKEA is not set up as a traditional furniture store, the company does provide several added amenities. IKEA rents car racks that customers can use to get bulky items to their homes. IKEA also provides child-care services to give parents time to shop. Once their children are in a safe place, parents will delegate more time to browsing and purchasing IKEA furniture and accessories. The company also provides restaurants in some of its stores to encourage customers to stay a little longer. Offering breakfast, lunch, and dinner, the restaurants also generate strong profits for the company each year. Customers can also schedule consultations with professional designers. In sum, the IKEA experience is designed to make the stores destinations in themselves. IKEA wants the customer to feel as if there is not a rush to leave the store and customers can do more than just shop for furniture.

Brand Image   There is no denying that brand image is a key strength for IKEA. Even if they have not been in a store, most people around the globe recognize the blue and yellow logo as a symbolic representation of trendy, modern, and fashionable furniture. Customers flock to the furniture giant to experience what *BusinessWeek* has referred to as "IKEA world, a state of mind which revolves around contemporary design, low prices, wacky promotions, and an enthusiasm that few institutions can muster."

Part of IKEA's brand strength comes from its wide array of products that exude a high-quality, low-cost focus. The company offers home furnishings and appliances for the bedroom, bathroom, and kitchen, as well as furniture for business offices. In addition to home furnishings, the company sells accent pieces and everyday products such as rugs, linens, and kitchen utensils. Some of the company's newest ventures include home building materials. Customers can build an IKEA home with reasonably priced, environmentally friendly materials.

Strong Focus on Sustainability   IKEA considers the environmental impact of every step in its business processes by making products that are environmentally conscientious and cost-effective. Suppliers are required to comply with strict environmental standards and to use as much renewable, reusable, and recycled materials as possible. With wood as a primary source of material, IKEA also employs field specialists to ensure the wood obtained comes from responsibly managed forests. From product design to disposal, the organization truly practices what it preaches in terms of its environmental responsibilities.

IKEA's Weaknesses

Do-It-Yourself Approach   Some customers may not appreciate IKEA's do-it-yourself approach. IKEA targets young, cost-conscious customers who want stylish furniture. However, these same consumers also like convenience and usually have the money to pay for it. For them, the time and effort involved in shopping for furniture, bringing it home, and assembling it may not be worth it. Furthermore, some customers enjoy having a conversation with a salesperson and getting individual ideas and advice from employees. These customers may continue to buy furniture from traditional retailers.

Limited Customization   To ensure alignment with its low cost structure and easy-assembly promise, IKEA's products are very basic and simple in terms of both structure and design. The ability for individualized customization is limited. Many American consumers prefer items with more style, accent, and color options.

Limited Promotional Expenditures   IKEA does not spend an enormous amount of money on promotion. Instead, the company depends on word of mouth and catalogs to generate a buzz among customers. Sadly, most U.S. consumers are not highly responsive to catalog marketing, making IKEA's bread-and-butter promotion less efficient and cost-effective for the U.S. market. American consumers also watch television and use the Internet more often than consumers in other countries. However, most of IKEA's television commercials are unknown outside of the United Kingdom. Further, many of the company's ads are controversial and not suitable for a U.S. audience. As a result of these issues, IKEA may be missing out on a larger potential customer base.

Weak Online Support Many aspects of the company's website leave much to be desired. Although product descriptions are available, many of the items shown cannot be ordered online. IKEA basically forces consumers to shop at their nearest brick-and-mortar locations. Because IKEA's physical presence in the U.S. market is small, the company is losing valuable sales due to its lack of online buying options.

IKEA's Market Opportunities

Economic Conditions IKEA's low-cost, high-quality strategy fits with the relatively weak state of the U.S. economy. As many consumers look for ways to cut personal spending, IKEA is well positioned to be a logical choice for home furnishings for the cost-conscious customer. Most American consumers still ascribe to a value-dominant logic when it comes to purchasing goods and services. However, these customers want not only high quality at a good price but also convenient access and timesaving services. IKEA can play into this buying logic but may have to expand its service offerings to increase customer convenience.

Demand for Convenience The number of consumers shopping online continues to rise. With the average schedule getting busier, technically savvy consumers increasingly enjoy the convenience and ease of online shopping. Comparison shopping is also a convenience afforded by the Internet that could allow IKEA to dominate the low-cost, quality furnishing sector. Offering convenient online shopping experiences would fit well with IKEA's low cost structure because it would allow them to sell items using a distribution network instead of a complete reliance on physical stores and their higher overhead costs. Convenience factors within IKEA's stores, such as restaurants and daycare, are already well suited to customer needs.

Popularity of Stylish, but Sustainable, Products Swedish design—the simple, futuristic, edgy, and fashionable designs offered by IKEA—is popular among consumers overall. In addition to style, consumers are also interested in "green" products that enhance the sustainability of natural resources. The recent corporate movement toward "green" practices is becoming more prevalent, and consumers are becoming more aware of a company's carbon footprint. IKEA is well positioned to take advantage of this trend.

IKEA's Market Threats

Competition Several other large retailers are vying for the do-it-yourself furniture segment. As consumers become more cost conscious in today's economy, the offerings of traditional bricks-and-mortar stores such as Home Depot, Target, and Walmart become more acceptable. IKEA also faces online competitors such as BluDot.com and Furniture.com. BluDot is a direct IKEA brand competitor that also claims to offer quality, unassembled furniture at low prices. It too offers simply designed and modern furniture. Furniture.com is a product competitor that uses the traditional furniture store concept but offers the ease and convenience of online price and product comparison.

Changing Customer Needs/Tastes   Customers' needs and tastes constantly change. At some point, customer interest in Swedish design and do-it-yourself furniture will wane. This is especially true as the U.S. population continues to age. The typical baby-boomer consumer demands quality, values his or her time, and appreciates convenience more than saving a few dollars. Overall, there are relatively fewer younger customers— IKEA's main target market—as compared to baby boomers. The end result is a likely decline in demand for trendy, low-cost furniture. IKEA's low-cost and high-quality designs might appeal to some baby boomers, but the inconveniences associated with the company's DIY approach probably send them looking elsewhere.

Mature Market Preferences   Most American consumers have preconceived notions of what the "best of the best" is when it comes to specialty furniture and furnishings purchases. For example, the average consumer may not purchase a mattress from IKEA because it is not a Select Comfort, Sealy, or Simmons mattress. Although IKEA focuses strongly on high-quality products, in the U.S. market the company must compete with well-established companies that have earned significant brand awareness.

Questions for Discussion

1. Given the SWOT analysis presented in the case, what are IKEA's key competitive advantages? What strategic focus should the company take as it looks to further expand into the U.S. market?
2. What factor is the biggest reason for IKEA's growth and popularity: value or image? Which is more important in the U.S. market? Why?
3. What strategic alternatives would you suggest IKEA employ to further penetrate the U.S. market?
4. Speculate on what will happen at IKEA stores as they are adapted to fit local tastes. Is the company's trade-off of service for low cost sustainable in the long term?

Sources

The facts of this case are from Roberto Baldwin, "IKEA's Augmented Reality Catalog Will Let You Peek Inside Furniture," *Gadget Lab*, July 20, 2012 (http://www.wired.com/gadgetlab/2012/07/ikeas-augmented-reality-catalog-lets-you-peek-inside-the-malm); Meera Bhatia and Armorel Kenna, "IKEA Has Slowest Sales Growth in More Than a Decade," *Bloomberg*, September 17, 2009 (http://www.bloomberg.com/apps/news?pid=20601085& sid=aSvPmp60dCL8); "Business: Flat-Pack Accounting; IKEA," *The Economist*, May 13, 2006, p. 76; Kerry Capell, "IKEA: How the Swedish Retailer Became a Global Cult Brand," *BusinessWeek*, November 13, 2005 (http://www.businessweek.com/stories/2005-11-13/ikea); Kerry Capell, "Online Extra: Sweden's Answer to Sam Walton," *BusinessWeek*, November 13, 2005 (http://www.businessweek.com/stories/2005-11-13/online-extra-swedens-answer-to-sam-walton); Cora Daniels, "Create IKEA, Make Billions, Take Bus," *CNNMoney*, May 3, 2004 (http://money.cnn.com/magazines/fortune/fortune_archive/2004/05/03/368549/index.htm); Sarah Fir-shein, "IKEA Unleashes Brand-New Graffiti-Art Campaign in Italy," *Curbed*, April 23, 2012 (http://curbed. com/archives/2012/04/23/ikea-unleashes-new-graffitiart-campaign-in-milan-subway.php); IKEA website (http://www.ikea.com), accessed August 14, 2012; IKEA San Diego Facebook Page (http://www.ikea.com/us/ en/store/san_diego), accessed August 14, 2012; IKEA 2011 Yearly Summary (http://www.ikea.com/ms/ en_US/pdf/yearly_summary/Welcome_inside_2011.pdf), accessed August 14, 2012; Inter IKEA Systems B.V. website (http://franchisor.ikea.com/index.asp), accessed August 14, 2012; Erika Kinetz, "IKEA to Invest $1.9B in India to Open 25 Stores," *BusinessWeek*, June 22, 2012 (http://www.businessweek.com/ap/2012-06-22/ikea-to-invest-1-dot-2b-in-india-to-open-25-stores); Philip Reynolds, "IKEA Cleans House," *Forbes*, June 25, 2009 (http://www.forbes.com/2009/06/25/ikea-redudancies-furniture-markets-equities-retail.html); Casey Ross, "IKEA Pulls Plan for Somerville Store in Assembly Square," *Boston.com*, July 20, 2012 (http://www. boston.com/businessupdates/2012/07/19/ikea-pulls-plan-for-somerville-store/PfHS9vViEaT8p5rcBmWuxO/ story.html); "Sweden's IKEA Posts Record Earnings, Growth Slows," *Bay Ledger News Zone*, September 16, 2009 (http://www.blnz.com/news/2009/09/17/Swedens_Ikea_posts_record_earnings_8604.html); and Swed-span website (http://www.swedspan.com), accessed August 14, 2012.

IVEY CASE **18**

Richard Ivey School of Business
The University of Western Ontario

Sushilicious: Standing Out In A Crowded Field

Ken Mark wrote this case under the supervision of Professors Dante Pirouz and Raymond Pirouz solely to provide material for class discussion. The authors do not intend to illustrate either effective or ineffective handling of a managerial situation. The authors may have disguised certain names and other identifying information to protect confidentiality.

Introduction

In a nondescript strip mall facing a farmer's field and power transmission lines, starting from the shell of a recently-shuttered sushi restaurant, entrepreneur Daniel Woo started Sushilicious, a different take on the concept. It was February 1, 2011, nearing the first-year anniversary of the restaurant's opening, and Woo was excited about the next stage of development.

Sushilicious had defied the odds as a new restaurant, drawing in both sushi aficionados and newcomers with its modern, Apple-store inspired design and its excellent food. Instead of spending marketing dollars in traditional advertising to increase business, Woo relied on a combination of social media tools — Facebook and Twitter — to drive awareness and interest.

Woo had not spent a single dollar on advertising, a remarkable feat considering that prospective diners needed to drive to Sushilicious; its location in the Irvine Village Shopping Center was not readily accessible on foot. Not content to sit on his laurels, Woo was considering three options to make Sushilicious's second year even more successful: franchising the concept, opening a second store in a different neighbourhood or focusing all effort on growing the customer base for his single restaurant.

Daniel Woo and the Sushilicious Concept

Originally from Seattle, Washington, Woo relocated to Irvine, California in 2008. In the process of looking at several business opportunities, he came up with the idea of opening a sushi restaurant geared towards families and customers who were new to sushi.

Sushi Competitors in Irvine

Sushi was a popular part of Japanese cuisine, introduced to the West in the early 1960s. It featured various combinations of cooked rice rolled or topped with sliced raw fish and other ingredients, and was served cold with soy dipping sauce and wasabi. While its appeal was initially limited to an audience familiar with Japanese cuisine, sushi was becoming popular on the West Coast due to the proliferation of sushi restaurants.

There were 10 sushi restaurants in Irvine — a city of 218,000 people. Most of the competition was sushi restaurants in the traditional style: they bore Japanese names and featured Japanese chefs. Their internal decor was either utilitarian — furnished with simple square tables and dark wood chairs — or Japanese, with light, unpainted pine furniture, latticed dividers and at least one wall that was painted red, which is an important colour in Japanese culture, carrying a number of symbolic meanings depending on the shade of the color and the shape used to represent it. The better restaurants were family-owned and managed by Japanese-born chefs.

Selecting a Location: The Former Gen Kai Japanese Cuisine Restaurant

The location Woo had chosen for his new restaurant had most recently housed a failed sushi restaurant, Gen Kai Japanese Cuisine (Gen Kai) (see Exhibits 1 and 2). Gen Kai was a traditional Japanese-style sushi restaurant, serving a variety of popular and exotic sushi and sashimi. The owners employed an *itamae* (a Japanese chef) who was in charge of food preparation.

EXHIBIT 1   Location

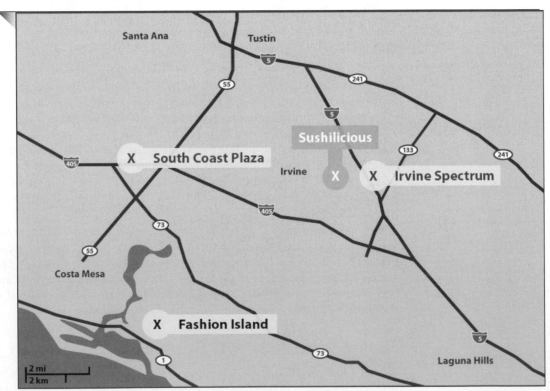

Source: Case writer.

EXHIBIT 2   Gen Kai Japanese Cuisine

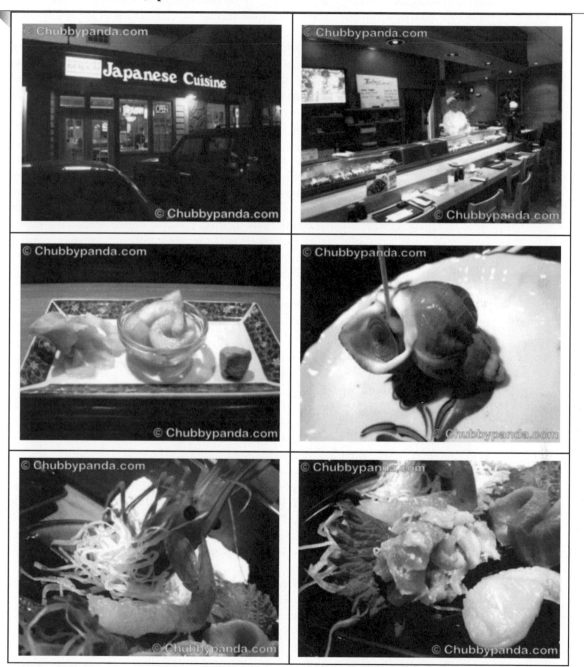

Source: "Gen Kai Japanese Cuisine – Irvine, CA," *Chubbypanda.com*, May 4, 2008, www.chubbypanda.com/2008/05/gen-kai-japanese-cuisine-irvine-ca.html, accessed May 25, 2011.

As was typical of Japanese sushi restaurants, the chef at Gen Kai was stationed in front of the diners, standing behind refrigerated glass shelves stocked with raw fish and other items such as fish roe and seafood. At Gen Kai, its red wall served as a general pantry and liquor cabinet. In between the bottles of sake and wine, a flat screen television showed sports programs.

Diners sat along the varnished pine bar, perching on wooden stools and facing the chef. Each setting included two bottles of soy sauce and a set of chopsticks. The restaurant had another 15 square tables, with total seating capacity at about 50 at any time. Gen Kai was located in the Irvine Village Shopping Center, to the right of Curves — a health fitness centre for women — and around establishments such as Papa John's Pizza, Pho Coffee Factory, the Irvine Dance Academy and Irvine Kid's Dentist. The shopping centre was on the edge of a residential area at the crossroads of Irvine Center Drive and Jeffrey Road. Unlike Irvine's downtown core, there was almost no foot traffic around the shopping centre.

Gen Kai's quality varied over the years depending on the skill and dedication of the chef employed. In the year before it closed, Gen Kai had an excellent Japanese chef named Juuji. An example of the exotic cuisine Juuji was able to prepare included octopus served in ribbons, whole poached sea snail, live prawns, monkfish liver and fried shrimp heads. Guests ordered from typical laminated paper menus with the list of dishes in black text (with no accompanying pictures). The names of the various dishes were in Japanese, with English translations. Dishes, whether hot or cold, were served on simple glass or ceramic plates. Despite its well-prepared authentic Japanese cuisine, Gen Kai was usually half-empty, even on its busiest nights. Gen Kai was open six days per week and was closed on Mondays and holidays. The restaurant closed its doors in early 2009.

In May 2009, as he looked at the restaurant space he had just rented, Woo could envision a different sushi concept.

The Sushilicious Concept

As he embarked on his new venture, Woo asked his five-year old daughter Hannah for help with the concept: "If I created a sushi restaurant, what should I name it?" "Sushi Delicious," Hannah replied. Woo combined both words and Sushilicious was created.

Woo drew upon his experience as a promotional executive to design a restaurant concept that stood apart. Woo had various inspirations for the Sushilicious concept, including Walt Disney World, Apple Inc. and Nordstrom (see Exhibit 3). He wanted to attract a target audience aged 14 to 34 who were interested in a casual, fun and affordable dining experience and would pay $15 to $30 for a meal, as well as families who were looking for dinner in a comfortable setting. This target audience was different from that of the other sushi restaurants in the area, most of which were either focused on high-end sushi enthusiasts or customers looking for low-cost, quick service food.

Sushilicious's logo featured lower-case sans serif font on a backdrop of brightly-coloured circles. It looked like a typical logo found on the latest electronic gadgets. Woo opted for a modern look to the store, sketching with a palette of cool colours: light green glass walls, white leather match couches for seating, white laminated table tops and bright steel counters. Sushilicious was deliberately designed to look like the restaurant version of an Apple Inc. retail store (see Exhibit 4).

In the centre of the restaurant was an elongated preparation area ringed by a conveyor belt circulating covered plates of foods from which diners could select. Called *kaiten*, this self-service feature was usually found in lower-end sushi restaurants. Woo intended to elevate the concept, designing lively containers in shades of yellow, pink and green to hold the sushi. He developed evocative names for the dishes, including Irrational Exuberance, Sushicalifragilistic and United Colors of Sushi; each dish ranged from $1.50 to $4.00. There were 50 dining seats in total and all booths were located next to the conveyor belt.

EXHIBIT 3   Inspirations for Sushilicious

Source: Company files.

Sushilicious had 11 full-time and 11 part-time employees. The full-time staff included one manager, five chefs, three waiters and waitresses, one dishwasher and one employee working in food preparation. Two chefs working in the middle of the restaurant refreshed the stock of food on the kaiten conveyor belt. Each plate of prepared sushi had a radio frequency identification (RFID) tag affixed to it that monitored how long the food had been on the belt; if more than a programmed number of minutes had passed, the dish was pulled off and the food discarded. If dining guests wished to order other items such as drinks or hot dishes, they had access to an application on an Apple iPod Touch that contained an electronic menu and ordering instructions. In addition, if customers wished to order freshly-prepared sushi or to make a custom order for sushi not found on the plates, the sushi chef could prepare a meal made to order.

EXHIBIT 4   Inside Sushilicious

Source: Company files and www.bighdesign.com/2010/04/sushilicious-sushi-with-a-side-of-social-media/, accessed May 30, 2011.

Instead of having limited opening hours, Woo elected to keep Sushilicious open seven days per week, even during most holidays. He commented on this decision:

> *Traditional Japanese restaurants are usually closed between 2:30 p.m. and 5:00 p.m. And they are shut at least one day a week, on either a Sunday or Monday. One of the reasons why I chose to keep Sushilicious open seven days a week was that our average customer bill, at $15 to $30, was lower than at other Japanese restaurants. Since I had a lower ring per customer, I wanted to ensure that we were attracting as many clients as possible. Our experience thus far is that there is a market for sushi in the afternoon.*

Marketing Sushilicious

Woo began his marketing campaign for the restaurant as the construction phase began. He opened Twitter and Facebook accounts and started posting news about his new restaurant. He sent messages to local food bloggers and Orange County news magazines. As the restaurant was built, he uploaded images of the work in progress (see Exhibit 5).

In the midst of the development, Woo began striking up conversations with Sushilicious's followers, not only describing his restaurant's concept but also speaking about local or state issues and discussing related topics such as exotic food or cool design concepts. Woo was unconventional in how he spent his marketing funds. He provided one example:

EXHIBIT 5   **Construction at Sushilicious**

Source: Company files.

I knew that I had to reach out to potential customers but I had a tight PR [public relations] budget. Near the restaurant, there is a college with a four-storey tall parking structure in which performance artists — dancers — would hold late night practices from 10:00 p.m. to 3 a.m. or 4 a.m. in the morning. I found out where these dancers were practicing and I decided to surprise them with free pizza. I ordered 10 boxes worth and had the delivery driver take them to one of their practice sessions. Inside each box was a note from me and it said, "From your friends at Sushilicious. Enjoy." I had thought about promoting my restaurant through the student newspaper but it would have cost me hundreds of dollars. Instead, I spent $90 on pizza and I had 40 kids who were delighted by the gesture. They put the story on their Facebook pages, on Twitter and on other social media outlets. We garnered a lot of publicity from that one gesture.

Woo discussed his reason for relying on social media to build awareness of his new restaurant: "I had enough money to open a restaurant but I had not budgeted for PR or for marketing. I was the PR, I had to do everything in-house. So, in a sense, social media was my only option at the start."

Prior to the opening of his restaurant in March 2010, Woo had nearly 1,000 followers on Twitter, many of whom were responding on a daily basis to his tweets about the restaurant and life in general (see Exhibit 6). Many brands establish a social media presence

---

EXHIBIT 6   A Selection of Daniel Woo's Sushilicious Tweets

- @raisamama Tell your friend I would sing Happy Birthday to him but, when I sing…. people leave the room.
- Come and watch the Giants vs Phillies at @sushilicious! Eat sushi, drink beer, watch baseball, and be merry. Sat Oct 16 2010 21:21:57 (Eastern Daylight Time) via web
- What did I say? Everyone un~followed me at the same time! ={
- Come celebrate the hottest day EVAR…. with some sushi from @sushilicious.
- @raymondpirouz sorry I missed you. I would loved to have chatted with you.12:43 AM Sep 26th, 2010 via Twitter for iPhone in reply to raymondpirouz
- @raymondpirouz did you stop by today?12:38 AM Sep 26th, 2010 via Twitter for iPhone in reply to raymondpirouz
- Please call 949.552.2260 for priority seating.6:19 PM Sep 24th, 2010 via web
- @dopeysang Thank you for the RT! Don't forget the FREE sushi plate offer if you come in b4 9/26.3:05 PM Sep 22nd, 2010 via web
- RT "@raymondpirouz: "Company owns the trademark, customers own the brand" http://www.vimeo.com/14798603" Wed Sep 15 2010 13:53:50 (Eastern Daylight Time) via Twitter for iPhone
- Yo @BigHeadAsian the bigger you get, the less I see you. Don't forget us little peeps !Fri Sep 10 2010 17:40:52 (Eastern Daylight Time) via web
- Don't have plans for dinner yet? Come in for some sushi tonight! We're open for Labor Day! Mon Sep 06 2010 18:30:05 (Eastern Daylight Time) via CoTweet
- You're still alive @raymondpirouz. Can't wait til you get back! 2:27 PM Aug 31st, 2010 via web
- staceysoleil @sushilicious we are raving about how awesome your#SocialMedia strategy is…expect LOTS of new fans ;) #SMMOC // *blushing*Sat Aug 28 2010 13:05:32 (Eastern Daylight Time) via web
- you had me at sushiTue Aug 10 2010 20:31:02 (Eastern Daylight Time) via web
- @kylezimmerman Thank you for coming! Sorry I didn't get a chance to say hi. I was a professional dishwasher yesterday.2:57 PM Jun 16th, 2010 via web in reply to kylezimmerman
- I can't vote ten times for myself….. so I need your help. http://www2.ocregister.com/voteocbest/ Sat Jun 12 2010 21:29:19 (Eastern Daylight Time) via web
- wow… people really read my tweets… now I just have to figure out something important to say. Sun May 30 2010 00:19:53 (Eastern Daylight Time) via web
- **KELLYCHOI** RT @sushilicious: If it's your Birthday today.. come in for FREE SUSHI! #fbFri May 28 2010 19:16:23 (Eastern Daylight Time) via UberTwitterRetweeted by sushilicious and 1 other
- @ohheylinds I'll have a nice cup of miso soup waiting for you the next time you come in.11:42 PM May 24th, 2010 via web in reply to Ohheylinds
- @shopeatsleep Thank you for coming…. I wanted to say hi. next time you come let me know. Sun May 23 2010 01:41:44 (Eastern Daylight Time) via web in reply to shopeatsleep
- My followers list is like the stock market…. up then down… up and then down….10:31 PM May 18th, 2010 via web
- Wow! So many new followers…. oh wait… it's spammers.. nevermind11:01 PM May 17th, 2010 via web
- Random Weekend Picture 10: http://bit.ly/a1NchKSat May 01 2010 03:34:29 (Eastern Daylight Time) via twitterfeed
- WARNING: if you are easily hypnotized… do not read this tweet! COME TO SUSHILICIOUS. COME TO SUSHILICIOUS. COME TO SUSHILICIOUS8:18 PM Apr 23rd, 2010 via web\
- I have been lacking in my twitter skillz lately.Wed Apr 21 2010 16:12:55 (Eastern Daylight Time) via web
- Attention all @UCIrvine students!!!! @sushilicious will be giving out a THOUSAND DOLLARS of gift cards between 12 & 3! Be sure to find us!Tue Mar 30 2010 23:29:55 (Eastern Daylight Time) via web
- We are in front of American Red Cross truck on Ring Road giving gift cards! 2:44 PM Mar 31st, 2010 via Twitter for iPhone
- Tyrant Habanero Wasabi Sticks: http://bit.ly/cQ7Pyt2:42 AM Mar 24th, 2010 via twitterfeed
- "@ElizaMichelleHo: @sushilicious my article with sushilicious in it came out today and I heard students talking about sushilicious!!" Fri Jun 04 2010 20:39:49 (Eastern Daylight Time) via Twitter for iPhone
- If you work at FedEx free sushi for you today! (First 10) Come between 1-3pm. Bring your appetite.9:27 AM Mar 18th, 2010 via web
- RT @ayoodanny Hella grubbed at @sushilicious! Hella good sushi and great customer service! The owner knows what he's doin.Mon Mar 15 2010 16:38:35 (Eastern Daylight Time) via web
- Chef Maekawa is in da house… Come on down for dinner… Holla! *Sun Mar 14 2010 19:49:51 (Eastern Daylight Time)* via Twitter for iPhone
- **sheryllalexande** @sushilicious You ROCK Daniel! LOVE your new kaiten sushi restaurant. Writing your www.Gayot.com review now. Eat sushilicious, #OC!4:40 PM Mar 11th, 2010 via web in reply to sushiliciousRetweeted by sushilicious

Source: Company files.

and immediately begin posting promotional messages advertising their products, services and prices (among other self-serving content). Woo intuitively understood how to engage with the community by becoming an active participant; sharing interesting stories and links while slowly building relationships with others in the community. Eventually, Woo held a soft opening of his restaurant for family and friends, followed by a public grand opening of the restaurant to great fanfare.

Woo used Facebook to post updates and pictures (see Exhibit 7) and Twitter to maintain a real-time link with Sushilicious's followers. Many followers would make themselves known to Woo in his restaurant, and he would reciprocate by offering them a free dish or acknowledging their visit via a tweet.

EXHIBIT 7   Sushilicious's Facebook Page

Source: Company files.

(Continued)

EXHIBIT 7 Sushilicious's Facebook Page (*Continued*)

Source: Company files.

Sushilicious seemed to be a hit with the Orange County crowd. The restaurant was at capacity during the busy nights (Thursday through Saturday) and had a strong lunchtime crowd. Looking to draw even more customers during the slow periods, Woo often tweeted about specials such as "kids eat free Tuesdays," "free sushi between 5-8 p.m. on Tuesday," "$2 specials" and even "Fed Ex employees eat free." He even tweeted in advance of his arrival on a local college campus to hand out Sushilicious coupons.

As part of his marketing for Sushilicious, Woo participated in promotional features on the Internet and on radio. Sushilicious was the "Deal of the Day," an online promotion Woo held with the Orange County Register, a regional newspaper. He explained:

*This was an online promotion that I feel generated value for Sushilicious.
look at "group buy deals" from the wrong perspective. It is not about whethe
make money on the deal; it is clear that they are designed as loss leaders. I see it
advertising tool. With the Deal of the Day, I was getting over $17,000 worth of adv
for no up-front money. In fact, I got paid for the deal. We were offering "$20 for $11
certificates, which allowed participants to purchase $20 worth for $11. I earned 50 per ce
of the revenues from the deal, or $5.50 per certificate sold. Now my food costs are 30 per
cent of the bill, so I was able to break even on it, cost-wise. I did find, however, that most
people using the certificates came to the restaurant on Thursdays and Fridays, which had
an impact on my regular sales and profits.*

In the radio promotion, Woo partnered with 95.9 FISH FM, a local radio station, to
sell gift certificates at 50 per cent off. The radio station promoted the deal with 30-
second radio spots, each of which was estimated to reach an audience of 250,000 listen-
ers. Woo repeated the promotion another three times over the next few months. Similar
to the Deal of the Day promotion, Woo did not have to pay for the radio spots.

Over the next 10 months, Woo averaged 800 tweets per month. As he became more
busy with the restaurant, he started to rely on a combination of social media tools to
help him with his Twitter updates. He was familiar with a few popular food and
Japanese-related blogs and had subscribed to them. Using tools such as Twitter Feed,
he set up search functions to parse selected blogs for interesting posts about sushi or
Japanese food. Once a relevant blog post was found, Twitter Feed would send a tweet
to alert Sushilicious's followers. Woo also relied on CoTweet, which allowed him to
develop content at once but space his tweets out (via a time delay).

Some of the regular topics (tweets and retweets) that appeared on Sushilicious' Twitter
feed included "random picture" which, as the titled implied, featured a random picture of
food or other items, or postings about unique Japanese foods such as "Shogoin (Red Bean)
Yatsuhashi" or "Pringles Mayonnaise Potato." Woo managed the direct tweets that
reminded patrons that Sushilicious was an option for lunch or dinner and acknowledging
visits by regular followers. He was often working in his office during his restaurant's busiest
times. If he saw that a customer was present and tweeting about it, he would often send an
immediate tweet offering that customer a free dessert item. As Woo learned more about the
benefits and drawbacks of various social media tools, he developed a comprehensive new
media marketing strategy that was different for each tool.

Sushilicious's New Media Marketing Strategy

Prior to Sushilicious, Woo had no experience using social media tools. He recalled: "I
stumbled upon social media by accident, but then started to realize what an incredible
tool it was to promote a business." He quickly learned that each of the tools was suited
for a different purpose. Woo commented on various social media tools:

Twitter

*A year before the restaurant opened, I grabbed the @sushilicious name and sat on it. In
August 2009, I started using Twitter to tell people about our opening in March 2010. Initially,
I expected to connect with a younger, 14 to 21 year-old college audience. But then I realized
that this younger audience tends to use Twitter as a way to let their network of friends know
where they are — or what they are doing — at that very instant. Their tweets typically start
with the words "I am." And their profiles are typically locked. At the same time, I noticed
that, in Orange County, there is a group of perhaps 500 to 1,000 people whom I call
"connectors."*

...connectors) are young professionals — realtors, lawyers, small business owners — ...and older and they are interested in reaching out and networking with others, ...roviding relevant information. So if one is a realtor, she might be talking about ...ing market going up or down in the near future, for example. And when they ...out something they like, I get to reach an extended audience through these ...s.

...to become part of this network slowly. At first, I was sending tweets and ...my Twitter timeline, seeing who would respond. As a follow-up, I would try to think of relevant things to say that would form a connection with one or two of the responders. Sometimes, my messages were retweeted to a wider audience, piquing the curiosity of another few hundred people. I try to keep my tweets unisex as a way to reach out to as wide an audience as possible.

To manage our Twitter account, I rely on tools such as Hootsuite, Twitter Feed, CoTweet and bit.ly.[1] It has been clear to me that this group of 500 people has been crucial to my success thus far. Without them, I could not have made it this far. For the first few months of my business, it was this group of 500 who packed the opening, who kept coming back, who brought five to 10 family members or friends to the restaurant. They are my core group of clients even today. Every time I see someone I recognize, I go over and offer to buy them a small dish, a green tea ice cream or a sushi plate. I estimate that, overall, 30 per cent of my customers account for 70 per cent of my volume.

Facebook

I use my Facebook page primarily to reach out to the younger age group. The majority of my Facebook followers are females, aged 18-24. As you can see, I do not really post directive messages that say "come to Sushilicious." Instead, I try to provide content that followers might find interesting. I hope they will like it and pass it on to their friends. With this younger demographic, the key to success is to be intriguing or funny. For example, I might post a picture of sushi-shaped earrings or sushi graffiti. On Facebook, July 2010, I had 760 page views and 598 monthly active users. In January 2011, I had 808 visits to the site and 406 monthly users. I try to reply to 90 per cent of the posts on my wall. We have close to 2,400 users who "like" us and we have about 2,000 of those users in the vicinity.

Yelp

On Yelp, which is an online directory, for the week of September 6, 2010, Sushilicious was viewed a total of 15 times and users checked in 11 times. The comparative figures for January 31, 2011 were 236 and 20.

Foursquare

I have not really used Foursquare but I know who my Mayors are. Mayors are people who visit a locale most frequently. Once at the restaurant, the user typically presses a button on his or her iPhone, adding another "visit" to the tally. Visitors with the most visits are named "Mayors."

---

[1]These tools are, respectively, a social media communications dashboard, a tool that links to tweets from multiple Twitter accounts, a tracking and analyzing tool and a URL shortener.

Website

The big reason why my website is not built up is because it is not in my budget. But many social media observers have written about the higher importance of tools such as Facebook and Twitter, versus a static website. Here is what I do instead to combine all three tools: I put up links to Facebook and Twitter. In fact, Facebook is really my unofficial webpage.

YouTube

I do not really utilize YouTube because I feel that if people can see a video of Sushilicious and our operations, some of the "magic" of discovery will be lost. There are certainly many who are interested in us because of our unique name, and I want these curious individuals to visit us in person.

Assessing the Strategy

The social media marketing seemed to pay off. In June 2010, Sushilicous was voted one of Orange County's best sushi restaurants by the Orange County Register. In encouraging followers to vote for Sushilicious, Woo jokingly tweeted: "I can't vote ten times for myself… so I need your help." Sushilicious was the feature of several blog posts by prominent bloggers.

Thinking About the Next Step

In February 2011, Woo looked at Sushilicious's one-year anniversary with pride. He had a dedicated group of over 1,800 followers on Twitter, many of whom were regulars he knew by name. He was achieving 80 per cent utilization in a (comparatively speaking) low-rent locale, making it one of the highest turning sit-down restaurants in Irvine.

With Sushilicious's social media strategy, modern decor and its affordable yet high quality food, Woo had overcome the fact that it was located far away from local hot-spots, had no traditional marketing budget and was competing in a crowded market with 10 other sushi restaurants (and six new Irvine restaurants). Woo could claim that Sushilicious had developed its own brand, and that its brand set it apart from any other sushi restaurant he had ever come across.

Woo continued to keep his restaurant open seven days per week to be accessible to customers. He wondered if he should franchise the concept, open another venue in Irvine or if he should continue to work on improving his single location. He commented on these options:

The Sushilicious concept is not that expensive, as far as franchises go. Potential franchisees would have to pay between $300,000 to $700,000 for a restaurant,[2] and recurring five per cent franchise fees and two per cent marketing fees. In exchange, franchisees will have access to me and the Sushilicious business model, and an exclusive territory in which to grow. Alternatively, I could use the profits from this first restaurant and build my own chain of sushi restaurants, starting with the rest of California.

Another option Woo was considering was to maintain all of his focus on his current restaurant. Revenues were trending at about $100,000 per month. Sushilicious's food costs were about 30 per cent of revenues and staff salaries and wages varied between $22,000 and $25,000 per month. All other restaurant-related variable costs — rent, natural gas, utilities and insurance, to name a few items — were $15,000 per month.

---

[2]All figures have been disguised.

However, Sushilicious continued to have low numbers of customers on Mondays and Tuesdays, despite Woo's efforts. He stated: "In the early days, it was relatively easy to connect to people on a personal level via Twitter or Facebook. But the busier I got, the more my tweets risked becoming automated or robotic." Woo noted that on his Google Analytics page for the week of January 24, 2011, there were 3,764 impressions and 1,053 actions. The comparative figures for September 8, 2010, were 4,000 impressions and 832 actions (see Exhibit 8).

> *The biggest key to social media, at least according to my experience, is that people do not want to be tweeted at; they want to be tweeted with. If I am following a local blogger after he or she has written about my restaurant, it is of no use to me to send him or her a "every Tuesday kids eat free" tweet. That is not really relevant. It would be better if I said something like, "I just read your article and I love it. I can't wait to read about your next post."*

EXHIBIT 8   Selected Web Analytics

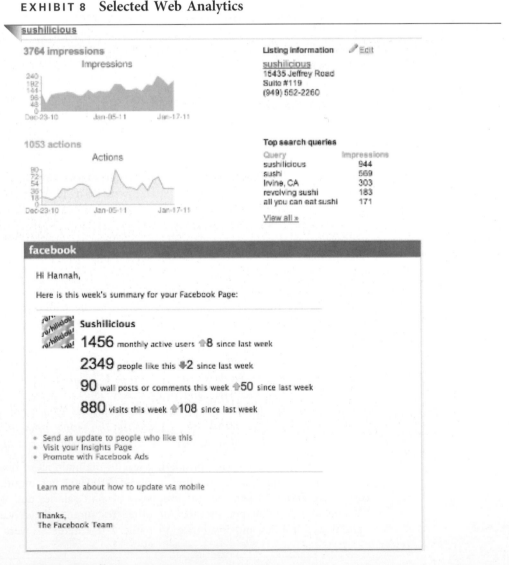

Source: Company files.

I've suddenly made a connection with that writer and he or she will look at Sushilicious in a more positive light. As we grow, how do we maintain that online personal touch? And is there something else we can do to increase our utilization rate from 80 per cent to close to 100 per cent?

Woo thought about whether he should take steps to develop Sushilicious's social marketing campaign (see Exhibit 9). He also wondered whether he should broaden Sushilicious's entire marketing strategy to include traditional marketing; for example, direct mail was another opportunity Woo wanted to explore. He thought about the potential of sending flyers to every one of Irvine's households. Delivering the flyer to doorsteps would cost Woo about $0.09 each. He was excited by the potential to take Sushilicious to the next level, but was unsure of which path to take.

EXHIBIT 9   Website

Source: Company files.

IVEY CASE 19

Richard Ivey School of Business
The University of Western Ontario

Trouble Brews at Starbucks[1]

Lauranne Buchanan and Carolyn J. Simmons wrote this case solely to provide material for class discussion. The authors do not intend to illustrate either effective or ineffective handling of a managerial situation. The authors may have disguised certain names and other identifying information to protect confidentiality.

Copyright © 2009, Ivey Management Services Version: (A) 2009-01-22

Starbucks was the darling of Wall Street, with a strong balance sheet and double-digit growth since going public in 1992. By 2007, it had more than 15,000 stores around the world[2] and projected that the number would eventually grow to 40,000 stores, half of them outside the United States.[3] But suddenly, performance slipped so seriously that the board ousted CEO Jim Donald and brought back Howard Schultz — Starbucks' visionary leader and CEO from 1987 to 2000 and current chairman and chief global strategist — to re-take the helm.

Despite the furor, the company was hardly in dire financial straits. In 2007, it had revenues of $9.4 billion, double-digit earnings growth and 2500 new store openings.[4] But its share price had fallen almost 50 per cent as Wall Street became increasingly worried that the chain had run out of room for further U.S. expansion. In November, the company reported its first-ever decline in customers' visits to U.S. stores.[5] Insiders and analysts alike questioned whether the brand had been irreparably damaged by a single-minded focus on

---

[1]This case has been written on the basis of published sources only. Consequently, the interpretation and perspectives presented in this case are not necessarily those of Starbucks or any of its employees.

[2]Janet Adamy, "Schultz Takes Over To Try to Perk Up Starbucks," *Wall Street Journal*, January 8, 2008, B1.

[3]Janet Adamy, "Starbucks Sets Ambitious Goal of 40,000 Stores," *Wall Street Journal*, October 6, 2006, B3.

[4]Jonathan Birchall and Jenny Wiggins, "The Starbucks Romantic," *Financial Times*, January 12, 2008, p. 7.

[5]Ibid.

growth and short-term profitability at the expense of the brand. It was a fear that Howard Schultz himself had written about as the "commoditization of the Starbucks experience."[6]

The Beginning[7]

The Starbucks Coffee, Tea, and Spice Company was founded in Seattle in 1971 by Jerry Baldwin, Gordon Bowker and Zev Siegl, three guys with a passion for dark-roasted, European-style coffee. Coffee, they felt, was so much more than the bland beverage offered by Folgers and Maxwell House; coffee had rich, sensuous flavors if roasted and brewed correctly. Their vision was to educate consumers about fine coffees the way a sommelier educates diners about fine wines. To this end, Starbucks sold only dark-roast, whole-bean coffee from places like Sumatra, Kenya, Ethiopia and Costa Rica — no ground or prepared coffee. And it sold only manual coffee pots and equipment needed to grind and brew coffee correctly at home — no electric coffeemakers that would mask the coffee's flavor.

The Seattleites successfully developed a devoted, local customer base, but it took Howard Schultz, who joined the company in 1982, to see the potential for bigger things. Schultz had grown up in the Bayview Projects, federally subsidized housing in Canarsie, Brooklyn. His father had quit school to help support the family, served in World War II and worked a series of blue-collar jobs. As Schultz recalls, his father "never found himself, never had a plan for his life."[8] One of his most vivid childhood memories was when his father, then a delivery truck driver, broke his foot and couldn't work. Without health insurance or worker's compensation, the family had nothing to fall back on. This childhood event made an indelible imprint on Schultz, and he became determined to make something of his life. He went to Northern Michigan University on a football scholarship. He majored in communications, taking courses in public speaking, interpersonal communications and business. After a short stint in sales at Xerox, he joined Hammarplast, a Swedish manufacturer of stylish kitchen equipment and housewares. By the age of 28, he was promoted to vice-president and general manager.

While at Hammarplast, Schultz noticed that a Seattle retailer with only four stores was buying more of a particular drip coffeemaker than the department store Macy's. Curious, he went to Seattle, visited the store — Starbucks — and was instantly hooked on the "romance" of fine coffee. The owners appreciated his conversion to the real thing, but they initially rejected his offer to join their crusade, perhaps worrying that his hard-hitting New York style was unsuited to laid-back West Coast culture and that his ideas for expansion were incompatible with their mission of enlightenment. It took Schultz more than a year to convince them, but he finally won the position of Starbucks marketing director.

Schultz's Vision for Starbucks

Soon after joining Starbucks, Schultz visited Milan for a trade show. There, he saw coffee bars packed with customers on every block. Baristas and customers were laughing and talking, enjoying the moment and the espresso together. As Schultz later described it, "It was on that day that I discovered the ritual and romance of coffee bars in Italy. I saw how popular they were, and how vibrant. Each one had its own unique character, but there was one common thread: the camaraderie between the customers, who knew

---

[6]Howard Schultz, "The Commoditization of the Starbucks Experience," Internal E-mail, February 14, 2007, http://starbucksgossip.typepad.com/_/2007/02/starbucks_chair_2.html, accessed December 30, 2008.

[7]Howard Schultz and Dori Jones Yang, *Pour Your Heart Into It*, 1997.

[8]Ibid., p. 13.

each other well, and the barista, who was performing with flair.... 'This is so powerful!' I thought. 'This is the link.' The connection to the people who love coffee did not have to take place only in their homes, where they ground and brewed whole-bean coffee. What we had to do was unlock the romance and mystery of coffee, firsthand, in coffee bars. The Italians understood the personal relationship that people could have to coffee, its social aspect. I couldn't believe that Starbucks was in the coffee business, yet was over-looking so central an element of it."[9]

But his bosses weren't interested. Cash was tight. Besides, Starbucks was a retailer, not a restaurant or a bar; serving espresso drinks would put it in the beverage business. When Schultz pressured Baldwin to expand the Starbucks vision, Baldwin would argue, "Howard, listen to me. It's just not the right thing to do. If we focus too much on serving coffee, we'll become just another restaurant or cafeteria. It may seem reasonable, each step of the way, but in the end, we'll lose our coffee roots."[10]

Creating His Own Story

Not willing to abandon his dream, Schultz departed Starbucks and opened *Il Giornale*, Italian for *daily*. His plan was to re-create the Italian espresso bar experience. To his surprise, Starbucks was his first investor, supplying $150,000. "It isn't a business we want to go into ourselves," Baldwin explained, "but we'll support you."[11] It was a start, but Schultz needed $1.7 million: $400,000 for the initial store, to demonstrate the practical operation and consumer appeal of an Italian espresso bar, and $1.3 million for eight additional espresso bars, to show that the idea would work on a larger scale. In the first year, Schultz spoke to 242 potential investors; 217 said "no."[12] Their arguments became all too familiar: "Coffee is a commodity." "Coffee consumption in the U.S. has been trending down since the mid-1960s." "Coffee shops are everywhere." "Americans will never pay $1.50 for a cup of coffee." Still, he persisted.

By 1987, Schultz had acquired the seed capital and opened three espresso bars. Then, in an unexpected twist of fate, Starbucks' owners decided to sell — six stores, the roasting plant and the name. Schultz had to go for it. He raised four million dollars, acquired Starbucks, adopted its name and began to expand. Fifteen new stores were opened in fiscal year 1988; 20 in 1989; 30 in 1990; 31 in 1991; and 53 in 1992; all company-owned.[13] Schultz explained, "We're so fanatical about quality control that we keep coffee in our hands every step of the way from raw green beans to the steaming cup. We buy and roast all our own coffee, and we sell it in company-owned stores.... Why? The answer can be found in the last cup of lousy coffee you drank. Unlike shoes, or books, or soft drinks, coffee can be ruined at any point from its production to consumption.... Coffee is a product so perishable that building a business on it is fraught with peril. The minute we hand our coffee over to someone else, we're extremely vulnerable to its quality being compromised."[14]

But Starbucks wasn't just about the coffee. It was also about recreating the Italian coffee bar culture. Schultz wanted Starbucks to become the "Third Place," the place between home and work where people gather, relax and interact with one another. To encourage customers to linger over a cup of coffee, Starbucks paid a great deal of attention to the details of the store — everything from the layout, to the furniture, to the music. Even more important

---

[9]Ibid., pp. 51-52.

[10]Ibid., p. 61.

[11]Ibid., p. 66.

[12]Ibid., p. 73.

[13]Ibid., p. 114.

[14]Ibid., pp. 171-172.

were the baristas, whose ability to engage the customer was the heart of the Starbucks experience. Understanding the difficulty of managing human capital, especially when two thirds of workers were part-time, Schultz felt he had to make employees "partners" in his vision. He had to infuse them with the Starbucks culture, reward them with a sense of personal security and give them a reason to be involved in the success of the business.

To instill the requisite coffee knowledge in recruits, Starbucks developed a 24-hour training program covering Coffee Knowledge (four hours), Brewing the Perfect Cup (four hours), Customer Service (four hours) and basic retail skills. To provide personal security, Schultz fought with his board to offer health insurance to all partners, even the part-timers. "Treat people like family, and they will be loyal and give their all. Stand by people, and they will stand by you," he argued. The math made sense; at the time, it cost $1,500 a year to provide an employee with full benefits, compared with $3,000 to train a new hire.[15]

And to increase involvement in the success of the business, he offered Bean Stocks — a pseudo stock option plan for partners with at least six months at the store.[16] As "stock holders," store partners had an incentive to participate in decision-making, to suggest cost-cutting measures to increase profitability and to help maintain the integrity of the brand. If they felt that management was straying from the Starbucks vision, they had the right and responsibility to call them on it. The result of these initiatives was a more satisfied partner base. For baristas, turnover averaged 60 to 65 per cent, compared to 150 to 400 per cent in the average retail or fast-food chain. For store managers, turnover was around 25 per cent compared to 50 per cent for other retailers.[17]

Starbucks Goes Public

With just over 100 stores in four states and Vancouver, British Columbia, Starbucks went public in 1992. Initially priced at $17 a share, the stock jumped to $21 at the opening bell. By the end of the day, the initial public offering (IPO) had raised $29 million for the company — $5 million more than expected — and Starbucks' market capitalization stood at $273 million.[18] Being a public company took Starbucks into the big leagues; it made millions for the believers who invested in the company, provided critical funds for future expansion and helped attract talented new people.

But Wall Street can be a fickle master. As Schultz described it, "Alongside the exhilaration of being a public company is the humbling realization, every quarter, every month, and every day, that you're a servant to the stock market.... Running a public company is an emotional roller coaster. In the beginning, you accept the congratulations as if you really deserve them. Then, when the stock price falls, you feel you have failed. When it bounces back, it leaves you dizzy. At some point, you have to divorce yourself from the stock price and just focus on running the business."[19]

Expanding the Business Model

To satisfy Wall Street and stave off competitive threats, Starbucks made growth its mantra. Starbucks was in a race to establish national dominance before other emerging specialty coffee bars and yet trying to fly under the radar of the "big boys" — such as Procter & Gamble, who had purchased Millstone Coffee, the largest whole-bean supplier

---

[15]Ibid., p. 127.

[16]Ibid., p. 134.

[17]Ibid., p. 128.

[18]Ibid., p. 185.

[19]Ibid., pp. 188-189.

to grocers. To grow and claim leadership in the category, Starbucks focused on a strategy of new products, a stronger connection with customers as the Third Place and expanding store locations in the United States and abroad.

Developing New Products

One of the first additions to the management team after the company went public was Howard Behar, who had 25 years of retail experience in the furniture business and in resort development. While many people inside Starbucks have had a lasting impact on its success, it was Behar who actually changed the way the company thought. Time and again, he argued that it wasn't just about the coffee or about the brand, it was about the customer. Behar's crusade was not always met with open minds, as Schultz recalled in his book, *Pour Your Heart into It*:

> Howard had been at Starbucks less than a month when he came to me one day and asked, "Have you been reading the customer comment cards?"
>
> "Sure," I said, "I read them. I read them all."
>
> "Well," he replied, "how come you're not responding?"
>
> "Responding to what?"
>
> "Look at all the people who want nonfat milk."
>
> "Well," I explained, "I did a formal tasting a number of times this year of lattes and cappuccinos made with nonfat milk and they just didn't taste good."
>
> "To whom?" Howard was clearly growing impatient with my answers.
>
> "To me…"
>
> "Well, read the customer comment cards. Our customers want nonfat milk! We should give it to them."
>
> I answered — and Howard never lets me forget it — "We will never offer nonfat milk. It's not who we are."[20]

The nonfat milk question led to one of the biggest debates in Starbucks' history. Coffee purists were scandalized. Store managers were frustrated — how could they handle more than one type of milk without slowing store operations? Still Behar persisted, eventually getting Schultz to authorize an in-store test. The stores didn't fall apart, customers got what they wanted and Starbucks stopped losing sales to more accommodating competitors. Nonfat milk was in.

The Frappuccino story is similar. Starbucks management refused to consider a cold blended beverage on principle — it wasn't a true coffee drink. This time, it was a couple of store managers in southern California who took the initiative after seeing their afternoon and evening customers defect to competitors who offered cooler, more refreshing coffee beverages. They began experimenting with different recipes and ingredients; they varied the blending time; they changed the ratio of ice to liquid. They tested their concoction with customers, and again, customers approved. Corporate came around. Within a year of rolling out Frappuccinos nationally, store sales of Frappuccinos were $52 million, seven per cent of total annual revenues.[21]

The success of the Frappuccino inspired more new products, many developed at local stores, then refined and disseminated nationally by corporate. Seasonal offerings, such as a strawberry and cream Frappuccino in the summer and gingerbread latte at Christmas,

---

[20]Ibid., pp.166-167.

[21]Ibid., pp. 208-209.

were introduced. Food items such as cookies and pastries began to make their way into the store. "Food is a big part of where we are going…" said Orin Smith, a member of Starbucks' senior management team. "It is not going to be a lot of any one thing. It will be food that makes sense and complements the customers and their choice of beverages."[22] Starbucks would later introduce cold sandwiches and salads for lunch as well as hot breakfast sandwiches.

As the company became more comfortable in expanding beyond its traditional roots, it developed products with other companies — a bottled Frappuccino with Pepsi, a coffee-flavored ice cream with Dreyer's and a coffee liqueur with Jim Beam. The extensive distribution networks of these companies afforded Starbucks access to supermarkets and restaurants with their broader customer base. But even in negotiations with much larger and more experienced partners, Starbucks took care to protect its brand. The partnership with Pepsi — a company 100 times the size of Starbucks at the time — was a fifty-fifty arrangement, in which Pepsi ceded Starbucks a high degree of control over its brand equity and product formulas.[23]

Location, Location, Location

At the same time, Starbucks was adding new stores at a rapid clip. Its sophisticated model for store expansion was based on a matrix of regional demographic profiles and an analysis of how best to leverage operational infrastructure. For each region, a large city was targeted to serve as a "hub," where teams of professionals could be located to serve as support for new stores. Markets were entered with the goal of expanding out to 20 or more stores in the first two years. From the core, it branched out to nearby "spoke" markets, including smaller cities and suburban locations with demographics similar to the typical customer mix.

Starbucks didn't advertise when entering a new market; it didn't have the funds. Instead the store devised a grassroots campaign, beginning with the selection of a highly visible location — such as DuPont Circle in Washington, D.C., or Astor Place in New York — for the flagship store. Artwork was designed to celebrate each city's personality, and it was used on commuter mugs and T-shirts. In each market, Starbucks planned at least one big community event to celebrate its arrival, with the proceeds going to a local charity. Local "ambassadors" were recruited from new partners and from customers whose names were part of Starbucks' database of catalog customers. They were given tickets to the grand-opening event and two free-drink coupons with a note asking them to "Share Starbucks with a Friend."[24]

As Starbucks expanded its business, the company sometimes perplexed onlookers with its store placement strategy, for stores were oftentimes opened across the street from one another. But Starbucks had learned that nearby stores didn't necessarily hurt one another's sales and in fact could actually help. Early on, it had opened a large store 30 yards from a tiny but top-performing store tucked in a building that was to be closed for remodeling. To the company's amazement, the two stores not only coexisted; they thrived. Dense store placement became the model for store location throughout the country — with similar, profitable results.[25] (Coca-Cola and PepsiCo Inc. have experienced similar results in placing a new vending machine next to an existing one; initially, sales of the first one drop but rebound quickly as more customers drink more soft drinks.)

[22]Sarah E. Lockyer, "Full Steam Ahead," *Nation's Restaurant News*, May 3, 2004, p. 4.

[23]Howard Schultz and Dori Jones Yang, *Pour Your Heart Into It*, 1997, p. 222.

[24]Ibid., p. 255.

[25]Dina ElBoghdady, "Pouring It On," *The Washington Post*, August 25, 2002, H1.

When Starbucks entered new markets, these store clusters acted as billboards, creating awareness. And as demand grew, clustered stores helped to manage store traffic, particularly in the crucial hours before 10 a.m. when as much as 60 per cent of a store's sales occur.[26] During this period, it's not uncommon for customers who perceive the wait time to be too long — due to long lines, parking difficulties or any other problem — to leave without their coffee. More stores meant a better chance for customers to find a short line or empty parking space and for Starbucks to capture the sale.

The ubiquity of the stores also helped drive sales throughout the day. "Where a lot of our growth is, is driving that incremental cup that someone may not have planned to buy," said Doug Satzman, a director of new store development in California. Standing on the corner of Mission and Fourth Streets in San Francisco — where there is a Starbucks on three of the four street corners — Satzman explained: "If you're over here [referring to the Metreon, an entertainment mall on his right] you are not likely to cross the street. If you're in the hotel, you might be going to the right to Market Street" to the shopping area.[27] The people in the complex on the third corner might not bother to go outside at all. But with a store on each corner, it was easy to grab a cup of Starbucks from any direction.

Once the company realized that convenience drove sales, it was only a matter of time until the company added drive-through service. Initially targeted to parents with young children, the drive-through windows quickly became a hit with a broader market, resulting in average annual sales of around $1.3 million — compared to $1 million at stores without a window.[28] The downside of the drive-through locations was the cost of real estate and additional partners needed to operate the window. In addition, the bottlenecks in the drive-through could be far worse than those in the store, even though the average time to serve customers was about the same. "In the store, it's an issue of queuing — someone can have a complex order and step aside while it's being made," said John Glass, an industry analyst with CIBC World Markets.[29] But a drive-through customer could not step aside, and all the cars behind that customer could do was wait. To address these problems, baristas' headphones were set to "ding" when a car pulled into the drive-through chute and a digital timer measured service times. The stores also added order confirmation screens to improve order accuracy and additional pastry racks to reduce time to serve.

To add new locations in areas otherwise inaccessible to the chain, Starbucks ventured into licensing. Airports were a natural venue for Starbucks, but all U.S. airport retail locations were run by concessionaires — in the case of food and beverages, Host Marriott. Licensing went against the chain's belief that it needed to control the customer's experience, but the additional exposure seemed worth the risk. Initially, the Host Marriott venues did not fully meet Schultz's expectations, but the partners cooperated to make the relationship work. Licensing, Schultz found, was like a marriage: "Whether it works is a matter of whom you choose as a partner, the amount of due diligence you do beforehand, and how things go during the courtship. If you jump in with little preparation, you risk setting yourself up for failure."[30]

Following the success of its relationship with Host Marriott, Starbucks initiated partnerships with retailers such as Safeway and Barnes & Noble. These licensing agreements created greater customer convenience in established markets, but they also gave

---

[26]Barbara Kiviat, "The Big Gulp at Starbucks," *Time*, December 18, 2006, p. 124.

[27]"Why Did Starbucks Cross the Road?" *Wall Street Journal*, April 3, 2007, B1.

[28]Steven Gray, "Fill 'er Up — with Latte," *Wall Street Journal*, January 6, 2006, A9.

[29]Ibid.

[30]Howard Schultz and Dori Jones Yang, *Pour Your Heart Into It*, 1997, p. 174.

Starbucks a way of entering new markets when it could not afford to build company-owned stores. Licensees agreed to build in-store coffee bars at their own expense and to provide the employees who operated the counter. Starbucks trained the baristas and the drinks were prepared with Starbucks ingredients and recipes. In selecting licensees, Starbucks carefully considered whether the image and goals of the licensee would be consistent with those of Starbucks. Target made the cut; Wal-Mart didn't.

Connecting with Customers

To create the sense of community that is central to the Third Place, Starbucks added music, books and movies to its product mix. "The overall strategy is to build Starbucks into a destination," explained Kenneth Lombard, then president of Starbucks Entertainment.[31] "We know there are going to be endless opportunities as this strategy continues to grow, and we're going to look at each and every opportunity."[32] Added Schultz, "Starbucks isn't an entertainment company. But we want to have an entertainment strategy that supports the foundation of the coffee experience that our customers have come to expect and enjoy."[33]

Hear the Music   Music had always been a part of the Starbucks environment, with stores playing primarily jazz and classical instrumentals and eventually adding jazz vocals to the mix. Time and again, customers asked Starbucks where they could buy what they heard there. So when Schultz stumbled upon a music store called *Hear Music* in the Stanford Shopping Center in California, he was intrigued. At Hear Music, customers could come in, listen to any one of more than 150,000 titles and create a custom mixed CD complete with personalized title, liner notes and artwork on the disc and jacket in just five minutes. Even more impressive were the people, who were as knowledgeable and passionate about music as Schultz was about coffee. It was clear that their vision for Hear Music was similar to his vision for Starbucks. "When I think about the average music-shopping experience, what I would call the sense of romance about music is gone," Schultz recalled. "But when I saw Hear Music that first time, it was clear that they had cracked the code on the sense of discovery that music should have."[34] He was so impressed he bought the company.

Soon after, Starbucks began offering compilations from Hear Music in its stores, launching a popular series of CDs called "Artist's Choice." The series included musicians as diverse as Yo-Yo Ma, Tony Bennett, Lucinda Williams and the Rolling Stones, all sharing their favorite songs. But the breakout success for Starbucks came when Hear Music co-produced and distributed Ray Charles' posthumously released album *Genius Loves Company*, a collection of duets between Charles and performers such as Norah Jones, James Taylor and B.B. King. The CD — boosted by the biographical film *Ray* and the artist's death — sold nearly three million copies, a quarter of those through Starbucks; no new Ray Charles release had come close to that level in years.[35] To make the success of the store's investment even sweeter, the CD won eight Grammy awards.

Starbucks' success with CDs — at a time when veteran music retailers like Tower Records were filing for bankruptcy — did not escape the attention of the recording industry. With guaranteed in-store play and a built-in distribution network of thousands of

---

[31]Eunjung Ariana Cha, "DVDs and Fries," *The Washington Post*, August 28, 2005, A1.

[32]Steven Gray and Kate Kelly, "Starbucks Plans to Make Debut in Movie Business," *Wall Street Journal*, January 12, 2006, A1.

[33]Ibid.

[34]Alison Overholt, "Listening to Starbucks," *Fast Company*, July 2004, p. 50.

[35]Steven Gray and Ethan Smith, "New Grind: At Starbucks, a Blend of Coffee and Music Creates a Potent Mix," *Wall Street Journal*, July 19, 2005, A1.

outlets, recording companies began to compete fiercely to supply one of the handful of CDs sold at any given time in Starbucks stores. Heritage artists such as Carole King, James Taylor, Paul McCartney and Joni Mitchell signed exclusive deals for the initial distribution of new recordings. And Starbucks helped introduce little known groups such as the rock band Antigone Rising and international artists such as Italian pop singer Zucchero. Concord Records President Glen Barros said he turned to Starbucks for the final say on whether to sign a new singer: "If they'll be our partner, we'll do it." Added another record-label executive, Starbucks is the "new cute girl that everyone wants to take to the dance."[36]

From offering CDs, Starbucks began to experiment with in-store personalized CDs. It introduced kiosks called Media Bars that let customers listen to music and create their own digital compilations while sitting in comfortable lounge chairs waiting for their latte. The bill — 99 cents a song — was paid with a Starbucks card or credit card.[37] "Our customers respond to music," said Anne Saunders, then senior vice-president of marketing. "Part of why they come is as an entertainment destination, for a respite, a break with friends, as a place for community gathering. The idea for the music service is very grounded in why people come to Starbucks."[38]

The Readers' Corner In an early misstep, Starbucks offered a literary magazine called *Joe* — it lasted only six months before Schultz decided, based on slow sales, that the product "didn't add any value."[39] But with its success in the music arena, Starbucks began to think about how it might extend its entertainment platform. The store chose Mitch Albom's *For One More Day* as its first book. To kick off sales and spark a communitywide dialogue, 25 Starbucks stores around the country offered discussion groups of the book, complete with free coffee. Publishers looked on with interest. "One of the big problems in the book industry is that outside of Oprah, there's no really widely accepted authority to recommend books," said Laurence Kirshbaum, founder of LJK Literary Management agency. Starbucks was beginning to see itself as that authority. "Customers say one of the reasons they come [to Starbucks] is because they can discover new things — a new coffee from Rwanda, a new food item. So extending that sense of discovery into entertainment is very natural for us. That's all part of the Starbucks experience," said Saunders.[40]

And On to the Red Carpet In 2006, Starbucks took the leap from music into movies through a promotional deal with Lions Gate Entertainment for *Akeelah and the Bee*. The movie was about an 11-year-old African-American girl from south Los Angeles who discovered a passion for words and, with the help of her teacher, reached the National Spelling Bee. Because of its largely African-American cast and urban setting, Lions Gate feared that the movie would only appeal to a narrow audience. A connection with Starbucks would guarantee broader exposure as well as provide an endorsement for the movie. As Jon Feltheimer, CEO of Lions Gate, saw it, "[Starbucks] is a company with a pristine brand putting their brand on the line and saying, 'You should go to this movie.'"[41]

Starbucks promoted the film aggressively, putting movie-related trivia games on its chalk boards and coffee-cup sleeves, as well as distributing the soundtrack. It held advance

[36]Ibid.

[37]Stanley Homes, "First the Music, Then the Coffee," November 22, 2004, p. 66.

[38]Alison Overholt, "Listening to Starbucks," *Fast Company*, July 2004, p. 50.

[39]Susan Dominus, "The Starbucks Aesthetic," *New York Times*, October 22, 2006, p. 1.

[40]Ibid.

[41]Steven Gray and Kate Kelly, "Starbucks Plans to Make Debut in Movie Business," *Wall Street Journal*, January 12, 2006, A1.

screenings for its baristas and holders of Starbucks cards. "The baristas want to tell their customers about the things they get excited about, and we're convinced this movie is going to be one of those things," said Anne Saunders, who had been promoted to Starbucks' senior vice-president for global brand strategy and communications. For its part, the deal included an undisclosed share of the movie's box-office proceeds. It also gave Starbucks an opportunity to broaden the use of its in-store Wi-Fi network by running trailers for the movie. "We've known for quite some time that the Wi-Fi opportunity in our stores [is] the perfect place for shorts, documentaries and other things that wouldn't be seen on the big screen," Schultz said.[42] The box office receipts, however, were disappointing.

Starbucks tried again the next year with a nature documentary, *Arctic Tale,* from Paramount Classics and National Geographic Films. The film was about a walrus pup and a polar bear who grew up and found their frozen environment melting beneath them. This time, in-store promotions were supplemented with Starbucks-hosted discussions on climate change.[43] "We introduced *Arctic Tale* to our customers because we want to spark a dialogue about environmental issues," Lombard said. "The coffeehouse is a great place to inspire such discussion. There is no more important issue facing our planet today than climate change." Starbucks' promotion was an "avenue to get people of all ages to talk … and hopefully be inspired to be a part of the solution."[44] Box office sales for "Arctic Tale" were again disappointing and failed to leverage Starbucks' "voice as a cultural arbiter."[45] But both Paramount and National Geographic Films executives said they were pleased with the Starbucks effort. "They were great partners and awesome to work with," said a National Geographic executive. "They did everything they said they would do. I'd work with them again in a heartbeat."[46]

Global Expansion

Starbucks began its expansion outside North America in 1995 with a partnership with SAZABY Inc. to open Starbucks coffeehouses in Japan. Skeptics initially doubted whether the Starbucks formula would play in countries that did not have a coffee culture. But since that time, Starbucks has invaded nearly every corner of the world — either through its "living-room-in-a-coffee-house" format or through its "corners" concept or through mini-outlets placed in airline offices, sports stadiums, airports, hotels and bookshops. By 2008, Starbucks had 4500 locations in 43 countries outside the United States.[47] Its overseas menus were anchored by the same lattes, cappuccinos and drip coffees as in the United States, with some modification for local tastes. In Athens, for example, local patrons find a thick layer of fine residue at the bottom of their coffee, and in the United Kingdom, customers can have a cheese and marmite sandwich. (Marmite is a black yeast spread favored only by the British and a few of its former colonies.) For the most part, the formula has worked. Even in the United Kingdom, where high tea is sacrosanct and a "nice cuppa tea" is the remedy for almost anything, Starbucks was thriving. In London, there were more Starbucks locations than in New York City.[48]

[42]Ibid.

[43]Janet Adamy, "Starbucks Sticks with Film-Promotion Plan," *Wall Street Journal*, June 28, 2007, B2.

[44]Marc Graser, "Rough Start for Starbucks," Variety.com, August 23, 2007, www.variety.com/article/VR1117970763.html?categoryid=13.

[45]Janet Adamy, "Starbucks Sticks with Film-Promotion Plan," *Wall Street Journal*, June 28, 2007, B2.

[46]Marc Graser, "Rough Start for Starbucks," Variety.com, August 23, 2007, www.variety.com/article/VR1117970763.html?categoryid=13.

[47]Janet Adamy, "Starbucks Brews Growth Abroad," *Wall Street Journal*, June 12, 2008, B2.

[48]Ibid.

Overall, the expense of building stores and other infrastructure in overseas locations meant that Starbucks global operations were not yet a major contributor to the company's bottom line. In addition, there have been challenges; the most public of these was Starbucks' withdrawal from the historical grounds of the Forbidden City in China after a ground swell of negative public opinion developed. Starbucks also delayed its entry into India and Russia, a move that some have said put Starbucks at a disadvantage. Such delays gave local competitors time to prepare for the onslaught and move into prime locations. And real estate prices continued to rise while the company waited.[49]

But Starbucks executives stressed that the chain was welcomed in the overwhelming majority of places it opened. "What we've found everywhere we've opened is we become a landmark overnight," said Martin Coles, president of Starbucks Coffee International. And, he continued, "We do not spend a great deal of time focusing on our competition."[50] In fact, Starbucks insisted that competition brought out the best in the company and helped grow the overall coffee market.

A Perfect Storm

By 2007, Starbucks had become one of the most widely recognized and admired global brands. Consistent with Schultz's memory of espresso bars on every corner in Milan and with his belief that a public company must grow robustly to please Wall Street, Starbucks seemed to be everywhere. But growth had had unintended consequences. And Starbucks was about to be challenged by a shifting competitive environment and a difficult economy.

Incremental Decisions and Unintended Consequences

From the very beginning, Starbucks had added stores at a rapid pace, so it surprised many analysts when the company announced in 2004 that it intended to double its pace of expansion. To meet this promise to Wall Street, "there was a little bit of a frenzy to get locations open," recalled Matt Dougherty, a real estate broker with Nevada Commercial. A Florida broker who worked with Starbucks agreed, "We pumped it up, we accelerated, but when you do that you sacrifice real estate. There was a disconnect somewhere in Seattle between those decisions and what the reality was on the ground. The opportunity was not always there."[51] Other analysts suggested that the company — swayed by the perks offered by landlords eager to bring Starbucks' cachet to their neighborhoods — simply ignored its own winning store location formula.[52]

The net results of expansion were a larger customer base and a changed profile for the "average" Starbucks customer. In 2000, about three per cent of Starbucks customers were between the ages of 18 and 24; 16 per cent were people of color; 78 per cent had college degrees, and the average annual income was $81,000. By 2005, 13 per cent of customers were between 18 and 24; 37 per cent were people of color; 56 per cent were college graduates, and the average income was $55,000.[53]

In addition, the increased accessibility of Starbucks — through store openings as well as licensees — had also changed consumers' perceptions of Starbucks. The store wasn't

---

[49]Janet Adamy, "From Seattle, with Lattes," *Wall Street Journal*, August 31, 2007, B1.

[50]Ibid.

[51]Brad Stone, "The Empire of Excess," *New York Times*, July 4, 2008.

[52]Andrew Bordeaux, "Is It Possible to Grow Too Fast?" July 9, 2008, *Growthink Blog*, www.growthink.com/content/it-possible-grow-too-fast.

[53]Steven Gray and Ethan Smith, "New Grind: At Starbucks, a Blend of Coffee and Music Creates a Potent Mix," *Wall Street Journal*, July 19, 2005, A1.

so much a destination or the Third Place as it was an "affordable luxury" — a little treat to get the morning started or a pick-me-up in the afternoon. Customer behavior reflected this as well, with 80 per cent of orders being consumed outside the store.[54]

At the same time, the increasing number of drive-through windows and in-store food items took Starbucks a step closer to fast food, which led to an internal rift between headquarters and store personnel. Store managers without drive-through windows felt their sales were being cannibalized by locations offering greater access, while managers of drive-through locations had more difficulty in generating impulse purchases for whole-bean coffee, CDs and other merchandise. Baristas resented having to cross-sell food items, a fast-food tactic. And even customers complained that cooking odors from hot breakfast sandwiches changed the "Starbucks experience." As noted by Jim Romenesko on Starbucks Gossip, an online Internet site not affiliated with the company, "If I go in there first thing in the morning, it smells like McDonald's, not a coffee shop."[55]

Efforts to increase operational efficiencies also affected the customer experience. To reduce wait time, Starbucks brought in the Verismo 801 automated espresso machines, which dispensed hot espresso at the touch of a button and allowed baristas to make drinks 40 per cent faster, but the machines were so tall that customers could no longer see the coffee being made or interact with the barista. The adoption of Flavorlock sealed bags of pre-ground coffee eliminated the step of grinding the coffee, but the stores lost the aroma of freshly ground coffee. And in an effort to reduce maintenance costs, stores were re-configured with fewer comfy chairs and less carpeting — making Starbucks a less inviting place in which to linger over a cup of coffee.[56]

By February 2007, Schultz was questioning whether the company was on the right path. The product mix — which included non-coffee drinks, food items, music, books, movies and even teddy bears — had expanded tremendously; locations — both company-owned and licensees — seemed to be everywhere. In a memo to the company's top execs, Schultz wrote, "…we have had to make a series of decisions that, in retrospect, have led to the watering down of the Starbucks experience, and, what some might call the commoditization of our brand."[57] The company, he lamented, had lost the "romance and theatre" of coffee-making with its meteoric expansion.

Competitors Collide

For years, the line between retailers of brewed coffee had been clearly defined. Starbucks, with its $3-plus espresso-based drinks, was in a different league from Dunkin' Donuts and McDonald's. One Starbucks marketing executive went so far as to characterize the competition as "selling hot, brown liquid masquerading as coffee."[58] But by mid-decade, their parallel worlds began to collide. Starbucks, with its drive-through window, was beginning to look a lot more like a fast-food restaurant. Dunkin' Donuts and McDonald's, seeing the profits in specialty coffee, began their own efforts to join the high-end coffee market. As Jon Luther, chief executive of Dunkin' Donuts' parent company, the U.K. group Allied Domecq PLC, said, "Espresso has become mainstream in America. And who does mainstream better than Dunkin' Donuts?"[59]

[54]Janet Adamy, "McDonald's Takes on a Weakened Starbucks," *Wall Street Journal*, January 7, 2008, A1.
[55]Barbara Kiviat, "Wake Up and Sell the Coffee," *Time*, April 7, 2008, p. 46.
[56]Ibid.
[57]Howard Schultz, "The Commoditization of the Starbucks Experience," Internal E-mail, February 14, 2007, http://starbucksgossip.typepad.com/_/2007/02/starbucks_chair_2.html.
[58]Janet Adamy, "McDonald's Takes on a Weakened Starbucks," *Wall Street Journal*, January 7, 2008, A1.
[59]Deborah Ball and Shirley Leung, "Latte Versus Latte," *Wall Street Journal*, February 10, 2004, B1.

Dunkin' Donuts was the largest seller in America of regular, non-flavored, brewed coffee through fast food outlets. Its stores were found throughout the United States, with the largest concentration in the Northeast, many in blue-collar neighborhoods. The chain rolled out its line of espresso drinks in 2003, claiming it could deliver its Italian brews "faster, cheaper, and simpler": faster, by working with a Swiss equipment manufacturer to provide real espresso and fresh steamed milk in less than a minute; cheaper, by offering drinks at prices 20 per cent lower than Starbucks; and simpler, by communicating in plain English, labeling its coffee sizes as "small," "medium" and "large," rather than the "tall," "grande" and "venti" preferred by Starbucks. In doing so, the chain hoped to "democratize" the espresso drink or as one billboard read: "Latte for Every Tom, Dick and Lucciano."

Not all Dunkin' Donuts regulars were impressed. Pat Kelly, a 26-year-old Boston police recruit who drank Dunkin' Donuts coffee daily, refused to try the new Dunkin' products. The only guy among his buddies to try a latte "got a razzing" he said. "I'm not really a latte sort of guy. Those are yuppie drinks." But some of Starbucks' yuppies took notice. Kathleen Brown, a 30-year-old Boston lawyer, used to treat herself to a $4 Starbucks Caramel Macchiato but switched to Dunkin' Donuts. "I can order a plain medium caramel latte and not deal with all that fancy stuff," she said.[60] The fact that it also costs less just made it that much sweeter.

McDonald's was slower to get into high-end specialty coffee. But this changed in 2004 when its share of breakfast traffic slipped 1.6 per cent — in large part due to declining coffee sales; coffee, it seems, drives consumers' choice of breakfast sandwiches, not the other way around. And McDonald's coffee sales had dropped 36 per cent over the past decade, while Dunkin' Donuts' and Starbucks' sales were growing.[61]

To remedy the situation, McDonald's management moved to overhaul the stores. It developed a "Plan to Win," which emphasized a shift "from growing by being bigger to growing by being better."[62] The stores would be refurbished — replacing molded plastic booths with oversized chairs, changing to softer lighting and repainting the restaurants with muted tones instead of the bright colors previously used. Wireless Internet was added. "We began to realize that we could definitely sell coffee in this environment," said Don Thompson, president of the chain's U.S. business.[63]

In 2006, McDonald's changed its drip coffee to a stronger blend and began marketing it as "premium" roast — which Consumer Reports rated "better" than Starbucks. Emboldened, the company developed an espresso line of drinks under the name McCafe. Like Dunkin' Donuts, it used a more automated process than Starbucks; instead of steaming milk in pitchers and then combining it with the espresso, McDonald's used a single machine to make all the components of each drink. And the McDonald's added flavors were limited to vanilla, caramel and mocha, significantly fewer than the thousands of combinations offered by Starbucks. Prices were also lower — $1.99 to $3.29 — $0.60 to $0.80 less than Starbucks.[64]

---

[60]Ibid.

[61]Steven Gray and Deborah Ball, "McDonald's Sees Rivals Bite Into Breakfast," *Wall Street Journal*, April 8, 2005, B1.

[62]Neil Buckley, "McDonald's Returns to Profit after Revamp Restaurants," *Financial Times*, January 2004, p. 21.

[63]Janet Adamy, "McDonald's Takes on a Weakened Starbucks," *Wall Street Journal*, January 7, 2008, A1.

[64]Ibid.

It's the Economy!

In 2007, the U.S. economy was hit with increasing prices. A barrel of oil almost doubled in price,[65] and gasoline prices climbed from around $2.00 to $3.00 a gallon.[66] Starbucks, like many retailers, felt consumers' pain. "They finally got to the point where their customer base was so broad it wasn't recession-proof," according to Joseph Buckley of a major investment bank and brokerage firm.[67] And as gas prices continued to rise all across the United States, the $3.50 average price of a cup of Starbucks coffee now stood in direct competition with the less discretionary gallon of gas, a crucial comparison when consumers' budgets were already pinched.

As if that were not enough, the economy was further hit by the fallout of the subprime mortgage lending crisis. Because Starbucks had expanded in the South and in Southern California, regions hit hard by the housing crisis, many new stores performed below expectation. In some cases, store locations had been chosen because the population was projected to grow rapidly with new development; that development did not occur and so the expected sales did not materialize.[68] In other cases, the population was there, but sales were not.

The Fall from Grace

Confirmation of trouble within Starbucks came in 2007 when the company experienced two quarters of flat growth in same-store sales, then reported its first ever decline in the fourth quarter. Same-store sales — a measure of sales in locations open at least a year — had hovered in the mid-single-digit range all year, after years of growing at a high single-digit or double-digit rate each quarter.[69]

To beat the economic woes being touted daily in the national press, CEO Jim Donald reacted by tinkering with lower-priced product offerings. Starbucks began testing a $1 coffee and free refills on traditional-brewed coffee to attract the price-conscious consumers amid a weak economy. At $1, Starbucks would undercut the price of competitors such as McDonald's and Dunkin' Donuts. Although most sit-down restaurants top off customers' coffee free of charge, fast-food convenience restaurants have traditionally stayed away from the practice.

And during the 2007 holiday season, Starbucks ran its first national television campaign — something that Wall Street had long advocated it was time to do. The ads used "animatics" — a crisper, less-cartoonish form of animation. In one TV spot, a bearded skier and a reindeer are stuck in a ski lift and the skier offers the reindeer a cup of Starbucks coffee. Ideas for future advertising efforts were decidedly more edgy. One proposed campaign showed Americans discussing issues of importance to them — such as the war in Iraq and health care or even pop culture — and depicted Starbucks as the "living room" of the national conversation. The images would shift from inside a Starbucks store to pictures of an American soldier or, on the lighter side, Britney Spears on the day she shaved her head.[70]

---

[65]*Weekly United States Spot Price FOB Weighted by Estimated Import Volume (Dollars per Barrel)* http://tonto.eia.doe.gov/dnav/pet/hist/wtotusaw.htm.

[66]Gasbuddy.com, www.gasbuddy.com/gb_retail_price_chart.aspx?time=24.

[67]Barbara Kiviat, "Wake Up and Sell the Coffee," *Time*, April 7, 2008, p. 46.

[68]Brad Stone, "Lax Real Estate Decisions Hurt Starbucks," *New York Times*, July 4, 2008.

[69]Janet Adamy, "Schultz Takes Over to Try to Perk Up Starbucks," *Wall Street Journal*, January 8, 2008, B1.

[70]Stephanie Kang, Janet Adamy and Suzanne Vrancia, "TV Campaign Is Culture Shift for Starbucks," *Wall Street Journal*, November 17, 2007, A1.

But by the end of 2007, Starbucks' stock had lost much of its luster. In early January, the company's share price was $18, down from $35 the previous year. Deciding that it was time to act, on January 7, 2008, the board brought back Howard Schultz as CEO. And Schultz came back determined to restore Starbucks' cachet as a premier brand: "I came back because it's personal; I came back because I love this company and our people and feel a deep sense of responsibility to 200,000 people and their families."[71]

Investors hailed his resumption of the CEO position, hoping that, like Steve Jobs's homecoming to Apple in 1997, it would portend a return to healthier days. But many analysts warned that investors should not expect an immediate reversal of company fortunes. "Many [investors] don't realize how long it can take to right the ship and how rocky the sailing can be during that time. Companies like Gap Inc. and Home Depot Inc. have spent several years trying to get back on track after losing their way."[72]

Schultz himself recognized that it would not be a quick fix and that choices would not be easy. In comments to the press, he warned, "We want to have the courage to do the things that support the core purpose and the reason for being and not veer off and get caught up in chasing revenue, because long-term value for the shareholder can only be created if you create long-term value for the customer and your people. We have to get back to what we do."[73]

---

[71]Barbara Kiviat, "Wake Up and Sell the Coffee," *Time*, April 7, 2008, p. 46.

[72]Janet Adamy, "With Starbucks, Investors Need Patience," *Wall Street Journal*, February 2, 2008, B1.

[73]Barbara Kiviat, "Wake Up and Sell the Coffee," *Time*, April 7, 2008, p. 46.

IVEY

Richard Ivey School of Business
The University of Western Ontario

CASE 20

Groupon[1]

Sayan Chatterjee, Sarah O'Keeffe and Alison Streiff wrote this case solely to provide material for class discussion. The authors do not intend to illustrate either effective or ineffective handling of a managerial situation. The authors may have disguised certain names and other identifying information to protect confidentiality.

Introduction

In December 2010, Groupon's 30-year-old chief executive officer (CEO), Andrew Mason, and his company leaders met with Google representatives to talk about the future of Groupon, the fast-growing online coupon company. In the two years since its launch, Groupon had reached 35 million users and was earning annual revenues of around $1 billion.[2] Google was now offering to buy out Mason and his partners. It was obvious that Groupon had hit upon a desirable business model. Would it be better for Groupon to continue on its own, trying to maintain the edge it had created — possibly even going public — or should Mason quit while he was ahead and sell out to Google?

What Is Groupon?

A Groupon was an online coupon that allowed a consumer, upon subscribing to Groupon.com, to purchase a specific service from a local business at a discount rate of 50 per cent to 90 per cent off the regular price. A new Groupon was sent to online subscribers each day; it had to be bought within the time limit specified (usually that day), and it had to have a minimum number of purchasers before "the deal [was] on"[3] and the purchase of the Groupon was truly completed (see Exhibit 1). Each deal was set up through Groupon with a business or organization that was tied to a particular market

---

[1]This case has been written on the basis of published sources only. Consequently, the interpretation and perspectives presented in this case are not necessarily those of Groupon or any of its employees.

[2]Evelyn Rusli and Jenna Wortham, "Groupon Said to Reject Google's Offer," *NY Times DealBook,* December 3, 2010, http://dealbook.nytimes.com/2010/12/03/groupon-said-to-reject-googles-offer/. accessed February 20, 2011.

[3]"How It Works," www.groupon.com, accessed February 28, 2011.

EXHIBIT 1 Flow Chart

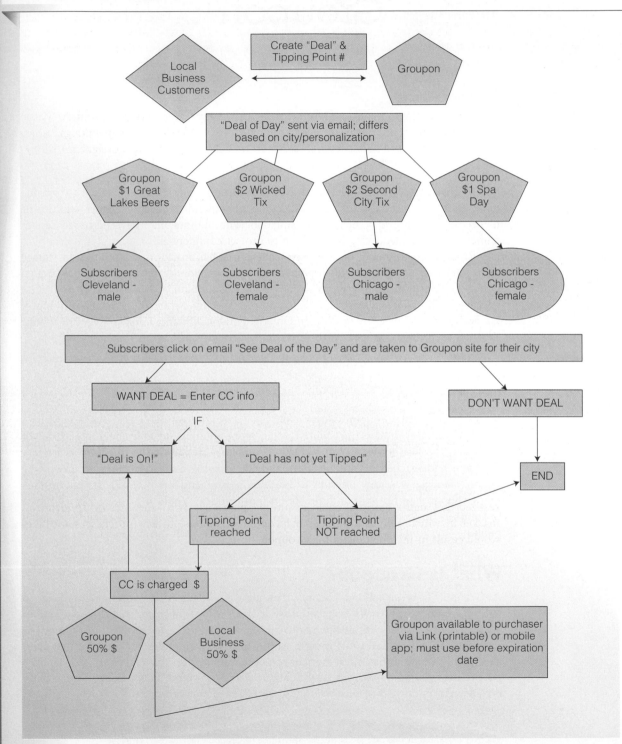

Source: "Frequently Asked Questions," www.kgbdeals.com/company/faq, accessed February 6, 2011.

city. Subscribers signed up for their city of choice (usually the one in which they lived), and in turn, they received an e-mail with the Featured Deal of the Day plus a few "side deals" for that city; they were encouraged to share the deal with friends. Deals were personalized by gender and by any other personal details that a subscriber was willing to provide. As the subscriber purchased deals on an ongoing basis, Groupon further personalized or targeted future deals based on past purchase preferences.

The Beginning

In 2003, as a recent graduate of Northwestern University's music program, Andrew Mason went to work for well-known Chicago entrepreneur Eric Lefkofsky at Innerworkings,[4] where he was employed as a self-styled web designer. In 2006, Mason left web designing to attend Chicago University's Harris School of Public Policy Studies. During this timeframe, a frustrating experience with his cell phone contract inspired Mason to experiment with a web-based platform for organizing collective action. As Mason's former employer and mentor, Lefkofsky offered to bankroll the burgeoning platform project, leading Mason to quit school in order to focus full time on his brainchild, which, by November 2007, became known as The Point.

The Point: Make Something Happen

Mason wanted to use his new web-based platform to offer organizations and individuals a place to campaign for a cause. Through The Point, anyone could start a campaign and anyone could pledge support to that campaign. Individuals only tentatively joined a cause, and monetary pledges were not collected until the campaign's predetermined tipping point — the amount of people needed to make it successful — was reached.[5] Early examples of successful campaigns on The Point were "Buy a Wii for The Point Office" (posted by Andrew Mason, who collected $350 for this campaign), "Chicago Wiffleball Tournament" (which raised $600), and the petition "Save your dog! Stop DC Bill 17-089!" in Washington, D.C. (which tipped at 75 concerned citizens). While these early successes made great use of Mason's platform, they did not generate income.

A year or so after The Point launched, Lefkofsky pushed Mason to think about how to make money with his concept. "[The Point] was too abstract and complex. So we said let us take one application of that — group buying — and focus on that and see what happens. So we started [Groupon] as this side project"[6] in November 2008. The partners realized they had a tool that could inspire people to act. Next, they needed to identify a market in which getting a number of people (consumers) to act (purchase something) would result in income dollars for Groupon.

Groupon Model

Early Days of Groupon - Finding What Worked

Until it launched in a second city in March of 2009, Groupon offered its group-coupons from Chicago businesses only, while it continued to tinker with its deal-offering formula. One key to success came from figuring out what would be a truly popular deal and who would be interested in buying those deals.

---

[4]Marcia Froelke Coburn, "On Groupon and its Founder, Andrew Mason," *Chicago Magazine*, August, 2010, www.chicagomag.com/Chicago-Magazine/August-2010/On-Groupon-and-its-founder-Andrew-Mason/index.php?cparticle=2&siarticle=1#artanc, accessed February 12, 2011.

[5]"Campaigns," www.thepoint.com, accessed March 9, 2011.

[6]"Andrew Mason, Interview with Charlie Rose," *Charlie Rose Show*, PBS, December 9, 2010, www.charlierose.com/view/interview/11338#frame_top, accessed February 12, 2011.

In a 2010 interview,[7] Andrew Mason described these early days as a time when Groupon "still hadn't quite figured out our stride yet, what worked and what didn't." Each day was a first for Groupon, as it offered deals from businesses in different sectors and in turn judged the subscribers' reactions. Deals for a sensory-deprivation tank session sold extremely well, while a bus tour of Michael Jackson's childhood haunts in Gary, Indiana, failed to catch on. Mason said the deprivation tank deal helped him to recognize "the potential of Groupon to … help people … have all kinds of experiences they might not otherwise have."[8] Through these early endeavors, Groupon learned to offer interesting, experiential deals to its users and to vet businesses in each market city that could deliver these types of deals. The tipping-point software allowed the company to automatically measure which deals were most popular, and a basic feedback tool was made available for both subscribers and businesses to report back on their Groupon experiences. Groupon developed into a veritable city guide for its users, serving as "a way for people to discover interesting, hidden gems in the city"[9] and encouraging them to try something fun and new at a discounted rate.

Along with these successful sales to Groupon buyers came a flood of businesses that could not wait to add their names to Groupon's stable of experience providers. In fact, Groupon soon boasted waiting lists that were "hundreds of businesses long" in the larger city markets.[10] The most typical Groupon deals came from the entertainment and restaurant sectors. Yet, as it expanded, Groupon continued to experiment with its offerings and began to include deals such as a Donors Choose Groupon, where a New York philanthropist donated matching funds for certificates sold at $20 for a $40 value, and a $10 Groupon for a copy of *Delivering Happiness*, a book by Zappos.com CEO Tony Hsieh.[11]

Attracting both businesses and subscribers initially required a lot of footwork by the Groupon staff. The sales team hit the pavement to get businesses to provide coupons, and the initial subscriber list consisted of the e-mail addresses of Groupon workers' friends and family. Early revenues plus $30 million in investment funds from ACCEL Partners went towards hiring a more experienced sales force that possessed a skill set in face-to-face selling. Meanwhile, e-mail subscriptions were increased through e-mail newsletters, deal sharing on social media and, finally, through the purchase of subscribers from other companies' client lists at $3 per e-mail address.[12]

The Journey Towards Expansion: Groupon's Working Formula

Once the model was set, Mason and his group used the social media infrastructure, built around sites like Facebook and Twitter, and an impressively skilled sales force in order to scale it to new cities. The sales force at Groupon, as discussed on Quora.com, numbered 2,000 after just two short years and was described as having "a core of really good and street savvy salespeople."[13] One contributor suggested that Groupon may have inherited its skilled sales culture by being another project funded Lefkofsky's Lightbank VC firm.

[7]"Groupon's CEO on Coupons and Start-Ups," *Wall Street Journal Blogs, Digits,* June 9, 2010, http://blogs.wsj. com/digits/2010/06/09/groupons-ceo-on-online-coupons-and-start-up-success/, accessed February 20, 2011.

[8]Ibid.

[9]Ibid.

[10]Ibid.

[11]Ibid.

[12]Chris McCoy, "How Did Groupon Scale Their Sales Team So Quickly?" January 25, 2011, www.quora.com/ How-did-Groupon-scale-their-sales-team-so-quickly, accessed May 11, 2011.

[13]Brian Roemmele and Jeff Domoracki, "How did Groupon Build a 2,000+ Person Sales Force in Two Years?" February 4, 2011, www.quora.com/How-did-Groupon-build-a-2-000+-person-salesforce-in-2-years, accessed May 11, 2011.

Other Lightbank companies, Echo Global Logistics, MediaBank and Mason's former employer, Innerworkings, were all sales-oriented. Another contributor attributed Groupon's ability to bolster its sales force to generous commission compensation, which sometimes hit the mid-six figures, and to a poor economy that made finding willing high producers much easier.

Groupon opened in New York, its third city, in mid-2009 and became available in 70 American cities and 80 European cities by June of 2010. The company perfected the model for the collective buying industry,[14] with many competitors following suit with their own subtle spins on deal-making and new competitors sprouting up as a result of Groupon's success. By February 2011, Groupon operated in 39 countries, including the United States, Canada, 16 European countries, and four Asian countries, with offices in each city or region it served.

Setting Up the Deal

Discount amounts, as well as the minimum and maximum number of deals available, were contracted between Groupon and the business before the deal was published. At this time, Groupon made money by taking a 50 per cent cut of all revenues generated from the daily deal.[15] The day after a deal, Groupon sent a cheque to each participating business for the business's cut of the money made on the daily deal. The business did not expend any financial resources until the Groupon was redeemed by the purchaser. According to research reports,[16] many analysts felt that Groupon's take of 40 per cent to 50 per cent of the revenue generated by each deal was unsustainable.[17]

Once a deal had been posted, subscribers had a time period during which they could purchase it. If the pre-set minimum number of subscribers purchased the deal, then the deal became valid, purchasers' credit cards were charged and they received their Groupon discount by e-mail or mobile phone application. Alternatively, for subscribers who purchased a deal that failed to reach the minimum, their credit cards were not charged, and the deal was off the table[18] (see Exhibit 1).

In July of 2010, Groupon began to offer personalized options to its consumers. Deals were tailored to each subscriber based on what that user had entered into their profile and on what deals they had already purchased. For example, two co-workers who subscribed to Cleveland Groupon might each have a different main deal, but the main deal of one may be the side deal of the other. And, while the deals were personalized in this way, there was still an option for subscribers to share the deal with a friend.

Marketing

In addition to the basic formula above, Groupon had a unique style to its brand that helped sell its services to both subscribers and businesses. Groupon marketed itself mainly through its subscribers by encouraging them to share deals through social media, including e-mail,

---

[14]"Amazon Flings Money at Groupon Rival LivingSocial," December 2, 2010, http://money.cnn.com/2010/12/02/technology/Amazon_invests_LivingSocial/index.htm, accessed February 19, 2011.

[15]"GrouponWorks For Businesses," www.grouponworks.com/, accessed February 26, 2011.

[16]Sandra Guy, "Groupon Poised for Growth, Possible IPO," *Chicago Sun-Times*, February 22, 2011, www.suntimes.com/business/3935658-420/groupon-poised-for-growth-possible-ipo.html, accessed February 27, 2011.

[17]Scott Austin, "Facebook, Groupon, Zynga: Off-the-chart Revenue," *WSJ Blogs*, February 26, 2011, http://blogs.wsj.com/venturecapital/2011/02/26/facebook-groupon-zynga-off-the-chart-revenue/?mod=google_news_blog, accessed February 27, 2011.

[18]"FAQ," www.groupon.com/faq, accessed February 26, 2011.

EXHIBIT 2 Copy from Groupon — Featured Daily Deal for Cleveland, March 25, 2011

"Though soy sauce is commonly believed to be of Asian origin, several linguists have unearthed its true Iberian beginnings by decoding the hidden Spanish translation. Celebrate the intriguing international condiment with the help of today's Groupon: for $15, you get $30 worth of Chinese cuisine and drinks at Hunan Solon in Solon.

The recipient of Cleveland Magazine's 2008 Silver Spoon Award for Best Chinese, Hunan Solon's multiple menus chronicle an eclectic array of traditional Chinese and pan-Asian cuisine. A vast lunch selection pits the Sino-centric Hunan chicken combo platter ($7) against the Southeast Asian pad Thai ($6) in a gustatory battle of poultry/noodle supremacy.

An encyclopedic dinner menu doles out international appetizers such as the Korean-inspired beef rib strips ($7), which serve as a prelude to an oeuvre of entrees, including the basil chicken, sliced with a flavorful textured mix of bell peppers, bamboo shoots, Spanish onions, and basil ($10). The authentic Chinese menu indexes various regional dishes such as salt-baked pork chops ($10) and a potpourri of seafood, vegetable, and meaty hot-pot combos ($10—$15).

Guests can nosh on Chinese delicacies and tipple from Hunan Solon's full bar in between vibrant jade-green wall sconces and Warhol-inspired canvas photographs. A five-foot-wide live lobster and Dungeness crab tank serves to show off the seafood goods and serves as mid-meal lecture material for adjunct marine-biology professors."

Source: www.groupon.com, accessed March 25, 2011.

Facebook and Twitter.[19] Groupon also rewarded its subscribers in Groupon dollars if they referred a non-subscriber friend to Groupon and that friend then purchased a deal.

Groupon hired creative writers and copy editors to highlight and deliver the message of product uniqueness on Groupon's website as well as in daily e-mails and advertisements. These writers were guided by an inch-thick manual, with the famous Chicago-style improvisational humor as a core element.[20] Then, they would let the Groupon speak for itself (see Exhibit 2).

In 2010, Groupon opened an office in Silicon Valley and hired Mark Johnson, former ad executive at Netflix. The company aired its very first television advertisements in January 2011, during Super Bowl XLV.

Customers: Individual Subscriber Demographics

Among Groupon's estimated 40 million subscribers in more than 170 cities in North America,[21] the core demographics reflected an extremely desirable market (see Exhibit 3). The typical Groupon subscriber was a young, single, educated, urban woman, employed and with significant earning power.

Women accounted for 77 per cent of Groupon subscribers in 2011, and more than two thirds of this customer segment fell between the ages of 18 and 34.[22] According to ComScore, a marketing research firm, women were more likely than men to visit coupon sites and to use coupons. Women also spent more time than men in the process of searching online for discounted retail offerings.

Groupon subscribers tended to be well-educated. Half of Groupon's subscribers held a bachelor's degree, with an additional 30 per cent holding a graduate degree.[23] By

---

[19]Jere Doyle, "How Big Brands Can Harness the Group-buying Craze," June 1, 2010, www.imediaconnection.com/content/26855.asp. accessed February 20, 2011.

[20]Marcia Froelke Coburn, "On Groupon and its founder, Andrew Mason," *Chicago Magazine*, August 2010, www.chicagomag.com/Chicago-Magazine/August-2010/On-Groupon-and-its-founder-Andrew-Mason/index.php?cparticle=2&siarticle=1#artanc, accessed February 20, 2011.

[21]www.grouponworks.com/, accessed February 28, 2011.

[22]Ibid.

[23]Ibid.

EXHIBIT 3   Demographic Data of Groupon's Individual Customers (March 2011)

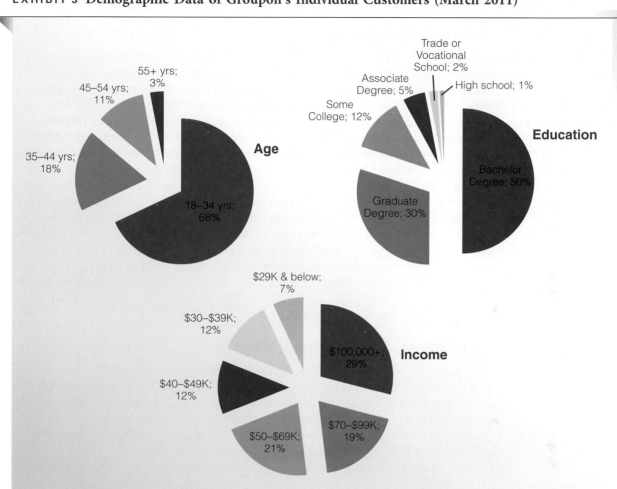

Source: All graphs in this exhibit based on data from "GrouponWorks for Businesses," www.grouponworks.com/, accessed February 26, 2011.

comparison, according to the 2010 U.S. Census, only slightly more than one in four Americans had a bachelor's or higher degree.[24]

The vast majority of Groupon subscribers were employed and— 75 per cent held full time jobs.[25] Twenty-nine per cent of Groupon subscribers had an annual income of more than $100,000,[26] and 69 per cent earned more than the national average income, i.e., slightly less than $50,000 for an American household in 2009.[27]

In a recent interview, Andrew Mason, founder of Groupon, stated,

Part of what makes Groupon really fun for consumers is this element of discovery, finding new things, being surprised every morning [to find out] what the deal is. And we try to remain surprising and we try to do things, whether it's the deal you're getting or whether

---

[24]www.census.gov, accessed February 28, 2011.

[25]www.grouponworks.com/, accessed February 28, 2011.

[26]Ibid.

[27]www.census.gov, accessed February 28, 2011.

it's the way we're writing about the deal or whether it's the brand and the culture of the company, that's constantly surprising people, because that's kind of the spice of life.[28]

Customers: Businesses

Typical profile — local, small to mid-sized, retail services, restaurants, health and beauty, etc. Groupon's chief operating officer (COO), Rob Solomon, maintained that the real *modus operandi* of Groupon was to wipe out perishability for small businesses.[29] Groupon was selling these businesses new customers by helping them to gain exposure through daily e-mailed deals, delivering Groupon customers literally to the door of each participating business. Groupons could drive a large number of visitors to a store location with a single event if the Groupon Deal was really popular.[30] For example, at Salon de la Mer in Mayfield, Ohio, the owners offered a Groupon for a manicure and pedicure for $25; more than 1,000 people bought that particular Groupon. The deal was so successful that the owners went on to offer a tanning Groupon.[31]

Mason stated, "It's for the first time local businesses get performance-based marketing. They only pay when these customers walk in the door. We get them in the door and then it's up to them to give them an amazing experience…." He also went so far as to say that Groupon was the "small business savior."[32] Others disagreed. While this model worked well for many customers, studies showed that up to 32 per cent of companies lose money on Groupon deals.[33] Small-business blog sites have told cautionary tales of how Groupons adversely affected business owners and have, as a result, offered guides on how to use Groupons effectively (or not at all).[34]

Collective Buying Industry

Early collective buying sites such as Mercata and MobShop attempted to use collective buying for consumer goods, but they simply could not compete with the likes of Amazon in driving down prices. Their goods could be bought other places and often more quickly. "Mason took what he gleaned from the failed collective buying sites, switched the concept from goods to services and married it to the basic premise of The Point."[35]

Thus, for a time, the collective buying industry became defined by Groupon,[36] with the core concepts involving the following elements: A local business offered its good or

[28]"Andrew Mason, Interview with Charlie Rose. Charlie Rose Show," PBS, December 9, 2010, www.charlierose.com/view/interview/11338#frame_top, accessed February 12, 2011.

[29]Sandra Guy, "Groupon poised for growth, possible IPO," *Chicago Sun-Times*, February 22, 2011, www.suntimes.com/business/3935658-420/groupon-poised-for-growth-possible-ipo.html. accessed March 6, 2011.

[30]Diana Marszalek, "Groupon: Good Relationships Spur Success," *NetNewsCheck*, March 4, 2011, www.netnewscheck.com/article/2011/03/04/9592/groupon-good-relationships-spur-success, accessed March 7, 2011.

[31]Personal Interview. Gabby at Salon de la Mer. Mayfield, OH, February 26, 2011.

[32]"Andrew Mason, Interview with Charlie Rose. Charlie Rose Show," PBS, December 9, 2010, www.charlierose.com/view/interview/11338#frame_top, accessed February 12, 2011.

[33]Utpal M. Dholakia, "How Effective Are Groupon Promotions For Businesses?" Rice University, September 10, 2010, www.ruf.rice.edu/~dholakia/Groupon%20Effectiveness%20Study,%20Sep%2028%202010.pdf, accessed February 5, 2011.

[34]Goeff Williams, "How to Avoid a Groupon Disaster," *AOL Small Business Blog*, December 2, 2010, http://smallbusiness.aol.com/2010/12/02/how-to-avoid-a-groupon-disaster/, accessed February 19, 2011.

[35]Marcia Froelke Coburn, "On Groupon and its founder, Andrew Mason," *Chicago Magazine*, August 2010, www.chicagomag.com/Chicago-Magazine/August-2010/On-Groupon-and-its-founder-Andrew-Mason/index.php?cparticle=2&siarticle=1#artanc, accessed February 12, 2011.

[36]Laurie Segall, "Amazon Flings Money at Groupon Rival LivingSocial," *CNNMoney*, December 2, 2010, http://money.cnn.com/2010/12/02/technology/Amazon_invests_LivingSocial/index.htm, accessed February 19, 2011.

services for a discounted rate in an attempt to attract new clients. Usually these deals were highly attractive to consumers in that they offered deep discounts on products or services that consumers might have been interested in buying or using but had not done so due to the cost. A website like Groupon offered or exposed the limited time deals to its members. The website members took advantage of the offer as well as communicated the offer by word of mouth to other potential like-minded consumers.

Collective buying or group buying has shown itself to be very compelling from a marketing standpoint," according to Sucharita Mulpuru, a retail analyst with Forrester Research. "It resonates with people and gets them to make a purchase quickly. And it's a great way for businesses to drive new customer acquisition."[37] In the case of Groupon, peer pressure has been a key factor in order to achieve the tipping point and ultimate purchase of the deal, "So if [a consumer] really wants the Groupon [then they should] be sure to either beg or threaten [their] friends [to sign up]."[38]

Groupon's particular collective-buying model resembled a Dutch auction with some significant changes. A Dutch auction is described as a public auction where the price of a collection of the same item is set after all the bids have been offered. The highest bid at which all the items in the collection can be sold will be the final bid price. (This price will not necessarily be the highest bid offered.) Those participants with bids matching the minimum price or higher will be awarded items from the collection. The allocation of the items starts with the quantity request of the highest bidder over the winning price and continues down until all the items have been allocated amongst the winners.[39] If a buyer bid $10 for a set of 10 T-shirts and the last accepted bid was $5, that buyer would get all 10 T-shirts but would pay $5 a shirt.

Groupon took the Dutch auction concept and twisted it. Instead of the price going up with the highest bidder, the quantity of coupons being sold climbed up with each person wanting to take advantage of the deal. Instead of the items in the collection staying constant, the price stayed constant, as it was predetermined by the vendor. Lastly, instead of the allotment being distributed to the winning bidders based on the individual bids from highest to lowest, coupons were given to all bidders until either all the available coupons had been distributed or until the deal's timeframe expired, whichever occurred first.

Consumers have been warned by the Better Business Bureau to do their due diligence to understand the restrictions and stipulations of group-buying deals in order to avoid the unexpected.[40] Groupon had a section called *The Fine Print* listed on each deal, and potential purchasers were reminded to review this section to ensure that the restrictions put in place by the vending business would not interfere with their use of the Groupon. A review of this section on several deals listed restrictions such as: limit one per visit; 24-hour cancellation policy or fees may apply; valid only at specific locations; limit one per table; dine-in only; not valid at happy hour; by appointment only; not available until a certain future date; shipping fees not included in discount and valid at certain times during the day.[41] Groupon also had what could be considered an escape clause that could help a purchaser out of a situation where s/he felt that the deal was not good. The Groupon Promise, (see Exhibit 4) which was displayed on Groupon deal pages, stated, "If you ever feel like Groupon let you down, give us a call and we'll return your purchase — simple as that."[42]

---

[37]David Gelles, "Collective buying takes off," *SLOW Movement*, February 15, 2010, http://chutzpah.typepad.com/slow_movement/2010/02/ft-collective-buying-takes-off.html, accessed February 20, 2011.

[38]"Groupon FAQ," www.groupon.com/faq, accessed March 26, 2011.

[39]"Dutch Auction," *Investopia*, www.investopedia.com/terms/d/dutchauction.asp, accessed March 26, 2011.

[40]"BBB Advice for Getting Deals on Collective Buying Sites," *Better Business Bureau*, May 3, 2010, www.bbb.org/us/article/bbb-advice-for-getting-deals-on-collective-buying-sites-19247, accessed February 20, 2011.

[41]"Groupon, Various deal pages," www.groupon.com/akron-canton/, accessed March 26, 2011.

[42]"Groupon,"www.groupon.com/akron-canton/, accessed March 26, 2011.

EXHIBIT 4 Groupon's Promises to Its Users

"…you should feel comfortable venturing out and trying something new - just because it's featured on Groupon."

"No BS. We really want you to love Groupon. 'Gotchas' and buried conditions that sour the experience are a terrible way to accomplish that goal. We want each Groupon purchase to feel too good to be true, from the moment you buy to the day you use it. If there's anything unusual about a deal (e.g., an inconvenient location), we go out of our way to point it out."

"…..If you contact us, we'll do what it takes to make things right - and we'll do it fast. Email us, or speak with a human (during normal business hours): (877) 788-7858

Source: www.groupon.com, accessed February 20, 2011.

Competition

Many new companies entered the competitive landscape in order to replicate the same success that Groupon and Groupon's initial competitors had enjoyed, and as a result, the market started to become quite crowded. Although a multitude of Groupon competitors emerged, many catered only to niche buying pockets, such as cosmetics or travel. Firms in the marketplace most similar in scope and structure to Groupon are tabulated in Exhibit 5.

It is evident that many competitors' deals were comparable to Groupon with regards to offer timing, the local businesses promoted, and the means through which that local business would reach out to a group-coupon company, such as a Groupon, in order to publicize and push its business into the spotlight. The largest contrast can be found in the way each competitor put its own spin on how daily deals became available to the people who purchased them.

Groupon Growth

Growth Initiatives

Groupon acquired several clone sites such as Citydeal (May 2010) in Europe, adding 16 countries to its roster.[43] Groupon then acquired Qpod (Japan), Darberry (Russia),[44] SoSasta (India), Grouper (Israel), and Twangoo (South Africa).[45] Groupon also started operations in Hong Kong, Taiwan, the Philippines, and Singapore in December 2010, through acquisition of deals sites Ubuyibuy, Beeconomic, and Atlaspost.[46]

The firm considered a joint venture to allow expansion into China, giving Groupon access to China's 450 million internet subscribers. According to Bloomberg, Groupon had plans to have a workforce of 1,000 employees in China by summer 2011.[47]

---

[43]"Groupon expands by acquiring Citydeal of Europe," *Chicago Tribune*, May 16, 2010, http://articles.chicagotribune.com/2010-05-16/business/ct-biz-0517-groupon-20100516_1_samwer-brothers-expands-acquiring, accessed February 12, 2011.

[44]"Groupon Makes Leap Into Japan and Russia With Latest Acquisitions," http://techcrunch.com/2010/08/17/groupon-manfest-destiny/, accessed March 27, 2011.

[45]Stan Schroeder, "Groupon Buys Local Competitors, Expands to South Africa, India and Israel," http://mashable.com/2011/01/11/groupon-south-africa-india-israel/, accessed March 27, 2011.

[46]Adaline Lau, "Groupon Expands Asia Footprint With 3 Acquisitions," www.clickz.asia/1946/groupon-expands-asia-footprint-with-3-acquisitions, accessed March 27, 2011.

[47]Mark Lee, "Groupon Starts China Service; Tencent, Alibaba's Jack Ma Among Investors," Bloomberg, February 27, 2011, www.bloomberg.com/news/2011-02-28/groupon-starts-china-service-tencent-alibaba-s-jack-ma-among-investors.html, accessed March 27, 2011.

EXHIBIT 5 Competitors of Groupon

Firm	How it Works	Geography	Products	Timing	Merchant Affiliates
Living Social	One coupon listed per day with discounts of up to 90 per cent in some cases. A user clicks the offer to purchase the deal. If the user forwards the deal link to three or more other users (and they subsequently purchase the deal too), the deal then becomes free to the originating user.	USA, Canada, UK, Ireland, Australia	Includes, but not limited to: restaurants, spas, theaters and bars within a city region	Daily. Users can go directly to LivingSocial. com for the deal or sign up for the daily email to participate in the deal of the day.	Selected by staff on the LivingSocial team
Buy-WithMe[48]	One coupon listed per day with discounts from 50 to 90 per cent off. The coupon is active for seven days for the deal to gather enough users to become active. Once the deal becomes active, users signing up for a deal receive an e-voucher to go towards their purchase. If not enough people purchase the deal, the user, subsequently, is not charged for the deal purchase. If a user refers a friend, the referring user gets a $10 credit on their next BuyWithMe purchase.	USA — however, not all cities/ regions are represented	Retail, restaurants, salons, recreation and more within a city region.	Daily. Users can go directly to BuyWithMe.com for the deal or sign up for the daily email to participate in the deal of the day.	A merchant goes to the BuyWithMe website to register their business for possible promotion. If interested, a BuyWithMe representative follows up with the merchant about a potential deal.[49]
DealOn[50]	A user signs up for a deal at a given sale price. As more users sign up for a deal throughout the day, the price is driven down, until midnight, when the deal ends. The price of the deal at midnight is what all users will pay, regardless of what they may have paid earlier in the day.	USA	Includes, but not limited to: restaurants, spas and entertainment venues within a city region	Daily. Users can go directly to DealOn.com for the deal or sign up for the daily email to participate in the deal of the day.	A merchant goes to the DealOn website to register their business for possible promotion. If interested, a DealOn representative follows up with the merchant about a potential deal.[51]

(Continued)

---

[48]"You've got Questions? We have Answers," www.buywithme.com/pages/faq, accessed February 6, 2011.
[49]"BoostYourBusiness with BuyWithMe," www.buywithme.com/boostyourbusiness/#, accessed February 6, 2011.
[50]"Frequently Asked Questions," www.kgbdeals.com/company/faq, accessed February 6, 2011.
[51]"How DealOn Works," www.dealon.com/featureyourbusiness/howdealonworks, accessed February 6, 2011.

EXHIBIT 5 Competitors of Groupon (Continued)

Home Run[52]	One coupon (50 per cent to 90 per cent off in most instances) listed per day. A user clicks the offer to purchase the deal. If enough users purchase the deal, all users receive the deal.	USA — however, not all cities/regions are represented	Includes, but not limited to spas, restaurants, event venues and salons within a city region	Daily. Users can go directly to HomeRun.com for the deal or sign up for the daily email to participate in the deal of the day.	Merchants register on HomeRun.com and are immediately able to advertise their first deal and have access to a merchant dashboard.[53]
KGB Deals[54]	Depending on availability, a user simply has between one or multiple days to purchase a coupon and is able to use the coupon immediately, regardless of how many others are interested in the deal. More often than not, deals last one day.	UK, Italy, France, USA — however, not all cities/regions in the USA are represented	Includes eateries, retail, and entertainment venues/activities within a city region.	Daily. Users receive deals via email.	A merchant goes to the KGB Deals website to register their business for possible promotion. If interested, a KGB Deals representative follows up with the merchant about a potential deal.
Tippr[55] [56] [57]	A user registers for the Tippr daily newsletter and receives three deals per day by e-mail. Each deal (lasting 2 to 5 days) starts off at a certain discount level, but when enough people show interest in the deal, it hits the tipping point and the deal accelerates to an even better savings level for those signed up for the deal. Refer a friend to a Tippr sponsored deal and the friend immediately enjoys a $5 credit. Once the friend uses the $5 credit, the referring user receives a $5 credit.	A select number of U.S. cities	Includes, but not limited to salons, entertainment, retail, fitness, restaurants and bars within a city region	Daily. Users receive deals by e-mail.	A merchant goes to the Tippr website to register their business for possible promotion. If interested, a Tippr representative follows up with the merchant about a potential deal.[58]

(Continued)

---

[52]"How HomeRun Works," http://homerun.com/how-it-works, accessed February 6, 2011.

[53]"Sign up for HomeRun and Submit Your First Offer," http://homerundelivers.com/signup, accessed February 6, 2011.

[54]"Frequently Asked Questions," www.kgbdeals.com/company/faq, accessed February 6, 2011.

[55]"How Does Tippr Differ from Other Group Buying Sites," http://support.tippr.com/entries/110989-how-does-tippr-differ-from-other-group-buying-sites, accessed February 6, 2011.

[56]"What is an Accelerated Deal," http://support.tippr.com/entries/111029-what-is-an-accelerated-deal, accessed February 6, 2011.

[57]"What is Tippr," http://support.tippr.com/entries/111012-what-is-tippr, accessed February 6, 2011.

[58]"Contact Us," www.poweredbytippr.com/contact-us, accessed February 6, 2011.

EXHIBIT 5 Competitors of Groupon (Continued)

Twangoo[59]	One coupon listed per day. A user clicks the offer to "purchase" the deal. If enough users purchase the deal, all users receive the deal.	Southeast Asia, Australia	Includes, but not limited to entertainment, retail and eating establishments within a city region	Daily. Users can go directly to Twangoo.com for the deal or sign up for the daily email to participate in the deal of the day.	A user or business suggests a business to feature. If interested, Twangoo works with the business to develop a deal that benefits both parties.[60]
Google Offers[61]	Currently in the testing phase	Not clear	Instantly post discounts and other types of special offers across Google properties		Interested businesses can fill out a contact form

Source: Created by author

Conclusion

Groupon had found a revolutionary niche in the coupon market. Using connections in social media and the Internet, Groupon had gone from a concept of collective action to one of the fastest growing companies in America. It succeeded by partnering with local small business as well as by offering deals that were convenient, consistent and valuable. Groupon face many obstacles ahead, with intense competition and stricter legislation. However, Groupon managed to capture and engage an important customer demographic that was sought after by many businesses. Would its seemingly winning combination continue to allow the business to excel and expand in this increasingly contested market on its own, or did Groupon need the resources and capabilities that Google could bring to the table?

[59]"FAQ," www.twangoo.com/hong-kong/en/page,3,faq, accessed February 6, 2011.

[60]"Twangoo for Businesses," www.twangoo.com/hong-kong/en/page,5,twangoo-for-businesses, accessed February 6, 2011.

[61]"Thank You for Your Interest in Google Offers," www.google.com/landing/offers/index.html, accessed March 12, 2011.

Marketing Plan Worksheets

These worksheets will assist you in writing a formal marketing plan. Worksheets are a useful planning tool because they help to ensure that important information is not omitted from the marketing plan. Answering the questions on these worksheets will enable you to:

1. Organize and structure the data and information you collect during the situation analysis.
2. Use this information to better understand a firm's strengths and weaknesses, and to recognize the opportunities and threats that exist in the marketing environment.
3. Develop goals and objectives that capitalize on strengths.
4. Develop a marketing strategy that creates competitive advantages.
5. Outline a plan for implementing the marketing strategy.

These worksheets are available in electronic format on our text's website at www. cengagebrain.com. By downloading these worksheets, you will be able to change the outline or add additional information that is relevant to your situation. Remember that there is no one best way to organize a marketing plan. We designed our outline to serve as a starting point and to be flexible enough to accommodate the unique characteristics of your situation.

As you complete the worksheets, it might be useful to refer back to the text of the chapters. In completing the situation analysis section, be sure to be as comprehensive as possible. The viability of your SWOT analysis depends on how well you have identified all of the relevant environmental issues. Likewise, as you complete the SWOT analysis, you should be honest about the firm's characteristics. Do not depend on strengths that the firm really does not possess. Honesty is also important for your listing of weaknesses.

I. Executive Summary

The executive summary is a synopsis of the overall marketing plan. It should provide an overview of the entire plan including goals/objectives, strategy elements, implementation issues, and expected outcomes. The executive summary should be the last part of the marketing plan that you write.

II. Situation Analysis

A. The Internal Environment (refer to Exhibit 3.3)

Review of marketing goals and objectives

Identify the firm's current marketing goals and objectives.

Explain how these goals and objectives are being achieved.

Explain how these goals and objectives are consistent or inconsistent with the firm's mission, recent trends in the external environment, and recent trends in the customer environment.

Review of current marketing strategy and performance

Describe the firm's current marketing strategy with respect to products, pricing, distribution, and promotion. Which elements of the strategy are working well? Which elements are not?

Describe the firm's current performance (sales volume, market share, profitability, awareness, brand preference) compared to other firms in the industry. Is the performance of the industry as a whole improving or declining? Why?

If the firm's performance is declining, what is the most likely cause (e.g., environmental changes, flawed strategy, poor implementation)?

Review of current and anticipated organizational resources

Describe the current state of the firm's organizational resources (e.g., financial, capital, human, experience, relationships with key suppliers or customers). How are the levels of these resources likely to change in the future?

If resource levels are expected to change, how can the firm leverage additional resources to meet customer needs better than competitors?

If additional resources are not available, how can the firm compensate for future resource constraints (lack of resources)?

Review of current and anticipated cultural and structural issues

In terms of marketing strategy development and implementation, describe the positive and negative aspects of the current and anticipated culture of the firm. Examples could include:

> The firm's overall customer orientation (or lack thereof)
> The firm's emphasis on short-term versus long-term planning
> Willingness of the firm's culture to embrace change
> Internal politics and power struggles
> The overall position and importance of the marketing function
> Changes in key executive positions
> General employee satisfaction and morale

Explain whether the firm's structure is supportive of the current marketing strategy.

B. The Customer Environment (refer to Exhibit 3.4)

Who are the firm's current and potential customers?

Describe the important identifying characteristics of the firm's current and potential customers with respect to demographics, geographic location, psychographic profiles, values/lifestyles, and product usage characteristics (heavy vs. light users).

Identify the important players in the purchase process for the firm's products. These might include purchasers (actual act of purchase), users (actual product user), purchase influencers (influence the decision, make recommendations), and the bearer of financial responsibility (who pays the bill?).

What do customers do with the firm's products?

How are the firm's products connected to customer needs? What are the basic benefits provided by the firm's products?

How are the firm's products purchased (quantities and combinations)? Is the product purchased as a part of a solution or alongside complementary products?

How are the firm's products consumed or used? Are there special consumption situations that influence purchase behavior?

Are there issues related to disposition of the firm's products, such as waste (garbage) or recycling, which must be addressed by the firm?

Where do customers purchase the firm's products?

Identify the merchants (intermediaries) where the firm's products are purchased (e.g., store-based retailers, ecommerce, catalog retailers, vending, wholesale outlets, direct from the firm).

Identify any trends in purchase patterns across these outlets (e.g., how has e-commerce changed the way the firm's products are purchased?).

When do customers purchase the firm's products?

How does purchase behavior vary based on different promotional events (communication and price changes) or customer services (hours of operation, delivery)?

How does purchase behavior vary based on uncontrollable influences such as seasonal demand patterns, time-based demand patterns, physical/social surroundings, or competitive activities?

Why (and how) do customers select the firm's products?

Describe the advantages of the firm's products relative to competing products. How well do the firm's products fulfill customers' needs relative to competing products?

Describe how issues such as brand loyalty, value, commoditization, and relational exchange processes affect customers' purchase behaviors.

Describe how credit or financing is used in purchasing the firm's products. Also, do customers seek long-term relationships with the firm, or do they buy in a transactional fashion (based primarily on price)?

Why do potential customers not purchase the firm's products?

Identify the needs, preferences, and requirements of non-customers that are not being met by the firm's products.

What are the features, benefits, and advantages of competing products that cause non-customers to choose them over the firm's products?

Explain how the firm's pricing, distribution, and/or promotion are out of sync with non-customers. Outside of the product, what causes non-customers to look elsewhere?

Describe the potential for converting non-customers into customers.

C. The External Environment (refer to Exhibit 3.5)

Competition

Identify the firm's major competitors (brand, product, generic, and total budget).

Identify the characteristics of the firm's major competitors with respect to size, growth, profitability, target markets, products, and marketing capabilities (production, distribution, promotion, pricing).

What other major strengths and weaknesses do these competitors possess?

List any potential future competitors not identified above.

Economic Growth and Stability

Identify the general economic conditions of the country, region, state, or local area where the firm's target customers are located. How are these economic conditions related to customers' ability to purchase the firm's products?

Describe the economics of the industry within which the firm operates. These issues might include the cost of raw materials, patents, merger/acquisition trends, sales trends, supply/demand issues, marketing challenges, and industry growth/decline.

Political Trends

Identify any political activities affecting the firm or the industry with respect to changes in elected officials (domestic or foreign), potential regulations favored by elected officials, industry (lobbying) groups or political action committees, and consumer advocacy groups.

What are the current and potential hot button political or policy issues at the national, regional, or local level that may affect the firm's marketing activities?

Legal and Regulatory Issues

Identify any changes in international, federal, state, or local laws and regulations affecting the firm's or industry's marketing activities with respect to recent court decisions, recent rulings of federal, state, or local government entities, recent decisions by regulatory and self-regulatory agencies, and changes in global trade agreements or trade law.

Technological Advancements

How have recent technological advances affected the firm's customers with respect to needs/wants/preferences, access to information, the timing and location of purchase decisions, the ability to compare competing product offerings, or the ability to conduct transactions more effectively and efficiently?

Have customers embraced or rejected these technological advances? How is this issue related to customers' concerns over privacy and security?

How have recent technological advances affected the firm or the industry with respect to manufacturing, process efficiency, distribution, supply chain effectiveness, promotion, cost-reduction, or customer relationship management?

What future technologies offer important opportunities for the firm? Identify any future technologies that may threaten the firm's viability or its marketing efforts.

Sociocultural Trends

With respect to the firm's target customers, identify changes in society's demographics, values, and lifestyles that affect the firm or the industry.

Explain how these changes are affecting (or may affect) the firm's products (features, benefits, branding), pricing (value), distribution and supply chain (convenience, efficiency), promotion (message content, delivery, feedback), and people (human resource issues).

Identify the ethical and social responsibility issues that the firm or industry faces. How do these issues affect the firm's customers? How are these issues expected to change in the future?

III. SWOT Analysis (refer to Exhibit 4.4)

A. Strengths

Strength 1: _____

Strength 2: _____

(Repeat as needed to develop a complete list of strengths)

How do these strengths enable the firm to meet customers' needs?

How do these strengths differentiate the firm from its competitors?

B. Weaknesses

Weakness 1: _____

Weakness 2: _____

(Repeat as needed to develop a complete list of weaknesses)

How do these weaknesses prevent the firm from meeting customers' needs?

How do these weaknesses negatively differentiate the firm from its competitors?

C. Opportunities (external situations independent of the firm—not strategic options)

Opportunity 1: _____

Opportunity 2: _____

(Repeat as needed to develop a complete list of opportunities)

How are these opportunities related to serving customers' needs?

What is the time horizon of each opportunity?

D. Threats (external situations independent of the firm)

Threat 1: _____

Threat 2: _____

(Repeat as needed to develop a complete list of threats)

How are these threats related to serving customers' needs?

What is the time horizon of each threat?

E. The SWOT Matrix (refer to Exhibit 4.5 and Exhibit 4.6)

Strengths: • • • • •	Opportunities: • • • • •
Weaknesses: • • • •	Threats: • • • •

F. Developing Competitive Advantages (refer to Exhibit 4.7)

Describe ways that the firm can match its strengths to its opportunities to create capabilities in serving customers' needs.

Are these capabilities and competitive advantages grounded in the basic principles of operational excellence, product leadership, and/or customer intimacy? If so, how are these capabilities and advantages made apparent to customers?

Can the firm convert its weaknesses into strengths or its threats into opportunities? If not, how can the firm minimize or avoid its weaknesses and threats?

Does the firm possess any major liabilities (unconverted weaknesses that match unconverted threats) or limitations (unconverted weaknesses or threats that match opportunities)? If so, are these liabilities and limitations apparent to customers?

Can the firm do anything about its liabilities or limitations, especially those that impact the firm's ability to serve customers' needs?

G. Developing a Strategic Focus

What is the overall strategic focus of the marketing plan? Does the strategic focus follow any particular direction, such as aggressiveness, diversification, turnaround, defensiveness, or niche marketing?

Describe the firm's strategic focus in terms of a strategy canvas. How does the firm's strategic thrust provide sufficient focus and divergence from other firms in the industry?

IV. Marketing Goals and Objectives

A. Marketing Goal A: _____
(should be broad, motivational, and somewhat vague)

Objective A1: _____
(must contain a specific and measurable outcome, a time frame for completion, and identify the person/unit responsible for achieving the objective)

Objective A2: _____
(must contain a specific and measurable outcome, a time frame for completion, and identify the person/unit responsible for achieving the objective)

B. Marketing Goal B: _____
(should be broad, motivational, and somewhat vague)

Objective B1: _____
(must contain a specific and measurable outcome, a time frame for completion, and identify the person/unit responsible for achieving the objective)

Objective B2: _____
(must contain a specific and measurable outcome, a time frame for completion, and identify the person/unit responsible for achieving the objective)

(Can be repeated as needed to develop a complete list of goals and objectives. However, having one goal and two or three objectives is advisable to greatly reduce the complexity of the marketing strategy.)

V. Marketing Strategy

A. Primary (and Secondary) Target Market

Primary target market

Identifying characteristics (demographics, geography, values, psychographics):
Basic needs, wants, preferences, or requirements:
Buying habits and preferences:
Consumption/disposition characteristics:

Secondary target market (optional)

Identifying characteristics (demographics, geography, values, psychographics):
Basic needs, wants, preferences, or requirements:
Buying habits and preferences:
Consumption/disposition characteristics:

B. Product Strategy

Brand name, packaging, and logo design:
Major features and benefits:
Differentiation/positioning strategy:
Supplemental products (including customer service strategy):
Connection to value (core, supplemental, experiential/symbolic attributes):

C. Pricing Strategy

Overall pricing strategy and pricing objectives:
Price comparison to competition:
Connection to differentiation/positioning strategy:
Connection to value (monetary costs):
Profit margin and breakeven:
Specific pricing tactics (discounts, incentives, financing, etc.):

D. Distribution/Supply Chain Strategy

Overall supply chain strategy (including distribution intensity):
Channels and intermediaries to be used:
Connection to differentiation/positioning strategy:
Connection to value (nonmonetary costs):
Strategies to ensure channel support (slotting fees, guarantees, etc.):
Tactics designed to increase time, place, and possession utility:

E. Integrated Marketing Communication (Promotion) Strategy

Overall IMC strategy, IMC objectives, and budget:

Consumer promotion elements

Advertising strategy:
Public relations/publicity strategy:
Personal selling strategy:
Consumer sales promotion (pull) strategy:

Trade (channel) promotion elements

Advertising strategy:
Public relations/publicity strategy:
Personal selling strategy:
Trade sales promotion (push) strategy:

VI. Marketing Implementation

A. Structural Issues

Describe the overall approach to implementing the marketing strategy.

Describe any changes to the firm's structure needed to implement the marketing strategy (e.g., add/delete positions, change lines of authority, change reporting relationships).

Describe any necessary internal marketing activities in the following areas: employee training, employee buy-in and motivation to implement the marketing strategy, overcoming resistance to change, internal communication and promotion of the marketing strategy, and coordination with other functional areas.

B. Tactical Marketing Activities (be *very* specific—this lays out the details of the marketing strategy and how it will be executed)

Specific Tactical Activities	Person/Department Responsible	Required Budget	Completion Date
Product Activities 1. 2. 3.			
Pricing Activities 1. 2. 3.			
Distribution/Supply Chain Activities 1. 2. 3.			
IMC (Promotion) Activities 1. 2. 3.			

VII. Evaluation and Control (refer to Exhibit 9.5)

A. Formal Controls

Describe the types of **input controls** that must be in place *before* the marketing plan can be implemented. Examples include financial resources, capital expenditures, additional research and development, and additional human resources.

Describe the types of **process controls** that will be needed *during* the execution of the marketing plan. Examples include management training, management commitment to the plan and to employees, revised employee evaluation/compensation systems, enhanced employee authority, and internal communication activities.

Describe the types of **output controls** that will be used to measure marketing performance and compare it to stated marketing objectives *during and after* the execution of the marketing plan.

Overall performance standards (these will vary based on the goals and objectives of the marketing plan). Examples include dollar sales, sales volume, market share, share of customer, profitability, customer satisfaction, customer retention, or other customer-related metrics.

Product performance standards (these are optional and will vary based on the product strategy). Examples include product specifications, core product quality, supplemental product quality, experiential quality, new product innovation, branding, and positioning.

Price performance standards (these are optional and will vary based on the pricing strategy). Examples include revenue targets, supply/demand balance, price elasticity, yield management, or metrics based on specific price adjustments.

Distribution performance standards (these are optional and will vary based on the distribution strategy). Examples include distribution effectiveness/efficiency, supply chain integration, value (time, place, and possession utility), relationship maintenance (collaboration, conflict), outsourcing, or direct distribution performance.

IMC (promotion) performance standards (these are optional and will vary based on the IMC strategy). Examples include communication objectives; brand awareness, recognition, or recall; campaign reach, frequency, and impressions; purchase intentions; and public relations, sales, and sales promotion effectiveness.

B. **Informal Controls**

Describe issues related to **employee self-control** that can influence the implementation of the marketing strategy. Examples include employee satisfaction, employee commitment (to the firm and the marketing plan), and employee confidence in their skills. If any of these controls are lacking, how can they be enhanced to support the implementation of the marketing plan?

Describe issues related to **employee social control** that can influence the implementation of the marketing strategy. Examples include shared organizational values, workgroup relationships, and social or behavioral norms. If any of these controls are lacking, how can they be enhanced to support the implementation of the marketing plan?

Describe issues related to **cultural control** that can influence the implementation of the marketing strategy. Examples include organizational culture and organizational rituals. If any of these controls are lacking, how can they be enhanced to support the implementation of the marketing plan?

C. **Marketing Audits (refer to Exhibit 9.6)**

Explain how marketing activities will be monitored. What are the specific profit- and time-based measures that will be used to monitor marketing activities?

Describe the marketing audit to be performed, including the person(s) responsible for conducting the audit.

If it is determined that the marketing strategy does not meet expectations, what corrective actions might be taken to improve performance (overall or within any element of the marketing program)?

If the marketing plan, as currently designed, shows little likelihood of meeting the marketing objectives, which elements of the plan should be reconsidered and revised?

D. Implementation Schedule and Timeline (refer to Exhibit 9.7)

Activities	Month Week	1	2	3	4	1	2	3	4	1	2	3	4
Product Activities													
Pricing Activities													
Distribution Activities													
IMC Activities													

Brands and Companies Index

A

Aapri, 483
Abbey Belgian Style Alc, 358
Abbey Grand Cru, 352
Abby, 352
ABC (American Broadcasting Company), 4, 444, 476
Abercrombie & Fitch (A&F), 136
ABI/INFORM®, 70
ACCEL Partners, 536
Ace, 153
Acer, 98, 332
Adobe, 41
Advertising Age, 465
Adweek, 79
Aflac Incorporated, 20–21
Agent Orange, 340
AIG (American International Group), 203–204
Aim Star, 389
Airstream, Inc., 362
AirTran Airways, 2
Air Wick, 205
All-American Soap Box Derby, 412
Allegiant Air, 94, 214
Allied Domecq PLC, 528
Allstate Corporation, 120, 207, 432
Alpha, 215
Altria Group, Inc., 103
Amalgamated, Inc., 363, 364
Amazon.com, Inc., 3, 5, 8–9, 11, 18, 46–47, 64, 86, 98, 100, 102, 116, 134, 150, 150–151, 169, 178, 203, 207, 208, 211–212, 214, 217, 292, 324, 330, 332, 379, 452, 456, 457, 471, 476, 490
  Instant Video, 476, 478
  Kindle, 5, 46, 47, 150–151, 207, 324
  Kindle Fire, 47, 330, 332, 476
  Kindle Store, 47

  1-Click, 11
  Prime, 28, 47, 150, 292
  Prime Instant Video, 476
Ambassador, 178
AMD (Advanced Micro Devices, Inc.), 288
American Airlines, Inc., 18, 32, 93–94
American Antitrust Institute, 346
American Banking Association, 44
American Cancer Society (ACS), 11
American Express Company (AmEx), 20, 73, 180
American Girl doll, 372–373
American Girl Place, 372
American Idol: The Search for a Superstar, 180, 319
American Legacy Foundation (ALF), 11
American Marketing Association, 79, 245
American Red Cross (ARC), 1, 11, 34
Amway (Thailand) Co., Ltd., 386, 389
Android, 28, 47, 121, 180, 332–333, 367, 475, 477
Angie's List, 156
Anglo-Persian Oil Company, 394
Angry Birds Lite, 41
Anheuser-Busch Companies, Inc., 23, 157, 363, 430, 432
ANZ (Australia and New Zealand Banking Group Limited), 177
AOL Inc. (American Online), 18, 60
Apollo 13, 471
Applebee's International, Inc., 302
Apple Inc. (Apple Computer, Inc.), 1, 2, 10, 16, 18, 20, 23, 41, 47, 86, 89, 151, 178, 180, 201, 203–204, 207–208, 213, 217, 241, 265, 287, 289, 302, 327–336, 367, 471–472, 476, 478, 501, 504
Apple I, 328
Apple Lisa and Cube, 328
Apple Newton, 328
Apple Retail Store, 201, 331

Apple TV, 41, 329, 476
App Store, 10, 86, 98, 330
iBooks, 5, 150
iMac, 329
iOS, 332
iPad, 1, 41, 47, 86, 98, 150, 180, 204, 324, 328-333,
   336, 476-477
iPhone, 1, 28, 41, 86, 121, 150, 201, 204, 207, 219,
   319, 324, 328-330, 332-335, 475-477, 512
iPod, 5, 41, 86, 180, 222, 293, 328-330, 334-335,
   476, 505
iTunes Music Store, 5, 23, 41, 47, 98, 201,
   328-329, 476-477
iTunesU, 11
MacBook, 1, 41, 207, 212-213, 239, 329
Apple Jacks, 131
Aquafina, 59
Arbitron, 80
Archway Cookie Bakery, 462
Ariel, 153, 205
Arista, 34
Arizona, 205
Arm & Hammer Baking Soda, 131
Armor All, 131
Art Academy™, 222
ASI (Advertising Specialty Institute), 466-467,
   469
Association of Southeast Asian Nations (ASEAN),
   383, 389
AstraZeneca plc, 217
Asus, 332
ATI, 288-289
Atlanta Motor Speedway, 437
Atlantic Southeast, 94
Atlaspost, 542
Atra, 483-484
Atra-Plus, 483
AT&T, 201, 208
Audit Bureau of Circulations, 80
Auto Club Speedway, 445
AutoPilot, 324
Auto Press, 410
Auto Shack, 207
AutoZone, 35, 175, 207
Avalanche, 88, 407
Avengers, The, 180
Avery Dennison, 101
Avis, 214, 294
AVON Cosmetics (Thailand) Co., Ltd., 386, 389
AVON Products Inc., USA, 178, 386

B

Baidu, 208
Ball Park, 205
Baltimore Grand Prix, 448
Banana Republic, 298
Band-Aid, 208
Bank of America, 15, 180, 203
Barbie, 371, 372-373, 378
Barbie.com, 379
Bare Elegance, 483

Barnes and Noble, Inc., 5, 47, 150-151, 175,
   211-212, 214-215, 240, 523
Baseball Weekly, 318
Battleground, 15
Bayer, 206, 236
Baymont Inns & Suites, 420
BBMG, 248
Beckett Ridge Innovation Center, 86
Beeconomic, 542
Beerdream, 362
Beer Stream, 353
Beijing Innovation Center (BJIC), 487
Belgo IPA, 352
Ben and Jerry's, 33, 201-202, 343
Best Buy, 15, 64, 169, 175, 178, 186, 330, 471
Better Business Bureau (BBB), 237, 243, 541
Better Way, 381-390
Betty Crocker, 206
Beyond Petroleum (BP), 203, 236, 393-402
   Alternative Energy, 396, 398
   Biofuels, 397
   Educational Service, 398
   Target Neutral, 398
   Wind Energy, 396
   Zhuhai (BPZ) PTA, 397-398
Bic, 206, 482-483, 489
Biere de Mars, 352
Big Brain Academy, 222
Bill Blass, 206
Biota Water, 209
BizRate.com, 10
BlackBerry, 47, 330
Blemish Balm (BB), 382, 384, 388
Blockbuster, 28, 216, 471-476, 476
Bloomberg, 542
BluDot, 499
Blue Paddle, 352, 358, 361
Blue- Scope Steel, 78
Bluetooth, 408
BMW, 47, 86, 90, 173, 208, 214
Boeing, 31
Bold, 153, 205
Bono, 20
Books-A-Million, 214-215
Boost Mobile, 443
Boots, 383
Borden, Inc., 464
Borders, 5, 150
Bose, 173
Boston Beer Company, 359, 361
Boston Brewing Company, 363, 367
Boston piano, 200
Bounce, 153
Bounty, 153, 213
Boy Scouts of America, 446
Brain Age, 222
Bratz, 57, 372, 378
Braun, 483-484, 486
Bravo's Top Chef, 180
Breville, 256
Bristol Motor Speedway, 437

British Olympic Association, 398
Budweiser, 157, 214
Buick, 153, 180, 406
Build-A-Bear Workshop, 133
Burger King, 132, 184, 189
Burgerville, 246
Burlington, 32
Busch Grand National Series, 432
Business Ethics Magazine, 256, 358
Business Objects, 132
BusinessWeek, 2, 79, 86, 101, 458, 498
Buxton Leather goods, 483
Buy-WithMe, 543
BYD, 86

C

Cabbage Patch Kids, 371, 373–374
Cabela's, 178
Cadillac, 153, 215, 406
Calvin Klein, 206
Cambridge Group, The, 477
Cameron International Corp., 400–401
Campbell Soup, 180, 205, 214
Canon, 89, 141, 215
Canvas Holidays, 420
Carbon Disclosure Institute, 228
Carbon Footprint Toolkit, 398
Carbon Trust, 233
Carnett's, 15
Carnival Cruise Lines, 157
Car of Tomorrow, 435
Carpet Fresh, 131
Cars, 206, 376–377
CarsDirect, 3, 9
Carson Pirie Scott & Company, 463
Cartoon Network, The, 433
"Car Town," 447
Cascade, 153
Cascade Farms, 234
Case IH/Case Construction, 466
Casella Wines, 66
CBS Broadcasting Inc., 4, 180, 477
CBSSports.com, 180
Celestial Seasonings, 31
Cendant Corp., 420
Chain Store Age, 79
Champ Car's, 444
Channel, 7, 384
Chardonnay, 106
Charles Schwab, 89
Charlotte Street Computers, 231
Charmin, 153, 207
Chase for the Cup, 433
Chateau Ste. Michelle Wine Estates, 103
Cheer, 153, 205
Chevrolet, 88–89, 153, 405–414, 436, 446
    Astra, 413
    Aveo, 413
    Camaro, 213, 223, 407, 408, 413
    Captiva, 413
    Cobalt, 409

Corvair, 407
Corvette, 88, 153, 407–408
Cruze, 407, 409, 413
Cruze Eco, 409
Equinox, 68, 410
Impala, 88, 407–409
Lumina, 413
Malibu, 407
Meriva, 413
Optra, 413
Orlando, 413
Prisma, 413
Sail, 413
Silverado, 291, 409–410
Sonic, 413
Spark, 413
S10, 413
Suburban, 410
Tahoe, 88–89, 407, 410
Trailblazer, 410
Traverse, 410
Vega, 407
Volt, 407, 411, 413–414
Zafira, 413
Chevrolet Detroit Belle Isle Grand Prix, 445
Chevron, 203
Chicago Unviersity, 535
Chick-fil-A, 2
Chili's, 302
China Construction Bank, 208
China Mobile, 208
China's General Administration of Quality Super-
    vision and Inspection and Quarantine, 377
Chiquita, 233
Christel House, 424
Chrysler, 203, 223, 265, 412, 414, 430, 436–437
Cibc World Markets, 523
Cie Games, 447
Cirque du Soleil, 106
Cisco Systems, 333
Citigroup, Inc., 199, 203
Citydeal, 542
Clarity braces, 101
Clearasil, 205
Cleveland Groupon, 537
Cleveland Magazine, 538
Clinique, 173
Clorox, 157, 180
Club Med, 168
CNBC, 321
CNH, 466
CNN, 318
Coca-Cola Company, The, 1, 2, 59, 86, 131, 140,
    143, 164, 180, 188, 203, 207–210, 232, 264, 287,
    293, 335, 340, 432, 436, 446, 522
    Diet Coke, 68, 206
    Vanilla Coke, 154
    Zero, 68, 206
Coinstar, 28, 475
Colgate Palmolive, 240
Coloradan Coors, 352

Colorado, 407
Columbia, 34
Columbia Tri-Star, 34, 473
Comcast, 203, 237
Comedy Central, 476
Commodity Futures Trading Commission, 396
Comphanhia Nacional de Acucar e Alcool, 397
CompuServe Network, 318
Computer Cool School, 373
ComScore, 538
Conrad, 154
Consumer Financial Protection Bureau (CFPB),
    244
Consumer Product Safety Commission, 244
Consumer Reports, 120, 158, 333, 484, 488, 529
Consumers International, 377
Container Store, The, 21
Converse, 20
Coors, 363, 436
Copenhagen, 103
Costco, 175, 294–295
cottages4you, 420
Countrywide Financial, 235
Cover Girl, 54, 205
Craftsman, 204
Craigslist, 322
CR Brands, 223
Crest, 143, 154
Cricket, 483
Crown Cork, 482
Crown Royal, 209
CUC International, 420
Cuisinart, 256
Curves, 106, 132, 504
Cute Press, 387
CVS, 15

D

Daewoo, 413
Daisy, 483
Dancing with the Stars, 443
Darberry, 542
Dasani, 59, 209
Dawn, 153
Dayne Printing Company, 461
Days Inn, 419–420, 422, 427
Daytona, 500, 12, 436–437
Daytona International Speedway, 430, 434–435
Daytonal Beach International Airport, 436
DealOn, 543
DECTRON, 425
Deepwater Horizon, 393–402
DeKalb, 346
Deli Select, 209
Dell Inc., 19, 64, 100, 133–134, 201, 228, 261, 295,
    328, 332
Del Monte Foods, 171
Delta Airlines, 27, 93–94, 206
Delta Land and Pine, 346
Deutsche Telecom, 208
DHL, 100

Dig, 352
Dillard's, 168
Direct Selling Association, 231
Discover Card, 190
Discovery Channel, 4
Discovery Toys, 178
Dismal Scientist, 79
Disney-ABC Television Group, 15, 476
Ditch Witch, 466
DiversityInc., 426
Dr. Pepper, 154, 180
Dollar Shave Club, 488–490
Domino's Pizza, 18
Domino Sugar, 464
Dongxin, 377
Do Not Call Registry, 81
Dora the Explorer, 373
Doritos, 319
Dove, 54
Dow Jones & Co Inc., 321
Downy, 153
Dream Hotels, 420
DreamWorks, 446, 477
Dreft, 153
Dreyer's, 522
"Drive for Diversity" program, 436
Dry Idea, 483
DSi, 222
DS Lite, 222
DTAC, 385
Duet, 221
Duke University, 54
Duncan Hines, 206
Dunkin' Donuts, 256, 528–530
DuPont, 345–346, 397, 432
Duracell, 130–131, 153–154, 205, 484

E

Early Light Industrial Co., 376–377
EarthSmart®, 425
EA SPORTS Champions of Gaming Tournament,
    485
eBay, 3, 8, 10–11
EBSCO, 70
Echo Global Logistics, 537
Econolodge, 292
Economist Intelligence Unit, New York, 160
Edgar Database, 79
Edmonton Indy, 445
Electronic Manufacturers Recycling Management
    Company, 64
Electronic Recyclers International, 64
Electroplankton, 222
Element, 138
Eli Lilly, 343
Elmo, 373
Elysian Brewing Company, 352
Embassy Suites, 154
Energizer, 484
ENERGY STAR®, 425
Enron, 20, 71, 234

Enterprise Leasing, 466
E-ONE, 469
Epic, 34
Epinions.com, 10
Equate, 15, 204
Equinox, 407
Era, 153
Eraser Mate, 483
ESPN, 4, 259, 442, 444–445
Essex piano, 200
Ethisphere, 426, 458
Ethisphere Institute, 228
EU Ecolabel, 233
Eve of Roma, 483
E-waste, 64
Expedia, 4, 200
Explore Series, 352
Express, 407
ExpressJet, 94
Extreme Makeover: Home Edition, 180
Exxon, 32
Exxon Mobil Corporation, 203
EZ-Pass, 73

F

Facebook, 2, 5, 18, 23, 116–117, 207–208, 210, 229, 236, 324, 353, 366–367, 447, 453, 455, 486–487, 496, 501, 506–507, 509, 512–514, 536, 538
Faded Glory, 15
Fair Trade Certified™, 256
Family Fun Magazine, 373
Fam Safety 4 Just Kids, 347
Faris by Naris, 382, 388
Fast Company, 458
Fat Tire Amber Ale, 351–353, 362, 364–365
Fat Tire Brewery, 352
Febreze, 153
Federal Emergency Management Agency, 401
Federal Express, 32
Federal Trade Commission (FTC), 79, 184, 233–234, 236, 241–242
FedEx, 13, 109, 153–154, 156–157, 180, 208, 219, 259, 265, 398, 442, 465, 510
    Express, 153
    Freight, 153
    Ground, 153
    SameDay®, 305
FedWorld, 79
Felicity, 373
FHM, 443
Fiat, 116
Fidelity Investments, 465
"Fiesta Menu," 130
FiOS Internet, 237
Firefox, 218
Firestone, 236, 446
Firestone, 550, 445
Fisher-Price, 371, 373
Flavorlock, 528
Flickr, 447
Florida's Natural, 210

Florida State University, 68
Folgers, 518
Follett Corporation, 143
Food Markets, 21
Food & Wine Magazine, 180
Ford Motor Company, 27, 47, 86, 120, 223, 405–406, 411–414, 430, 436–437
    Escape, 68
    Focus, 409
    Model T, 405–406, 412
    Mustang, 223, 408, 412
Forest Stewardship Council (FSC), 468, 495
Forest Trust, 229
Formula One, 373, 413, 433, 443, 448
Forrester Research, 541
Forties Field, 395
Fortune magazine, 21, 79, 228, 256, 264, 372, 426, 431, 458, 471
Fosamax, 103
Foursquare, 512
FOX, 431, 438, 444, 476
Foxconn, 334
Fox Entertainment Group, 15, 476
Franklin Computer Corporation, 333
French's, 205
Fresh Rewards, 284
Frito-Lay, 59, 143
Frosted Flakes, 135
Fruity Pebbles, 131, 135
Fuji, 89
Furniture.com, 499
Fuzzy Vodka, 446

G

Gaffarine Skyline Unity Co., Ltd., 386
Gain, 153, 205
GameBoy, 222
Gamecube, 222
Gannett Co., Inc., 313–325
Gap Inc., 20, 54, 118, 204, 234, 531
Garmin, 156–157
Gatorade, 59, 69
GEICO Insurance, 178, 200
General Electric (GE), 12, 86, 208, 264
General Mills, 135, 206, 231, 234
General Motors, 88, 153, 233, 272, 405–408, 410–414, 430, 436–437
General Motors (GM), 23, 27, 47, 103, 154, 223, 234. *See also* Chevrolet
Gen Kai Japanese Cuisine, 502–504
GeoVALS, 139
GfK Mediamark Research and Intelligence, 80
Giffarine, 386
Gillette Safety Razor Company, 158, 432, 481–490
    Fusion, 158, 184, 481, 484–485, 489
    Fusion Power, 485, 489
    Fusion ProGlide, 485–486, 488–489
    Guard, 487
    Hair Care and Body Wash, 485
    Mach3, 481, 484, 489–490
    ProGlide, 486, 490

Sensor, 483–484, 486
  Team Gillette, 486
  Venus, 484, 486, 489
  Young Guns, 486
Gillette Stadium, 185, 486
Girogio Armani S.P.A., 20
Glad Products Company, 209
GladWare, 209
GlaxoSmithKline, 227
Glee, 476
Global Fund to fight AIDS in Africa, 20
Gmail, 103
GMC, 199, 406
GMM Grammy Music Records, 387
Go Daddy, 443, 448
  IndyCar Challenge, 448
Goldman Sachs, 203
Good News!, 483–484
Goodwill Industries, 64
Goodyear Tire & Rubber, 241, 430
Google, 2, 5, 6, 18, 21, 30, 47, 86, 98, 103, 116, 150–
    151, 200, 203, 208, 230, 259, 262, 320–321, 327,
    330, 332–333, 468, 471, 477, 533
  Docs, 86, 103
  Google+, 18
  Offers, 545
  Play, 476–478
  Plus, 103
  Voice, 86, 103
Goshen North Wind Farm, 396
Grand Prix, 443, 445
Great Value, 15
Green Fuel Technolgoies, 446
Green Mountain Coffee Roasters, Inc., 256
Greenpeace, 342
Green Seal, 233
Grey's Anatomy, 476
Grouper, 542
Groupon, 2, 533–545
G-series, 69
Guinness, 201

H

Habitat for Humanity, 1
Halliburton, 399–401
Hallmark Gold Crown Card, 178, 190
Hammarplast, 518
Hampton Hotels, 324
Hampton Inn, 17, 154
Hanes, 205
HANS, 435
Happy Meal, 190
Harley Davidson, 286, 335
Harrah's Entertainment, 116
Harris School of Public Policy Studies, 535
Harry Potter, 68, 206, 372
Harvard Business Review, 79
Harvard Business School, 363
Harvard University, 48
Hasbro, 373
HBO, 476–477

Hear Music, 524
Heinz, 209
Henkel, 240
Hershey Foods, 5, 206, 240–241
Hertz, 214, 294
Hewlett Packard (HP), 86, 186, 332, 334, 472
HGTV, 4
Highlander, 154
Hilfiger, 204
Hi-Liter markers, 101
Hilton, Inc., 154, 292
Hilton Garden Inn, 154
Hoffman LaRoche, Inc., 466
Home Depot Inc., 54, 107–108, 127–128, 167, 174,
    203, 233, 240, 294, 531
Home Run, 544
Home Shopping Network, 178
HomeTrends, 15
Honda, 12, 54, 138, 157, 199, 203, 212, 214–215,
    442, 446
  Accord, 69
  Acura, 180
  Civic, 120, 157
  CR-V, 68–69
  Grand Prix of St. Petersburg, 445
  Indy 200 at Mid-Ohio, 445
  Indy Grand Prix of Alabama, 445
  Indy Toronto, 445
  Pilot SUV, 69
Honeycomb, 207
Hoover, 70, 79
Hoseasons, 420
Host Marriott, 523
Hot Wheels, 371, 373–374, 446
Howard Johnson, 419–420, 422, 427
H&R Block, 156
HTC Corporation, 332–333
Huffington Post, 321
Hulu, 14–15, 471, 476
Hummer, 23, 103, 154, 410, 414
Hunan Solon, 538
Hush Puppies, 236
Hyatt, 292, 297
Hyundai, 12, 86, 140, 207, 297, 409

I

IBM, 18, 78, 86, 202, 208, 244, 264
iBooks Author, 47
ICBC, 208
IHS Screen Digest, 474
IKEA, 167, 178, 201, 233, 493–500
  Card, 496
  Concept, 494, 496
  Group, 496–497
  of Sweden, 496
ImClone, 20
Inc. Magazine, 452
Incivek, 103
Indianapolis, 500, 442–443, 445, 447
Indianapolis Motor Speedway, 441–442, 446–445
"INDY-CAR 36," 446

IndyCar.com, 447
IndyCar Series, 433, 441–449
   Grand Prix of Sonoma, 445
   Nation, 447
IndyQingdao, 600, 445
Indy Racing League (IRL), 406, 431, 442–444, 447
Indy Racing League and Champ Car (CART), 441–442, 444
InfoTrac, 70
Ingeo, 209
INGKA Holding B.V., 496
Innerworkings, 535
Instagram, 353, 367
Institute for Brewing Studies, 358
Institute of Medicine, 135
Intel Corporation, 31, 86, 100, 201, 212, 288–289
Intensive Care Vaseline, 131
International Paper Company, 466
International Reciprocal Trade Association, 65
International Visual Communications Association (IVCA), 398
Iowa Corn Indy, 250, 445
Irvine Dance Academy, 504
Irvine Kid's Dentist, 504
Irvine Village Shopping Center, 501, 504
Ivey Management Services, 501, 517
Ivey Publishing, 501, 517, 533
iVillage, 9
IZOD IndyCar Series, 445–447

J

J. Crew, 178
Jabil Circuit, 241
Jack Daniels, 206
Jafra Cosmetics, 483
Jaguar, 120, 173
James Villa Holidays, 420
J.C. Penney, 204–205, 215
Jeep Compass, 68
Jell-O, 221
JetBlue, 2, 94, 100, 214
Jim Beam, 206, 522
Jimmy Dean, 205
Joe, 525
John Middleton, 103
Johnson & Johnson, 33–34, 203, 207, 215, 239
Josephina, 373
JPMorgan Chase, 203
Justice Department, 230, 240, 400

K

Kangaroo, 28, 475
Kashi, 135
Kawai, 200
Kelley Blue Book, 410
Kellogg Company, 131, 135, 205
   Froot Loops, 135
   Frosted Flakes, 205
   Honey Smacks, 135
   Rice Krispies, 205
Kenmore, 214

Keurig®, 256
KGB Deals, 544
Khan Academy, 11
Kia, 120, 124, 140, 158, 207, 215, 297
   Forte, 158
   Optima, 158, 207
   Rio, 158
   Soul, 124, 158
Kick, 352
Kit-Kat, 229
Kix, 131
Kleenex, 208
Klomar Korea Co., Ltd., 382
Knights Inn, 420
Kodak, 5, 89, 333
Kohl's, 234
Konica Minolta, 89, 215
Kraft Foods, 75, 131, 176, 203, 221, 247
Kroger, 15, 28, 343, 475

L

LaFace, 34
La Folie, 352, 358
Landal Greenparks, 420
Lands' End, 178
La Quinta, 214
Las Vegas Convention and Visitors Authority, 446
Lava Soap, 131
Learning.com, 319
Lee Der Industrial Co., 376–377
L'eggs, 205
Lehman Brothers, 235
Lenovo, 117
Leo Burnett Company, 31
Lexmark, 276
Lexus, 120, 136
LG Electronics, 86, 89, 302
Life, 131
Lightbank VC firm, 536–537
LinkedIn, 18
Lions Gate, 525
Lips of Faith, 352
Liquid Paper, 483
Listerine, 207
Little Gym, The, 132
Little People, 373
Littmann Stethoscopes, 101, 143
LIVESTRONG Day, 456
Living Social, 543
Liz Claiborne, 205
LJK Literary Management, 525
Lockheed Martin, 231, 276
Lotus, 383, 446
Louis Vuitton, 208
Lowe's, 127–128, 167, 240, 294
LSU, 68
Lucky Charms, 135

M

Mac, 16
Macondo, 399

Macworld Expo, 201
Macy's, 298, 518
Magellan, 156
Magnetica, 222
Major League Baseball (MLB), 437, 486
March Madness, 180
Marks-A-Lot pens, 101
Marlboro, 103, 208
Marriot Hotels, 424
Marvel, 180
Mary Kay, 207
Massachusetts Institute of Technology (MIT), 487
MasterCard, 73, 206
Matchbox, 371
Mattel, Inc., 57, 371–379, 446
   Children's Foundation, 375
   Children's Hospital, 375–376
Maxwell House, 131, 154, 518
McAfee, 41
McCafé, 263
McDonald's, 18–19, 23, 28, 130, 168, 173, 184,
    189–190, 199–200, 207–208, 235–236, 256,
    263, 475, 528–530
   Arch Deluxe, 18–19
   Big Mac, 184
McNeilab, 33
MediaBank, 537
Media Bars, 525
Men's Health, 485
Mercedes-Benz USA, 12, 21, 120, 173, 214, 293
Merck, 103, 217
Metreon, 523
MGA Entertainment Inc., 57, 378
MGM, 473, 476
   Mirage, 424
   Resorts, 446
Michelin, 140, 207, 214
Michigan International Speedway, 442
Microsoft, 41, 86, 100, 121, 151, 201, 203, 207–208,
    332–333, 336, 451
   Legal and Corporate Affairs Group (LCA), 77
   Windows, 16, 121, 151, 332, 373, 477
   Xbox, 41, 162, 222, 477
Midas, 156, 305
Midwest Roadside Safety Facility, 435
Miller, 206, 363, 365
MillerCoor's New Moon Belgian White, 359
Millstone Coffee, 520
Milwaukee Electric Tool Corporation, 466
Milwaukee IndyFest, 445
Minerals Management Service (MMS), 400
Mingdai, 377
Mink Difference, 483
Minute Maid, 210
Mircrotel Inns & Suites, 420
Misfits, 15
Mrs. Fields Cookies, 5
Mr. Clean, 15, 153
Mr. Coffee, 256
Mistine, 381–390
MOJO HD, 319

Mojo Tree, 3
Monsanto Chemical Company, 339–348
Monster, 8
Monte Carlo, 408
Moody's, 70, 79
Motel, 6, 214, 292, 297
Mothers Against Drunk Drivers, 11
Motorola, 20, 47, 89, 98, 302, 443
Motor Trend, 410
Motrin, 34
Mountain Dew, 188
Movie Gallery, 216
Mozilla, 218
MSL Cup, 486
MSN, 18
MTV, 476
My Scene, 372
MySpace, 18, 117

N

Nabisco Brands, Inc., 131, 465–466
NASA's Mission Control Center, 412
NASCAR (National Association for Stock Car Auto
    Racing), 185, 373, 408, 413, 429–438, 441–444,
    448–449, 486
   Budweiser Late Model Sportsman Series, 430
   Camping World Cup Series, 429, 443
   Fan Council, 438
   K&N Pro Series, 436
   Nationwide Series, 429, 432–433, 435, 443
   Nextel Cup, 431
   Sprint Cup Series,
    429–431, 433, 435–436, 438, 443–444
   Whelen All-American Series, 436
   Winston Cup, 431
National Advertising Division (NAD), 237
National Basketball Association (NBA), 437, 442
National Commission, 401
National Fish and Wildlife Foundation, 395
National Football League (NFL), 429, 435, 437, 442,
    444, 486
National Geographic, 319, 526
National Guard, The, 446
National Highway Traffic Safety Administration
    (NHTSA), 410, 435
National Hockey League (NHL), 437
National Quality Research Center, 22
National SAFE KIDS Campaign, 435
NatureWorks LLC, 209
NBC Broadcasting Company, 4, 431, 445, 476
NBCUniversal, 15, 228, 476–477
NCAA, 180, 293
NCR, 28, 476
Neosporin, 207
Nestlé, 229
Netflix, 5, 18, 28, 216, 471–478, 538
Nevada Childhood Cancer Foundation, 456
Nevada Commercial, 527
New Belgium Brewing Company (NBB), 8, 142,
    184–185, 259, 351–359, 352, 361–368
New England Patriots, 185, 486

New England Revolution, 486
New Holland Agricultural/New Holland Construction, 466
Newman'sOwn®Organics, 256
New Mexico University, 68
News Corp, 203
Newsweek, 426
New United Motor Manufacturing, Inc., 406
New York Medical College, 342
New York Times, 4, 116, 314, 316, 317, 320–322, 335
Nexus, 47, 330
Nickelodeon, 4, 373, 476
Nicorette, 207
Nielson Company, The, 79, 80, 438, 477
Night Hotels, 420–421, 427
Nike, 18, 154, 165, 180, 199, 201, 204, 241, 287, 335
Nikon, 89, 215
Nintendo, 86, 221–222
Nintendogs, 222
Ninth U.S. Circuit Court of Appeals, 378
Nissan, 2, 15, 47, 158, 411
Nokia, 89, 265, 302
Nook, 47, 150
Nordstrom, 100, 102, 214, 261, 298, 504
Northern Michigan University, 518
Northwest, 27
Northwestern University, 535
Norton, 41
Novation, 241
NVIDIA, 289
NYTimes.com, 321

O

Oak State Products, 462
Occupational Safety and Health Administration (OSHA), 399
O-Cel-O sponges, 101
Odyssey, 54, 69
Office, The, 476
Office Depot, 175, 436
Oldsmobile, 23, 223
Olive Garden, 302
Ol' Roy, 15, 204
1-800-Flowers.com, 133, 283–284
One Hundred Years of Solitude, 399
1554, 352
OnStar, 408
Oracle, 132
Oral-B, 484
Orange County Register, 510, 513
Orbitz, 446
Oriental Princess, 387
Oxford, 363
Oxydol, 223
Ozone Laundry system, 425

P

Pace, 205
Pac-Man, 222
Pampered Chef, 178

Panasonic, 64
Pandora, 353
Papa John's Pizza, 12, 504
Paper Mate Pen, 482–483
Paramount, 477, 526
Parents Magazine, 373
Parsons, Inc., 186
Patagonia, 232
Patriot American Hospitality, Inc., 420
Patron, 207
Peak Performance Motor Oil, 446
Pepperidge Farm, 205
PepsiCo., Inc., 59, 62, 68–69, 164, 188, 210, 227, 430, 522
   Diet Pepsi, 68, 206
   Diet Pepsi Vanilla, 154
Pfizer, 100, 207, 217
Pharmacia Corporation, 340
Philip Morris Capital Corporation, 103
Philip Morris USA, 103
Philips, 446
Pho Coffee Factory, 504
Pier, 1, 497
PINK, 426
Pinterest, 18, 117
Pioneer, 472
Pizza Hut, 10, 119
Planet Hollywood, 419–420
PlantBottle, 209
Playdom, Inc., 5–6
Pleasant Company, 372
Point, The, 535, 540
PointRoll, 318
Polaroid, 89
Polo, 204
Polo Ralph Lauren, 205
Pong, 222
Pontiac, 27, 103, 154, 414
Pop-Tarts, 176
Porsche, 142
Posilac, 342–343
Post-It Notes, 101
Powerade, 59, 69
Power Wheels, 373
Pret a Manger, 124
Priceline.com, 3, 10
Prince Albert, 103
Princess Cruises, 214
Pringles, 153, 209
Printing Industry of Illionois, 464
Prius, 86
Procter & Gamble (P&G), 14, 23, 41, 62, 86, 142–143, 153, 157, 184, 203, 205, 223, 240, 481, 484–487, 490, 520
Program for the Endorsement of Forest Certification (PEFC), 468
Propel, 69
Prudential, 199
Puffs, 153
Pure Premium, 210

Q

Qpod, 542
Quaker, 59, 180
Qualcomm, 228
Quora.com, 536
QVC, 178
Qwikster, 474–475, 477–478

R

R. J. Reynolds Tobacco Company, 430–432
Radio Shack, 207
Rainforest Alliance, 233
Ralph Lauren, 206
Ramada, 419–420
Ranger IPA, 352, 366
Ranger Team, 362, 365
Ray-Ban, 142
RazWar.com, 490
RCI, 420
Realtor.com, 12
Reckitt Benckiser, 205
Recreation Equipment, Inc. (REI), 233
Redbox, 28, 216, 223, 471, 475–476, 478
Red brand, 20
Red Cross, 231
Red Lobster, 302
Redox Brands, 223
Reebok, 184, 241
Regions Financial Corporation, 287–288
Registry Collections, The, 420
Research and Design Center, 435
Research in Motion (RIM), 86, 98, 302
Reuters, 321
Reviewed.com, 319
Richard Ivey School of Business, 501, 517, 533
Richard Ivey School of Business Foundation, 501
Ridgeline Energy, LLC., 69, 396
Ritz-Carlton Hotels, 100, 102, 167, 214, 261, 266, 293
Rock-a-Stack, 373
Rocky Mountain National Park, 354
Roku, 476
Rolex, 293
Rolling Stone, 366
Roundup, 340, 342–344, 347–348
Royal Caribbean, 265–266
RSA, 364
RS Entertainment, 384
Rubbermaid, 127–128
Ruth's Chris Steak House, 12, 293, 304

S

S. T. Dupont, 483
Saab, 103, 414
SABMiller, 77–78, 103
Safeway, 523
St. John's Bay, 205
Saks, 298
Salah Gas Field, 397
Sales and Marketing Executives, 79
Salesforce.com, 187, 228

Salon de la Mer, 540
Sam Adams, 361, 363, 367
Sam's Choice, 15, 204
Sam's Club, 172, 176, 294–295
Samsung, 86, 89, 98, 203, 207, 265, 302, 332–333
Sandals, 168
Sanka, 131
Santa Fe, 32
Sao Paulo Indy, 300, 445
SAP, 132, 208
Sara Lee, 205
Saturn, 23, 103, 154, 272, 414
SAZABY Inc., 526
Schering-Plough, 103
Schick, 158, 484
    Hydro, 158, 489–490
    Intuition Plus, 489
    Quattro, 158, 481, 484, 489
    Silk Effects Plus, 489
Schwab.com, 12
Science Diet, 173
Scion, 158
Scope, 205
Scotch Tape, 101, 208
Screen Actors Guild, 473
Sealy, 500
Sears, 32, 104, 119, 180, 203, 214
Seat Geek, 319
Seattle's Best, 2
Sea World, 167
Secret, 136
Securities and Exchange Commission (SEC), 344–345
Sedgwick Group, 132
Select Comfort, 500
Seminis, Inc., 340
Sempra U.S. Gas & Power, 396
Sequoia Capital, 456–457
SeriousFun Children's Network, 424
Serta Mattress, 464
Sesame Street, 373
7-Eleven, 199, 474–475
7-Up, 188, 207
Sharp, 64
Shift, 352
Shiraz, 106
Shoebox Greetings card, 178
ShoeSite.com, 451
Shredded Wheat, 131
Sierra Nevada, 359, 361, 367
Sigma Marketing, 461–470
Silkience, 483
Silverado, 407, 409–410
Simmons, 500
Simmons Abramson Marketing, 442–443
Sims, The, 222
Singulair, 103
Siri, 329
Sirius/XM, 321
Skechers, 184
Skoal, 103

Skype, 207
SkyRadio, 318
Sloan Management Review, 79
SmartMoney, 321
Snacktime Kids, 373–374
Snow Day, 352
Society of Human Resource Management, 256
Soft & Dri, 483
Sonic, 407
Sony, 34, 41, 47, 86, 89, 118, 154, 168, 203, 215, 336, 472, 476–477
  BMG, 5
  Financial Holdings, 34
  Mobile Communications, 34
  Music Entertainment, 34
  Pictures Entertainment, 34
  PlayStation, 41, 162, 222, 476
Sorento, 158, 207
SoSasta, 542
Southwest Airlines, 2, 19, 32–33, 94, 100, 105, 105–106, 165, 167, 258, 294
Spark, 407
Special K, 135
Speedway Motorsports, 437
Spirit, 94
Sports Illustrated, 443
Sports Science Institute, 69
Sports Weekly, 318
Spotify, 23
SpreadFirefox.com, 218
Sprint, 201, 432
Sprite Zero, 154
SPSS, 116
SSUP Company, 387, 389
Standard & Poor's (S&P), 79, 248, 264, 351
Stanford Shopping Center, 524
Starbucks, 2, 62, 95, 169, 256, 287, 319, 343, 517–531
  Coffee, Tea, and Spice Company, 518
  Coffee International, 527
  Entertainment, 524
  Gossip, 528
Starlight Children's Foundation, 424
Star Trek, 68
Starwood Resorts, 424
Starz, 477
State Administration for Commerce and Industry (SACI), 377
State Administration for Quality Supervision and Inspection and Quarantine (AQSIQ), 377
State Farm, 89, 140
Steel And Foam Energy Reduction (SAFER) barriers, 435
Steinway and Sons, 199–200
Sterilite, 127–128
Sterilon hospital razors, 483
Stichting INGKA Foundation, 496
Stumble Upon, 324
Subaru, 140
Suburban, 407
Sudafed, 207
Sudoku Gridmaster, 222

Sunbeam, 264
Sunoco, 432, 435
Sunshine Wheat, 352, 361
Super Bowl, 12, 183, 293
Super, 8, 419–420, 422, 427
Surface, 151, 332
Surveys.com, 80
Sushilicious, 501–515
Sustainable Forestry Initiative (SFI), 468
Suvarnabhumi Airport, 383
Swanson, 205
Swedspan, 496
Swedwood, 496
Swiffer, 153
Swiss Miss, 256
Symantec, 228
SymphonyIRI Group, 80

T

Talladega Nights, 433
Talladega Superspeedway, 430, 435
Tandy Corporation, 207
Target, 5, 7, 15, 20, 116, 175, 178, 379, 471, 497, 524
Tata Group, 86
Tazo, 256
TED Talks, 11
Tesco, 77, 383
TET propane, 396
Tetris DS, 222
Texas Instruments (TI), 30, 249
30 Rock, 476
3-IN-ONE Oil, 131
3M (Minnesota Mining and Manufacturing), 35, 92, 100–101, 143
3PLs, 177
Tide, 15, 86, 153, 205, 209
Time Life, 178
Time Warner Cable, 28, 60, 203, 471
Tippr, 544
T-Mobile, 203
Tommy Hilfiger, 173, 206
TomTom, 156
Toro Company, 174
Toshiba, 64, 332, 472
Total, 131
Tour de Fat, 357, 362
Tour de France, 185, 293
Toyota, 23, 46–47, 86, 154, 180, 212, 215, 406, 442
  Camry, 154
  Corolla, 409
  Grand Prix Long Beach, 445
Toys "R" Us, 7, 374, 379
Trac II, 483–484
Trans-Alaska pipeline system, 395
Transocean, Ltd., 399–401
Travelocity, 4
Travelodge, 420, 422
Traverse, 407
Tree Ripe, 210
Tri-County Speedway, 436
Trim Nutrition, 446

TripAdvisor, 422
Trippel, 352
Tropical Energia S.A., 397
Tropicana, 59, 210
True Swing Golf, 222
TRYP, 420–421, 427
Tully's, 256–257
Tupperware, 178
"Turbo," 446
Twangoo, 542, 545
20th Century Fox, 28, 477
24-hour Mistine Call Center, 385
Twilight, 68
Twitter, 2, 9, 18, 117, 201, 210, 324, 353, 367, 447,
    453, 455–456, 486–487, 501, 506–507, 509,
    511–514, 536, 538
2000 Flushes, 131
Tyco, 71, 371
Tylenol, 33–34, 239

U

Ubuyibuy, 542
Ultrabooks, 239
UNICEF, 372
Union, 76, 430
Union Pacific, 32
Unisource, 466
United, 94
United States Auto Club (USAC), 441, 443
U.S. Army, 256
U.S. Consumer Product Safety Commission,
    373–374
U.S. Department of Justice (DOJ), 344–345
U.S. Environmental Protection Agency, 64, 342–343,
    358, 425, 435
U.S. Food and Drug Administration, 217, 227, 239,
    342–343, 382
U.S. International Trade Commission, 333
U.S. Justice Department, 227
U.S. Patent and Trademark Office, 207
U.S. Postal Inspection Consumer Fraud Fund, 396
U.S. Postal Service, 305, 472
U.S. Small Business Administration, 79
U.S. Smokeless Tobacco Company, 103
U.S. Supreme Court, 209, 346
US Airways, 93–94
United Way, 12, 231
Universal Studios, 12, 28, 167
University of California, Los Angeles (UCLA), 375
    Children's Hospital, 375–376
University of Michigan, 22
University of Nebraska, 435
University of Western Ontario, 501, 517, 533
Unsafe at Any Speed, 407
UPS, 66, 154, 203, 208, 432, 436
USA Today, 313–325, 409
    International, 317
    Live, 319
    Online, 318
    Open Air, 318
    USAToday.com, 313–314, 318–321, 324

    USA Today + Me Social News, 324
U*Star, 386–387, 389

V

Vaseline, 131
Vault, 188
V8, 205
Verenium Corporation, 397
Verismo, 801, 528
Verizon, 28, 201, 208, 237, 291, 476
Versus, 319
Viacom, 476
Victoria's Secret, 298
Vioxx, 103
Virgin America, 94
Virgin Group Limited, 458
Virginia Slims, 103
VirPharm, 98
Visa, 73, 206, 208
Visine, 207
Vitamin Water, 1, 18, 69
Vodafone, 208
Volkswagen, 86, 158, 215
Volvo, 466
Vue Packs, 256

W

Waldenbooks, 150
Walgreens, 15, 28, 475
Wall Street Journal, 79, 314, 316–317, 320–321, 358
Wal-Mart, 5, 7, 14, 15, 20, 28, 34–35, 62, 92, 100,
    127–128, 138, 167, 169, 171, 174, 176, 178, 200,
    204, 208, 233–234, 240, 261, 268, 343, 379, 397,
    471, 473, 475, 497, 524
Walt Disney Company, The, 5–6, 203, 371, 373, 477
Walt Disney World, 12, 13, 167, 206, 214, 293, 504
Warner Brothers, 477
Warner Home Video, 473
Waste Management, 64
WD-40 Company, 131, 199
Weakest Reputations, The, 203
Wegman's, 21
Welcome Wagon, Inc., 483
Wellbutrin, 227
Wells Fargo, 89, 203, 208
Weston Laboratories, 461–462
White Rain, 483
Whirlpool, 221
Whole Foods Market, 203
WiFi, 263
Wilkinson Sword-Schick Company, 481–482
Wine.com, 4
Wingate, 420
Winn-Dixie, 28, 475
Winnie the Pooh, 373
Winston, 430
Wired, 366
Woolite, 205
WorldCom, 20, 71, 234
World Cup, 486
World Health Organization, 135

WorldMark, 420
World Trade Organization, 72
World Wildlife Federation, 495
Worthington, 205
Write Brothers, 483
Wyndham Hotel & Resorts, 419–422, 425
  Club, 420
  Exchange & Rentals, 419, 423
  Garden, 420, 422
  Grand Collection, 420, 422
  Hawthorne Suites by, 420, 425
  International, 420
  Vacation Ownership, 419, 423, 425
  Vacation Rentals, 420
  Vacation Resorts Asia Pacific, 420
  Worldwide, 419–427
  Worldwide University, 423
Wynn Resorts, 424

X

Xerox, 208, 264, 305, 518
X14 Cleaner, 131

Xinhua, 377
XM Radio, 443
xpedx, 466

Y

Yahoo!, 18, 116, 320
Yamaha, 200
Yellow Frieght Systems, 466
Yelp, 512
YouCanDo.net, 386
YouTube, 5, 103, 353, 366, 447, 476–477, 513
Yuban, 131

Z

Zappos, 207, 451–459, 536
  Family, 452, 455
  Insights, 458
  Leading Environmental Awareness for the Future
    (L.E.A.F.), 456
  Recycling Day, 456
Zhongxin, 377
Zocor, 103

Name Index

A

Adamy, Janet, 517, 526–531
Adkins, Craig, 453
Akerson, Dan, 414
al-Gaddafi, Muammar, 394–395
Allen, Booz, 264
Allen, Tim, 409
Andretti, Michael, 447
Anthony, Carmelo, 442
Antioco, John, 473–474
Arkus-Duntov, Zora, 407
Aurand, Timothy, 429
Austin, Scott, 537

B

Baird, Harper, 313, 327, 419, 451
Baldwin, Jerry, 518
Ball, Deborah, 528–529
Banhart, Devendra, 365
Barad, Jill, 371
Barros, Glen, 525
Behar, Howard, 521
Benjamin, André 3000, 486
Bennett, Tony, 524
Bergh, Chip, 485
Bernal, Gael García, 486
Bernard, Randy, 445, 448
Berry, Leonard L., 289, 299
Bezos, Jeff, 21, 454
Bhasin, Chandani, 419
Biden, Joe, 407
Birchall, Jonathan, 517
Bitner, Mary Jo, 289
Bowker, Gordon, 518
Breiding, Daniel, 481
Brody, Adrian, 486
Brown, Kathleen, 529
Bryant, Carter, 378
Buchanan, Lauranne, 517
Buckley, Neil, 529
Burton, Jeff, 435

Busch, Kurt, 431
Busch, Kyle, 486
Byron, Red, 430

C

Carroll, Archie, 230
Carson, Johnny, 407
Castroneves, Helio, 443
Cha, Eunjung Ariana, 524
Charles, Ray, 524
Chatterjee, Sayan, 533
Cherry, Michael, 436
Chevrolet, Louis, 405–406
Chokwatana, Boonyakiat, 381
Churchill, Winston, 394
Clinton, Bill, 14, 472
Coburn, Marcia Froelke, 535, 538, 540
Coles, Martin, 527
Cook, David, 473
Cook, Tim, 201, 336
Copeland, Christin, 493
Crow, Trammel, 420
Curley, Tom, 316

D

D'Arcy, William, 393–394
Daley, Clayton C. Jr., 485
Danziger, Eric, 421
Davis, Edward W., 171, 177
Davis, Leanne, 481
Deerojanawong, Amornthep, 381, 384, 390
Deerojanawong, Danai, 390
Dell, Michael, 328
DeLorenzo, Tony, 406
Dempsey, Patrick, 442
Deschanel, Zooey, 201
Dholakia, Utpal M., 540
Dominus, Susan, 525
Domoracki, Jeff, 536
Donald, Jim, 517, 530
Donohue, Mark, 406

Dougherty, Matt, 527
Doyle, Jere, 538
Dubow, Craig, 318, 324
Dudley, Bob, 401, 402
Dunlap, Al, 264
Durant, William, 405–406
Dyche, Nicole, 481

E

Earnhardt, Dale, 406, 435, 443
Earnhardt, Dale Jr., 429, 433, 435, 443–444
Eckert, Robert, 371, 376
Edgar, David, 358
Eggelston, William, 364
ElBoghdady, Dina, 522

F

Fain, Richard, 266
Feltheimer, Jon, 525
Ferrell, Linda, 381, 419, 451
Ferrell, O. C., 152, 188, 217, 327, 339, 351, 371, 381, 393, 405, 419, 451, 461, 471
Fields, Bill, 473
Flock brothers, 430
Force, John, 413
Ford, Henry, 20, 413
Fraedrich, John, 371
France, Brian, 432–433, 436, 438
France, William Henry, 430, 434
France, William Jr., 430, 434
Franchitti, Dario, 448

G

Gaciolosi, Matthew, 481
Gallegos, Bernadette, 451
Gay, Tyson, 486
Gelles, David, 541
George, Anton H. "Tony", 441–442, 444
Gerstner, Lou, 264
Gillette, King Camp, 482
Glass, John, 523
Glueck, William F., 260
Goizueta, Roberto, 264
Gonzalez, Carlos, 486
Gordon, Jeff, 406–407, 412, 429, 432, 443
Gordon, Robby, 448
Gordon, Tina, 431
Grant, Hugh, 340, 341, 346–347
Grant, Mauricia, 436
Graves, Michael, 421
Gray, Steven, 523–525, 527, 529
Gremler, Dwayne, 289
Guy, Sandra, 537, 540

H

Hair, Joseph F. Jr., 138
Hamlin, Denny, 486
Handler, Ruth and Elliot, 371–372
Harbaugh, Jim, 442
Hartline, Michael, 471, 481, 493
Hastings, Reed, 471–472, 474
Hayward, Tony, 400–401

Herrman, Kurt, 367
Holmes, Stanley, 525
Holmes, Stephen, 420–421
Holt, Douglas, 353, 363, 366
Hornish, Sam Jr., 448
Hsieh, Tony, 451–458, 536
Huizenga, Warne, 473

I

Iacocca, Lee, 265
Irwin, Kenny, 435
Ittiwattanakorn, Nuntiya, 381
Izral, Joe, 429

J

Jackson, Jennifer, 339, 371
Jackson, Michael, 536
Jackson, Samuel L., 201
Jaunch, Lawrence R., 260
Jaworski, Bernard J., 271
Jenkins, George W., 305
Jobs, Steve, 201, 265, 327–328, 336, 531
Johnson, Jimmie, 412, 444
Johnson, Junior, 406
Johnson, Mark, 538
Jones, Norah, 524
Jones, Patricia, 5
Jordan, Kim, 352, 354, 359, 365, 368
Judson, Kimberly, 429
Juuji, 504

K

Kahaner, Larry, 5
Kahne, Kasey, 444
Kamprad, Ingvar, 493
Kang, Stephanie, 530
Kaplan, Robert, 22–23
Keller, Kevin, 202
Kelly, Kate, 524–525
Kelly, Pat, 529
Kemp, Dave, 359
Kendall, Tom, 413
Keys, James, 474
Kim, W. Chan, 104, 106
King, B. B., 524
King, Carole, 525
Kirshbaum, Laurence, 525
Kiviat, Barbara, 523, 528, 530–531
Koch, Jim, 363
Kotler, Philip, 202
Kramer, Larry, 323

L

Lamb, Charles W. Jr., 138
Larian, Isaac, 378
Lau, Adaline, 542
Lebesch, Jeff, 352, 354, 359, 361, 365
Lee, Mark, 542
Leno, Jay, 407
Letterman, David, 442
Leung, Shirley, 528
Lin, Alfred, 454, 457

Lochte, Ryan, 486
Lockyer, Sarah E., 522
Lombard, Kenneth, 524
Longoria, Evan, 486
Lopez, Cassondra, 419
Lovelock, Christopher, 166
Luther, Jon, 528
Lynch, Mike, 436

M

Mark, Ken, 501
Marquez, Gabriel Garcia, 399
Marszalek, Diana, 540
Mason, Andrew, 533, 535–537, 539–540
Matson, Matt, 371
Mauborgne, Renee, 104, 106
Mbuthia, Alex, 429
McCann, Jim, 284
McCartney, Paul, 525
McCormick, Rhonda, 429
McCoy, Chris, 536
McDaniel, Carl, 138
Mekwichai, Rawadee, 381
Mihaly, Kevin, 313
Mikulay, Bob, 365
Miller, Robert K., 437
Ming, Choi Chee, 376
Mitchell, Joni, 525
Mockler, Colman, 483
Montoya, Juan Pablo, 433, 436
Mulcahy, Anne, 264
Mulpuru, Sucharita, 541
Myers, James H., 299

N

Nader, Ralph, 407
Neuharth, Allen H., 313–317
Newman, Paul, 413
Newman, Ryan, 431, 444
Nickerson, William, 482
Nooyi, Indra, 227
Norton, David, 22–23

O

O'Keeffe, Sarah, 533
Obama, Barack, 319
Overholt, Alison, 524–525
Owsley, Greg, 353, 362–363, 366–368

P

Palin, Sarah, 319
Parasuraman, A., 289, 299
Patrick, Danica, 436, 443, 448
Petty, Adam, 435
Petty, Kyle, 431
Petty, Lee, 430
Piercy, Nigel, 91, 96, 269
Pirouz, Dante, 501
Pirouz, Raymond, 501
Pisano, Bob, 473
Pride, William M., 152, 188, 217

Q

Queeny, John F., 340
Queeny, Olga Monsanto, 340

R

Randolph, Marc, 471
Reddick, Kelsey, 471
Renshaw, Deborah, 431
Reynolds, George, 394
Rice, Ray, 486
Rihanna, 12
Roberts, Fireball, 430
Roddy, Colin, 481
Roemmele, Brian, 536
Rolling Stones, 524
Romenesko, Jim, 528
Roper, Tony, 435
Rose, Charlie, 535, 540
Roy, Don, 441
Rusli, Evelyn, 533
Ryan, Matt, 486

S

Sajjamanochai, Supishsha, 381
Sapit, Don, 461–465, 468
Sapit, Jeff, 468
Sapit, Mike, 461, 465, 468
Satzman, Doug, 523
Saunders, Anne, 525–526
Sawayda, Jennifer, 327, 339, 351, 361, 371, 381, 393, 405, 419, 461, 471
Scherz, Brent, 481
Schreyer, Peter, 158
Schroeder, Stan, 542
Schultz, Howard, 2, 95, 517–521, 523–524, 526–528, 531
Schwarzkopf, Norman, 317
Scott, Jake, 364
Scott, Jamie, 429
Sculley, John, 330
Segall, Laurie, 540
Shapiro, Benson, 487
Shelton, Beau, 451
Shepard, Alan, 407
Siegl, Zev, 518
Simkin, Lyndon, 45
Simmons, Carolyn J., 517
Simmons, Gene, 442–443
Simpson, Bryan, 361, 366
Smith, Ethan, 524, 527
Smith, Fred, 157, 265
Smith, Orin, 522
Spears, Britney, 530
Speckman, Robert E., 171, 177
Srbecky, Charles, 364
Stewart, Tony, 448
Stone, Brad, 527, 530
Streiff, Alison, 533
Sutton, Kelly, 431
Swasey, Steve, 473
Swinmurn, Nick, 451

T

Taylor, James, 524–525
Thompson, Don, 529
Thorne, Debbie, 371
Three Doors Down, 433
Treacy, Michael, 102
Trent, Jacqueline, 471

V

Vervier, Jenn, 368
Villa, Felix, 429
Villeneuve, Jacques, 413
Vrancia, Suzanne, 530

W

Wach, Ryan, 481
Walton, Sam, 268
Wangprapa, Ekachai, 381
Warren, Elizabeth, 244
Watson, Robyn, 313
Webber, Jeff, 319
Welch, Jack, 264
Wendling, Larry, 101

Wheldon, Dan, 448
Wiersema, Fred, 102
Wiggins, Jenny, 517
Williams, Goeff, 540
Williams, Lucinda, 524
Winfrey, Oprah, 525
Winton, Alexander, 413
Witt, James Lee, 401
Woo, Daniel, 501, 502, 504, 506, 508–511, 513–514
Woo, Hannah, 504
Wood, Celeste, 313
Wortham, Jenna, 533
Wozniak, Steve, 328, 336

Y

Yang, Dori Jones, 518, 522–523
Yo-Yo Ma, 524

Z

Zeithaml, Valerie, 289, 299
Ziegler, Vincent, 482–483
Zucchero, 525

Subject Index

A

academic journals, 79
accessory equipment, 152
achievers, 139
action, 181
advantages, 212–213
advertising
    of brand/branding, 363–365
    cooperative, 191
    direct response, 178
    direct-to-consumer, 66
    integrated marketing communications and, 182–184
    Internet, 183
    media, 180
advocacy, 286
aggressiveness, 103
AIDA model, 181
alliances, 206
allowances, 169
alternatives, evaluation of, 121
Amazon, Zappos merger with, 456–457
American Customer Satisfaction Index, 22–23
American Girl, 372–373
Amway (Thailand) Co., Ltd., 386
Apple, 327–336
    App Store, 330
    corporate culture of, 331–332
    future of, 336
    history of, 328
    iPad, 330
    iPhone, 329
    iPod, 329
    iTunes, 329
    Mac computers, 329
    marketing for, 330–336
    products of, 328–330
assessment, 69
assortment, 154
attainability, 107–108
attention, 181
audience, media fragmentation and, 4

Average Order Value (AOV), 306
Avon, 386
awareness, 286

B

baby boomers, 54
backstage technology, 72–73
balanced performance scorecard, 49
balanced strategic planning, 48–50
Barbie, 372
barters, 169
base prices/pricing, 166–169
behavioral segmentation, 136–137
believers, 139
benefits, 213
    segmentation of, 138
    sought out, 141
Beyond Petroleum (BP), 393–402
    branding of, 396–398
    code of conduct of, 398
    ethical conduct of, 395–398
    history of, 394–395
    marketing strategy of, 402
    social conduct of, 395–398
bids, 128
biofuels, 397
biotechnology
    bovine growth hormone, 342–343
    environmental effects of, 343–344
    genetically modified food, 342
    herbicides, 344
    Monsanto, 341–344
    pesticides, 344
Blockbuster, 473–474
blue ocean strategy, 106
book sources, 79
bovine growth hormone, 342–343
BP oil spill, 399–400
    initial explosion, 399
    recovery following, 401–402
    repercussions of, 400
    risks, failure to manage, 400

brand/branding
  advantages of, 204
  attributes of, 202
  of BP, 396–398
  of Chevrolet, 411–412
  of competitors, 68–69
  concept of, 199
  corporate, 202–203
  decisions for, 204–206
  decline stage of, 223–224
  development stage of, 217–218
  of equity, 207, 434
  growth stage of, 219–220
  of IKEA, 498
  insistence of, 207
  introduction stage of, 218–219
  labeling and, 209
  loyalty to, 206–207, 434
  management of, 215–224
  manufacturer *vs.* private-label, 205
  marketing strategy decisions on, 19–20
  maturity stage of, 220–221
  of NASCAR, 431–434
  of New Belgium Brewing, 363–366
  packaging and, 209
  positioning and, 199–224
  preferences to certain, 206
  recognition of, 206
  strategic alliances and, 206
  strategic issues in, 202–209
  technical aspects of, 199–202
  value of, 206–208
  Wyndham Worldwide, 421
branding equity, 207
branding license, 206
Bratz, 378
breakeven analysis, 159–161
bribery, 344–345
bulk breaking, 172
business buying process, 128–129, 141
  bids, 128
  consumer, 125
  order processing, 128
  problem recognition, 128
  product development, 128
  proposals, 128
  for vendor, 128
business customers, for Groupon, 540
business markets/marketing, 7
  business buying process in, 128–129
  buyer behavior in, 125–129
  characteristics of, 126–128
  customer relationships in, 288–290
  fundamental changes to, 3–7
  segmentation of, 141–142
  types of, 126
business model
  customer-focused, 452–454
  of Netflix, 474–475
    of Starbucks, 520–527
  of Zappos, 452–456

business partners, with Mattel, 374–375
business practices, 375
business products, 151–152
business publications, 79
business purchases, 128
business relationships, 290
business sales promotions, 191–192
business services, 152
business-unit strategy, 34–35
buyer behavior
  in business markets, 125–129
  in consumer markets, 117–125
buyers roles, 290
buying center, 126–127

C

Cabbage Patch Kids, 373–374
capabilities, 69
carbon sequestration, 397
carbon storage, 397
cash flow, 163, 220
catalog marketing, 178
cause-related marketing, 231
CEO's, 264
cereal markets, 135
change, marketing implementation through, 263–265
channel functions, outsourcing of, 175–177
channel intermediaries, 172
characteristics, 69
Chevrolet, 405–414
  branding strategy of, 411–412
  Camaro, 408
  challenges of, 414
  Corvette, 407–408
  Cruze, 409
  Ford, rivalry with, 412–413
  history of, 405–406
  Impala, 408–409
  international marketing of, 413–414
  product mix of, 406–411
  recovery of, 414
  Silverado, 409–410
  SUVs/Crossover vehicles, 410
  Volt, 411
Children's Online Privacy Protection Act (COPPA),
    5–6
Children's Online Privacy Protection Rule, 6
client-based relationships, 155
co-branding, 431–432
codes of conduct, 243–245, 398
codes of ethics, 244–245
coercive power, 174
cognitive dissonance, 123
collaboration, 87, 89–90, 170
collective buying industry, 540–542
commercial markets, 126
commercial sources, 79–80
commoditization, 2
commodity hell, 2
communication
  about risk, 277
  corporate, 77

during exchange, 10
social, 307
communities
customer relationship management within, 286
extended enterprise in, 170
stakeholders, relationship with, 424
comparison shopping, 204
competition
with Apple, 332
in external environment, 66–70
with Groupon, 542
with IKEA, 499
SWOT analysis and, 89
in today's society, 1
types of, 68
with *USA Today*, 321–322
competitive advantage
defined, 16, 34
developing, 98–100
leveraging, 98–100
in marketing, 16–17
realization of, 35
sources of, 99
strategic focus and, 85–111
strategies for, 99–100
competitive advantage strategies, 102
competitive analysis, 69
competitive intelligence, 16
competitive matching, 163, 167
complementary products, 164
compliance programs, 426
component parts, 152
comprehensiveness, 107–108
connectivity, 170
consensus, marketing implementation through, 265–266
consistency, 107
consumer buyer process, 117–123
alternatives evaluation, 121
factors affecting, 123–125
information search, 120–121
postpurchase evaluation, 122–123
purchasing decisions, 121–122
recognition, need for, 119–120
stages of, 118
consumer markets, 137
buyer behavior in, 117–125
consumer buyer process in, 117–123
customer relationships in, 286–288
prices/pricing in, 168
consumers
products for, 151–152
sales promotions for, 189–191
wants of, 120
consumption, 155
contests, 191
continuity, 108–109
control
cultural, 276
formal, 554–555
input, 272, 554

marketing implementation and, 20–21, 255–279
of marketing plan/planning, 36, 42
output, 272–275, 555
social, 276
worksheet for, 554–556
convenience products, 152
cooperative advertising, 191
corporate affairs, 77
corporate branding, 202–203
corporate codes of ethics, 245
corporate communication, 77
corporate culture
of Apple, 331–332
of IKEA, 497
of Zappos, 454–456
corporate philanthropy, 77, 231–232
corporate social responsibility
of Monsanto, 346–347
pyramid of, 230
of Zappos, 456
corporate strategy, 34–35
corporate sustainability, 77
cost structure of firm, 159–161, 223
counterfeit products, 239
countertrade, 169
coupons, 189
cultural control, 276
cultural management risk, 277
cultural values, 76
culture, corporate, 331–332, 454–456, 497
current customers, 62
customer focus. *See also* SWOT analysis
competitive advantage and, 105–111
establishing, 100–105, 104
identifying, 105
marketing plan/planning and, 45–50
SWOT analysis and, 88–89
customer-focused business model, 452–454
customer-focused mission statement, 33–34
customer-focused planning, 46–47
customer market segmentation, 136–141
behavioral segmentation, 136
demographic segmentation, 136–138
geographic segmentation, 140–141
psychographic segmentation, 138–140
customer relationship management (CRM), 285–286
customer relationships. *See also* customer satisfaction
in business markets, 288–290
in consumer markets, 286–288
developing, 283–308
introduction to, 283–284
maintaining, 283–308
managing, 284–290
in marketing, 21–22
quality of, 290–299
value of, 290–299
customers, 285
acquisition of, 285, 307
attrition rate of, 307
benefits of, 161

complaints by, 306
conversion rate for, 307
current, 62
delight of, 123, 300
dissatisfaction of, 301
environment for, 55–57, 60–66
expectations of, 293, 299–303, 305, 307
5W model for analysis of, 61
focus of, 45–50
of Groupon, 538–540
of IKEA, 500
intimacy of, 100, 102
maintaining, 285
perception of, 158
performance of, 307
potential, 62
power shift to, 3
privacy of, 332–333
recovery rate of, 307
relationships with, 289
repeat, 286
retention of, 299–308
share of, 220, 287
stakeholders, relationship with, 422
of Starbucks, 524–526
strengths of, 91
of *USA Today*, 320–321
weaknesses of, 91
customer satisfaction, 301
customer expectations and, 299–303
customer retention and, 299–308
loyalty *vs.*, 302
measurement of, 306–308
quality *vs.*, 303–304
value *vs.*, 303–304
customer service
efficiency *vs.*, 294–295
at Zappos, 453–454
customer support services, 213–214
customization, 498

D

data mining, 116
data *vs.* information, 56
decisions/decision-making process
for brand/branding, 204–206
consumer buyer process and, 123
marketing and, 14–22
in marketing program, 18–19
team-based buying, 290
decline stage of brand/branding, 223–224
defensiveness, 103
demands, 5, 120
demographic changes, 74–75
demographic segmentation, 136–138
desirable exchange, 10–11
desire, 181
development stage of brand/branding, 217–218
differential advantage, 34
differentiated marketing, 131–132
differentiation, 210–215, 432–433

digital competitors, 476–477
direct mail, 191
direct marketing, 178
direct observation, 80
direct response advertising, 178
direct selling, 178, 384–385
direct-to-consumer (DTC) advertising, 66
discounts/discounting, 168–169
dissatisfaction, 123
distribution
of Apple, 331
exclusive, 173
intensive, 173
of Mistine, 383
at Netflix, 473
physical, 169–170
selective, 173
strategy for, 217
supply chain management and, 19
of *USA Today*, 317
diversification/diversity, 103
in NASCAR, 436
of population, 75, 130
divesting option, 223
do-it-yourself approach, 497–498

E

economic buyer, 126
economic growth, 70–71
economic mission statement, 33
economic responsibilities, 229
economic stability, 70–71
efficiency
customer service *vs.*, 294–295
shopping, 204
elected officials, 71
employee relations, 185
employees, 285
commitment of, 262
compensation for, 262
evaluation of, 262
motivation of, 262
satisfaction of, 262
selection of, 262
self-control of, 275–276
stakeholders, relationship with, 422–423
training of, 262
environment. *See also* specific types of
for customers, 55–57, 60–66
external, 66–76
internal, 58–60
scanning of, 16
sociocultural, 74
stakeholders, relationship with, 424–425
ethical climate, 246–247
ethical leadership, 245–246
ethical misconduct, 234–237
ethical responsibilities, 229–231
ethical sourcing, 241
ethics
BP, conduct of, 395–398
business practices and, 375

challenges of, 236–237
codes of, 244
controlling, 242–246
managing, 242–246
marketing, 20, 233–236, 238
in marketing program, 237–242
of marketing strategies, 229–250
Mattel, responsibility of, 374–376
Monsanto, issues of, 344–345
pricing-related, 239–240
product-related, 238–239
promotion-related, 241–242
social responsibility and, 20, 229–232, 233–236
strategic planning and, 249–250
supply chain, 241
supply chain-related, 240–241
sustainability and, 232–233
training on, 244
Wyndham Worldwide, programs for, 426
event sponsorship, 185
evolution, 258
e-waste, 64
exchange
communication during, 10
defined, 9–11
desirable, 10–11
rejection of, 10
two-party, 9
value of, 9–10
exclusive distribution, 173
executive summary, 34, 37–39
expectations
of customers, 293, 299, 305, 307
experience-based, 299
ideal, 299
experience-based expectations, 299
experiencers, 139
experiential quality, 296–297
experiments, 81
extended enterprise, 170
external environment, 66–76
competition in, 66–70
economic growth in, 70–71
economic stability in, 70–71
legal issues in, 71–72
political trends in, 71
regulatory issues in, 71–72
sociocultural trends in, 73–76
SWOT analysis of, 55–57
technological advancements in, 72–73
worksheet for, 549–551
external stakeholders, 285

F

Facebook, as media marketing strategy, 512
feature articles, 185
financial performance, 246–248
financial resources, 92
Fisher-Price, 373
flexibility, 37, 87
focus groups, 80, 308

Ford, rivalry with Chevrolet, 412–413
formal marketing controls, 271–275
Formula 1, 443
form utility, 12
Foursquare, as media marketing strategy, 512
fragmentation, 180
fraudulent activity, 242
free merchandise, 191
frontstage technology, 72, 73
functional strategies, 35–36

G

generalizations, 288
generic competitors, 68
genetically modified food, 342
geographic pricing, 169
geographic segmentation, 137, 140–141
Giffarine Skyline Unity Co., Ltd., 386
Gillette, 481–490
future of, 490
innovation at, 482–483, 485–486
marketing strategies of, 486–490
razors of, 483–484
global expansion
of Gillette, 487
of Starbucks, 526–527
global manufacturing, of Mattel, 376
global sourcing, 290
government markets, 126
government relations, 77
government sources, 78–79
Great Recession, 4
green marketing, 233
green products, 233–234
greenwashing, 233
Groupon, 533–545
collective buying industry of, 540–542
competition with, 542
customers of, 538–540
deals for, 537
defined, 533–535
expansion of, 536–537
growth of, 542–545
historical beginning of, 535, 535–536
marketing of, 537–538
model for, 535–540
Point, The, 535
growth stage of brand/branding, 219–220

H

hard costs, 127
harvesting approach, 223
Hear Music, 524–525
herbicides, 344
heterogencity, 155
Hispanic population, 75
home shopping networks, 178
Hot Wheels, 373
"how" question, 65
human resources, 92, 261–263
Hurricane Katrina, 34

Hurricane Rita, 34
Hurricane Wilma, 34

I

ideal expectations, 299
identification, 69
IKEA, 493–500
  added amenities of, 497–498
  brand image, 498
  concept of, 494–496
  corporate culture of, 497
  customization and, 498
  do-it-yourself approach of, 497, 498
  low cost structure of, 497
  marketing of, 495–496, 499–500
  online support of, 499
  production, 494–495
  promotional expenditures of, 498–499
  strengths, 497–498
  sustainability of, 498
  U.S. expansion of, 496–500
  weaknesses, 498–499
in-depth information, 115
individual influences, 124
IndyCar, 441–449
  motorsports market and, 443–444
  reunification of, 444–445
  U.S. open-wheel racing and, 441–443
informal marketing controls, 275–276
information. *See also* marketing information
  data *vs.*, 56
  in-depth, 115
  power of, 174
  searching for, 120–121
  secondary sources of, 76–80
  synthesis of, 85
informational resources, 92
initial purchase, 286
innovation
  at Gillette, 482–483, 485–486
  marketing, 15
  of marketing strategies, 15
innovators, 139
input controls, 272, 554
installations, 152
institutional markets, 126
intangibility, 108, 155
intangibles, 70
integrated marketing communications (IMC), 19,
    179–192
  advertising and, 182–184
  personal selling and, 186–188
  public relations and, 184–186
  sales management and, 186–188
  sales promotion and, 188–192
  strategic issues in, 181–182
  worksheet for, 554–556
integration, 87
intellectual property, 333–334
intellectual resources, 92
intended marketing strategies, 257

intensive distribution, 173
interdependency, 258
interest, 181
internal analysis, 16
internal data sources, 76–78
internal environment, 55–60
  worksheet for, 547–548
internal marketing, 268–270
international marketing, with Chevrolet, 413–414
Internet advertising, 183
introduction stage of brand/branding, 218–219
investor relations, 77
Irvine, 502

L

labeling, 209
leadership, 100, 102, 245–246, 263
Leadership in Energy and Environmental Design
    (LEED), 232–233
legal business practices, 375
legal issues
  in external environment, 71–72
  with Monsanto, 344–346
legal jurisdiction, 6–7
legal resources, 92
legal responsibilities, 229
legitimate power, 174
life cycle costs, 297
lifetime value (LTV), 288, 306
local touch, 365–366
location
  channel intermediaries and, 172
  of Starbucks, 522–524
  of Sushilicious, 502–504
loyalty
  to brand/branding, 206–207, 434
  to products, 204
loyalty programs, 190

M

maintenance inventories, 172
maintenance products, 152
major trade associations, 79
makers, 140
Malcolm Baldrige Award, 109–110
managerial clichés, 91
manufacturer brand/branding, 205
market concentration approach, 131–132
marketing. *See also* specific types of
  of Apple, 330–336
  challenges of, 3–7
  concepts of, 7–14
  decision-making and, 14–22
  defined, 7–8
  ethical issues in, 233–236, 238
  as function of business, 7
  fundamental changes to, 3–7
  goals of, 7
  of Groupon, 537–538
  of IKEA, 495–500
  introduction to, 1
  of Mistine, 382–387

objectives of, 40, 108–110
opportunities in, 3–7
standard of living, link to, 8
stimuli in, 120
strategic planning and, 14, 16
strategies of, 15, 22–23
structure of, 260–261
of Sushilicious, 506–511
in today's economy, 1–23
traditional view of, 227
of *USA Today*, 316–317
value and, connections between, 296
marketing activities
  controlling, 270–279
  evaluating, 270–279
  in marketing, 14–22
  planning of, 13–14
  scheduling, 276–279
  strategic, 13–14
marketing audit, 273–275, 555
marketing challenges
  of Apple, 332–335
  of Zappos, 456–458
marketing channels
  functions of, 170–172
  structure of, 173
  supply chain management in, 169
marketing control, 42, 271
marketing ethics, 20, 233–236, 242–243
marketing goals
  attainability, 107
  comprehensiveness, 107–108
  consistency, 107
  developing, 105–111
  intangibility, 108
  marketing plan/planning and, 40
  moving beyond, 111
marketing implementation, 20. *See also* marketing
    activities
  advantages of, 267
  approaches to, 263–268
  by command, 263
  control and, 20–21, 255–279
  defined, 255
  disadvantages of, 267
  elements of, 259–263
  of functional strategies, 36
  human resources and, role of, 262
  internal marketing and, 268–270
  marketing plan/planning and,
    36, 40–41, 45, 257–259
  as organizational culture, 266–268
  planning and, 257–259
  scheduling, 556
  strategic issues in, 257–263
  target markets for, 36
  through change, 263–265
  through consensus, 265–266
  worksheet for, 554
marketing information, 53–82
  customer environment, 60–66
  external environment, 66–76

  information collection, 76–82
  internal environment, 58–60
  introduction to, 53–55
  market data collection, 76–82
  situational analysis, 55–57
marketing mix, 7
marketing objectives
  developing, 105–111
  marketing plan/planning and, 40
  moving beyond, 111
marketing plan/planning, 14, 27–50
  business-unit strategy for, 34–35
  comprehension of, 37
  consistency of, 37
  control of, 36, 42
  corporate strategy for, 34–35
  development of, 16, 37, 43, 45
  evaluation of, 36, 42
  executive summary and, 37–39
  flexibility of, 37
  focus and, 45–50
  functional goals of, 35
  functional strategy of, 35
  introduction to, 27
  logical manner of, 37
  marketing activities and, 14
  marketing goals and, 40
  marketing implementation and,
    36, 40–41, 45, 257–259
  marketing objectives and, 40
  marketing strategy for, 40
  objective goals of, 35
  organizational aspects of, 44–45
  of organizational mission, 30–34
  of organizational vision, 30–34
  process for, 27, 29–36
  purpose of, 44
  requirements for, 27
  significance of, 44
  situation analysis of, 39
  structure of, 37–42
  SWOT analysis of, 39–40
  tactical, 13–14
  worksheets for, 547–556
marketing program, 149–192
  decision-making and, 18–19
  defined, 149
  integrated marketing communications in,
    179–192
  introduction to, 149–151
  pricing strategy in, 158–169
  product strategy in, 151–158
  supply chain strategy in, 169–178
marketing strategies, 227–250
  BP, 402
  decisions about, 17–20
  development of, 1
  ethics in, 229–237
  financial performance and, 247–248
  Gillette, 486–490
  implementation of, 1, 20–21

innovative, 15
intended, 257
introduction to, 227–229
marketing and, 246–248
for marketing plan/planning, 40
market specialization as, 143
mass market targeting as, 142–143
Netflix, 477–478
New Belgium Brewing, 362–363
people-driven, 22
planning of, 1
product specialization as, 143
selective targeting as, 142
Sigma Marketing, 463–469
single segment targeting as, 142
social responsibility in, 229–237
stakeholder orientation and, 247
targeting, 142–143
traditional ideas about, 3
worksheet for, 553–554
market-oriented firms, 46
market primary data collection, 80–81
markets
    data collection in, 81–82
    defined, 8–9
    demand within, 163
    deterioration of, 223
    four P's of, 7
    specialization in, 143
market segmentation, 129–134
    criteria for, 134
    defined, 17, 129
    identification of, 135–142
    individualized approaches to, 132–134
    potential of, 223
    target marketing and, 17–18
    traditional approaches to, 129–132
market share, 163. 220
marketspace, 8–9
mass customization, 133
mass fragmentation, 4
mass marketing, 130–131
mass market targeting, 142–143
Mattel, 371–379
    Bratz, intellectual property fight with, 378
    ethical responsibilities of, 374–376
    future of, 378–379
    product recalls faced by, 376–377
    products of, 372–374
    social responsibilities of, 374–376
Mattle Children's Foundation, 375–376
maturity stage of brand/branding, 220–221
media, for New Belgium Brewing, 366–367
media advertising, 180
media fragmentation, 4
media marketing strategy, 511–513
media usage, changes in, 4
metamarket, 9–10
metamediary, 9
minimum tolerable expectations, 299
mission statement, 31–34

Mistine, 381–390
    future of, 390
    marketing program for, 382–387
    strategic assessment of, 387–390
monetary costs, 297–298
monetary life cycle costs, 296
monetary transactional costs, 296
Monsanto, 339–348
    biotechnology of, 341–344
    corporate responsibility at, 346–347
    ethical issues surrounding, 344–345
    future of, 347–348
    history of, 340–341
    legal issues surrounding, 344–345
motorsports market, 443–444
movie rental business, 475–477
multisegment approach, 131
mutual dependence, 127–128

N

NASCAR (National Association for Stock Car Auto
        Racing), 429–438
    branding strategy of, 431–434
    challenges of, 434–438
    history of, 430–431
    motorsports market for, 443–444
National Quality Research Center at the University
        of Michigan, 22
near field communication (NFC), 73
necessities, 119, 164
needs, 119–120
negative feedback, 302
Netflix, 471–478
    competition with movie rental business, 475–477
    future of, 478
    history of, 471–475
    marketing strategy of, 477–478
New Belgium Brewing, 351–359
    brand/branding of, 363–366, 367–368
    history of, 352–353
    marketing strategies of, 362–363
    media, consistent messaging of, 366–367
    social responsibility of, 354–358
new products, developing, 156–158
news releases, 185
New York Times, 321–322
niche marketing, 132
nonmonetary costs, 296, 297–298
non-price strategies, 167
nontraditional channels, 178
normative expectations, 299
North American Free Trade Agreement (NAFTA),
        72

O

objectives, 59, 109, 163
odd pricing, 168
older population, growth in, 75
on-demand information, 318–319
on-demand news, 318–319
one-size-does-not-fit-all recognition, 302

one-time purchases, 186
one-to-one marketing, 132–133
online social networking, 18
online support, 499
operating products, 152
operational excellence, 99–100, 102
opinion leaders, 124
order processing, 128
organizational characteristics, 141
organizational culture, 60, 266–268
organizational factors, 129
organizational mission, 30–34
organizational resources, 92
organizational structures, 48
organizational vision, 30–34
organizations, types of, 141
output controls, 272–275, 555
outside management, 302
outsourcing, 175–177
overpromising, 295

P

packaging, 209
patents, 345
people, 261–263
people-driven marketing strategies, 22
perceived differential advantages, 219
perceived necessities, 164
perceived product benefits, 164
perceived value, 161
perception of customer, 158
perceptual map, 211, 212
periodical sources, 79
perishability, 155
permission marketing, 133–134
personal characteristics, 141
personalization, 302
personal selling, 186–188, 242
pesticides, 344
philanthropy
    corporate, 77, 231–232
    of Monsanto, 347
    responsibilities and, 231–232
    strategic, 231–232
physical distribution, 169–170
Point, The, 535
point-of-purchase promotion, 190
policy analysis, 77
political trends, 71
population diversity, 130
portfolio, 151–154
positioning
    bases for, 212–214
    brand/branding and, 199–224
    defined, 210
    differentiation and, 210–215
    strategies for, 214–215
possession utility, 13
postpurchase doubt, 123
postpurchase evaluation, 122–123
potential customers, 62

power shift to customer, 3
predatory pricing, 240
premiums, 190
press conferences, 185
press releases, 185
prestige, 163
prestige pricing, 167
price lining, 168
prices/pricing
    of Apple, 330
    around the world, 160
    base, 166–169
    bundling of, 168
    in business markets, 168–169
    comparisons of, 163–164
    in consumer markets, 168
    cutting of, 162
    decisions about, 19
    differences in, 163
    discrimination of, 169, 239–240
    elasticity of, 162–165
    ethics of, 239–240
    fixing, 240
    of Gillette, 487–490
    of Mistine, 383
    myths about, 161
    objectives of, 162–163
    odd, 168
    penetration of, 167
    predatory, 240
    prestige, 167
    revenue and, 161–162
    service, 165
    skimming of, 167
    structure of, 223
pricing strategy, 158–169, 217
    for base price, 166–169
    key issues in, 159–165
    for service products, 165–166
primary data collections, 80–81
privacy, 5–6, 374
private-label brand/branding, 205
problem recognition, 128
process controls, 272, 554
product competitors, 68
product descriptors, 212–213
product leadership, 100, 102
product line depth, 154
product mission statement, 33
product mix, 153
    of Chevrolet, 406–411
    of Mistine, 382
products
    acceptance of, 204
    Apple, 328–330
    business, 151–152
    classifying, 11–12
    complementary, 164
    consumer, 151–152
    convenience, 152
    counterfeit, 239

defined, 11, 11–14
development of, 158
differentiation between, 164
digital, 11
ethics and, 238–239
events as, 12
experiences as, 12
features of, 212
financial property as, 12
four P's of, 17
goods as, 11
green, 233, 234
ideas as, 11
identification of, 204
IKEA, 494–495
information as, 11
interrelated dimensions of, 291
life cycle of, 216–217
loyalty to, 204
maintenance of, 152
market position of, 223
Mattel, 372–374
new, strategic options for, 157
operating, 152
organizations as, 12
people as, 11
places as, 12
portfolio for, 151–154
positioning of, 19–20
purchase of, 63–66
quality of, 296, 333
real property as, 12
recalls on, 376–377
repair of, 152
selecting, 65
selection of, 3–4
services as, 11
shopping for, 152
specialization in, 143
specialty, 152
specifications for, 128
Starbucks, 521–522
stylish, but sustainability, 499
substitute, 162, 164
supplemental, 296
unsought, 152
USA Today, 316
use of, 62–63
utilities of, 12–13
values of, 297
product strategy, 151–158, 217
    for new products, 156–158
    for product portfolio, 151–154
    for service products, 154–156
profit-oriented objectives, 163
promotion
    of Apple, 330–331
    ethics of, 241–242
    of Mistine, 383–384
    strategies for, 217
    of *USA Today*, 317

promotional expenditures, 498–499
proposals, 128
provided services, 172
psychographic segmentation, 137, 138–140
psychological characteristics, 141
psychological utility, 13
public relations, 184–186
purchasing decisions, 121–122

Q

quality
    defined, 290
    experiential, 296
    experimental attributes of, 292–293
    of product, 291–292
    standards of, 295
    superior, 293–295
    supplemental product, 292, 296
    symbolic attributes of, 292–293
    understanding role of, 290–293
    value *vs.*, 303–304

R

radio frequency identification (RFID), 17, 73, 175
raison d'etre, 291
raw materials, 152
readers' corner, 525
realism, 108–109
reality, 214
realized marketing strategy, 257
real necessities, 164
rebates, 189–190
reciprocity, 127
recognition, need for, 119–120
recruitment, 187
Redbox, 475–476
red carpet, 525–526
reference groups, 124
reference pricing, 168
referent power, 174
referrals, 307
regulatory issues, 71–72
relational resources, 92
relationship marketing, 21–22
relationships
    business, 290
    client-based, 155
    with customers, 289
    intensity of, 141
    programs for building, 306
relative position, 210–211
repair products, 152
repeat customer, 286
reputational resources, 92
research and analysis, 16
reseller markets, 126
resources, 92, 261
response, 69
revenue, prices and, 161–162
reward power, 174
risk cultures, 277
risks, 204, 277

S

sale management, strategic implementation of, 187
sales force, 187–188
sales incentives, 191–192
sales management, 186–188
sales promotions
  business, 191–192
  in business markets, 191–192
  for consumer, 189–191
  integrated marketing communications and, 188–192
  trade, 191–192
  types of, 189–191
Sarbanes-Oxley Act, 71
satisfaction, 123
satisfaction guarantees, 305
secondary information sources, 76–80
security, 5
segmentation, 137. *See also* specific types of
selective distribution, 173
selective targeting, 142
self-control of employee, 275–276
self-image, 204
self-regulatory association, 243
sellers roles, 290
separation, 92–93, 258–259
service characteristics, 155
service pricing, 165
service products, 154–156, 165–166
shared goals, 259–260
shared values, 259–260
shareholders, relationship with stakeholders, 423–424
share of customer, 220, 287
shipping, 453
shopping efficiency, 204
shopping products, 152
Sigma Marketing, 461–470
  desk calendar of, 462–463
  marketing strategies of, 463–469
  total service package of, 465–467
simplicity, 87
simultaneous production, 155
single segment targeting, 142
situational analysis, 16, 29, 53
  conducting, 55–57
  of marketing plan/planning, 39
  of strategic planning, 29
  SWOT for, 55–57, 85–87
situational influences, 124–125, 164
slotting allowances, 175
social communication, 307
social conduct, of BP, 395–398
social control, 276
social influences, 124
social mission statement, 33
social responsibility
  challenges of, 236–237
  concept of, 229
  dimensions of, 229–232

ethics and, 20, 229–236
marketing strategies and, 229–237
of Mattel, 374–376
of New Belgium Brewing, 354–358
strategic planning and, 249–250
sustainability and, 232–233
worksheet for, 551
sociocultural environment, 74
sociocultural trends, 73–76
soft costs, 127
solar power, 397
sole sourcing, 290
sorting, 172
specialty products, 152
stakeholders
  financial performance, relationship to, 247
  marketing strategies and, 247
  of Wyndham Worldwide, 421–425
standard of living, 8
Starbucks, 517–531
  business model for, 520–527
  fall of, 530–531
  going public, 520
  growth of, 527–530
  historical beginnings of, 518
  Schultz's vision for, 518–520
status quo, 163
strategic business unit (SBU), 34
strategic philanthropy, 231–232
strategic planning
  marketing and, 14, 16
  opportunities for, 95
  situation analysis of, 29
  social responsibility and, 249–250
  strengths of, 93–94
  SWOT analysis and, 93–98
  SWOT matrix and, 96–98
  threats and, 95
  weaknesses of, 93–94
  worksheet for, 547, 551
strategy, defined, 14
strategy canvas, 104–105, 211–212
strivers, 140
stylish, but sustainability products, 499
subscription services, 79
substitute products, 162, 164
superficial discounting, 240
supplemental product, 296–297
supply chain, 19
  defined, 170
  ethics in, 241
  management of, 169–171, 334–335
  power in, 174–175
supply chain partners, 285
supply chain strategy, 169–178
  issues with, 170–175
  for power, 174–175
  trends in, 175–178
surveys, 80–81
survivors, 140

Sushilicious, 501–515
  concept of, 501–506
  future of, 513–515
  marketing of, 506–513
sustainability
  of Apple, 335
  corporate, 77
  ethics and, 232–233
  of IKEA, 498
  of Monsanto, 346–347
  social responsibility and, 232–233
sweepstakes, 191
SWOT analysis
  benefits of, 87
  directives for, 88
  effectiveness of, 85–87
  issues to be considered in, 55–57
  marketing plan/planning and, 39–40
  potential issues to consider in, 94
  productive, 87–93
  situation analysis and, 85
  strategic planning and, 93–98
  strategy canvas and, combination
    of, 105
  worksheet for, 547, 551–552
SWOT matrix, 97
  worksheet for, 551
synthesis, 87

T

tactical planning, 13–14
tangibles-dominant economy, 70
target markets
  defined, 17
  for market implementation, 36
  selection of, 142
  strategies for, 142–143
team-based buying decisions, 290
technical buyers, 126–127
television, brand/branding on, 431
thinkers, 139
time utility, 12–13
total budget competitors, 68
total distribution costs, 172
total expenditures, 163
total product offering, 291
total service package, of Sigma Marketing,
    465–467
trade allowances, 191
trade discounts, 168–169
trade sales promotions, 191–192
training
  assistance with, 191–192
  of salespeople, 187
transactional costs, 297
transactional marketing, 21, 186
transfer pricing, 169
transparency, 455–456
trial offers, 41
turnaround, 103

Twitter, as media marketing strategy, 511–512
two-party exchange, 9

U

U.S. open-wheel racing, 441–443
unsought products, 152
USA Today, 313–325
  competition of, 321–322
  customers of, 320–321
  growth of, 313–319
  history of, 313–319
  information provided by, 318–319
  launching of, 314–316
  marketing of, 316–317
  news provided by, 318–319
  online, 317–318
  present day and future of, 320–325

V

VALS (values and lifestyles), 138–139
value-based pricing (EDLP), 167
value proposition, 4–5
values
  of brand/branding, 206–208
  competing on, 298–299
  cultural, 76
  defined, 161
  of exchange, 9–10
  experiential quality and, 297
  marketing and, connections between, 296
  monetary costs and, 297–298
  nonmonetary costs and, 297–298
  perceived, 161
  of product, 297
  quality *vs.*, 303–304
  shared, 259–260
  of supplemental product, 297
  understanding role of, 295–298
vending, 178
vendor, 128
vision, 30
vision statement, 30
volume-oriented objectives, 163

W

Wall Street Journal, 321
wants of consumer, 120
websites, as media marketing
    strategy, 513
"when" question, 63–65
"where" question, 63
white papers, 185
"why" question, 65
wind, 396
work environment, of Zappos, 454–456
work-life integration, of Zappos, 455
Wyndham Worldwide, 419–427
  background on, 420–421
  branding strategy of, 421
  compliance programs of, 426
  ethical programs of, 426

future of, 426–427
history of, 420–421
stakeholder orientation of, 421–425

Y

Yelp, as media marketing strategy, 512
yield management, 165–166
YouTube, as media marketing strategy, 513

Z

Zappos, 451–459
  business model of, 452–456
  future of, 458–459
  history of, 451–452
  marketing of, 456–458
  operating philosophy of, 452–456
zone of tolerance, 300, 300–301